Oracle Tuning
The Definitive Reference

Oracle In-Focus Series

Donald K. Burleson
Alexey B. Danchenkov

I dedicate this book to my wife, Julie, and my sons, Michael and Daniel. I always feel their unceasing love for me and their understanding of all my thoughts. Without support of my family, I don't know whether I would have ever finished this book.

~Alexey Danchenkov

Oracle Tuning
The Definitive Reference

By Donald K. Burleson and Alexey B. Danchenkov

Copyright © 2005 by Rampant TechPress. All rights reserved.

Printed in the United States of America.

Published in Kittrell, North Carolina, USA.

Oracle In-focus Series: Book 24

Series Editor: Don Burleson

Editors: Janet Burleson, John Lavender, Robin Haden, and Cindy Cairns

Production Editor: Teri Wade

Cover Design: Bryan Hoff

Printing History: July 2005 for First Edition; December 2006 for Second Edition

ISBN: 0-9744486-2-1

ISBN 13: 978-0974448626

Library of Congress Control Number: 2005901261

Table of Contents

Using the Online Code Depot

Purchase of this book provides complete access to the online code depot that contains the sample code scripts and a free copy of WISE software to help plot performance data. All of the code depot scripts in this book are located at the following URL:

rampant.cc/tuning_awr.htm

All of the code scripts in this book are available for download in zip format, ready to load and use. If technical assistance is needed with downloading or accessing the scripts, please contact Rampant TechPress at info@rampant.cc.

Purchase of this book includes a free copy of the WISE Oracle tool and the Oracle10g reference poster. Instructions for obtaining the poster and WISE Oracle software can be found at this URL:

www.rampant.cc/10g_customer

Coupon code is: *wisese*

Got Scripts?

Mike Ault offers a complete collection of 670 working Oracle scripts, a real timesaver and an indespensible tool for all Oracle DBAs.

www.oracle-script.com

Conventions Used in this Book

It is critical for any technical publication to follow rigorous standards and employ consistent punctuation conventions to make the text easy to read. However, this is not an easy task. Within Oracle there are many types of notation that can confuse a reader. Some Oracle utilities such as STATSPACK and TKPROF are always spelled in CAPITAL letters, while Oracle parameters and procedures have varying naming conventions in the Oracle documentation. It is also important to remember that many Oracle commands are case sensitive, and are always left in their original executable form, and never altered with italics or capitalization.

Hence, all Rampant TechPress books follow these conventions:

Parameters - All Oracle parameters will be *lowercase italics*. Exceptions to this rule are parameter arguments that are commonly capitalized (KEEP pool, TKPROF), these will be left in ALL CAPS.

Variables – All PL/SQL program variables and arguments will also remain in *lowercase italics* (*dbms_job*, *dbms_utility*).

Tables & dictionary objects – All data dictionary objects are referenced in lowercase italics (*dba_indexes*, *v$sql*). This includes all *v$* and *x$* views (*x$kcbcbh*, *v$parameter*) and dictionary views (*dba_tables*, *user_indexes*).

SQL – All SQL is formatted for easy use in the code depot, and all SQL is displayed in lowercase. The main SQL terms (select, from, where, group by, order by, having) will always appear on a separate line.

Programs & Products – All products and programs that are known to the author are capitalized according to the vendor specifications (IBM, DBXray, etc). All names known by Rampant TechPress to be trademark names appear in this text as initial caps. References to UNIX are always made in uppercase.

Acknowledgements

This type of highly technical reference book requires the dedicated efforts of many people. Even though we are the authors, our work ends when we deliver the content. After each chapter is delivered, several Oracle DBAs carefully review and correct the technical content. After the technical review, experienced copy editors polish the grammar and syntax..

The finished work is then reviewed as page proofs and turned over to the production manager, who arranges the creation of the online code depot and manages the cover art, printing distribution, and warehousing.

In short, the authors play a small role in the development of this book, and we need to thank and acknowledge everyone who helped bring this book to fruition:

Dr. Tim Hall – For content from his wonderful book Oracle Job Scheduling

John Lavender, for the production management, including the coordination of the cover art, page proofing, printing, and distribution.

Teri Wade, for her help in the production of the page proofs.

Bryan Hoff, for his exceptional cover design and graphics.

Janet Burleson, for her assistance with the web site, and for creating the code depot and the online shopping cart for this book.

My wife, Julia Danchenkova, for her constant support of me.

With our sincerest thanks,

Alexey Danchenkov
Don Burleson

Supplemental Materials

Purchase of this book includes free copies of important supplemental materials that will help with Oracle tuning and management:

- Free Oracle10g DBA Reference Poster (an $8.95 value)

- Free copy of the Workload Interface Statistical Engine (WISE) for Oracle10g (a $9.95 value)

 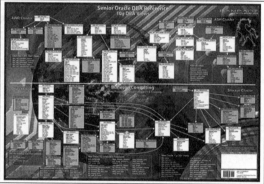

These reference tools are designed to provide assistance to quickly accessing the complex Oracle10g workload structures.

The WISE software download is available immediately. The cost for shipping and handling of the poster is only $5.99.

Follow this link to get the poster and WISE Oracle software:

www.rampant.cc/10g_customer

Note: The coupon code is: wisese

Preface

Oracle tuning has always been a complex task; however, it has become even more complex as Oracle evolves and yields new techniques for achieving optimal performance in the stressed production environment of today's high-tech world. Increasingly robust versions of Oracle continue to drive up the expectations of the business world to new heights and end-users no longer tolerate slow access to data. Oracle is the central component of today's world, and DBA's are in-charge of the mission-critical data.

Today's end users demand database that support thousands of transactions per second with sub-second response time, and the job of the Oracle tuning professional is learning the complexities of high-speed Oracle processing.

The key to success is to leverage the performance history in Oracle to locate and fix bottlenecks and plan for changes in processing requests. The central features of our book are the Automatic Workload Repository (AWR), an exciting new feature introduced in Oracle10g that is a gold-mine of performance insights. The AWR history is crucial for analysis and tuning, and the AWR forms a knowledge base for other Oracle10g intelligent tools such as ADDM.

There are three catchphrases that apply to this book:

- Time takes Time.

- Those who cannot remember the past are condemned to repeat it.

- You eat an Elephant one bite at a time.

This book strives to show how to leverage upon the Oracle performance information to create a robust Oracle engine that maximize the computing resources while minimizing the overhead to process SQL statements and updates.

Those who forget the past are condemned to repeat it.

George Santanaya

Trends are important to Oracle tuning, and this book contains helpful advice and scripts to get tuning information from AWR and the data dictionary views.

But it's not just DBA's who need to understand Oracle tuning. Oracle application developers need to know where to look for information and how to use automated tuning tools in conjunction with AWR to quickly find and correct performance bottlenecks.

This book is intended to be an adjunct to the Oracle documentation collection and it leverages on decades of real-world Oracle tuning experience. Focus is placed on those tools and techniques that have a proven track record of improving performance and the goal is to show how to find and resolve acute performance problems and predict future database workload for capacity planning; using the AWR time-series approach.

Great effort has been taken to ensure this book is error free in all text and script sections, but Oracle is constantly changing, so not all of the techniques in this book will apply to your specific release and version. We strive to improve this book with each re-printing and we welcome your feedback, so please let us know if you find any errors in our book.

Don Burleson
Alexey Danchenkov

Introduction to Oracle Tuning

Oracle Tuning

Oracle tuning is a complex endeavor and Oracle is changing constantly. Transactions come-and-go at lightening speed and Oracle tuning is often compared to trying to tune a car while it's flying down the highway at 80 miles per hour. Even the automated tuning tools within Oracle10g are not always sufficient to tune large, complex Oracle databases. There are many approaches to tuning, and while every method seeks to remedy a bottleneck, each approach is very different.

There are two ways to address Oracle performance, proactively and reactively. Time-based proactive tuning is a proven approach to long term success. In proactive tuning, the goal is to set a baseline for immutable database settings (e.g. tablespace options, initialization parameters) and the tuning of all SQL.

Once the baselines and signatures (repeating patterns) are determined for the important performance metrics, time-based tuning becomes the pursuit, recognizing that the Oracle database's needs may change dramatically depending on the time of day, day of the week, and week of the month. This chapter will cover the following topics:

- The Reactive Tuning Approach
- The Proactive Tuning Approach
- The Oracle Tuning Hierarchy
- The External Review
- The Instance Review
- Tuning the Instance
- Tuning Objects
- Tuning SQL

A review of the reactive Oracle tuning approach is a good place to start the exploration of Oracle tuning.

Reactive Oracle Tuning

As one might surmise, reactive Oracle tuning is very different from proactive Oracle tuning. While there is a methodology associated with proactive Oracle tuning, reactive Oracle tuning usually takes place during an emergency. The end-users are complaining, Oracle is slow, and DBAs must rely on tools such as Enterprise Manager (EM) to quickly diagnose and solve an acute performance problem.

As noted in the preface, Oracle DBAs are charged with ensuring that the Oracle database performs at optimal levels and that the database fully utilized all hardware while using the hardware efficiently. Historically, DBAs would monitor their databases and when a problem occurred, they would be powerless to fix it because many Oracle tuning actions cannot be done in real-time. Hence, the DBA would note the issue and schedule the appropriate action such as SQL Tuning, parameter adjustment, etc., during a scheduled maintenance window.

This *wait until the problem occurs* approach is generally limited in benefit, yet it is practiced widely. In reactive tuning, the Oracle DBA is overworked and without time or options for fixing the database. This means that fixes for a problem will have to be made at a later time, after the end-users have been inconvenienced.

Proactive Oracle Tuning

With the incorporation of the Automated Workload Repository (AWR) into the Oracle database kernel, Oracle tuning professionals have been given a gold-mine data repository that allows the leisurely analysis of Oracle performance statistics and trends over time. The AWR allows DBAs to devise a general tuning strategy that addresses the different kinds of processing that take place within all Oracle applications. When history repeats itself and the DBA can see it coming, corrective actions can be taken before the database is crippled.

In proactive tuning, the Oracle DBA's goal is to tune the Oracle database by finding the optimal global parameter settings that will maximize Oracle throughput and minimize hardware resources. By using a proactive approach to Oracle tuning, the Oracle DBA can ensure that the database is optimally tuned for any type of processing that is demanded of it.

The ability to dynamically change the System Global Area (SGA) with *alter* commands (starting in Oracle9i) allows AWR information to be used as input and justification for dynamic SGA reconfiguration. For example, if the AWR shows that the demands on the shared pool become very high between 1:00 pm and 2:00 pm, the DBA might trigger a dynamic decrease of *db_cache_size* and a corresponding increase of the *shared_pool_size* parameter during this time period.

Inside AWR

The AWR tables are quite simple, extensions of the ancient bstat-estat utilities and the successor to STATSPACK. Whenever an AWR snapshot is requested, Oracle interrogates the in-memory *x$* and *v$* structures and stores the information in the appropriate Oracle *dba_hist* views. Having a historical collection over long periods of time gives the DBA the opportunity to accurately simulate and implement an optimal overall performance plan for the database instance.

Moreover, Oracle DBAs have the unique ability to visually represent AWR information using Excel spreadsheet graphics or with the Workload Interface Statistics Engine (WISE) tool. WISE provides DBAs with a convenient framework within which they can work with AWR performance data and produce charts to support proactive tuning.

After a decade of tuning Oracle systems, Alexey Danchenkov developed the WISE software to aid in his Oracle tuning, and a free copy of this software is provided with this book. WISE instantly captures Oracle AWR and STATSPACK data easily and allow the visualization of the data aggregated by averages for day-of-the-week and hour-of-the day.

www.wise-oracle.com

The WISE Oracle tool is becoming a popular tool for proactive Oracle tuning in Oracle10g.

WISE provides a great time-saving tool for plotting Oracle performance trends. WISE also identifies repeating signatures for important performance metrics.

Throughout the remainder of this book, details will be provided that will show how the AWR tables can be used to gain insight into the where, what, and how of the tuning plan that is best suited for the database in question.

The next section will start an overview of Oracle tuning by exploring some of the most common causes of poor performance, starting with general issues such as poor design and sub-optimal applications and moving into Oracle-specific areas.

Poor Design and Poor System Performance

Application design is the single most important factor in run-time Oracle performance. Sadly, most Oracle DBAs are unable to change a poor application design, either because the application is proprietary software or because the application is already implemented in a production environment.

This and other common external causes of poor Oracle performance are often out of reach of the DBA and poor design is responsible for poor performance, at several levels:

- **Poor Schema Design**: Legacy databases from the early 1990s were designed to minimize data redundancy through high normalization forcing Oracle to perform unnecessary table joins. While materialized views may offer some relief, legacy schemas are often unchangeable for economic reasons.

- **Poor Application Design**: Many serious performance problems may lie at the application level, outside the scope of the Oracle database. If poorly designed PL/SQL is encountered, users might be able to tune the database by using array processing such as bulk collect, forall and ref cursors, but the application code is often out of reach, especially when Oracle calls are placed inside procedural code such as C++.

Because the DBA cannot alter the design of a system, Oracle design issues are not addressed in this book and O'Reilly offers several excellent books on Oracle design. DBAs must work within the bounds of the existing database and may not have the luxury of re-design. However, this does not mean that the Oracle DBA is helpless. When re-design of the application is not economically feasible, the

DBA may choose to employ tools such as materialized views or improved performance through the addition of faster hardware.

Enough about what cannot be changed. The following is an exploration of the things that can be changed and starts with the Oracle tuning hierarchy, a top-down approach to Oracle tuning.

The Proactive Oracle Tuning Hierarchy

The following is a top-down approach to Oracle tuning that has been very successful for tuning Oracle systems, large and small alike. It is an approach that starts with the review of external and instance bottlenecks and then the application of solutions, moving from global to specific. As previously noted, the assumption is made that the design and application performance is untouchable and thus restricts tuning to the Oracle database boundary.

The main categories of Oracle tuning include:

Review the External Environment: This is a review of the server, disk and network environment to ascertain when hardware components are over-stressed or under-utilized.

Review the Instance Metrics: This is a review of the specific events and metrics within AWR over a period of time to understand repeating patterns and the exact nature of a performance problem.

Perform the Instance Tuning: This is the adjustment of system-wide parameters that affect the behavior of the whole database. Since any Oracle database is in a constant state of flux, it is critical to identify the best overall setting for each of Oracle's 250+ initialization parameters and develop bi-modal instances when necessary.

Perform the Object Tuning: This is a review of specific wait events that are closely tied to data files, tablespaces, tables and indexes. The source of the stress is examined for each object and then the object characteristics are adjusted in order to remove the bottleneck.

Perform the SQL Tuning: This is the most time-intensive of the tuning tasks. The *dba_hist* tables are used to extract sub-optimal SQL and search for sub-optimal table join order, unnecessary large-table full-table scans, or inefficient execution plans. The SQL is then tuned manually, by using hints, or with the Oracle10g SQL Tuning Advisor where SQL Profiles can be used to alter execution plans.

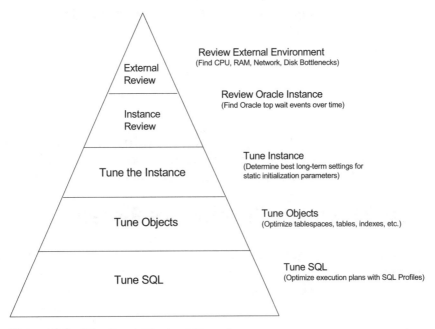

Figure 1.1: *The Oracle Tuning Hierarchy*

Tune the instance first!

Remember that the instance configuration parameters have a profound impact on SQL execution plans and overall performance.

Code Depot Username = reader, Password = tuning

The following is a quick overview of these proactive tuning steps, and a subsequent chapter is dedicated to each of these topics later in the book.

Proactive tuning differs from ordinary Oracle tuning because of the time dimension that allows the observation of performance in a real-world fashion. Proactive tuning yields complete signatures or patterns of behavior for all performance metrics. This is invaluable information that allows the prediction of the future through the examination of the past. As George Santayana said:

> Those who forget the past are doomed to repeat it.

The following continues the exploration of how the external environment impacts Oracle performance and how CPU, disk, and network affect different areas of Oracle content delivery.

External Hardware Performance Review

Oracle does not run in a vacuum. The performance of Oracle databases depends heavily on external considerations, namely the Oracle server, disk, and network. The first tasks when tuning a database are to identify the external bottleneck conditions, which may include:

CPU Bottleneck: A shortage of CPU cycles can slow down SQL. Whenever the run queue exceeds the number of CPUs on the Oracle server in the absence of high idle times, the system is said to be CPU-bound. CPU consumption can be reduced by a variety of methods, such as tuning SQL and reducing library cache contention, but a CPU shortage may indicate a need to add more, or faster, processors to the Oracle server.

RAM Bottleneck: The amount of available RAM memory for Oracle can affect the performance of SQL, especially in the regions that control the data buffers and in-memory sorts and hash joins.

Network Bottleneck: Large amounts of Oracle*Net traffic contribute to slow SQL performance.

Disk Bottleneck: Disk bottlenecks can be identified by the fact that updates are slow due to channel contention, such as using RAID5 for high update systems.

There are several simple items that can be monitored when checking the external Oracle environment:

CPU Run Queue Waits: When the number of run queue waits exceeds the number of CPUs on the server, the server is experiencing a CPU shortage. The remedy is the addition of CPUs on the server or the disabling of high CPU consumers such as Oracle Parallel Query.

RAM Page Ins: When RAM page-in operations are noted along with a prior increase in scan-rate, the non-virtual RAM memory has been exceeded and memory pages are moving into RAM from the swap disk. The remedy for excessive wrapping is to add more RAM, reduce the size of the Oracle SGAs, or turn-on Oracle's multi-threaded server.

Disk Enqueues: Enqueues on a disk device may indicate that the channels are saturated or that the read-write heads cannot move fast enough to keep up with data access requirements.

Network Latency: Volume-related network latency may indicate either the need to tune the application so that it will make fewer requests. High latency may also indicate a need for faster network hardware.

Finding Database Bottlenecks

Every Oracle database has at least one physical constraint, and it is not always the disks. The best way to isolate the constraints in the system is to analyze the *top five wait events* for the database and look for any external waits that might be associated with disk, CPU and network. The best way to see system-level wait summaries is to run the *awrrpt.sql* script from the $ORACLE_HOME/rdbms/admin directory. This will yield the *top 5 timed events* for the specific interval between AWR snapshots.

Top wait events can also be quickly identified by using the Top Wait Events report in WISE:

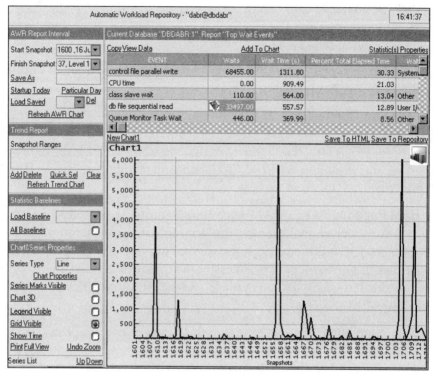

Figure 1.2: *Top Wait Events report in WISE*

Disk Constrained Database

In a disk-bound database, the majority of the wait time is spent accessing data blocks. This can be *db file sequential read* waits, usually index access, and *db file scattered read* waits, usually full-table scans, similar to the following section of a sample AWR report:

```
Top 5 Timed Events
                                                    % Total
Event                      Waits   Time (s) Ela Time
-------------------------- ------- -------- --------
db file sequential read      2,598    7,146    48.54
db file scattered read      25,519    3,246    22.04
library cache load lock        673    1,363     9.26
CPU time                        44    1,154     7.83
log file parallel write     19,157      837     5.68
```

CPU Constrained Database

In Oracle, the majority of wait time is spent waiting on I/O or performing computations. As previously indicated, CPU enqueues can be observed when the CPU run queue exceeds the number of CPUs on the database server, and this can be seen by looking at the "r" column in the *vmstat* UNIX/Linux utility or within the Windows performance manager. If the system is already optimized, having CPU time as a top wait event is a positive because the addition of faster CPUs or more CPUs will relieve the bottleneck.

However, high CPU usage is also indicative of excessive logical I/O (*consistent gets*) against the data buffers which might indicate the need for SQL tuning or shared pool and library cache tuning. High CPU usage will be reported as a top 5 timed even in any AWR report as shown below:

```
Top 5 Timed Events
                                                    % Total
Event                      Waits    Time (s) Ela Time
-------------------------- -------- -------- --------
CPU time                      4,851    4,042    55.76
db file sequential read       1,968    1,997    27.55
log file sync               299,097      369     5.08
db file scattered read       53,031      330     4.55
log file parallel write     302,680      190     2.62
```

Network Constrained Database

Network bottlenecks are common in distributed systems and those with high network traffic. Such bottlenecks manifest as SQL*Net wait events as evidenced by this mockup AWR report:

```
Top 5 Wait Events
                                                          % Total
Event                              Waits    Time (cs)  Wt Time
--------------------------------  ------------  ------------  -------
SQL*Net more data to client     3,914,935    9,475,372   99.76
db file sequential read         1,367,659        6,129     .06
db file parallel write              7,582        5,001     .05
rdbms ipc reply                        26        4,612     .05
db file scattered read             16,886        2,446     .03
```

Server statistics can be viewed in a variety of ways using standard server-side UNIX and Linux tools such as *vmstat*, *glance*, *top* and *sar*. The goal is to ensure that the database server has enough CPU and RAM resources at all times in order to manage the Oracle requests.

Server stress can change radically over time. The system might be CPU-bound in the morning and network-bound in the afternoon. The challenge is to identify server stress over time and learn to interpret any trends in hardware consumption. For example, Oracle10g Enterprise Manager tracks server run queue waits over time and combines the CPU and Paging display into a single OEM screen so that DBAs can tell when the system is experiencing server-side waits on hardware resources. Figure 1.3 shows the CPU run queue trends over time.

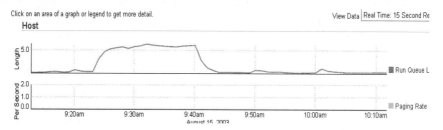

Figure 1.3: *Server CPU run queue and RAM paging values over time*

This time-based display is important because it illustrates how Oracle performance issues can be transient with short spikes of excessive hardware consumption. Due to the super-fast nature of CPU dispatching, a database might be CPU constrained for a few minutes at a time several times per day. The time series OEM display gives a quick visual clue about those times when the system is experiencing a CPU or RAM bottleneck.

Using Hardware to Correct a Sub-Optimal Oracle Database

While an excessive amount of resource consumption may be due to a poorly optimized Oracle database, the perceptive Oracle tuning professional knows that the addition of faster hardware to a poorly tuned database is sometimes a legitimate tuning solution, especially when management considers the low cost and low risk of faster hardware, relative to a database re-design. It not elegant, or even correct, but it's a common choice by managers who need quick, low-risk performance improvements.

For example, tuning 5,000 SQL statements might cost $100,000 in human resources, but moving to faster 64-bit processors might only cost $20,000. Another example is a system that is heavily I/O bound due to a poorly written application. Rebuilding the application might cost millions of dollars and take months, yet a move to super-fast solid-state disk can happen overnight at less cost and risk. The application is still poorly written, but it runs many times faster.

It may not be elegant to throw hardware at an Oracle performance problem, but it can often be a safe, cost-effective and timely solution to an acute Oracle performance issue.

The next step in the process involves drilling down to look at the overall tuning of the Oracle instance.

Oracle Instance Tuning

As a quick review, an Oracle instance is the allocated RAM region on the server, which is called the System Global Area (SGA). Individual Program Global Areas (PGA's, for each session) are a set of running programs that do the work for the instance and are referred to as processes.

Instance tuning will be discussed in great detail in the chapter titled *Oracle Instance Tuning*, but this will provide a quick overview.

Oracle instance tuning consists of the adjustment of the static global parameters that affect Oracle performance. The process begins with an examination of the instance to locate bottlenecks and sub-optimal settings.

The rules for instance tuning vary greatly, depending on the release of the Oracle database software. With each subsequent release, more of the initialization parameters become changeable via *alter system* commands. The following is a presentation of the distinction between parameters.

Dynamic Instance Parameters

Starting in Oracle9i, it became possible to adjust the values of several important SGA parameters:

- *shared_pool_size:* The memory region allocated for the library cache and internal control structures.

- *pga_aggregate_target:* A shared RAM area, outside the SGA, where Oracle performs sorting and hash joins.

- *db_cache_size* (and *db_2k_cache_size* . . . *db_32k_cache_size*): The number of data buffers to allocate for the instance.

Oracle10g users can employ the Oracle10g Automatic Memory Management (AMM) facility for this area of instance tuning. Remember, the more processes that can be automated, the easier it will be to control time-based performance. Many DBA's create their own ad-hoc triggers using *dbms_scheduler* to change these dynamic parameter values, depending on upcoming database stress loads.

The following section is an introduction to the non-changeable parameters.

Static Instance Parameters

The most important parameters for instance tuning are those that are immutable, because they cannot be changed without starting and

---

stopping the instance or using *alter session* commands or SQL hints, in some cases. Because they survive for the entire existence of an instance run, these parameters must be carefully set in order to accommodate the average load on the database during its uptime. The most important of these parameters include:

- *db_file_multiblock_read_count:* When set to a high value, the CBO recognizes that scattered (multi-block) reads may be less expensive than sequential reads. This makes the CBO friendlier to full-table scans.

- *parallel_automatic_tuning:* When set to ON, full-table scans are parallelized. Since parallel full-table scans are very fast, the CBO will give a higher cost to index access and be friendlier to full-table scans.

- *optimizer_mode:* The optimal baseline setting for this important parameter can affect the execution plans for thousands of SQL statements.

- *optimizer_index_cost_adj:* This parameter controls the relative costs of full-table scans versus index scans.

- *optimizer_index_caching:* This parameter allows DBAs to tell Oracle, on average, how much of an index resides in the RAM data buffer cache. This is an important clue when the optimizer makes an access decision.

The next section will provide information on how schema statistics affect SQL execution speed.

Statistics for the Oracle SQL Optimizer

The quality of the execution plans made by the CBO is only as good as the statistics available to it. The old-fashioned *dbms_utility* method for generating CBO statistics is obsolete and somewhat dangerous. The *dbms_stats* package is now the de facto way to get good optimizer statistics.

The better the quality of the statistics, the better the job that the CBO will do when determining SQL execution plans. Unfortunately, doing a complete analysis on a large database could take days, and most shops must sample their database to get CBO statistics. The goal is to take a large enough sample of the database to provide top-quality data for the CBO and to choose the best sampling parameters for the *dbms_stats* utility.

In Oracle10g, statistics collections are automated, but users may still need to selectively add histograms and other specialized optimizer statistics.

In Chapter 12, *Server & Network Tuning with AWR*, the process for getting the average load values for these important parameters will be presented. By setting the most appropriate baseline values for static initialization parameters, a huge amount of work can be saved when detailed SQL tuning is undertaken. A quick look at object tuning follows in the next section.

Oracle Object Tuning

Oracle object tuning is the process of setting characteristics for data files, tablespaces, tables, indexes, hash cluster tables and IOTs to achieve optimal performance. Each new release of Oracle introduces new object-level features for the DBA to use:

- **Oracle 7** - *Bitmap Indexes*

- **Oracle8** - *Locally Managed Tablespaces (LMTs)*

- **Oracle9i** – *Automatic Segment Space Management (ASSM)*

- **Oracle10g** - *Automatic Storage Management (ASM)*

Object tuning can be vital to overall system performance because major system wait events such as buffer busy waits are closely tied to the internal structure of the database objects.

For example, the following object level adjustments might be called for:

- **Tablespaces**: There are many tablespace options including dictionary-managed tablespaces, locally-managed tablespaces, and

---

special tablespace options such as Automatic Segment Space (ASS) managed tablespaces, internally represented by bitmap freelists.

- **Indexes**: Users can now choose between b*tree, bitmap and bitmap join indexes.

- **Tables/Indexes**: Users can adjust the number of freelists, freelist groups, and the freelist unlink threshold (PCTFREE) for any table or index. Hash cluster tables and index-organized tables can also be used to reduce I/O for SQL requests.

Adjusting the structure of Oracle objects can help to remove system bottlenecks. The value of removing these bottlenecks will be presented in subsequent chapters.

Oracle SQL Tuning

SQL tuning is a complex subject and entire books have been dedicated to the endeavor. In essence, SQL tuning activities have the following goals:

- **Eliminate sub-optimal large-table full-table scans**: Ensure that the fastest access path to the data is chosen.

- **Ensure fastest table join method**: The optimizer must choose intelligently between nested loop joins, hash joins and star transformation join methods.

- **Ensure optimal table-joining order**: SQL will run fastest when the first table joins deliver the smallest result set.

In Oracle10g, the new SQL profiles and the SQL Access advisor can be used to help identify sub-optimal SQL statements. Once identified, the new Oracle10g SQL profile utility will allow changes to execution plans without adding hints. SQL tuning will be covered in greater detail in Chapter 15, *SQL Tuning with AWR*.

Another type of Oracle tuning is the Oracle emergency tuning model. Time is of the essence and the DBA must act quickly to relive an acute performance problem. This will be examined more closely in the following section.

Emergency Oracle Tuning Support

Huge stress levels and late night hours are an inevitable part of life for an emergency support DBA. Most of the databases will be unfamiliar and there will only be a few minutes to view the problem and create a plan to quickly relieve bottleneck.

Only when the easy remedies have failed is the emergency support DBA called in because when a production database is in crisis, minimizing downtime is critical. At this point, cost is not an issue, but the clients demand quick fixes, and this often requires unconventional methods.

There are many Silver Bullets for Oracle performance tuning. Silver Bullets are defined as a single action or small set of commands that quickly relieves an acute performance bottleneck. Some of these just-in-time tuning techniques have been codified in Oracle10g via the Automatic Memory Management (AMM) facility, in which the SGA regions are changed dynamically to meet changing demands of processing. The following are fictionalized stories that have been gleaned from the personal accounts of Oracle emergency support professionals. In the following examples, a quick fix was used to relieve an acute performance problem.

Testing a hypothesis on a large active database is like trying to tune a car while it's flying down the freeway at 75 miles per hour. It is impossible to reproduce the conditions of a complex performance breakdown in a test environment, so the emergency support DBA must depend on experience and anecdotal evidence to guide their plan of action.

The following examples will show how a well-placed Silver Bullet can save the day.

Fix Missing CBO Statistics

A client had just moved their system into production and they were experiencing a serious performance problem. The emergency support DBA found that the *optimizer_mode=choose* and there was only one table with statistics. The client was running cost-based but seemed completely unaware of the necessity to analyze the schema for CBO statistics.

The trouble began when the DBA wanted to know the average row length for a table. The DBA then went to MetaLink and learned that an *analyze table* command would fill-in the *avg_row_len* column.

Unfortunately, the CBO will dynamically estimate statistics for all tables with missing statistics and when using *optimizer_mode=choose* with only one table analyzed, any SQL that touches the analyzed table will be optimized as a cost-based query. In this case, a multi-step Silver Bullet did the trick:

```
exec dbms_stats.delete_table_stats(owner,table);
```

When the system immediately returned to an acceptable performance level, the importance of providing complete and timely statistics for the CBO using the *dbms_stats* utility became apparent.

Repair CBO Statistics

In this example, a client expressed confusion as to why their Oracle system was grinding to a halt. There was a serious degradation in SQL performance immediately after the implementation of partitioned tablespaces in a 16-CPU Solaris 64-bit Oracle 9i database. The

---

changes had been thoroughly tested in their development and QA instances so everyone was confused about the slowdowns.

As it turned out, *analyze table* and *analyze index* commands had been used to gather the CBO statistics, a very bad choice for partitioned tables since only the *dbms_stats* utility gathers partition-wise statistics. There was not time to pull a deep-sample collection, so a *dbms_stats* was issued with a 10 percent sample size. Note that is the full-table scans are parallelized with 15 parallel query processes to speed-up the statistics collection:

```
exec dbms_stats.gather_schema_stats( -
   ownname          => 'SAPR4', -
   options          => 'GATHER AUTO', -
   estimate_percent => 10, -
   method_opt       => 'for all columns size repeat', -
   degree           => 15 -
)
```

In less than 30 minutes, the improved CBO statistics tripled the performance of the entire database.

Set Missing Initialization Parameters

A call came in from a client who reported that system performance was growing progressively worse as more customers accessed the Oracle database. Upon examination, the *db_cache_size* parameter was not present in the *init.ora* file. A quick instance bounce to reset *sga_max_size* and *db_cache_size* resulted in a 400 percent performance improvement.

In another case, a data warehouse client called and complained that performance degraded as the database grew. A quick study revealed the *sort_area_size* parameter was missing and defaulting to a tiny value. With a change of *sort_area_size*=1048575, a quick bounce of the instance, and overall database performance improved by more than 50 percent.

Adding Missing Indexes

When an Oracle site DBA called and reported that their performance degraded as more data was entered into the tables, a quick check of *v$sql_plan* using the *plan9i.sql* script from the code depot revealed a huge number of large-table, full-table scans, which is one symptom of suboptimal SQL. Looking into *v$sql* revealed that the rows returned by each query were small, and a common WHERE clause for many queries looked like this:

```
WHERE customer_status = ':v1' and customer_age > :v2;
```

Creation of a concatenated index on *customer_status* and *customer_age* resulted in a 50x performance improvement and a reduction in disk I/O by over 600 percent.

Change CBO Parameters

There was an emergency involving an Oracle client who was experiencing steadily degrading performance. They had a large number of large-table full-table scans which were suspected to be unnecessary. This suspicious information was found by a quick look into *v$sql_plan* view using the *plan9i.sql* script.

The top SQL was extracted from *v$sql* and timed as-is and with an index hint. While it was unclear why the CBO was not choosing the index, the query with the index hint ran almost 20x faster. After acting fast and running a script against *v$bh* and *user_indexes*, the DBA discovered that approximately 65 percent of the indexes were currently inside the data buffer cache.

Based on similar systems, the next step was to lower *optimizer_index_cost_adj* to a value of 20 in hopes of forcing the CBO to lower the relative costs of index access.

```
optimizer_index_cost_adj=20
optimizer_index_caching=65
```

Some parameters can be dynamically altered in versions of Oracle9i and newer.

```
alter system set optimizer_index_cost_adj=20 scope = pfile;
```

The execution plans for over 350 SQL statements were changed and the overall system response time was cut in half.

Employ *cursor_sharing*=force

An Oracle9i database had experienced poor performance immediately after a new manufacturing plant was added to the existing database. Since the AWR was not available in version 9i, a standard STATSPACK report was used to isolate the top five wait events which looked similar to this:

```
Top 5 Wait Events
~~~~~~~~~~~~~~~~~~                                  Wait      % Total
Event                               Waits      Time (cs)  Wt Time
-------------------------------- ------------ ------------ -------
enqueue                               25,901      479,654   46.71
db file scattered read            10,579,442      197,205   29.20
db file sequential read              724,325      196,583    9.14
latch free                         1,150,979       51,084    4.97
log file parallel write              148,932       39,822    3.88
```

A review of the SQL section of the STATSPACK report revealed that almost all of the SQL used literals in the WHERE clause of all queries.

```
WHERE customer_state = 'Alabama' and customer_type = 'LAWYER';
```

The *cursor_sharing* parameter was the only fast solution because the application was a vendor package with dynamically generated SQL and it could not easily be changed without using Optimizer Plan Stability (Stored Outlines), a very time-consuming task.

Setting *cursor_sharing*=force greatly reduced the contention on the library cache and reduced CPU consumption. The end users reported a 75 percent improvement in overall performance.

Implement the KEEP Pool

A client was running Oracle on a system that had a 16 CPU Solaris server with 8GB of RAM. The client complained that performance had been degrading since the last production change. A STATSPACK top five timed events report showed that more than 80 percent of system waits were related to *db file scattered reads*.

A quick review of *v$sql_plan* using *plan9i.sql* showed a number of small-table full-table scans, with many of the tables not assigned to the KEEP pool. Tables assigned to the KEEP pool are denoted in the "K" column in the listing below):

```
                        Full table scans and counts

OWNER      NAME                     NUM_ROWS C K   BLOCKS   NBR_FTS
---------- ------------------------ -------- - - -------- --------
APPLSYS    FND_CONC_RELEASE_DISJS         39 N          44   98,864
APPLSYS    FND_CONC_RELEASE_PERIODS      39 N K         21   78,232
APPLSYS    FND_CONC_RELEASE_STATES        1 N K          2   66,864
APPLSYS    FND_CONC_PP_ACTIONS        7,021 N        1,262   52,036
APPLSYS    FND_CONC_REL_CONJ_MEMBER       0 N K        322   50,174
APPLSYS    FND_FILE_TEMP                  0 N          544   48,611
APPLSYS    FND_RUN_REQUESTS              99 N           98   48,606
INV        MTL_PARAMETERS                 6 N K         16   21,478
APPLSYS    FND_PRODUCT_GROUPS             1 N           23   12,555
APPLSYS    FND_CONCURRENT_QUEUES_TL      13 N K         10   12,257
AP         AP_SYSTEM_PARAMETERS_ALL       1 N K          6    4,521
```

Rows fetched into the *db_cache_size* from full-table scans are not pinged to the Most-Recently-Used (MRU) end of the data buffer upon re-reads. Running a *buf_blocks.sql* script confirmed that the FTS blocks were falling off the least-recently-used end of the buffer and had to be frequently reloaded into the buffer.

```
                       Contents of Data Buffers
                              Number of Percentage
                              Blocks in of object
            Object        Object    Buffer   Buffer  Buffer     Block
Owner       Name          Type      Cache    Blocks  Pool        Size
------      --------------  --------- --------- ------- -------   -------
DW01        WORKORDER     TAB PART   94,856        6 DEFAULT     8,192
DW01        HOUSE         TAB PART   50,674        7 DEFAULT    16,384
ODSA        WORKORDER     TABLE      28,481        2 DEFAULT    16,384
DW01        SUBSCRIBER    TAB PART   23,237        3 DEFAULT     4,096
ODS         WORKORDER     TABLE      19,926        1 DEFAULT     8,192
DW01        WRKR_ACCT_IDX INDEX       8,525        5 DEFAULT    16,384
DW01        SUSC_SVCC_IDX INDEX       8,453       38 KEEP       32,768
```

Therefore, running a *buf_keep_pool.sql* script to reassign all tables that experienced small-table full-table scans into the KEEP pool was required. The output looks like this, and can be fed directly into SQL*Plus:

```
alter TABLE BOM.BOM_OPERATIONAL_ROUTINGS storage (buffer_pool keep);
alter INDEX BOM.CST_ITEM_COSTS_U1 storage (buffer_pool keep);
alter TABLE INV.MTL_ITEM_CATEGORIES storage (buffer_pool keep);
alter TABLE INV.MTL_ONHAND_QUANTITIES storage (buffer_pool keep);
alter TABLE INV.MTL_SUPPLY_DEMAND_TEMP storage (buffer_pool keep);
alter TABLE PO.PO_REQUISITION_LINES_ALL storage (buffer_pool keep);
alter TABLE AR.RA_CUSTOMER_TRX_ALL storage (buffer_pool keep);
alter TABLE AR.RA_CUSTOMER_TRX_LINES_ALL storage (buffer_pool keep);
```

In less than one hour, the problem was fixed via more efficient buffer caching and overall database performance more than doubled.

Employ Materialized Views

A point-of-sale Oracle data warehouse had a system that was largely read-only with a short batch window for nightly updates. It soon became apparent that nearly every query in the system was performing a sum() or avg() function against several key tables.

The *v$sql_plan* view via *plan9i.sql* showed a considerable number of very-large-table full-table scans, and the system was virtually crippled by *db file scattered read waits*.

```
Top 5 Timed Events
                                                      % Total
Event                        Waits    Time (s) Ela Time
-----------------------  ------------ ----------- --------
db file scattered read       325,519     3,246     82.04
library cache load lock        4,673     1,363      9.26
db file sequential read      534,598     7,146      4.54
CPU time                       1,154       645      3.83
log file parallel write       19,157       837      1.68
```

Once the problem was identified as unnecessary disk reads, it was easily fixed by the creation of three materialized views and the employment of Oracle's automatic query rewrite. This reduced physical disk I/O by over 2,000 percent and improved performance by more than 30x — a real Silver Bullet!

Implement Bitmap Indexes

An ad-hoc query system was experiencing slow query performance. The system was read-only except for a 30-minute window at night for data loading. Inspection of the SQL showed complex combinational WHERE clauses like:

```
WHERE color='BLU' and make='CHEVY' and year=1997 and doors=2;
```

Concatenated B-tree indexes were being used and the distinct values for each of these columns numbered less than 200. By replacing the b-tree indexes with bitmap indexes, the overall performance improvement of the system was incredible.

Queries that had taken as much as three seconds to run were reduced to runtimes of under one-tenth of a second.

Be Careful with bitmap indexes!

Bitmap indexes do not update quickly, so the best approach is to only use them in database that update all rows in a nightly "batch". In this fashion, the bitmap is dropped, changes applied to the table, and the bitmap rebuilt.

Adding Freelists

An order processing center was unable keep up with their new orders and Oracle was blamed. The VP reported that 400 order-entry clerks were experiencing 30-second response times and were forced to manually write-down order information. It came to light that the client had just expanded the telephone order processing department and had doubled the order processing staff to meet a surge in market interest.

A *v$session* check found over 400 connected users, and a quick scan of *v$sql* revealed that nearly all the Data Manipulation Locks (DML) were inserts into a *customer_order* table. The top timed event was *buffer busy wait* and it was clear that there were enqueues on the segment header blocks for the table and its indexes.

The next step to correcting this problem was to create a new tablespace for the table and index using Automatic Segment Space Management (ASSM), also known as bitmap freelists. This allows the table to be reorganized online with the *dbms_redefinition* utility and alter index *cust_pk* rebuild the index into the new tablespace. In this situation, it would have taken several hours to build and execute the jobs and the VP said that he was losing over $500 per minute.

Since the system was on Oracle9i, it was easy to immediately relieve the segment header contention with the following commands:

```
alter table customer_order freelists 5;
alter index cust_pk freelists 5;
```

Without knowing the length of the enqueues on the segment header, it was necessary to add the additional freelists, one at a time until the buffer busy waits disappeared.

The additional freelists were the key to the solution and the segment header contention disappeared. This was only a stop-gap fix and as soon as the weekly purge was run, only one of the five freelists would get the released blocks which would cause the table to extend unnecessarily.

Summary of Silver Bullet Tuning Techniques

Functioning as an emergency Oracle support DBA can be great fun for any adrenaline junky. As illustrated in the many scenarios above, this kind of support often requires a unique set of techniques:

- **Fix the symptom first**: The root cause can always be addressed later.

- **Time is critical**: When a quick fix is required, instance-wide adjustments are often the best hope.

- **Be creative**: Traditional (i.e., time consuming) tuning methods do not apply in an emergency.

Once the Silver Bullets have done their job and minimized the bottlenecks, the Emergency Oracle support DBA can only hope that the client will dedicate resources to the identification and long-term correction of the root cause of the problem.

Conclusion

This chapter focused on a basic overview of reactive, proactive and emergency Oracle tuning. The proactive tuning model will serve as the foundation for the later chapters where the value of time-series tuning for the overall health of databases will be addressed. The main points of this chapter include:

- Reactive tuning is too little, too late. The end-user is already experiencing a loss of service.

- Proactive tuning assumes that DBAs take advantage of the Oracle dynamic tuning features and change the system configuration just in time to meet the change in processing demand.

- All tuning activities start with a global review of the server (e.g. CPU, network, disk) to isolate the current hardware bottleneck.

- Global tuning is performed through a review of the instance configuration such as initialization parameters and CBO statistics. After the review, the challenge becomes choosing the best overall settings.

- Detailed tuning is performed by tuning the individual SQL statements. Ongoing tuning is the process of adjusting the dynamic Oracle parameters in anticipation of changes in processing profiles.

At this point, it should be clear that the only way to achieve effective Oracle tuning over time is to develop a strategy for monitoring performance trends. The following chapter provides a closer look at time-series tuning and details on how it provides an overall methodology for tuning any database.

Time-Series Oracle Tuning

Everyone demands fast response time

Introduction to Time Series Analysis

One of the most common comments from novice Oracle professionals relates to the complexity of the Oracle software. Many of these professionals learned relational database management in College using a simple relational product, and they are overwhelmed at the power and complexity of Oracle.

From its humble beginning in the early 1990s, Oracle has become a very complex and powerful database. Whenever there is a complaint like *"Why does Oracle have to be so hard?"*, it is important to remember that along with complexity comes flexibility and power.

Unlike other relational products, Oracle gives the database professional complete control over every aspect of the database. The DBA can

---

control the physical layout of the data on disk and almost every aspect of the Oracle instance.

Leveraging the power and sophistication of Oracle are important to tuning efforts. The Oracle DBA has complete control over the database, so there is no excuse for not making maximum use of the server resources. However, tuning an Oracle database with over 250 initialization parameters and dozens of object configuration options can be overwhelming, especially to a beginner.

Oracle has started to address the complexity issue with special advisory utilities. Starting in Oracle9i, advisory utilities were developed that can be used to predict the marginal benefits of changes to System Global Area (SGA) memory region parameters such as *db_cache_size*, *pga_aggregate_target* and *shared_pool_size*.

This advisory approach has been refined in Oracle10g where the automatic management make Oracle10g an extremely simple and yet complex engine, all in the same package. Oracle can be simplified if the DBA uses only a few tuning parameters and allows Oracle to automate storage and memory management. This automation approach is how Oracle competes successfully in the smaller database market. For more details, see Dr. Arun Kumar's book *Easy Oracle Automation*.

As a small database grows, the broad brush automation features can be selectively turned off, eventually allowing the DBA full control over every aspect of the database.

The following section will provide a quick tour of time-series tuning.

Time-Series Tuning Guidelines

There are three main areas that affect the decision to resize the Oracle RAM regions. While this book has been devoted to advanced scripts for detecting specific Oracle resource problems, all SGA self-tuning is generally done in one of these areas:

- *shared_pool_size*: A high value for any of the library cache miss ratios may signal the need to allocate more memory to the shared pool.

- *db_cache_size:* When the data buffer hit ration falls below a predefined threshold, it might be useful to add RAM to the data buffer cache.

- *pga_aggregate_target:* When there are high values for multi-pass executions, it may be desirable to increase the available PGA memory.

The shops that will benefit most from automated self-tuning are those shops with the following characteristics:

- **Bi-modal systems**: Systems that alternate between OLTP and Data Warehouse processing modes will especially benefit from self-tuning RAM regions

- **32-bit shops**: Those shops that are running 32-bit servers are constrained by the size of their RAM regions. This constraint consists of a maximum limit of about 1.7 Gigabytes. For these shops, making the most effective use of RAM resources is especially important.

The following section provides detail on each of these conditions.

Measuring Behavior over Short Periods

To optimally cache the working set of frequently accessed data, the data buffers can be monitored for short periods of time. An experienced DBA can measure the buffer efficiency with either the Automated Workload Repository (AWR) or STATSPACK with the script below. An overall system-wide data buffer hit ratio is not much help.

The shorter the time interval, the more variation will exist in the Data Buffer Hit Ratio (DBHR). For example, the hourly DBHR might be 94%, but when measured every minute, it might range from 35% to 99%, depending on the activity within each data buffer.

The following scripts can be used to get an idea what is happening "right now" in the database. It prompts the DBA for a wait period, takes two STATSPACK snapshots and then does a quick time period summary of database changes.

This is just a quick overview of SGA tuning. Chapter 14, *Instance Tuning with AWR* provides significantly more detail on the subject.

Before revealing the script, the following is a sample of the output:

```
*************************************************************
This will identify any single file whose read I/O
is more than 10% of the total read I/O of the database.

*************************************************************


MYDATE              FILE_NAME                                    READS
----------------    ----------------------------------------    ---------
2000-12-20 11       /u03/oradata/PROD/pod01.dbf                  1,766


*************************************************************
When the data buffer hit ratio falls below 90%, you
should consider adding to the db_block_buffer init.ora parameter

*************************************************************

MYDATE              phys_writes  BUFFER HIT RATIO
----------------    ------------ ----------------
20 Dec 11:23:47       101,888           91


*************************************************************
When there are high disk sorts, you should investigate
increasing sort_area_size, or adding indexes to force index_full
scans
*************************************************************


MYDATE              SORTS_MEMORY   SORTS_DISK          RATIO
----------------    ------------   ------------   ---------------
20 Dec 11:23:47          109             1     .0091743119266


*************************************************************
Buffer busy wait most frequently signal incorrectly configured
database writer (DBWR) or freelist cointention. This event means
simply that another session has the buffer pinned and that the
session recording this event must wait.

*************************************************************
```

```
MYDATE             BUFFER_BUSY_WAIT
----------------   ----------------
20 Dec 11:23:47                  20


***********************************************************
Table fetch continued row indicates chained rows, or fetches of
long datatypes (long raw, blob)

Investigate increasing db_block_size or reorganizing tables
with chained rows.
***********************************************************


MYDATE             TABLE_FETCH_CONTINUED_ROW
----------------   -------------------------
20 Dec 11:23:47                        1,551


***********************************************************
Long-table full table scans might indicate a need to:

- Make the offending tables parallel query
(alter table xxx parallel degree yyy;)
- Place the table in the RECYCLE pool
- Build an index on the table to remove the FTS

To locate the table, run access.sql

See Oracle Magazine September 2000 issue for details
***********************************************************


MYDATE                  FTS
----------------   ------------
20 Dec 11:23:47            148
```

The listing above shows the significant value of this report. The DBA can see a time-series report of Oracle behavior and even gets choose the time interval. An experienced DBA would likely run the quick.ksh script below using a five minute time interval.

💾 oracle10g_quick.ksh

```
spool rpt_last.lst

set pages 9999;
set feedback on;
set verify off;

column reads  format 999,999,999
column writes format 999,999,999

select
   to_char(sn.end_interval_time,'yyyy-mm-dd HH24'),
   (newreads.value-oldreads.value) reads,
   (newwrites.value-oldwrites.value) writes
from
   dba_hist_sysstat oldreads,
   dba_hist_sysstat newreads,
   dba_hist_sysstat oldwrites,
   dba_hist_sysstat newwrites,
   dba_hist_snapshot   sn
where
   newreads.snap_id = (select max(sn.snap_id)
from dba_hist_snapshot)
   and newwrites.snap_id = (select max(sn.snap_id)
from dba_hist_snapshot)
   and oldreads.snap_id = sn.snap_id-1
   and oldwrites.snap_id = sn.snap_id-1
   and oldreads.stat_name = 'physical reads'
   and newreads.stat_name = 'physical reads'
   and oldwrites.stat_name = 'physical writes'
   and newwrites.stat_name = 'physical writes'
;

prompt ************************************************************
prompt  This will identify any single file who's read I/O
prompt  is more than 10% of the total read I/O of the database.
prompt
prompt  The "hot" file should be examined, and the hot table/index
prompt  should be identified using STATSPACK.
prompt
prompt  - The busy file should be placed on a disk device with
prompt    "less busy" files to minimize read delay and channel
prompt    contention.
prompt
prompt  - If small file has a hot small table, place the table
prompt    in the KEEP pool
prompt
prompt  - If the file has a large-table full-table scan, place
prompt    the table in the RECYCLE pool and turn on parallel query
prompt    for the table.
prompt ************************************************************

column mydate format a16
column file_name format a40
column reads  format 999,999,999

select
   to_char(sn.end_interval_time,'yyyy-mm-dd HH24')  mydate,
```

```
      new.filename                              file_name,
      new.phyrds-old.phyrds                     reads
from
   dba_hist_filestatxs old,   dba_hist_filestatxs new,
dba_hist_snapshot   snwhere   sn.snap_id = (select max(snap_id) from
dba_hist_snapshot) and    new.snap_id = sn.snap_id
and
   old.snap_id = sn.snap_id-1
and
   new.filename = old.filename
--and
--   new.phyrds-old.phyrds > 10000
and
   (new.phyrds-old.phyrds)*10 >
(
select
   (newreads.value-oldreads.value) reads
from
   dba_hist_sysstat oldreads,
   dba_hist_sysstat newreads,
   dba_hist_snapshot   sn1
where
   sn.snap_id = sn1.snap_id
and newreads.snap_id = sn.snap_id
and oldreads.snap_id = sn.snap_id-1
and oldreads.stat_name = 'physical reads'
and newreads.stat_name = 'physical reads'
and (newreads.value-oldreads.value) > 0)
;

prompt ***********************************************************
prompt  This will identify any single file who's write I/O
prompt  is more than 10% of the total write I/O of the database.
prompt
prompt  The "hot" file should be examined, and the hot table/index
prompt  should be identified using STATSPACK.
prompt
prompt  - The busy file should be placed on a disk device with
prompt    "less busy" files to minimize write delay and channel
prompt    channel contention.
prompt
prompt  - If small file has a hot small table, place the table
prompt    in the KEEP pool
prompt
prompt ***********************************************************

column mydate format a16
column file_name format a40
column writes  format 999,999,999

select
   to_char(sn.end_interval_time,'yyyy-mm-dd HH24')  mydate,
   new.filename                              file_name,
   new.phywrts-old.phywrts                   writes
from
   dba_hist_filestatxs old,
   dba_hist_filestatxs new,
```

```
   dba_hist_snapshot    sn
where
   sn.snap_id = (select max(snap_id) from dba_hist_snapshot)
and new.snap_id = sn.snap_id
and old.snap_id = sn.snap_id-1
and new.filename = old.filename
--and
----    new.phywrts-old.phywrts > 10000
and (new.phywrts-old.phywrts)*10 >
(select(newwrites.value-oldwrites.value) writes
from
   dba_hist_sysstat oldwrites,
   dba_hist_sysstat newwrites,
   dba_hist_snapshot    sn1
where
   sn.snap_id = sn1.snap_id
and newwrites.snap_id = sn.snap_id
and oldwrites.snap_id = sn.snap_id-1
and oldwrites.stat_name = 'physical writes'
and newwrites.stat_name = 'physical writes'
and (newwrites.value-oldwrites.value) > 0)
;

prompt ***********************************************************
prompt  The data buffer hit ratio is controlled by the
db_block_buffer or db_cache_size parameters.
prompt ***********************************************************

column logical_reads  format 999,999,999
column phys_reads     format 999,999,999
column phys_writes    format 999,999,999
column "BUFFER HIT RATIO" format 999

select
   to_char(sn.end_interval_time,'dd Mon HH24:mi:ss') mydate,
   d.value            "phys_writes",
   round(100 * (((a.value-e.value)+(b.value-f.value))-(c.value-
g.value)) /
((a.value-e.value)+(b.value-f.value)))
        "BUFFER HIT RATIO"
from
   dba_hist_sysstat a,
   dba_hist_sysstat b,
   dba_hist_sysstat c,
   dba_hist_sysstat d,
   dba_hist_sysstat e,
   dba_hist_sysstat f,
   dba_hist_sysstat g,
   dba_hist_snapshot    sn
where
--    (round(100 * (((a.value-e.value)+(b.value-f.value))-(c.value-
g.value))
--/ ((a.value-e.value)+(b.value-f.value)))  ) < 90
--and sn.snap_id = (select max(snap_id) from dba_hist_snapshot)
and a.snap_id = sn.snap_id
and b.snap_id = sn.snap_id
and c.snap_id = sn.snap_id
```

```
and d.snap_id = sn.snap_id
and e.snap_id = sn.snap_id-1
and f.snap_id = sn.snap_id-1
and g.snap_id = sn.snap_id-1
and a.stat_name = 'consistent gets'
and e.stat_name = 'consistent gets'
and b.stat_name = 'db block gets'
and f.stat_name = 'db block gets'
and c.stat_name = 'physical reads'
and g.stat_name = 'physical reads'
and d.stat_name = 'physical writes'
;

column mydate heading 'Yr.  Mo Dy  Hr.' format a16
column reloads        format 999,999,999
column hit_ratio      format 999.99
column pin_hit_ratio format 999.99

break on mydate skip 2;

select
   to_char(sn.end_interval_time,'yyyy-mm-dd HH24')  mydate,
   new.namespace,
   (new.gethits-old.gethits)/(new.gets-old.gets) hit_ratio,
   (new.pinhits-old.pinhits)/(new.pins-old.pins) pin_hit_ratio,
   new.reloads
from
   dba_hist_librarycache old,
   dba_hist_librarycache new,
   dba_hist_snapshot      sn
where
   new.snap_id = sn.snap_id
and old.snap_id = new.snap_id-1
and old.namespace = new.namespace
and new.gets-old.gets > 0
and new.pins-old.pins > 0
;

prompt ************************************************************
prompt  When there are high disk sorts, you should investigate
prompt  increasing sort_area_size, or adding indexes to force
index_full scans
prompt ************************************************************

column sorts_memory  format 999,999,999
column sorts_disk    format 999,999,999
column ratio format .9999999999999

select
   to_char(sn.end_interval_time,'dd Mon HH24:mi:ss') mydate,
   newmem.value-oldmem.value sorts_memory,
   newdsk.value-olddsk.value sorts_disk,
   (newdsk.value-olddsk.value)/(newmem.value-oldmem.value) ratio
from
   dba_hist_sysstat oldmem,
   dba_hist_sysstat newmem,
   dba_hist_sysstat newdsk,
```

```
      dba_hist_sysstat olddsk,
      dba_hist_snapshot    sn
where
   -- Where there are more than 100 disk sorts per hour
--    newdsk.value-olddsk.value > 100
--and
   sn.snap_id = (select max(snap_id) from dba_hist_snapshot)
and newdsk.snap_id = sn.snap_id
and olddsk.snap_id = sn.snap_id-1
and newmem.snap_id = sn.snap_id
and oldmem.snap_id = sn.snap_id-1
and oldmem.stat_name = 'sorts (memory)'
and newmem.stat_name = 'sorts (memory)'
and olddsk.stat_name = 'sorts (disk)'
and newdsk.stat_name = 'sorts (disk)'
and newmem.value-oldmem.value > 0
;


prompt ************************************************************
prompt  When there is high I/O waits, disk bottlenecks may exist
prompt  Run iostats to find the hot disk and shuffle files to
prompt  remove the contention
prompt
prompt  See p. 191 "High Performance Oracle8 Tuning" by Don Burleson
prompt
prompt ************************************************************

break on snapdate skip 2

column snapdate format a16
column filename format a40

select
   to_char(sn.end_interval_time,'dd Mon HH24:mi:ss') mydate,
   old.filename,
   new.wait_count-old.wait_count waits
from
   dba_hist_filestatxs old,
   dba_hist_filestatxs new,
   dba_hist_snapshot   sn
where
   sn.snap_id = (select max(snap_id) from dba_hist_snapshot)
and new.wait_count-old.wait_count > 0
and new.snap_id = sn.snap_id
and old.filename = new.filename
and old.snap_id = sn.snap_id-1
;

prompt ************************************************************
prompt  Buffer Bury Waits may signal a high update table with too
prompt  few freelists.  Find the offending table and add more
freelists.
prompt ************************************************************

column buffer_busy_wait format 999,999,999

select
```

```
      to_char(sn.end_interval_time,'dd Mon HH24:mi:ss') mydate,
      avg(new.buffer_busy_wait-old.buffer_busy_wait) buffer_busy_wait
from
   dba_hist_buffer_pool_stat old,
   dba_hist_buffer_pool_stat new,
   dba_hist_snapshot    sn
where
   sn.snap_id = (select max(snap_id) from dba_hist_snapshot)
and new.snap_id = sn.snap_id
and new.snap_id = sn.snap_id
and old.snap_id = sn.snap_id-1
--having
--   avg(new.buffer_busy_wait-old.buffer_busy_wait) > 100
group by
   to_char(sn.end_interval_time,'dd Mon HH24:mi:ss')
;

prompt ***********************************************************
prompt  High redo log space requests indicate a need to increase
prompt  the log_buffer parameter
prompt ***********************************************************

column redo_log_space_requests  format 999,999,999

select
   to_char(sn.end_interval_time,'dd Mon HH24:mi:ss') mydate,
   newmem.value-oldmem.value redo_log_space_requests
from
   dba_hist_sysstat oldmem,
   dba_hist_sysstat newmem,
   dba_hist_snapshot    sn
where
   sn.snap_id = (select max(snap_id) from dba_hist_snapshot)
--and
--   newmem.value-oldmem.value > 30
and newmem.snap_id = sn.snap_id
and oldmem.snap_id = sn.snap_id-1
and oldmem.stat_name = 'redo log space requests'
and newmem.stat_name = 'redo log space requests'
and newmem.value-oldmem.value > 0
;

prompt ***********************************************************
prompt   Table fetch continued row indicates chained rows, or
prompt   fetches of long datatypes (long raw, blob)
prompt
prompt   Investigate increasing db_block_size or reorganizing tables
prompt   with chained rows.
prompt
prompt ***********************************************************

column table_fetch_continued_row  format 999,999,999

select
   to_char(sn.end_interval_time,'dd Mon HH24:mi:ss') mydate,
   avg(newmem.value-oldmem.value) table_fetch_continued_row
from
```

```
   dba_hist_sysstat oldmem,
   dba_hist_sysstat newmem,
   dba_hist_snapshot    sn
where
   sn.snap_id = (select max(snap_id) from dba_hist_snapshot)
and newmem.snap_id = sn.snap_id
and oldmem.snap_id = sn.snap_id-1
and oldmem.stat_name = 'table fetch continued row'
and newmem.stat_name = 'table fetch continued row'
--and
--    newmem.value-oldmem.value > 0
--having
--    avg(newmem.value-oldmem.value) > 10000
group by
   to_char(sn.end_interval_time,'dd Mon HH24:mi:ss')
;

prompt ***********************************************************
prompt   Enqueue Deadlocks indicate contention within the Oracle
prompt   shared pool.
prompt
prompt   Investigate increasing shared_pool_size
prompt ***********************************************************

column enqueue_deadlocks       format 999,999,999

select
   to_char(sn.end_interval_time,'dd Mon HH24:mi:ss') mydate,
   a.value enqueue_deadlocks
from
   dba_hist_sysstat       a,
   dba_hist_snapshot    sn
where
   sn.snap_id = (select max(snap_id) from dba_hist_snapshot)
and a.snap_id = sn.snap_id
and a.stat_name = 'enqueue deadlocks'
;

prompt ***********************************************************
prompt   Long-table full table scans can indicate a need to:
prompt
prompt          - Make the offending tables parallel query
prompt            (alter table xxx parallel degree yyy;)
prompt          - Place the table in the RECYCLE pool
prompt          - Build an index on the table to remove the FTS
prompt
prompt To locate the table, run access.sql
prompt
prompt ***********************************************************

column fts  format 999,999,999

select
   to_char(sn.end_interval_time,'dd Mon HH24:mi:ss') mydate,
   newmem.value-oldmem.value fts
from
   dba_hist_sysstat oldmem,
```

```
    dba_hist_sysstat newmem,
    dba_hist_snapshot    sn
where
  sn.snap_id = (select max(snap_id) from dba_hist_snapshot)
and newmem.snap_id = sn.snap_id
and oldmem.snap_id = sn.snap_id-1
and oldmem.stat_name = 'table scans (long tables)'
and newmem.stat_name = 'table scans (long tables)'
;

spool off;
```

The following is a similar script that was designed for the Oracle9i version:

💾 oracle9i_quick.ksh

```
-- ****************************************************
-- Copyright © 2005 by Rampant TechPress
-- This script is free for non-commercial purposes
-- with no warranties.  Use at your own risk.
--
-- To license this script for a commercial purpose,
-- contact info@rampant.cc
-- ****************************************************

#!/bin/ksh

# First, we must set the environment . . . .
ORACLE_SID=$ORACLE_SID
export ORACLE_SID
ORACLE_HOME=`cat /etc/oratab|grep ^$ORACLE_SID:|cut -f2 -d':'`
export ORACLE_HOME
PATH=$ORACLE_HOME/bin:$PATH
export PATH

echo "Please enter the number of seconds between snapshots."
read elapsed

$ORACLE_HOME/bin/sqlplus -s perfstat/perfstat<<!
execute statspack.snap;
exit
!

sleep $elapsed

$ORACLE_HOME/bin/sqlplus -s perfstat/perfstat<<!
execute statspack.snap;

select
   name,
   snap_id,
   to_char(snap_time,' dd Mon YYYY HH24:mi:ss')
```

```
from
   stats\$snapshot,
   v\$database
where
   snap_id > (select max(snap_id)-2 from stats\$snapshot)
;
```

Here is the SQL script invoked by *quick.ksh*. Again, the script can easily be modified to make it work against Oracle 10g AWR tables.

💾 oracle9i_rpt_last.sql

```
-- **************************************************
-- Copyright © 2005 by Rampant TechPress
-- This script is free for non-commercial purposes
-- with no warranties.  Use at your own risk.
--
-- To license this script for a commercial purpose,
-- contact info@rampant.cc
-- **************************************************

spool rpt_last.lst

set pages 9999;
set feedback on;
set verify off;

column reads  format 999,999,999
column writes format 999,999,999

select
   to_char(snap_time,'yyyy-mm-dd HH24'),
   (newreads.value-oldreads.value) reads,
   (newwrites.value-oldwrites.value) writes
from
   perfstat.stats$sysstat oldreads,
   perfstat.stats$sysstat newreads,
   perfstat.stats$sysstat oldwrites,
   perfstat.stats$sysstat newwrites,
   perfstat.stats$snapshot   sn
where
   newreads.snap_id = (select max(sn.snap_id) from stats$snapshot)
and newwrites.snap_id = (select max(sn.snap_id) from stats$snapshot)
and oldreads.snap_id = sn.snap_id-1
and oldwrites.snap_id = sn.snap_id-1
and oldreads.statistic# = 40
and newreads.statistic# = 40
and oldwrites.statistic# = 41
and newwrites.statistic# = 41
;

prompt ****************************************************************
prompt  This will identify any single file who's read I/O
```

```
prompt  is more than 10% of the total read I/O of the database.
prompt
prompt  The "hot" file should be examined, and the hot table/index
prompt  should be identified using STATSPACK.
prompt
prompt  - The busy file should be placed on a disk device with
prompt    "less busy" files to minimize read delay and channel
prompt    contention.
prompt
prompt  - If small file has a hot small table, place the table
prompt    in the KEEP pool
prompt
prompt  - If the file has a large-table full-table scan, place
prompt    the table in the RECYCLE pool and turn on parallel query
prompt    for the table.
prompt  **************************************************************

column mydate     format a16
column file_name  format a40
column reads      format 999,999,999

select
   to_char(snap_time,'yyyy-mm-dd HH24')  mydate,
   new.filename                          file_name,
   new.phyrds-old.phyrds                 reads
from
   perfstat.stats$filestatxs old,
   perfstat.stats$filestatxs new,
   perfstat.stats$snapshot    sn
where
   sn.snap_id = (select max(snap_id) from stats$snapshot)
and new.snap_id = sn.snap_id
and old.snap_id = sn.snap_id-1
and new.filename = old.filename
--and
--   new.phyrds-old.phyrds > 10000
and
   (new.phyrds-old.phyrds)*10 >
(
select
   (newreads.value-oldreads.value) reads
from
   perfstat.stats$sysstat oldreads,
   perfstat.stats$sysstat newreads,
   perfstat.stats$snapshot    sn1
where
   sn.snap_id = sn1.snap_id
and newreads.snap_id = sn.snap_id
and oldreads.snap_id = sn.snap_id-1
and oldreads.statistic# = 40
and newreads.statistic# = 40
and (newreads.value-oldreads.value) > 0
)
;

prompt  **************************************************************
prompt  This will identify any single file who's write I/O
```

```
prompt  is more than 10% of the total write I/O of the database.
prompt
prompt  The "hot" file should be examined, and the hot table/index
prompt  should be identified using STATSPACK.
prompt
prompt  - The busy file should be placed on a disk device with
prompt    "less busy" files to minimize write delay and channel
prompt    channel contention.
prompt
prompt  - If small file has a hot small table, place the table
prompt    in the KEEP pool
prompt
prompt  ************************************************************

column mydate format a16
column file_name format a40
column writes  format 999,999,999

select
   to_char(snap_time,'yyyy-mm-dd HH24')  mydate,
   new.filename                          file_name,
   new.phywrts-old.phywrts               writes
from
   perfstat.stats$filestatxs old,
   perfstat.stats$filestatxs new,
   perfstat.stats$snapshot    sn
where
   sn.snap_id = (select max(snap_id) from stats$snapshot)
and new.snap_id = sn.snap_id
and old.snap_id = sn.snap_id-1
and new.filename = old.filename
--and
----   new.phywrts-old.phywrts > 10000
and
   (new.phywrts-old.phywrts)*10 >
(
select
   (newwrites.value-oldwrites.value) writes
from
   perfstat.stats$sysstat oldwrites,
   perfstat.stats$sysstat newwrites,
   perfstat.stats$snapshot    sn1
where
   sn.snap id = sn1.snap id
and newwrites.snap_id = sn.snap_id
and oldwrites.snap_id = sn.snap_id-1
and oldwrites.statistic# = 40
and newwrites.statistic# = 40
and (newwrites.value-oldwrites.value) > 0
)
;

prompt  ************************************************************
prompt  When the data buffer hit ratio falls below 90%, you
prompt  should consider adding to the db_block_buffer init.ora
parameter
prompt  ************************************************************
```

```
column logical_reads   format 999,999,999
column phys_reads      format 999,999,999
column phys_writes     format 999,999,999
column "BUFFER HIT RATIO" format 999

select
   to_char(snap_time,'dd Mon HH24:mi:ss') mydate,
   d.value              "phys_writes",
   round(100 * (((a.value-e.value)+(b.value-f.value))-(c.value-
g.value)) / ((a.value-e.value)+(b.value-f.value)))
        "BUFFER HIT RATIO"
from
   perfstat.stats$sysstat a,
   perfstat.stats$sysstat b,
   perfstat.stats$sysstat c,
   perfstat.stats$sysstat d,
   perfstat.stats$sysstat e,
   perfstat.stats$sysstat f,
   perfstat.stats$sysstat g,
   perfstat.stats$snapshot   sn
where
--   (round(100 * (((a.value-e.value)+(b.value-f.value))-(c.value-
g.value)) / ((a.value-e.value)+(b.value-f.value)))  ) < 90
--and
   sn.snap_id = (select max(snap_id) from stats$snapshot)
and a.snap_id = sn.snap_id
and b.snap_id = sn.snap_id
and c.snap_id = sn.snap_id
and d.snap_id = sn.snap_id
and e.snap_id = sn.snap_id-1
and f.snap_id = sn.snap_id-1
and g.snap_id = sn.snap_id-1
and a.statistic# = 39
and e.statistic# = 39
and b.statistic# = 38
and f.statistic# = 38
and c.statistic# = 40
and g.statistic# = 40
and d.statistic# = 41
;

column mydate heading 'Yr.  Mo Dy  Hr.' format a16
column reloads       format 999,999,999
column hit_ratio     format 999.99
column pin_hit_ratio format 999.99

break on mydate skip 2;

select
   to_char(snap_time,'yyyy-mm-dd HH24')  mydate,
   new.namespace,
   (new.gethits-old.gethits)/(new.gets-old.gets) hit_ratio,
   (new.pinhits-old.pinhits)/(new.pins-old.pins) pin_hit_ratio,
   new.reloads
from
   stats$librarycache old,
```

```
     stats$librarycache new,
     stats$snapshot       sn
where
   new.snap_id = sn.snap_id
and old.snap_id = new.snap_id-1
and old.namespace = new.namespace
and new.gets-old.gets > 0
and new.pins-old.pins > 0
;

prompt ***************************************************************
prompt   When there are high disk sorts, you should investigate
prompt   increasing sort_area_size, or adding indexes to force
index_full scans
prompt ***************************************************************

column sorts_memory  format 999,999,999
column sorts_disk    format 999,999,999
column ratio format .9999999999999

select
   to_char(snap_time,'dd Mon HH24:mi:ss') mydate,
   newmem.value-oldmem.value sorts_memory,
   newdsk.value-olddsk.value sorts_disk,
   (newdsk.value-olddsk.value)/(newmem.value-oldmem.value) ratio
from
   perfstat.stats$sysstat oldmem,
   perfstat.stats$sysstat newmem,
   perfstat.stats$sysstat newdsk,
   perfstat.stats$sysstat olddsk,
   perfstat.stats$snapshot   sn
where
   -- Where there are more than 100 disk sorts per hour
--    newdsk.value-olddsk.value > 100
--and
   sn.snap_id = (select max(snap_id) from stats$snapshot)
and newdsk.snap_id = sn.snap_id
and olddsk.snap_id = sn.snap_id-1
and newmem.snap_id = sn.snap_id
and oldmem.snap_id = sn.snap_id-1
and oldmem.name = 'sorts (memory)'
and newmem.name = 'sorts (memory)'
and olddsk.name = 'sorts (disk)'
and newdsk.name = 'sorts (disk)'
and newmem.value-oldmem.value > 0
;

prompt ***************************************************************
prompt   When there is high I/O waits, disk bottlenecks may exist
prompt   Run iostats to find the hot disk and shuffle files to
prompt   remove the contention
prompt
prompt   See p. 191 "High Performance Oracle8 Tuning" by Don Burleson
prompt
prompt ***************************************************************

break on snapdate skip 2
```

```
column snapdate format a16
column filename format a40

select
   to_char(snap_time,'dd Mon HH24:mi:ss') mydate,
   old.filename,
   new.wait_count-old.wait_count waits
from
   perfstat.stats$filestatxs old,
   perfstat.stats$filestatxs new,
   perfstat.stats$snapshot    sn
where
   sn.snap_id = (select max(snap_id) from stats$snapshot)
and new.wait_count-old.wait_count > 0
and new.snap_id = sn.snap_id
and old.filename = new.filename
and old.snap_id = sn.snap_id-1
;

prompt ***********************************************************
prompt  Buffer Bury Waits may signal a high update table with too
prompt  few freelists.  Find the offending table and add more
freelists.
prompt ***********************************************************

column buffer_busy_wait format 999,999,999

select
   to_char(snap_time,'dd Mon HH24:mi:ss') mydate,
   avg(new.buffer_busy_wait-old.buffer_busy_wait) buffer_busy_wait
from
   perfstat.stats$buffer_pool_statistics old,
   perfstat.stats$buffer_pool_statistics new,
   perfstat.stats$snapshot    sn
where
   sn.snap_id = (select max(snap_id) from stats$snapshot)
and new.snap_id = sn.snap_id
and new.snap_id = sn.snap_id
and old.snap_id = sn.snap_id-1
--having
--   avg(new.buffer_busy_wait-old.buffer_busy_wait) > 100
group by
   to_char(snap_time,'dd Mon HH24:mi:ss')
;

prompt ***********************************************************
prompt  High redo log space requests indicate a need to increase
prompt  the log_buffer parameter
prompt ***********************************************************

column redo_log_space_requests  format 999,999,999

select
   to_char(snap_time,'dd Mon HH24:mi:ss') mydate,
   newmem.value-oldmem.value redo_log_space_requests
from
```

```
   perfstat.stats$sysstat oldmem,
   perfstat.stats$sysstat newmem,
   perfstat.stats$snapshot   sn
where
   sn.snap_id = (select max(snap_id) from stats$snapshot)
--and
--   newmem.value-oldmem.value > 30
and newmem.snap_id = sn.snap_id
and oldmem.snap_id = sn.snap_id-1
and oldmem.name = 'redo log space requests'
and newmem.name = 'redo log space requests'
and newmem.value-oldmem.value > 0
;

prompt ***********************************************************
prompt  Table fetch continued row indicates chained rows, or
prompt  fetches of long datatypes (long raw, blob)
prompt
prompt  Investigate increasing db_block_size or reorganizing tables
prompt  with chained rows.
prompt
prompt ***********************************************************

column table_fetch_continued_row  format 999,999,999

select
   to_char(snap_time,'dd Mon HH24:mi:ss') mydate,
   avg(newmem.value-oldmem.value) table_fetch_continued_row
from
   perfstat.stats$sysstat oldmem,
   perfstat.stats$sysstat newmem,
   perfstat.stats$snapshot   sn
where
   sn.snap_id = (select max(snap_id) from stats$snapshot)
and newmem.snap_id = sn.snap_id
and oldmem.snap_id = sn.snap_id-1
and oldmem.name = 'table fetch continued row'
and newmem.name = 'table fetch continued row'
--and
--   newmem.value-oldmem.value > 0
--having
--   avg(newmem.value-oldmem.value) > 10000
group by
   to_char(snap_time,'dd Mon HH24:mi:ss')
;

prompt ***********************************************************
prompt  Enqueue Deadlocks indicate contention within the Oracle
prompt  shared pool.
prompt
prompt  Investigate increasing shared_pool_size
prompt ***********************************************************

column enqueue_deadlocks      format 999,999,999

select
   to_char(snap_time,'dd Mon HH24:mi:ss') mydate,
```

```
   a.value enqueue_deadlocks
from
   perfstat.stats$sysstat      a,
   perfstat.stats$snapshot    sn
where
   sn.snap_id = (select max(snap_id) from stats$snapshot)
and a.snap_id = sn.snap_id
and a.statistic# = 24
;

prompt  ***************************************************************
prompt  Long-table full table scans can indicate a need to:
prompt
prompt          - Make the offending tables parallel query
prompt            (alter table xxx parallel degree yyy;)
prompt          - Place the table in the RECYCLE pool
prompt          - Build an index on the table to remove the FTS
prompt
prompt To locate the table, run access.sql
prompt
prompt  ***************************************************************

column fts   format 999,999,999

select
   to_char(snap_time,'dd Mon HH24:mi:ss') mydate,
   newmem.value-oldmem.value fts
from
   perfstat.stats$sysstat oldmem,
   perfstat.stats$sysstat newmem,
   perfstat.stats$snapshot    sn
where
   sn.snap_id = (select max(snap_id) from stats$snapshot)
and newmem.snap_id = sn.snap_id
and oldmem.snap_id = sn.snap_id-1
and oldmem.statistic# = 140
and newmem.statistic# = 140
;

spool off;
```

💾 oracle10g_rpt_last.sql

```
-- ***************************************************
-- Copyright © 2005 by Rampant TechPress
-- This script is free for non-commercial purposes
-- with no warranties.  Use at your own risk.
--
-- To license this script for a commercial purpose,
-- contact info@rampant.cc
-- ***************************************************

spool rpt_last.lst

set pages 9999;
set feedback on;
set verify off;

column reads   format 999,999,999
column writes  format 999,999,999

select
   to_char(sn.end_interval_time,'yyyy-mm-dd HH24'),
   (newreads.value-oldreads.value) reads,
   (newwrites.value-oldwrites.value) writes
from
   dba_hist_sysstat oldreads,
   dba_hist_sysstat newreads,
   dba_hist_sysstat oldwrites,
   dba_hist_sysstat newwrites,
   dba_hist_snapshot    sn
where
   newreads.snap_id = (select max(sn.snap_id)
      from dba_hist_snapshot)
   and newwrites.snap_id = (select max(sn.snap_id)
      from dba_hist_snapshot)
   and oldreads.snap_id = sn.snap_id-1
   and oldwrites.snap_id = sn.snap_id-1
   and oldreads.stat_name = 'physical reads'
   and newreads.stat_name = 'physical reads'
   and oldwrites.stat_name = 'physical writes'
   and newwrites.stat_name = 'physical writes'
;

prompt **********************************************************
prompt  This will identify any single file who's read I/O
prompt  is more than 10% of the total read I/O of the database.
prompt
prompt  The "hot" file should be examined, and the hot table/index
prompt  should be identified using STATSPACK.
prompt
prompt  - The busy file should be placed on a disk device with
prompt    "less busy" files to minimize read delay and channel
prompt    contention.
prompt
prompt  - If small file has a hot small table, place the table
prompt    in the KEEP pool
```

```
prompt
prompt    - If the file has a large-table full-table scan, place
prompt      the table in the RECYCLE pool and turn on parallel query
prompt      for the table.
prompt    *************************************************************

column mydate    format a16
column file_name format a40
column reads     format 999,999,999

select
   to_char(sn.end_interval_time,'yyyy-mm-dd HH24')   mydate,
   new.filename                          file_name,
   new.phyrds-old.phyrds                 reads
from
   dba_hist_filestatxs  old,
   dba_hist_filestatxs  new,
   dba_hist_snapshot    sn
where
   sn.snap_id = (select max(snap_id) from dba_hist_snapshot)
and new.snap_id = sn.snap_id
and old.snap_id = sn.snap_id-1
and new.filename = old.filename
--and
--   new.phyrds-old.phyrds > 10000
and (new.phyrds-old.phyrds)*10 >
(select(newreads.value-oldreads.value) reads
from
   dba_hist_sysstat oldreads,
   dba_hist_sysstat newreads,
   dba_hist_snapshot    sn1
where
   sn.snap_id = sn1.snap_id
and newreads.snap_id = sn.snap_id
and oldreads.snap_id = sn.snap_id-1
and oldreads.stat_name = 'physical reads'
and newreads.stat_name = 'physical reads'
and (newreads.value-oldreads.value) > 0)
;

prompt    *************************************************************
prompt    This will identify any single file who's write I/O
prompt    is more than 10% of the total write I/O of the database.
prompt
prompt    The "hot" file should be examined, and the hot table/index
prompt    should be identified using STATSPACK.
prompt
prompt    - The busy file should be placed on a disk device with
prompt      "less busy" files to minimize write delay and channel
prompt      channel contention.
prompt
prompt    - If small file has a hot small table, place the table
prompt      in the KEEP pool
prompt
prompt    *************************************************************

column mydate    format a16
```

```
column file_name format a40
column writes   format 999,999,999

select
   to_char(sn.end_interval_time,'yyyy-mm-dd HH24')   mydate,
   new.filename                              file_name,
   new.phywrts-old.phywrts                   writes
from
   dba_hist_filestatxs old,
   dba_hist_filestatxs new,
   dba_hist_snapshot    sn
where
   sn.snap_id = (select max(snap_id) from dba_hist_snapshot)
and new.snap_id = sn.snap_id
and old.snap_id = sn.snap_id-1
and new.filename = old.filename
--and
----    new.phywrts-old.phywrts > 10000
and (new.phywrts-old.phywrts)*10 >
(select (newwrites.value-oldwrites.value) writes
from
   dba_hist_sysstat oldwrites,
   dba_hist_sysstat newwrites,
   dba_hist_snapshot    sn1
where
   sn.snap_id = sn1.snap_id
and newwrites.snap_id = sn.snap_id
and oldwrites.snap_id = sn.snap_id-1
and oldwrites.stat_name = 'physical writes'
and newwrites.stat_name = 'physical writes'
and (newwrites.value-oldwrites.value) > 0)
;

prompt **************************************************************
prompt  When the data buffer hit ratio falls below 90%, you
prompt  should consider adding to the db_block_buffer init.ora
parameter
prompt **************************************************************

column logical_reads  format 999,999,999
column phys_reads     format 999,999,999
column phys_writes    format 999,999,999
column "BUFFER HIT RATIO" format 999

select
   to_char(sn.end_interval_time,'dd Mon HH24:mi:ss') mydate,
   d.value          "phys_writes",
   round(100 * (((a.value-e.value)+(b.value-f.value))-(c.value-
g.value)) /
((a.value-e.value)+(b.value-f.value)))
        "BUFFER HIT RATIO"
from
   dba_hist_sysstat a,
   dba_hist_sysstat b,
   dba_hist_sysstat c,
   dba_hist_sysstat d,
   dba_hist_sysstat e,
```

```
   dba_hist_sysstat f,
   dba_hist_sysstat g,
   dba_hist_snapshot    sn
where
--    (round(100 * (((a.value-e.value)+(b.value-f.value))-(c.value-
g.value))
--/ ((a.value-e.value)+(b.value-f.value)))  ) < 90
--and
   sn.snap_id = (select max(snap_id) from dba_hist_snapshot)
and a.snap_id = sn.snap_id
and b.snap_id = sn.snap_id
and c.snap_id = sn.snap_id
and d.snap_id = sn.snap_id
and e.snap_id = sn.snap_id-1
and f.snap_id = sn.snap_id-1
and g.snap_id = sn.snap_id-1
and a.stat_name = 'consistent gets'
and e.stat_name = 'consistent gets'
and b.stat_name = 'db block gets'
and f.stat_name = 'db block gets'
and c.stat_name = 'physical reads'
and g.stat_name = 'physical reads'
and d.stat_name = 'physical writes'
;

column mydate heading 'Yr.  Mo Dy  Hr.' format a16
column reloads        format 999,999,999
column hit_ratio      format 999.99
column pin_hit_ratio format 999.99

break on mydate skip 2;

select
   to_char(sn.end_interval_time,'yyyy-mm-dd HH24')  mydate,
   new.namespace,
   (new.gethits-old.gethits)/(new.gets-old.gets) hit_ratio,
   (new.pinhits-old.pinhits)/(new.pins-old.pins) pin_hit_ratio,
   new.reloads
from
   dba_hist_librarycache old,
   dba_hist_librarycache new,
   dba_hist_snapshot      sn
where
   new.snap_id = sn.snap_id
and old.snap_id = new.snap_id-1
and old.namespace = new.namespace
and new.gets-old.gets > 0
and new.pins-old.pins > 0
;

prompt *************************************************************
prompt  When there are high disk sorts, you should investigate
prompt  increasing sort_area_size, or adding indexes to force
index_full scans
prompt *************************************************************

column sorts_memory  format 999,999,999
```

```
column sorts_disk    format 999,999,999
column ratio format .9999999999999

select
   to_char(sn.end_interval_time,'dd Mon HH24:mi:ss') mydate,
   newmem.value-oldmem.value sorts_memory,
   newdsk.value-olddsk.value sorts_disk,
   (newdsk.value-olddsk.value)/(newmem.value-oldmem.value) ratio
from
   dba_hist_sysstat oldmem,
   dba_hist_sysstat newmem,
   dba_hist_sysstat newdsk,
   dba_hist_sysstat olddsk,
   dba_hist_snapshot   sn
where
   -- Where there are more than 100 disk sorts per hour
--    newdsk.value-olddsk.value > 100
--and
   sn.snap_id = (select max(snap_id) from dba_hist_snapshot)
and newdsk.snap_id = sn.snap_id
and olddsk.snap_id = sn.snap_id-1
and newmem.snap_id = sn.snap_id
and oldmem.snap_id = sn.snap_id-1
and oldmem.stat_name = 'sorts (memory)'
and newmem.stat_name = 'sorts (memory)'
and olddsk.stat_name = 'sorts (disk)'
and newdsk.stat_name = 'sorts (disk)'
and newmem.value-oldmem.value > 0
;

prompt ************************************************************
prompt  When there is high I/O waits, disk bottlenecks may exist
prompt  Run iostats to find the hot disk and shuffle files to
prompt  remove the contention
prompt
prompt  See p. 191 "High Performance Oracle8 Tuning" by Don Burleson
prompt
prompt ************************************************************

break on snapdate skip 2

column snapdate format a16
column filename format a40

select
   to_char(sn.end_interval_time,'dd Mon HH24:mi:ss') mydate,
   old.filename,
   new.wait_count-old.wait_count waits
from
   dba_hist_filestatxs old,
   dba_hist_filestatxs new,
   dba_hist_snapshot   sn
where
   sn.snap_id = (select max(snap_id) from dba_hist_snapshot)
and new.wait_count-old.wait_count > 0
and new.snap_id = sn.snap_id
and old.filename = new.filename
```

```
and old.snap_id = sn.snap_id-1
;

prompt ***************************************************************
prompt  Buffer Bury Waits may signal a high update table with too
prompt  few freelists.  Find the offending table and add more
freelists.
prompt ***************************************************************

column buffer_busy_wait format 999,999,999

select
   to_char(sn.end_interval_time,'dd Mon HH24:mi:ss') mydate,
   avg(new.buffer_busy_wait-old.buffer_busy_wait) buffer_busy_wait
from
   dba_hist_buffer_pool_stat old,
   dba_hist_buffer_pool_stat new,
   dba_hist_snapshot    sn
where
   sn.snap_id = (select max(snap_id) from dba_hist_snapshot)
and new.snap_id = sn.snap_id
and new.snap_id = sn.snap_id
and old.snap_id = sn.snap_id-1
--having
--   avg(new.buffer_busy_wait-old.buffer_busy_wait) > 100
group by
   to_char(sn.end_interval_time,'dd Mon HH24:mi:ss')
;

prompt ***************************************************************
prompt  High redo log space requests indicate a need to increase
prompt  the log_buffer parameter
prompt ***************************************************************

column redo_log_space_requests  format 999,999,999

select
   to_char(sn.end_interval_time,'dd Mon HH24:mi:ss') mydate,
   newmem.value-oldmem.value redo_log_space_requests
from
   dba_hist_sysstat oldmem,
   dba_hist_sysstat newmem,
   dba_hist_snapshot    sn
where
   sn.snap_id = (select max(snap_id) from dba_hist_snapshot)
--and
--   newmem.value-oldmem.value > 30
and newmem.snap_id = sn.snap_id
and oldmem.snap_id = sn.snap_id-1
and oldmem.stat_name = 'redo log space requests'
and newmem.stat_name = 'redo log space requests'
and newmem.value-oldmem.value > 0
;

prompt ***************************************************************
prompt  Table fetch continued row indicates chained rows, or fetches
of
```

```
prompt   long datatypes (long raw, blob)
prompt
prompt   Investigate increasing db_block_size or reorganizing tables
prompt   with chained rows.
prompt
prompt   ************************************************************

column table_fetch_continued_row  format 999,999,999

select
   to_char(sn.end_interval_time,'dd Mon HH24:mi:ss') mydate,
   avg(newmem.value-oldmem.value) table_fetch_continued_row
from
   dba_hist_sysstat oldmem,
   dba_hist_sysstat newmem,
   dba_hist_snapshot    sn
where
   sn.snap_id = (select max(snap_id) from dba_hist_snapshot)
and newmem.snap_id = sn.snap_id
and oldmem.snap_id = sn.snap_id-1
and oldmem.stat_name = 'table fetch continued row'
and newmem.stat_name = 'table fetch continued row'
--and
--    newmem.value-oldmem.value > 0
--having
--    avg(newmem.value-oldmem.value) > 10000
group by
   to_char(sn.end_interval_time,'dd Mon HH24:mi:ss')
;

prompt   ************************************************************
prompt   Enqueue Deadlocks indicate contention within the Oracle
prompt   shared pool.
prompt
prompt   Investigate increasing shared_pool_size
prompt   ************************************************************

column enqueue_deadlocks       format 999,999,999

select
   to_char(sn.end_interval_time,'dd Mon HH24:mi:ss') mydate,
   a.value enqueue_deadlocks
from
   dba_hist_sysstat      a,
   dba_hist_snapshot    sn
where
   sn.snap_id = (select max(snap_id) from dba_hist_snapshot)
and a.snap_id = sn.snap_id
and a.stat_name = 'enqueue deadlocks'
;

prompt   ************************************************************
prompt   Long-table full table scans can indicate a need to:
prompt
prompt           - Make the offending tables parallel query
prompt             (alter table xxx parallel degree yyy;)
prompt           - Place the table in the RECYCLE pool
```

```
prompt             - Build an index on the table to remove the FTS
prompt
prompt To locate the table, run access.sql
prompt
prompt ************************************************************

column fts  format 999,999,999

select
   to_char(sn.end_interval_time,'dd Mon HH24:mi:ss') mydate,
   newmem.value-oldmem.value fts
from
   dba_hist_sysstat oldmem,
   dba_hist_sysstat newmem,
   dba_hist_snapshot    sn
where
  sn.snap_id = (select max(snap_id) from dba_hist_snapshot)
and newmem.snap_id = sn.snap_id
and oldmem.snap_id = sn.snap_id-1
and oldmem.stat_name = 'table scans (long tables)'
and newmem.stat_name = 'table scans (long tables)'
;

spool off;
```

Building on the information on how to capture performance metrics, the following section will provide some details about the shared pool.

Rules for adjusting *shared_pool_size*

From Oracle8 onward, there are several queries used for determining when the Oracle shared pool is too small. The *library cache miss ratio* tells the DBA whether to add space to the shared pool, and it represents the ratio of the sum of library cache reloads to the sum of pins.

In general, if the library cache miss ratio is greater than one, the DBA should consider adding to the *shared_pool_size*. Library cache misses occur during the parsing and preparation of the execution plans for SQL statements.

The compilation of an SQL statement consists of two phases: the parse phase and the execute phase. When the time comes to parse an SQL statement, Oracle checks to see if the parsed representation of the statement already exists in the library cache. If not, Oracle will

---

Time-Series Tuning Guidelines

allocate a shared SQL area within the library cache and then parse the SQL statement. At execution time, Oracle checks to see if a parsed representation of the SQL statement already exists in the library cache. If not, Oracle will reparse and execute the statement.

The following script will compute the library cache miss ratio. The script sums all of the values for the individual components within the library cache and provides an instance-wide view of the health of the library cache.

```
set lines 80;
set pages 999;

column mydate heading 'Yr.  Mo Dy  Hr.'           format a16
column c1 heading "execs"                         format 9,999,999
column c2 heading "Cache Misses|While Executing"  format 9,999,999
column c3 heading "Library Cache|Miss Ratio"      format 999.99999

break on mydate skip 2;

select
   to_char(snap_time,'yyyy-mm-dd HH24')   mydate,
   sum(new.pins-old.pins)                 c1,
   sum(new.reloads-old.reloads)           c2,
   sum(new.reloads-old.reloads)/
   sum(new.pins-old.pins)                 library_cache_miss_ratio
from
   stats$librarycache old,
   stats$librarycache new,
   stats$snapshot      sn
where
   new.snap_id = sn.snap_id
and old.snap_id = new.snap_id-1
and old.namespace = new.namespace
group by
   to_char(snap_time,'yyyy-mm-dd HH24')
;
```

The following is the 10g version of the script:

```
set lines 80;
set pages 999;

column mydate heading 'Yr.  Mo Dy  Hr.'            format a16
column c1 heading "execs"                          format 9,999,999
column c2 heading "Cache Misses|While Executing"   format 9,999,999
column c3 heading "Library Cache|Miss Ratio"       format 999.99999

break on mydate skip 2;

select
   to_char(sn.end_interval_time,'yyyy-mm-dd HH24')  mydate,
   sum(new.pins-old.pins)              c1,
   sum(new.reloads-old.reloads)        c2,
   sum(new.reloads-old.reloads)/
   sum(new.pins-old.pins)              library_cache_miss_ratio
from
   dba_hist_librarycache old,
   dba_hist_librarycache new,
   dba_hist_snapshot      sn
where
   new.snap_id = sn.snap_id
and old.snap_id = new.snap_id-1
and old.namespace = new.namespace
group by
   to_char(sn.end_interval_time,'yyyy-mm-dd HH24')
;
```

The output is shown below. This report can easily be customized to alert the DBA when there are excessive executions or library cache misses.

```
                     Cache Misses   Library Cache
Yr.  Mo Dy  Hr.        execs  While Executing   Miss Ratio
---------------    ----------  ---------------   ----------------------
2001-12-11 10          10,338        3                 .00029
2001-12-12 10         182,477      134                 .00073
2001-12-14 10         190,707      202                 .00106
2001-12-16 10           2,803       11                 .00392
```

Once this report identifies a time period where there may be a problem, STATSPACK provides the ability to run detailed reports to show the behavior of the objects within the library cache.

In the preceding example, there is clearly a RAM shortage in the shared pool between 10:00 a.m. and 11:00 a.m. each day. In this case, the shared pool could be reconfigured dynamically with additional RAM memory from the *db_cache_size* during this period.

Sizing the Shared Pool with the New Advisory Utility

Oracle9i release 2 included a new advice called *v$shared_pool_advice*, and there is talk of expanding the advice facility to all SGA RAM areas in future releases of Oracle. It is also included in the standard AWR reports, $ORACLE_HOME/rdbms/admin/awrrpt.sql.

Starting in Oracle9i release 2, the *v$shared_pool_advice* view shows the marginal difference in SQL parses as the shared pool changes in size from 10% of the current value to 200% of the current value.

The Oracle documentation contains a complete description for the set-up and use of shared pool advice, and it is very simple to configure. Once it is installed, a simple script can be run to query the *v$shared_pool_advice* view and locate the marginal changes in SQL parses for different *shared_pool* sizes.

```
set lines   100
set pages   999

column      c1      heading 'Pool |Size(M)'
column      c2      heading 'Size|Factor'
column      c3      heading 'Est|LC(M)  '
column      c4      heading 'Est LC|Mem. Obj.'
column      c5      heading 'Est|Time|Saved|(sec)'
column      c6      heading 'Est|Parse|Saved|Factor'
column      c7      heading 'Est|Object Hits'   format 999,999,999

SELECT
   shared_pool_size_for_estimate    c1,
   shared_pool_size_factor          c2,
   estd_lc_size                     c3,
   estd_lc_memory_objects           c4,
   estd_lc_time_saved               c5,
   estd_lc_time_saved_factor        c6,
   estd_lc_memory_object_hits       c7
FROM
   v$shared_pool_advice;
```

The following is a sample of the output:

Pool Size(M)	Size Factor	Est LC(M)	Est LC Mem. Obj.	Est Time Saved (sec)	Est Parse Saved Factor	Est Object Hits
48	.5	48	20839	1459645	1	135,756,032
64	.6667	63	28140	1459645	1	135,756,101
80	.8333	78	35447	1459645	1	135,756,149
96	1	93	43028	1459645	1	135,756,253
112	1.1667	100	46755	1459646	1	135,756,842
128	1.3333	100	46755	1459646	1	135,756,842
144	1.5	100	46755	1459646	1	135,756,842
160	1.6667	100	46755	1459646	1	135,756,842
176	1.8333	100	46755	1459646	1	135,756,842
192	2	100	46755	1459646	1	135,756,842

The statistics for the shared pool in this example fall in a wide range from 50% of the current size to 200% of the current size. These statistics can give a great idea about the proper size for the *shared_pool-size*. If the SGA region sizes are selected automatically with the alter system commands, creating this output and writing a program to interpret the results is a great way to ensure that the shared pool and library cache always have enough RAM.

The next section will provide information on the Program Global Area (PGA) RAM regions.

Rules for adjusting *pga_aggregate_target*

The DBA may wish to consider dynamically changing the *pga_aggregate_target* parameter when any one of the following conditions are true:

- Whenever the value of the *v$sysstat* statistic *estimated PGA memory for one-pass* exceeds *pga_aggregate_target*, the *pga_aggregate_target* should be increased.

- Whenever the value of the *v$sysstat* statistic "*workarea executions – multipass*" is greater than 1 percent, the database may benefit from additional RAM memory.

- It is possible to over-allocate PGA memory, and the DBA might want to consider reducing the value of *pga_aggregate_target* whenever the value of the *v$sysstat* row *workarea executions—optimal* consistently measures 100 percent.

Rules for Adjusting the Data Buffer Sizes

The following report can be used to alert the DBA when the data buffer hit ratio falls below the preset threshold. It is very useful for pinpointing those times when decision support type queries are being run, since a large number of large-table, full-table scans may make the data buffer hit ratio drop. This script also reports on all three data buffers, including the KEEP and RECYCLE pools, and it can be customized to report on individual pools.

The KEEP pool should always have enough data blocks to cache all table rows, while the RECYCLE pool should get a very low buffer hit ratio, since it seldom rereads data blocks. If a low data buffer hit ratio is combined with expressive disk I/O, the DBA may want to increase *db_cache_size* (*db_block_buffers* in Oracle8i and earlier).

```
yr.  mo dy Hr.   Name    bhr
------------ -------- -----
2001-01-27 09 DEFAULT   45
2001-01-28 09 RECYCLE   41
2001-01-29 10 DEFAULT   36
2001-01-30 09 DEFAULT   28
2001-02-02 10 DEFAULT   83
2001-02-02 09 RECYCLE   81
2001-02-03 10 DEFAULT   69
2001-02-03 09 DEFAULT   69
```

These results indicate those times when the DBA might want to dynamically increase the value of the *db_cache_size* parameter. In the case of the preceding output, the *db_cache_size* could be increased each day between 8:00 a.m. and 10:00 a.m., stealing RAM memory from *pga_aggregate_target*.

With Oracle9i came the important ability to dynamically modify almost all of the Oracle parameters. This gives the Oracle professional the ability to dynamically reconfigure the Oracle instance while it is running, whether in reaction to a current performance problem or in anticipation of an impending performance problem.

Since everything within the SGA can now be modified dynamically, it is critical that the Oracle professional understands how to monitor the Oracle database. It is important to learn to recognize trends and patterns with the system and proactively reconfigure the database in anticipation of regularly scheduled resource needs.

With respect to ongoing database tuning activities, the Oracle DBA generally looks at these three areas:

- **Normal scheduled re-configuration**: A bimodal instance that performs OLTP and DSS during regular hours will benefit from a scheduled task to reconfigure the SGA and PGA.

- **Trend-based dynamic reconfiguration**: STATSPACK can be used to predict those times when the processing characteristics change. The *dbms_job* or *dbms_scheduler* packages can be used to fire ad-hoc SGA and PGA changes.

- **Reactive reconfiguration**: Just as Oracle9i dynamically redistributes RAM memory for tasks within the *pga_aggregate_target* region, the Oracle DBA can write scripts that steal RAM from an under-utilized area and reallocate these RAM pages to another RAM area.

Scheduling an SGA Reconfiguration

One of the most common techniques for reconfiguring an Oracle instance is to use a shell script. To illustrate a simple example, consider a database that runs in OLTP mode during the day and data warehouse mode at night. For this type of bi-modal database, the Oracle DBA can schedule a job to reconfigure the instance to the most appropriate configuration for the type of processing that is being done.

Oracle professionals generally use two tools for scheduling a dynamic reconfiguration. The most common approach is to use a UNIX cron job in order to schedule a periodic reconfiguration, while some other Oracle professionals prefer to use the Oracle *dbms_job* (Oracle9i) or *dbms_scheduler* (Oracle10g) utility. Both of these approaches allow the Oracle professional to schedule a reconfiguration.

In the following example there is a UNIX script that can be used to reconfigure Oracle for decision support processing. One must note the important changes to the configuration in the *shared_pool*, *db_cache_size*, and *pga_aggregate_target* in order to accommodate data warehouse activity.

The following script changes Oracle into DSS-mode each evening at 6:00 PM

```
#!/bin/ksh

# First, we must set the environment . . . .
ORACLE_SID=$1
export ORACLE_SID
ORACLE_HOME=`cat /etc/oratab|grep ^$ORACLE_SID:|cut -f2 -d':'`
#ORACLE_HOME=`cat /var/opt/oracle/oratab|grep ^$ORACLE_SID:|cut -f2
-d':'`
export ORACLE_HOME
PATH=$ORACLE_HOME/bin:$PATH
export PATH

$ORACLE_HOME/bin/sqlplus -s /nologin<<!
connect system/manager as sysdba;
alter system set db_cache_size=1500m;
alter system set shared_pool_size=500m;
alter system set pga_aggregate_target=4000m;
exit
!
```

This example shows that writing scripts to reconfigure the SGA is easy. The next section presents information on how to use buffer trend reports from Oracle STATSPACK or AWR to predict those times when the data buffers need additional RAM.

Trend-based Oracle Reconfiguration

A common approach to trend-based reconfiguration is to use historical data to proactively reconfigure the database. A good analogy is just-in-time manufacturing, where parts appear on the plant floor just as they are needed for assembly. Time series tuning enables the DBA to anticipate processing needs and regularly schedule appropriate intervention, insuring that SGA resources are delivered just-in-time for processing tasks.

For those who would like to investigate STATSPACK features and abilities at a deeper level, two informative books are available from Oracle Press:

- *Oracle High-performance Tuning with STATSPACK* - Oracle Press, by Donald K. Burleson.

- *Oracle9i High-performance Tuning with STATSPACK* - Oracle Press, by Donald K. Burleson.

This section will focus on the examination of STATSPACK reports that indicate trends in the behavior of the data buffer pools. Average values for Oracle performance metrics can be generated along two dimensions:

- Averages by day of the week

- Averages by hour of the day

Either of these reports will supply invaluable information for spotting usage trends in the Oracle database. Change occurs in the data buffers rapidly, and sometimes a long-term analysis will provide clues to processing problems within the database. Almost every Oracle database exhibits patterns that are linked to regular processing schedules, called signatures. These signatures allow the DBA to plan long-term solutions based on a database's documented performance over time. Specific details about procedures are presented later in this chapter.

When to Trigger a Dynamic Reconfiguration

The DBA must choose which RAM region to borrow memory from whenever the scripts indicate an overstressed RAM region. Table 2.1 displays the threshold condition for triggering a dynamic memory change.

RAM AREA	OVERSTRESSED CONDITION	OVER-ALLOCATED CONDITION
Shared pool	Library cache misses	No misses
Data buffer cache	Hit ratio < 70%*	Hit ratio > 95%
PGA aggregate	High multi-pass exec	100% optimal executions

Table 2.1: *Threshold Conditions for Dynamic RAM Reallocation*

* The data buffer cache behavior may be meaningless for some applications where data is not re-read frequently.

It is easy to schedule tasks that change the RAM memory configuration as the processing needs change on a UNIX platform. For example, it is common for Oracle databases to operate in OLTP mode during normal work hours and to perform the database services memory-intensive batch reports at night. An OLTP database needs a large *db_cache_size* value. Memory-intensive batch tasks require additional RAM in the *pga_aggregate_target* parameter.

The UNIX scripts given below can be used to reconfigure the SGA between the OLTP and DSS without stopping the instance. The example assumes an isolated Oracle server with 8 Gigabytes of RAM, with 10 percent of RAM reserved for UNIX overhead, leaving 7.2 Gigabytes for Oracle and Oracle connections. The scripts are intended either for HP-UX or Solaris and accept the $ORACLE_SID as an argument.

This script will be run at 6:00 p.m. each evening in order to reconfigure Oracle for the memory-intensive batch tasks.

```ksh
#!/bin/ksh

# First, we must set the environment . . . .
ORACLE_SID=$1
export ORACLE_SID
ORACLE_HOME=`cat /etc/oratab|grep ^$ORACLE_SID:|cut -f2 -d':'`
#ORACLE_HOME=`cat /var/opt/oracle/oratab|grep ^$ORACLE_SID:|cut -f2
-d':'`
export ORACLE_HOME
PATH=$ORACLE_HOME/bin:$PATH
export PATH
```

```
$ORACLE_HOME/bin/sqlplus -s /nologin<<!
connect system/manager as sysdba;
alter system set db_cache_size=1500m;
alter system set shared_pool_size=500m;
alter system set pga_aggregate_target=4000m;
exit
!
```

The script below will be run at 6:00 a.m. each morning to reconfigure Oracle for the OLTP usage during the day.

```
#!/bin/ksh

# First, we must set the environment . . . .
ORACLE_SID=$1
export ORACLE_SID
ORACLE_HOME=`cat /etc/oratab|grep ^$ORACLE_SID:|cut -f2 -d':'`
#ORACLE_HOME=`cat /var/opt/oracle/oratab|grep ^$ORACLE_SID:|cut -f2
-d':'`
export ORACLE_HOME
PATH=$ORACLE_HOME/bin:$PATH
export PATH

$ORACLE_HOME/bin/sqlplus -s /nologin<<!
connect system/manager as sysdba;

alter system set db_cache_size=4000m;
alter system set shared_pool_size=500m;
alter system set pga_aggregate_target=1500m;

exit
!
```

Again, the *dbms_job* or *dbms_scheduler* packages can also be used to schedule the SGA reconfigurations.

It should now be clear that the Oracle database administrator can develop mechanisms to constantly monitor the processing demands on the database and issue the alter system commands to dynamically respond to these conditions.

Approaches to Self-tuning Oracle Databases

The Oracle administrator must adjust the RAM configuration according to the types of connections the database experiences.

Generally, queries against the *v$* structures and STATSPACK will pinpoint those times when Oracle connections change their processing characteristics. There are three approaches to automated tuning:

Normal scheduled reconfiguration -A bimodal instance that performs OLTP and DSS during regular hours will benefit from a scheduled task to reconfigure the SGA and PGA.

Trend-based dynamic reconfiguration - STATSPACK can be used to predict those times when the processing characteristics change and use the *dbms_job* or *dbms_scheduler* packages to fire ad-hoc SGA and PGA changes.

Dynamic reconfiguration -Just as Oracle dynamically redistributes RAM memory for tasks within the *pga_aggregate_target* region, the Oracle DBA can write scripts that take RAM from an under-utilized area and reallocate these RAM pages to another RAM area.

The following section will show how Oracle may evolve to allow super-fast dynamic reconfiguration.

Tuning a constantly changing database

Oracle has recognized that it is impossible to create a one-size-fits-all approach to tuning a database. The database is in a constant state of flux and the ideal tuning approach will react to changes in processing demands, reallocating resources in real-time.

To the small business user, Oracle10g automation regulates data file and storage management, changes the sizes of the SGA regions and REACTIVELY self-tunes performance issues.

But is a reactive approach enough? It is often too late to make changes after the end user has suffered from poor response time. The real goal of Oracle tuning is to anticipate changes in processing and reallocate resources just-in-time.

Can Oracle possess psychic abilities?

Just as the name implies, Oracle can indeed predict the future, sometimes with remarkable accuracy. Instead of relying on mystic or spiritual sources, Oracle can learn from experience, and use this experience to predict the future.

This is the core of time-series tuning. Almost all Oracle databases experience repeating patterns of usage, predictable by hour-of-the-day and day-of-the-week. Once Oracle detects a statistically valid pattern of events, the DBA can schedule a reconfiguration, just-in-time to meet the change in requirements and before the end user experiences degradation in response time. Information in the following section will show how this works.

Capturing time-series metrics

The focus of this chapter is the fact that the Oracle DBA now has a wealth of Oracle performance information at their fingertips, with more than 100 new dynamic performance tables stored in the Automatic Workload Repository (AWR).

These AWR tables feed data to the totally reworked Oracle Enterprise Manager (OEM) to produce stunning time-series displays. AWR data is also used by the Automatic Database Diagnostic Monitor (ADDM), the SQL Tuning Advisor, or by the *dbms_sqltune* package to make intelligent performance recommendations.

Instead of running complex scripts to track database performance over time, the Oracle10g DBA now has detailed time-series performance data immediately available for detailed analysis within OEM.

These industrial strength AWR tables are a true blessing for the Oracle tuning DBA. Oracle10g has new DBMS packages (*dbms_sqltune*, *dbms_mview.explain_rewrite* packages) that read the *wrh$* tables and perform sophisticated performance analysis. While not artificial intelligence in the truest sense, these sophisticated tools help simplify the complex task of Oracle tuning.

Before delving into the AWR tables in detail, it is first important to be familiar with the Oracle licensing requirements.

AWR Licensing Options

Oracle Corporation invested millions of dollars to create the Automated Workload Repository (AWR) and the self-tuning features of ADDM and the SQL tuning advisor. As of February 2004, Oracle is requiring extra licensing to access AWR and ADDM view information, even if queries are run directly from SQL*Plus.

Some Oracle licensing agreements give Oracle Corporation the right to audit user databases to ensure that they have paid for all of the Oracle optional tools that are in use.

This might include the extra-cost Database Diagnostic Pack that covers access to the AWR and the Automatic Database Diagnostic Monitor (ADDM) including use of the following:

- The *dbms_advisor* package with ADDM as the value to the *advisor_name* parameter.

- Access to views starting with *dba_advisor_** of all tasks generated by ADDM (i.e. tasks with ADDM as the *advisor_name* column in *dba_advisor_tasks* view).

- Use of the *dbms_workload_repository* package.

- Running the *awrrpt.sql* and *awrrpti.sql* reports.

- Querying the *dba_hist_** and *v$active_session_history* views.

The extra-cost Database Tuning Pack that is required if the SQL Tuning Advisor PL/SQL Packages located in the $ORACLE_HOME/rdbms/admin directory is accessed by the user. This includes use of the following:

- The *dbms_advisor* package with "SQL Tuning Advisor" as the value to the "*advisor_name*" parameter.

- Using the *addmrpt.sql* or *addmrpti.sql* reports.

- Invoking the *dbms_sqltune* package.

These features can get expensive. According to oraclestore.oracle.com in July 2004, in the U.S., the costs are:

- Oracle Diagnostics pack - $3,000/processor

- Oracle Tuning pack - $3,000/processor

So, if both products are used on a 16 CPU server, the costs for Oracle Performance Pack and Oracle Tuning Pack would be $96,000, a significant sum.

Check your License!

Oracle frequently changes licensing options and you should consult your support representative for details about your specific Oracle license options.

Tracking Oracle Option Usage

Oracle10g has auditing functions to inform DBA's if they have been querying the Oracle10g Automated Session History (ASH) views, an extra cost option according to sources at Oracle. The following Oracle 10g views can be used to to tell if specific extra cost Oracle features have been used:

- *dba_feature_usage_statistics*

- *dba_high_water_mark_statistics*

To see details on how Oracle tracks extra cost feature usage, the *dba_feature_usage_statistics* view can be queried to see usage for the following:

Automatic Database Diagnostic Monitor: A task for the Automatic Database Diagnostic Monitor has been executed.

Segment Space Management: The new Oracle10g features where extents of locally managed tablespaces are managed automatically by Oracle. This is an Oracle9i feature where bitmap freelists replace traditional one-way linked-list freelists.

Automatic SQL Execution Memory: This feature allows automatic sizing of work areas for all dedicated sessions in the PGA.

Automatic Storage Manager: This is a new Oracle10g feature for the elimination of traditional data file and tablespace allocation.

Automatic Undo Management: Oracle automatically manages undo data using an UNDO tablespace.

Automatic Workload Repository: This event fires when an Automatic Workload Repository (AWR) snapshot was taken in the last sample period.

Change-Aware Incremental Backup: Track blocks that have changed in the database.

Locally Managed Tablespaces: This indicates tablespaces that are locally managed within the in the database. This is an Oracle feature where the tablespace metadata is moved from the data dictionary into the tablespace segment header.

SQL Access Advisor: This indicates that any task related to the SQL Access Advisor has been executed.

SQL Tuning Advisor: This indicates that any task relating to the SQL Tuning Advisor has been used.

If the source for the *dba_feature_usage_statistics* view is examined, it becomes apparent that it is composed from three *wri$* tables: *wri$_dbu_usage_sample*; *wri$_dbu_feature_usage*; and *wri$_dbu_feature_metadata*.

```
select samp.dbid, fu.name, samp.version, detected_usages,
total_samples,
  decode(to_char(last_usage_date, 'MM/DD/YYYY, HH:MI:SS'),
       NULL, 'FALSE',
       to_char(last_sample_date, 'MM/DD/YYYY, HH:MI:SS'), 'TRUE',
       'FALSE')
  currently_used, first_usage_date, last_usage_date, aux_count,
  feature_info, last_sample_date, last_sample_period,
```

```
  sample_interval, mt.description
from wri$_dbu_usage_sample samp, wri$_dbu_feature_usage fu,
    wri$_dbu_feature_metadata mt
where
 samp.dbid    = fu.dbid and
 samp.version = fu.version and
 fu.name      = mt.name and
 fu.name not like '_DBFUS_TEST%' and  /* filter out test features
*/
 bitand(mt.usg_det_method, 4) != 4    /* filter out disabled
features */
```

Now that the licensing issues have been presented, it is time to take a look at how customized queries can be written against the *wri$* tables.

Customized AWR Tuning Reports

To better explain custom AWR reports, a simple example using a couple of the most popular views, the *dba_hist* view and *dba_hist_sysstat* view, will be used. The *dba_hist_sysstat* view is one of the most valuable uses of the AWR history tables because it contains instance-wide summaries of many important performance metrics. The following are the most commonly used statistics for Oracle exception reporting:

```
STATISTIC_NAME
-------------------------------------------------------
cluster wait time
concurrency wait time
application wait time
user I/O wait time
enqueue waits
enqueue deadlocks
db block gets
consistent gets
physical reads
physical read IO requests
db block changes
physical writes
DBWR buffers scanned
DBWR checkpoints
hot buffers moved to head of LRU
shared hash latch upgrades - wait
redo log space requests
redo log space wait time
table scans (short tables)
table scans (long tables)
table fetch continued row
leaf node splits
leaf node 90-10 splits
index fast full scans (full session cursor cache hits)
```

```
buffer is not pinned count
workarea executions - multipass
parse time cpu
parse time elapsed
parse count (total)
SQL*Net roundtrips to/from client
sorts (memory)
sorts (disk)
sorts (rows)
```

The following custom AWR query starts with a simple query to plot the *user I/O wait time* statistic for each AWR snapshot. From this script, it is easy to extract the physical read counts from the AWR.

```
break on begin_interval_time skip 2

column phyrds               format 999,999,999
column begin_interval_time format a25

select
   begin_interval_time,
   filename,
   phyrds
from
   dba_hist_filestatxs
natural join
   dba_hist_snapshot
;
```

Below is running total of Oracle physical reads from *phys_reads.sql*. The snapshots are collected every half-hour in this example, and many DBAs will increase the default collection frequency of AWR snapshots. Starting from this script, a where clause criteria could easily be added to create a unique time-series exception report.

```
SQL> @phys_reads

BEGIN_INTERVAL_TIME       FILENAME                                  PHYRDS
------------------------- ----------------------------------------- -------
24-FEB-04 11.00.32.000 PM E:\ORACLE\ORA92\FSDEV10G\SYSTEM01.DBF     164,700
                          E:\ORACLE\ORA92\FSDEV10G\UNDOTBS01.DBF      26,082
                          E:\ORACLE\ORA92\FSDEV10G\SYSAUX01.DBF      472,008
                          E:\ORACLE\ORA92\FSDEV10G\USERS01.DBF         1,794
                          E:\ORACLE\ORA92\FSDEV10G\T_FS_LSQ.ORA        2,123
```

Now that the basic idea behind custom AWR scripts has been presented, the next step is to look at how the Oracle10g Enterprise Manager (EM) can be used to produce powerful exception reports and create even more powerful exception reports with SQL*Plus.

Exception Reporting with OEM

Oracle10g OEM has a fantastic interface for easily creating exception alerts and mailing them directly to the Oracle professional; however, the OEM has limitations. Until OEM evolves into a true Decision Support System (DSS) for the Oracle DBA, the DBA will still need to use the workload information in the AWR for:

- Complex exception reporting

- Correlation analysis

- Data Mining

- Developing metric signatures

- Hypothesis testing

There are more sophisticated exception reports that cannot be provided by OEM. The data inside the AWR *dba_hist* views can be used by the senior DBA to perform sophisticated exception and correlation analysis. For example:

Signature Analysis: The AWR data can be used to plot values of many important performance metrics, averaged by hour-of-the-day and day-of-the-week. For example, plotting physical reads and writes signatures will give the DBA insights into the regular variations in database stress. This information is critical to scheduling just-in-time changes to SGA resources, which is the foundation of creating a self-tuning database.

Hypothesis testing: The DBA can easily run correlation analysis scripts to detect correlations between important performance metrics. Queries can be developed to show the correlation between buffer busy waits and DML per second for specific tables, all averaged over long periods of time.

Comparing a single value to a system-wide value: Custom scripts can easily be written to compare the relationship between performance values. For example, it can issue an alert when the physical writes for any data files exceeds 25% of total physical writes.

The next section provides information on how the Oracle professional can get valuable exception reports from the AWR.

Exception Reporting with the AWR

Oracle performance exception reporting involves adding a *where* clause to a query to eliminate any values that fall beneath a predefined threshold in the AWR script. For example, this can be done quite easily with a generic script to read *dba_hist_sysstat*. The following is a simple script that displays a time-series exception report for any statistic in *dba_hist_sysstat*. This script accepts the statistics number and the value threshold for the exception report as supplied parameters.

```
prompt
prompt  This will query the dba_hist_sysstat to display all values
prompt  that exceed the value specified in
prompt  the "where" clause of the query.
prompt

set pages 999

break on snap_time skip 2

accept stat_name   char    prompt 'Enter Statistic Name:  ';
accept stat_value  number  prompt 'Enter Statistics Threshold value:
';

col snap_time      format a19
col value          format 999,999,999

select
   to_char(begin_interval_time,'yyyy-mm-dd hh24:mi') snap_time,
   value
from
   dba_hist_sysstat
  natural join
   dba_hist_snapshot
where
   stat_name = '&stat_name'
and
  value > &stat_value
order by to_char(begin_interval_time,'yyyy-mm-dd hh24:mi');
```

Note: On 10.2 the above script requires SYSDBA connection.

The following script can be run at this point. It will prompt for the statistic name and threshold value:

```
SQL> @rpt_sysatst

This will query the dba_hist_sysstat view to display all values
that exceed the value specified in
the "where" clause of the query.

Enter Statistic Name:  physical writes
Enter Statistics Threshold value:  200000

SNAP_TIME                    VALUE
------------------     ------------
2004-02-21 08:00           200,395
2004-02-27 08:00           342,231
2004-02-29 08:00           476,386
2004-03-01 08:00           277,282
2004-03-02 08:00           252,396
2004-03-04 09:00           203,407
```

The listing above indicates a repeating trend where physical writes seem to be high at 8:00 AM on certain days. This powerful script will allow the DBA to quickly extract exception conditions from any instance-wide Oracle metric and see the values changes over time.

The next section examines an even more powerful exception report that compares system-wide values to individual snapshots.

Exception reporting with *dba_hist_filestatxs*

The *dba_hist_filestatxs* view contains important file-level information about Oracle I/O activities. Because most Oracle databases perform a high amount of reading and writing from disk, the *dba_hist_filestatxs* view can be very useful for identifying high-usage data files.

If the Oracle10g Automated Storage Management (ASM) is in use, all disks will be striped with the Stripe and Mirror Everywhere (SAME) approach. In ASM, this view is indispensable for locating and isolating "hot" data files. Many Oracle shops will isolate hot data files onto high-speed solid-state disk (SSD) or relocate the hot files to another physical disk spindle.

If the *dba_hist_filestatxs* table is described as shown in Table 2.2, the important information columns can be viewed. The important

---

information relates to physical reads and writes, the actual time spent performing reads and writes, and the wait count associated with each data file, for each snapshot.

COLUMN	DESCRIPTION
snap_id	Unique snapshot ID
filename	Name of the datafile
phyrds	Number of physical reads done
phywrts	Number of times DBWR is required to write
singleblkrds	Number of single block reads
readtim	Time, in hundredths of a second, spent doing reads if the timed_statistics parameter is TRUE; 0 if timed_statistics is FALSE
writetim	Time, in hundredths of a second, spent doing writes if the timed_statistics parameter is TRUE; 0 if timed_statistics is FALSE
singleblkrdtim	Cumulative single block read time, in hundredths of a second
phyblkrd	Number of physical blocks read
phyblkwrt	Number of blocks written to disk, which may be the same as PHYWRTS if all writes are single blocks
wait_count	Wait Count

Table 2.2: *Important metrics on file-level I/O in dba_hist_filestatxs*

The following is another example of a quickly written custom exception report. In this report, the *dba_hist_filestatxs* table is queried to identify hot write datafiles where the file consumed more than 25% of the total physical writes for the instance.

A close look at the query reveals that it compares the physical writes (the *phywrts* column of *dba_hist_filestatxs*) with the instance-wide physical writes (statistic# = 55 from *dba_hist_sysstat*).

This simple, yet powerful, script allows the Oracle professional to track hot write datafiles over time, thereby gaining important insights into the status of the I/O sub-system over time.

```
prompt
prompt   This will identify any single file who's write I/O
prompt   is more than 25% of the total write I/O of the database.
prompt

set pages 999

break on snap_time skip 2

col filename        format a40
col phywrts         format 999,999,999
col snap_time       format a20

select
   to_char(begin_interval_time,'yyyy-mm-dd hh24:mi') snap_time,
   filename,
   phywrts
from
   dba_hist_filestatxs
natural join
   dba_hist_snapshot
where
   phywrts > 0
and
   phywrts * 4 >
(
select
   avg(value)              all_phys_writes
from
   dba_hist_sysstat
  natural join
   dba_hist_snapshot
where
   stat_name = 'physical writes'
and
  value > 0
)
order by
   to_char(begin_interval_time,'yyyy-mm-dd hh24:mi'),
   phywrts desc;
```

The following is the sample output from this script. This is a useful report because the high-write datafiles are shown as well as those times at which they are hot.

```
SQL> @hot_write_files

This will identify any single file who's write I/O
is more than 25% of the total write I/O of the database.

SNAP_TIME          FILENAME                               PHYWRTS
---------------    ------------------------------------   -------
2004-02-20 23:30   E:\ORACLE\ORA92\FSDEV10G\SYSAUX01.DBF   85,543
2004-02-21 01:00   E:\ORACLE\ORA92\FSDEV10G\SYSAUX01.DBF   88,843
```

```
2004-02-21 08:31   E:\ORACLE\ORA92\FSDEV10G\SYSAUX01.DBF    89,463
2004-02-22 02:00   E:\ORACLE\ORA92\FSDEV10G\SYSAUX01.DBF    90,168
2004-02-22 16:30   E:\ORACLE\ORA92\FSDEV10G\SYSAUX01.DBF   143,974
                   E:\ORACLE\ORA92\FSDEV10G\UNDOTBS01.DBF    88,973
```

This type of time-series exception reporting is extremely useful for detecting those times when an Oracle10g database is experiencing I/O related stress. Many Oracle professionals will schedule these types of exception reports using *dbms_scheduler* and send them via automatic e-mail every day.

Now that information on the concept of trend identification has been covered, it is time to move on to an examination of a more sophisticated type of report where repeating trends in the data can be identified.

Trend identification with the AWR

Once the creation of simple *dba_hist* queries has been mastered, the DBA should be prepared to move on to trend identification with the AWR views. The Oracle professional knows that aggregating important Oracle performance metrics over time (day-of-the-week and hour-of-the-day) allows them to see hidden signatures.

These signatures are extremely important for proactive tuning because they show regularly occurring changes in processing demands. This knowledge allows the DBA to anticipate upcoming changes and reconfigure Oracle just-in-time to meet the changes.

The following report shows the signature for any Oracle system statistic, averaged by hour-of–the-day.

```
prompt  This will query the dba_hist_sysstat view to
prompt  display average values by hour of the day

set pages 999

break on snap_time skip 2

accept stat_name char prompt 'Enter Statistics Name:  ';

col snap_time   format a19
col avg_value   format 999,999,999
```

```
select
   to_char(begin_interval_time,'hh24')  snap_time,
   avg(value)                           avg_value
from
   dba_hist_sysstat
  natural join
   dba_hist_snapshot
where
   stat_name = '&stat_name'
group by
   to_char(begin_interval_time,'hh24')
order by
   to_char(begin_interval_time,'hh24');
```

In the output, there is an average for every hour of the day. This information can be easily pasted into an MS Excel spreadsheet and plotted with the chart wizard or the WISE tool, which is included free with this book:

```
SQL> @rpt_sysstat_hr
```

This will query the dba_hist_sysstat view to display average values by hour of the day

Enter Statistics Name: physical reads

SNAP_TIME	AVG_VALUE
00	120,861
01	132,492
02	134,136
03	137,460
04	138,944
05	140,496
06	141,937
07	143,191
08	145,313
09	135,881
10	137,031
11	138,331
12	139,388
13	140,753
14	128,621
15	101,683
16	116,985
17	118,386
18	119,463
19	120,868
20	121,976
21	112,906
22	114,708
23	116,340

Figure 2.1 shows the data after it has been pasted into an MS Excel spreadsheet and plotted with the Excel chart wizard:

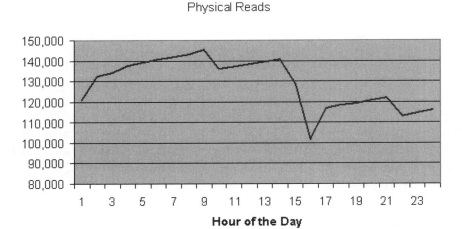

Figure 2.1: *An hourly Signature can show hidden trends*

For details on the procedure for plotting Oracle performance data, see the OTN article titled "Perfect Pitch." Open source products such as RRDtool and WISE can also be used to automate the plotting of data from the AWR and ASH.

The WISE tool is a great way to quickly plot Oracle time series data and gather signatures for Oracle metrics. Figure 2.2 shows how the WISE tool displays this data. WISE is also able to plot performance data on daily or monthly average basis. See www.wise-oracle.com for details.

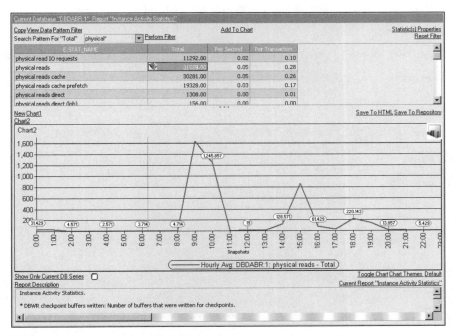

Figure 2.2: *Output from the WISE viewer*

The same types of reports aggregated by day-of-the week can also be used to see ongoing daily trends. Over long periods of time, almost all Oracle databases will develop distinct signatures that reflect the regular daily processing patterns of the end user community.

The following script will accept any of the values from *dba_hist_sysstat* and plot the average values by hour-of-the-day.

```
prompt
prompt   This will query the dba_hist_sysstat view to display
prompt   average values by day-of-the-week
prompt

set pages 999

accept stat_name char prompt 'Enter Statistic Name:  ';
```

---

*   See the code depot page for instructions on downloading a free copy of WISE

Capturing time-series metrics

```
col snap_time     format a19
col avg_value     format 999,999,999

select
    to_char(begin_interval_time,'day')    snap_time,
    avg(value)                            avg_value
from
    dba_hist_sysstat
natural join
    dba_hist_snapshot
where
    stat_name = '&stat_name'
group by
    to_char(begin_interval_time,'day')
order by
    decode(
    to_char(begin_interval_time,'day'),
     'sunday',1,
     'monday',2,
     'tuesday',3,
     'wednesday',4,
     'thursday',5,
     'friday',6,
     'saturday',7
    )
;
```

The following is the output from this script:

```
SQL> @rpt_sysstat_dy

This will query the dba_hist_sysstat view to display
average values by day-of-the-week

Enter Statistics Name:  physical reads

SNAP_TIME            AVG_VALUE
------------------- ------------
sunday                 190,185
monday                 135,749
tuesday                 83,313
wednesday              139,627
thursday               105,815
friday                 107,250
saturday               154,279
```

These results provide an average for every day of the week as shown graphically in Figure 2.3. These types of signatures will stabilize for most Oracle databases and can be used to develop a predictive model for proactive tuning activities.

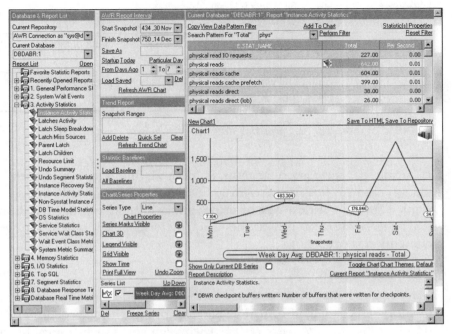

Figure 2.3: *A Signature for average physical reads by day of the week*

The next step is to explore correlation analysis using AWR data.

Correlation analysis reports with the AWR and ASH views

The Oracle Wait Interface (OWI) in version 10g automatically collects interesting statistics that relate to system-wide wait events from *dba_hist_waitstat* with detailed wait event information from *dba_hist_active_sess_history*.

COLUMN	DESCRIPTION
snap_id	Unique snapshot ID
Dbid	Database ID for the snapshot
instance_number	Instance number for the snapshot

COLUMN	DESCRIPTION
Class	Class of the block
wait_count	Number of waits by the operation for this class of block
Time	Sum of all wait times for all the waits by the operation for this class of block

Table 2.3: *The dba_hist_waitstat statistics used to wait event analysis*

If advanced correlation analysis is desired, the DBA can seek to identify correlations between instance-wide wait events and block-level waits. This is a critical way of using human insight and the AWR and ASH information to isolate the exact file and object where the wait contention is occurring.

The ASH *wrh$* tables store the history of a recent session's activity in *dba_hist_active_sess_history* and this data is designed as a rolling buffer in memory and earlier information is overwritten when needed. To do this, the *dba_hist_active_sess_history* view which contains historical block-level contention statistics is needed. The contents are shown in Table 2.4.

COLUMN	DESCRIPTION
snap_id	Unique snapshot ID
sample_time	Time of the sample
session_id	Session identifier
session_serial#	Session serial number which is used to uniquely identify a session's objects
user_id	Oracle user identifier
current_obj#	Object ID of the object that the session is currently referencing
current_file#	File number of the file containing the block that the session is currently referencing
current_block#	ID of the block that the session is currently referencing

COLUMN	DESCRIPTION
wait_time	Total wait time for the event for which the session last waited. 0 if currently waiting.
time_waited	Time that the current session actually spent waiting for the event. This column is set for waits that were in progress at the time the sample was taken.

Table 2.4: *Selected columns from the dba_hist_active_sess_history view*

In the following script, the wait event values from *dba_hist_waitstat* and *dba_hist_active_sess_history* are compared. This comparison allows the identification of the exact objects that are experiencing wait events.

```
prompt
prompt   This will compare values from dba_hist_waitstat with
prompt   detail information from dba_hist_active_sess_history.
prompt

set pages 999
set lines 80

break on snap_time skip 2

col snap_time      heading 'Snap|Time'    format a20
col file_name      heading 'File|Name'    format a40
col object_type    heading 'Object|Type'  format a10
col object_name    heading 'Object|Name'  format a20
col wait_count     heading 'Wait|Count'   format 999,999
col time           heading 'Time'         format 999,999

select
   to_char(begin_interval_time,'yyyy-mm-dd hh24:mi') snap_time,
--   file_name,
   object_type,
   object_name,
   wait_count,
   time
from
   dba_hist_waitstat                wait,
   dba_hist_snapshot                snap,
   dba_hist_active_sess_history     ash,
   dba_data_files                   df,
   dba_objects                      obj
where
   wait.snap_id = snap.snap_id
and wait.snap_id = ash.snap_id
and df.file_id = ash.current_file#
```

```
and obj.object_id = ash.current_obj#
and wait_count > 50
order by
   to_char(begin_interval_time,'yyyy-mm-dd hh24:mi'),
   file_name
;
```

This script is also enabled to join into the *dba_data_files* view if the goal is to get the file names associated with the wait event. This is a very powerful script that can be used to quickly drill-in to find the cause of specific waits. Below is a sample output from *wait_time_detail*:

```
SQL> @wait_time_detail

This will compare values from dba_hist_waitstat with
detail information from dba_hist_active_sess_hist.

Snap                  Object      Object            Wait
Time                  Type        Name              Count     Time
--------------------  ----------  ----------------  --------  --------
2004-02-28 01:00      TABLE       ORDOR              4,273         67
                      INDEX       PK_CUST_ID        12,373        324
                      INDEX       FK_CUST_NAME       3,883         17
                      INDEX       PK_ITEM_ID         1,256        967
2004-02-29 03:00      TABLE       ITEM_DETAIL           83         69
2004-03-01 04:00      TABLE       ITEM_DETAIL        1,246         45
2004-03-01 21:00      TABLE       CUSTOMER_DET       4,381        354
                      TABLE       IND_PART             117         15
2004-03-04 01:00      TABLE       MARVIN            41,273         16
                      TABLE       FACTOTUM           2,827         43
                      TABLE       DOW_KNOB             853          6
                      TABLE       ITEM_DETAIL           57        331
                      TABLE       HIST_ORD           4,337        176
```

This simple example should demonstrate how the AWR and ASH data can be used to create an almost infinite number of sophisticated custom performance reports.

The wealth of metrics within the AWR can be greatly useful for getting detailed correlation information between any of the 500+ performance metrics captured by the AWR.

The AWR repository can also be used for Oracle Data Mining. If the Oracle10g Data Mining (ODM) option is used, the AWR can be automatically scanned to seek statistically significant correlations between metrics using multivariate Chi-Square techniques to reveal hidden patterns within the performance information. The Oracle10g

ODM uses sophisticated Support Vector Machines (SVM) algorithms for binary, multi-class classification models and has built-in linear regression functionality.

The AWR and ASH are arguably the most exciting performance optimization tools in Oracle's history. They can provide the foundation for the use of artificial intelligence techniques to be applied to Oracle performance monitoring and optimization. As Oracle evolves, DBA's expect that the AWR and ASH will largely automate the tedious and time-consuming task of Oracle tuning.

The following section provides some more generalized guidelines for self-tuning an Oracle10g database.

There are dozens of self-tuning parameters that are considered immutable that may be found to be changeable. The *optimizer_index_cost_adj* parameter is one good example.

Oracle Corporation has invested millions of dollars in making the Cost-based SQL optimizer (CBO) one of the most sophisticated tools ever created. The job of the CBO is to always choose the most optimal execution plan for any SQL statements, and allow the DBA to define optimal as fast row delivers (*first_rows*) or minimization of computing resources (*all_rows*).

However, there are some things that the CBO cannot detect. The type of SQL statements, the speed of the disks, and the load on the CPUs all affect the "best" execution plan for an SQL statement. For example, the best execution plan at 4:00 AM, when 16 CPUs are idle, may be quite different from the same query at 3:00 PM, when the system is 90% utilized.

The CBO is not actually psychic, and it can never know, in advance, the exact load on the system. Hence, the Oracle professional must adjust the CBO behavior. Most Oracle professionals adjust the CBO with two parameters: *optimizer_index_cost_adj* and *optimizer_index_caching*.

The *optimizer_index_cost_adj* parameter controls the CBO's propensity to favor index scans over full-table scans. In a dynamic system, the ideal value for *optimizer_index_cost_adj* may change radically in just a few minutes as the type of SQL and load on the database changes.

Is it possible to query the Oracle environment and intelligently determine the optimal setting for *optimizer_index_cost_adj*? The *optimizer_index_cost_adj* parameters default to a value of 100 and can range in value from 1 to 10,000. A value of 100 means that equal weight is given to index versus multi-block reads. In other words, *optimizer_index_cost_adj* can be thought of as a "how much do I like full-table scans?" parameter.

With a value of 100, the CBO likes full-table scans and index scans equally, and a number lower than 100 tells the CBO that index scans are faster than full-table scans. However, even with a super-low setting (*optimizer_index_cost_adj*=1), the CBO will still choose full-table scans against no-brainers, like tiny tables that reside on two blocks.

In sum, the *optimizer_index_cost_adj* parameter is a weight that can be applied to the relative cost of physical disk reads for two types of block access:

- A single-block read (i.e. index fetch by ROWID)

- A multi-block read (i.e. a full-table scan, OPQ, sorting)

Physical disk speed is an important factor in weighing these costs. As disk access speed increases, the costs of a full-table scan versus single block reads can become negligible. For example, the new TMS RamSan-210 solid-state disk provides up to 100,000 I/Os per second, six times faster than traditional disk devices. In a solid-state disk environment, disk I/O is much faster, and multi-block reads are far cheaper than traditional disks.

The speed of performing a full-table (SOFTS) scan depends on many factors:

- The number of CPUs on the system

- The setting for Oracle Parallel query (parallel hints, alter table)

- Table partitioning

- The speed of the disk I/O sub-system (e.g. hardware cached I/O, solid-state disk RAM-Disk)

With all of these factors, it may be impossible to determine the exact best setting for the weight in *optimizer_index_cost_adj*. In the real world, the decision to invoke a full-table scan is heavily influenced by run-time factors such as:

- The availability of free blocks in the data buffers

- The amount of TEMP tablespace (if the FTS has an order by clause)

- The current demands on the CPUs

Hence, it follows that the *optimizer_index_cost_adj* should be changing frequently, as the load changes on the server.

However, is it safe to assume that all of the SOFTS factors are reflected in the relative I/O speed of FTS versus index access? If this assumption is made, the relative speed in *v$system_event* has be measured and there has to be a foundation for creating a self-tuning parameter. To do this, several assumptions must be made and accepted.

No systems are alike, and a good DBA must adjust *optimizer_index_cost_adj* according to the configuration and data access patterns. The SOFTS is measurable, and it is reflected in the wait times in *v$system_event*

The overall amount of time spent performing full-table scans is equal to the percentage of *db file sequential read* waits as a percentage of total I/O waits from *v$system_event*.

The following is a script that interrogates the *v$system_event* view and displays a suggested starting value for *optimizer_index_cost_adj*.

```
col c1 heading 'Average Waits for|Full Scan Read I/O'       format
9999.999
col c2 heading 'Average Waits for|Index Read I/O'           format
9999.999
col c3 heading 'Percent of| I/O Waits|for Full Scans'       format
9.99
col c4 heading 'Percent of| I/O Waits|for Index Scans'      format
9.99
col c5 heading 'Starting|Value|for|optimizer|index|cost|adj' format
999

select
   a.average_wait                                   c1,
   b.average_wait                                   c2,
   a.total_waits /(a.total_waits + b.total_waits)   c3,
   b.total_waits /(a.total_waits + b.total_waits)   c4,
   (b.average_wait / a.average_wait)*100            c5
from
   v$system_event   a,
   v$system_event   b
where
   a.event = 'db file scattered read'
and
   b.event = 'db file sequential read'
;
```

The listing from this script appears below.

				Starting Value for optimizer index cost adj
Average Waits for Full Scan Read I/O	Average Waits for Index Read I/O	Percent of I/O Waits for Full Scans	Percent of I/O Waits for Index Scans	
1.473	.289	.02	.98	20

The suggested starting value for *optimizer_index_cost_adj* may be too high because 98% of data waits are on index (sequential) block access. How can this starting value be weighted for *optimizer_index_cost_adj* to reflect the reality that this system has only 2% waits on full-table scan reads like a typical OLTP system with few full-table scans? As a practical matter, the automated value for *optimizer_index_cost_adj* should not be less than 1, nor more than 100.

Also, these values change constantly. As the I/O waits accumulate and access patterns change, this same script may give a very different result at a different time of the day.

```
                                                                    Starting
                                                                       Value
                                                                         for
                                                                   optimizer
                                          Percent of     Percent of     index
                   Average Waits for Average Waits for  I/O Waits      I/O Waits      cost
                   Full Scan Read I/O   Index Read I/O for Full Scans for Index Scans   adj
                   ------------------ ------------------ -------------- --------------- ---------
                            1208.249           212.676           .08             .92        18
```

This example has served to show the dynamic nature of an active database and demonstrate the value of being able to dynamically change important parameters as the processing load on the system changes.

Conclusion

As people get more sophisticated in their self-tuning endeavors, many more Oracle metrics may become self-tuning. In Oracle10g, the self-tuning capability increases greatly, and it becomes even easier to write detection scripts and schedule tasks to adjust Oracle based on the processing needs.

One easy feature that many shops implement is the intelligent detection of repeating signatures and the ability to schedule reconfigurations using the *dbms_scheduler* utility.

Unlike the existing Oracle10g AMM, a proactive approach re-configures the instance immediately before the change, thereby ensuring minimum interruption.

These are the common steps:

- Collect an "Hourly signature analysis" or "Daily signature analysis"
- Gather averages for the most important instance metrics. These might include:
  - Buffer cache performance
  - PGA multi-pass executions
  - Library cache miss ratio

- Use a mathematical formula to seek:

    - Times when a region should be increased

    - Identification of another region that can lose RAM for the increase

- Finally, display intelligent recommendations about changes and display a set of *dbms_scheduler* syntax that the DBA may use to implement the change

As Oracle10g continues to evolve, Oracle will continue to enhance the mechanisms for analyzing the valuable performance information in AWR. At the present rate, future releases of Oracle may have true artificial intelligence built-in to detect and correct even the most challenging Oracle optimization issues.

The next chapter will introduce details about the internals of the AWR tables and show how these structures can be used for complex reporting.

References

Oracle10g documentation library:
otn.oracle.com/pls/db10g/portal.portal_demo3?selected=1

Analyzing Oracle performance data on OTN:
otn.oracle.com/oramag/webcolumns/2003/techarticles/
burleson_wait.html

Oracle10g reference manual:
download-west.oracle.com/docs/cd/B12037_01/server.101/
b10755/toc.htm

Using the RRDtool:
www.rrdtool.com

Creating a self-tuning Oracle database:
www.rampant-books.com/book_2003_1_oracle9i_sga.htm

Oracle10g new DBA Features:
www.rampant-books.com/book_2003_2_oracle10g.htm

Oracle Data Mining (ODM):
otn.oracle.com/products/bi/odm/odmining.html

Solid-state RAM disk with Oracle:
www.storagesearch.com/texasmemsysart1.pdf

WISE – Workload Interface Statistical Engine
www.wise-oracle.com

Oracle10g Automated Workload Structures

The Many Faces of Oracle10g

The *dba_hist* views that comprise AWR are built from their underlying *wrh$* equivalents. These views serve to provide the data source a wealth of customizable reports for identification of trends and time-series performance optimization.

This type of proactive tuning includes the process of identifying signatures, which are regularly repeating patterns that are unique to every Oracle database instance. Once the DBA understands the signatures of the important metrics in the database, the Oracle10g scheduler, the *dbms_scheduler* package can be used to re-allocate system resources just-in-time to anticipate a repeating event.

All custom queries that are written against the *dba_hist* views require a join into the *dba_hist_snapshot* view, which is the main anchor for the

AWR history views. Figure 3.1 shows the anchor *dba_hist_snapshot* view and samples of summary and detail *dba_hist* views.

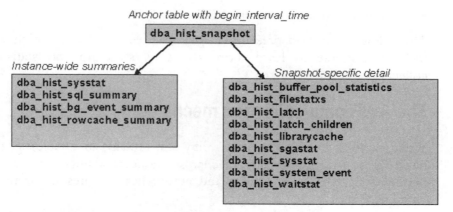

Figure 3.1: *A sample of the dba_hist views for the AWR*

With 64 new *dba_hist* views and thousands of possible statistics to examine, the focus of this chapter will be narrowed to some commonly used tuning approaches and data sources. To start, a quick look at the following AWR *dba_hist* views is in order:

- *dba_hist_sysstat*

- *dba_hist_filestatxs*

- *dba_hist_waitstat*

As customization of the AWR reports is covered, these *dba_hist* views will be examined as simple AWR reports. From there, more sophisticated reports will be examined such as exception reporting, trend identification, correlation analysis, and hypothesis testing.

The following topics are integral to obtaining a full understanding of time-series tuning with AWR:

- The AWR data collection mechanism

- The AWR as a replacement for STATSPACK

- Use of the *dba_hist* views

- Writing exception reports from the AWR

- Trend identification with the AWR

- Hypothesis testing with the AWR

The following section presents an overview of the AWR, which will make it possible to learn more about its structure and statistics collection mechanism.

The AWR data collection mechanism

While the Oracle STATSPACK utility still remains in Oracle10g, the new 10g automating polling mechanism collects a huge amount of performance data from Oracle and automatically stores it for time-based analysis.

The AWR data collection process involves the transfer of in-memory statistics from the *x$* fixed tables into the *wrh$* tables. Oracle10g also has a new Manageability Monitor (MMON) background process does the data collection.. In addition to the automatic collections, the new Automatic Session History (ASH) component samples time-based wait collections every 60 seconds, collecting critical time wait event information.

Furthermore, Oracle10g automatically collects new metrics showing the rate of change of important wait events such as consistent gets per second or user calls per transaction.

There are approximately 180 metrics that are computed by Oracle10g automatically. These metrics are instantly available by querying new *v$* dynamic views such as *v$sysmetric_history* or *v$sysmetric_summary*. The AWR keeps the history for metrics in its special *wrh$* internal tables and provides *dba_hist* views to access them. These wait event metrics are presented in more detail later in this book.

Armed with information on AWR data collection, the following section will delve into custom AWR scripts.

Customizing AWR Scripts for Proactive Tuning

 Adjustments must be made in the AWR in order to perform time-based tuning since the default retention period for AWR data is only seven days. The adjustment to increase the storage of detail information over longer time periods can be made by using the new database procedure called *dbms_workload_repository.modify_snapshot_settings*.

The *recodify_snapshot_settings* procedure will change the AWR retention period and collection frequency to make the date available for longer periods of time. For example:

```
execute dbms_workload_repository.modify_snapshot_settings (
    interval => 60,
    retention => 43200);
```

In this example the retention period is specified as 30 days (43,200 minutes) and the interval between each snapshot is 60 minutes. If the *dba_hist_wr_control* view is queried after this procedure is executed, the changes to these settings will be evident.

The architecture of the AWR is quite simple, as shown in Figure 3.2. The MMON background process polls the *x$* fixed tables from the SGA region and stores them in the AWR tables. From there, the performance data is instantly available for analysis. The Enterprise Manager can be used for graphical data display. Alternatively, the Automatic Database Diagnostic Monitor (ADDM) can be used for automated tuning analysis, or SQL*Plus can be used if customized Oracle tuning size reports are desired.

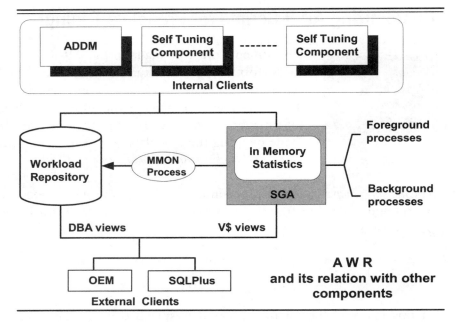

Figure 3.2: *The AWR architecture*

The AWR is very comprehensive and there are literally thousands of distinct metrics that can be examined. For example, the *dba_hist_systat* view contains over 300 individual performance metrics.

The following section provides a brief overview of the AWR tables and then introduces ways that customized reports can be extracted from the AWR views.

The Mysterious AWR Performance Tables

The Oracle10g dynamic performance tables constitute the foundation of sophisticated automations such as Automatic Memory Management (AMM) as well as intelligent advisory tools such as ADDM and the SQL Tuning Advisor.

The AWR is a core feature of the 10g database kernel and automatically collects and stores important run-time performance information for historical analysis.

The tables that store this information are prefixed with *wrh$* and are very similar in function to the STATSPACK tables. This could make STATSPACK appear somewhat obsolete, although it is still available in the $ORACLE_HOME/rdbms/admin directory.

Unlike the more cumbersome STATSPACK utility, which requires knowledge of the table structure and creation of complex query scripts, the 10g Enterprise Manager (OEM) automatically displays and interprets this valuable time-series performance data.

The *wrh$* AWR tables store important historical statistical information about the database in the form of periodic snapshots. Each snapshot is a capture of the in–memory *x$* fixed view and other control structures at a certain point in time. Each of the AWR table names is prefixed with *wrm$* (Metadata tables), *wrh$* (History tables), or *wri$* (Advisory tables).

- The *wrm$* tables store metadata information for the Workload Repository.

- The *wrh$* tables store historical data or snapshots.

- The *wri$* tables: These 49 tables store data related to advisory functions.

The next section provides a closer look at the underlying data structures so that how the AWR tables store important time-series performance data becomes more evident.

AWR vs. STATSPACK

The first effective proactive time-series method for Oracle performance appeared in Oracle7 and used begin and end snapshots, using the *utlbstat* and *utlestat* utilities, and the data was stored inside temporary DBA-defined storage tables. Staring with Oracle8i and

---

back-portable to Oracle8, Oracle Corporation codified the snapshot approach with the STATSPACK utility.

While many important time-series reports are now instantly created within Oracle10g Enterprise Manager, the senior Oracle DBA may want to go beyond the recommendations of ADDM and the SQL Tuning Advisor. Complex time series analysis, such as hypothesis testing and correlation analysis, still require that custom queries be written against the *wrh$* tables. Table 3.1 below shows the comparison of Oracle8i and Oracle9i STATSPACK tables to their AWR equivalents. Fortunately, many of the names of the *wrh$* tables are identical to their *stats$* equivalents making it easy to migrate STATSPACk scripts to AWR.

DBA HIST VIEW	WRH$TABLE	STATSPACK TABLE
dba_hist_event_summary	*wrh$_bg_event_summary*	*stats$bg_event_summary*
dba_hist_buffer_pool_statistics	*wrh$_buffer_pool_statistics*	*stats$buffer_pool_statistics*
dba_hist_filestatxs	*wrh$_filestatxs*	*stats$filestatxs*
dba_hist_latch	*wrh$_latch*	*stats$latch*
dba_hist_latch_children	*wrh$_latch_children*	*stats$latch_children*
dba_hist_librarycache	*wrh$_librarycache*	*stats$librarycache*
dba_hist_rowcache_summary	*wrh$_rowcache_summary*	*stats$rowcache_summary*
dba_hist_sgastat	*wrh$_sgastat*	*stats$sgastat*
dba_hist_sql_summary	*wrh$_sql_summary*	*stats$sql_summary*
dba_hist_sysstat	*wrh$_sysstat*	*stats$sysstat*
dba_hist_system_event	*wrh$_system_event*	*stats$system_event*
dba_hist_waitstat	*wrh$_waitstat*	*stats$waitstat*

Table 3.1: *STATSPACK, DBA HIST and wrh$ equivalencies*

It is fortunate for the seasoned DBA that the column definitions and contents of these tables are almost identical. This allows easy porting of the STATSPACK time-series scripts to be run against the *wrh$* tables with a minimum of modification.

The script below gathers physical disk read counts, the *phyrds* column of *dba_hist_filestatxs*. It then joins this data into the *dba_hist_snapshot* view to get the *begin_interval_time* column.

```
break on begin_interval_time skip 2

column phyrds   format 999,999,999
column begin_interval_time format a25

select
   begin_interval_time,
   filename,
   phyrds
from
   dba_hist_filestatxs
   natural join
   dba_hist_snapshot;
```

When this script is executed, a display of the running total of physical reads, organized by datafile is shown below. In this case, the AWR snapshots are collected every half-hour, and the DBA is free to adjust the snapshot collection interval depending on data needs.

```
SQL> @reads

BEGIN_INTERVAL_TIME          FILENAME                                            PHYRDS
-------------------------    -----------------------------------------------    ----------
24-FEB-04 11.00.32.000 PM    E:\ORACLE\ORA92\FSDEV10G\SYSTEM01.DBF              164,700
                             E:\ORACLE\ORA92\FSDEV10G\UNDOTBS01.DBF              26,082
                             E:\ORACLE\ORA92\FSDEV10G\SYSAUX01.DBF              472,008
                             E:\ORACLE\ORA92\FSDEV10G\USERS01.DBF                 1,794
                             E:\ORACLE\ORA92\FSDEV10G\T_FS_LSQ.ORA                2,123


24-FEB-04 11.30.18.296 PM    E:\ORACLE\ORA92\FSDEV10G\SYSTEM01.DBF              167,809
                             E:\ORACLE\ORA92\FSDEV10G\UNDOTBS01.DBF              26,248
                             E:\ORACLE\ORA92\FSDEV10G\SYSAUX01.DBF              476,616
                             E:\ORACLE\ORA92\FSDEV10G\USERS01.DBF                 1,795
                             E:\ORACLE\ORA92\FSDEV10G\T_FS_LSQ.ORA                2,244


25-FEB-04 12.01.06.562 AM    E:\ORACLE\ORA92\FSDEV10G\SYSTEM01.DBF              169,940
                             E:\ORACLE\ORA92\FSDEV10G\UNDOTBS01.DBF              26,946
                             E:\ORACLE\ORA92\FSDEV10G\SYSAUX01.DBF              483,550
                             E:\ORACLE\ORA92\FSDEV10G\USERS01.DBF                 1,799
                             E:\ORACLE\ORA92\FSDEV10G\T_FS_LSQ.ORA                2,248
```

Where clause criteria can easily be added to this script to create a unique time-series exception report on specific data file or specific time periods.

Of course, with a few minor adjustments to this script, physical writes, read time, write time, single block reads, and a host of other neat metrics from the *dba_hist_filestatxs* view can also be displayed.

Now that general information has been presented on the AWR concept, the following section will provide details about the new AWR table contents.

Inside the AWR Tables

Due to the transient nature of the data in the *x$* fixed tables, the goal in the development of Oracle10g was to make this information persistent; hence, the introduction of the *wrh$* tables. Much of the information collected by the AWR comes from the *x$* fixed table structures in the Oracle heap.

As part of Oracle's commitment to time-series tuning, 10g contains major changes in the *x$* structures as well as many new and modified *v$* performance views. Figure 3.3 shows the 10g *v$* views relating to database events.

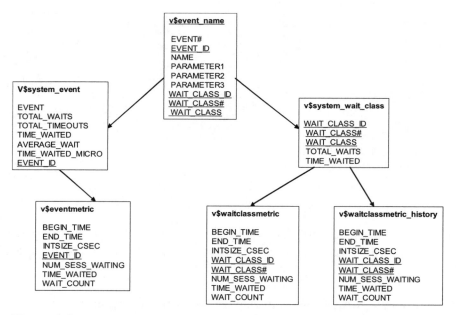

Figure 3.3: *The Oracle 10g v$ system event structure*

Prior to Oracle10g, no *v$* views captured time-series performance data. To get proactive tuning data, the DBA was forced to take snapshots with BSTAT-ESTAT with Oracle6 and Oracle7 or STATSPACK with Oracle8 and Oracle9i in order to see performance over time.

Best of all, in Oracle10g there are new *v$* metric tables including *v$eventmetric*, *v$waitclassmetric* and *v$waitclassmetric_history*, which offer persistent storage of elapsed time Oracle performance data. The metrics tables are easy to identify because they contain *begin_time* and *end_time* data columns. As a standard in Oracle10g, any *v$* views that contain these columns are used to store proactive time-series performance information.

The following section presents information on the *wrh$* wait event structure.

The Oracle10g Wait Event Tables

Prior to Oracle10g, capturing wait event information was a cumbersome process involving the setting of special events (e.g. the 10046 trace dump) and the reading of complex trace dumps. Fortunately, Oracle10g has simplified the way that wait event information is captured and there is a wealth of new *v$* and *wrh$* views relating to Oracle wait events.

Oracle10g has introduced brand new wait events and the database kernel and Oracle's Automatic Session History (ASH) now captures statistics on more than 800 specific wait events. These new wait events are the result of Oracle breaking out their latch waits into their individual components and breaking out enqueue waits (locks) into a finer level of granularity.

The foundation concept of the ASH architecture is called the time model, and Oracle10g has introduced several important new wait event v$ views as shown in Table 3-2:

v$ VIEW	dba_hist VIEW
v$active_sess_hist	*dba_hist_active_sess_history*
v$sys_time_model	*dba_hist_sys_time_model*

v$ VIEW	dba_hist VIEW
v$active_session_history	dba_hist_active_sess_history
v$event_histogram	No equivalent DBA view

Table 3.2: *The new Oracle10g wait event v$ views*

Unlike the old-fashioned *v$session* and *v$session_wait* views, where waits could only be seen at the exact instant in which they occurred, the new *v$session_wait_history* and *v$sys_time_model* views allow Oracle10g to capture system waits details in a time-series mode. The following section provides an overview of the new ASH table structures.

A Kick in the ASH

One of the most important areas of Oracle10g wait event tuning is the Oracle10g Active Session History (ASH). ASH data is visualized through the *v$active_sess_hist* view and the *wrh$active_session_history* tables.

At a basic level, ASH stores the history of a recent session's activity and facilitates the analysis of the system performance at the current time. ASH is designed as a rolling buffer in memory, and earlier information is overwritten when needed. ASH uses the memory of the SGA. Figure 3.4 shows the relationships between the ASH structures.

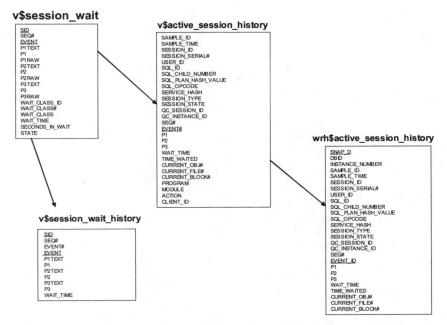

Figure 3.4: *The relationship between v$ views and wrh$ event tables*

Another innovation is the ability to use the new Oracle10g "hash key" for tracking session identification. This new hash key allows the DBA to track common session processes and allows inter-cal session tracking in cases like Oracle Call Interface (OCI) session bouncing where each call to Oracle is a different session ID.

The ASH samples for wait events every second and tracks the waits in the new *v$active_sess_hist* view. New data values are written to the *wrh$* tables every hour, or when a new AWR snapshot is taken. The following are the Oracle10g *wrh$* wait event tables.

- *wrh$_active_session_history*

- *wrh$_active_session_history_bl*

- *wrh$_bg_event_summary*

- *wrh$_event_name*

- *wrh$_metric_name*

- *wrh$_sessmetric_history*

- *wrh$_sys_time_model*

- *wrh$_sys_time_model_bl*

- *wrh$_sysmetric_history*

- *wrh$_sysmetric_summary*

- *wrh$_sysstat*

- *wrh$_sysstat_bl*

- *wrh$_system_event*

- *wrh$_system_event_bl*

- *wrh$_waitclassmetric_history*

- *wrh$_waitstat*

- *wrh$_waitstat_bl*

Following that look at the basics, the following section will detail the new Oracle10g *dba_hist* views that are used to create time-series performance reports, both manually and within Oracle Enterprise Manager (EM). The information will start with an overview of the *dba_hist* views and move on to examples of custom Oracle10g performance exception reports that can be easily generated from these views with SQL*Plus.

Inside the *dba_hist* Views

Oracle10g has added 64 *dba_hist_ xxx* views, each one mapping to underlying *x$* and *wrh$* component fixed tables.

For example, the listing below shows the internal creation syntax for the *dba_hist_sysstat* view. The *dba_hist_sysstat* view is built from several workload repository tables; *wrm$_snapshot*, *wrh$_sysstat*, and *dba_hist_stat_name*.

```
select s.snap_id, s.dbid, s.instance_number, s.statistic#,
s.statistic_hash, nm.statistic_name, value
from WRM$_SNAPSHOT sn, WRH$_SYSSTAT s, DBA_HIST_STAT_NAME nm
where s.statistic_hash = nm.statistic_hash
and s.statistic# = nm.statistic#
and s.dbid = nm.dbid
and s.snap_id = sn.snap_id
and s.dbid = sn.dbid
and s.instance_number = sn.instance_number
and sn.status = 0
and sn.bl_moved = 0
union all
select s.snap_id, s.dbid, s.instance_number, s.statistic#,
s.statistic_hash, nm.statistic_name, value
from WRM$_SNAPSHOT sn, WRH$_SYSSTAT_BL s, DBA_HIST_STAT_NAME nm
where s.statistic_hash = nm.statistic_hash
and s.statistic# = nm.statistic#
and s.dbid = nm.dbid
and s.snap_id = sn.snap_id
and s.dbid = sn.dbid
and s.instance_number = sn.instance_number
and sn.status = 0
and sn.bl_moved = 1
```

Due to the overwhelming amount of data captured by AWR, the information presented on some *dba_hist* views that may already be familiar from the older STATSPACK utility. Table 3.3 lists a few of the more familiar views.

The column names in the *dba_hist* tables are different from the STATSPACK tables, but the types of performance data collected by these STATSPACK tables is essentially the same as that found inside the dba_hist views.

dba_hist VIEW	STATSPACK TABLE
dba_hist_bg_event_summary	*stats$bg_event_summary*
dba_hist_buffer_pool_statistics	*stats$buffer_pool_statistics*
dba_hist_filestatxs	*stats$filestatxs*
dba_hist_latch	*stats$latch*
dba_hist_latch_children	*stats$latch_children*
dba_hist_librarycache	*stats$librarycache*
dba_hist_rowcache_summary	*stats$rowcache_summary*
dba_hist_sgastat	*stats$sgastat*
dba_hist_sql_summary	*stats$sql_summary*

dba_hist VIEW	STATSPACK TABLE
dba_hist_sysstat	stats$sysstat
dba_hist_system_event	stats$system_event
dba_hist_waitstat	stats$waitstat

Table 3.3: *STATSPACK vs. dba_hist name equivalencies*

For reference, these views are fully documented in the Oracle 10g Database Reference Manual. The next area of focus will be some of the most important *dba_hist* views for time-series and exception reporting.

Conclusion

Once the DBA understands the AWR table data and inter-table relationships between AWR and performance metrics, the foundation is set for learning how the *wrh$* tables are used as input to the AMM, the ADDM, and the SQL Tuning Advisor.

The main points of this chapter include:

- The creation of AWR and ASH provides a complete repository for diagnosing and fixing any Oracle performance issue.

- The AWR *dba_hist* views are similar to well-known STATSPACK tables, making it easy to migrate existing performance reports to Oracle10g. The *dba_hist* views are fully-documented and easy to use for writing custom scripts.

- The AWR provides the foundation for sophisticated performance analysis including exception reporting, trend analysis, correlation analysis, hypothesis testing and data mining.

With that basic information on AWR, it's time to dive deeper into the new AWR *dba_hist* tables and get detailed information on how they can be used to improve Oracle performance by showing impending problems before they cripple an Oracle database.

Investigating the *dba_hist* Views

Know the History

The previous chapter introduced the concept and role of the Automatic Workload Repository (AWR) feature in Oracle10g. The next step is to learn more about key views which form the AWR repository.

As a quick review, Oracle stores the AWR internal data structures in schema *sys* which is physically located in the tablespace *sysaux*. The DBA can, however, access any AWR historical data directly by using the AWR internal tables prefixed *wrx_*.

Oracle provides DBAs with a set of data dictionary views prefixed with *dba_hist* to be used to access AWR information via queries. The Workload Interface Statistical Engine (WISE) tool uses the *dba_hist*

---

dictionary views intensively in order to generate chart reports for AWR data, and WISE is a handy way to realize trends.

This chapter will present an overview of various categories of *dba_hist* views and types of statistics collected. The following points will be covered:

- Access paths to AWR data.
- *dba_hist* data dictionary views.

Access Paths to AWR data

Typically, Oracle DBAs can access AWR historical data using the Oracle Enterprise Manager (EM), AWR standard report, or by using WISE tool reports.

Oracle OEM 10g allows access to AWR data through a web browser interface. The Oracle documentation can be referenced for details on using OEM to generate reports for AWR historical data.

An AWR standard report can be generated using the *awrrpt.sql* script located in $ORACLE_HOME/rdbms catalog. This script generates its report in either HTML or TEXT formats, depending on user specified parameters. Users must have a DBA role granted in order to successfully run this script. Furthermore, a script called *awrrpt1.sql*, which is located in $ORACLE_HOME/rdbms catalog, asks for a database identifier *dbid* and *instance number* and generates the AWR report for the specified database.

The WISE tool was initially designed and developed by author Alexey B. Danchenkov to provide a convenient graphical interface for Oracle STATSPACK and AWR data. The WISE tool is available for free download at www.wise_oracle.com.

The WISE tool's role has been extended to support work with the Oracle10g AWR by providing an advanced set of useful features. The WISE tool provides users with a convenient GUI framework that allows quick and easy navigation through AWR snapshots. It also allows the retrieval of historical data in text or chart formats for any snapshot ranges specified. The main advantages of WISE tool when compared to OEM are:

- The ability to quickly build a historical or trend chart for any AWR statistic.

- The ability to automate chart report generation on a schedule basis.

- The ability to easily write custom AWR reports.

The WISE tool and its features will be presented in detail later in this book and it is available for download free.

Oracle gives users the option of accessing AWR metadata or historical data manually using any ad-hoc query tool like SQL*Plus by performing queries against the following database objects:

- *The dba_hist* dictionary views provide access to historical statistical data stored in the AWR. The AWR stores cumulative values available through dynamic performance views like *v$sysstat*. Instance restart resets these cumulative values in *v$* memory views. However, the AWR keeps cumulative statistics as well as delta values that show the change of statistics over time.

- *The v$* metric views provide metric statistics which show users the rate of change of some particular statistic. The metrics in Oracle can be measured against such units as time, transaction number, database or user calls, etc. One specific example would be the parse number per second. The metric views are organized by Oracle in groups as system, session, file, event, tablespace, etc. These metric v$ views are presented in a later chapter in this book.

- *The v$active_session_history* view provides access to a sampled data. The sampled data shows the activity status of all active database sessions at the given moment. The content of v$active_session_history view is also preserved by the AWR.

The following section will explore the intervals of the *dba_hist* tables so custom reports can be created.

Inside the *dba_hist* Data Dictionary Views

Oracle10g provides the following *dba_hist* data dictionary views to access AWR data:

AWR Data Dictionary Views

DBA_HIST_ACTIVE_SESS_HISTORY
DBA_HIST_BASELINE
DBA_HIST_BG_EVENT_SUMMARY
DBA_HIST_BUFFER_POOL_STAT
DBA_HIST_CLASS_CACHE_TRANSFER
DBA_HIST_CR_BLOCK_SERVER
DBA_HIST_CURRENT_BLOCK_SERVER
DBA_HIST_DATABASE_INSTANCE
DBA_HIST_DATAFILE
DBA_HIST_DB_CACHE_ADVICE
DBA_HIST_DLM_MISC
DBA_HIST_ENQUEUE_STAT
DBA_HIST_EVENT_NAME
DBA_HIST_FILEMETRIC_HISTORY
DBA_HIST_FILESTATXS
DBA_HIST_INSTANCE_RECOVERY
DBA_HIST_JAVA_POOL_ADVICE
DBA_HIST_LATCH
DBA_HIST_LATCH_CHILDREN
DBA_HIST_LATCH_MISSES_SUMMARY
DBA_HIST_LATCH_NAME
DBA_HIST_LATCH_PARENT
DBA_HIST_LIBRARYCACHE
DBA_HIST_LOG
DBA_HIST_METRIC_NAME
DBA_HIST_MTTR_TARGET_ADVICE
DBA_HIST_OPTIMIZER_ENV
DBA_HIST_OSSTAT
DBA_HIST_OSSTAT_NAME
DBA_HIST_PARAMETER
DBA_HIST_PARAMETER_NAME
DBA_HIST_PGASTAT
DBA_HIST_PGA_TARGET_ADVICE
DBA_HIST_RESOURCE_LIMIT
DBA_HIST_ROWCACHE_SUMMARY

DBA_HIST_SEG_STAT
DBA_HIST_SEG_STAT_OBJ
DBA_HIST_SERVICE_NAME
DBA_HIST_SERVICE_STAT
DBA_HIST_SERVICE_WAIT_CLASS
DBA_HIST_SESSMETRIC_HISTORY
DBA_HIST_SGA
DBA_HIST_SGASTAT
DBA_HIST_SHARED_POOL_ADVICE
DBA_HIST_SNAPSHOT
DBA_HIST_SNAP_ERROR
DBA_HIST_SQLBIND
DBA_HIST_SQLSTAT
DBA_HIST_SQLTEXT
DBA_HIST_SQL_PLAN
DBA_HIST_SQL_SUMMARY
DBA_HIST_SQL_WORKAREA_HSTGRM
DBA_HIST_STAT_NAME
DBA_HIST_SYSMETRIC_HISTORY
DBA_HIST_SYSMETRIC_SUMMARY
DBA_HIST_SYSSTAT
DBA_HIST_SYSTEM_EVENT
DBA_HIST_SYS_TIME_MODEL
DBA_HIST_TABLESPACE_STAT
DBA_HIST_TBSPC_SPACE_USAGE
DBA_HIST_TEMPFILE
DBA_HIST_TEMPSTATXS
DBA_HIST_THREAD
DBA_HIST_UNDOSTAT
DBA_HIST_WAITCLASSMET_HISTORY
DBA_HIST_WAITSTAT
DBA_HIST_WR_CONTROL

Figure 4.1: *AWR data dictionary list*

The *dba_hist* views below are grouped by the types of performance data available through them. The Oracle10g AWR repository collects the history for the following types of database statistics:

- Database wait events.

- Metric statistics.

- Time model statistics.

- System statistics.

- Operating system statistics.

- SQL statistics.

- Segment statistics.

- Datafile I/O statistics.

The usage of the types of statistics in the time-series tuning approach was introduced earlier in this book, and it is now time to take a deeper look. The following is a basic overview of parent *dba_hist* views containing the corresponding statistic history and basic reports, which retrieve statistic history for a particular AWR snapshot interval.

The following section presents more details about the concrete statistics provided by particular *dba_hist* views.

Database Wait Events in the *dba_hist* Views

Database wait event statistics show how much and how long Oracle processes had to wait for a particular type of database resource in order to process their work. These wait events are grouped by Oracle into several categories including Administrative, Application, Cluster, Commit, Concurrency, Configuration, Idle, Network, Other, Scheduler, System I/O, and User I/O.

Wait event data can be used effectively if the wait events are ordered by wait time. This way, the most significant wait events are found first which makes them the lead candidates for further investigation.

Even though there is a standard AWR report which contains a Wait Events section that displays top wait events, the following query can also be used to retrieve the top wait events for a particular AWR snapshot interval:

```
select event
     , waits "Waits"
     , time "Wait Time (s)"
     , pct*100 "Percent of Tot"
     , waitclass "Wait Class"
from (select e.event_name event
                  , e.total_waits - nvl(b.total_waits,0)   waits
                  , (e.time_waited_micro -
nvl(b.time_waited_micro,0))/1000000  time
                  , (e.time_waited_micro -
nvl(b.time_waited_micro,0))/
                  (select sum(e1.time_waited_micro -
nvl(b1.time_waited_micro,0)) from dba_hist_system_event b1 ,
dba_hist_system_event e1
                  where b1.snap_id(+)          = b.snap_id
                    and e1.snap_id             = e.snap_id
                    and b1.dbid(+)             = b.dbid
                    and e1.dbid                = e.dbid
                    and b1.instance_number(+)  =
b.instance_number
                    and e1.instance_number     =
e.instance_number
                    and b1.event_id(+)         = e1.event_id
                    and e1.total_waits         >
nvl(b1.total_waits,0)
                    and e1.wait_class          <> 'Idle'
   )  pct
                  , e.wait_class waitclass
            from
              dba_hist_system_event b ,
              dba_hist_system_event e
          where b.snap_id(+)           = &pBgnSnap
            and e.snap_id              = &pEndSnap
            and b.dbid(+)              = &pDbId
            and e.dbid                 = &pDbId
            and b.instance_number(+)   = &pInstNum
            and e.instance_number      = &pInstNum
            and b.event_id(+)          = e.event_id
            and e.total_waits          > nvl(b.total_waits,0)
            and e.wait_class           <> 'Idle'
      order by time desc, waits desc
   )
```

The sample output of this query looks like:

```
SQL> @ wt_events_int_10g.sql

EVENT                         Waits Wait Time(s) Percent of Tot Wait Class
----------------------------- ----- ------------ -------------- -------------
control file parallel write   11719      119.13  34,1611762     System I/O
class slave wait                 20      102.46  29,3801623     Other
Queue Monitor Task Wait          74       66.74  19,1371008     Other
log file sync                   733       20.60   5,90795938    Commit
db file sequential read        1403       14.27   4,09060416    User I/O
log buffer space                178       10.17   2,91745801    Configuration
process startup                 114        7.65   2,19243344    Other
db file scattered read          311        2.14    ,612767501   User I/O
control file sequential read   7906        1.33    ,380047642   System I/O
latch free                      254        1.13    ,324271668   Other
log file switch completion       20        1.11    ,319292495   Configuration
```

The output of the script displays the wait events ordered by wait times in seconds.

The WISE tool has a report named Top Wait Events that yields a chart for top wait events that occurred for the particular snapshot interval.

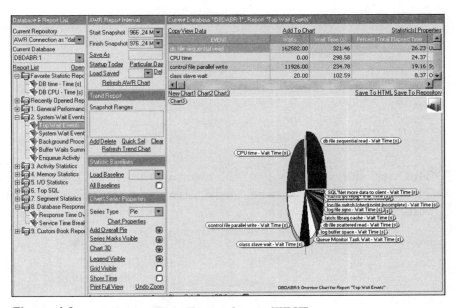

Figure 4.2: *AWR Top Wait Events chart in WISE.*

---

* See the code depot page for instructions on downloading a free copy of WISE

Database Wait Events in the dba_hist Views

Figure 4.2 contains a WISE pie chart for wait events. This chart allows the DBA to quickly identify the wait events that database waited for the most. With the WISE tool, graphing wait events is a simple exercise.

The following *dba_hist* views are available for accessing wait events statistics in the AWR.

dba_hist_system_event

The *dba_hist_system_event* view displays information about the count of total waits and time waited in microseconds.

```
SQL> desc DBA_HIST_SYSTEM_EVENT

Name                                      Null?    Type
----------------------------------------- -------- ----------------
SNAP_ID                                            NUMBER
DBID                                               NUMBER
INSTANCE_NUMBER                                    NUMBER
EVENT_ID                                           NUMBER
EVENT_NAME                                         VARCHAR2(64)
WAIT_CLASS_ID                                      NUMBER
WAIT_CLASS                                         VARCHAR2(64)
TOTAL_WAITS                                        NUMBER
TOTAL_TIMEOUTS                                     NUMBER
TIME_WAITED_MICRO                                  NUMBER
```

This view stores snapshots of the *v$system_event* system dynamic view. The following query can be used to retrieve wait events data for a particular snapshot interval:

```
select
    event "Event Name",
    waits "Waits",
    timeouts "Timeouts",
    time "Wait Time (s)",
    avgwait "Avg Wait (ms)",
    waitclass "Wait Class"
from
    (select e.event_name event
        , e.total_waits - nvl(b.total_waits,0)  waits
        , e.total_timeouts - nvl(b.total_timeouts,0) timeouts
        , (e.time_waited_micro -
nvl(b.time_waited_micro,0))/1000000  time
        ,  decode ((e.total_waits - nvl(b.total_waits, 0)), 0,
```

```
to_number(NULL),
            ((e.time_waited_micro -
nvl(b.time_waited_micro,0))/1000) / (e.total_waits -
nvl(b.total_waits,0)) ) avgwait
        , e.wait_class waitclass
    from
        dba_hist_system_event b ,
        dba_hist_system_event e
    where
                    b.snap_id(+)            = &pBgnSnap
            and e.snap_id               = &pEndSnap
            and b.dbid(+)               = &pDbId
            and e.dbid                  = &pDbId
            and b.instance_number(+)    = &pInstNum
            and e.instance_number       = &pInstNum
            and b.event_id(+)           = e.event_id
            and e.total_waits           > nvl(b.total_waits,0)
            and e.wait_class            <> 'Idle' )
order by time desc, waits desc
```

In the above and some subsequent queries the following parameters need to have appropriate values substituted for them:

- BgnSnap: the start snapshot number for the AWR snapshot interval of interest.

- EndSnap: the finish snapshot number for the AWR snapshot interval of interest.

- DbId: the database identified of the target database.

- InstNum: the instance number of the target database.

The sample output for this query looks like following:

```
SQL> @ Sys_event_int_10g.sql

Event Name                      Waits Timeouts Wait Time (s) Avg Wait (ms) Wait Class
------------------------------- ----- -------- ------------- ------------- ----------
control file parallel write     11719        0        119.13         10.17 System I/O
class slave wait                   20       20        102.46      5,122.91 Other
Queue Monitor Task Wait            74        0         66.74        901.86 Other
log file sync                     733        6         20.60         28.11 Commit
db file sequential read          1403        0         14.27         10.17 User I/O
log buffer space                  178        0         10.17         57.16 Configuration
process startup                   114        0          7.65         67.07 Other
db file scattered read            311        0          2.14          6.87 User I/O
control file sequential read     7906        0          1.33           .17 System I/O
latch free                        254        0          1.13          4.45 Other
log file switch completion         20        0          1.11         55.67 Configuration
```

The WISE tool has a report named System Wait Events that runs the above query with some additional information:

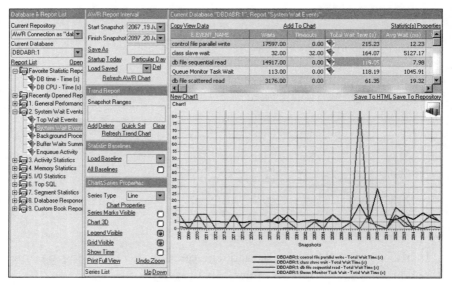

Figure 4.3: *AWR System Wait Events chart in WISE*

Figure 4.3 is a WISE screenshot that shows database wait event details for a particular time period. The above chart was produced using the System Wait Events report and shows how and when particular wait events stressed the database the most during observed snapshot interval.

Using the above chart, it is a quick task to identify instances when the database spent the most wait time and what particular wait events caused the wait.

The *dba_hist_event_name* view can be used to help tune Oracle and that topic will be presented next.

---

dba_hist_event_name

The *dba_hist_event_name* view shows information about all wait events available in the database. This view contains the history of snapshots for *v$event_name* view.

```
SQL> desc DBA_HIST_EVENT_NAME
Name                                     Null?    Type
---------------------------------------- -------- ----------------
DBID                                     NOT NULL NUMBER
EVENT_ID                                 NOT NULL NUMBER
EVENT_NAME                               NOT NULL VARCHAR2(64)
WAIT_CLASS_ID                                     NUMBER
WAIT_CLASS                                        VARCHAR2(64)
```

This view allows users to find out the wait class to which every wait event belongs.

dba_hist_bg_event_summary

The *dba_hist_bg_event_summary* data dictionary view is very similar to the *dba_hist_system_event* view. The difference is that the *dba_hist_bg_event_summary* view displays historical information about wait events caused by Oracle background process activities. Oracle background processes form a kernel of Oracle instance with SGA memory region and perform many types of important jobs.

During their job in a concurrent access environment, these Oracle background processes cause some contention for system resources in much the same way as do the foreground user processes serving end users. Thus, Oracle DBAs may want to know what part of database waits are caused by background Oracle processes.

```
SQL> desc DBA_HIST_BG_EVENT_SUMMARY

Name                                     Null?    Type
---------------------------------------- -------- ----------------
SNAP_ID                                  NOT NULL NUMBER
DBID                                     NOT NULL NUMBER
INSTANCE_NUMBER                          NOT NULL NUMBER
EVENT_ID                                 NOT NULL NUMBER
EVENT_NAME                               NOT NULL VARCHAR2(64)
WAIT_CLASS_ID                                     NUMBER
WAIT_CLASS                                        VARCHAR2(64)
```

```
TOTAL_WAITS                                          NUMBER
TOTAL_TIMEOUTS                                       NUMBER
TIME_WAITED_MICRO                                    NUMBER
```

The following query can be used to retrieve background wait event data for a particular snapshot interval:

```
select
    event       "Event Name",
    waits       "Waits",
    timeouts    "Timeouts",
    time        "Wait Time (s)",
    avgwait     "Avg Wait (ms)",
    waitclass   "Wait Class"
from
    (select e.event_name event
          , e.total_waits - nvl(b.total_waits,0)  waits
          , e.total_timeouts - nvl(b.total_timeouts,0) timeouts
          , (e.time_waited_micro -
nvl(b.time_waited_micro,0))/1000000  time
          , decode ((e.total_waits - nvl(b.total_waits, 0)), 0,
to_number(NULL),
            ((e.time_waited_micro -
nvl(b.time_waited_micro,0))/1000) / (e.total_waits -
nvl(b.total_waits,0)) ) avgwait
          , e.wait_class waitclass
        from
          dba_hist_bg_event_summary b ,
          dba_hist_bg_event_summary e
        where
                    b.snap_id(+)            = &pBgnSnap
            and e.snap_id               = &pEndSnap
            and b.dbid(+)               = &pDbId
            and e.dbid                  = &pDbId
            and b.instance_number(+)    = &pInstNum
            and e.instance_number       = &pInstNum
            and b.event_id(+)           = e.event_id
            and e.total_waits           > nvl(b.total_waits,0)
            and e.wait_class            <> 'Idle' )
order by time desc, waits desc
```

The WISE tool has a corresponding report named Background Process Wait Events that allows users to build time-series charts for background wait events.

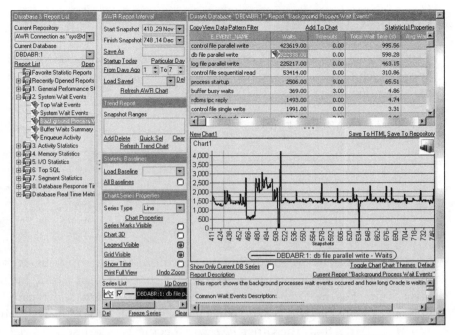

Figure 4.4: *AWR Background Process Wait Events chart in WISE*

Figure 4.4 is a WISE screenshot that shows database background wait events details for a particular time period. The above chart was produced using the Background Process Wait Events report and shows how and when particular background wait events stressed the database most during the observed snapshot interval.

The output of the script looks similar to the output of the script shown in the previous *dba_hist_system_event* section with the exception that wait events are displayed for background processes.

---

* See the code depot page for instructions on downloading a free copy of WISE

---

dba_hist_waitstat

The *dba_hist_waitstat* view displays historical statistical information about block contention, and the AWR stores this information from the *v$waitstat* dynamic view.

```
SQL> desc DBA_HIST_WAITSTAT

Name                                      Null?    Type
----------------------------------------- -------- -------------
 SNAP_ID                                            NUMBER
 DBID                                               NUMBER
 INSTANCE_NUMBER                                    NUMBER
 CLASS                                              VARCHAR2(18)
 WAIT_COUNT                                         NUMBER
 TIME                                               NUMBER
```

This view is useful in the following situation. If the top wait events query as described above reveals the fact that the wait event buffer busy waits has a large wait time, the *dba_hist_waitstat* view can be queried to investigate what particular type of block caused this situation. After that, the other *dba_hist* specific views described below can be used to drill down to find out additional information.

For example, the *dba_hist_active_sess_history* view can be queried to identify particular sessions and objects that caused the high contention. The datafile and objects ids can be found in the *v$session_wait* dynamic view. The following query can be used to retrieve historical block contention statistics:

```
select e.class                                "E.CLASS"
     , e.wait_count   - nvl(b.wait_count,0)   "Waits"
     , e.time         - nvl(b.time,0)         "Total Wait Time
(cs)"
     , (e.time        - nvl(b.time,0)) /
       (e.wait_count  - nvl(b.wait_count,0))  "Avg Time (cs)"
  from dba_hist_waitstat b
     , dba_hist_waitstat e
 where b.snap_id          = &pBgnSnap
   and e.snap_id          = &pEndSnap
   and b.dbid             = &pDbId
   and e.dbid             = &pDbId
   and b.dbid             = e.dbid
   and b.instance_number  = &pInstNum
   and e.instance_number  = &pInstNum
   and b.instance_number  = e.instance_number
   and b.class            = e.class
```

```
   and b.wait_count    < e.wait_count
order by 3 desc, 2 desc
```

The sample query output looks like:

```
SQL> @Wait_stat_int_10g.sql

E.CLASS                    Waits Total Wait Time (cs) Avg Time (cs)
------------------ ---------- -------------------- -------------
undo header                   97                  121  1,24742268
file header block              2                  114           57
```

The output of the script shows which particular buffer wait events play a significant role.

The WISE tool has a corresponding report named Buffer Waits Summary that generates time-series charts for the block contention statistics.

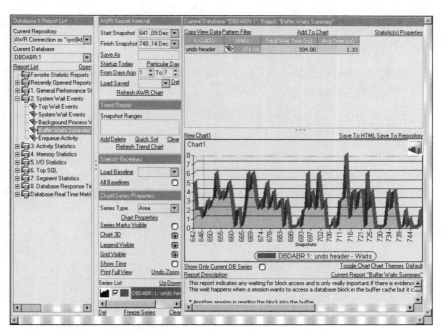

Figure 4.5: *AWR Buffer Waits Summary chart in WISE.*

---

*   See the code depot page for instructions on downloading a free copy of WISE

Figure 4.5 shows a WISE chart that allows the DBA to see how the database waited for particular types of buffers during the observed snapshot interval.

dba_hist_enqueue_stat

The *dba_hist_enqueue_stat* view displays statistical information about requests for various types of enqueues or locks. This view stores snapshots of *v$enqueue_statistics* dynamic performance view.

Enqueues provide a lock mechanism for the coordination of concurrent access to numerous database resources. The name of the enqueue is included as part of the wait event name and takes the form enq: enqueue_type - related_details. There are several types of enqueues available. Some examples are:

- ST enqueues control dynamic space allocation.

- HW enqueues are used to serialize the allocation of space beyond the high water mark (HWM).

- Waits for TM locks are usually caused by missing indexes on foreign key constraints.

TX locks are placed in various modes on data blocks when a transaction modifies data within this block. There are several types of TX locks: enq: TX - allocate ITL entry; enq: TX – contention; enq: TX - index contention; enq: TX - row lock contention.

```
SQL> desc DBA_HIST_ENQUEUE_STAT
```

Name	Null?	Type
SNAP_ID	NOT NULL	NUMBER
DBID	NOT NULL	NUMBER
INSTANCE_NUMBER	NOT NULL	NUMBER
EQ_TYPE	NOT NULL	VARCHAR2(2)
REQ_REASON	NOT NULL	VARCHAR2(64)
TOTAL_REQ#		NUMBER
TOTAL_WAIT#		NUMBER
SUCC_REQ#		NUMBER
FAILED_REQ#		NUMBER
CUM_WAIT_TIME		NUMBER
EVENT#		NUMBER

If wait events with enqueue in their name, like *enqueue wait* wait event, have significant wait time, the *dba_hist_enqueue_stat* view can be used to drill down to details about what particular enqueue has a long wait time. This script can be used to query this view:

```
select
  ety "Enqueue",
  reqs "Requests",
  sreq "Successful Gets",
  freq "Failed Gets",
  waits "Waits",
  wttm "Wait Time (s)",
  awttm "Avg Wait Time(ms)"
from (
select /*+ ordered */
        e.eq_type || '-' || to_char(nvl(l.name,' '))
     || decode( upper(e.req_reason)
                , 'CONTENTION', null
                , '-',          null
                , ' ('||e.req_reason||')')            ety
    , e.total_req#   - nvl(b.total_req#,0)           reqs
    , e.succ_req#    - nvl(b.succ_req#,0)            sreq
    , e.failed_req#  - nvl(b.failed_req#,0)          freq
    , e.total_wait#  - nvl(b.total_wait#,0)          waits
    , (e.cum_wait_time - nvl(b.cum_wait_time,0))/1000  wttm
    , decode( (e.total_wait#  - nvl(b.total_wait#,0))
              , 0, to_number(NULL)
              , ( (e.cum_wait_time - nvl(b.cum_wait_time,0))
                / (e.total_wait#  - nvl(b.total_wait#,0))
              )
            )                                      awttm
  from dba_hist_enqueue_stat e
     , dba_hist_enqueue_stat b
     , v$lock_type           l
where b.snap_id(+)            = &pBgnSnap
  and e.snap_id              = &pEndSnap
  and b.dbid(+)              = &pDbId
  and e.dbid                 = &pDbId
  and b.dbid(+)              = e.dbid
  and b.instance_number(+)   = &pInstNum
  and e.instance_number      = &pInstNum
  and b.instance_number(+)   = e.instance_number
  and b.eq_type(+)           = e.eq_type
  and b.req_reason(+)        = e.req_reason
  and e.total_wait# - nvl(b.total_wait#,0) > 0
  and l.type(+)              = e.eq_type
 order by wttm desc, waits desc)
```

The output will look like the following:

```
SQL> @Enq_stat_int_10g.sql

Enqueue                    Requests Successful Gets Failed Gets Waits Wait Time (s) Avg Wait Time(ms)
-------------------------- -------- --------------- ----------- ----- ------------- -----------------
RO-Multiple Object             1806            1806           0   153         4,554        29,7647059

TC-Tablespace Checkpoint         81              81           0    27         4,016       148,740741

TQ-Queue table enqueue        19878           19878           0    16         3,596            224,75

CF-Controlfile Transaction   308733          308732           1     2          ,692               346
```

The script output shows activity statistics for particular types of enqueues which allows users to find the enqueues that cause most waits and wait times.

The WISE tool has a special report named Enqueue Activity that is used to retrieve and chart AWR data from *dba_hist_enqueue_stat* view.

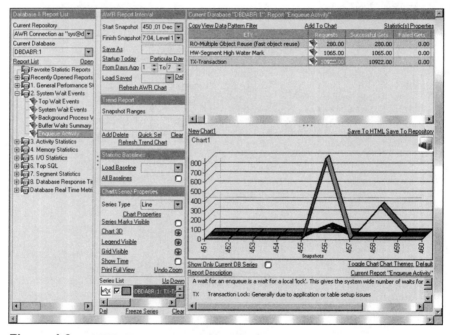

Figure 4.6: *AWR Enqueue Activity chart in WISE*

Figure 4.6 is a WISE screenshot. From the figure, it is possible to see how particular enqueue types placed overhead on the database during the selected snapshot interval.

Metric *dba_hist* Views

The metric *dba_hist* data dictionary views are organized into several groups: system; session; service; file; tablespace; and event metrics. All available metric groups can be found in the *v$metricgroup* dynamic view:

```
SQL> select * from V$METRICGROUP;

GROUP_ID NAME                             INTERVAL_SIZE MAX_INTERVAL
-------- -------------------------------- ------------- ------------
       0 Event Metrics                             6000            1
       1 Event Class Metrics                       6000           60
       2 System Metrics Long Duration              6000           60
       3 System Metrics Short Duration             1500           12
       4 Session Metrics Long Duration             6000           60
       5 Session Metrics Short Duration            1500            1
       6 Service Metrics                           6000           60
       7 File Metrics Long Duration               60000            6
       9 Tablespace Metrics Long Duration          6000            0
```

All available metrics for which the AWR keeps history are in the *dba_hist_metric_name* view that stores snapshots for the *v$metric_name* view. There are approximately 184 different metrics available.

Metrics are actively used by sophisticated automation features of Oracle10g such as the Automatic Memory Management (AMM) and advisory engines such as Automatic Database Diagnostic Monitor (ADDM), SQL Advisor, etc. For example, the ADDM uses a goal-based algorithm designed to minimize *db time*. This metric is computed as a cumulative time spent.

```
SQL> select METRIC_NAME  from DBA_HIST_METRIC_NAME;
```

The following is a list of several metrics that are computed by the AWR snapshot engine; however, the list is not exhaustive.

```
METRIC_NAME
------------------------------------
Average File Read Time (Files-Long)
Average File Write Time (Files-Long)
```

```
Average Users Waiting Counts
Background Checkpoints Per Sec
Blocked User Session Count
Branch Node Splits Per Sec
Branch Node Splits Per Txn
Buffer Cache Hit Ratio
CPU Time (Session)
CPU Time Per User Call
CPU Usage Per Sec
```

The usage of metric statistics in time-series tuning approach will be presented later in this book. This chapter provides a general overview of metric *dba_hist* views that are available and a short description of information they provide.

dba_hist_filemetric_history

The *dba_hist_filemetric_history* view collects metrics history for datafile I/O related activity such as average file read/write times, number of physical read/write operations, and blocks.

```
SQL> desc DBA_HIST_FILEMETRIC_HISTORY

Name                                       Null?      Type
------------------------------------------ ---------- -------
SNAP_ID                                    NOT NULL   NUMBER
DBID                                       NOT NULL   NUMBER
INSTANCE_NUMBER                            NOT NULL   NUMBER
FILEID                                     NOT NULL   NUMBER
CREATIONTIME                               NOT NULL   NUMBER
BEGIN_TIME                                 NOT NULL   DATE
END_TIME                                   NOT NULL   DATE
INTSIZE                                    NOT NULL   NUMBER
GROUP_ID                                   NOT NULL   NUMBER
AVGREADTIME                                NOT NULL   NUMBER
AVGWRITETIME                               NOT NULL   NUMBER
PHYSICALREAD                               NOT NULL   NUMBER
PHYSICALWRITE                              NOT NULL   NUMBER
PHYBLKREAD                                 NOT NULL   NUMBER
PHYBLKWRITE                                NOT NULL   NUMBER
```

Along with this *dba_hist_filemetric_history* view, there is an AWR data dictionary view called *dba_hist_sysmetric_summary* that contains several useful datafile I/O related metrics.

```
SQL> select metric_name from dba_hist_metric_name where group_name
like 'File Metrics%';
```

```
METRIC_NAME
-----------------------------------
Physical Block Writes (Files-Long)
Physical Block Reads (Files-Long)
Physical Writes (Files-Long)
Physical Reads (Files-Long)
Average File Write Time (Files-Long)
Average File Read Time (Files-Long)
```

The above query output shows all of the metrics available for datafile I/O activity.

dba_hist_sessmetric_history

The *dba_hist_sessmetric_history* view collects history information for important session related metrics such as:

```
SQL> select metric_name from dba_hist_metric_name where group_name
like 'Session Metrics%';

METRIC_NAME
----------------------------------------
Blocked User Session Count
Logical Reads Ratio (Sess/Sys) %
Physical Reads Ratio (Sess/Sys) %
Total Parse Count (Session)
Hard Parse Count (Session)
PGA Memory (Session)
Physical Reads (Session)
CPU Time (Session)
User Transaction Count (Session)
```

The *dba_hist_sessmetric_history* view can be queried to find additional metric details about particular sessions of interest.

```
SQL> desc DBA_HIST_SESSMETRIC_HISTORY

Name                                     Null?    Type
---------------------------------------- -------- ----------
SNAP_ID                                  NOT NULL NUMBER
DBID                                     NOT NULL NUMBER
INSTANCE_NUMBER                          NOT NULL NUMBER
BEGIN_TIME                               NOT NULL DATE
END_TIME                                 NOT NULL DATE
SESSID                                   NOT NULL NUMBER
SERIAL#                                  NOT NULL NUMBER
INTSIZE                                  NOT NULL NUMBER
GROUP_ID                                 NOT NULL NUMBER
METRIC_ID                                NOT NULL NUMBER
METRIC_NAME                              NOT NULL VARCHAR2(64)
```

```
VALUE                                     NOT NULL NUMBER
METRIC_UNIT                               NOT NULL VARCHAR2(64)
```

This view contains a *metric_unit* column that helps identify the units of measure for every metric.

dba_hist_sysmetric_history

The *dba_hist_sysmetric_history* view collects history for all system-wide metrics which belong to such metric groups as System Metrics Long Duration and System Metrics Short Duration. This view stores snapshots of *v$sysmetric_history* dynamic view.

```
SQL> desc DBA_HIST_SYSMETRIC_HISTORY

Name                                      Null?    Type
----------------------------------------- -------- ----------
SNAP_ID                                   NOT NULL NUMBER
DBID                                      NOT NULL NUMBER
INSTANCE_NUMBER                           NOT NULL NUMBER
BEGIN_TIME                                NOT NULL DATE
END_TIME                                  NOT NULL DATE
INTSIZE                                   NOT NULL NUMBER
GROUP_ID                                  NOT NULL NUMBER
METRIC_ID                                 NOT NULL NUMBER
METRIC_NAME                               NOT NULL VARCHAR2(64)
VALUE                                     NOT NULL NUMBER
METRIC_UNIT                               NOT NULL VARCHAR2(64)
```

This *dba_hist_sysmetric_history* view contains important metrics for database time-series tuning approach such as:

- Buffer Cache Hit Ratio

- Database CPU Time Ratio

- Database Time Per Sec

- Database Wait Time Ratio

- Physical Reads Per Sec

- Response Time Per TXN

- SQL Service Response Time.

This view also contains a *metric_unit* column that helps identify measure units for every metric.

dba_hist_sysmetric_summary

The *dba_hist_sysmetric_summary* view shows a history for system-wide metrics that belong to the System Metrics Long Duration metric group. This view stores snapshots for the *v$sysmetric_summary* dynamic view.

```
SQL> desc DBA_HIST_SYSMETRIC_SUMMARY

Name                                      Null?     Type
----------------------------------------- --------- ----------
SNAP_ID                                   NOT NULL  NUMBER
DBID                                      NOT NULL  NUMBER
INSTANCE_NUMBER                           NOT NULL  NUMBER
BEGIN_TIME                                NOT NULL  DATE
END_TIME                                  NOT NULL  DATE
INTSIZE                                   NOT NULL  NUMBER
GROUP_ID                                  NOT NULL  NUMBER
METRIC_ID                                 NOT NULL  NUMBER
METRIC_NAME                               NOT NULL  VARCHAR2(64)
METRIC_UNIT                               NOT NULL  VARCHAR2(64)
NUM_INTERVAL                              NOT NULL  NUMBER
MINVAL                                    NOT NULL  NUMBER
MAXVAL                                    NOT NULL  NUMBER
AVERAGE                                   NOT NULL  NUMBER
STANDARD_DEVIATION                        NOT NULL  NUMBER
```

The following simple query can be used to retrieve metrics for a particular snapshot.

```
select
  metric_name "Metric Name",
  metric_unit "Metric Unit",
  minval "Minimum Value",
  maxval "Maximum Value",
  average "Average Value"
from
  DBA_HIST_SYSMETRIC_SUMMARY
where
      snap_id           = &pEndSnap
  and dbid              = &pDbId
  and instance_number   = &pInstNum
```

This view contains pre-computed metric values as they appeared in *v$sysmetric_summary* dynamic view. The sample output of the   script looks like:

```
SQL> @ metric_summary.sql

Metric Name             Metric Unit             Minimum Value Maximum Value Average Value
----------------------- ----------------------- ------------- ------------- -------------
Host CPU Utilization (%) % Busy/(Idle+Busy)                 1            55            16
Database Time Per Sec    CentiSeconds Per Second            0             9             0
Txns Per Logon           Txns Per Logon                     1            17             4
Executions Per Sec       Executes Per Second                0            17             1
Executions Per Txn       Executes Per Txn                  10           357            28
Session Limit %          % Sessions/Limit                  10            12            10
Process Limit %          % Processes/Limit                  9            12            10
PGA Cache Hit %          % Bytes/TotalBytes                97            97            97
Shared Pool Free %       % Free/Total                      10            11            10
Library Cache Miss Ratio % Misses/Gets                      0             6             0
Library Cache Hit Ratio  % Hits/Pins                       93           100            99
Row Cache Miss Ratio     % Misses/Gets                      0            24             1
```

The output shows that database workload statistics can be easily retrieved directly from the AWR for any time interval, without any additional computing overhead.

The WISE tool has a report called System Metric Summary History that allows the production of time-series charts for all of the metrics available.

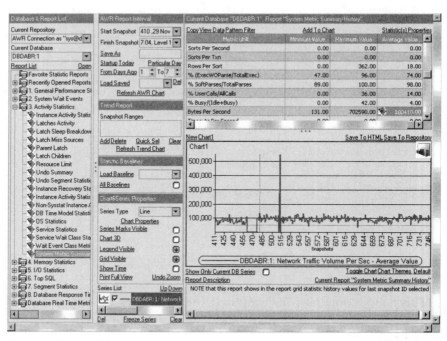

Figure 4.7: *AWR System Metric Summary History chart in WISE*

Figure 4.7 shows a chart produced for a particular system metric, Network Traffic Volume Per Second. This chart allows the quick identification of the times when the database experienced the most network traffic workload.

dba_hist_waitclassmet_history

The *dba_hist_waitclassmet_history* view displays the metric history for wait event classes such as application, commit, concurrency, configuration, and other.

```
SQL> desc  DBA_HIST_WAITCLASSMET_HISTORY

Name                                     Null?     Type
---------------------------------------- --------  ----------
SNAP_ID                                  NOT NULL  NUMBER
DBID                                     NOT NULL  NUMBER
INSTANCE_NUMBER                          NOT NULL  NUMBER
WAIT_CLASS_ID                            NOT NULL  NUMBER
WAIT_CLASS                                         VARCHAR2(64)
BEGIN_TIME                               NOT NULL  DATE
END_TIME                                 NOT NULL  DATE
INTSIZE                                  NOT NULL  NUMBER
GROUP_ID                                 NOT NULL  NUMBER
AVERAGE_WAITER_COUNT                     NOT NULL  NUMBER
DBTIME_IN_WAIT                           NOT NULL  NUMBER
TIME_WAITED                              NOT NULL  NUMBER
WAIT_COUNT                               NOT NULL  NUMBER
```

The metrics stored in this view include average waiter count, database time spent in the wait, time waited, and number of wait times.

Time Model Statistics *dba_hist* Views

Time model statistics show the amount of CPU time that it takes to complete each type of database processing work. Examples include SQL execute elapsed time, parse time elapsed and PL/SQL execution elapsed time statistics. The time model statistics allow the identification of points at which the Oracle database spends the most CPU time for processing.

The most important time model statistic is *db time*, which represents the total time spent by Oracle in processing all database calls; thus, it describes the total database workload. *db time* is calculated by aggregating the CPU and all non-idle wait times for all sessions in the database after last startup. Since it is an aggregate values, it is possible that the *db time* statistic could be larger than the total instance runtime.

One common objective in Oracle performance tuning is the reduction of database workload or *db time* by minimizing specific components such as the session's SQL parse and processing times, session's wait times, and so on.

dba_hist_sys_time_model

The *dba_hist_sys_time_model* view displays snapshots for the *v$sys_time_model* dynamic view and stores history for system time model statistics.

```
SQL> desc DBA_HIST_SYS_TIME_MODEL
```

Name	Null?	Type
SNAP_ID		NUMBER
DBID		NUMBER
INSTANCE_NUMBER		NUMBER
STAT_ID		NUMBER
STAT_NAME		VARCHAR2(64)
VALUE		NUMBER

The statistic names are also available in the *dba_hist_stat_name* view that displays all the statistic names gathered by the AWR and stores snapshots for the *v$statname* dynamic view. The *dba_hist_stat_name* view is also used with the *dba_hist_sysstat* view described below.

The query below can be used to retrieve information from *dba_hist_sys_time_model* view for a particular AWR snapshot interval.

```
column "Statistic Name" format A40
column "Time (s)" format 999,999
column "Percent of Total DB Time" format 999,999

select e.stat_name "Statistic Name"
     , (e.value - b.value)/1000000        "Time (s)"
     , decode( e.stat_name,'DB time'
             , to_number(null)
             , 100*(e.value - b.value)
```

```
            ) /
    ( select nvl((e1.value - b1.value),-1)
    from dba_hist_sys_time_model  e1
       , dba_hist_sys_time_model  b1
    where b1.snap_id              = b.snap_id
    and e1.snap_id                = e.snap_id
    and b1.dbid                   = b.dbid
    and e1.dbid                   = e.dbid
    and b1.instance_number        = b.instance_number
    and e1.instance_number        = e.instance_number
    and b1.stat_name              = 'DB time'
    and b1.stat_id                = e1.stat_id
)
    "Percent of Total DB Time"
  from dba_hist_sys_time_model e
     , dba_hist_sys_time_model b
 where b.snap_id                  = &pBgnSnap
   and e.snap_id                  = &pEndSnap
   and b.dbid                     = &pDbId
   and e.dbid                     = &pDbId
   and b.instance_number          = &pInst_Num
   and e.instance_number          = &pInst_Num
   and b.stat_id                  = e.stat_id
   and e.value - b.value > 0
 order by 2 desc;
```

The output of this query looks like:

```
SQL> @Sys_time_model_int_10g.sql

Statistic Name                         Time (s) Percent of Total DB Time
-------------------------------------- -------- ------------------------
DB time                                     169
sql execute elapsed time                    156                       93
DB CPU                                      153                       90
PL/SQL execution elapsed time                77                       46
background cpu time                           53                       31
parse time elapsed                            6                        4
hard parse elapsed time                       4                        3
connection management call elapsed time       0                        0
Java execution elapsed time                   0                        0
PL/SQL compilation elapsed time               0                        0
sequence load elapsed time                    0                        0
hard parse (sharing criteria) elapsed ti      0                        0
hard parse (bind mismatch) elapsed time       0                        0
```

This simple script provides valuable information about the percentage of total database processing time and actual time in seconds each metric takes. With this query, users can quickly identify the areas in which the database consumes processing, not wait, time and thus isolate the most resource intensive tasks.

The WISE tool has a report for the *dba_hist_sys_time_model* view called DB Time Model Statistics which allows users to quickly build time-series charts for time model statistics. The time-series charts for *db time* model statistics allow easy identification of the hot time periods of the database workload. Figure 4.8 is a representation of the WISE tool report for Time Model Statistics.

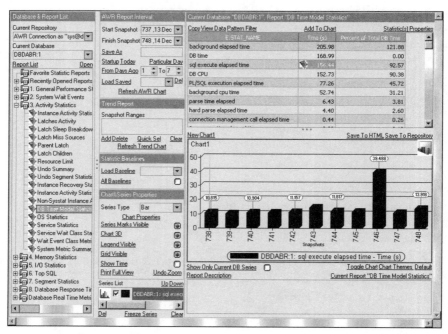

Figure 4.8: *Time Model Statistics chart in WISE.*

Figure 4.8 shows a sample WISE screenshot where a chart has been produced for a particular time model statistic called *sql execute elapsed time*. This sample chart allows us the quick identification of the points in time at which this time model statistics consumed the most database processing time. Using this information, the DBA will be able to drill

---

*   See the code depot page for instructions on downloading a free copy of WISE

down to particular SQL statements to find those that caused this long processing time.

The next section will provide an overview of performance information that the AWR stores about instance-wide system activity.

System statistics

The AWR stores history for a large number of instance cumulative statistics. These statistics are generally available through the *v$sysstat* dynamic view. The AWR stores snapshots for this view in the *dba_hist_sysstat* view. The following sections provide more details on these system statistics AWR views.

dba_hist_sysstat

The *dba_hist_sysstat* view contains a history for system statistics from the *v$sysstat* view. Statistic names can be retrieved from the *dba_hist_statname* view where more than 300 statistics are available.

```
SQL> desc  DBA_HIST_SYSSTAT

Name                 Null?    Type
-----------------    -------- -----------
SNAP_ID                       NUMBER
DBID                          NUMBER
INSTANCE_NUMBER               NUMBER
STAT_ID                       NUMBER
STAT_NAME                     VARCHAR2(64)
VALUE                         NUMBER
```

System statistics for a particular snapshot interval can be viewed using the following query.

```
select e.stat_name        "Statistic Name"
     , e.value - b.value   "Total"
     , round((e.value - b.value)/
     ( select
       avg( extract( day from (e1.end_interval_time-
b1.end_interval_time) )*24*60*60+
            extract( hour from (e1.end_interval_time-
b1.end_interval_time) )*60*60+
            extract( minute from (e1.end_interval_time-
b1.end_interval_time) )*60+
```

```
              extract( second from (e1.end_interval_time-
b1.end_interval_time)) )
      from dba_hist_snapshot  b1
          ,dba_hist_snapshot  e1
    where b1.snap_id          = b.snap_id
      and e1.snap_id          = e.snap_id
      and b1.dbid             = b.dbid
      and e1.dbid             = e.dbid
      and b1.instance_number = b.instance_number
      and e1.instance_number = e.instance_number
      and b1.startup_time     = e1.startup_time
      and b1.end_interval_time < e1.end_interval_time ),2) "Per
Second"
 from  dba_hist_sysstat  b
    ,  dba_hist_sysstat  e
 where b.snap_id           = &pBgnSnap
   and e.snap_id           = &pEndSnap
   and b.dbid              = &pDbId
   and e.dbid              = &pDbId
   and b.instance_number = &pInstNum
   and e.instance_number = &pInstNum
   and b.stat_id           = e.stat_id
   and e.stat_name not in (  'logons current'
                          , 'opened cursors current'
                          , 'workarea memory allocated'
                          )
   and e.value             >= b.value
   and e.value             >  0
 order by 1 asc
```

The query output will look like:

```
SQL> @Sys_stat_int_10g.sql

Statistic Name                                Total Per Second
------------------------------------- ---------- ----------
CPU used by this session                      4,307          1
CPU used when call started                    4,307          1
CR blocks created                               200          0
DB time                                     959,909        115
DBWR checkpoint buffers written               3,228          0
DBWR checkpoints                                  9          0
DBWR object drop buffers written                 75          0
DBWR tablespace checkpoint buffers written       71          0
DBWR transaction table writes                    92          0
DBWR undo block writes                          822          0
IMU CR rollbacks                                 20          0
IMU Flushes                                     103          0
IMU Redo allocation size                    761,060         92
IMU commits                                     383          0
IMU contention                                    0          0
IMU ktichg flush                                  4          0
IMU pool not allocated                        1,702          0
IMU undo allocation size                  1,772,624        213
```

This script allows users to easily identify all instance activity statistics for a particular snapshot interval in two representations: cumulative and per second.

The WISE tool also has a report named Instance Activity Statistics that is based on *dba_hist_sysstat* view.

dba_hist_latch

The *dba_hist_latch* view contains historical latch statistics from the *v$latch* dynamic performance view. The statistics in the *dba_hist_latch* view are grouped by latch names and allow users to tune applications if wait events show significant latch contention. For example, latch resource usage can be greatly reduced if the application is properly tuned and shared pool is used. Methods for reducing latch contention will be covered in a later chapter of this book.

```
SQL> desc DBA_HIST_LATCH

Name                  Null?      Type
-----------------     --------   -----------
SNAP_ID                          NUMBER
DBID                             NUMBER
INSTANCE_NUMBER                  NUMBER
LATCH_HASH                       NUMBER
LATCH_NAME                       VARCHAR2(64)
LEVEL#                           NUMBER
GETS                             NUMBER
MISSES                           NUMBER
SLEEPS                           NUMBER
IMMEDIATE_GETS                   NUMBER
IMMEDIATE_MISSES                 NUMBER
SPIN_GETS                        NUMBER
SLEEP1                           NUMBER
SLEEP2                           NUMBER
SLEEP3                           NUMBER
SLEEP4                           NUMBER
WAIT_TIME                        NUMBER
```

The following query can be used to retrieve historical data about latches from AWR.

```
select e.latch_name "Latch Name"
     , e.gets      - b.gets  "Get Requests"
     , to_number(decode(e.gets, b.gets, null,
       (e.misses - b.misses) * 100/(e.gets - b.gets)))    "Percent
Get Misses"
     , to_number(decode(e.misses, b.misses, null,
       (e.sleeps - b.sleeps)/(e.misses - b.misses)))    "Avg Sleeps
/ Miss"
     , (e.wait_time - b.wait_time)/1000000 "Wait Time (s)"
     , e.immediate_gets - b.immediate_gets "No Wait Requests"
     , to_number(decode(e.immediate_gets,
                 b.immediate_gets, null,
                  (e.immediate_misses - b.immediate_misses) * 100
/
                  (e.immediate_gets   - b.immediate_gets)))
"Percent No Wait Miss"
 from  dba_hist_latch  b
     , dba_hist_latch  e
 where b.snap_id         = &pBgnSnap
   and e.snap_id         = &pEndSnap
   and b.dbid            = &pDbId
   and e.dbid            = &pDbId
   and b.dbid            = e.dbid
   and b.instance_number = &pInstNum
   and e.instance_number = &pInstNum
   and b.instance_number = e.instance_number
   and b.latch_hash      = e.latch_hash
   and e.gets - b.gets   > 0
 order by 1, 4
```

The results of the query show latch activity statistics and identify the particular type of latch that produces miss events that cause processes to wait.

```
SQL> @latch_int_10g.sql

Latch Name                     Get Requests
------------------------- ------------
Percent Get Misses Avg Sleeps / Miss Wait Time (s) No Wait Requests
------------------ ----------------- ------------- ----------------
Percent No Wait Miss
-------------------
Consistent RBA             5,670           0              0                0

FOB s.o list latch           203           0              0                0

In memory undo latch      22,929           0              0            5,163

JOX SGA heap latch         1,173           0              0                0
```

Figure 4.9 is a representation of the WISE tool's latch activity.

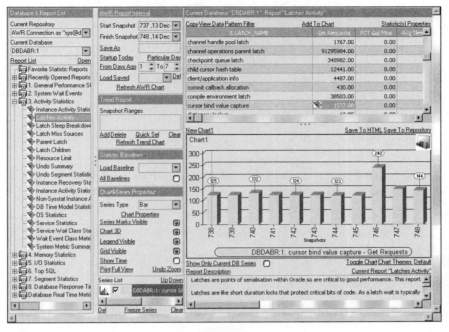

Figure 4.9: *Latch Activity chart in WISE*

This WISE screenshot shows a chart that was produced using the Latch Activity report. This report allows the quick identification of the times when particular latches experienced the most waits. Using this report together with Latch Miss Sources report and others allows the identification of the root cause of latch misses/sleeps.

dba_hist_latch_misses_summary

The *dba_hist_latch_misses_summary* view displays historical summary statistics about missed attempts to get latches.

```
SQL> desc DBA_HIST_LATCH_MISSES_SUMMARY

Name                    Null?     Type
------------------      --------  ------------
SNAP_ID                           NUMBER
DBID                              NUMBER
INSTANCE_NUMBER                   NUMBER
PARENT_NAME                       VARCHAR2(50)
WHERE_IN_CODE                     VARCHAR2(64)
NWFAIL_COUNT                      NUMBER
SLEEP_COUNT                       NUMBER
WTR_SLP_COUNT                     NUMBER
```

The following query can be used to get statistics on latch misses for a particular snapshot interval.

```
select    latchname "Latch Name",
          nwmisses "No Wait Misses",
          sleeps "Sleeps",
            waiter_sleeps "Waiter Sleeps"
From (
select e.parent_name||' '||e.where_in_code  latchname
    , e.nwfail_count - nvl(b.nwfail_count,0) nwmisses
    , e.sleep_count - nvl(b.sleep_count,0)  sleeps
    , e.wtr_slp_count - nvl(b.wtr_slp_count,0)   waiter_sleeps
  from dba_hist_latch_misses_summary  b
    , dba_hist_latch_misses_summary   e
 where b.snap_id(+)          = &pBgnSnap
   and e.snap_id             = &pEndSnap
   and b.dbid(+)             = &pDbId
   and e.dbid                = &pDbId
   and b.dbid(+)             = e.dbid
   and b.instance_number(+)  = &pInstNum
   and e.instance_number     = &pInstNum
   and b.instance_number(+)  = e.instance_number
   and b.parent_name(+)      = e.parent_name
   and b.where_in_code(+)    = e.where_in_code
   and e.sleep_count         > nvl(b.sleep_count,0)
)
 order by 1, 3 desc
```

The output of the query provides additional details about sleeps that occur while the database attempts to acquire a particular latch.

```
SQL> @latch_miss_int_10g.sql

Latch Name                                  No Wait Misses  Sleeps Waiter Sleeps
------------------------------------------- --------------- ------ -------------
KWQMN job cache list latch kwqmnuji: update job it  0            8        0
cache buffers chains kcbgcur: kslbegin              0            2        0
cache buffers chains kcbgtcr: fast path             0            2        0
cache buffers lru chain kcbzgws_1                   0            1        1
latch wait list No latch                            0        1,163    1,163
library cache kgldti: 2child                        0            3        0
```

```
library cache kglhdgc: child:                        0         1      0
library cache kglic                                  0         3      0
library cache kglobld                                0         1      2
library cache kglobpn: child:                        0        11     15
library cache kglpin                                 0         4      0
library cache kglpnc: child                          0        51  1,606
library cache kglpndl: child: after processing       0         7      0
library cache kglpndl: child: before processing      0     1,016     40
```

The WISE tool contains several reports for analyzing latch related statistics such as Latches Activity, Latch Sleep Breakdown, Parent Latch, Latch Children, and Latch Miss Sources.

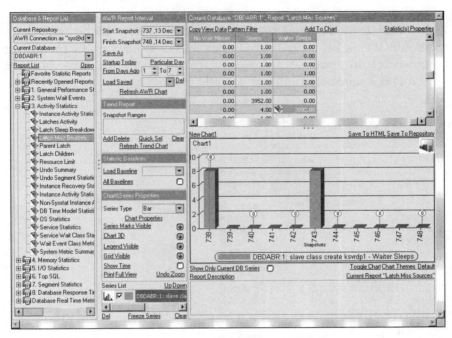

Figure 4.10: *AWR Latch Miss Sources chart in WISE*

The above figure shows a sample WISE screenshot with a chart produced by the Latch Miss Sources report.

*   See the code depot page for instructions on downloading a free copy of WISE

dba_hist_librarycache

The *dba_hist_librarycache* view contains the statistical history for library cache activity. This view stores snapshots for the *v$librarycache* dynamic view. The library cache stores SQL cursors, Java classes, and PL/SQL programs in executable form. If library cache contention is significant, this view can be queried to get more details about particular library objects that may cause such a contention. These details will give users hints about ways to potentially reduce library cache contention.

In order to understand the importance of library cache tuning, users should always be aware that a library and dictionary cache miss is more expensive in terms of resources than data buffer miss because it involves a significant amount of CPU work.

```
SQL> desc DBA_HIST_LIBRARYCACHE

Name                     Null?      Type
------------------       --------   ------------
SNAP_ID                  NOT NULL   NUMBER
DBID                     NOT NULL   NUMBER
INSTANCE_NUMBER          NOT NULL   NUMBER
NAMESPACE                NOT NULL   VARCHAR2(15)
GETS                                NUMBER
GETHITS                             NUMBER
PINS                                NUMBER
PINHITS                             NUMBER
RELOADS                             NUMBER
INVALIDATIONS                       NUMBER
DLM_LOCK_REQUESTS                   NUMBER
DLM_PIN_REQUESTS                    NUMBER
DLM_PIN_RELEASES                    NUMBER
DLM_INVALIDATION_                   NUMBER
REQUESTS
DLM_INVALIDATIONS                   NUMBER
```

The following query can be used to get a report for library cache statistics.

```
select b.namespace "Name Space"
     , e.gets - b.gets   "Get Requests"
     , to_number(decode(e.gets,b.gets,null,
       100 - (e.gethits - b.gethits) * 100/(e.gets - b.gets))) "Get
Pct Miss"
     , e.pins - b.pins "Pin Requests"
     , to_number(decode(e.pins,b.pins,null,
```

```
        100 - (e.pinhits - b.pinhits) * 100/(e.pins - b.pins))) "Pin
Pct Miss"
      , e.reloads - b.reloads
"Reloads"
      , e.invalidations - b.invalidations
"Invalidations"
  from dba_hist_librarycache  b
     , dba_hist_librarycache  e
 where b.snap_id            = &pBgnSnap
   and e.snap_id            = &pEndSnap
   and b.dbid               = &pDbId
   and e.dbid               = &pDbId
   and b.dbid               = e.dbid
   and b.instance_number    = &pInstNum
   and e.instance_number    = &pInstNum
   and b.instance_number    = e.instance_number
   and b.namespace          = e.namespace
```

The following is a possible result of this query.

```
SQL> @ Lib_cache_int_10g.sql

Name Space       Get Requests Get Pct Miss Pin Requests Pin Pct Miss   Reloads
Invalidations
---------------- ------------ ------------ ------------ ------------ ---------- ------
BODY                    1840  5,76086957          3117  4,39525184        24       0
CLUSTER                  216  2,31481481           532  1,12781955         1       0
INDEX                     37  97,2972973            41  87,804878          0       0
JAVA DATA                  3  33,3333333             5          40         0       0
JAVA RESOURCE              0                         0                     0       0
JAVA SOURCE                0                         0                     0       0
OBJECT                     0                         0                     0       0
PIPE                       0                         0                     0       0
SQL AREA               31706   7,459156        120148  2,84482472       495      60
TABLE/PROCEDURE        13926  17,6576188        83460  5,5415768        425       0
TRIGGER                  119  14,2857143           488  3,89344262         2       0
```

The report shows what particular types of library cache contents have
the highest miss percentage. This means that these objects require
additional work to reload them back into library cache, thereby causing
CPU overhead.

The WISE tool has a report named Library Cache, represented in
Figure 4.11, which generates charts against the *dba_hist_librarycache*
view.

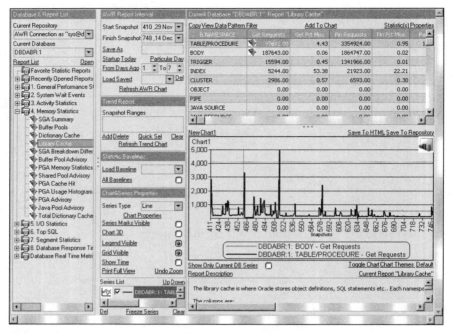

Figure 4.11: *AWR Library Cache chart in WISE*

The above WISE screenshot displays a sample chart produced for particular types of library cache objects. This chart shows an activity history of how the database requested particular types of objects during the selected snapshot interval.

dba_hist_rowcache_summary

The *dba_hist_rowcache_summary* view stores history summary statistics for data dictionary cache activity. This view contains snapshots for the *v$rowcache* dynamic view. The data dictionary cache stores metadata information about schema objects that participate in SQL parsing or compilation of PL/SQL programs.

---

*   See the code depot page for instructions on downloading a free copy of WISE

```
SQL> desc DBA_HIST_ROWCACHE_SUMMARY

Name                    Null?     Type
-----------------       --------  -------------
SNAP_ID                           NUMBER
DBID                              NUMBER
INSTANCE_NUMBER                   NUMBER
PARAMETER                         VARCHAR2(32)
TOTAL_USAGE                       NUMBER
USAGE                             NUMBER
GETS                              NUMBER
GETMISSES                         NUMBER
SCANS                             NUMBER
SCANMISSES                        NUMBER
SCANCOMPLETES                     NUMBER
MODIFICATIONS                     NUMBER
FLUSHES                           NUMBER
DLM_REQUESTS                      NUMBER
DLM_CONFLICTS                     NUMBER
DLM_RELEASES                      NUMBER
```

The following query can be used to retrieve historical statistical data for data dictionary cache:

```
select
  param    "Parameter",
  gets     "Get Requests",
  getm     "Pct Miss"
From
(select lower(b.parameter)
param
     , e.gets - b.gets
gets
     , to_number(decode(e.gets,b.gets,null,
       (e.getmisses - b.getmisses) * 100/(e.gets - b.gets)))
getm
     , e.scans - b.scans
scans
     , to_number(decode(e.scans,b.scans,null,
       (e.scanmisses - b.scanmisses) * 100/(e.scans - b.scans)))
scanm
     , e.modifications - b.modifications
mods
     , e.usage
usage
  from dba_hist_rowcache_summary  b
     , dba_hist_rowcache_summary  e
 where b.snap_id          = &pBgnSnap
   and e.snap_id          = &pEndSnap
   and b.dbid             = &pDbId
   and e.dbid             = &pDbId
   and b.dbid             = e.dbid
   and b.instance_number  = &pInstNum
   and e.instance_number  = &pInstNum
   and b.instance_number  = e.instance_number
```

```
    and b.parameter       = e.parameter
    and e.gets - b.gets   > 0    )
 order by param;
```

The following is a sample output from this script that displays details about dictionary cache activity for a particular snapshot interval.

```
SQL> @rowcache_int_10g.sql

Parameter                          Get Requests    Pct Miss
--------------------------------   ------------   -----------
dc_awr_control                           23,167          .00
dc_constraints                              558        33.51
dc_files                                  2,748          .00
dc_global_oids                        3,018,842          .00
dc_histogram_data                        55,080        15.47
dc_histogram_defs                       225,507        16.29
dc_object_ids                         3,269,890          .05
dc_objects                              265,208         1.34
dc_profiles                              29,205          .00
dc_rollback_segments                    155,231          .00
dc_segments                             348,808          .31
dc_sequences                                763         1.31
dc_table_scns                                38       100.00
dc_tablespace_quotas                          6          .00
dc_tablespaces                          582,952          .00
dc_usernames                             65,451          .02
dc_users                              3,753,587          .00
outstanding_alerts                       13,822         3.43
```

The WISE tool has a report named Dictionary Cache, represented in Figure 4.12, which generates charts against the *dba_hist_rowcache_summary* view.

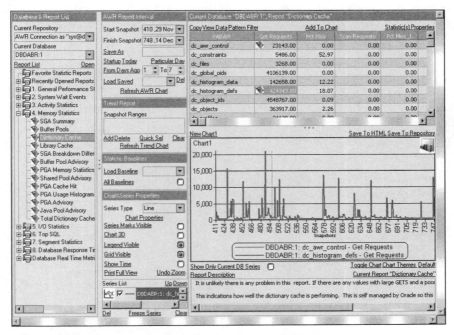

Figure 4.12: *AWR Dictionary Cache chart in WISE*

The above figure presents a WISE screenshot with a sample chart produced for particular data dictionary objects activity during the snapshot interval observed.

dba_hist_buffer_pool_stat

The *dba_hist_buffer_pool_stat* view contains statistical history for all buffer pools configured for the instance. Additional non-default buffer caches can be used as keep and recycle caches in order to address atypical access patterns to data segments.

```
SQL> desc DBA_HIST_BUFFER_POOL_STAT

Name                                        Null?      Type
----------------------------------------    --------   ----------
SNAP_ID                                     NOT NULL   NUMBER
DBID                                        NOT NULL   NUMBER
INSTANCE_NUMBER                             NOT NULL   NUMBER
ID                                          NOT NULL   NUMBER
NAME                                                   VARCHAR2(20)
BLOCK_SIZE                                             NUMBER
SET_MSIZE                                              NUMBER
CNUM_REPL                                              NUMBER
CNUM_WRITE                                             NUMBER
CNUM_SET                                               NUMBER
BUF_GOT                                                NUMBER
SUM_WRITE                                             NUMBER
SUM_SCAN                                              NUMBER
FREE_BUFFER_WAIT                                      NUMBER
WRITE_COMPLETE_WAIT                                   NUMBER
BUFFER_BUSY_WAIT                                      NUMBER
FREE_BUFFER_INSPECTED                                 NUMBER
DIRTY_BUFFERS_INSPECTED                               NUMBER
DB_BLOCK_CHANGE                                       NUMBER
DB_BLOCK_GETS                                         NUMBER
CONSISTENT_GETS                                       NUMBER
PHYSICAL_READS                                       NUMBER
PHYSICAL_WRITES                                      NUMBER
```

This query can be used to review the statistical history of buffer pools for a particular snapshot interval:

```
select
     name
     , numbufs    "Number of Buffers"
     , buffs      "Buffer Gets"
     , conget     "Consistent Gets"
     , phread     "Physical Reads"
     , phwrite    "Physical Writes"
     , fbwait     "Free Buffer Waits"
     , bbwait     "Buffer Busy Waits"
     , wcwait   "Write Complete Waits"
     , poolhr   "Pool Hit %"
From
(select e.name
     , e.set_msize
numbufs
     , decode(   e.db_block_gets      - nvl(b.db_block_gets,0)
            +  e.consistent_gets   - nvl(b.consistent_gets,0)
           , 0, to_number(null)
           , (100* (1 - (  (e.physical_reads -
nvl(b.physical_reads,0))
                        / (  e.db_block_gets     -
nvl(b.db_block_gets,0)
                          + e.consistent_gets    -
nvl(b.consistent_gets,0))
```

```
                    )
               )
          )
     )                                              poolhr
  ,     e.db_block_gets      - nvl(b.db_block_gets,0)
    +   e.consistent_gets    - nvl(b.consistent_gets,0)     buffs
  ,   e.consistent_gets      - nvl(b.consistent_gets,0)     conget
  ,   e.physical_reads       - nvl(b.physical_reads,0)
phread
  ,   e.physical_writes      - nvl(b.physical_writes,0)
phwrite
  ,   e.free_buffer_wait     - nvl(b.free_buffer_wait,0)    fbwait
  ,   e.write_complete_wait  - nvl(b.write_complete_wait,0) wcwait
  ,   e.buffer_busy_wait     - nvl(b.buffer_busy_wait,0)    bbwait
  from dba_hist_buffer_pool_stat  b
  ,    dba_hist_buffer_pool_stat  e
 where b.snap_id(+)             = &pBgnSnap
   and e.snap_id                = &pEndSnap
   and b.dbid(+)                = &pDbId
   and e.dbid                   = &pDbId
   and b.dbid(+)                = e.dbid
   and b.instance_number(+)     = &pInst_Num
   and e.instance_number        = &pInst_Num
   and b.instance_number(+)     = e.instance_number
   and b.id(+)                  = e.id)
 order by 1
```

The output of the query looks like:

```
SQL> @Buf_pool_int_10g.sql

NAME                 Number of Buffers Buffer Gets Consistent Gets
-------------------- ----------------- ----------- ----------
Physical Reads Physical Writes Free Buffer Waits Buffer Busy Waits
-------------- --------------- ----------------- -------------
Write Complete Waits Pool Hit %
-------------------- ----------

DEFAULT                           8016     5,354,123      4,347,376
       100,070          41,865                 0              24
              0 98.1309731
```

The script output provides users with valuable history information about activity in configured data buffers. Analysis of this information will determine if pools are configured correctly and whether or not tables need to be re-assigned to a particular cache.

The WISE tool contains a report named Buffer Pools that shows history charts for buffer pools statistics.

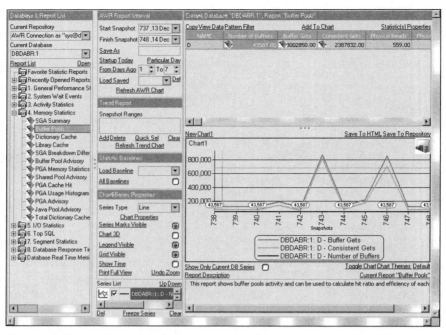

Figure 4.13: *AWR Buffer Pools chart in WISE*

In Figure 4.13, a sample WISE screenshot that displays a sample activity chart for a particular buffer cache is shown. This chart allows the visual identification of times when a buffer pool experienced high workload activity.

The next section provides more details about a *dba_hist* view that exposes operating system performance statistics gathered by database server.

---

* See the code depot page for instructions on downloading a free copy of WISE

Operating System Statistics in AWR

Operating system (OS) statistics such as CPU, disk input/output (I/O), virtual memory, and network statistics help identify possible bottlenecks where system hardware is stressed.

The AWR has a view called *dba_hist_osstat* that stores snapshots of the *v$osstat* dynamic view. OS statistics indicate how the hardware and OS are working, and thus, they reflect the workload placed on the database. These statistics can give an indication of where to first search the database for possible hot spots.

The structure of *dba_hist_osstat* view is:

```
SQL> desc DBA_HIST_OSSTAT

Name                                     Null?    Type
---------------------------------------- -------- ----------
SNAP_ID                                           NUMBER
DBID                                               NUMBER
INSTANCE_NUMBER                                    NUMBER
STAT_ID                                            NUMBER
STAT_NAME                                          VARCHAR2(64)
VALUE                                              NUMBER
```

To view history statistics for a particular snapshot interval, the following query can be used:

```
select e.stat_name "Statistic Name"
     , decode(e.stat_name, 'NUM_CPUS', e.value, e.value - b.value)
"Total"
     , decode( instrb(e.stat_name, 'BYTES'), 0, to_number(null)
          , round((e.value - b.value)/( select
       avg( extract( day from (e1.end_interval_time-
b1.end_interval_time) )*24*60*60+
          extract( hour from (e1.end_interval_time-
b1.end_interval_time) )*60*60+
          extract( minute from (e1.end_interval_time-
b1.end_interval_time) )*60+
          extract( second from (e1.end_interval_time-
b1.end_interval_time)) )
    from dba_hist_snapshot  b1
        ,dba_hist_snapshot  e1
   where b1.snap_id        = b.snap_id
     and e1.snap_id        = e.snap_id
     and b1.dbid           = b.dbid
     and e1.dbid           = e.dbid
```

```
         and b1.instance_number = b.instance_number
         and e1.instance_number = e.instance_number
         and b1.startup_time     = e1.startup_time
         and b1.end_interval_time < e1.end_interval_time ),2)) "Per
Second"
  from   dba_hist_osstat  b
       , dba_hist_osstat  e
  where  b.snap_id          = &pBgnSnap
    and  e.snap_id          = &pEndSnap
    and  b.dbid             = &pDbId
    and  e.dbid             = &pDbId
    and  b.instance_number  = &pInstNum
    and  e.instance_number  = &pInstNum
    and  b.stat_id          = e.stat_id
    and  e.value           >= b.value
    and  e.value           >  0
  order by 1 asc;
```

The query output looks like the following:

```
SQL> @os_stat_int_10g.sql

Statistic Name                        Total    Per Second
------------------------------  -----------   -----------
AVG_BUSY_TICKS                    1,974,925
AVG_IDLE_TICKS                    7,382,241
AVG_IN_BYTES                  2,236,256,256   23,881.91
AVG_OUT_BYTES                   566,304,768      6047.8
AVG_SYS_TICKS                       727,533
AVG_USER_TICKS                    1,247,392
BUSY_TICKS                        1,974,925
IDLE_TICKS                        7,382,241
IN_BYTES                      2,236,256,256   23,881.91
NUM_CPUS                                  1
OUT_BYTES                       566,304,768     6,047.8
SYS_TICKS                           727,533
USER_TICKS                        1247,392
```

This script allows a view of OS statistics in two forms: cumulative and per second. Thus, users are able to identify hot areas in the OS and hardware.

The WISE tool has a corresponding report called OS Statistics that is used to produce history charts. Figure 4.14 is a representation of the results of the OS Statistics from the AWR interval.

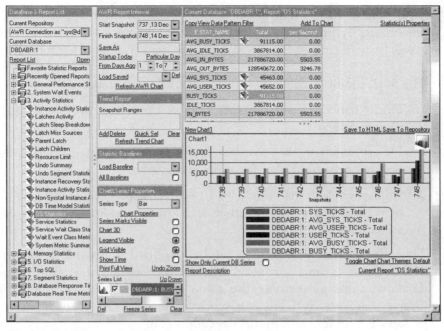

Figure 4.14: *AWR OS Statistics chart in WISE*

The above sample WISE screenshot displays a sample chart produced by the OS Statistics report. This chart allows the identification of times when operating system experienced the most workload and overhead during the snapshot interval observed.

The next section describes the very important *dba_hist* views that contain performance history information for SQL statements executed in the Oracle10g database.

SQL Statistics

SQL statements are the only way to access data in an Oracle database; therefore, it is nearly impossible to overestimate the importance of

---

See the code depot page for instructions on downloading a free copy of WISE

SQL tuning work. Most performance problems in an Oracle database are caused by poor SQL statements. It is important to learn how the AWR helps identify SQL statements that are candidates for tuning.

The SQL tuning process usually consists of three steps:

1. Find "bad" SQL statements that place a high workload on an Oracle database.

2. Determine that the cost-based optimizer (CBO) created a sub-optimal execution plan for those statements.

3. Implement actions which lead to alternative execution plans that provide better response times and lower workload for poor SQL statements.

Thus, the goals of SQL tuning can be identified as the minimization of SQL response time or reduction of the workload on an Oracle database while performing the same amount of work. In previous Oracle releases, SQL tuning work was mostly a manual iterative process for finding an optimal execution plan.

Fortunately, Oracle10g introduces automated SQL tuning tools in the form of the SQL Tuning Advisor and the SQL Access Advisor. These intelligent tools give Oracle tuning experts recommendations and advice. Recommendations may take the form of ideas on the collection of additional object statistics, creation or removal of indexes, restructuring of SQL statements, etc. Furthermore, all resulting recommendations contain an estimated benefit of its implementation.

Oracle DBAs have several options available for the identification of poorly performing SQL statements:

- Use of the AWR.

- Use of the STATSPACK utility.

- Use of SQL related *v$* dynamic performance views as *v$sql*.

- Use of the SQL trace facility.

The AWR can be used to find resource-intensive SQL statements. The AWR repository contains several SQL statistics related views:

- *dba_hist_sqlstat* view contains a history for SQL execution statistics and stores snapshots of *v$sql* view.

- *dba_hist_sqltext* view stores actual text for SQL statements captured from *v$sql* view.

- *dba_hist_sql_plan* view stores execution plans for SQL statements available in *dba_hist_sqlstat* view.

The *dba_hist_sqlstat* is the view that helps identify SQL statements that are candidates for tuning. A study of the structure of *dba_hist_sqlstat* view and the information available through it will further aid users in the identification of poor SQL statements.

The *dba_hist_sqlstat* View

This view contains more than 20 statistics related to SQL statements. The structure of the *dba_hist_sqlstat* view is:

```
SQL> desc DBA_HIST_SQLSTAT

Name                                     Null?     Type
---------------------------------------- --------- -----------------
SNAP_ID                                            NUMBER
DBID                                               NUMBER
INSTANCE_NUMBER                                    NUMBER
SQL_ID                                             VARCHAR2(13)
PLAN_HASH_VALUE                                    NUMBER
OPTIMIZER_COST                                     NUMBER
OPTIMIZER_MODE                                     VARCHAR2(10)
OPTIMIZER_ENV_HASH_VALUE                           NUMBER
SHARABLE_MEM                                       NUMBER
LOADED_VERSIONS                                    NUMBER
VERSION_COUNT                                      NUMBER
MODULE                                             VARCHAR2(64)
ACTION                                             VARCHAR2(64)
SQL_PROFILE                                        VARCHAR2(64)
PARSING_SCHEMA_ID                                  NUMBER
FETCHES_TOTAL                                      NUMBER
FETCHES_DELTA                                      NUMBER
END_OF_FETCH_COUNT_TOTAL                           NUMBER
END_OF_FETCH_COUNT_DELTA                           NUMBER
SORTS_TOTAL                                        NUMBER
SORTS_DELTA                                        NUMBER
EXECUTIONS_TOTAL                                   NUMBER
EXECUTIONS_DELTA                                   NUMBER
LOADS_TOTAL                                        NUMBER
LOADS_DELTA                                        NUMBER
INVALIDATIONS_TOTAL                                NUMBER
INVALIDATIONS_DELTA                                NUMBER
```

```
PARSE_CALLS_TOTAL                        NUMBER
PARSE_CALLS_DELTA                        NUMBER
DISK_READS_TOTAL                         NUMBER
DISK_READS_DELTA                         NUMBER
BUFFER_GETS_TOTAL                        NUMBER
BUFFER_GETS_DELTA                        NUMBER
ROWS_PROCESSED_TOTAL                     NUMBER
ROWS_PROCESSED_DELTA                     NUMBER
CPU_TIME_TOTAL                           NUMBER
CPU_TIME_DELTA                           NUMBER
ELAPSED_TIME_TOTAL                       NUMBER
ELAPSED_TIME_DELTA                       NUMBER
IOWAIT_TOTAL                             NUMBER
IOWAIT_DELTA                             NUMBER
CLWAIT_TOTAL                             NUMBER
CLWAIT_DELTA                             NUMBER
APWAIT_TOTAL                             NUMBER
APWAIT_DELTA                             NUMBER
CCWAIT_TOTAL                             NUMBER
CCWAIT_DELTA                             NUMBER
DIRECT_WRITES_TOTAL                      NUMBER
DIRECT_WRITES_DELTA                      NUMBER
PLSEXEC_TIME_TOTAL                       NUMBER
PLSEXEC_TIME_DELTA                       NUMBER
JAVEXEC_TIME_TOTAL                       NUMBER
JAVEXEC_TIME_DELTA                       NUMBER
```

The statistics for every SQL statement are stored in two separate columns:

- *<Statistic Name>_total* column stores the total values of statistics since the last instance startup;

- *<Statistic Name>_delta* column reflects the change in a statistic's value between *end_interval_time* and *begin_interval_time* that is stored in the *dba_hist_snapshot* view.

Using this core *dba_hist_sqlstat* view, poor SQL statements can be identified using such criteria as:

- High number of buffer gets.

- High number of physical reads.

- Large execution count.

- High shared memory usage.

- High version count.

- High parse count.

- High elapsed time.

- High execution CPU time.

- High number of rows processed.

- High number of sorts, etc

This view does not contain the actual text of SQL statements; however, it does contain a *sql_id* column. The SQL text can be retrieved by joining *dba_hist_sqlstat* with *dba_hist_sqltext* view. For example, the *high_sql_buf_gets.sql* script below retrieves high buffer gets SQL statements for a particular snapshot interval.

💾 high_sql_buf_gets.sql

```
-- *************************************************
-- Copyright © 2005 by Rampant TechPress
-- This script is free for non-commercial purposes
-- with no warranties.  Use at your own risk.
--
-- To license this script for a commercial purpose,
-- contact info@rampant.cc
-- *************************************************

select
          sql_id
        , buffer_gets_total                     "Buffer Gets"
        , executions_total                      "Executions"
        , buffer_gets_total/executions_total "Gets / Exec"
        , pct*100                               "% Total"
        , cpu_time_total/1000000                "CPU Time (s)"
        , elapsed_time_total/1000000            "Elapsed Time (s)"
        , module                                "SQL Module"
        , stmt                                  "SQL Statement"
from
(select
            e.sql_id sql_id
          , e.buffer_gets_total - nvl(b.buffer_gets_total,0)
buffer_gets_total
          , e.executions_total - nvl(b.executions_total,0)
executions_total
          , (e.buffer_gets_total - nvl(b.buffer_gets_total,0))/
          (  select e1.value - nvl(b1.value,0)
            from dba_hist_sysstat b1 , dba_hist_sysstat e1
                where b1.snap_id(+)         = b.snap_id
                and e1.snap_id              = e.snap_id
                and b1.dbid(+)              = b.dbid
                and e1.dbid                 = e.dbid
                and b1.instance_number(+)   =
b.instance_number
```

```
                        and e1.instance_number      =
e.instance_number
                        and b1.stat_id              = e1.stat_id
                        and e1.stat_name            = 'session
logical reads'

) pct
            , e.elapsed_time_total - nvl(b.elapsed_time_total,0)
elapsed_time_total
            , e.cpu_time_total - nvl(b.cpu_time_total,0)
cpu_time_total
            , e.module
            , t.sql_text   stmt
      from dba_hist_sqlstat   e
         , dba_hist_sqlstat   b
         , dba_hist_sqltext   t
     where b.snap_id(+)           = @pBgnSnap
       and b.dbid(+)              = e.dbid
       and b.instance_number(+) = e.instance_number
       and b.sql_id(+)           = e.sql_id
       and e.snap_id             = &pEndSnap
       and e.dbid                = &pDBId
       and e.instance_number     = &pInstNum
       and (e.executions_total - nvl(b.executions_total,0)) > 0
       and t.sql_id              = b.sql_id
)
      order by 2 desc;
```

The WISE tool has several reports which allow the retrieval of top
SQL statements from the AWR based on various criteria.

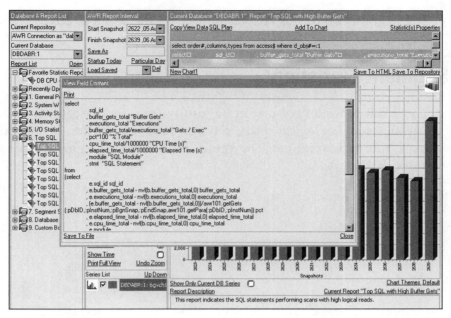

Figure 4.15: *AWR Top SQLs With High Buffer Gets Report in WISE.*

The above sample WISE screenshot presents a *TOP SQL's With High Buffer Gets* report that retrieves a list of SQL statements that had the most number of buffer gets during execution phase.

Furthermore, the WISE tool allows users to quickly drill down to execution plan details for particular SQL statements. In addition, the WISE tool allows the easy creation and viewing of SQL Advisor recommendations in a GUI environment.

Thus, the *dba_hist_sqlstat* view provides valuable information about SQL statements that are querying the database. By regularly checking this view, the primary causes of most performance problems can easily be identified.

---

*   See the code depot page for instructions on downloading a free copy of WISE

The next section of this chapter introduces the segment access related *dba_hist* views.

Segment Statistics

The AWR repository also stores a history for a set of segment related statistics such as logical reads, physical reads and writes, buffer busy waits, row lock waits, etc. The kernel AWR view for segment statistics is *dba_hist_seg_stat*.

```
SQL> desc DBA_HIST_SEG_STAT

Name                                     Null?    Type
---------------------------------------- -------- ----------
SNAP_ID                                           NUMBER
DBID                                              NUMBER
INSTANCE_NUMBER                                   NUMBER
TS#                                               NUMBER
OBJ#                                              NUMBER
DATAOBJ#                                          NUMBER
LOGICAL_READS_TOTAL                               NUMBER
LOGICAL_READS_DELTA                               NUMBER
BUFFER_BUSY_WAITS_TOTAL                           NUMBER
BUFFER_BUSY_WAITS_DELTA                           NUMBER
DB_BLOCK_CHANGES_TOTAL                            NUMBER
DB_BLOCK_CHANGES_DELTA                            NUMBER
PHYSICAL_READS_TOTAL                              NUMBER
PHYSICAL_READS_DELTA                              NUMBER
PHYSICAL_WRITES_TOTAL                             NUMBER
PHYSICAL_WRITES_DELTA                             NUMBER
PHYSICAL_READS_DIRECT_TOTAL                       NUMBER
PHYSICAL_READS_DIRECT_DELTA                       NUMBER
PHYSICAL_WRITES_DIRECT_TOTAL                      NUMBER
PHYSICAL_WRITES_DIRECT_DELTA                      NUMBER
ITL_WAITS_TOTAL                                   NUMBER
ITL_WAITS_DELTA                                   NUMBER
ROW_LOCK_WAITS_TOTAL                              NUMBER
ROW_LOCK_WAITS_DELTA                              NUMBER
GC_CR_BLOCKS_SERVED_TOTAL                         NUMBER
GC_CR_BLOCKS_SERVED_DELTA                         NUMBER
GC_CU_BLOCKS_SERVED_TOTAL                         NUMBER
GC_CU_BLOCKS_SERVED_DELTA                         NUMBER
SPACE_USED_TOTAL                                  NUMBER
SPACE_USED_DELTA                                  NUMBER
SPACE_ALLOCATED_TOTAL                             NUMBER
SPACE_ALLOCATED_DELTA                             NUMBER
TABLE_SCANS_TOTAL                                 NUMBER
TABLE_SCANS_DELTA                                 NUMBER
```

This view contains historical snapshots for the *v$segstat* dynamic performance view. Oracle10g also has a more user friendly dynamic view called *v$segment_statistics* which shows the same statistics along with additional owner and segment names, tablespace name, etc. Available segment-level statistics can be selected from the *v$segstat_name* view:

```
SQL> select name from V$SEGSTAT_NAME;

NAME
------------------------------------
logical reads
buffer busy waits
gc buffer busy
db block changes
physical reads
physical writes
physical reads direct
physical writes direct
gc cr blocks received
gc current blocks received
ITL waits
row lock waits
space used
space allocated
segment scans
```

Reviewing the segment-level statistics history helps to identify hot segments in the database such as tables and indexes, which possibly play a significant role in performance problems. For example, if the database has a high value of TX enqueue waits, the *dba_hist_seg_stat* view can be queried to find actual segments experiencing high row lock activity.

Users can query the *dba_hist_seg_stat* view using various criteria to identify hot segments. For example, the *seg_top_logreads_10g.sql* script retrieves top segments that have high logical reads activity:

💾 seg_top_logreads_10g.sql

```
-- ***************************************************
-- Copyright © 2005 by Rampant TechPress
-- This script is free for non-commercial purposes
-- with no warranties.  Use at your own risk.
--
-- To license this script for a commercial purpose,
```

```
-- contact info@rampant.cc
-- ****************************************************

select
    object_name "Object Name"
  , tablespace_name "Tablespace Name"
  , object_type "Object Type"
  , logical_reads_total "Logical Reads"
  , ratio "%Total"
from(
select
n.owner||'.'||n.object_name||decode(n.subobject_name,null,null,'.'||
n.subobject_name) object_name
    , n.tablespace_name
    , case when length(n.subobject_name) < 11 then
              n.subobject_name
           else
              substr(n.subobject_name,length(n.subobject_name)-9)
      end subobject_name
    , n.object_type
    , r.logical_reads_total
    , round(r.ratio * 100, 2) ratio
  from dba_hist_seg_stat_obj  n
     , (select *
          from (select e.dataobj#
                     , e.obj#
                     , e.dbid
                     , e.logical_reads_total -
nvl(b.logical_reads_total, 0) logical_reads_total
                     , ratio_to_report(e.logical_reads_total -
nvl(b.logical_reads_total, 0)) over () ratio
                  from dba_hist_seg_stat  e
                     , dba_hist_seg_stat  b
                 where b.snap_id  = 2694
                   and e.snap_id  = 2707
                   and b.dbid        = 37933856
                   and e.dbid        = 37933856
                   and b.instance_number  = 1
                   and e.instance_number  = 1
                   and e.obj#           = b.obj#
                   and e.dataobj#          = b.dataobj#
               and e.logical_reads_total -
nvl(b.logical_reads_total, 0)  > 0
                 order by logical_reads_total desc) d
          where rownum <= 100) r
 where n.dataobj# = r.dataobj#
   and n.obj#       = r.obj#
   and n.dbid       = r.dbid
)
order by logical_reads_total desc;
```

This script allows the identification of hot segments which experience high logical reads activity. This information may help with the selection of tuning actions such as the optimization of corresponding queries that access these segments, re-distribute segments across different disks, etc.

```
SQL> @seg_top_logreads.sql

Object Name                     Tablespace Object Type Logical Reads %Total
------------------------------  ---------- ----------- ------------- ------
SYSMAN.MGMT_METRICS_RAW_PK      SYSAUX     INDEX              46,272   8.68
SYS.SMON_SCN_TIME               SYSTEM     TABLE              43,840   8.23
SYS.JOB$                        SYSTEM     TABLE              30,640   5.75
SYS.I_SYSAUTH1                  SYSTEM     INDEX              27,120   5.09
PERFSTAT.STATS$EVENT_HISTOGRAM  SYSAUX     INDEX              26,912   5.05
```

The WISE tool also has several reports for the retrieval of hot segments using the following criteria:

- Top logical reads.

- Top physical reads.

- Top physical writes.

- Top buffer busy waits.

- Top row lock waits.

- Top block changes.

The *dba_hist_seg_stat* view has two columns for each statistic: total and delta. The total column shows the cumulative value of the statistic and the delta column shows change in the statistic value between *begin_interval_time* and *end_interval_time* in the *dba_hist_snapshot* view for the corresponding *snap_id* in the *dba_hist_seg_stat* view.

The next chapter section introduces the *dba_hist* views that are related to the I/O activity of the database.

Datafile I/O Statistics

Oracle10g database significantly improves the I/O subsystem through the addition of such great features as the Automatic Storage Management (ASM) facility. It is important to constantly monitor the I/O workload on the database because in a well tuned application, I/O remains a bound factor that can cause significant wait times in data access. I/O layout design is a complex process and includes consideration of the following points:

- Sufficient disk capacity for business needs.

- Appropriate data protection level using RAID levels, hardware, LVM, etc.

- Sufficient I/O throughput that does not exceed disk I/O bandwidth.

The AWR has several views that can be used to isolate datafile I/O related statistics as well as tablespace space usage statistics.

The *dba_hist_filestatxs* and *dba_hist_tempstatxs* views display information about I/O activity for data and temporary database files, respectively.

```
SQL> desc DBA_HIST_FILESTATXS

Name                 Null?    Type
-----------------    -------- ------------
SNAP_ID                       NUMBER
DBID                          NUMBER
INSTANCE_NUMBER               NUMBER
FILE#                         NUMBER
CREATION_CHANGE#              NUMBER
FILENAME                      VARCHAR2(513)
TS#                           NUMBER
TSNAME                        VARCHAR2(30)
BLOCK_SIZE                    NUMBER
PHYRDS                        NUMBER
PHYWRTS                       NUMBER
SINGLEBLKRDS                  NUMBER
READTIM                       NUMBER
WRITETIM                      NUMBER
SINGLEBLKRDTIM                NUMBER
PHYBLKRD                      NUMBER
PHYBLKWRT                     NUMBER
WAIT_COUNT                    NUMBER
TIME                          NUMBER
```

The *dba_hist_tempstatxs* view has the identical structure. Both views can be queried to monitor overall database I/O activity for a particular snapshot interval grouped by tablespaces using the *db_tbsp_io_10g.sql* query.

🖫 db_tbsp_io_10g.sql

```
-- ****************************************************
-- Copyright © 2005 by Rampant TechPress
-- This script is free for non-commercial purposes
-- with no warranties.  Use at your own risk.
--
-- To license this script for a commercial purpose,
-- contact info@rampant.cc
-- ****************************************************

select tbsp "Tablespace"
     , ios "I/O Activity"
From (
select e.tsname tbsp
     , sum (e.phyrds  - nvl(b.phyrds,0))  +
       sum (e.phywrts - nvl(b.phywrts,0)) ios
  from dba_hist_filestatxs  e
     , dba_hist_filestatxs  b
 where b.snap_id(+)          = &pBgnSnap
   and e.snap_id             = &pEndSnap
   and b.dbid(+)             = &pDbId
   and e.dbid                = &pDbId
   and b.dbid(+)             = e.dbid
   and b.instance_number(+)  = &pInstNum
   and e.instance_number     = &pInstNum
   and b.instance_number(+)  = e.instance_number
   and b.file#               = e.file#
   and ( (e.phyrds  - nvl(b.phyrds,0) ) +
         (e.phywrts - nvl(b.phywrts,0)) ) > 0
 group by e.tsname
union
select e.tsname tbsp
     , sum (e.phyrds  - nvl(b.phyrds,0))  +
       sum (e.phywrts - nvl(b.phywrts,0)) ios
  from dba_hist_tempstatxs  e
     , dba_hist_tempstatxs  b
 where b.snap_id(+)          = &pBgnSnap
   and e.snap_id             = &pEndSnap
   and b.dbid(+)             = &pDbId
   and e.dbid                = &pDbId
   and b.dbid(+)             = e.dbid
   and b.instance_number(+)  = &pInstNum
   and e.instance_number     = &pInstNum
   and b.instance_number(+)  = e.instance_number
   and b.file#               = e.file#
   and ( (e.phyrds  - nvl(b.phyrds,0) ) +
         (e.phywrts - nvl(b.phywrts,0) ) ) > 0
 group by e.tsname
)
```

This script allows users to look at the I/O activity on a per tablespace basis. It assists in finding hot tablespaces that experienced a large workload and may be candidates for further tuning consideration.

```
SQL> @db_tbsp_io.sql

Tablespace                      I/O Activity
------------------------------- ------------
SYSAUX                                  9630
SYSTEM                                  3658
UNDOTBS1                                1104
USERS                                     14
```

The WISE tool offers the following I/O related reports that build time-series charts for I/O database activity:

- I/O by datafiles.

- I/O by tablespaces.

- Total database I/O activity.

- Total tablespace I/O activity.

The screenshots below demonstrate sample chart reports available in WISE. These screenshots show a database's I/O activity by particular datafiles, tablespaces, or total database I/O. WISE also allows a view of I/O statistics averaged by hour of day, day of week, or month of year.

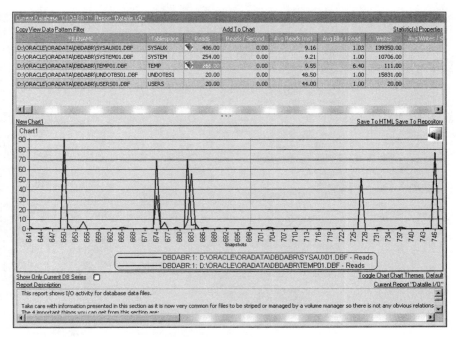

Figure 4.16: *AWR I/O by datafiles chart in WISE*

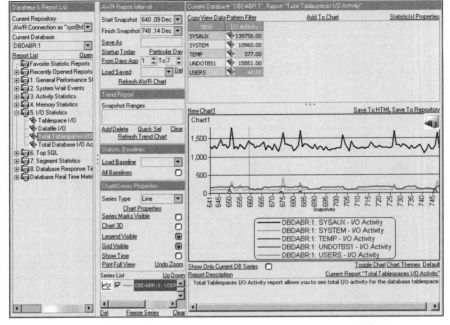

Figure 4.17: *AWR Total Tablespace I/O Activity chart in WISE*

The WISE screenshots in Figures 4.16 and 4.17 present charts produced for I/O activity for particular datafiles and tablespaces. These time-based charts allow the identification of time periods when the database experienced the heaviest I/O workload.

---

*   See the code depot page for instructions on downloading a free copy of WISE

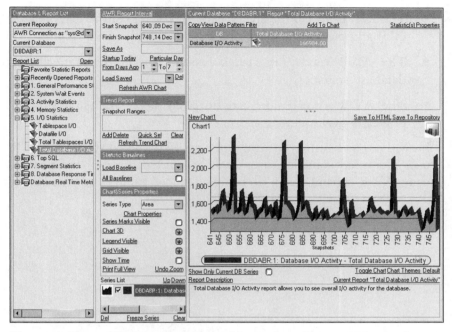

Figure 4.18: *AWR Total Database I/O Activity chart in WISE*

The WISE screenshot in Figure 4.18 displays the total database I/O activity chart that gives an overview of database I/O workload during the selected snapshot time period.

Conclusion

This chapter provided a familiarization with the structures of important AWR data dictionary views. In addition, it presented the statistic types available in AWR views and guidance on how to retrieve statistic history for a particular time interval. The main points of this chapter include:

- Oracle provides DBAs with a set of data dictionary views prefixed with *dba_hist* to access AWR information via queries.

---

* See the code depot page for instructions on downloading a free copy of WISE

- The WISE tool intensively uses AWR repository to visualize in GUI and plot performance history information in different forms.

- The AWR repository stores history for all major performance database statistics.

- The AWR information can be easily accessed using simple but powerful SQL queries.

Now that basic history information can be retrieved from the AWR for user identified statistics, users will be guided through the process of using AWR capabilities to do more advanced tuning and trend analysis.

References

Oracle10g documentation library:
otn.oracle.com/pls/db10g/portal.portal_demo3?selected=1

Oracle10g reference manual:
download-west.oracle.com/docs/cd/B12037_01/server.101/
b10755/toc.htm

Oracle Diagnostic Pack and Oracle Tuning Pack:
download-west.oracle.com/docs/cd/B12037_01/license.101/
b13552/options.htm

WISE site: www.wise-oracle.com

AWR vs. STATSPACK

Why Such a Difference?

The internal structures of the Oracle10g Automatic Workload Repository (AWR) and the information it stores have already been presented, but it is important to understand how the AWR evolved from STATSPACK. The AWR is similar to STATSPACK in that it takes time-based snapshots of all important performance tuning *v$* dynamic views and stores these snapshots in its repository.

Along with the AWR, Oracle10g delivers a new version of STATSPACK; the utility that is well known and highly recommended from previous releases of Oracle starting with 8.1.6.

Introduced in Oracle 10g, the AWR is a more advanced and convenient feature that has many additional, useful features. It is much like a next generation of STATSPACK. Of course, AWR is more automated and stores more information than STATSPACK.

Furthermore, performance data gathered by the AWR is extensively used by a number of automatic facilities such as the Automatic Database Diagnostic Monitor (ADDM), SQL Tuning Advisor, etc. Thus, Oracle Corporation documentation recommends the use of the AWR functionality over that of STATSPACK in Oracle10g databases.

The STATSPACK utility is still functional and can be used by Oracle DBAs the same way it has been used in previous releases. A look at the structure of the last version of STATSPACK and its general differences from the AWR is a good place to start.

Files Delivered with STATSPACK

In Oracle10g, STATSPACK utility consists of 20 SQL scripts located in the $ORACLE_HOME/rdbms/admin directory where the important database scripts are usually located. The following files form STATSPACK as distributed in Oracle10g:

- The *spcreate.sql* script is a main script for STATSPACK utility installation and should be run by user *sys*. This script calls some of the other creation scripts described below.

- The *spcusr.sql* script creates the *perfstat* schema. *perfstat* is the owner of all STATSPACK database objects that form the STATSPACK repository. This script also grants all the necessary authorities to user *perfstat*.

- The *spctab.sql* script creates all the STATSPACK objects under schema *perfstat*.

- The *spcpkg.sql* script creates a special statistics package that is necessary for snapshot and report generation.

- The *spdrop.sql* script uninstalls the STATSPACK utility from the database. This script calls the scripts: *spdtab.sql* and *spdusr.sql*

- The *spauto.sql* script is used to schedule the STATSPACK procedure called *statspack.snap* that gathers STATSPACK snapshots. In the AWR, this job performs a new background process called the Manageability Monitor (MMON).

- The *sppurge.sql* script purges old STATSPACK data from the repository. The snapshot range for the data to be cleared must be specified by the user.

- The *sprepcon.sql* is a new script in STATSPACK that is used to specify selected parameters that are related to report generation invoked by spreport.sql script.

- The *spreport.sql* and *sprepins.sql* are the scripts used for report generation. The *spreport.sql* script must be called to produce the STATSPACK report for a specified snapshot range.

- The *sprepsql.sql* and *sprsqins.sql* scripts are used to generate the STATSPACK report for SQL statements, statistics and plan usage.

- The *sptrunc.sql* script can be used to clear all the STATSPACK tables, thereby reclaiming space for the database.

- The *spuexp.par* is the name of the export parameter file which is used to export the whole STATSPACK user.

- The *sp*.sql* scripts are the upgrade scripts used to convert existing STATSPACK repository information to the latest Oracle10g version.

There are only two AWR installation scripts, which are also located in the $ORACLE_HOME/rdbms/admin directory:

- *catawr.sql* script creates data dictionary catalog objects for the AWR.

- *dbmsawr.sql* script creates the *dbms_workload_repository* package for database administrators.

By design, the AWR is created at the same time the database is created and is included in the data dictionary. This shows that the AWR is in the kernel part of the database that cannot function properly without it, while STATSPACK is a stand-alone utility that can be installed or removed from the database at any time. By default, the STATSPACK utility is not installed in the Oracle database. STATSPACK must be manually loaded into the database to start monitoring performance and gathering statistic history.

In Oracle10g, STATSPACK is shipped without the *spdoc.txt* file, which was a guide for working with STATSPACK that was included in previous versions. This is another mechanism by which Oracle Corporation urges the use of the AWR for performance tuning purposes rather than STATSPACK.

A look at the commonalities and differences between STATSPACK and AWR repository structures will be helpful at this point.

STATSPACK and AWR Statistics Comparison

In a previous chapter, it was shown that many of the internal AWR tables have similar structure to the corresponding STATSPACK tables that store snapshots of the same *v$* dynamic views. This supports the statement that the AWR is the next evolution of the STATSPACK utility. This similarity enables the easy conversion of existing performance reports originally designed for STATSPACK to new AWR views. Table 3.1 from Chapter 3 of this book contains a list of equivalent tables in the STATSPACK and AWR repositories.

The AWR repository holds all of the statistics available in STATSPACK as well as some additional statistics which are not. The following information on statistics is specific to those stored in the AWR that are not part of the STATSPACK.

STATSPACK does not store the Active Session History (ASH) statistics available in the AWR *dba_hist_active_sess_history* view. The ASH allows DBAs to perform time-series analyses of wait events for a particular session history.

An important difference between STATSPACK and the AWR is that STATSPACK does not store history for new metric statistics introduced in Oracle10g. The key AWR views, *dba_hist_sysmetric_history* and *dba_hist_sysmetric_summary*, help the DBA build time-series reports for important database performance metrics such as *Total Time Waited or Response Time Per Txn*.

The AWR also contains views such as *dba_hist_service_stat*, *dba_hist_service_wait_class* and *dba_hist_service_name*, which store history for performance cumulative statistics tracked for specific services.

The latest version of STATSPACK included with Oracle10g contains a set of specific tables, which track history of statistics that reflect the performance of the Oracle Streams feature. These tables are *stats$streams_capture*, *stats$streams_apply_sum*, *stats$buffered_subscribers*, *stats$rule_set*, *stats$propagation_sender*, *stats$propagation_receiver* and *stats$buffered_queues*. The AWR does not contain the specific tables that reflect Oracle Streams activity; therefore, if a DBA relies heavily on the Oracle Streams feature, it would be useful to monitor its performance using STATSPACK utility.

The WISE tool combines support for both STATSPACK and AWR features. It is able to generate time-series reports for both repositories at the same time. All the DBA needs to do is target the STATSPACK or AWR repositories for which time-series analysis is desired, and that's it! All of the reports available in the standard AWR and STATSPACK text reports are also contained in the WISE tool for charting. In addition, the WISE tool includes a number of valuable reports that are not included in the standard AWR and STATSPACK reports.

For example, the WISE tool has such useful reports as the Database Response Time Overview report and the Database Summary I/O report. The WISE tool has approximately 70 reports for the STATSPACK and AWR repositories.

Furthermore, the WISE tool is able to monitor most of the AWR metrics and performance statistics in real time charts. A sample real time monitor chart is shown below.

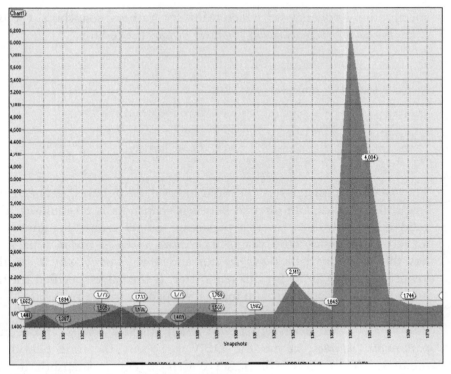

Figure 5.1: *Real time chart in The WISE tool.*

Now that the basic functionality of the AWR and the STATSPACK utility have been introduced, it will be helpful to see how database statistics are managed in each.

Statistic Management in AWR and STATSPACK

Both STATSPACK and AWR take a snapshot of the *v$* dynamic view and store it in repositories.

The AWR has a special background process, MMON, which is responsible for gathering regular snapshots. The DBA is able to

---

*   See the code depot page for instructions on downloading a free copy of WISE

---

specify the frequency at which MMON gathers snapshots via the *dbms_workload_repository.modify_snapshot_settings* procedure:

```
SQL> desc dbms_workload_repository

PROCEDURE MODIFY_SNAPSHOT_SETTINGS

Argument Name      Type              In/Out  Default?
----------------   ---------------   ------  --------
RETENTION          NUMBER            IN      DEFAULT
INTERVAL           NUMBER            IN      DEFAULT
DBID               NUMBER            IN      DEFAULT
```

The *interval* parameter sets the time interval, in minutes, between the snapshots. The default interval between snapshots is 60 minutes. The valid range of values for this parameter ranges from 10 minutes to 52,560,000 minutes (100 years). The *dbms_workload_repository* package has the global variables *min_interval* and *max_interval*, which set the lower and upper limits for this parameter. If the value specified for the interval is zero, automatic and manual snapshots will be prohibited.

The first *dbms_workload_repository.modify_snapshot_settings* procedure parameter, *retention*, allows the DBA to specify the time period, in minutes. The AWR will preserve that particular snapshot in the repository. The default value for this parameter is 10,080 minutes (seven days). The valid range of values for this parameter also ranges from 10 minutes to 52,560,000 minutes (100 years). The *dbms_workload_repository* package has global variables *min_retention* and *max_retention*, which set up the lower and upper limits for the *retention* parameter. If a zero value is specified for retention, snapshots will be stored for an unlimited time.

The current settings for AWR *retention* and *interval* parameters can be viewed using *dba_hist_wr_control* data dictionary view using this script:

```
select
     extract( day from snap_interval) *24*60+
     extract( hour from snap_interval) *60+
     extract( minute from snap_interval ) "Snapshot Interval",
     extract( day from retention) *24*60+
     extract( hour from retention) *60+
     extract( minute from retention ) "Retention Interval"
from dba_hist_wr_control;
```

This script returns the current AWR interval values in minutes:

```
Snapshot Interval Retention Interval
----------------- ------------------
             60              10080
```

The WISE tool provides a GUI interface, shown in Figure 5.2, which can be used to set the AWR interval parameters:

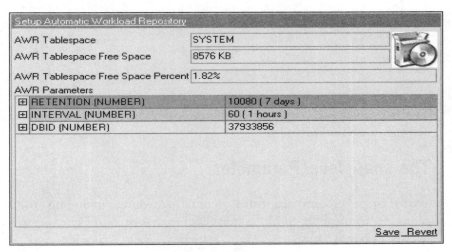

Figure 5.2: *Setting AWR parameters in the WISE tool.*

STATSPACK has many more settings that can be configured. These are kept in the *stats$statspack_parameter* table. This table stores a single row for the database parameters with the corresponding STATSPACK settings. These settings influence the amount of information STATSPACK gathers from the *v$* views.

---

*   See the code depot page for instructions on downloading a free copy of WISE

```
SQL> desc stats$statspack_parameter

 Name                                        Null?    Type
 ------------------------------------------- -------- -------------
 DBID                                        NOT NULL NUMBER
 INSTANCE_NUMBER                             NOT NULL NUMBER
 SESSION_ID                                  NOT NULL NUMBER
 SNAP_LEVEL                                  NOT NULL NUMBER
 NUM_SQL                                     NOT NULL NUMBER
 EXECUTIONS_TH                               NOT NULL NUMBER
 PARSE_CALLS_TH                              NOT NULL NUMBER
 DISK_READS_TH                               NOT NULL NUMBER
 BUFFER_GETS_TH                              NOT NULL NUMBER
 SHARABLE_MEM_TH                             NOT NULL NUMBER
 VERSION_COUNT_TH                            NOT NULL NUMBER
 PIN_STATSPACK                               NOT NULL VARCHAR2(10)
 ALL_INIT                                    NOT NULL VARCHAR2(5)
 LAST_MODIFIED                                        DATE
 UCOMMENT                                             VARCHAR2(160)
 JOB                                                  NUMBER
```

The *stats$statspack_parameter* configuration table stores the following settings for STATSPACK:

The *snap_level* Parameter

Snapshot level zero captures general statistics, including rollback segment, row cache, SGA, system events, background events, session events, system statistics, wait statistics, lock statistics and latch information.

- Level 5 includes the capture of high resource usage SQL Statements along with all data captured by lower levels.

- Level 6, only available in version 9.0.1 or later, includes the capture of SQL plan and SQL plan usage information for high resource usage SQL Statements, in addition to all data captured by lower levels.

- Level 7, also only available in version 9.0.1 or later, captures segment level statistics, including logical and physical reads, row lock, itl and buffer busy waits, as well as all data captured by lower levels.

- Level 10 includes the capture of child latch statistics, along with all data captured by lower levels.

session_id

This is the Session ID of the Oracle session for which session granular data is captured. The valid value is from the *sid* column in *v$* session. The default value is zero, which means no session.

num_sql

This is the number of SQL statements to be gathered for TOP Resource SQL reports. The default value is 50.

STATSPACK Collection Thresholds

The *executions_th*, *parse_calls_th*, *disk_read_th*, *buffer_gets_th*, *sharable_mem_th*, and *version_count_th* settings allow the DBA to set thresholds for SQL statements. If any of the thresholds are exceeded, the information will be stored by STATSPACK in the repository.

The above STATSPACK parameters can be set manually using the *statspack.modify_statspack_parameter* procedure:

```
SQL> desc statspack

PROCEDURE MODIFY_STATSPACK_PARAMETER

 Argument Name          Type           In/Out  Default?
 --------------------   -------------  ------  --------
 I_DBID                 NUMBER         IN      DEFAULT
 I_INSTANCE_NUMBER      NUMBER         IN      DEFAULT
 I_SNAP_LEVEL           NUMBER         IN      DEFAULT
 I_SESSION_ID           NUMBER         IN      DEFAULT
 I_UCOMMENT             VARCHAR2       IN      DEFAULT
 I_NUM_SQL              NUMBER         IN      DEFAULT
 I_EXECUTIONS_TH        NUMBER         IN      DEFAULT
 I_PARSE_CALLS_TH       NUMBER         IN      DEFAULT
 I_DISK_READS_TH        NUMBER         IN      DEFAULT
 I_BUFFER_GETS_TH       NUMBER         IN      DEFAULT
 I_SHARABLE_MEM_TH      NUMBER         IN      DEFAULT
 I_VERSION_COUNT_TH     NUMBER         IN      DEFAULT
 I_ALL_INIT             VARCHAR2       IN      DEFAULT
 I_PIN_STATSPACK        VARCHAR2       IN      DEFAULT
 I_MODIFY_PARAMETER     VARCHAR2       IN      DEFAULT
```

The WISE tool has a GUI interface that can be used to configure STATSPACK settings.

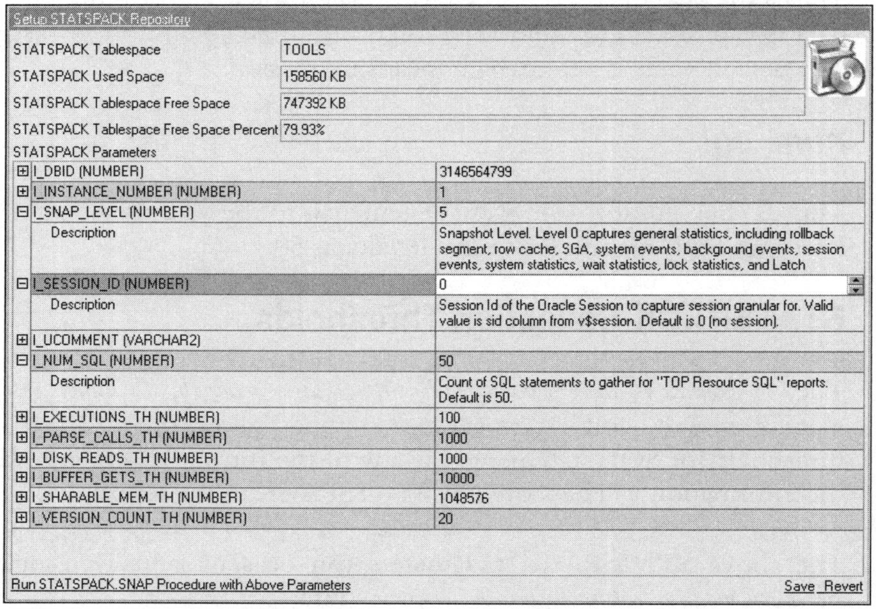

Figure 5.3: *Setting up STATSPACK parameters in The WISE tool.*

In Oracle10g, the use of STATSPACK requires more configuration settings than with the AWR. By default, the AWR requires no DBA intervention. STATSPACK has to be configured to work properly.

While the AWR is fully automated with regard to statistic history storage, it also allows the DBA to take new snapshots manually using the *dbms_workload_repository.create_snapshot* procedure:

---

*   See the code depot page for instructions on downloading a free copy of WISE

```
SQL> desc dbms_workload_repository
...
PROCEDURE CREATE_SNAPSHOT
 Argument Name                    Type          In/Out Default?
 -----------------------------    ------------  ------ --------
 FLUSH_LEVEL                       VARCHAR2      IN     DEFAULT
FUNCTION CREATE_SNAPSHOT RETURNS NUMBER
 Argument Name                    Type          In/Out Default?
 -----------------------------    ------------  ------ --------
 FLUSH_LEVEL                       VARCHAR2      IN     DEFAULT
```

The single parameter, *flush_level*, establishes the amount of information the AWR gathers. This parameter can have either the default value of TYPICAL or a value of ALL. When the statistics level is set to ALL, the AWR gathers the maximum amount of performance data. Usually, the TYPICAL level is quite enough for performance analysis and tuning purposes. The AWR uses the SPFILE initialization parameter, *statistics_level*, which specifies the level for snapshots gathered by the MMON process. The possible values for this parameter are the same, TYPICAL and ALL.

The package, *dbms_workload_repository*, also has the overloaded function, *create_snapshot*, which has the same parameter level and performs the same job as *create_snapshot* procedure except that it only returns the number of the newly created snapshot.

In the STATSPACK utility, the *statspack.snap* procedure must be executed manually as an Oracle job in order to gather history for *v$* statistics on a regular basis. The *statspack.snap* procedure must be called to take a new STATSPACK snapshot:

```
SQL> desc statspack

PROCEDURE SNAP

 Argument Name         Type          In/Out Default?
 -------------------   ------------  ------ --------
 I_SNAP_LEVEL          NUMBER        IN     DEFAULT
 I_SESSION_ID          NUMBER        IN     DEFAULT
 I_UCOMMENT            VARCHAR2      IN     DEFAULT
 I_NUM_SQL             NUMBER        IN     DEFAULT
 I_EXECUTIONS_TH       NUMBER        IN     DEFAULT
 I_PARSE_CALLS_TH      NUMBER        IN     DEFAULT
 I_DISK_READS_TH       NUMBER        IN     DEFAULT
 I_BUFFER_GETS_TH      NUMBER        IN     DEFAULT
 I_SHARABLE_MEM_TH     NUMBER        IN     DEFAULT
```

```
I_VERSION_COUNT_TH   NUMBER       IN    DEFAULT
I_ALL_INIT           VARCHAR2     IN    DEFAULT
I_PIN_STATSPACK      VARCHAR2     IN    DEFAULT
I_MODIFY_PARAMETER   VARCHAR2     IN    DEFAULT
```

The parameters for the *statspack.snap* procedure allow the DBA to specify the level of statistics gathered and the specific thresholds for the new snapshot. The settings specified in the call of statspack.snap procedure will be valid only for this single new snapshot.

The WISE tool provides the ability to submit the *statspack.snap* procedure as an Oracle job as well as take new snapshots with non-default threshold values and levels.

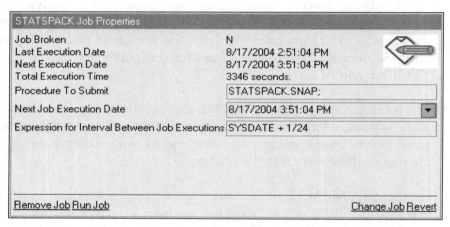

Figure 5.4: *Submitting STATSPACK as an Oracle job in WISE.*

Another essential difference between AWR and STATSPACK is the way that old statistical history is removed from the database. The AWR removes old snapshots from its repository based on the *retention* parameter, which specifies the length of time that any snapshot is stored in the database. DBAs do not need to manually clear the database of old information.

Thus, the total space consumed by the AWR remains relatively constant depending on the *statistics_level* parameter. However, the AWR also has a procedure for the manual removal of historical data called *dbms_workload_repository.drop_snapshot_range*.

```
SQL> desc dbms_workload_repository

PROCEDURE DROP_SNAPSHOT_RANGE

Argument Name        Type           In/Out Default?
------------------   ------------   ------ --------
LOW_SNAP_ID          NUMBER         IN
HIGH_SNAP_ID         NUMBER         IN
DBID                 NUMBER         IN     DEFAULT
```

STATSPACK, on the other hand, does not automatically remove its old data from the database. DBAs must manually remove old STATSPACK data from the database using either *sppurge.sql* script or the WISE tool, which supports a process that will automatically remove STATSPACK data on a specified schedule.

The summary reports for the AWR and STATSPACK can be built using SQL scripts such as *awrrpt.sql* for the AWR and *spreport.sql* for STATSPACK. In addition, the AWR is able to produce summary reports in HTML format. Fortunately, The WISE tool supports the conversion of summary text report files produced by STATSPACK to HTML format with the addition of some valuable performance tuning hints and tips based on an analysis of the processed STATSPACK report. Figure 5.5 is a sample HTML report produced from the source STATSPACK report:

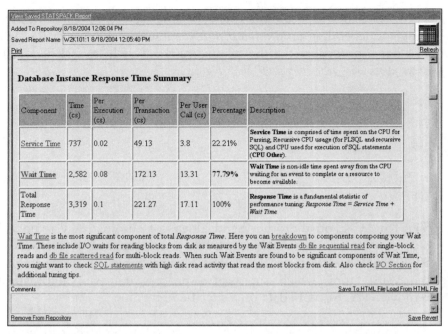

Figure 5.5: *STATSPACK report analysis in The WISE tool.*

The WISE tool is able to produce both AWR and STATSPACK reports and store them in its repository.

Another interesting point in the comparison of AWR and STATSPACK is that both utilities support the ability to store historical performance information from several databases in a single repository. This can be checked using *dba_hist* views or the underlying *wrh$* data dictionary tables. Each table contains *dbid* and *instance_number* columns, which are included as primary keys on *wrh$* data dictionary tables.

In the case of STATSPACK, most *stats$* repository tables contain *dbid* and *instance_number* columns, which are included as primary keys. This process allows the storage of different subsets of performance history

---

* See the code depot page for instructions on downloading a free copy of WISE

data from different databases in a single repository. However, the current release of Oracle10g does not support any documented method of exporting/importing AWR data between databases. Perhaps this functionality will be provided in a future release of the Oracle software.

As shown in Figure 5.6, the WISE tool can be used to facilitate the task of moving STATSPACK data to another database. All the DBA needs to do is specify the source and target databases and the snapshots to be moved. That's it! All the remaining work is performed automatically by the WISE tool.

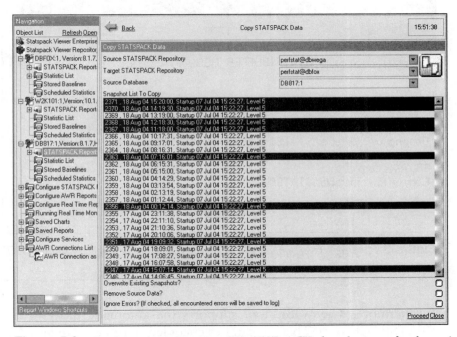

Figure 5.6: *Configuration of moving STATSPACK data between databases in The WISE tool.*

The STATSPACK utility has a documented method for moving data between different repositories using Oracle Export/Import utilities. A special parameter file, *spuexp.par*, is delivered with STATSPACK as a sample export parameter file. However, moving STATSPACK data between databases using the Export/Import approach is a complex process.

While the data is being moved, the WISE tool displays a work progress dialog box that shows the status of current process as shown in Figure 5.7 below:

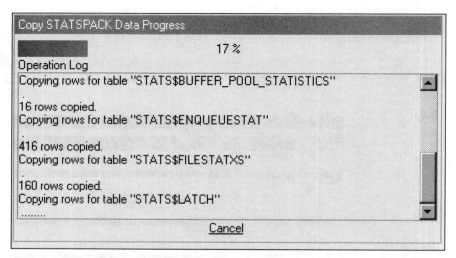

Figure 5.7: *Progress of moving STATSPACK data between databases in The WISE tool.*

Furthermore, The WISE tool supports the automatic movement of STATSPACK data. This job can be scheduled to run on a regular basis for automatic execution and the WISE tool will move data from the STATSPACK repositories to a single place without manual intervention.

<hr />

STATSPACK's ability to store performance data from multiple databases allows DBAs to establish a single STATSPACK storage database that will store data from all Oracle databases. The WISE tool supports the analysis and charting of historical data for different databases stored in a single place.

There is one more significant difference between the AWR and STATSPACK. The AWR supports the creation and ability to work with baselines. A baseline is a set of statistics that is defined by a beginning and ending pair of snapshots. A baseline can be created using the *dbms_workload_repository.create_baseline* procedure:

```
SQL> desc dbms_workload_repository

PROCEDURE CREATE_BASELINE

Argument Name        Type                     In/Out Default?
----------------     ----------------------   ------ --------
START_SNAP_ID        NUMBER                   IN
END_SNAP_ID          NUMBER                   IN
BASELINE_NAME        VARCHAR2                 IN
DBID                 NUMBER                   IN     DEFAULT

FUNCTION CREATE_BASELINE RETURNS NUMBER

Argument Name        Type                     In/Out Default?
----------------     ----------------------   ------ --------
START_SNAP_ID        NUMBER                   IN
END_SNAP_ID          NUMBER                   IN
BASELINE_NAME        VARCHAR2                 IN
DBID                 NUMBER                   IN     DEFAULT
```

All of the baselines that are created are visible in the *dba_hist_baselines* view:

```
SQL> desc dba_hist_baseline

Name                 Null?      Type
----------------     --------   ----
DBID                 NOT NULL   NUMBER
BASELINE_ID          NOT NULL   NUMBER
BASELINE_NAME                   VARCHAR2(64)
START_SNAP_ID                   NUMBER
START_SNAP_TIME                 TIMESTAMP(3)
END_SNAP_ID                     NUMBER
END_SNAP_TIME                   TIMESTAMP(3)
```

After two baselines have been created, statistics related to those two baselines can be compared. The AWR automatically preserves the snapshots, which are part of any existing baseline.

STATSPACK does not support the functionality of baselines; however, the WISE tool provides Oracle DBAs with the ability to create and work with baselines. Using the WISE GUI interface, a current statistic's behavior can be compared with a baseline.

Conclusion

In this chapter, the comparison of the AWR to the STATSPACK utility shows that the AWR presents a much more comprehensive and advanced tool when compared with STATSPACK.

The AWR gathers and stores history for an extended set of performance data that is available in Oracle10g. The main points of this chapter include:

- The great benefit of the AWR is that it requires minimal administration efforts from the Oracle DBA.

- The AWR gives Oracle DBAs a powerful tool for performance tuning and trend analysis. It is simple enough to be used as a monitoring tool by junior DBAs yet powerful enough to be used as an advanced data mining source for detailed time-series analysis, trend identification and capacity planning.

- The AWR forms an analysis base for Oracle10g intelligent self-tuning features such as ADDM, the SQL Tuning Advisor, Automatic Segment Management and ASM

Now that the similarities and differences between the AWR and the STATSPACK utility have been introduced, the next chapter will provide a detailed look into Oracle10g *v$* views.

Inside Oracle10g v$ Views

The Secret World of the *v$* Views

The previous chapter provided information on the new capabilities and major enhancements of AWR as compared to the traditional STATSPACK utility that is still available for free in Oracle10g database.

The AWR takes and stores momentary snapshots of many *v$* dynamic performance views, and this technique allows the deep analysis of database behavior using a time-series approach.

There are over 300 *v$* views available within the data dictionary, but not all of them are directly related to performance. For example, the *v$controlfile* view displays information about the status of database control files, and *v$version* shows details about core components of the

---

database server. These views play a significant role in the performance tuning job.

Significant changes and improvements in *v$* dynamic performance views have been introduced in Oracle10g. This chapter will present some of the enhancements as well as information on how the information available in the views can be used:

- There are new columns present in the *v$session* and *v$session_wait* views that track the resources for which sessions are waiting.

- A history of waits per session is collected. This enables the diagnosis of performance problems for a desired time frame and period. This sampled data is gathered by the Active Session History (ASH), which samples the current state of all active sessions. This data is available through the *v$active_session_history* view.

- There are new *v$* views that show new time model statistics. Time model statistics describe the total time spent by the database for each particular type of work. For example, the *sql execute elapsed time* statistic shows the elapsed time spent by the database to process SQL statements.

- There are new *v$* views that display a new type of statistic known as a metric. Metrics track the rates of change of activities in the database.

- Oracle10g maintains wait statistics for each SQL statement in the library cache.

- Oracle10g can create histograms of wait durations rather than a simple accumulated average.

This list is not exhaustive, but it reflects some major changes in the *v$* views that are of the most interest.

Changes in Wait Event v$ Views

All of the wait event columns from the *v$session_wait* view have been added to the Oracle10g *v$session* view. This facilitates the identification of waiting sessions without the need to join the *v$session* and *v$session_wait* views, which can be quite costly in terms of resources.

The statement below can be used to determine the wait events that affect the most sessions.

```
SQL> SELECT wait_class, count(username)
FROM v$session GROUP BY wait_class;
```

Table 6.1 contains several new columns that have been added to the *v$session* view:

NEW *v$session* VIEW COLUMNS
sql_child_number
blocking_session_status
seq#
event
wait_class
seconds_in_wait
service_name
prev_child_number
blocking_session
event#
wait_class#
wait_time
state

Table 6.1: *v$session new columns*

Two columns have been added to *v$event_name* view that display information about wait events: *wait_class#* and *wait_class*. These columns help to the DBA group related events while analyzing the wait issues. For example, to list the events related to I/O, the following statement can be used:

```
SQL> SELECT name, wait_class#, wait_class FROM v$event_name
WHERE wait_class IN ('System I/O',' User I/O');
```

The output of this query, showing I/O wait classes, might look like:

```
NAME                            WAIT_CLASS# WAIT_CLASS
------------------------------- ----------- -----------
ksfd: async disk IO                       9 System I/O
io done                                   9 System I/O
control file sequential read              9 System I/O
control file single write                 9 System I/O
control file parallel write               9 System I/O
recovery read                             9 System I/O
ARCH wait for pending I/Os                9 System I/O
LGWR sequential i/o                       9 System I/O
LGWR random i/o                           9 System I/O
RFS sequential i/o                        9 System I/O
RFS random i/o                            9 System I/O
ARCH sequential i/o                       9 System I/O
ARCH random i/o                           9 System I/O
log file sequential read                  9 System I/O
log file single write                     9 System I/O
log file parallel write                   9 System I/O
db file parallel write                    9 System I/O
kfk: async disk IO                        9 System I/O
```

There are several wait classes available within Oracle10g that allow the analysis of wait activities more conveniently and granularly. To group all events by class to get a quick idea of the performance issues, the following statement can be used:

```
SQL> SELECT e.wait_class, sum(s.total_waits), sum(s.time_waited)
FROM v$event_name e, v$system_event s WHERE e.name = s.event GROUP
BY e.wait_class;
```

The output will look like:

```
WAIT_CLASS           SUM(S.TOTAL_WAITS) SUM(S.TIME_WAITED)
-------------------- ------------------ ------------------
Application                         354                925
Commit                            10715              18594
Concurrency                      584360              16525
Configuration                     94415              28140
Idle                            2691962          911122390
Network                           99645               2278
Other                            225773             445863
System I/O                       467075             275631
User I/O                         298723             335344
```

The *wait_class#* and *wait_class* columns have been added to the *v$session_wait* view. This view displays information about resources or events for which active sessions are waiting.

There are several new views introduced in Oracle10g which assist the DBA in the analysis of wait related statistics in more complex way:

- *v$system_wait_class*: This view provides the instance-wide time totals for each class of wait events.

- *v$session_wait_class*: This view provides the time totals spent in each class of wait event on a per session basis. This view can be useful as the first source of identifying where a particular session waits the largest amount of time.

- *v$event_histogram*: This view displays a histogram of the number of waits, the maximum wait, and total wait time on a wait event basis. Using this view, a histogram showing the frequency of wait events for a range of durations can be created. This information assists in the determination of whether a wait event is a frequent problem that needs addressing or a unique event. The following query, which filters out idle events, can be used to view this type of information:

```
SQL> SELECT  event,
        wait_time_milli,
        wait_count
FROM    v$event_histogram
WHERE   event in
        (SELECT name
         FROM    v$event_name
         WHERE   wait_class NOT IN ('Idle'))
ORDER BY 1,2
```

- *v$session_wait_history* – This view displays the last ten wait events for each active session. A query like the one below can be used to retrieve the last ten wait events for all sessions, as they occurred, for every session:

```
SELECT  a.sid,
        b.username,
        a.seq#,
        a.event,
        a.wait_time
FROM    v$session_wait_history a,
        v$session b
WHERE   a.sid = b.sid AND
        b.username is not null
ORDER BY 1,3
```

- *v$file_histogram* – This view displays a histogram of all single block reads on a per-file basis. To provide more in-depth data, the *v$file_histogram* view shows the number of I/O wait events over a range of values. The histogram can be used to determine if the bottleneck is a regular or a unique problem.

- *v$temp_histogram* – This view displays a histogram of all single block reads on a per-tempfile basis.

The *v$system_wait_class* view can be useful as the first source of information about where database spends the most time waiting. The following query can be used to take a quick look at system-wide wait activity and to quickly identify possible problem areas:

```
column TOTAL_WAITS format 999,999,999
column PCT_WAITS format 99.99
column TIME_WAITED format 999,999,999
column PCT_TIME format 99.99
column WAIT_CLASS format A20

SELECT   wait_class,
         total_waits,
         ROUND(100 * (total_waits / sum_waits),2) pct_waits,
         time_waited,
         ROUND(100 * (time_waited / sum_time),2) pct_time
FROM
(SELECT wait_class,
        total_waits,
        time_waited
FROM    v$system_wait_class
WHERE   wait_class != 'Idle'),
(SELECT   SUM(total_waits) sum_waits,
          SUM(time_waited) sum_time
FROM     v$system_wait_class
WHERE    wait_class != 'Idle')
ORDER BY 5 DESC;
```

The sample output of the above query is presented below:

WAIT_CLASS	TOTAL_WAITS	PCT_WAITS	TIME_WAITED	PCT_TIME
Other	747,485	4.50	957,039	50.37
System I/O	4,182,722	25.18	771,654	40.62
User I/O	188,448	1.13	81,534	4.29
Commit	341,861	2.06	53,797	2.83
Application	1,216,251	7.32	15,341	.81
Configuration	262,214	1.58	7,640	.40
Network	9,664,173	58.17	7,623	.40
Concurrency	10,618	.06	5,279	.28

The above listing summarizes the wait events information by wait classes and provides an overview of the contribution of every wait class to the total database response time. For example, in the listing above, the wait events that belong to other wait class caused the most database wait time than any other wait classes. The most important wait events that belong to other wait class are:

- log writer (LGWR) waits for redo copy

- latch free

- latch: redo allocation

- enq: TX – contention

New Active Session History *v$* View

Oracle10g introduces the *v$active_session_history* view that keeps a history for recent active sessions' activity. Oracle takes snapshots of active database sessions every second without placing serious overhead on the system. A database session is considered active by Oracle when it is consuming CPU time or waiting for an event that does not belong to the idle wait class. This view contains a considerable amount of information that is available in the *v$session* view, but it also has the *sample_time* column that points to a time in the past when a session was doing some work or waiting for a resource. *v$active_session_history* view contains a single row for each session when sampling was performed.

An interesting possibility becomes available with the introduction of the *v$active_session_history* view in Oracle10g. With this tool, Oracle DBAs are now able to trace sessions without the need to use the well known 10046 event to perform extended tracing. All tracing can be performed now using only SQL queries without the need to review raw trace files and format them using the TKPROF utility.

Oracle keeps session history in the circular memory buffer in the SGA. This means that the greater the database activity is, the smaller the amount of time session history available in the ASH view is. In this instance, it might help that the AWR *dba_hist_active_sess_history* view stores the ASH history for a longer time; however, the *dba_hist_active_sess_history* view stores ASH data snapshots only for the times the AWR snapshots were taken.

How can the information available through the *v$active_session_history* view be used?. If a session that is experiencing delays or hangs has been identified and the goal is to identify the SQL statement(s) the session is issuing, along with the wait events being experienced for a particular time period, a query similar to this one can be issued:

```
SELECT   C.SQL_TEXT,
         B.NAME,
         COUNT(*),
         SUM(TIME_WAITED)
FROM     v$ACTIVE_SESSION_HISTORY A,
         v$EVENT_NAME B,
         v$SQLAREA C
WHERE    A.SAMPLE_TIME BETWEEN '10-JUL-04 09:57:00 PM' AND
                              '10-JUL-04 09:59:00 PM' AND
         A.EVENT# = B.EVENT# AND
         A.SESSION_ID= 123 AND
         A.SQL_ID = C.SQL_ID
GROUP BY C.SQL_TEXT, B.NAME
```

The *current_obj#* column can be joined with the *dba_objects* view to get name of the object, or it can be joined with the current_file# column using dba_data_files to see the name of datafile that was accessed. Even a particular block that caused a wait event can be identified using the *current_block#* column.

It is also possible to identify hot datafiles, objects, or even data blocks that are being accessed by sessions more frequently than others and thus could be candidates for additional investigations. This query shows hot datafiles that caused the most wait times during session access:

```
SELECT
  f.file_name        "Data File",
  COUNT(*)           "Wait Number",
  SUM(h.time_waited) "Total Time Waited"
FROM
  v$active_session_history h,
  dba_data_files           f
WHERE
  h.current_file# = f.file_id
GROUP BY f.file_name
ORDER BY 3 DESC
```

The sample output looks like:

```
Data File                              Wait Number Total Time Waited
-------------------------------------- ----------- -----------------
D:\ORACLE\ORADATA\DBDABR\SYSAUX01.DBF         5514         994398837
D:\ORACLE\ORADATA\DBDABR\SYSTEM01.DBF         2579         930483678
D:\ORACLE\ORADATA\DBDABR\UNDOTBS01.DBF         245           7727218
D:\ORACLE\ORADATA\DBDABR\USERS01.DBF          141           1548274
```

To be fair to the 10046 trace, the *v$active_session_history* does not catch session activity that is extremely fast, but it should catch activity that causes the most waits and resource consumption and will, therefore, be useful to the DBA. Statistically, the *v$active_session_history* does catch extremely fast operations if they occur sufficiently often to contribute to user time.

The following text includes several helpful queries that run against the *v$active_session_history* view. The first query reports a list of resources that were in high demand in the last hour. This query does not reflect Idle wait events.

```
SELECT
   h.event "Wait Event",
   SUM(h.wait_time + h.time_waited) "Total Wait Time"
FROM
   v$active_session_history h,
   v$event_name e
WHERE
      h.sample_time BETWEEN sysdate - 1/24 AND sysdate
   AND h.event_id = e.event_id
   AND e.wait_class <> 'Idle'
GROUP BY h.event
ORDER BY 2 DESC
```

The output looks like the following:

```
Wait Event                     Total Wait Time
------------------------------ ---------------
Queue Monitor Task Wait             10,256,950
class slave wait                    10,242,904
log file switch completion           5,142,555
control file parallel write          4,813,121
db file sequential read                334,871
process startup                        232,137
log file sync                          203,087
latch free                              36,934
```

```
log buffer space                        25,090
latch: redo allocation                  22,444
db file parallel write                     714
db file scattered read                     470
log file parallel write                    182
direct path read temp                      169
control file sequential read               160
direct path write temp                     112
```

The following query exposes database users who experienced the most wait times in the last hour. Idle wait events are also not counted.

```
SELECT
   s.sid,
   s.username,
   SUM(h.wait_time + h.time_waited) "total wait time"
FROM
  v$active_session_history h,
  v$session               s,
  v$event_name            e
WHERE
     h.sample_time BETWEEN sysdate - 1/24 AND sysdate
  AND h.session_id = s.sid
  AND e.event_id = h.event_id
  AND e.wait_class <> 'Idle'
  AND s.username IS NOT NULL
GROUP BY
  s.sid, s.username
ORDER BY 3
```

The output looks like the following:

```
      SID USERNAME                        Total Wait Time
---------- ------------------------------ ---------------
      137 DABR                                     17,955
      144 SPV                                      12,334
      152 SCOTT                                     3,449
```

The next useful query against the *v$active_session_history* view retrieves the SQL statements that experienced high wait time during last hour:

```
SELECT
   h.user_id,
   u.username,
   sql.sql_text,
   SUM(h.wait_time + h.time_waited) "total wait time"
FROM
  v$active_session_history h,
  v$sqlarea sql,
  dba_users u,
  v$event_name e
```

```
WHERE
    h.sample_time BETWEEN sysdate - 1/24 AND sysdate
 AND h.sql_id = sql.sql_id
 AND h.user_id = u.user_id
 AND h.sql_id is not null
 AND e.event_id = h.event_id
 AND e.wait_class <> 'Idle'
GROUP BY
  h.user_id,sql.sql_text, u.username
ORDER BY 4 DESC
```

The output of the query, showing the SQL with the highest wait time, looks like the following:

```
USER_ID USERNAME   SQL_TEXT                                                    total wait time
---------- ---------- ------------------------------------------------------- ---------------
       0 SYS        begin prvt_hdm.auto_execute( :db_id, :inst_id, :en             37107
                    d_snap ); end;

       0 SYS              begin          dbms_rcvman.setDatabase(upper            35378
                    (:dbname:dbname_i),
                       :rlgscn,                                    :rlgt
                    ime,                            :fhdbi:fhdbi
                    _i);         end;

      69 DABR       select    h.history.user_id,    u.username,    sql            8004
                    .sql_text,    sum(h.wait_time + h.time_waited) "To
                    tal Wait Time" from    v$active_session_history h,
                       v$sqlarea sql,    dba_users u where        h.sample
                    _time between sysdate - 1/24 and sysdate  and h.sq
                    l_id = sql.sql_id  and h.user_id = u.user_id  and
                    h.SQL_ID is not null group by    h.user_id,sql.sql_
                    text, u.username order by 4

       0 SYS        select pos#,intcol#,col#,spare1,bo#,spare2 from ic             594
                    ol$ where obj#=:1

       0 SYS        select /*+ rule */ bucket_cnt, row_cnt, cache_cnt,             142
                       null_cnt, timestamp#, sample_size, minimum, maxim
                       um, distcnt, lowval, hival, density, col#, spare1,
                       spare2, avgcln from hist_head$ where obj#=:1 and
                       intcol#=:2

      69 DABR       select    h.user_id,    u.username,    sql.sql_tex            121
                    t,    sum(h.wait_time + h.time_waited) "Total Wait
                    Time" from    v$active_session_history h,    v$sqla
                    rea sql,    dba_users u where        h.sample_time be
                    tween sysdate - 1/24 and sysdate  and h.sql_id = s
                    ql.sql_id  and h.user_id = u.user_id  and h.SQL_ID
                       is not null group by    h.user_id,sql.sql_text, u.
                    username order by 4

      69 DABR       select    s.sid,    s.username,    sum(h.wait_time             11
                       + h.time_waited) "Total Wait Time" from    v$activ
                    e_session_history h,    v$session s,    v$event_name
                    e where       h.sample_time between sysdate - 1/2
                    4 and sysdate  and h.session_id = s.sid    and e.E
                    VENT_ID = h.EVENT_ID   and e.WAIT_CLASS <> 'Idle'
                       and s.username is not null group by    s.sid, s.u
                    sername order by 3
```

Finally, the last sample query against the ASH view displays a list of database objects that caused the most wait times during the last hour. Idle wait times are not computed.

```
SELECT
  o.owner,
  o.object_name,
  o.object_type,
  SUM(h.wait_time + h.time_waited) "total wait time"
FROM
  v$active_session_history h,
  dba_objects o,
  v$event_name e
WHERE
      h.sample_time BETWEEN sysdate - 1/24 AND sysdate
  AND h.current_obj# = o.object_id
  AND e.event_id = h.event_id
  AND e.wait_class <> 'Idle'
GROUP BY
  o.owner, o.object_name, o.object_type
ORDER BY 4 DESC
```

With the WISE tool, the ASH can be monitored in real time using a GUI form like the representation in Figure 6.1 below:

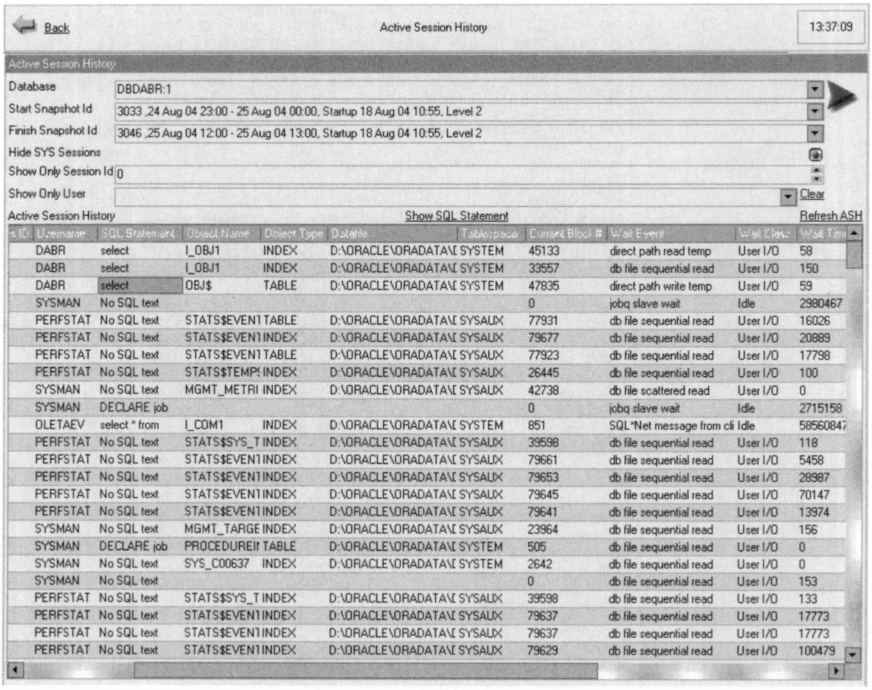

Figure 6.1: *Accessing ASH in the WISE tool*

New Time Model v$ Views

Oracle10g introduces a time modeling approach that allows the DBA to have a single scale by which to compare statistics in terms of time. Oracle10g measures cumulative processing times for the following database operations:

- DB CPU

- DB time

- Java execution elapsed time

- PL/SQL compilation elapsed time

- PL/SQL execution elapsed time

- Background CPU time

- Background elapsed time

- Connection management call elapsed time

- Failed parse (out of shared memory) elapsed time

- Failed parse elapsed time

- Hard parse (bind mismatch) elapsed time

- Hard parse (sharing criteria) elapsed time

- Hard parse elapsed time

- Inbound PL/SQL rpc elapsed time

- Parse time elapsed

- Sequence load elapsed time

- SQL execute elapsed time

There are two time model statistic *v$* views available: *v$sess_time_model* displays accumulated times per session basis; and *v$sys_time_model* shows system-wide cumulative processing times.

The time reported in both views is expressed in microseconds and represents the total elapsed or CPU time of operations. Background processing times are not computed for cumulative times except for statistics such as background CPU time and background elapsed time.

The most important statistics within the time model views are *DB time* and *DB CPU*. The DB time statistic in the *v$sess_time_model* view determines the total elapsed processing time spent by database for a particular session. The same statistic in the *v$sys_time_model* view represents the total cumulative time spent by Oracle for all sessions' CPU times and wait times spent for non-idle wait events. Therefore, the system-wide DB time can exceed the elapsed time since the last instance startup.

One great benefit of using the *v$sess_time_model* view is that it allows the quick identification of what part of the session's processing work spends most time. If a user is complaining about poor response times, once the SID for the user session has been grabbed, a query like this can be used to find out exactly what areas of work are causing the degradation:

```
SELECT  b.username,
        a.stat_name,
        round((a.value / 1000000),3) time_secs
FROM    v$sess_time_model a,
        v$session b
WHERE   a.sid = b.sid AND
        b.sid = 123
ORDER BY 3 DESC
```

The sample output looks like the following:

```
USERNAME    STAT_NAME                                           TIME_SECS
----------  ------------------------------------------------    ---------
SPV         DB time                                                23,133
SPV         sql execute elapsed time                                6,035
SPV         DB CPU                                                   3,399
SPV         parse time elapsed                                      3,205
SPV         hard parse elapsed time                                 2,976
SPV         connection management call elapsed time                  ,168
SPV         background elapsed time                                      0
SPV         PL/SQL execution elapsed time                               0
SPV         PL/SQL compilation elapsed time                             0
SPV         Java execution elapsed time                                 0
SPV         inbound PL/SQL rpc elapsed time                             0
SPV         hard parse (bind mismatch) elapsed time                     0
SPV         background cpu time                                         0
SPV         failed parse elapsed time                                   0
```

```
SPV        hard parse (sharing criteria) elapsed time       0
SPV        failed parse (out of shared memory) elapsed time 0
SPV        sequence load elapsed time                       0
```

New Database Metric v$ Views

In Oracle database releases prior to 10g, Oracle DBAs were often tasked to compute numerous statistics like ratios that give an overview of database performance and workload at a glance. For example, database buffer hit ratio, library cache hit ratio, or physical reads per second, etc. In order to compute such statistics, Oracle DBAs were required to write complex queries, which joined several *v$* views like *v$sysstat* and *v$statname*. These queries were quite resource costly and placed additional overhead on the database.

Now, nearly all significant database statistics such as those mentioned above are already automatically pre-computed by the database and are available for immediate use. The Oracle10g database introduces a new type of statistic known as a database metric. There are several database metric-related *v$* views available. The most interesting and valuable views will be presented in the following text.

All database metrics are grouped into two categories: long duration; and short duration. The long duration database metrics are computed by Oracle every 60 seconds, and short duration metrics are computed every 15 seconds. Furthermore, all metrics are grouped by their meaning. The available metric groups are available in the *v$metricgroup* view:

```
SQL> SELECT name,interval_size FROM v$metricgroup ORDER BY
interval_size;
```

The *interval_size* column specifies the sampling frequency, in hundredths of seconds, for every metric group. The names of the metric groups are self explanatory and identify each group as a long or short duration group.

```
NAME                                                INTERVAL_SIZE
-------------------------------------------------- -------------
System Metrics Short Duration                               1500
Session Metrics Short Duration                              1500
Event Metrics                                               6000
Event Class Metrics                                         6000
Service Metrics                                             6000
Tablespace Metrics Long Duration                            6000
Session Metrics Long Duration                               6000
System Metrics Long Duration                                6000
File Metrics Long Duration                                 60000
```

The available database metrics computed by Oracle can all be viewed through the *v$metricname* view. There are more than 180 metrics available. This view displays information such as metric name, corresponding metric group, and metric unit that exposes the meaning of the particular metric.

```
SQL> SELECT group_name, metric_name, metric_unit FROM v$metricname
ORDER BY group_name, metric_name;
```

The truncated output of this query shows the different metrics available:

```
GROUP_NAME                     METRIC_NAME                         METRIC_UNIT
------------------------------ ----------------------------------- ------------------------
Event Class Metrics            Average Users Waiting Counts        Users
                               Database Time Spent Waiting(%)      % TimeWaited / DBTime)
                               Total Time Waited                   CentiSeconds
                               Total Wait Counts                   Waits
Event Metrics                  Number of Sessions Waiting (Event)  Sessions
                               Total Time Waited                   CentiSeconds
                               Total Wait Counts                   Waits
File Metrics Long Duration     Average File Read Time (Files-Long) CentiSeconds Per Read
                               Average File Write Time (Files-Long CentiSeconds Per
Write
                               Physical Block Reads (Files-Long)   Blocks
                               Physical Block Writes (Files-Long)  Blocks
                               Physical Reads (Files-Long)         Reads
                               Physical Writes (Files-Long)        Writes
Service Metrics                CPU Time Per User Call              Microseconds Per Call
                               Elapsed Time Per User Call          Microseconds Per Call
Session Metrics Long Duration  Blocked User Session Count          Sessions
Session Metrics Short Duration CPU Time (Session)                  CentiSeconds
                               Hard Parse Count (Session)          Parses
                               Logical Reads Ratio (Sess/Sys) %    %
SessLogRead/SystemLogRead
                               PGA Memory (Session)                Bytes
                               Physical Reads (Session)            Reads
                               Physical Reads Ratio (Sess/Sys) %   %
SessPhyRead/SystemPhyRead
                               Total Parse Count (Session)         Parses
                               User Transaction Count (Session)    Transactions
System Metrics Long Duration   Background Checkpoints Per Sec      Check Points Per Second
                               Branch Node Splits Per Sec          Splits Per Second
                               Branch Node Splits Per Txn          Splits Per Txn
                               Buffer Cache Hit Ratio            % (LogRead -
PhyRead)/LogRead
                               CPU Usage Per Sec                   CentiSeconds Per Second
                               CPU Usage Per Txn                   CentiSeconds Per Txn
                               CR Blocks Created Per Sec           Blocks Per Second
```

```
CR Blocks Created Per Txn              Blocks Per Txn
CR Undo Records Applied Per Sec    Undo Records Per Second
CR Undo Records Applied Per Txn       Records Per Txn
Consistent Read Changes Per Sec      Blocks Per Second
```

Oracle keeps a history for database metrics in a circular memory buffer. This history is available through several *v$* metric views. This history is periodically saved to the AWR repository by MMON process as well. By default, Oracle retains database metrics history for one hour duration.

A rolling forward history for database metrics can be exposed through the use of such *v$* views as *v$sysmetric_history*, *v$waitclassmetric_history*, and *v$filemetric_history*.

The *v$sysmetric_history* view displays the history kept in memory for all system database metrics that for the last hour. The *begin_time* and *end_time* columns identify the time of interval for which a metric was computed. Only a single row for each metric per every interval exists in this view. Once Oracle adds a new metric value for a particular metric to the memory buffer, it removes the oldest row from memory buffer for the same metric at the same time. A query like the one that follows can be used to see a metric's behavior for the recent time period. For example, the following query shows data buffer hit ratio history for last hour:

```
SELECT
   'Buffer Cache Hit Ratio' "Metric Name",
   to_char(begin_time,'hh24:mi:ss') "Begin",
   to_char(end_time,'hh24:mi:ss') "End",
   round(value,2) "Value"
FROM
  v$sysmetric_history
WHERE
 Metric_name = 'Buffer Cache Hit Ratio'
ORDER BY
  Begin_time DESC;
```

The following is a sample of the output:

```
Metric Name           Begin    End         Value
--------------------- -------- -------- ----------
Buffer Cache Hit Ratio 13:56:15 13:56:32         99
                       13:56:00 13:56:15        100
                       13:55:45 13:56:00        100
```

New Database Metric v$ Views

```
13:55:32 13:56:32        99
13:55:32 13:55:45       100
13:55:17 13:55:32       100
13:55:02 13:55:17       100
13:54:46 13:55:02       100
13:54:31 13:55:32       100
13:54:31 13:54:46       100
13:54:15 13:54:31       100
13:54:03 13:54:15       100
13:53:45 13:54:03       100
13:53:32 13:54:31       100
13:53:32 13:53:45       100
13:53:17 13:53:32       100
13:52:31 13:53:32       100
13:51:33 13:52:31        99
13:50:31 13:51:33       100
13:49:33 13:50:31       100
13:48:31 13:49:33       100
13:47:32 13:48:31       100
13:46:32 13:47:32        99
13:45:33 13:46:32       100
13:44:31 13:45:33       100
13:43:30 13:44:31       100
13:42:31 13:43:30       100
13:41:32 13:42:31       100
13:40:31 13:41:32        99
13:39:33 13:40:31       100
13:38:31 13:39:33       100
13:37:33 13:38:31       100
13:36:31 13:37:33        99
13:35:33 13:36:31       100
```

Based on the information in the *v$sysmetric_history* view, the WISE tool allows the construction of charts for any database metric in real time. Furthermore, time series charts can be built for database metrics using the AWR repository as a data source. The screen shot below, Figure 6.2, is a representation of database metric charts which were built real time based on information in the AWR.

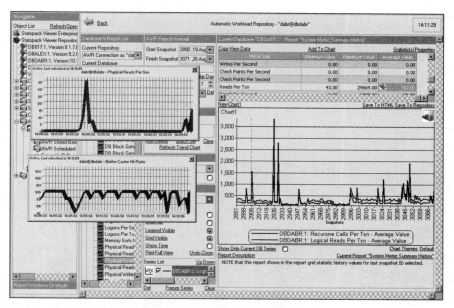

Figure 6.2: *Accessing database metrics in the WISE tool[*]*

Another metric view, *v$waitclassmetric_history*, allows an overview of the totals of wait database metrics for wait classes. The following metrics are available in this view:

- *average_waiter_count* shows the average number of waiters for wait class events for the sample time interval.

- *db_time_in_wait* reports total database wait time spent for the particular wait class.

- *time_waited* shows time waited during the sample interval.

- *wait_count* displays the number of waits that occurred during the sample interval.

By querying *v$waitclassmetric_history*, the history for recent database wait activity can be reconstructed. The query below can be used to view recent history for a particular wait class:

---

*   See the code depot page for instructions on downloading a free copy of WISE

```
SELECT
  c.wait_class                        "Wait Class",
  to_char(h.begin_time,'hh24:mi:ss')  "Begin",
  to_char(h.end_time,'hh24:mi:ss')    "End",
  h.average_waiter_count,
  h.time_waited,
  h.wait_count
FROM
  v$waitclassmetric_history h,
  v$system_wait_class c
WHERE
      c.wait_class_id = h.wait_class_id
  AND c.wait_class = 'User I/O'
ORDER BY
  h.begin_time DESC
```

The output looks like the following:

```
Wait Class              Begin     End       AVERAGE_WAITER_COUNT
TIME_WAITED WAIT_COUNT
-------------------- -------- -------- ------ ----------- -----------
ser I/O                 15:39:31 15:40:30      0          24          15
                        15:38:30 15:39:31      0           0           0
                        15:37:32 15:38:30      0           0           1
                        15:36:30 15:37:32      0           3           7
                        15:35:32 15:36:30      0           8         125
                        15:34:30 15:35:32      0          66          63
                        15:33:32 15:34:30      0           0           0
                        15:32:30 15:33:32      0           0           1
                        15:31:32 15:32:30      0           2           5
                        15:30:31 15:31:32      0           1           8
                        15:29:32 15:30:31      0           0           0
                        15:28:31 15:29:32      0           3           2
                        15:27:32 15:28:31      0           0           0
                        15:26:32 15:27:32      0           0           1
                        15:25:32 15:26:32      0           0           0
                        15:24:31 15:25:32      0           0           0
                        15:23:32 15:24:31      0           0           8
                        15:22:31 15:23:32      0           0           1
                        15:21:33 15:22:31      0           1           9
                        15:20:31 15:21:33      0           2          77
                        15:19:33 15:20:31      0           0           5
                        15:18:32 15:19:33      0        2117         944
                        15:17:30 15:18:32      1        3210        2310
```

The view *v$filemetric_history* reports such I/O metrics as averages for
file read and write times and the number of physical reads and writes
for both operations and blocks. This view allows the DBA to estimate
datafile I/O activity that occurred during the last hour. For example,
the following query retrieves the I/O metrics for a particular datafile:

```
SELECT
  f.file_name,
  to_char(h.begin_time,'hh24:mi:ss') "Begin",
  to_char(h.end_time,'hh24:mi:ss') "End",
  h.AVERAGE_READ_TIME,
  h.PHYSICAL_READS
 FROM
  v$filemetric_history h,
  dba_data_files f
WHERE
      h.file_id = f.file_id
  AND f.file_id = 3
ORDER BY
  h.begin_time DESC
```

The output looks like the following:

```
FILE_NAME                    Begin    End       AVERAGE_READ_TIME PHYSICAL_READS
-------------------------    -------- --------  ----------------- --------------
D:\ORACLE\SYSAUX01.DBF       15:46:30 15:56:33                  0              6
D:\ORACLE\SYSAUX01.DBF       15:36:30 15:46:30                  0              2
D:\ORACLE\SYSAUX01.DBF       15:26:32 15:36:30                  0             16
D:\ORACLE\SYSAUX01.DBF       15:16:31 15:26:32                  1           2156
D:\ORACLE\SYSAUX01.DBF       15:06:32 15:16:31                  0            314
D:\ORACLE\SYSAUX01.DBF       14:56:32 15:06:32                  1            821
D:\ORACLE\SYSAUX01.DBF       14:46:30 14:56:32                  0              0
```

Now that some of the new *v$* views have been introduced, the next section will present information on changes to existing SQL related v$ views.

Changes to SQL Related v$ Views

There are several significant changes made to the SQL related *v$* views. The following text addresses some of the most interesting and important changes that were introduced in the Oracle10g database.

Oracle10g includes changes to the *v$sqlarea* view that contains statistics for SQL statements which are already in memory, parsed and ready for execution and reuse. The following columns have been added to this view: *application_wait_time*, *concurrency_wait_time*, *cluster_wait_time*, *user_io_wait_time*, *plsql_exec_time*, and *java_exec_time*. These columns report different wait times that occurred during SQL execution. The following SQL query can be issued to get SQL statements that have high wait time for I/O:

```
SELECT sql_text, user_io_wait_time
FROM (select * from v$sqlarea ORDER BY user_io_wait_time DESC)
WHERE rownum <= 10;
```

The following is a sample output:

```
SQL_TEXT                                                 USER_IO_WAIT_TIME
------------------------------------------------------   -----------------
select obj#,type#,ctime,mtime,stime,status,dataobj               1670
#,flags,oid$, spare1, spare2 from obj$ where owner
#=:1 and name=:2 and namespace=:3 and remoteowner
is null and linkname is null and subname is null

select object_name, owner object_owner, status, ob                828
ject_type, created, last_ddl_time from sys.dba_obj
ects where object_type = :object_type and (owner =
user)

DECLARE JOBHNDL NUMBER;      BEGIN      :JOBHNDL :=          765
SYS.DBMS_DATAPUMP.OPEN(
operation =>:OPERATION,                              j
ob_mode => :JOB_MODE,                              rem
ote_link => :REMOTE_LINK,
 job_name => :JOB_NAME,                              v
ersion =>  :VERSION);        END;

BEGIN          SYS.DBMS_DATAPUMP.GET_STATUS(              517
               handle => :JOBHNDL,
          mask => :MASK,
     timeout => :TIMEOUT,
 job_state => :JOB_STATE,
status => :STATUS);      END;

select grantee#,privilege#,nvl(col#,0),max(mod(nvl          326
(option$,0),2))from objauth$ where obj#=:1 group b
y grantee#,privilege#,nvl(col#,0) order by grantee
#

select owner#,name,namespace,remoteowner,linkname,          154
p_timestamp,p_obj#, nvl(property,0),subname,d_attr
s from dependency$ d, obj$ o where d_obj#=:1 and p
_obj#=obj#(+) order by order#

select /*+ rule */ bucket, endpoint, col#, epvalue         142
 from histgrm$ where obj#=:1 and intcol#=:2 and ro
w#=:3 order by bucket
```

A new interesting view, *v$sql_bind_capture*, has been introduced to report information on bind variables used by SQL cursors. This view allows the retrieval of the actual values of bind variables for a given SQL cursor. The script below can be used to retrieve list of bind variables and the corresponding actual values used for a particular SQL statement. This query uses the *sql_id* address that should be specified for each unique SQL statement:

```
SELECT a.sql_text, b.name, b.position, b.datatype_string, b.value_string FROM
   v$sql_bind_capture b,
   v$sqlarea a
WHERE
      b.sql_id = 'dpf3w96us2797'
   AND b.sql_id = a.sql_id
```

The following is a sample output:

```
SQL_TEXT                                           NAME       POSITION DATATYPE_STRING
VALUE_STRING
-------------------------------------------------- ---------- ------- --------------- --
select owner, object_type, count (*) from all_obje :PAR            1 VARCHAR2(4000)  SYS%
cts where owner not like :par and object_type = :o
bjtype group by owner,object_type order by 1,2,3

select owner, object_type, count (*) from all_obje :OBJTYPE         2 VARCHAR2(4000)  TABLE
cts where owner not like :par and object_type = :o
bjtype group by owner,object_type order by 1,2,3
```

The changes to the SQL related *v$* views enhance the DBA's ability to evaluate the impact of SQL statements on the database. Overall, Oracle10g enhancements to the *v$* views provide new and exciting tools for the DBA to use in the evaluation of database performance.

Tips for v$data buffer contents

As noted in Chapter 14, *Oracle Insrance Tuning*, the *v$bh* view is very useful for examining the contents of the buffers. Several scripts have been referenced that can be used to display the data buffer contents with this powerful *v$* view.

Conclusion

The *v$* dynamic views play a significant role in database monitoring and tuning processes. They serve as sources for real time estimation of current database workload and health. The Oracle10g database introduced many great improvements to data dictionary dynamic performance views.

In this chapter, information was presented that will allow the DBA to make use of such new capabilities as the wait event interface *v$* views. Details were included on the active session history view called *v$active_session_history* as well as the valuable performance reports can run against it. The new Oracle time model approach and corresponding *v$* views yield information about where the database spends its processing time. Also, database metrics were introduced as a new database statistic type.

The *v$* dynamic views play significant role in database monitoring and tuning processes. They serve as sources for real time estimation of current database workload and health. Oracle10g database introduced a lot of great improvements and changes to data dictionary dynamic performance views.

The next chapter will explore the new Oracle10g metrics and how they can help in the tuning of an Oracle database.

Understanding the Oracle 10g Metrics

Oracle10g Metrics have a lot to say about performance

Inside Oracle10g Metrics

The dynamic *v$* views that were introduced or changed in the Oracle10g database were presented in another chapter of this book. This chapter covers, in more detail, the important database statistics known as metrics. Database metrics were introduced in version 10g of the Oracle database. Metrics represent various database performance statistics as rates.

These rates are measured using units such as time, number of database calls, number of transactions, etc. Metrics show the rate of change of cumulative database statistics. For example, the Hard Parse Count Per Txn metric reports the number of hard parses per transaction. The Total Table Scans Per Sec metric describes database full table scan activity per second.

One great benefit of metrics is that they are automatically computed by Oracle with minimal overhead placed on the database server. In previous Oracle releases, Oracle DBAs manually computed similar metrics using *v$* views like *v$sysstat*. With the release of Oracle10g, database metrics have become immediately available for use. Database metrics are perfect candidates for assisting the DBA with database monitoring tasks such as system health monitoring, database workload monitoring, problem detection and alerting, and self-tuning. Metrics are intensively used by internal Oracle10g clients for self-tuning purposes.

The server alert mechanism introduced in Oracle10g also uses database metrics for alerting DBAs when certain metrics violate their thresholds. The Manageability Monitor (MMON) background process, during its work, performs threshold verification and alert generation, if required. Using Advanced Queuing, the alerts generated are queued to a special alert queue owned by SYS. The Oracle10g Enterprise Manager (OEM) console provides access to the alert queue and notifies the DBA by e-mail or pager. Server generated alerts are always visible through OEM.

Custom thresholds for the database metrics that are available can be easily defined and activated using the OEM console. Furthermore, the DBA can create custom metrics and have MMON monitor them the same way it does the pre-defined metrics. Below is a sample OEM screen that provides access to database metrics.

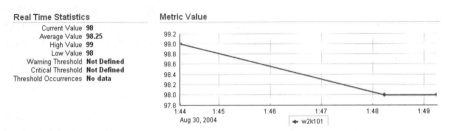

Figure 7.1: *Access database metrics in the OEM Console.*

Database metrics are not computed by Oracle when the initialization parameter called *statistics_level* is set to BASIC. In this event, Oracle does not collect AWR or metric statistics at all. The *statistics_level* parameter must be set to the default setting of TYPICAL, or it can be set to a value of ALL if the DBA wants to view and monitor database metrics.

The v$metric Tables

The MMON is the new background process that is responsible for gathering database metrics. MMON computes short duration metrics every 15 seconds and long duration metrics every 60 seconds. Database metrics are grouped by their meaning and duration. The available metric groups are available in the *v$metricgroup* view:

```
SELECT
   name,interval_size
FROM
   v$metricgroup
ORDER BY
   interval_size;
```

The *interval_size* column specifies the sampling frequency in hundredths of a second for every metric group.

Some of these metric values are more important than others, so the details on the most important metrics are presented in groups as follows:

- User Metrics are useful for getting details on total user waits and PGA usage.

```
METRIC_NAME                               METRIC_UNIT
----------------------------------------- ---------------------
Average Users Waiting Counts              Users
Blocked User Session Count                Sessions
PGA Memory (Session)                      Bytes
```

- Wait Metrics are useful for getting details on total waits and total session waits. These metrics are also very valuable in the AWR trend identification process as they can serve as a baseline value to compare with other AWR data. For example, a query could be written to determine the long-term relationship between Database Time Spent Waiting and suspected bottleneck events such as physical reads, CPU, Network waits, etc.

```
METRIC_NAME                                METRIC_UNIT
-----------------------------------------  ---------------------
Database Time Spent Waiting (%)            % (TimeWaited /
Total Time Waited                          CentiSeconds
Total Wait Counts                          Waits
Number of Sessions Waiting (Event)         Sessions
Total Time Waited                          CentiSeconds
Total Wait Counts                          Waits
```

- I/O Metrics are valuable for any I/O-bound Oracle database, and they show the overall performance of the disk I/O sub-system. Tracking these events is especially useful when determining where to replace platter disks with solid-state disks.

```
METRIC_NAME                                METRIC_UNIT
-----------------------------------------  ---------------------
Average File Read Time (Files-Long)        CentiSeconds Per Read
Average File Write Time (Files-Long)       CentiSeconds Per Write
Physical Block Reads (Files-Long)          Blocks
Physical Block Writes (Files-Long)         Blocks
Physical Reads (Files-Long)                Reads
Physical Writes (Files-Long)               Writes
Physical Reads (Session)                   Reads
Physical Reads Ratio (Sess/Sys) %          %
Logical Reads Ratio (Sess/Sys) %           %
```

- CPU Metrics are especially valuable since Oracle's SQL costing algorithm has shifted from I/O costing to CPU costing. Oracle has recognized that large data buffer caches such as *db_cache_size* and *db_keep_cache_size* have reduced overall disk I/O and driven up CPU consumption on the typical Oracle 10g database. These CPU metrics are also valuable for trend analysis in which overall "CPU Time (Session)" might be compared with consistent gets from the RAM data buffers.

```
METRIC_NAME                                METRIC_UNIT
-----------------------------------------  ---------------------
CPU Time Per User Call                     Microseconds Per Call
Elapsed Time Per User Call                 Microseconds Per Call
CPU Time (Session)                         CentiSeconds
CPU Usage Per Sec                          CentiSeconds Per
CPU Usage Per Txn                          CentiSeconds Per Txn
```

The AWR stores metrics history for those times when MMON takes the corresponding snapshot. The AWR does not retain all of the database metric history as it occurred over the course of time.

Database Workload Metrics

Database workload metrics describe different aspects of database workload activity. Two examples are the number of calls per second and the physical reads per transaction. These metrics help the DBA monitor the database and estimate how effectively it operates at any given moment in time. The *v$sysmetric_history*, *v$sysmetric*, and *v$sysmetric_summary* dynamic performance views allow access to information about these metrics.

The AWR captures snapshots of *v$sysmetric_history* which are available through the *dba_hist_sysmetric_history* view.

One great benefit of the *v$sysmetric_history* view is that it helps monitor the database workload in real time. It is very simple to build real time charts based on this view. For example, the Statspack Viewer (SV) tool provides such functionality as the plotting of real time charts for metrics with both short and long durations. The example in Figure 7.2 shows how SV monitors metrics in real time:

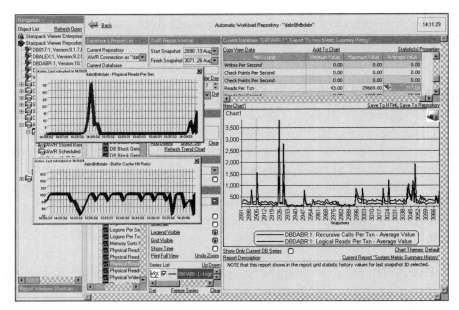

Figure 7.2: *Monitoring workload database metrics in real time using Statspack Viewer.*

Using a visual representation of database workload, it is simple to find correlations between the behaviors of database workload metrics and wait events that are caused by database processing. For example, if there are high values for log file switch completion or log file sync wait events, it is worth the DBA's time to view the workload for the Redo Generated Per Second metric in order to estimate the impact of the redo workload on these wait events.

The *v$sysmetric* view is similar to the *v$sysmetric_history* view, but it reports metric values for only the most current time sample. Both long and short duration metrics are available in the *v$sysmetric* view.

The *v$sysmetric_summary* view is also similar to the *v$sysmetric_history* view, but it has additional columns and it displays such summary information as minimum, maximum, and average values of database metrics as well as their standard deviations. These summary values are computed for the number of sample intervals included in the *num_intervals* column. The *v$sysmetric_summary* view reports data only for database metrics that belong to the System Metrics Long Duration metric group. This view can be used to build alert reports. For example, the following query shows database metrics that have more than 15 percent growth in their current value compared to average value:

```
SELECT
    to_char(m.begin_time,'hh24:mi')  "start time",
    to_char(m.end_time,'hh24:mi')    "end time",
    m.value                          "current value",
    s.average                        "average value",
    m.metric_name,
    m.metric_unit
FROM
    v$sysmetric          m,
    v$sysmetric_summary s
WHERE
        m.metric_id = s.metric_id
    AND s.average > 0
    AND ((m.value - s.average)/s.average)*100 >= 10
    AND lower(m.metric_name) NOT LIKE '%ratio%';
```

The following output shows the current and average values for metrics of interest to the DBA:

```
Start End T Curr Val Avg Val METRIC_NAME            METRIC_UNIT
----- ----- -------- ------- ---------------------- ---------------------
15:42 15:43       29      18 User Calls Per Txn     Calls Per Txn
15:42 15:43       63      31 Rows Per Sort          Rows Per Sort
15:42 15:43        5       3 CPU Usage Per Sec      CentiSeconds Per Second
15:42 15:43      294     180 CPU Usage Per Txn      CentiSeconds Per Txn
15:42 15:43       29      26 Current Logons Count   Logons
15:42 15:43      301     225 Response Time Per Txn  CentiSeconds Per Txn
15:42 15:43       17      15 Process Limit %        % Processes/Limit
15:42 15:43       18      16 Session Limit %        % Sessions/Limit
15:42 15:43        5       3 Database Time Per Sec  CentiSeconds Per Second
15:43 15:43       21      18 User Calls Per Txn     Calls Per Txn
15:43 15:43        7       3 Database Time Per Sec  CentiSeconds Per Second
```

Using the above script output, the DBA is able to identify the database metrics that have significantly changed from their average values. This report can point a DBA to some exceptional activity occurring in the database.

The AWR also takes snapshots for the *v$sysmetric_summary* view that are available through the *dba_hist_sysmetric_summary* view.

It is also possible to monitor database metrics on a per session basis. The *v$sessmetric* view contains a single row per current session and reports the following metrics:

- CPU usage by session.

- Number of physical reads.

- PGA memory consumption.

- Numbers of hard and soft parses.

- Physical and logical read ratios.

Using this view, database sessions can be monitored for extra resource consumption. For example, the query below returns a list of sessions which consume CPU time more than one percent of total database CPU time:

```
select
   s.sid,
   s.username
FROM
  v$sessmetric sm,
  v$session      s
WHERE
     s.sid = sm.session_id
AND
   (sm.cpu/(SELECT decode(value,0,-1)
    FROM
       v$sysmetric
    WHERE
      metric_name = 'cpu usage per sec')
*100) > 1;
```

The output of this query might look like:

```
SID     USERNAME
------  --------------------------
33      SCOTT
19      SYSTEM
```

Using the above output, a DBA is able to quickly identify sessions consuming extra CPU resources.

Now that database metrics used to describe database workload activity have been introduced, it is time to look at the metrics available in Oracle10g that show times database was waiting for something.

Database Wait Metrics

Database wait metrics describe database wait activity that occurred in the recent past. A list of the overall wait metrics is available in the *v$sysmetric* view:

```
SELECT
    group_name,
    metric_name,metric_unit
FROM
    v$metricname
WHERE
    group_name IN ('Event Metrics', 'Event Class Metrics');
```

The following is a sample output:

```
GROUP_NAME           METRIC_NAME                        METRIC_UNIT
-------------------  ---------------------------------  ----------------------
Event Metrics        Total Wait Counts                  Waits
Event Metrics        Total Time Waited                  CentiSeconds
Event Metrics        Number of Sessions Waiting(Event)  Sessions
Event Class Metrics  Total Wait Counts                  Waits
Event Class Metrics  Total Time Waited                  CentiSeconds
Event Class Metrics  Database Time Spent Waiting (%)    % (TimeWaited / DBTime)
Event Class Metrics  Average Users Waiting Counts       Users
```

The metrics listed in the output above give an overview of database waits that occurred. More detailed information about wait activity is available through the views presented below.

The wait metric view called *v$waitclassmetric_history* helps the DBA to get an overview of the totals of wait database metrics for wait classes. The following metrics are available in this view:

- Column *average_waiter_count* reports the average number of individual waits for the particular wait class during the sample time interval.

- Column *db_time_in_wait* reports the total database wait time spent for the particular wait class.

- Column *time_waited* shows the time waited during the sample interval.

- Column *wait_count* displays the number of waits that occurred during the sample interval.

The *v$waitclassmetric_history* view helps the DBA monitor the total wait activity by grouping wait events to specific wait classes. The query below can be used to view the recent history for a particular wait class named APPLICATION:

```
SELECT
   c.wait_class                        "Wait Class",
   to_char(h.begin_time,'hh24:mi:ss') "Begin",
   to_char(h.end_time,'hh24:mi:ss')   "End",
   h.average_waiter_count,
   h.time_waited,
   h.wait_count
FROM
   v$waitclassmetric_history h,
   v$system_wait_class        c
WHERE
   c.wait_class_id = h.wait_class_id
AND
   c.wait_class = 'Application' -- plug-in your metric name here
ORDER BY
   h.begin_time DESC;
```

The output is a running count of total user I/O for each snapshot interval:

Wait Class	Begin	End	AVERAGE_WAITER_COUNT	TIME_WAITED	WAIT_COUNT
Application	16:47:58	16:48:56	0	0	4
	16:46:56	16:47:58	0	0	26
	16:45:58	16:46:56	0	0	4
	16:44:57	16:45:58	0	0	4
	16:43:58	16:44:57	0	0	4
	16:42:57	16:43:58	0	0	4
	16:41:58	16:42:57	0	0	10
	16:40:57	16:41:58	0	0	4
	16:39:55	16:40:57	0	0	2
	16:38:57	16:39:55	0	0	4
	16:37:56	16:38:57	0	1	30
	16:36:57	16:37:56	0	0	4
	16:35:56	16:36:57	0	0	4
	16:34:58	16:35:56	0	0	4
	16:33:56	16:34:58	0	0	4
	16:32:58	16:33:56	0	0	4
	16:31:57	16:32:58	0	0	8
	16:30:59	16:31:57	0	0	4
	16:29:57	16:30:59	0	0	4
	16:28:58	16:29:57	0	0	4
	16:27:58	16:28:58	0	0	4

```
16:26:56 16:27:58                    0              1             38
16:25:58 16:26:56                    0              0              4
16:24:58 16:25:58                    0              0              4
16:23:59 16:24:58                    0              0              4
16:22:58 16:23:59                    0              0              4
16:21:59 16:22:58                    0              2             30
```

The *v$waitclassmetric* view is similar to the *v$waitclassmetric_history* view except that it only shows wait class metrics for the most current sample.

Once a particular wait class that is consuming a lot of time or that has a large number of waits has been identified, the DBA can dive in deeper to review wait metrics for specific wait events which belong to an identified wait class.

The *v$eventmetric* reports wait metrics as the number of sessions waiting during the sample interval, the number of waits, and the wait time. This view contains a single row per every wait event. The following query returns a list of non-idle wait events that recently experienced the most wait time:

```
SELECT
    to_char(m.begin_time,'hh24:mi') "start time",
    to_char(m.end_time,'hh24:mi')   "end time",
    n.name,
    m.time_waited,
    m.num_sess_waiting,
    m.wait_count
FROM
    v$eventmetric m,
    v$event_name   n
WHERE
      m.event_id = n.event_id
  AND n.wait_class <> 'Idle'   -- add your event metric name here
  AND m.time_waited > 0
ORDER BY 4 DESC;
```

The following output has a breakdown, by time, of all of the wait events and the counts of the number of times waited during the AWR snapshot period:

```
start end t NAME                       TIME_WAITED NUM_SESS_WAITING WAIT_COUNT
----- ----- --------------------------- ----------- ---------------- --------
17:29 17:30 control file parallel write          29                0         19
17:29 17:30 latch free                            4                0          8
17:29 17:30 db file parallel write                1                0          7
```

Datafile Metrics

Oracle10g provides several database metrics for datafile access monitoring. There are two *v$* views that report datafile metrics. The *v$filemetric_history* view shows file metrics for samples that occurred on ten minute intervals during the preceding hour. The *v$filemetric* view provides the datafile metrics for the most recent sample. The following metrics are available for review:

- Average file read and write times

- Current numbers of physical read and write operations

- Current numbers of physical blocks reads and writes

The following query reports datafiles that experience a high current read/write I/O time that exceeds the average I/O time computed:

```
SELECT
  to_char(m.begin_time,'hh24:mi') "start time",
  to_char(m.end_time,'hh24:mi')   "end time",
  f.file_name,
  s.lstiotim                      "last i/o time",
  m.average_read_time + m.average_write_time "average i/o time"
FROM
  v$filemetric    m,
  dba_data_files  f,
  v$filestat      s
WHERE
    m.file_id = f.file_id
  AND s.file# = f.file_id
  AND s.lstiotim > (m.average_read_time + m.average_write_time);
```

The following is a result listing where the average I/O time and the last I/O time are shown:

```
start end t FILE_NAME                                Last I/O Time Average I/O
Time
----- ----- ---------------------------------------- ---- ----------------
12:36 12:46 D:\ORACLE\ORADATA\DBDABR\SYSTEM01.DBF       6               3
12:36 12:46 D:\ORACLE\ORADATA\DBDABR\UNDOTBS01.DBF      3               2
12:36 12:46 D:\ORACLE\ORADATA\DBDABR\SYSAUX01.DBF      12               5
12:36 12:46 D:\ORACLE\ORADATA\DBDABR\USERS01.DBF        4               7
```

Oracle captures snapshots of *v$filemetric_history* views in the corresponding AWR table, *wrh$_filemetric_history*. MMON does not write all datafile metric history to AWR repository. It only writes

---

snapshots of history that existed at the moment of the snapshots. Therefore, the DBA cannot reconstruct a sequential, all-inclusive file I/O access history using AWR views such as *dba_hist_filemetric_history*.

Database Service Metrics

Oracle tracks database metrics related to different services configured in the database. For example, several services could be configured for different applications accessing the database. The full list of services configured in the system can be accessed using the *v$services* dynamic view:

```
SELECT * FROM v$services;
```

The following is a sample output:

```
SERVICE_ID NAME                  NAME_HASH NETWORK_NAME
---------- -------------------- ---------- ------------
         5 dbdabr               3608862068 dbdabr
         1 SYS$BACKGROUND        165959219
         2 SYS$USERS            3427055676
```

From the above output, one is able to see the list of services configured in the database.

There are two *v$* views that can be used for reporting metrics for database services. The *v$servicemetric_history* view displays metrics for all samples during the last hour. The similar *v$servicemetric* view shows only the most recent samples for all services. This view contains a single row per every database service. The following metrics are gathered for services:

- Elapsed time per call issued through the given service.

- CPU time per call issued through the given service.

It is worth the DBA's time to use the *v$servicemetric_history* view to monitor database workload on a per instance basis. For example, the query below retrieves recent history for a particular network service configured:

```
SELECT
  to_char(m.begin_time,'hh24:mi')  "start time",
  to_char(m.end_time,'hh24:mi')    "end time",
  m.service_name,
  m.elapsedpercall                 "elapsed time",
  m.cpupercall                     "cpu time"
FROM
  v$servicemetric_history m
WHERE
  m.service_name = 'dbdabr'  - add your service name here
ORDER BY
  m.end_time DESC;
```

The sample output of this script is:

```
start end t SERVICE_NA Elapsed Time   CPU Time
----- ----- ---------- ------------ ----------
13:16 13:17 dbdabr                0          0
13:15 13:16 dbdabr             4532       3926
13:14 13:15 dbdabr             5478       4897
13:13 13:14 dbdabr                0          0
13:12 13:13 dbdabr           604549     408964
13:11 13:12 dbdabr            13901       3111
13:10 13:11 dbdabr             9687       5356
13:09 13:10 dbdabr             7296       6533
13:08 13:09 dbdabr                0          0
13:07 13:08 dbdabr                0          0
13:06 13:07 dbdabr                0          0
13:05 13:06 dbdabr                0          0
13:04 13:05 dbdabr                0          0
13:03 13:04 dbdabr                0          0
13:02 13:03 dbdabr                0          0
13:01 13:02 dbdabr                0          0
13:00 13:01 dbdabr             2160       2160
12:59 13:00 dbdabr            11080       5270
```

From the above output, a DBA is able to identify the particular database service which places a particular workload on the database. Using this approach, it is possible to localize the application that places burden on the database.

Conclusion

Database metrics introduced in Oracle10g give Oracle DBAs a powerful tool for real time database health monitoring by providing:

- Pre-computed values of significant database workload parameters ready for immediate usage.

- Metrics which place minimal overhead on the database and eliminate the need for manual data selection and computation.

- Active use of metrics gathered for self-tuning purposes.

- Server generated alerts initiated from within the database as a result of database metrics being checked against pre-defined or custom thresholds Such that the DBA receives a timely notification if workload exceptions occur.

The next chapter presents information on the new Database Management System (DBMS) packages that are provided in Oracle10g for tuning activities.

Oracle10g DBMS Tuning Packages

Don't get burned by failing to know the tuning packages

Packaging Oracle10g Tuning

This chapter focuses on the new packages introduced in Oracle10g database that facilitate the Automatic Workload Repository (AWR) configuration and data management. In addition, important information will be presented about the new DBMS packages such as *dbms_workload_repository* that allow the analysis of AWR data and generate intelligent recommendations and advice for database tuning and SQL optimization.

The packages described in this chapter are delivered with the Oracle10g software and are automatically installed to the data dictionary.

The *dbms_workload_repository* Package

The *dbms_workload_repository* package allows the DBA to manage the AWR using the PL/SQL API. This functionality can be used by Oracle DBAs to configure AWR settings such as snapshot interval and data retention, to create or remove baselines for trend performance analysis purposes, to gather AWR snapshots manually or programmatically, and to generate reports in various formats.

The *dbms_workload_repository.modify_snapshot_settings* procedure is used to configure snapshot intervals and AWR data retention in the database. The snapshot interval defines how often MMON background process are to take new snapshots. The retention interval determines the length of time that data will be preserved in the AWR. The default value of the snapshot interval is 60 minutes, and the default setting for retention is 10,080 minutes which is seven days.

```
desc dbms_workload_repository
PROCEDURE MODIFY_SNAPSHOT_SETTINGS
 Argument Name                    Type         In/Out Default?
 ------------------------------   ----------   ------ --------
 RETENTION                        NUMBER       IN     DEFAULT
 INTERVAL                         NUMBER       IN     DEFAULT
 DBID                             NUMBER       IN     DEFAULT
```

The range of valid values for the *interval* setting is 10 minutes to 52,560,000 minutes or 100 years. The *dbms_workload_repository* package contains global variables called *min_interval* and *max_interval*. These two variables set the lower and upper limits for the *interval*. If a zero value is specified for *interval*, automatic and manual snapshots will be prohibited.

An interesting fact about the AWR is that the base *wrh$_* history and *wrm$_* AWR data dictionary metadata tables support *dbid* and *instance_number* columns that store the current database identifier and the *instance* number. Furthermore, some procedures and functions in the *dbms_workload_repository* package contain the *dbid* parameter that defaults to the current database identifier and can be omitted. The popular theory is that these parameters are reserved for future use when a single AWR will be able to store data from multiple databases.

The *retention* parameter configures the time period, in minutes, that the AWR will preserve a particular set of snapshot data in the repository. The default value for this parameter is 10,080 minutes or seven days. The range of valid values for this parameter ranges from ten minutes to 52,560,000 minutes or 100 years.

The *dbms_workload_repository* package contains the global variables of *min_retention* and *max_retention*. These variables set the lower and upper limits for the *retention* parameter. If a zero value is specified for *retention*, snapshots will be stored for an unlimited amount of time.

The following script can be used to check the current settings for the AWR interval and retention settings:

```
select
      extract( day from snap_interval) *24*60+
      extract( hour from snap_interval) *60+
      extract( minute from snap_interval ) "Snapshot Interval",
      extract( day from retention) *24*60+
      extract( hour from retention) *60+
      extract( minute from retention ) "Retention Interval"
from dba_hist_wr_control;
```

The script returns the current AWR interval values in minutes:

```
Snapshot Interval Retention Interval
----------------- ------------------
               60              10080
```

The new MMON Oracle background process is responsible for the creation of new snapshots at the specified snapshot interval; however, the DBA is able to programmatically take new snapshots using the *dbms_workload_repository.create_snapshot* procedure. An overloaded function with the same name is also supported, which returns the number of the last snapshot taken:

```
SQL> desc dbms_workload_repository

PROCEDURE CREATE_SNAPSHOT

Argument Name                      Type                      In/Out Default?
---------------------------------- ------------------------- ------ --------
FLUSH_LEVEL                        VARCHAR2                  IN     DEFAULT
```

```
FUNCTION CREATE_SNAPSHOT RETURNS NUMBER

Argument Name                         Type                      In/Out Default?
------------------------------        ----------------------    ------ --------
FLUSH_LEVEL                           VARCHAR2                   IN     DEFAULT
```

The only parameter listed in the procedures is the *flush_level,* which configures the amount of information the AWR gathers. This parameter can have either the default value of TYPICAL or a value of ALL. When the statistics level is set to ALL, the AWR gathers the maximum amount of performance data. Usually, the TYPICAL level is quite enough for performance analysis and tuning purposes. The AWR uses the SPFILE initialization parameter *statistics_level* to specify the snapshots level for snapshots gathered by MMON process. The possible values for this parameter are also TYPICAL and ALL.

The MMON background process is also responsible for removing old historical data from the AWR. The amount of retention time after which data will be removed from database is determined by the *retention* setting. However, data can be cleared from the AWR tables by using the *dbms_workload_repository.drop_snapshot_range* procedure. The starting and ending snapshots for the history to be removed from the AWR will need to be set to run the following script,:

```
desc dbms_workload_repository

PROCEDURE DROP_SNAPSHOT_RANGE
  Argument Name                       Type                      In/Out Default?
------------------------------        --------------------      ------ --------
  LOW_SNAP_ID                         NUMBER                    IN
  HIGH_SNAP_ID                        NUMBER                    IN
  DBID                                NUMBER                    IN     DEFAULT
```

Using the *dbms_workload_repository* package, the DBA is able to create AWR baselines that identify a pair of snapshots to be used for subsequent performance analyses. The *dbms_workload_repository.create_baseline* procedure and the overloaded function that returns the baseline identifier are shown below. In order to create a baseline, specify the starting and ending snapshots as well as the baseline name:

```
desc dbms_workload_repository

PROCEDURE CREATE_BASELINE
```

The dbms_workload_repository Package   **243**

```
Argument Name                        Type                      In/Out Default?
------------------------------------ --------------------      ------ --------
START_SNAP_ID                        NUMBER                    IN
END_SNAP_ID                          NUMBER                    IN
BASELINE_NAME                        VARCHAR2                  IN
DBID                                 NUMBER                    IN     DEFAULT

FUNCTION CREATE_BASELINE RETURNS NUMBER
Argument Name                        Type                      In/Out Default?
------------------------------------ --------------------      ------ --------
START_SNAP_ID                        NUMBER                    IN
END_SNAP_ID                          NUMBER                    IN
BASELINE_NAME                        VARCHAR2                  IN
DBID                                 NUMBER                    IN     DEFAULT
```

The available baselines that have been created are visible in the *dba_hist_baselines* view:

```
desc dba_hist_baseline
Name                                          Null?     Type
--------------------------------------------- --------- -----------
DBID                                          NOT NULL  NUMBER
BASELINE_ID                                   NOT NULL  NUMBER
BASELINE_NAME                                           VARCHAR2(64)
START_SNAP_ID                                           NUMBER
START_SNAP_TIME                                         TIMESTAMP(3)
END_SNAP_ID                                             NUMBER
END_SNAP_TIME                                           TIMESTAMP(3)
```

After two baselines have been created, the DBA can compare statistics related to only those two baselines. The AWR automatically preserves the snapshots, from each existing baseline. One must bear in mind that MMON or *dbms_workload_repository.drop_snapshot_range* does not delete historical data from the AWR that is related to any existing baselines.

The *dbms_workload_repository.drop_baseline* procedure can be used to remove existing baselines from the data dictionary, and the *baseline_name* parameter identifies the baseline to be dropped. The default setting for the *cascade* parameter is FALSE, and in order to remove the snapshots associated with the baseline to be removed, the *cascade* parameter will have to be set to TRUE:

```
desc dbms_workload_repository

PROCEDURE DROP_BASELINE
```

```
Argument Name                            Type                  In/Out Default?
------------------------------           --------------------  ------ --------
BASELINE_NAME                            VARCHAR2              IN
CASCADE                                  BOOLEAN              IN     DEFAULT
DBID                                     NUMBER               IN     DEFAULT
```

This wraps up the explaination of how to invoke the workload repository packages directly. The following section will take a look at how to generate a standard AWR report with the *dbms_workload_repository* package.

Creating an AWR Report

The remaining procedures in the *dbms_workload_repository* package are *awr_report_text* and *awr_report_html*, which generate the AWR report for the specified snapshot range in text or HTML formats, respectively. The following script segment shows how to retrieve the AWR text report for any snapshot range or duration:

```
SELECT
    output
FROM    TABLE(dbms_workload_repository.awr_report_text
(37933856,1,2900,2911 ));
```

The sample output below shows the typical report generated for AWR data.   The output displays shows the four arguments to the *awr_report_text* stored procedure:

- The database ID is 37933856.

- The instance number for RAC is 1.

- The starting snapshot number is 2900.

- The ending snapshot number is 2911.

This standard Oracle elapsed time report has evolved over the past 12 years and had several names:

report.txt: In Oracle7 and Oracle8, this BSTAT-ESTAT was taken by running the *utlbstat.sql* followed by *utlestat.sql* in the $ORACLE-HOME/rdbms/admin directory.

---

spreport: From Oracle8i to Oracle10g, this is an enhanced BSTAT-ESTAT report where the user chooses the beginning and ending snapshot numbers.

AWR Report: In Oracle 10g, this is the latest time-series report, and it is produced by running a SQL*Plus script in the $ORACLE_HOME/rdbms/admin directory. *awrrpt.sql* is a text-based report. *awrrpti.sql* is a HTML-based report for online publishing of time-series reports.

```
OUTPUT
-----------------------------------------------------------------
WORKLOAD REPOSITORY report for

DB Name        DB Id     Instance     Inst Num Release
Cluster Host
------------   -----------  ------------  --------  -----------  ------
DBDABR         37933856 dbdabr                    1 10.1.0.2.0  NO
Host1

                 Snap Id      Snap Time        Sessions Curs/Sess
                 ---------  -------------------  --------  ---------
Begin Snap:        2900 19-Aug-04 11:00:29        18        5.2
  End Snap:        2911 19-Aug-04 22:00:16        18        4.6
   Elapsed:               659.78 (mins)
   DB Time:                10.08 (mins)

Cache Sizes (end)
~~~~~~~~~~~~~~~~~
Buffer Cache:       48M     Std Block Size:        8K
Shared Pool Size:   56M         Log Buffer:      256K

Load Profile
~~~~~~~~~~~~          Per Second       Per Transaction
                     --------------     -----------
        Redo size: 1,766.20             18,526.31
    Logical reads:    39.21                411.30
    Block changes:    11.11                116.54
   Physical reads:     0.38                  3.95
  Physical writes:     0.38                  3.96
       User calls:     0.06                  0.64
           Parses:     2.04                 21.37
      Hard parses:     0.14                  1.45
            Sorts:     1.02                 10.72
           Logons:     0.02                  0.21
         Executes:     4.19                 43.91
```

This is very similar to the old STATSPACK reports from Oracle9i, and it contains vital elapsed-time change information for what happened during the particular snapshot range.

More details on reading the standard AWR report are included later in this book.

The next step is to learn about the *dbms_advisor* package and see how it can yield important Oracle tuning insights.

The *dbms_advisor* Package

Oracle10g introduced several intelligent utilities that produce performance tuning advices and suggestions based on historical data stored in the AWR. These utilities are called advisors. The *dbms_advisor* package provides PL/SQL API to access the following advisors:

- The Automatic Database Diagnostic Monitor (ADDM) provides Oracle DBAs with performance data gathered by the AWR. The ADDM also identifies root causes of performance bottlenecks and generates a report containing recommendations or findings on how to improve database performance.

- The SQLAccess Advisor provides analysis and recommendations about indexes and materialized views which may improve system performance.

A list of the available advisors can be viewed using the *dba_advisor_definitions* data dictionary view:

```
select * from dba_advisor_definitions;

ADVISOR_ID ADVISOR_NAME                      PROPERTY
---------- ------------------------------- ----------
         1 ADDM                                     1
         2 SQL Access Advisor                      15
         3 Undo Advisor                             1
         4 SQL Tuning Advisor                       3
         5 Segment Advisor                          3
         6 SQL Workload Manager                     0
         7 Tune MView                              31
```

The above advisors are accessible through the Oracle10g Enterprise Manager (EM), and the WISE tool can also be used to access some advisors through its GUI interface. However, most senior Oracle DBAs work with advisors directly from PL/SQL Application

Programming Interface (API). The advisors' API is provided in the standard package *dbms_advisor* that is installed automatically to the data dictionary. The next step is to learn how this package can be used as a diagnostic aid for Oracle tuning.

The ADDM Advisor

Each analysis performed by the various advisors in Oracle10g is called a *task*. Tasks are storage objects within the data dictionary and are used to store everything about the task including the parameters, recommendations, internal data, etc. Tasks are private to the user who created the task, so there can be a separate set of advisors for each DBA.

When Oracle performs an ADDM analysis, it automatically creates a new task when the MMON takes a new AWR snapshot, storing the results of these analysis tasks into the data dictionary. The view called *dba_advisor_tasks* reports all the existing advisor tasks:

```
desc dba_advisor_tasks

 Name                      Null?     Type
 ----------------------    --------  -------------
 OWNER                               VARCHAR2(30)
 TASK_ID                   NOT NULL  NUMBER
 TASK_NAME                           VARCHAR2(30)
 DESCRIPTION                         VARCHAR2(256)
 ADVISOR_NAME                        VARCHAR2(30)
 CREATED                   NOT NULL  DATE
 LAST_MODIFIED             NOT NULL  DATE
 PARENT_TASK_ID                      NUMBER
 PARENT_REC_ID                       NUMBER
 EXECUTION_START                     DATE
 EXECUTION_END                       DATE
 STATUS                              VARCHAR2(11)
 STATUS_MESSAGE                      VARCHAR2(4000)
 PCT_COMPLETION_TIME                 NUMBER
 PROGESS_METRIC                      NUMBER
 METRIC_UNITS                        VARCHAR2(64)
 ACTIVITY_COUNTER                    NUMBER
 RECOMMENDATION_COUNT                NUMBER
 ERROR_MESSAGE                       VARCHAR2(4000)
 SOURCE                              VARCHAR2(30)
 HOW_CREATED                         VARCHAR2(30)
 READ_ONLY                           VARCHAR2(5)
 ADVISOR_ID                NOT NULL  NUMBER
```

This task contains information about all historical tasks and those that are still executing. The status of a particular task is determined by the *dba_advisor_tasks.status* column. The DBA can view the task name, advisor name that created this task, status task, error messages, etc. Since Oracle stores the results in internal data dictionary tables, everything the DBA needs can be accessed through these *dba_advisor* views. For example, the *dba_advisor_usage* view shows statistics about the advisors' usage through the following script:

```
SELECT
  d.advisor_name,
  u.last_exec_time,
  u.num_execs
FROM
  dba_advisor_usage u,
  dba_advisor_definitions d
WHERE
  u.advisor_id = d.advisor_id;
```

This is a great script for a DBA Manager to monitor the work of their DBA staff. The following is a sample output showing the times and number of executions of the 10g advisors:

```
ADVISOR_NAME                         LAST_EXE  NUM_EXECS
-----------------------------------  --------  ----------
ADDM                                 03.09.04          16
SQL Access Advisor                   10.03.04           0
Undo Advisor                         10.03.04           0
SQL Tuning Advisor                   12.08.04          16
Segment Advisor                      10.03.04           0
SQL Workload Manager                 10.03.04           0
Tune MView                           10.03.04           0
```

The *dba_advisor_log* view also allows the DBA to see historical log information about advisor activities, thereby providing a built-in audit.

The ADDM advisor screen within the Oracle Enterprise Manager (OEM) allows the DBA to easily view all of the tasks available and the recommendations contained in a particular ADDM task.

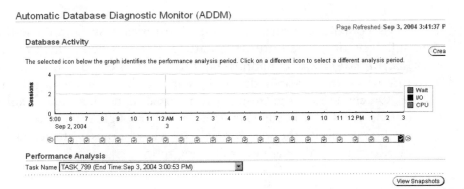

Figure 8.1: *Access ADDM Recommendations in OEM Console.*

The WISE tool also supports the creation and viewing of ADDM advisor tasks in its GUI:

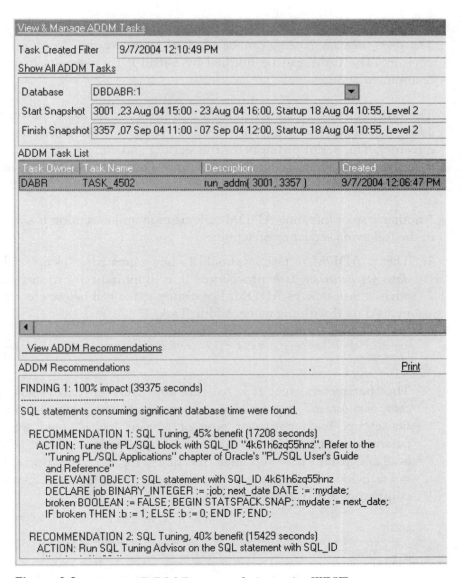

Figure 8.2: *Access ADDM Recommendations using WISE.*

It is useful for the DBA to know how to create custom ADDM advisor tasks in order to analyze the AWR snapshot interval and view their associated recommendations.

The *dbms_scheduler package* can be used to automate the execution of advisors. The DBA can be notified by e-mail if the advisors make a recommendation.

The DBA can also create an ADDM task manually by using the script *addmrpt.sql* which is located in the *$ORACLE_HOME/rdbms/admin* directory. This script prompts for the starting and ending snapshots of the interval to be analyzed and reports, and allows the output file name to be chosen.

Another way of initiating ADDM task creation and execution is shown in the following sequence of actions:

1. The ADDM task should be created using the *dbms_advisor.create_task* procedure. It is important to specify the advisor task type as ADDM. For example, the call below creates a new ADDM with the name Addm_Task_1:

```
execute dbms_advisor.create_task ( 'ADDM' , 'ADDM_TASK_1' , 'New
ADDM Task' );
```

The parameters required to run the ADDM task such as *start_snapshot, end_snapshot, days_to_expire, mode, time_limit*, etc. must be set up. Each particular type of advisor has its own set of parameters, and the Oracle documentation contains a full list of all available parameters and their meanings for every advisor. The query below can be used to see the parameters are available for configuring the ADDM task:

```
SELECT
   p.parameter_name, p.parameter_value , p.parameter_type ,
p.is_output
FROM
   dba_advisor_tasks t,
   dba_advisor_parameters p
WHERE
      t.owner = 'DABR'
   AND t.task_name = 'ADDM_TASK_1'
   AND t.task_id = p.task_id;
```

In this example showing the parameters for the ADDM tasks, by joining *dba_advisor_tasks* and *dba_advisor_parameters*, the output looks like the following.

```
PARAMETER_NAME     PARAMETER_VALUE                    PARAMETER_  I
----------------------------------------------------  ----------  -
ANALYSIS_TYPE      PERIOD                             STRING      N
DAYS_TO_EXPIRE     30                                 NUMBER      N
DBIO_EXPECTED      10000                              NUMBER      N
DB_ELAPSED_TIME    0                                  NUMBER      N
DB_ID              0                                  NUMBER      N
END_SNAPSHOT       UNUSED                             NUMBER      N
END_TIME           UNUSED                             UNKNOWN     N
HISTORY_TABLE      UNUSED                             STRING      N
INSTANCE           UNUSED                             NUMBER      N
JOURNALING         4                                  NUMBER      N
MODE               COMPREHENSIVE                      STRING      N
SCOPE_TYPE         UNUSED                             STRING      N
SCOPE_VALUE        UNUSED                             NUMBER      N
START_SNAPSHOT     UNUSED                             NUMBER      N
START_TIME         UNUSED                             UNKNOWN     N
TARGET_OBJECTS     UNUSED                             STRINGLIST  N
TIME_LIMIT         UNLIMITED                          NUMBER      N
```

2. At this point, the DBA should be ready to add the start and end snapshots, thereby specifying the width of the elapsed time sample. Comparing the point-in-time snapshot 1000 with snapshot 1050, the procedure below calls the configuration of *start_snapshot* and *end_snapshot* task parameters:

```
dbms_advisor.set_task_parameter('ADDM_TASK_1', 'START_SNAPSHOT',
1000 );
dbms_advisor.set_task_parameter('ADDM_TASK_1', 'END_SNAPSHOT',
1050 );
```

In the sample listing above, the two parameters *start_snapshot* and *end_snapshot* are configured for the particular task named ADDM_TASK_1.

3. After all of necessary task parameters have been configured, the ADDM task can be executed to produce recommendations using the following statement:

```
exec dbms_advisor.execute_task ('ADDM_TASK_1');
```

That's it! Now, everything is in place for the DBA to view the ADDM recommendations and start tuning their system. The following is an invocation for an ADDM session:

```
select dbms_advisor.get_task_report ('ADDM_TASK_1', 'TEXT',
'TYPICAL', 'ALL', 'DABR') FROM dual;
```

The *dbms_advisor.get_task_report* function is able to return reports in many forms including TEXT, XML, or HTML formats. The sample SELECT statement above returns advisor recommendations in the text format as specified by the second parameter of the function *dbms_advisor.get_task_report*. The level of detail to be retrieved in the report can be selected by specifying the parameter *level*, which can be set to BASIC, TYPICAL, or ALL. In most tuning cases it is sufficient to set the *level* parameter to the TYPICAL value because all the important information will be included in the report. It is important to note that the ALL value for this parameter retrieves all available information for the tuning task and it was designed for use by Oracle Support employees.

The ADDM recommendations can be retrieved directly from data dictionary views such as *dba_advisor_recommendations* and *dba_advisor_findings*. The *dba_advisor_recommendations* view contains the results of completed advisor tasks, and the recommendations for a particular task should be retrieved in the order contained in the *rank* column. This column reports the importance of every suggestion. For example, the query below can be used to show recommendations for the particular task:

```
SELECT
 r.type,
 r.Rank,
 r.benefit,
 f.impact_type,
 f.impact,
 f.message
FROM
 dba_advisor_recommendations r,
 dba_advisor_findings f
WHERE
      r.task_name = 'TASK_4502'
  AND r.finding_id = f.finding_id
  AND r.task_id = f.task_id
```

```
ORDER BY r.rank ASC, r.benefit DESC;
```

The following analysis report is a typical recommendation produced by the ADDM advisor, and it is worth a moment of time to read this listing of recommendations and justifications:

```
FINDING 3: 11% impact (4160 seconds)
------------------------------------
SQL statements were not shared due to the usage of literals. This resulted in
additional hard parses which were consuming significant database time.

   RECOMMENDATION 1: Application Analysis, 11% benefit (4160 seconds)
      ACTION: Investigate application logic for possible use of bind variables
         instead of literals. Alternatively, you may set the parameter
         "cursor_sharing" to "force".
      RATIONALE: SQL statements with PLAN_HASH_VALUE 2114039622 were found to
         be using literals. Look in V$SQL for examples of such SQL statements.
      RATIONALE: SQL statements with PLAN_HASH_VALUE 78517174 were found to be
         using literals. Look in V$SQL for examples of such SQL statements.
      RATIONALE: SQL statements with PLAN_HASH_VALUE 507465275 were found to
         be using literals. Look in V$SQL for examples of such SQL statements.
      RATIONALE: SQL statements with PLAN_HASH_VALUE 2816422638 were found to
         be using literals. Look in V$SQL for examples of such SQL statements.
      RATIONALE: SQL statements with PLAN_HASH_VALUE 1083969639 were found to
         be using literals. Look in V$SQL for examples of such SQL statements.

   SYMPTOMS THAT LED TO THE FINDING:
      Hard parsing of SQL statements was consuming significant database time.
      (14% impact [5305 seconds])
         Contention for latches related to the shared pool was consuming
         significant database time. (12% impact [4759 seconds])
         Waits for "latch: library cache" latch amounted to 1% of database
         time.  Waits for "library cache lock" latch amounted to 2% of
         database time.  Waits for "library cache pin" latch amounted to 8% of
         database time.  Waits for "library cache load lock" latch amounted to
         0% of database time.  Waits for "latch: shared pool" latch amounted
         to 0% of database time.
            Wait class "Concurrency" was consuming significant database time.
            (12% impact [4736 seconds])
```

The analysis report consists of the findings of the performance bottleneck analysis that have the most impact on database response time. Information on each finding includes its impact in seconds and the percentage from the total database processing time that is the ADDM's measurement of throughput. The target solution of the ADDM tuning analysis is to reduce the *Database Time* metric as much as possible.

The ADDM makes recommendations for tuning and includes the expected benefit associated with implementation of the recommendation. The expected benefit is expressed in terms of the reduction of total database response time if all of the

---

recommendations for that finding are implemented. Also, this report contains the description of the symptoms that led the ADDM to produce each finding.

Watch the time slices!

Elapsed time reports that span more than a few hours might not be as meaningful as shorter durations. Also, the DBA should never specify a start-stop snapshot range that spans a bounce, a shutdown and restart.

Many Oracle tuning professionals will temporarily collect snapshots every ten minutes while investigating a transient performance issue.

Each ADDM tuning task submitted for analysis has the potential to consume significant database time, and the last thing the DBA wants to create is a performance problem. It is recommended that the DBA execute the advisor tasks at times when the database workload is quite low, for example, at night. The *dbms_advisor* package contains a set of routines that allow tasks to be interpreted, reset, restarted, or deleted:

- Procedure *interrupt_task* stops the currently running task. Recommendations that have already been generated will be preserved in the database.

- Procedure *reset_task* allows the DBA to reset a task to its initial state by removing all the parameter and recommendation data from the database.

- Procedure *resume_task* resumes the previously interrupted task.

- Procedure *delete_task* completely removes a task and all its associated information from the database.

- Procedure *set_default_task_parameter* is useful for setting task parameter defaults for all subsequent advisor tasks. This allows the DBA to specify defaults for common task parameters of a particular advisor.

The ADDM Advisor can be extremely beneficial as a tuning tool when properly used. Now it's time to explore how to use the SQLAccess Advisor tool as a diagnostic aid for Oracle tuning.

Working with the SQLAccess Advisor

The SQLAccess Advisor tool produces intelligent recommendations for the proper usage of indexes and materialized views. The SQLAccess Advisor can recommend both bitmap and B-tree indexes to optimize access to data. It can also produce suggestions about how to tune with materialized views to take advantage of fast refresh and query rewrite features.

Materialized views (MV) are a blessing for poorly-designed schemas. An MV can be used to create a denormalized schema by pre-joining tables, and commonly referenced tasks can be pre-aggregated to eliminate redundant queries.

Generally, the SQLAccess Advisor is accessible through the Oracle *dbms_advisor* package. This package has a set of advisory and analysis functions and procedures that can be used to access the SQLAccess Advisor tool. The following information contains guidance on how to use *dbms_advisor* API to get recommendations from this advisor.

Through the *dbms_advisor,* the SQLAccess Advisor API supports the DBA by recommending new indexes or MVs:

- A real world or hypothetical workload can be used.

- It can assist in making a materialized view fast refreshable.

- It helps edit and change existing materialized views to improve query rewrite.

- It can save and manage historical workload data.

- It can update and remove recommendations.

- It can perform a quick tune operation using a single SQL statement as input.

Working with SQLAccess Advisor is very similar to working with the ADDM Advisor. The SQLAccess Advisor can be invoked using the following four steps:

1. Create an advisor task.

2. Configure advisor task parameters.

3. Run the analysis for the task.

4. Review and implement the recommendations.

The *dbms_advisor.create_task* procedure can be used to create an initial SQLAccess Advisor task. In the example below, a new SQLAccess Advisor task named SQL_ACC_TASK1 is created:

```
execute dbms_advisor.create_task ( 'SQL Access Advisor',
'SQL_ACC_TASK1' , 'New SQLAccess  Task' );
```

The next step is to configure the workload parameters for this task. In the case of the SQLAccess Advisor task, this step would involve the creation of a workload that will form the grounds for subsequent advisor analysis with ADDM. The workload consists of one or more SQL statements along with associated statistics and attributes that describe each statement. The *dbms_advisor.create_sqlwkld* procedure is used to create a new workload object that is independent from any tasks created earlier:

```
DECLARE
 W_name VARCHAR2(100);
BEGIN
 W_name := 'SQL_WRKLD_1';
 dbms_advisor.create_sqlwkld (W_name);
END;
/
```

After the workload object is created, it must be linked in to the SQLAccess Advisor task that was just created. The *dbms_advisor.add_sqlwkld_ref* procedure is used to link a workload with a task:

```
exec dbms_advisor. add_sqlwkld_ref('SQL_ACC_TASK1', 'SQL_WRKLD_1' );
```

The new workload object must now be populated with the SQL or DML statements to be analyzed. The following options are available for adding statements to the workload:

- Use the *dbms_advisor.import_sqlwkld_sqlcache* procedure to import data into a workload from the current SQL cache in the shared pool.

- Use the *dbms_advisor.add_sqlwkld_statement* procedure to add a single SQL statement to a workload.

- Use the *dbms_advisor.import_sqlwkld_sts* procedure to import SQL statements from an existing SQL Tuning Set.

- Use the *dbms_advisor.import_sqlwkld_user* procedure to import SQL statements from the specified user table.

For example, the call below imports all the SQL statements to the workload from the current contents of the library cache:

```
DECLARE
   Saved_rows number;
   Failed_rows number;
BEGIN
  Dbms_advisor.import_sqlwkld_sqlcache ('SQL_WRKLD_1', 'NEW', 2,
Saved_rows, Failed_rows);
END;
/
```

The next step is setting up the SQLAccess Advisor task parameters. The query below can be used to produce the list of parameters that can be configured:

```
SELECT
   p.parameter_name,
   p.parameter_value,
   p.parameter_type,
   p.is_output
FROM
   dba_advisor_tasks       t,
   dba_advisor_parameters p
WHERE
    t.owner = 'DABR'
AND
   t.task_name = 'SQL_ACC_TASK1'
AND
   t.task_id = p.task_id;
```

The Oracle documentation contains details about the wealth of parameters that can be configured for SQLAccess Advisor analysis. These parameters range from resource limits to choices about where new indexes and materialized views may be placed:

```
PARAMETER_NAME          PARAMETER_VALUE                      PARAMETER_ I
----------------------  -----------------------------------  ---------- -
ACTION_LIST             UNUSED                               STRINGLIST N
COMMENTED_FILTER_LIST   /* OPT_DYN_SAMP */,/* DS_SVC */      STRINGLIST N
CREATION_COST           TRUE                                 STRING     N
DAYS_TO_EXPIRE          30                                   NUMBER     N
DEF_EM_TEMPLATE         SQLACCESS_EMTASK                     STRING     N
DEF_INDEX_OWNER         UNUSED                               STRING     N
DEF_INDEX_TABLESPACE    UNUSED                               STRING     N
DEF_MVIEW_OWNER         UNUSED                               STRING     N
DEF_MVIEW_TABLESPACE    UNUSED                               STRING     N
DEF_MVLOG_TABLESPACE    UNUSED                               STRING     N
DML_VOLATILITY          TRUE                                 STRING     N
EM_DATA                 UNUSED                               STRING     N
END_SNAPSHOT            UNUSED                               NUMBER     N
END_TIME                UNUSED                               UNKNOWN    N
EVALUATION_ONLY         FALSE                                STRING     N
EXECUTION_TYPE          FULL                                 STRING     N
FAST_REFRESH            FALSE                                STRING     N
INDEX_NAME_TEMPLATE     <TABLE>_IDX$$_<TASK_ID><SEQ>         STRING     N
INSTANCE                UNUSED                               NUMBER     N
INVALID_TABLE_LIST      UNUSED                               TABLELIST  N
JOURNALING              4                                    NUMBER     N
MODE                    COMPREHENSIVE                        STRING     N
MODULE_LIST             UNUSED                               STRINGLIST N
MVIEW_NAME_TEMPLATE     MV$$_<TASK_ID><SEQ>                  STRING     N
ORDER_LIST              PRIORITY,OPTIMIZER_COST              STRINGLIST N
REFRESH_MODE            ON_DEMAND                            STRING     N
REFRESH_TIME            UNLIMITED                            NUMBER     N
REPORT_DATE_FORMAT      DD/MM/YYYY HH24:MI                   STRING     N
REPORT_SECTIONS         ALL                                  STRING     N
SQL_LIMIT               UNLIMITED                            NUMBER     N
START_SNAPSHOT          UNUSED                               NUMBER     N
START_TIME              UNUSED                               UNKNOWN    N
STORAGE_CHANGE          UNLIMITED                            NUMBER     N
TARGET_OBJECTS          UNUSED                               STRINGLIST N
TIME_LIMIT              UNLIMITED                            NUMBER     N
USERNAME_LIST           UNUSED                               STRINGLIST N
VALID_TABLE_LIST        UNUSED                               TABLELIST  N
WORKLOAD_SCOPE          PARTIAL                              STRING     N
```

For example, the following call script sets the parameter *mode* to the value COMPREHENSIVE, instructing the advisor to perform a detailed analysis:

```
SQL>exec dbms_advisor.set_task_parameter('SQL_ACC_TASK1', 'MODE', '
COMPREHENSIVE ');
```

In another option, the DBA can configure parameters for the SQL workload. To retrieve that parameter list for the workload created above, use the query below.

```
SELECT
    p.parameter_name,
    p.parameter_value,
    p.parameter_type
FROM
    dba_advisor_sqlw_parameters p
WHERE
  p.owner = 'DABR'
AND
    p.workload_name = 'SQL_WRKLD_1';
```

The output for this query, showing all workload parameters, looks like the following:

```
PARAMETER_NAME           PARAMETER_VALUE                    PARAMETER_
----------------------   --------------------------------   ----------
ACTION_LIST              UNUSED                             STRINGLIST
COMMENTED_FILTER_LIST    /* OPT_DYN_SAMP */,/* DS_SVC */    STRINGLIST
DAYS_TO_EXPIRE           30                                 NUMBER
DEF_DATA_SOURCE          UNUSED                             STRING
DEF_EM_TEMPLATE          SQLACCESS_EMWKLD                   STRING
END_SNAPSHOT             UNUSED                             NUMBER
END_TIME                 UNUSED                             UNKNOWN
INSTANCE                 UNUSED                             NUMBER
INVALID_TABLE_LIST       UNUSED                             TABLELIST
JOURNALING               4                                  NUMBER
MODE                     COMPREHENSIVE                      STRING
MODULE_LIST              UNUSED                             STRINGLIST
ORDER_LIST               PRIORITY,OPTIMIZER_COST            STRINGLIST
REPORT_DATE_FORMAT       DD/MM/YYYY HH24:MI                 STRING
REPORT_SECTIONS          ALL                                STRING
SQL_LIMIT                UNLIMITED                          NUMBER
START_SNAPSHOT           UNUSED                             NUMBER
START_TIME               UNUSED                             UNKNOWN
TARGET_OBJECTS           UNUSED                             STRINGLIST
TIME_LIMIT               UNLIMITED                          NUMBER
USERNAME_LIST            UNUSED                             STRINGLIST
VALID_TABLE_LIST         UNUSED                             TABLELIST
```

This shows that the *dbms_advisor.set_sqlwkld_parameter* procedure can be used to set all values for the required parameters. In-depth descriptions for every parameter are available in the Oracle documentation.

After configuring all necessary parameters, the DBA is ready to start the SQLAccess Advisor tool to search for recommendations. The *dbms_advisor.execute_task* is used to proceed to workload analysis:

```
exec dbms_advisor.execute_task ('SQL_ACC_TASK1');
```

During the analysis phase of work, the progress of the execution can be monitored using the *dba_advisor_log* view:

```
SELECT pct_completion_time
FROM dba_advisor_log WHERE task_name = 'SQL_ACC_TASK1';
```

Once the analysis has completed successfully, the DBA can proceed to review and evaluate the recommendations and then implement the changes necessary for improving performance.

To view the recommendations summary portion of the SQLAccess Advisor analysis report, the query below can be used:

```
SELECT
   a.rec_id,
   a.precost,
   a.postcost,
   (a.precost-a.postcost)*100/a.precost "Percent Benefit",
   s.sql_text
FROM
   dba_advisor_sqla_wk_stmts a,
   dba_advisor_sqlw_stmts s
WHERE
   a.task_name = 'SQL_ACC_TASK1'
AND
   a.workload_name = 'SQL_WRKLD_1'
AND
   a.sql_id = s.sql_id;
```

The sample output of the above script might look like:

```
REC_ID PRECOST POSTCOST Percent Benefit SQL_TEXT
------ ------- -------- --------------- ----------------------------------------------------
     3       3        2     33,3333333 select b.*,a.* from spv_alert_def a,spv_baselines b
                                        where a.dbid = :dbid and a.i
     2      16        6           62,5 SELECT NVL(MAX(BEGIN_TIME), TO_DATE('01011900',
                                        'DDMMYYYY')) FROM STATS$U
     0      12       12              0 INSERT INTO STATS$SNAPSHOT ( SNAP_ID, DBID,
                                        INSTANCE_NUMBER , SNAP_TIME,
     4       2        2              0 SELECT 1 FROM STATS$DATABASE_INSTANCE WHERE
                                        STARTUP_TIME = :B3 AND DBID
     1       2        2              0 SELECT NVL(:B4 , :B3 ) , NVL(:B2 , :B1 ) FROM
                                        STATS$STATSPACK_PARAMETER
     1       4        4              0 SELECT NVL(:B21 , SESSION_ID) , NVL(:B20 ,
                                        SNAP_LEVEL) , NVL(:B19 , UCOM
```

It is important that the DBA know that the *precost* and *postcost* columns are expressed in terms of optimizer cost, and they show the estimated SQL cost before and after the recommended changes. In the above listing, it is clear that optimizer cost was reduced by one from three to two.

The following query returns the particular actions that are suggested in order for the DBA to implement each recommendation:

```
SELECT
  rec_id, action_id, SUBSTR(command,1,30) AS command
FROM
  dba_advisor_actions
WHERE
  task_name = 'SQL_ACC_TASK1'
ORDER BY
  rec_id, action_id;
```

The output of the above script typically looks like this sample:

```
    REC_ID   ACTION_ID COMMAND
---------- ---------- ----------------
         1           5 RETAIN INDEX
         2           2 CREATE INDEX
         3           1 CREATE INDEX
         3           3 RETAIN INDEX
         4           4 RETAIN INDEX
```

The final step is the generation of a SQL script that implements changes according to the automatically generated recommendations. The *dbms_advisor.get_task_script* should be used to produce the script. Keep in mind that the following parameters have influence on the resulting script: *mview_name_template;* *index_name_template;* *def_index_owner;* *def_mview_owner;* *def_mview_tablespace;* and, *def_index_tablespace.* The SQL commands below can be used to save the SQL script to the SQL file:

```
CREATE DIRECTORY ADVISOR_RESULTS AS 'd:\temp\';
GRANT READ ON DIRECTORY ADVISOR_RESULTS TO PUBLIC;
GRANT WRITE ON DIRECTORY ADVISOR_RESULTS TO PUBLIC;
exec dbms_advisor.create_file (dbms_advisor.get_task_script
('SQL_ACC_TASK1'), -
     'ADVISOR_RESULTS', 'advscript.sql');
```

Working with the SQLAccess Advisor

The following is a sample result of the SQL script produced by the SQLAccess Advisor:

```
set feedback 1
set linesize 80
set trimspool on
set tab off
set pagesize 60

whenever sqlerror CONTINUE

CREATE BITMAP INDEX "SPV"."_IDX$$_11A40001"
    ON "SPV"."SPV_BASELINES"
    ("AWR")
    COMPUTE STATISTICS;

CREATE INDEX "PERFSTAT"."_IDX$$_11A40002"
    ON "PERFSTAT"."STATS$UNDOSTAT"
    ("DBID","INSTANCE_NUMBER")
    COMPUTE STATISTICS;

/* RETAIN INDEX "SPV"."SPV_ALERT_DEF_PK" */

/* RETAIN INDEX "PERFSTAT"."STATS$DATABASE_INSTANCE_PK" */

/* RETAIN INDEX "PERFSTAT"."STATS$STATSPACK_PARAMETER_PK" */

whenever sqlerror EXIT SQL.SQLCODE

begin
  dbms_advisor.mark_recommendation('SQL_ACC_TASK1',1,'IMPLEMENTED');
  dbms_advisor.mark_recommendation('SQL_ACC_TASK1',2,'IMPLEMENTED');
  dbms_advisor.mark_recommendation('SQL_ACC_TASK1',3,'IMPLEMENTED');
  dbms_advisor.mark_recommendation('SQL_ACC_TASK1',4,'IMPLEMENTED');
end;
/
```

The comprehensive analysis sessions can be very time consuming, but Oracle10g also offers quick analysis features that are less stressful on a production database.

Using the *quick_tune* option

The *dbms_advisor* package has a procedure called *dbms_advisor.quick_tune* that allows the DBA to quickly tune a single SQL statement with a single procedure call. This procedure performs all of the stages described above that are necessary to launch the SQLAccess Advisor, e.g. creating a task, creating and populating a workload, and executing the task. The sample call of this procedure is as follows:

```
VARIABLE task_name VARCHAR2(255);
VARIABLE sql_stmt VARCHAR2(4000);
exec :sql_stmt := 'SELECT COUNT(*) FROM all_objects WHERE
object_type = 'VIEW';
exec:task_name  := 'MY_QUICKTUNE_TASK';
exec DBMS_advisor.quick_tune (dbms_advisor.sqlaccess_advisor,
:task_name, :sql_stmt);
```

The *dbms_advisor* package provides a rich collection of managing tasks, workloads, and recommendations. These examples should give an overview of how to work with SQLAccess Advisor. Once armed with this information, the DBA should be able to be more flexible in the creation and configuration of tuning sessions.

Inside the *dbms_sqltune* Package

SQL tuning work is one of the most time-consuming and challenging tasks faced by Oracle DBAs and application developers. The Oracle10g SQL Tuning Advisor is intended to facilitate SQL tuning tasks and to help the DBA find the optimal SQL execution plan. The SQL Tuning Advisor can search the SQL cache, the AWR, or user inputs searching for inefficient SQL statements. The SQL Tuning Advisor is available through the OEM console, or the *dbms_sqltune* package can be invoked manually. Figure 8.3 is a representation of the SQL Tuning Advisor tool in the OEM console.

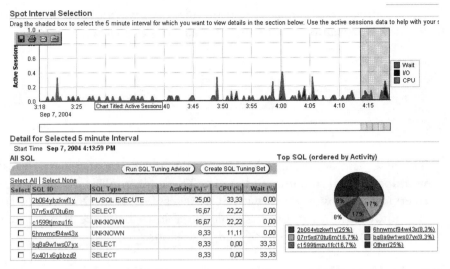

Figure 8.3: *Access SQL Tuning Advisor in the OEM Console*

The WISE tool, which has been provided free with the purchase of this book, also supports use of the SQL Tuning Advisor and allows the DBA to tune any SQL statement that is stored in the AWR. Figure 8.4 is a representation of the SQL Tuning Advisor in the WISE tool.

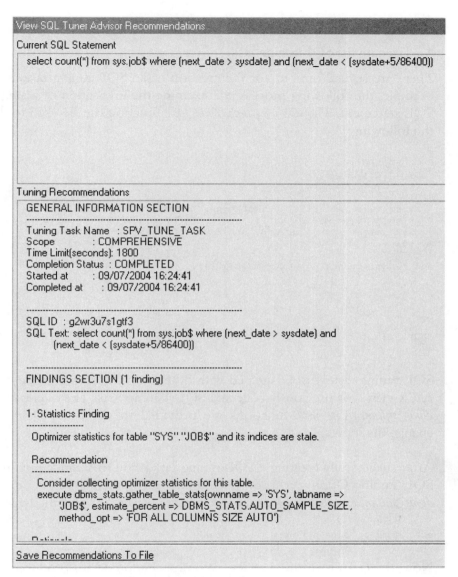

Figure 8.4: *Access SQL Tuning Advisor in WISE*

The *dbms_sqltune* package provides the DBA with a PL/SQL API for using the SQL Tuning Advisor tool. Running the SQL Tuning Advisor using PL/SQL API includes two steps:

- Create the SQL tuning task.

- Execute the SQL tuning task.

There are several options for the creation of an SQL tuning task. For example, the following process will examine the invocation of a single SQL statement. The *dbms_sqltune.create_task* function can be used to do the following:

```
DECLARE
  my_sqltext CLOB;
  task_name VARCHAR2(30);
BEGIN
  my_sqltext := 'SELECT object_type, count(*) FROM ';
  my_sqltext := my_sqltext || ' all_objects GROUP BY object_type';
  task_name := DBMS_SQLTUNE.CREATE_TUNING_TASK( sql_text =>
my_sqltext,
                                   bind_list =>
sql_binds(anydata.ConvertNumber(100)),
                                   user_name => 'DABR',
                                   scope => 'COMPREHENSIVE',
                                   time_limit => 60,
                                   task_name => 'sql_tuning_task1');

END;
/
```

SQL tuning tasks can be created with SQL from the cursor cache, the AWR views, or previously collected SQL Tuning Sets. The overloaded *dbms_sqltune.create_task* functions are provided to allow the DBA to change the inputs.

After successfully creating a SQL tuning task, the DBA can launch the SQL Tuning Optimizer to produce tuning recommendations. Use the *dbms_sqltune.execute_tuning_task* procedure to execute the specified task:

```
exec dbms_sqltune.execute_tuning_task ( 'sql_tuning_task1');
```

Now, the DBA is ready to review recommendation details produced by the SQL Tuning Advisor. A query like the one below can be used to retrieve the SQL analysis results:

```
select dbms_sqltune.report_tuning_task('sql_tuning_task1') from
dual;
```

The following is the resulting report.

```
DBMS_SQLTUNE.REPORT_TUNING_TASK('SQL_TUNING_TASK1')
-------------------------------------------------------------------
GENERAL INFORMATION SECTION
-------------------------------------------------------------------
Tuning Task Name     : SQL_TUNING_TASK1
Scope                : COMPREHENSIVE
Time Limit(seconds)  : 1800
Completion Status    : COMPLETED
Started at           : 09/07/2004 16:24:41
Completed at         : 09/07/2004 16:24:41


-------------------------------------------------------------------
SQL ID  : g2wr3u7s1gtf3
SQL Text: 'SELECT object_type, count(*) FROM
          all_objects GROUP BY object_type'


-------------------------------------------------------------------
FINDINGS SECTION (1 finding)
-------------------------------------------------------------------

1- Statistics Finding
---------------------
  Optimizer statistics for table "SYS"."OBJ$" and its indices are
stale.

  Recommendation
  --------------
    Consider collecting optimizer statistics for this table.
    execute dbms_stats.gather_table_stats(ownname => 'SYS',
```

The recommendation report contains problem findings and the corresponding recommendations for fixing them.

The analysis process could consume significant processing times. Therefore, the *dbms_sqltune* package provides an API to manage tuning tasks such as:

- The *interrupt_tuning_task* procedure is used to stop the executing task. Any results that have already been produced will be preserved.

- The *cancel_tuning_task* procedure terminates the task that is executing without preserving its results.

- The *reset_tuning_task* procedure is used to stop the running task and reset it to the initial state.

- The *drop_tuning_task* procedure can be used to remove the task from the database.

During tuning analysis, the SQL Tuning Advisor can recommend and automatically create SQL profiles. The SQL profile is a special object that is used by the optimizer. The SQL Profile contains auxiliary statistics specific to a particular SQL statement.

The SQL optimizer uses the information in the SQL profile to adjust the execution plan for the SQL statement that has the associated SQL profile. SQL profiles are great for SQL tuning because it is possible to tune SQL statements without any modification of the application source code or the text of SQL queries. The *dba_sql_profiles* view shows information about all existing SQL profiles.

The *dbms_sqltune* package can be used to manage SQL profiles. The SQL Tuning Advisor can recommend the use of a specific SQL Profile. This SQL profile can be associated with SQL statements that are being analyzed by accepting it using *dbms_sqltune.accept_sql_profile*:

```
DECLARE
   sqlprofile VARCHAR2(30);
BEGIN
   sqlprofile := dbms_sqltune.accept_sql_profile (
   task_name => 'sql_tuning_task1',
   name => 'sql_profile1');
END;
```

After the profile is defined, the DBA can alter any stored SQL profile attributes such as *status, name, description,* and *category* using *dbms_sqltune.alter_sql_profile*. The *category* attribute is used to limit user sessions that can use the particular SQL profile. There is an initialization parameter called *sqltune_category*, which allows the DBA to set up the default SQL profile category for the database.

The *dbms_sqltune.drop_sql_profile* procedure is used to remove the SQL profile from the database.

The *dbms_sqltune* package also provides a PL/SQL API to work with SQL Tuning Sets (STS). The STS is a database object that contains one or more SQL statements combined with their execution statistics and context such as particular schema, application module name, list of bind variables, etc. The STS also includes a set of basic execution statistics such as CPU and elapsed times, disk reads and buffer gets, number of executions, etc.

When creating a STS, the SQL statements can be filtered by different patterns such as application module name or execution statistics, such as high disk reads. Once created, STS can be an input source for the SQL Tuning Advisor.

Typically, the following steps are used to work with STS using the *dbms_sqltune* API:

1. STS is created using the dbms_sqltune.create_sqlset procedure. For example, the following script can be used to create a STS called SQLSET1:

```
exec dbms_sqltune.create_sqlset ( 'SQLSET1');
```

2. STS is loaded from such sources as the AWR, another STS, or the cursor cache. The following sample PL/SQL block loads STS from the current cursor cache:

```
DECLARE
  cur dbms_sqltune.sqlset_cursor;
BEGIN
OPEN cur FOR
SELECT VALUE(p)
FROM TABLE (dbms_sqltune.select_cursor_cache) p;
dbms_sqltune.load_sqlset(
sqlset_name => 'SQLSET1',
populate_cursor => cur);
END;
/
```

3. An SQL tuning task that uses STS as input can be created and executed like this:

```
exec dbms_sqltune.create_tuning_task (sqlset_name  => 'SQLSET1',
task_name => 'TASK1');
exec dbms_sqltune.execute_tuning_task ('TASK1');
```

4. The following syntax can be used to drop a SQL tuning set when finished:

```
exec dbms_sqltune.drop_sqlset ( 'SQLSET1' );
```

All SQL tuning sets created in the database by querying the *dba_sqlset, dba_sqlset_binds, dba_sqlset_definitions,* and *dba_sqlset_statements* views are reviewed. For example, the *dbms_sqltune_show_sts.sql* query below shows the particular SQL statements associated with STS:

```
SELECT
  s.sql_text,
  s.cpu_time
FROM
  dba_sqlset_statements s,
  dba_sqlset a
WHERE
  a.name = 'SQLSET1'
AND
  s.sqlset_id =   a.id
AND
  rownum <= 10
ORDER BY
  s.cpu_time DESC
```

Clearly, Oracle10g has introduced a rich set of powerful tools for the DBA to use to identify and resolve possible performance problems. While these advisors cannot yet replicate the behavior of a senior DBA, they promise to get more intelligent with each new release of Oracle.

Conclusion

Oracle10g database provides DBAs with a unique set of intelligent advisor tools that are able to significantly reduce analysis and tuning efforts. This chapter has given a high level overview for using these advisors and their associated packages.

This chapter did not cover the non-tuning related advisor tools available in Oracle10g such as the Segment Advisor, and the Undo Advisor, but more information regarding these advisors will be presented in subsequent chapters of this book.

The main points of this chapter include:

- The *dbms* packages in Oracle10g provide an easy interface to complex automation performance tools.

- The *dbms_workload_repository* package allows the DBA to manage the AWR, setting snapshot intervals and data retention periods.

- The *dbms_advisor* package provides PL/SQL API to access the Automatic Database Diagnostic Monitor (ADDM) and SQLAccess Advisor.

- ADDM is implemented with the powerful *dbms_advisor* package.

- The SQL Access advisor is implemented with the *dbms_sqltune* package.

- ADDM can be used to provide intelligent analysis of the changes that occur during a snapshot period and makes automated recommendations. ADDM does not replace the intelligence of the DBA, who must still understand Oracle10g tuning concepts.

- The SQLAccess advisor provides analysis of all SQL executions for the snapshot intervals and rudimentary suggestions to improve SQL execution speed using SQL profiles. The SQLAccess advisor does not perform advanced SQL tuning and the DBA still must understand SQL execution internals, hints and table join methods.

The next chapter will present information on the new time model tuning approach that is used by all tuning advisors and tools within Oracle.

The AWR Time Model
Approach

Time Model Tuning for Oracle

This chapter covers the new *time model* tuning approach introduced in the Oracle10g database. In plain English, the time model approach allows the DBA to identify where the Oracle database spends its CPU processing time, and the time model method reveals how much CPU time is consumed by each processing component of the database.

The greatest benefit of this approach is that every statistic is measured in terms of time, so that the DBA can evaluate CPU consumers on an equal basis. This approach is best suited for situations in which there is a CPU-bound system and the DBA needs to know what steps to take to remove or at least decrease this time dependence.

The Oracle10g database provides two basic *v$* time model performance views: *v$sys_time_model* and *v$sess_time_model*. These views report on cumulative database processing times for the whole instance, and on a per session basis.

```
desc v$sys_time_model

Name                 Null?      Type
----------------- --------   -----------
STAT_ID                        NUMBER
STAT_NAME                      VARCHAR2(64)
VALUE                          NUMBER

desc v$sess_time_model

Name                 Null?      Type
----------------- --------   -----------
SID                            NUMBER
STAT_ID                        NUMBER
STAT_NAME                      VARCHAR2(64)
VALUE                          NUMBER
```

The *v$sys_time_model* view displays cumulative times, expressed in microseconds, which are collected from all non-idle database sessions. Therefore, these cumulative times could be greater than the total time measured since instance startup.

This cumulative approach is not applicable to the times reported for session time model statistics presented in the *v$sess_time_model* view. The background process times are not included in the statistic values unless the statistic is specific for background processes. For example, the *background elapsed time* statistic shows database time spent for the background processes to run.

Use the following script to retrieve a list of time model statistics available in Oracle10g database:

```
SQL> select
  stat_name,
  Round(value/1000000) "Time (Sec)"
from v$sys_time_model;
```

The output of the above query shows many of the most important statistics and looks like the following:

```
STAT_NAME                                           Time (Sec)
-------------------------------------------------   ----------
DB time                                                515,178
DB CPU                                                 299,352
background elapsed time                                583,318
background cpu time                                    128,953
sequence load elapsed time                                  59
parse time elapsed                                      76,889
hard parse elapsed time                                 73,126
sql execute elapsed time                               505,637
connection management call elapsed time                    458
failed parse elapsed time                                9,503
failed parse (out of shared memory) elapsed time             0
hard parse (sharing criteria) elapsed time               1,382
hard parse (bind mismatch) elapsed time                    184
PL/SQL execution elapsed time                           36,788
inbound PL/SQL rpc elapsed time                              0
PL/SQL compilation elapsed time                          4,932
Java execution elapsed time                              1,949
```

The listing above confirms that Oracle computes elapsed times for various parts of both user and background processing. For example, the DBA can see how much time is consumed in the hard parsing of SQL statements. If this time component is large enough, the DBA might wish to consider investigating the application to find inefficient SQL statements that are causing the excessive hard parsing workload and perhaps implement *cursor_sharing=force*. If a high PL/SQL execution elapsed time is discovered, the system may benefit from optimization of the PL/SQL programs.

The most important time model statistics are *DB time* and *DB CPU*. The *DB time* statistic shows the elapsed processing time accumulated from the elapsed times of non-idle sessions. *DB CPU* presents the cumulative CPU time from all non-idle sessions. Both statistics directly show database workload and describe overall database response time.

Most of the Oracle advisors use the time model approach to perform their work, and *DB time* is a statistic used as a criterion for tuning and producing the recommendations. Of course, all database users want to get results as soon as possible. The goal of tuning for every particular session can be summarized as the minimization of database response time for the session or the whole system.

It is also useful to monitor *DB time* or *DB CPU* statistics in real time. This approach allows the DBA to immediately identify possible system overload or stress when an exceptional event occurs. For example, The WISE tool allows the DBA to monitor database time in real time as shown in Figure 9.1 below:

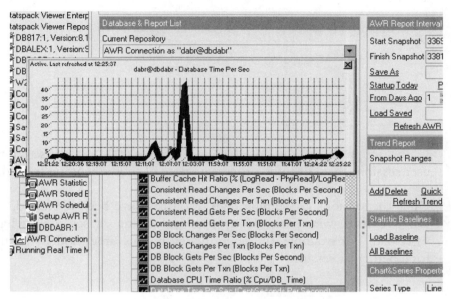

Figure 9.1: *Monitoring real-time database processing with the WISE tool.*

It is possible to write an exception script that will give a warning if the database workload exceeds some predefined threshold. For example, the script below lists sessions that experience high workload and consume significant processing resources:

```
SELECT
   s.sid,
   s.username,
   s.module,
   round(t.value/1000000,2) "Elapsed Processing Time (Sec)"
FROM
   v$sess_time_model t,
   v$session s
WHERE
   t.sid = s.sid
AND
   t.stat_name = 'DB time'
```

```
AND
    s.username IS NOT NULL
AND
    t.value/1000000 >= 1;
```

The output, showing the elapsed time used by specific modules, looks like the following:

```
SID USER  MODULE        Elapsed Processing Time (Sec)
--- ----- ------------- -----------------------------
137 DABR  SQL*Plus                              5,93
133 SPV   spvent.exe                           26,47
135 SYS   SQL*Plus                              6,36
141 DABR  SpMon.exe                            23,42
150 DABR  spvent.exe                            8,3
152 SYS   SQL*Plus                              8,13
156 SYS   SQL*Plus                              1,43
```

In the script above, the (WHERE t.value/1000000>1) clause shows user sessions that consume processing time of more than one second.

Once the sessions consuming high resources have been identified, the DBA reviews what particular type of processing causes such a high workload. For example, the query below reveals time model statistics for a particular session:

```
select
    *
from
    v$sess_time_model
where
    sid = 137
order by
    value desc;
```

The output of the above query, showing all important statistics for a particular session, might look like:

```
SID STAT_ID       STAT_NAME                                        VALUE
--- ------------- ------------------------------------------- ----------
137 3,649,082,374 DB time                                      7,244,647
137 2,821,698,184 sql execute elapsed time                     7,035,683
137 2,748,282,437 DB CPU                                       6,827,842
137 1,431,595,225 parse time elapsed                             529,294
137   372,226,525 hard parse elapsed time                       512,333
137 1,311,180,441 PL/SQL compilation elapsed time                65,472
137 1,990,024,365 connection management call elapsed time        18,180
137 2,643,905,994 PL/SQL execution elapsed time                   1,225
137 4,157,170,894 background elapsed time                             0
137   751,169,994 Java execution elapsed time                        0
```

```
137   290,749,718 inbound PL/SQL rpc elapsed time                      0
137   268,357,648 hard parse (bind mismatch) elapsed time              0
137 2,451,517,896 background cpu time                                  0
137 1,824,284,809 failed parse elapsed time                            0
137 3,138,706,091 hard parse (sharing criteria) elapsed time           0
137 4,125,607,023 failed parse (out of shared memory) elapsed time     0
```

From the listing above, it is apparent that a significant part of processing time for this database is consumed by SQL execution. This could clue the DBA that an investigation into SQL statements to identify high CPU consuming SQL statements is required. For example, such SQL statements could have a large number of buffer gets that were taken in *consistent mode*. This requires a large amount of CPU processing time to reconstruct data blocks from rollback segments or UNDO logs.

The DBA must remember that the Automated Workload Repository (AWR) stores history for only the *v$sys_time_model* view snapshots which are available through the *dba_hist_sys_time_model* view:

```
SQL> desc dba_hist_sys_time_model

Name                 Null?      Type
-----------------    --------   -----------
SNAP_ID                         NUMBER
DBID                            NUMBER
INSTANCE_NUMBER                 NUMBER
STAT_ID                         NUMBER
STAT_NAME                       VARCHAR2(64)
VALUE                           NUMBER
```

The AWR repository stores only snapshots of time model statistics that reflect its cumulative values at the time of its snapshots and comparisons between database shutdowns are meaningless. However, it is easy to build time-series trend charts of database workload and particular processing parts based on history stored in the AWR. These charts allow the DBA to get signatures of the database workload and identify hot periods when the database most stressed. For example, the query below displays the database workload for a particular snapshot interval using the *dba_hist_sys_time_model* view:

```
SELECT
    e.stat_name "E.STAT_NAME"
      , Round((e.value - b.value)/1000000,2)"Time (s)"
      , Round(decode( e.stat_name,'DB time'
```

```
            , to_number(null)
            , 100*(e.value - b.value)
            )/
   (SELECT NVL((e1.value - b1.value),-1)
      FROM dba_hist_sys_time_model   e1
         , dba_hist_sys_time_model   b1
      WHERE b1.snap_id               = b.snap_id
      AND e1.snap_id                 = e.snap_id
      AND b1.dbid                    = b.dbid
      AND e1.dbid                    = e.dbid
      AND b1.instance_number         = b.instance_number
      AND e1.instance_number         = e.instance_number
      AND e1.stat_name               = 'DB time'
      AND b1.stat_id                 = e1.stat_id ),2) "Percent of
Total DB Time"
  FROM dba_hist_sys_time_model e
     , dba_hist_sys_time_model b
 WHERE b.snap_id                  = &pBgnSnap
   AND e.snap_id                  = &pEndSnap
   AND b.dbid                     = &pDbId
   AND e.dbid                     = &pDbId
   AND b.instance_number          = &pInstNum
   AND e.instance_number          = &pInstNum
   AND b.stat_id                  = e.stat_id
   AND e.value - b.value > 0
 ORDER BY 2 DESC
```

The output of the above script, showing the time usage for all of the major activities, might look like:

```
E.STAT_NAME                               Time (s) Pct Tot DB Time
----------------------------------------- ---------- -------------
DB time                                   21,204.9
sql execute elapsed time                  20,934.21      98.72
background elapsed time                   16,202.46      76.41
DB CPU                                     8,761.48      41.32
parse time elapsed                         5,007.8       23.62
hard parse elapsed time                    4,788         22.58
background cpu time                         2,785.09      13.13
PL/SQL execution elapsed time              2,495.51      11.77
failed parse elapsed time                   933.21        4.4
PL/SQL compilation elapsed time             280.73        1.32
Java execution elapsed time                 123.52         .58
hard parse (sharing criteria) elapsed ti    84.84          .4
connection management call elapsed time      23.05         .11
hard parse (bind mismatch) elapsed time      10.75         .05
sequence load elapsed time                    2.21         .01
```

The above output reports the overall database workload activity and shows the particular part of database processing that consumes significant CPU resources.

This time-series database workload trend report is also available in WISE for immediate visualization so that the main bottlenecks in a database can be easily identified.

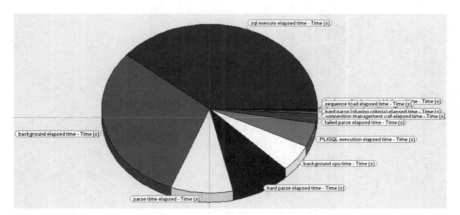

Figure 9.2: *Time model overview report (graph section) in the WISE tool.*

Using the *dba_hist_sys_time_model* view, the DBA can also write various trend reports describing database workload by hours of the day, days of the week, months, etc. For example, the query below returns the average database workload by hours of a day:

```
SELECT
    to_char(end_interval_time,'HH24') "Hour of Day",
    Round(avg(newtime.value-oldtime.value)/1000000,2) "Avg DB Time
(Sec)"
FROM
    dba_hist_sys_time_model oldtime,
    dba_hist_sys_time_model newtime,
    dba_hist_snapshot         sn
WHERE
    newtime.snap_id = sn.snap_id
AND
    oldtime.snap_id = sn.snap_id-1
AND
    newtime.stat_name = 'DB time'
AND
    oldtime.stat_name = 'DB time'
HAVING
    avg(newtime.value-oldtime.value) > 0
GROUP BY
    to_char(end_interval_time,'HH24');
```

The sample output, showing a signature of *DB time* by hour of the day, looks like the following:

```
Ho Avg DB Time (Sec)
-- -----------------
00              55.21
01              54.68
02              53.38
03              52.79
04               53.8
05              52.98
06              53.62
07              52.51
08              53.26
09              61.27
10             515.71
11             484.96
12             109.26
13              88.07
14             121.25
15             134.94
16              90.56
17              70.51
18              79.53
19              53.32
20              53.89
21              53.61
22              53.47
23              53.91
```

From the above listing, it appears that the database experiences the heaviest workload between the tenth and fifteen hours which corresponds with 10 am to 3 pm.

Trend charts of averages can easily be generated by hours of the day, days of the week, or months using the WISE tool. The following sample screen shows such a report in the WISE tool:

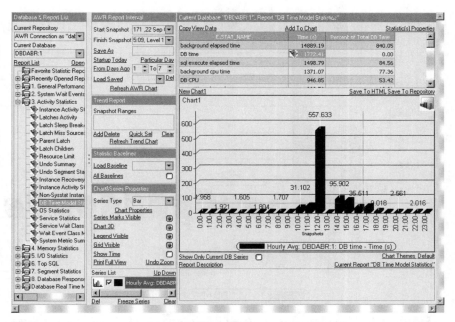

Figure 9.3: *Hourly averages for database time in the WISE tool.*

This information helps create a better understanding of the workload the database experiences during a day and helps the DBA undertake the appropriate tuning actions.

One example of an appropriate tuning action would be the redistribution of batch processing jobs or other CPU consuming jobs to a time of day that is different from the ones mentioned above. The WISE tool can be used to produce trend charts like the one below:

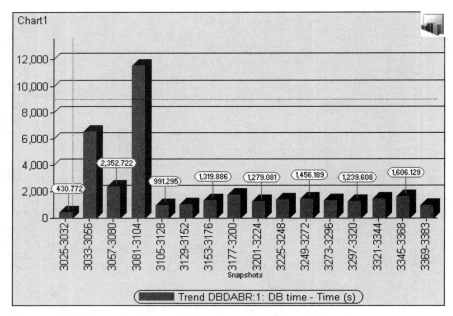

Figure 9.4: *Sample time model trend report in the WISE tool.*

The next step is to learn how to use the Active Session History (ASH) tables to determine the causes of buffer busy waits.

Finding the Cause of Buffer Busy Waits

The resolution of buffer busy wait events is one of the most confounding problems with Oracle. In an I/O-bound Oracle system, buffer busy waits are common, as evidenced by any system with read (sequential/scattered) waits in the top-five waits in the Oracle AWR report, like the following sample AWR report:

```
Top 5 Timed Events

                                                          % Total
Event                         Waits        Time (s)      Ela Time
----------------------------  ------------ -----------  -----------
db file sequential read        2,598        7,146         48.54
db file scattered read        25,519        3,246         22.04
library cache load lock          673        1,363          9.26
CPU time                       2,154          934          7.83
log file parallel write       19,157          837          5.68
```

Reducing *buffer busy waits* reduces the total I/O on the system. This can be accomplished by tuning the SQL to access rows with fewer block reads by adding indexes, adjusting the database writer, or adding freelsts to tables and indexes. Even if there is a huge *db_cache_size,* the DBA may still see *buffer busy waits* and, in this case, increasing the buffer size will not help.

Can Buffer Busy Waits be fixed?

The most common remedies for high buffer busy waits include database writer (DBWR) contention tuning, adding freelisys, implementing Automatic Segment Storage Management (ASSM, a.k.a bitmap freelists), and, of course, and adding a missing index to reduce buffer touches.

The *v$system_event* performance view can also be queried in order to look at system-wide wait events. Shown below, this view provides the name of the wait event, the total number of waits and timeouts, the total time waited, and the average wait time per event:

```
select *
from
    v$system_event
where
    event like '%wait%';
```

EVENT	TOTAL_WAITS	TOTAL_TIMEO	TIME_WAITED	AVERAGE_WAIT
buffer busy waits	636,528	1,557	549,700	.863591232
write complete waits	1,193	0	14,799	12.4048617
free buffer waits	1,601	0	622	.388507183

The type of buffer causing the wait can be queried using the *v$waitstat* view. This view lists the waits for each buffer type for buffer busy waits, where *count* is the sum of all waits for the class of block, and *time* is the sum of all wait times for that class:

```
select * from v$waitstat;

CLASS                  COUNT       TIME
------------------  ----------  ----------
data block          1,961,113   1,870,278
segment header         34,535     159,082
undo header           233,632      86,239
undo block              1,886       1,706
```

When an Oracle session needs to access a block in the buffer cache, but is unable to because the buffer copy of the data block is locked, a buffer busy wait occurs. This *buffer busy wait* condition happens for two reasons:

- Another session has the buffer block locked in a mode that is incompatible with the waiting session's request.

- The block is being read into the buffer by another session, so the waiting session must wait for the block read to complete.

Unfortunately, there's nothing the DBA can do until the blocks that are in conflict are identified along with the reasons that the conflicts are occurring, since buffer busy waits are due to contention between particular blocks. Therefore, this type of tuning involves identifying and eliminating the cause of the block contention.

Shown below, the *v$session_wait* performance view can offer some insight into what is being waited for and why the wait is occurring.

```
SQL> desc v$session_wait

Name                                     Null?     Type
---------------------------------------  --------  ----------------
SID                                                NUMBER
SEQ#                                               NUMBER
EVENT                                              VARCHAR2(64)
P1TEXT                                             VARCHAR2(64)
P1                                                 NUMBER
P1RAW                                              RAW(4)
P2TEXT                                             VARCHAR2(64)
P2                                                 NUMBER
P2RAW                                              RAW(4)
P3TEXT                                             VARCHAR2(64)
P3                                                 NUMBER
P3RAW                                              RAW(4)
WAIT_TIME                                          NUMBER
SECONDS_IN_WAIT                                    NUMBER
STATE                                              VARCHAR2(19)
```

There are three columns of the *v$session_wait* view that are of particular interest for a *buffer busy wait* event:

- P1: The absolute file number for the data file involved in the wait.

- P2: The block number within the data file referenced in P1 that is being waited upon.

- P3: The reason code describing why the wait is occurring.

The following is an Oracle data dictionary query for these values:

```
select
    p1 "File #".
    p2 "Block #",
    p3 "Reason Code"
from
    v$session_wait
where
    event = 'buffer busy waits';
```

The next query should show the name and type of the segment, but only if the output from repeatedly running the above query shows a block or range of blocks is experiencing waits:

```
select
    owner,
    segment_name,
    segment_type
from
    dba_extents
where
    file_id = &P1
and
    &P2 between block_id and block_id + blocks -1;
```

Once the segment is established, the *v$segment_statistics* performance view facilitates real-time monitoring of segment-level statistics. This enables a DBA to recognize performance issues related to individual tables or indexes, as shown below.

```
select
    object_name,
    statistic_name,
    value
```

```
from
   V$SEGMENT_STATISTICS
where
   object_name = 'SOURCE$';
```

The sample script output below shows various I/O related statistics against SOURCE$ table:

```
OBJECT_NAME    STATISTIC_NAME              VALUE
-----------    ------------------------    ----------
SOURCE$        logical reads               11,216
SOURCE$        buffer busy waits              210
SOURCE$        db block changes                32
SOURCE$        physical reads              10,365
SOURCE$        physical writes                  0
SOURCE$        physical reads direct            0
SOURCE$        physical writes direct           0
SOURCE$        ITL waits                        0
SOURCE$        row lock waits
```

By using the P1 value from *v$session_wait* to find the *file_id*, the *dba_data_files* can also be queried to determine the *file_name* for the file involved in the wait.

```
SQL> desc dba_data_files

Name                                    Null?      Type
-------------------------------------   --------   ----------------
FILE_NAME                                          VARCHAR2(513)
FILE_ID                                            NUMBER
TABLESPACE_NAME                                    VARCHAR2(30)
BYTES                                              NUMBER
BLOCKS                                             NUMBER
STATUS                                             VARCHAR2(9)
RELATIVE_FNO                                       NUMBER
AUTOEXTENSIBLE                                     VARCHAR2(3)
MAXBYTES                                           NUMBER
MAXBLOCKS                                          NUMBER
INCREMENT_BY                                       NUMBER
USER_BYTES                                         NUMBER
USER_BLOCKS                                        NUMBER
```

In Oracle10g, the same information can be found through the use of a new ASH view called *v$active_session_history*. This view shows the real time history for various session wait events including buffer busy waits that occurred in the recent past. The following Oracle10g query can be used as a substitute for all of the above queries:

```
select
    h.p3 "Reason Code",
    h.time_waited "Time Waited",
    o.object_name "Object",
    f.file_name "Datafile",
    h.current_block# "Block Waited"
from
    v$active_session_history h,
    dba_objects o,
    dba_data_files f
where
    h.event = 'buffer busy waits' and
    h.current_obj# = o.object_id and
    h.current_file# = f.file_id and
    h.session_state = 'WAITING';
```

Retrieving the reason code, P3, from the *v$session_wait* or ASH query for a *buffer busy wait* event, will give the DBA information as to why the session is waiting. The following table lists the P3 reason codes and their definitions.

CODE	REASON FOR WAIT
-	A modification is happening on a SCUR or XCUR buffer but has not yet completed.
0	The block is being read into the buffer cache.
100	The goal is to NEW the block, but the block is currently being read by another session, most likely for undo.
110	The goal is to have the CURRENT block either shared or exclusive, but the block is being read into cache by another session; therefore, one has to wait until it's read() is completed.
120	The goal is to get the block in current mode, but someone else is currently reading it into the cache. The solution is to wait for the user to complete the read. This occurs during buffer lookup.
130	The block is being read by another session, no other suitable block image was found, so one must wait until the read is completed. This may also occur after a buffer cache assumes deadlock. The kernel cannot get a buffer in a certain amount of time and assumes a deadlock; therefore, it will read the CR version of the block.
200	The goal is to NEW the block, but someone else is using the current copy; therefore, one has to wait for that user to finish.

CODE	REASON FOR WAIT
210	The session wants the block in SCUR or XCUR mode. If this is a buffer exchange or the session is in discrete TX mode, the session waits for the first time and the second time escalates the block as a deadlock, so it does not show up as waiting very long. In this case, the statistic exchange deadlocks is incremented, and the CPU for the buffer deadlock wait event is revealed.
220	During buffer lookup for a CURRENT copy of a buffer, the buffer has been found, but someone holds it in an incompatible mode, so one has to wait.
230	The systems is trying to get a buffer in CR/CRX mode, but a modification has started on the buffer that has not yet been completed.
231	CR/CRX scan found the CURRENT block, but a modification has started on the buffer that has not yet been completed.

Table 9.1: *Reason Codes*

To reiterate, *buffer busy waits* are prevalent in I/O-bound systems with high DML updates. I/O contention is sometimes the result of waiting for access to data blocks and can be caused by multiple Oracle tasks repeatedly reading the same blocks, as when many Oracle sessions scan the same index.

For resolving each type of contention situations, the following rules of thumb may be useful:

Undo header contention: Increase the number of rollback segments.

Segment header contention: Increase the number of *freelist*s and use multiple *freelist groups*, which can make a difference even within a single instance.

Freelist block contention: Again, increase the *freelists* value. Also, when using Oracle Parallel Server or Real Application Clusters, one must be certain that each instance has its own *freelist groups*.

Data block contention: Identify and eliminate *hot* blocks from the application via changing *pctfree* and or *pctused* values to reduce the number of rows per data block. Check for repeatedly scanned indexes. Since each transaction updating a block requires a transaction entry, we might increase the *initrans* value.

Oracle provides the *v$segment_statistics* view to help monitor *buffer busy waits*, and the *v$system_event* view is provided to identify the specific blocks for the buffer busy wait. The identification and resolution of buffer busy waits can be very complex and confusing. Determining and correcting the causes of buffer busy waits is not an intuitive process, but the results of the DBA's efforts can be quite rewarding.

For great scripts to interrogate *v$segment_statistics*, see the scripts in Chapter 14, *Oracle Instance Tuning*.

Conclusion

This chapter covered the basic concepts of the new time model tuning method and how to use timing statistics to quickly identify high resource consuming sessions and components.

The time model approach is a very powerful tool for finding and resolving performance issues, especially when a system is CPU-bound. Furthermore, the time model statistics allow the DBA to build sophisticated monitoring and analysis solutions based on real time data and history stored in the AWR.

The main points of this chapter include:

- The automatic Active Session History (ASH) data collection makes it easy to see recent database sessions and a breakdown of the response time waits for each session.

- The *dba_hist_sys_time_model* table provides valuable aggregate information on total database time spent in different phases of database processing. This is very helpful for implementing instance-wide features and adjusting initialization parameters.

- The session ID can be specified when querying *dba_hist_sys_time_model* to see specific details about individual session processing patterns.

The next chapter is one of the most important chapters in this text as it presents information on reading the AWR report. Despite the tools and tricks shared in this book, the DBA must still be able to understand the raw data, and reading an AWR report is an indispensable skill for any Oracle DBA.

Reading an AWR or STATSPACK Report

I'm here to divine the secret meaning within your AWR report

Listening to the Database

This chapter focuses on the skills required for reading and interpreting an Automated Workload Repository (AWR) report, which is very similar to the STATSPACK elapsed-time report. The AWR elapsed-time report contains valuable information regarding the health of the Oracle instance, but considerable skill is required to fully understand and interpret each section.

While there is only enough room in this chapter to cover the highlights, this important chapter should give users a good idea about what to look for in an AWR report and how to use this data to identify performance problems.

Generating the AWR Report

The procedure for creating a standard report provided by the STATSPACK utility in previous Oracle releases has already been introduced. The only way to get a final STATSPACK report is to manually run the *spreport.sql* script in an ad-hoc SQL environment like SQL*Plus. The procedure of report generation in Oracle10g is quite different with AWR. The final AWR report can be built by using the PL/SQL API provided in the *dbms_workload_repository* package.

Two procedures that generate AWR reports are *awr_report_text* and *awr_report_html*. These procedures generate the AWR report for the specified snapshot range in TEXT or HTML formats, respectively. The following script shows one way of retrieving the AWR text report for the particular snapshot range:

```
SELECT
   output
FROM
   TABLE
   (dbms_workload_repository.awr_report_text
      (37933856,1,2900,2911 )
   );

OUTPUT
-------------------------------------------------------------------
WORKLOAD REPOSITORY report for

DB Name      DB Id      Instance  Inst Num Release     Cluster Host
----------  -----------  --------- -------- ----------- ------- -----
DBDABR       37933856 dbdabr          1 10.1.0.2.0  NO      Host1

             Snap Id      Snap Time      Sessions Curs/Sess
             --------- ------------------- -------- ---------
Begin Snap:     2900 19-Aug-04 11:00:29       18       5.2
  End Snap:     2911 19-Aug-04 22:00:16       18       4.6
  Elapsed:            659.78 (mins)
  DB Time:             10.08 (mins)

Cache Sizes (end)
~~~~~~~~~~~~~~~~~
          Buffer Cache:      48M    Std Block Size:      8K
      Shared Pool Size:      56M       Log Buffer:    256K
```

```
Load Profile
~~~~                                Per Second         Per Transaction
                                    ---------          ---------------
             Redo size:            1,766.20               18,526.31
         Logical reads:               39.21                  411.30
         Block changes:               11.11                  116.54
        Physical reads:                0.38                    3.95
       Physical writes:                0.38                    3.96
            User calls:                0.06                    0.64
                Parses:                2.04                   21.37
           Hard parses:                0.14                    1.45
                 Sorts:                1.02                   10.72
                Logons:                0.02                    0.21
              Executes:                4.19                   43.91
```

The old-fashioned AWR report generation procedure has also been preserved from STATSPACK. The *awrrpt.sql* script in SQL*Plus can simply be run, and the parameters necessary to build the AWR report can be provided. In fact, the *awrrpt.sql* script calls the corresponding procedure from the *dbms_workload_repository* package and stores its output in the target report file.

The next section outlines the evolution of the STATSPACK report, *spreports*, into the Oracle10g AWR report.

Reading the AWR Report

This section contains detailed guidance for evaluating each section of an AWR report. An AWR report is very similar to the STATSPACK report from Oracle9i, and it contains vital elapsed-time information on what happened during the particular snapshot range. The data in an AWR or STATSPACK report is the delta, or changes, between the accumulated metrics within each snapshot.

The main sections in an AWR report include:

Report Summary: This gives an overall summary of the instance during the snapshot period, and it contains important aggregate summary information.

Cache Sizes (end): This shows the size of each SGA region after AMM has changed them. This information can be compared to the original *init.ora* parameters at the end of the AWR report.

Load Profile: This important section shows important rates expressed in units of per second and transactions per second.

Instance Efficiency Percentages: With a target of 100%, these are high-level ratios for activity in the SGA.

Shared Pool Statistics: This is a good summary of changes to the shared pool during the snapshot period.

Top 5 Timed Events: This is the most important section in the AWR report. It shows the top wait events and can quickly show the overall database bottleneck.

Wait Events Statistics Section: This section shows a breakdown of the main wait events in the database including foreground and background database wait events as well as time model, operating system, service, and wait classes statistics.

Wait Events: This AWR report section provides more detailed wait event information for foreground user processes which includes Top 5 wait events and many other wait events that occurred during the snapshot interval.

Background Wait Events: This section is relevant to the background process wait events.

Time Model Statistics: Time mode statistics report how database-processing time is spent. This section contains detailed timing information on particular components participating in database processing.

Operating System Statistics: The stress on the Oracle server is important, and this section shows the main external resources including I/O, CPU, memory, and network usage.

Service Statistics: The service statistics section gives information about how particular services configured in the database are operating.

SQL Section: This section displays top SQL, ordered by important SQL execution metrics.

- **SQL Ordered by Elapsed Time:** Includes SQL statements that took significant execution time during processing.

- **SQL Ordered by CPU Time:** Includes SQL statements that consumed significant CPU time during its processing.

- **SQL Ordered by Gets:** These SQLs performed a high number of logical reads while retrieving data.

- **SQL Ordered by Reads:** These SQLs performed a high number of physical disk reads while retrieving data.

- **SQL Ordered by Parse Calls:** These SQLs experienced a high number of reparsing operations.

- **SQL Ordered by Sharable Memory:** Includes SQL statements cursors which consumed a large amount of SGA shared pool memory.

- **SQL Ordered by Version Count:** These SQLs have a large number of versions in shared pool for some reason.

Instance Activity Stats: This section contains statistical information describing how the database operated during the snapshot period.

- **Instance Activity Stats** (Absolute Values): This section contains statistics that have absolute values not derived from end and start snapshots.

- **Instance Activity Stats** (Thread Activity): This report section reports a log switch activity statistic.

I/O Section: This section shows the all important I/O activity for the instance and shows I/O activity by tablespace, data file, and includes buffer pool statistics.

- Tablespace IO Stats

- File IO Stats

- Buffer Pool Statistics

Advisory Section: This section show details of the advisories for the buffer, shared pool, PGA and Java pool.

- Buffer Pool Advisory

- PGA Aggr Summary: PGA Aggr Target Stats; PGA Aggr Target Histogram; and PGA Memory Advisory.

- Shared Pool Advisory

- Java Pool Advisory

Buffer Wait Statistics: This important section shows buffer cache waits statistics.

Enqueue Activity: This important section shows how enqueue operates in the database. Enqueues are special internal structures which provide concurrent access to various database resources.

Undo Segment Summary: This section gives a summary about how undo segments are used by the database.

Undo Segment Stats: This section shows detailed history information about undo segment activity.

Latch Activity: This section shows details about latch statistics. Latches are a lightweight serialization mechanism that is used to single-thread access to internal Oracle structures.

- Latch Sleep Breakdown

- Latch Miss Sources

- Parent Latch Statistics

- Child Latch Statistics

Segment Section: This report section provides details about hot segments using the following criteria:

- **Segments by Logical Reads:** Includes top segments which experienced high number of logical reads.

- **Segments by Physical Reads:** Includes top segments which experienced high number of disk physical reads.

- **Segments by Buffer Busy Waits:** These segments have the largest number of buffer waits caused by their data blocks.

- **Segments by Row Lock Waits:** Includes segments that had a large number of row locks on their data.

- **Segments by ITL Waits:** Includes segments that had a large contention for Interested Transaction List (ITL). The contention for ITL can be reduced by increasing INITRANS storage parameter of the table.

Dictionary Cache Stats: This section exposes details about how the data dictionary cache is operating.

Library Cache Activity: Includes library cache statistics describing how shared library objects are managed by Oracle.

SGA Memory Summary: This section provides summary information about various SGA regions.

init.ora **Parameters:** This section shows the original *init.ora* parameters for the instance during the snapshot period.

The following section details what each report section contains and what valuable tuning information is available.

Report Summary

The first part of the report includes general information. The report summary section contains the identification of the database on which the AWR report was run along with the time interval of the AWR report.

```
WORKLOAD REPOSITORY report for

DB Name        DB Id       Instance      Inst Num Release      Cluster
Host
------------ ----------- ------------- -------- ----------- ------- -
LSQ            2787970997 lsq                   1 10.1.0.2.0  NO
BASK

                Snap Id        Snap Time      Sessions Curs/Sess
              --------- ------------------- -------- ---------
Begin Snap:     1355 24-Jun-04 18:00:10          29     14.8
  End Snap:     1356 24-Jun-04 19:00:39          28     15.0
  Elapsed:              60.49 (mins)
  DB Time:             121.24 (mins)
```

Cache Sizes

This report section contains the cache sizes at the end of the snapshot period. If Automatic Memory Management is being used, AMM may adjust sizes between snapshots. This information is valid for the time specific to the end snapshot of the snapshot interval observed. This is essential because the Automatic Memory Management activity could resize caches during the snapshot interval time or the DBA can do it manually.

```
Cache Sizes (end)
~~~~~~~~~~~~~~~~~
Buffer Cache:      48M    Std Block Size:       8K
Shared Pool Size:  56M       Log Buffer:      256K
```

Load Profile

This section gives a glimpse of the database workload activity that occurred within the snapshot interval. For example, the load profile below shows that an average transaction generates about 18K of redo data, and the database produces about 1.8K redo per second.

```
Load Profile
~~~~~~~~~~~~                Per Second      Per Transaction
                           ------------     ---------------
          Redo size:         1,766.20           18,526.31
      Logical reads:            39.21              411.30
      Block changes:            11.11              116.54
      Physical reads:            0.38                3.95
     Physical writes:           0.38                3.96
          User calls:           0.06                0.64
              Parses:           2.04               21.37
         Hard parses:           0.14                1.45
               Sorts:           1.02               10.72
              Logons:           0.02                0.21
            Executes:           4.19               43.91
```

The above statistics give an idea about the workload the database experienced during the time observed. However, they do not indicate what in the database is not working properly. For example, if there are a high number of physical reads per second, this does not mean that the SQLs are poorly tuned.

Perhaps this AWR report was built for a time period when large DSS batch jobs ran on the database. This workload information is intended to be used along with information from other sections of the AWR report in order to learn the details about the nature of the applications running on the system. The goal is to get a correct picture of database performance.

The following list includes detailed descriptions for particular statistics:

Redo size: The amount of redo generated during this report.

Logical Reads: Calculated as (Consistent Gets + DB Block Gets = Logical Reads).

Block changes: The number of blocks modified during the sample interval.

Physical Reads: The number of requests for a block that caused a physical I/O operation.

Physical Writes: Number of physical writes performed.

User Calls: Number of user queries generated.

Parses: The total of all parses; both hard and soft.

Hard Parses: The parses requiring a completely new parse of the SQL statement. These consume both latches and shared pool area.

Soft Parses: Soft parses are not listed but derived by subtracting the hard parses from parses. A soft parse reuses a previous hard parse; hence it consumes far fewer resources.

Sorts, Logons, Executes and Transactions: All self-explanatory.

Parse activity statistics should be checked carefully because they can immediately indicate a problem within the application. For example, a database has been running several days with a fixed set of applications, it should, within a course of time, parse most SQLs issued by the applications, and these statistics should be near zero.

If there are high values of Soft Parses or especially Hard Parses statistics, such values should be taken as an indication that the applications make little use of bind variables and produce large numbers of unique SQLs. However, if the database serves developmental purposes, high vales of these statistics are not bad.

The following information is also available in the workload section:

```
% Blocks changed per Read:   4.85   Recursive Call %:   89.89
Rollback per transaction %:  8.56      Rows per Sort:    13.39
```

The *% Blocks changed per Read* statistic indicates that only 4.85 percent of all blocks are retrieved for update. In this example, the *Recursive Call %* statistic is extremely high with about 90 percent. However, this fact does not mean that nearly all SQL statements executed by the database are caused by parsing activity, data dictionary management, space management, and so on.

Oracle considers all SQL statements executed within PL/SQL programs to be recursive. If there are applications making use of a large number of stored PL/SQL programs, this is good for performance. However, applications that do not widely use PL/SQL may indicate the need to further investigate the cause of this high recursive activity.

It is also useful to check the value of the *Rollback per transaction %* statistic. This statistic reports the percent of transactions rolled back. In a production system, this value should be low. If the output indicates a high percentage of transactions rolled back, the database expends a considerable amount of work to roll back changes made. This should be further investigated in order to see why the applications roll back so often.

Instance Efficiency Percentage

The Instance Efficiency Percentage report section contains ratios or calculations that may provide information regarding different structures and operations in the Oracle instance. Database tuning must never be driven by hit ratios. Hit ratios only provide additional information to help the DBA understand how the instance is operating.

For example, in the Decision Support System (DSS), a low cache hit ratio may be acceptable due to the amount of recycling needed due to the large volume of data accessed. If the size of the buffer cache is increased based on this number, the corrective action may not take affect and expensive RAM memory resources may be wasted. The following is a sample *Instance Efficiency Percentage* section of an AWR report:

```
Instance Efficiency Percentages (Target 100%)
~~~~~~~~~~~~~~~~~~~~~~~~~~~~~~~~~~~~~~~~~~~~~~~~
            Buffer Nowait %:   96.11      Redo NoWait %:   99.98
            Buffer  Hit   %:   66.52   In-memory Sort %:  100.00
            Library Hit   %:   98.42       Soft Parse %:   95.70
         Execute to Parse %:   80.96       Latch Hit %:   100.00
  Parse CPU to Parse Elapsd %:  3.13    % Non-Parse CPU:   97.75

  Shared Pool Statistics       Begin     End
                               ------    ------
            Memory Usage %:    92.70     92.49
    % SQL with executions>1:   86.73     84.20
  % Memory for SQL w/exec>1:   84.12     71.86
```

The following list includes the meanings of particular hit ratios:

Buffer Hit Ratio: Measures how many times a required block was found in memory rather than having to execute an expensive read operation on disk to get the block.

Buffer Nowait %: Shows the percentage of times when data buffers were accessed directly without any wait time.

Library Hit %: Shows the percentage of times when SQL statements and PL/SQL packages were found in the shared pool.

Execute to Parse %: Shows how often parsed SQL statements are reused without reparsing.

Parse CPU to Parse Elapsd %: Gives the ratio of CPU time spent to parse SQL statements.

Redo NoWait %: Shows whether the redo log buffer has sufficient size.

In-memory Sort %: Shows the percentage of times when sorts are performed in memory instead of using temporary tablespaces.

Soft Parse %: Shows how often sessions issued a SQL statement that is already in the shared pool and how it can use an existing version of that statement.

Latch Hit %: Shows how often latches were acquired without having to wait.

% Non-Parse CPU: Shows the percentage of how much CPU resources were spent on the actual SQL execution.

In the above list of statistics, special attention should be paid to parse-related statistics. The *Instance Efficiency Percentage* report provided previously shows that about 95 percent of the parses are soft as indicated by the *Soft Parse %*. This is good enough, indicating that the SQL statements are actively reused by Oracle.

The next interesting item to review is the *Parse CPU to Parse Elapsd %* statistic. In this case, it is about three percent, which is very low. This fact reveals that Oracle waits for some resources during parsing of SQL statements. This should be investigated further to find the cause.

In this case, *% Non-Parse CPU* statistic is about 97 percent, which is quite high. This indicates Oracle utilizes the CPU mostly for statement execution but not for parsing.

As a rule of thumb, one should always minimize the number of hard parses in a production database. This reduction yields the benefit of minimizing CPU overhead spent performing costly parse work.

This following sample report section shows shared pool related statistics:

```
Shared Pool Statistics          Begin     End
                                ------    ------
            Memory Usage %:     92.70     92.49
    % SQL with executions>1:    86.73     84.20
 % Memory for SQL w/exec>1:     84.12     71.86
```

In this example, the *Memory Usage %* statistic shows that almost all, approximately 92 percent, of the shared pool memory is consumed. This could indicate that the system experiences some overhead while aging out old shared memory structures like cursors, PL/SQL programs, and so on. This places additional overhead on the CPU to perform reparsing aging-out. The size of the shared pool should be increased appropriately to eliminate such overhead. In general, this statistic should be near 70 percent after the database has been running a long time. If it is quite low, memory is being wasted.

The *% SQL with executions>1* statistic indicates how many SQL statements are executed more than one time. This measures how well production applications are tuned and how well they make use of bind variables.

Top 5 Timed Events Section

The AWR report provides a super-detailed view of all elapsed-time metrics. The most important of these metrics is the *Top-5 timed events* as shown in the output below. This report is critical because it shows those database events that might constitute the bottleneck for the system.

```
Top 5 Timed Events
~~~~~~~~~~~~~~~~~~
                                              % Total
Event                      Waits   Time (s)  Ela Time
-------------------------  ------- ---------  --------
CPU time                    4,851     4,042     55.76
db file sequential read     1,968     1,997     27.55
log file sync             299,097       369      5.08
db file scattered read     53,031       330      4.55
log file parallel write   302,680       190      2.62
```

In the above example, it is clear that this system is clearly CPU-bound, with 55% of the processing time being spent in the CPU. One can also infer from the wait time that this server may be experiencing CPU enqueues, in which multiple processes must queue-up to be dispatched by the CPUs. As a general rule, a server is CPU-bound when the number of processes in the execution queue exceeds the number of CPUs on the server, the "r" value in *rmstat*.

The same phenomenon can also be observed in a system which is disk I/O bound. In the AWR sample report section below, one can see that the system is clearly constrained by disk I/O.

```
Top 5 Timed Events
~~~~~~~~~~~~~~~~~                                       %
Event                       Waits      Time (s)    Ela
                                                   Time
-------------------------  ----------  ----------  ----
db file sequential read        2,598      7,146    48.54
db file scattered read        25,519      3,246    22.04
library cache load lock          673      1,363     9.26
CPU time                       1,154      7.83
log file parallel write       19,157        837     5.68
```

Here, reads and writes constitute the majority of the total database time. In this case, one might consider increasing the RAM size of the *db_cache_size* to reduce disk I/O, tune the SQL to reduce disk I/O, or invest in a faster disk I/O sub-system.

In general, the causes of these top wait events should be investigated in order to minimize database wait time as much as possible. These top wait events are also available in the next report section called Wait Events.

Wait Events

This section shows a breakdown of the main wait events in the database, and it also shows the wait event details for foreground user processes.

The Wait Events report section displays all wait events that occurred during the snapshot interval. This section contains wait events statistics for only foreground end-user processes. All the IDLE events are placed at the end of this report. The following is a sample of the wait events section.

```
Wait Events  DB/Inst: LSQ/lsq  Snaps: 1355-1356
-> s  - second
-> cs - centisecond -     100th of a second
-> ms - millisecond -    1000th of a second
-> us - microsecond - 1000000th of a second
```

```
-> ordered by wait time desc, waits desc (idle events last)

                                                           Avg
                                    Total Wait      wait  Waits
Event                       Wts  Timeouts Time (s)  (ms)  /txn
-------------------------  ------ -------- -------- ----- -----
db file scattered read     23,611        0    3,453   146  36.1
read by other session      44,218        8    3,440    78  67.6
db file sequential read     5,227        0      466    89   8.0
db file parallel write      1,321        0      240   182   2.0
control file parallel write 1,113        0      121   109   1.7
log file parallel write       726        0       47    64   1.1
control file sequential rea   319        0       28    89   0.5
class slave wait                5        5       26  5116   0.0
log file sync                 368        0       22    59   0.6
```

Oracle has more than 200 specific wait events, and the description for every wait event is available in the Oracle documentation. Recall the old saying "time takes time" and recognize that any database will inevitably wait for some resources when running. The intention of this report is to provide important information for what a particular database is waiting, but it is only one clue. Other sections of the AWR report must be reviewed to find the real bottleneck in the system.

The following are the most common causes of wait events:

DB File Scattered Read: This wait event is usually caused by large full table scans. This is normal for DSS systems but is critical for OLTP systems. The DBA should consider the caching of small tables to eliminate file reads. Also, in the OLTP environment, consideration should be given to tuning SQL statements as well.

DB File Sequential Read: A high number of waits for this event indicates possible problems with join operations of SQLs or the existence of non-selective indexes. This wait is caused by a large number of single block reads.

Buffer Busy: This wait is caused by concurrent access to buffers in the buffer cache. This statistic should be correlated with the Buffer Waits section of the AWR report.

Free Buffer: This wait event indicates that Oracle waited many times for a free buffer in the buffer cache. This could be caused by the small size of buffer cache, or a large number of reads which populated the buffer cache with unnecessary data. In this case, the

SQLs and buffer contents should be examined. Also, slow work by the Database Writer (DBWR) process could cause such wait event.

Log Buffer Space: This wait event shows that the Log Writer (LGWR) process is not fast enough to free log cache for new blocks. This could be caused by slow log switches, slow disks serving redo logs, or a small size of the redo log buffer.

Latch Free: This wait event is often caused by not using bind variables in SQL statements. This fact is indicated by the *library cache latch* in the Latches section of the AWR report. There are other latches that can cause this wait event to be high: *redo allocation latch, cache buffers LRU chain, cache buffers chain,* etc.

The wait events for background processes are separated in the Background Wait Events section. In most cases, Oracle background processes place very little overhead on the system. However, it makes sense to monitor the database's wait events activity in order to see how they operate.

Time Model Statistics

The time model statistics give insight about where the processing time is actually spent during the snapshot interval.

```
Time Model Statistics   DB/Inst: LSQ/lsq   Snaps: 1355-1356
-> ordered by Time (seconds) desc

                                               Time        %
Total
Statistic Name                              (seconds)     DB
Time
------------------------------------------ -------------- -----------
DB time                                      7,274.60     100.00
sql execute elapsed time                     7,249.77      99.66
background elapsed time                        778.48      10.70
DB CPU                                         150.62       2.07
parse time elapsed                              45.52        .63
hard parse elapsed time                         44.65        .61
PL/SQL execution elapsed time                   13.73        .19
background cpu time                               8.90        .12
PL/SQL compilation elapsed time                  3.80        .05
connection management call elapsed time           .15        .00
Java execution elapsed time                       .05        .00
hard parse (bind mismatch) elapsed time           .00        .00
hard parse (sharing criteria) elapsed time        .00        .00
sequence load elapsed time                        .00        .00
```

```
failed parse (out of shared memory) elapsed          .00          .00
inbound PL/SQL rpc elapsed time                      .00          .00
failed parse elapsed time                            .00          .00
          -------------------------------------------------------
```

In the sample output of the AWR Time Model Statistics Report shown above, it can be seen that the system spends the most processing time on actual SQL execution but not on parsing. This is very good for production systems.

Operating System Statistics

The stress on the Oracle server is important, and this section explores the main external resources including I/O, CPU, memory, and network usage. This information helps the DBA view performance in a more complex way, thus providing more details about possible system bottlenecks.

In order to isolate a performance bottleneck at the database level, the information from the next section may be used.

Service Statistics

The service statistics section gives information about how particular services configured in the database are operating. A sample of the AWR Service Report may look like the following:

```
Service Statistics  DB/Inst: LSQ/lsq  Snaps: 1355-1356
-> ordered by DB Time
-> us - microsecond - 1000000th of a second

                                         Physical   Logical
Service Name   DB Time (s)   DB CPU (s)  Reads      Reads
-------------- ------------- ------------ ---------- ----------
SYS$USERS      3,715.8              67.7    191,654    525,164
LSQ            3,572.4              83.1    187,653    544,836
LSQXDB         0.0                   0.0          0          0
SYS$BACKGROUND 0.0                   0.0      1,927     70,537
               ----------------------------------------

Service Wait Class Stats  DB/Inst: LSQ/lsq  Snaps: 1355-1356

-> Wait Class info for services in the Service Statistics section.
-> Total Waits and Time Waited displayed for the following wait
   classes:  User I/O, Concurrency, Administrative, Network
-> Time Waited (Wt Time) in centisecond (100th of a second)
```

```
Service Name
-----------------------------------------------------------------
User I/O  User I/O Concurcy  Concurcy     Admin     Admin  Network   Network
Total Wts  Wt Time Total Wts  Wt Time Total Wts  Wt Time Total Wts  Wt
Time
---------  --------- -- --  ---------  ---------  ---------  ---------
SYS$USERS
    36370     360380 73 66          0          0       1313         4
LSQ
    35514     346409 85 95          0          0       8057         7
SYS$BACKGROUND
     1226      29322  4  4          0          0          0         0
        -----------------------------------------------
```

If particular production databases are configured for different database services, the above report section allows the DBA to quickly isolate which application places the most overhead on the system. Furthermore, the report indicates where the application waits most of the time. The report shows that that applications that use the SYS$USERS service is spending most of the time performing I/O operations.

It is necessary to notice that this SYS$USERS service is a default service for all applications. To take advantage of isolating applications performance, some DBAs will configure separate services for each kind of production application.

The DBA is now ready to find which particular SQL statements may cause that stress.

Top SQL

This section displays top SQL ordered by important SQL execution metrics. The top SQL section in the AWR report contains lists of SQL statements ordered by the following criteria:

Elapsed Time: Statements are ordered according to elapsed execution times.

CPU Time: Statements are ordered according to CPU time.

Buffer Gets: Statements are ordered according to logical reads number.

Physical Reads: Statements are ordered according to physical reads number.

Execution Number: Statements are ordered according to execution number.

Parse Calls: Statements are ordered according to parse number.

Version Count: Statements are ordered according to version number.

Sharable Memory: Statements are ordered according to sharable memory consumption.

Here is a sample of a Top SQL AWR report section:

```
  Elapsed       CPU                     Elap per  % Total
  Time (s)    Time (s)   Executions    Exec (s)  DB Time   SQL Id
---------- ----------  ------------  ---------- -------  ------------
     4,504         78            2      2251.9     61.9 6zmdns6h6xm5p
Module: SQL*Plus
DECLARE
feeval NUMBER;
BEGIN
  FS_LSQ.sp_funds_val(Feeval,'1003');
  dbms_output
.put_line('Feeval = '||TO_CHAR(Feeval));
END;

     3,434         62           74        46.4     47.2 dahmxun9ngx14
Module: SQL*Plus
SELECT NVL(SUM(PAYMENTS.AMT) * :B4 ,0) FROM PAYMENTS, TRANSACTIONS WHERE (
(TRAN
SACTIONS.TRANSKEY = PAYMENTS.TRANSKEY) AND (TRANSACTIONS.CLIENTKEY = :B3 ) AND
(
PAYMENTS.TYPE_ <> 7) AND PAYMENTS.AMT>0 AND (PAYMENTS.COLSTATUS = 2) AND
(PAYMEN
TS.POSTDATE=:B2 +:B1 ) )

     3,408         54           74        46.1     46.8 0fzfwb0szmgss
Module: SQL*Plus
SELECT PAYMENTS.POSTDATE FROM TRANSACTIONS, PAYMENTS WHERE (
(TRANSACTIONS.CLIEN
TKEY = :B3 ) AND (TRANSACTIONS.TRANSKEY = PAYMENTS.TRANSKEY) AND
(PAYMENTS.TYPE_
 <> 7) AND (PAYMENTS.COLSTATUS = 2) AND (PAYMENTS.POSTDATE=:B2 +:B1 )) GROUP
BY
PAYMENTS.POSTDATE

        87          2           56         1.6      1.2 6gvch1xu9ca3g
DECLARE job BINARY_INTEGER := :job; next_date DATE := :mydate;  broken BOOLEAN
:
= FALSE; BEGIN EMD_MAINTENANCE.EXECUTE_EM_DBMS_JOB_PROCS(); :mydate :=
next_date
; IF broken THEN :b := 1; ELSE :b := 0; END IF; END;

        74          2            1        74.1      1.0 d92h3rjp0y217
begin prvt_hdm.auto_execute( :db_id, :inst_id, :end_snap ); end;

        52          1            2        25.8      0.7 gfwfn87avpfq8
Module: SQL*Plus
DECLARE
checkval NUMBER;
BEGIN
```

Operating System Statistics

```
    FS_LSQ.Sp_get_res_checkval(checkval,'844');
  d
bms_output.put_line('checkval = '||TO_CHAR(checkval));
END;

        52        1        2      25.8     0.7 cv2n8rfpnzdza
Module: SQL*Plus
SELECT NVL(SUM(CHECKDTL.AMT),0) FROM CHECKHDR , CHECKDTL,ACCOUNTS WHERE
(CHECKDT
L.CHECKHDRKEY = CHECKHDR.CHECKHDRKEY) AND (CHECKDTL.ACCTNO = ACCOUNTS.ACCTNO)
AN
D (ACCOUNTS.ACCOUNTS = 5) AND CHECKTYPE<>1 AND CHECKTYPE<>2 AND CHECKTYPE<>12
AN
D CHECKTYPE<>5 AND CLIENTKEY=:B1 ORDER BY CHECKHDR.CHECKDATE ASC
```

The sample AWR *Top SQL by Elapsed Time* Report shown above is most useful when it is ordered according to the appropriate status. This information should be used in conjunction with other sections of the AWR report. For example, if the system experiences a high number of parses, the Top SQL should be checked by parse number section to find the particular statements with a large number of parses.

The Top SQL section alone cannot reveal which particular statements have sub-optimal execution. This decision is completely dependent on other factors and the DBAs knowledge about the system and applications.

The next AWR report section allows the DBA to acquire an overview the system in a more complex way.

Instance Activity Section

This section of the AWR report contains useful statistical information about the database.

```
Instance Activity Stats   DB/Inst: LSQ/lsq   Snaps: 1355-1356

Statistic                          Total    per Second    per Trans
-------------------------------  ---------  ----------  --------------
CPU used by this session            10,267        2.8            15.7
CPU used when call started          10,267        2.8            15.7
CR blocks created                      135        0.0             0.2
Cached Commit SCN referenced             0        0.0             0.0
Commit SCN cached                        0        0.0             0.0
DB time                          1,876,018      516.9         2,868.5
```

The information in the instance activity AWR report section is used to compute numerous ratios and percentages contained in other AWR report sections. For example, the statistics in this section are used to calculate hit ratios in the Instance Efficiency Load Profile report sections, and so on.

Additional attention should be paid to the *parse count (hard)* statistic. Too high a value of this statistic could indicate that the DBA should consider tuning SQL statements to make the SQL reentrant by using bind variables.

If the *Redo log space wait time* statistic is high enough, the DBA should consider tuning the redo log files.

High numbers of the statistics *table scans (long tables)* and *physical reads* may indicate that SQL statements perform a large number of unnecessary full table scans.

The following section allows the DBA to estimate how the I/O subsystem works, and gives the DBA a way to find possible hot spots in I/O operation.

I/O Reports Section

The following sections of the AWR report show the distribution of I/O activity between the tablespaces and data files.

```
Tablespace IO Stats  DB/Inst: LSQ/lsq  Snaps: 1355-1356
-> ordered by IOs (Reads + Writes) desc


Tablespace
------------------------------
                Av      Av      Av                         Av     Buffer Av Buf
        Reads Reads/s Rd(ms) Blks/Rd  Writes Writes/s   Waits Wt(ms)
-------------- ------- ------ ------- ------- - ---------- ------
T_FS_LSQ
        26,052       7  132.5    14.5       1 0      43,931   78.3
SYSAUX
         1,730       0  123.5     1.1   1,139 0           0    0.0
SYSTEM
           814       0  305.1     2.0      95 0           0    0.0
USERS
           262       0   15.2     1.0       1 0         290   12.1
UNDOTBS1
            14       0   86.4     1.0     129 0           3    0.0
```

```
TEMP
          1      0   80.0     1.0      0 0           0   0.0
        -------------------------------------------------------
```

Tablespace		Filename							
		Av	Av	Av			Av	Buffer	Av Buf
	Reads	Reads/s	Rd(ms)	Blks/Rd		Writes	Writes/s	Waits	Wt(ms)
SYSAUX		G:\ORACLE\LSQ\LSQ\SYSAUX01.DBF							
	1,730 0	123.5	1.1		1,139		0 0		0.0
SYSTEM		G:\ORACLE\LSQ\LSQ\SYSTEM01.DBF							
	814 0	305.1	2.0		95		0 0		0.0
TEMP		G:\ORACLE\LSQ\LSQ\TEMP01.DBF							
	1 0	80.0	1.0		0		0 0		
T_FS_LSQ		G:\ORACLE\LSQ\LSQ\T_FS_LSQ01.DBF							
	26,052 7	132.5	14.5		1		0	43,931	78.3
UNDOTBS1		G:\ORACLE\LSQ\LSQ\UNDOTBS01.DBF							
	14 0	86.4	1.0		129		0	3	0.0
USERS		G:\ORACLE\LSQ\LSQ\USERS01.DBF							
	262 0	15.2	1.0		1		0	290	12.1

In general, the information presented in the sample AWR I/O section shown above is intended to help the DBA identify hot spots of the database I/O subsystem.

Oracle considers average disk read times of greater than 20 milliseconds to be unacceptable. If data files, as in the example above, consistently have average read times of 20 ms or greater, a number of possible approaches can be followed:

SQL Management: A database with no user SQL being run generates little or no I/O. Ultimately all I/O generated by a database is directly or indirectly due to the nature and amount of user SQL being submitted for execution. This means that it is possible to limit the I/O requirements of a database by controlling the amount of I/O generated by individual SQL statements. This is accomplished by tuning SQL statements so that their execution plans result in a minimum number of I/O operations. Typically in a problematic situation, there will only be a few SQL statements with suboptimal execution plans generating a lot more physical I/O than necessary and degrading the overall performance for the database.

Using Memory Caching to Limit I/O: The amount of I/O required by the database is limited by the use of a number of memory caches;

e.g., the Buffer Cache, the Log Buffer, various Sort Areas etc. Increasing the Buffer Cache, up to a point, results in more buffer accesses by database processes (logical I/Os) being satisfied from memory instead of having to go to disk (physical I/Os). With larger Sort Areas in memory, the likelihood of them being exhausted during a sorting operation and having to use a temporary tablespace on disk is reduced.

Tuning the Size of Multi-Block I/O: The size of individual multi-block I/O operations can be controlled by instance parameters. Up to a limit, multi-block I/Os are executed faster when there are fewer larger I/Os than when there are many smaller I/Os.

Index Management: If the tablespace contains indexes, another option is to compress the indexes so that they require less space and hence, less I/O.

Optimizing I/O at the Operating System Level: This involves making use of I/O capabilities such as Asynchronous I/O or using File systems with advanced capabilities such as Direct I/O, bypassing the Operating System's File Caches. Another possible action is to raise the limit of maximum I/O size per transfer.

Load Balancing: Balancing the database I/O by use of Striping, RAID, Storage Area Networks (SAN) or Network Attached Storage (NAS). This approach relies on storage technologies such as Striping, RAID, SAN and NAS to automatically load balance database I/O across multiple available physical disks in order to avoid disk contention and I/O bottlenecks when there is still available unused disk throughput in the storage hardware.

I/O Management: Database I/O by manual placement of database files across different file systems, controllers and physical devices. This is an approach used in the absence of advanced modern storage technologies. Again, the aim is to distribute the database I/O so that no single set of disks or controller becomes saturated from I/O requests when there is still unused disk throughput. It is harder to get right than the previous approach and most often less successful.

Volume: Reducing the data volumes of the current database by moving older data out.

Hardware: Investing in more modern and faster hardware.

Advisory Section

This section shows details of the advisories for the buffer, shared pool, PGA and Java pool.

Buffer Pool Advisory

This section of the AWR report shows the estimates from the buffer pool advisory, which are computed based on I/O activity that occurred during the snapshot interval.

```
Buffer Pool Advisory
-> Only rows with estimated physical reads >0 are displayed
-> ordered by Block Size, Buffers For Estimate

          Size for  Size      Buffers for  Est Physical
Estimated
P   Estimate (M) Factr   Estimate   Read Factor    Physical Reads
--- ------------ -----  ----------  ------------- ------------------
D              4   .1        501         2.10         1,110,930
D              8   .2      1,002         1.84           970,631
D             12   .2      1,503         1.75           924,221
D             16   .3      2,004         1.62           857,294
D             20   .4      2,505         1.61           850,849
D             24   .5      3,006         1.59           837,223
D             28   .5      3,507         1.58           831,558
D             32   .6      4,008         1.57           829,083
D             36   .7      4,509         1.56           825,336
D             40   .8      5,010         1.56           823,195
D             44   .8      5,511         1.06           557,204
D             48   .9      6,012         1.01           534,992
D             52  1.0      6,513         1.00           527,967
D             56  1.1      7,014         0.78           411,218
D             60  1.2      7,515         0.35           186,842
D             64  1.2      8,016         0.28           148,305
D             68  1.3      8,517         0.26           134,969
D             72  1.4      9,018         0.23           123,283
D             76  1.5      9,519         0.23           121,878
D             80  1.5     10,020         0.23           120,317
          -------------------------------------------------------
```

In general, this report shows estimates of how physical read operations can be reduced if the buffer cashe is increased by some amount of memory. For example, the sample AWR Buffer Advisory Report above shows at the existing buffer cache size, there will likely be about 527,000 physical reads and that increasing the size by one-half (to 10,020) the physical reads drop to only 120,000.

The AWR report contains sections related to other advisories like PGA, Shared Pool, Java Pool advisories. Enabling the AMM feature of Oracle10g allows the DBA freedom from fine-grained tuning of components within SGA. Oracle now takes responsibility for automatically adjusting sizes of caches depending on its current needs. All the DBA has to do is specify the total SGA size target that is used by Oracle as upper limit of SGA size. This target is specified by the *init.ora* parameter *sga_target*.

Usage Note: In cases where *sga_target* is set, the *shared_pool_size* parameter serves as the minimum value and increasing *sga_target* causes the shared pool to be increased without re-setting the *shared_pool_size* parameter.

The following AWR report section gives details about data buffer cache waits.

Buffer Wait Statistics Section

This section of the AWR report exposes the wait activity that occurred within the data cache.

```
Buffer Wait Statistics   DB/Inst: LSQ/lsq   Snaps: 1355-1356
-> ordered by wait time desc, waits desc

Class                    Waits Total Wait Time (s)  Avg Time (ms)
------------------ ----------- -------------------- --------------
data block              44,213                3,445             78
segment header               1                    0             20
undo header                  2                    0              0
                        ------------------------------------------
```

In the above sample AWR Buffer Wait Report listing, one can see that the database experiences a large wait time waiting for *data blocks*. This may indicate that there are some hot blocks applications are concurrently using. The following actions can be considered in order to reduce such contention:

- Eliminate hot blocks from the application by redistributing the data.

- Check for repeatedly scanned / unselective indexes.

- Change *pctfree* / *pctused*.

- Check for right-hand-indexes. These are indexes that get inserted at the same point by many processes.

- Increase *initrans*. Reduce the number of rows per block.

- If there is a high number of waits for *segment header* blocks, the number of *freelist*s can be increased or use made of *freelist group*s.

- In the case of high *undo header* waits, one may want to increase the number of undo/rollback segments.

Enqueue Activity Section

This important section shows how enqueues operate in the database. Enqueues are special internal structures, which provide concurrent access to various database resources.

In general, this view can be used to determine how optimally applications are tuned for concurrent access of data. If there are a large number of waits for TX or TS, the applications may need to be revised to identify a reason for the frequent locks.

Undo Segment Summary Section

This section provides summary information about undo segments usage by Oracle. In this section, one can see how evenly Oracle distributes work between undo segments as along with statistics about the undo errors that occurred.

Undo Segment Stats Section

This section helps identify possible time periods when extra rollback activity occurred in the database. This could be very useful when the DBA has identified that the database sometimes experiences a large number of rollbacks. This section can help find exact times when such an activity took a place.

Latch Statistics Section

The latch statistics AWR report section shows the activity statistics of latches, which are lightweight serialization devices to provide concurrent access to the internal Oracle structures.

```
Latch Activity  DB/Inst: LSQ/lsq  Snaps: 1355-1356
-> "Get Requests", "Pct Get Miss" and "Avg Slps/Miss" are statistics
for
   willing-to-wait latch get requests
-> "NoWait Requests", "Pct NoWait Miss" are for no-wait latch get
requests
-> "Pct Misses" for both should be very close to 0.0
```

Latch Name	Pct Get Requests	Avg Get Miss	Wait Slps /Miss	Time (s)	NoWait Requests	Pct NoWait Miss
Consistent RBA	728	0.0		0	0	
FOB s.o list latch	86	0.0		0	0	
In memory undo latch	8,641	0.0		0	1,563	
JOX SGA heap latch	23	0.0		0	0	
JS queue state obj latch	24,588	0.0		0	0	
JS slv state obj latch	2	0.0		0	0	
KTF sga enqueue	10	0.0		0	977	

In this report, the *NoWait Get Miss* column should be checked carefully. This column indicates the percentage of requests to get a latch that were finished successfully. It also indicates which latch was acquired. For example, if the application does not widely use bind variables, there will be a low ratio in *Pct Get Miss* column for *library cache* latch.

The next report section allows the identification of hot segments by using the criteria described below.

Segment Statistics Section

The segment statistics section exposes the hot segments ordered by the following criteria:

- Top segments by logical reads.

- Top segments by physical reads.

- Top segments by buffer busy waits.

- Top segments row lock waits.

Owner	Tablespace Name	Object Name	Obj. Type	Logical Reads	%Total
FS_LSQ	T_FS_LSQ	PAYMENTS	TABLE	751,616	67.93
FS_LSQ	T_FS_LSQ	TRANSACTIONS	TABLE	113,696	10.28
FS_LSQ	T_FS_LSQ	CHECKHDR	TABLE	54,048	4.88
FS_LSQ	USERS	CHECKHDRKEY_1	INDEX	29,136	2.63
SYS	SYSAUX	SYS_IOT_TOP_8547	INDEX	22,560	2.04

Segments by Physical Reads   DB/Inst: LSQ/lsq   Snaps: 1355-1356

Owner	Tablespace Name	Object Name	Obj. Type	Physical Reads	%Total
FS_LSQ	T_FS_LSQ	PAYMENTS	TABLE	374,984	98.59
FS_LSQ	T_FS_LSQ	CHECKDTL	TABLE	1,210	.32
SYS	SYSTEM	TAB$	TABLE	801	.21
FS_LSQ	T_FS_LSQ	CHECKHDR	TABLE	763	.20
SYSMAN	SYSAUX	MGMT_METRICS_INDEX		498	.13

The top segments section allows the quick identification of segments which may pose a potential bottleneck or create a hot spot in the application. In the sample AWR Top Segments Report above, the PAYMENTS table experiences most physical reads and the DBA might want to investigate why this table has such a high number of physical reads.

Perhaps, the SQLs that retrieve data from it are not optimized, or this table has stale statistics that causes the optimizer to use a wrong execution plan. On the other hand, perhaps this table has a large number of analytic reports being run against it. In this case, the large number of physical reads might be normal.

This report section, in conjunction with other AWR report sections, should be used to identify the primary cause of really hot segments.

The next report section contains information about the data dictionary cache.

Dictionary Cache Stats Section

This section contains statistics describing the dictionary cache activity. In real life, a lot of useful information cannot be gained here since the dictionary cache is completely managed by Oracle and there is no direct mechanism available for tuning. The only way it can be managed is via the *init.ora* parameter, *shared_pool_size*.

The next section gives more useful information about the library cache.

Library Cache Activity Section

The library cache AWR report section provides details about the library cache activity. Oracle stores in the library cache, which is part of shared pool SGA component, many parsed objects such as cursors, packages, procedures, etc.

Below is a sample of the library cache report section:

```
Library Cache Activity  DB/Inst: LSQ/lsq  Snaps: 1355-1356
-> "Pct Misses"  should be very low

                  Get   Pct             Pin  Pct      Invalidations
Namespace         Requests Miss  Requests Miss Reloads
----------------- -------- ----- -------- ---- ------- -------------
BODY                   700   0.4    6,038  0.0       0             0
CLUSTER                 17   5.9       33  9.1       2             0
INDEX                   34  17.6       78  7.7       0             0
JAVA DATA                1   0.0        0            0             0
SQL AREA             3,777   3.4   37,955  1.2     107             9
TABLE/PROCEDURE        639   1.7   11,907  3.9     252             0
TRIGGER                 33   6.1    2,943  0.1       0             0
                  ---------------------------------------------
```

The most important information listed in this section is that the *Pct Miss* columns indicate how often Oracle finds cached objects in the cache. If there are enough high values in these columns, the DBA may want to increase shared pool size. If the AMM feature is being used, the DBA should consider increasing the values of the *sga_target* parameter.

The next report section gives more details about the SGA regions and their size.

SGA Memory Summary Section

This report section gives details about SGA components and their size. This section is mostly informational providing detailed size information of memory caches as shown below:

```
SGA regions                       Size in Bytes
----------------------------     ----------------
Database Buffers                     54,525,952
Fixed Size                              787,828
Redo Buffers                            262,144
Variable Size                        82,836,108

SGA breakdown difference   DB/Inst: LSQ/lsq   Snaps: 1355-1356

Pool    Name                              Begin value         End
value   % Diff
------  ------------------------------   ----------------   -------
java    free memory            2,675,264      2,675,264      0.00
java    joxlod exec hp         5,471,424      5,471,424      0.00
java    joxs heap                241,920        241,920      0.00
large   PX msg pool              206,208        206,208      0.00
large   free memory            3,988,096      3,988,096      0.00
shared  ASH buffers            2,097,152      2,097,152      0.00
shared  KGLS heap              1,669,884      2,272,852     36.11
shared  KQR L SO                 144,384        146,432      1.42
shared  KQR M PO               2,279,792      2,323,860      1.93
shared  KQR M SO                 610,864        610,864      0.00
shared  KQR S PO                 229,728        192,856    -16.05
shared  KQR S SO                   6,400          6,400      0.00
shared  KSPD key heap              4,220          4,220      0.00
shared  KSXR pending message    841,036        841,036      0.00
shared  KSXR receive buffer   1,033,000      1,033,000      0.00
shared  PL/SQL DIANA            861,124        932,120      8.24
shared  PL/SQL MPCODE         3,382,696      3,352,036     -0.91
shared  PLS non-lib hp           29,160         29,160      0.00
shared  PX subheap               68,668         68,668      0.00
shared  alert threshol              728            728      0.00
```

```
shared event statistics pe      2,966,080       2,966,080    0.00
shared fixed allocation ca            260             260    0.00
```

init.ora Parameters Section

Table 10.1 below shows the original *init.ora* parameters for the instance during the snapshot period. One interesting feature in AWR is the use of *begin values* and *end values* for those parameters that are changed dynamically or via the Automatic Memory Manager (AMM) facility in Oracle10g:

PARAMETER NAME	BEGIN VALUE	END VALUE (IF DIFFERENT)
background_dump_dest	D:\ORACLE\ADMIN\DBDABR\DUMP	
compatible	10.1.0.2.0	
db_block_size	8192	
db_cache_size	364904448	455210668
db_domain		
db_file_multiblock_read_count	8	
db_name	dbdabr	
db_recovery_file_dest	D:\oracle\flash_recovery_area	
db_recovery_file_dest_size	2147483648	
dispatchers	(protocol=TCP)(mul=ON)	
java_pool_size	8388608	2000000
pga_aggregate_target	104857600	2038570
shared_pool_size	138412032	
sga_max_size	578813952	
sga_target	524288000	
shared_servers	1	
sort_area_size	1500000	
undo_management	AUTO	

Table 10.1: *The original init.ora parameters for the instance during the snapshot period*

Conclusion

The AWR report is a great tool for use in monitoring day-to-day database activity. Careful usage of this report allows the DBA to quickly overview the health of the system and to identify possible hot spots, which stand out from the usual picture of the database workload.

It is very crucial to understand the information any particular AWR report section presents.

The main points of this chapter include:

- The AWR (STATSPACK) report has become the de-facto standard within Oracle for elapsed-time reports.

- The AWR and STATSPACK reports were originally designed for Oracle Technical Support Staff, and all of the metrics are not fully described in the Oracle documentation.

- The AWR and STATSPACK reports are invoked from the scripts in the $ORACLE_HOME/rdbms/admin directory.

- The AWR and STATSPACK reports provide detailed elapsed-time report to expose the root cause of Oracle performance slowdowns and bottlenecks.

- The shorter time elapsed time between AWR or STATSPACK snapshots, the finer the granularity. Hence, frequent snapshot collection is advised during those times when a performance problem manifests itself.

Of course, reading the AWR report is just the beginning, and the DBA must clearly understand what steps to undertake according to the information contained in the AWR report in order to pro-actively react to the problems identified by an AWR or STATSPACK report.

In the next chapter, several novel approaches and techniques of database tuning using trend analysis and prediction based on AWR data will be introduced.

Predictive Models with AWR

The trend is clear!

Tomorrow we will see lightly-scattered I/O bottlenecks clearing into afternoon latch contention.

Predicting the Future with AWR

Predictive modeling is one of the best ways to perform long-term Oracle instance tuning, and the AWR tables are very helpful in this pursuit. In the predictive model of Oracle tuning, the DBA is charged with taking the existing AWR statistics and predicting the future needs for all instance and I/O areas within the Oracle database. For example, the AWR *physical reads* could be analyzed and compared to the memory usage within the Oracle *db_cache_size*. The information from the comparison could be extrapolated and used to predict the times at which the Oracle data buffers would need to be increased in order to maintain the current levels of performance.

Those who forget the past are condemned to repeat it.

George Santanaya

The DBA can also make a detailed analysis of Oracle's data buffer caches, including the KEEP pool, DEFAULT pool, the RECYCLE pool, and the pools for multiple block sizes like *db_32k_cache_size*. With that information, the DBA can accurately measure the performance of each one of the buffer pools, summarized by day-of-the-week and hour-of-the-day over long periods of time. Based upon existing usage, the DBA can accurately predict at what time additional RAM memory is needed for each of these data buffers.

The AWR tables also offer the DBA an opportunity to slice off the information in brand new ways. In the real world, all Oracle applications follow measurable, cyclical patterns called signatures. For example, an Oracle Financials application may be very active on the first Monday of every month when all of the books are being closed and the financial reports are being prepared. Using AWR data, information can be extracted from every first Monday of the month for the past year which will yield a valid signature of the specific performance needs of the end of the month Oracle financials applications.

Starting with Oracle8i, DBAs could dynamically change the Oracle database RAM regions and other instance parameters depending upon the performance needs of the applications. By making many initialization parameters alterable, Oracle is moving towards a dynamic database configuration, whereby the configuration of the system can be adjusted according to the needs of the Oracle application. The AWR can identify these changing needs.

With Oracle9i r2, there were three predictive utilities included with the standard STATSPACK report:

PGA advice: Oracle9i introduced an advisory utility dubbed *v$pga_target_advice*. This utility shows the marginal changes in optimal, one-pass, and multipass PGA execution for different sizes of *pga_aggregate_target*, ranging from 10% to 200% of the current value.

Shared Pool advice - This advisory functionality was extended in Oracle9i r2 to include an advice called *v$shared_pool_advice*.

Data Cache advice - The *v$db_cache_advice* utility shows the marginal changes in physical data block reads for different sizes of *db_cache_size*. The data from STATSPACK can provide similar data as *v$db_cache_advice*, and most Oracle tuning professionals use STATSPACK and *v$db_cache_advice* to monitor the effectiveness of their data buffers.

These advisory utilities are extremely important for the Oracle DBA who must adjust the sizes of the RAM areas to meet processing demands. The following query can be used to perform the cache advice function once the *v$db_cache_advice* has been enabled and the database has run long enough to give representative results.

```
column c1    heading 'Cache Size (meg)'    format 999,999,999,999
column c2    heading 'Buffers'             format 999,999,999
column c3    heading 'Estd Phys|Read Factor' format 999.90
column c4    heading 'Estd Phys| Reads'    format 999,999,999

select
   size_for_estimate        c1,
   buffers_for_estimate     c2,
   estd_physical_read_factor c3,
   estd_physical_reads      c4
from
   v$db_cache_advice
where
   name = 'DEFAULT'
and
   block_size  = (SELECT value FROM V$PARAMETER
                  WHERE name = 'db_block_size')
and
   advice_status = 'ON';
```

The output from the script is shown below. The values range from ten percent of the current size to double the current size of the *db_cache_size*.

Cache Size (meg)	Buffers	Estd Phys Read Factor	Estd Phys Reads	
30	3,802	18.70	192,317,943	<== 10% size
60	7,604	12.83	131,949,536	
91	11,406	7.38	75,865,861	
121	15,208	4.97	51,111,658	
152	19,010	3.64	37,460,786	
182	22,812	2.50	25,668,196	
212	26,614	1.74	17,850,847	
243	30,416	1.33	13,720,149	
273	34,218	1.13	11,583,180	
304	38,020	1.00	10,282,475	Current Size
334	41,822	.93	9,515,878	
364	45,624	.87	8,909,026	
395	49,426	.83	8,495,039	
424	53,228	.79	8,116,496	
456	57,030	.76	7,824,764	
486	60,832	.74	7,563,180	
517	64,634	.71	7,311,729	
547	68,436	.69	7,104,280	
577	72,238	.67	6,895,122	
608	76,040	.66	6,739,731	<== 2x size

From the above listing, it is clear that increasing the *db_cache_size* from 304 Megabytes to 334 Megabytes would result in approximately 700,000 less physical reads. This can be plotted as a 1/x function and the exact optimal point computed as the second derivative of the function 1/x as shown in Figure 11.1:

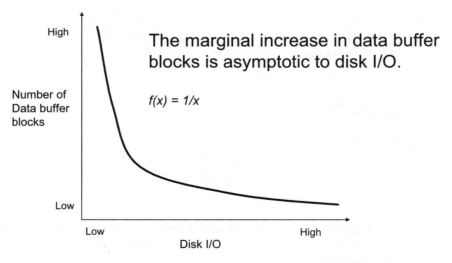

Figure 11.1: *The relationship between buffer size and disk I/O*

Once DBAs can recognize cyclic performance patterns in the Oracle database, they are in a position to reconfigure the database in order to meet the specific processing needs of that Oracle database.

While the predictive models are new, the technique dates back to Oracle6. Old-timer Oracle professionals would often keep several versions of their initialization parameter file and bounce in a new version when processing patterns were going to change.

For example, it was not uncommon to see a special Oracle instance configuration that was dedicated exclusively to the batch processing tasks that might occur on every Friday while another version of the *init.ora* file would be customized for OLTP transactions.

Additional *init.ora* files could be created that were suited to data warehouse processing that might occur on the weekend. In each of these cases, the Oracle database had to be stopped and restarted with the appropriate *init.ora* configuration file.

Starting with Oracle10g, the AWR tables can be used to identify all specific times when an instance-related component of Oracle is stressed, and the new *dbms_scheduler* package can be used to trigger a script to dynamically change Oracle during these periods. In sum, AWR data is ideally suited to work with the dynamic SGA features of Oracle10g.

Exception Reporting with the AWR

At the highest level, exception reporting involved adding a WHERE clause to a data dictionary query to eliminate values that fall beneath a pre-defined threshold. For a simple example, this can be done quite easily with a generic script to read *dba_hist_sysstat*.

The following simple script displays a time-series exception report for any statistic in *dba_hist_sysstat*. The script accepts the statistics number and the value threshold for the exception report.

```
prompt
prompt  This will query the dba_hist_sysstat view to display all
values
prompt  that exceed the value specified in
prompt  the "where" clause of the query.
prompt

set pages 999

break on snap_time skip 2

accept stat_name   char   prompt 'Enter Statistic Name:   ';
accept stat_value  number prompt 'Enter Statistics Threshold value:
';


col snap_time    format a19
col value        format 999,999,999

select
   to_char(begin_interval_time,'yyyy-mm-dd hh24:mi') snap_time,
   value
from
   dba_hist_sysstat
  natural join
   dba_hist_snapshot
where
   stat_name = '&stat_name'
and
  value > &stat_value
order by
   to_char(begin_interval_time,'yyyy-mm-dd hh24:mi')
;
```

This simple script will prompt for the statistic name and threshold
value which allow for ad-hoc AWR queries:

```
SQL> @rpt_sysatst

This will query the dba_hist_sysstat view to display all values
that exceed the value specified in
the "where" clause of the query.

Enter Statistic Name:  physical writes
Enter Statistics Threshold value:  200000

SNAP_TIME                  VALUE
-------------------  ------------
2004-02-21 08:00         200,395
2004-02-27 08:00         342,231
2004-02-29 08:00         476,386
2004-03-01 08:00         277,282
2004-03-02 08:00         252,396
2004-03-04 09:00         203,407
```

The listing above indicates a repeating trend where physical writes seem to be high at 8:00 AM on certain days. This powerful script will allow the DBA to quickly extract exception conditions from any instance-wide Oracle metric and see its behavior over time.

The next section provides a more powerful exception report that compares system-wide values to individual snapshots.

Exception reporting with *dba_hist_filestatxs*

The new 10g *dba_hist_filestatxs* table contains important file level information about Oracle I/O activities. Because most Oracle databases perform a high amount of reading and writing from disk, the *dba_hist_filestatxs* view can be very useful for identifying high use data files.

For Oracle10g customers who are not using the Stripe and Mirror Everywhere (SAME) approach, this view is indispensable for locating and isolating hot data files. Many Oracle shops will isolate hot data files onto high-speed solid-state disk (SSD), or relocate the hot files to another physical disk spindle.

If the *dba_hist_filestatxs* is described as shown in Table 11.1, the important information columns can be seen below. The important information relates to physical reads and writes, the actual time spent performing reads and writes, and the wait count associated with each data file, for each snapshot.

COLUMN	DESCRIPTION
snap_id	Unique snapshot ID
filename	Name of the datafile
phyrds	Number of physical reads done
phywrts	Number of times DBWR is required to write
singleblkrds	Number of single block reads

COLUMN	DESCRIPTION
readtim	Time, in hundredths of a second, spent doing reads if the *timed_statistics* parameter is TRUE; 0 if *timed_statistics* is FALSE
writetim	Time, in hundredths of a second, spent doing writes if the *timed_statistics* parameter is TRUE; 0 if *timed_statistics* is FALSE
singleblkrdtim	Cumulative single block read time, in hundredths of a second
phyblkrd	Number of physical blocks read
phyblkwrt	Number of blocks written to disk, which may be the same as *phywrts* if all writes are single blocks
wait_count	Wait Count

Table 11.1: *The metrics relating to file I/O in dba_hist_filestatxs*

It is easy to write a customized exception report with AWR data. In this simple report called *hot_write_files_10g.sql*, the *dba_hist_filestatxs* table is queried to identify hot write datafiles, which is any condition where any individual file consumed more than 25% of the total physical writes for the whole instance. Especially when RAID is not being used, identification of hot datafiles is important because the objects inside the file cache can be cached with the KEEP pool or by moving the hot data file onto high-speed solid-state RAM disks.

The query below compares the physical writes in the the *phywrts* column of *dba_hist_filestatxs* with the instance-wide physical writes *statistic#* = 55 from the *dba_hist_sysstat* table.

This simple yet powerful script allows the Oracle professional to track hot-write datafiles over time, thereby gaining important insight into the status of the I/O sub-system over time.

```
prompt   This will identify any single file who's write I/O
prompt   is more than 25% of the total write I/O of the database.
prompt
```

```
set pages 999

break on snap_time skip 2

col filename      format a40
col phywrts       format 999,999,999
col snap_time     format a20

select
   to_char(begin_interval_time,'yyyy-mm-dd hh24:mi') snap_time,
   filename,
   phywrts
from
   dba_hist_filestatxs
natural join
   dba_hist_snapshot
where
   phywrts > 0
and
   phywrts * 4 >
(
select
   avg(value)                all_phys_writes
from
   dba_hist_sysstat
  natural join
   dba_hist_snapshot
where
   stat_name = 'physical writes'
and
  value > 0
)
order by
   to_char(begin_interval_time,'yyyy-mm-dd hh24:mi'),
   phywrts desc
;
```

The following is the sample output from this powerful script. This is a useful report because the high-write datafiles are identified as well as those specific times at which they are hot.

```
SQL> @hot_write_files

This will identify any single file who's write I/O
is more than 25% of the total write I/O of the database.


SNAP_TIME          FILENAME                                PHYWRTS
----------------   -------------------------------------   --------
2004-02-20 23:30   E:\ORACLE\ORA92\FSDEV10G\SYSAUX01.DBF    85,540

2004-02-21 01:00   E:\ORACLE\ORA92\FSDEV10G\SYSAUX01.DBF    88,843

2004-02-21 08:31   E:\ORACLE\ORA92\FSDEV10G\SYSAUX01.DBF    89,463
```

```
2004-02-22 02:00   E:\ORACLE\ORA92\FSDEV10G\SYSAUX01.DBF     90,168

2004-02-22 16:30   E:\ORACLE\ORA92\FSDEV10G\SYSAUX01.DBF    143,974
                   E:\ORACLE\ORA92\FSDEV10G\UNDOTBS01.DBF    88,973
```

This type of time-series exception reporting is extremely useful for detecting those times when an Oracle database is experiencing I/O stress. Many Oracle professionals will schedule these types of exception reports for automatic e-mailing every day. AWR can also be used to aggregate this information to spot trends.

Now that the concept of trend identification has been introduced, it is time to move onto an examination of a more sophisticated type of report where repeating trends within the data can be identified.

General trend identification with the AWR

Once the *dba_hist* scripts have been mastered, the next step is to look at the more complex task of trend identification with the AWR tables. By now, it should be clear that aggregating important Oracle performance metrics over time, day-of-the-week and hour-of-the-day, allows the DBA to see the hidden signatures. These signatures are extremely important because they show regularly occurring changes in processing demands. This knowledge allows the DBA to anticipate upcoming changes and reconfigure Oracle just-in-time to meet the changes.

The following is a simple example. A script can be used to show the signature for any Oracle system statistic, averaged by hour of the day. Figure 11.2 shows how the output of such a script might appear.

Physical Reads

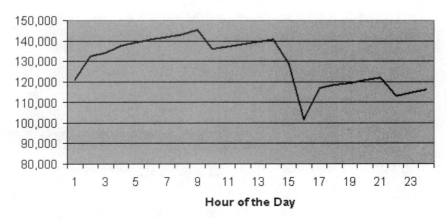

Figure 11.2: *An hourly Signature for physical disk reads*

Plotting the data makes it easy to find trends. Of course, open source products such as RRDTool can also be used to automate the plotting of data from the AWR and ASH tables and make nice web screens to see the data. Finally, the WISE tool can be used and with just a few clicks, comprehensive charts can be produced for any snapshot period as well as trend charts for month, day, or hourly periods. Figure 11.3 below shows a sample WISE view:

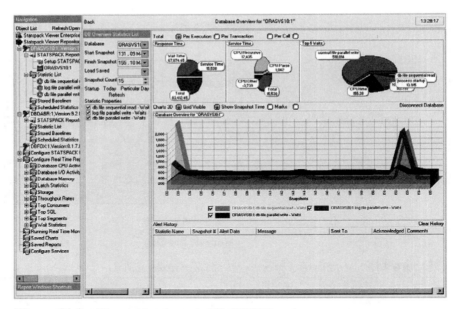

Figure 11.3: *Time series charts in The WISE tool*

The same types of reports, aggregated by day-of-the week, can be created to show daily trends. Over long periods of time, almost all Oracle databases will develop distinct signatures that reflect the regular daily processing patterns of the end-user community.

The script that was introduced in the section titled *Exception Reporting with the AWR* in Chapter 2 will accept any of the values from *dba_hist_sysstat*. This data can now be plotted for trend analysis as shown in Figure 11.4 below. These types of signatures will become very stable for most Oracle databases and can be used to develop a predictive model for proactive tuning activities.

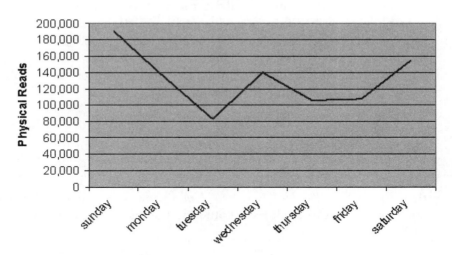

Average Physical Reads

Figure 11.4: *The signature for average physical reads by day of the week*

Correlation analysis with AWR and ASH

For those who like Oracle tuning with the Oracle Wait Interface (OWI), there are interesting statistics that relate to system-wide wait events from the *dba_hist_waitstat* table as shown in Table 11.2 that provide detailed wait event information from the *dba_hist_active_sess_history*.

COLUMN	DESCRIPTION
snap_id	Unique snapshot ID
dbid	Database ID for the snapshot
instance_number	Instance number for the snapshot
class	Class of the block
wait_count	Number of waits by the OPERATION for this CLASS of block
time	Sum of all wait times for all the waits by the OPERATION for this CLASS of block

Table 11.2: *The dba_hist_waitstat statistics used to wait event analysis*

To understand correlation analysis for an Oracle database, a simple example may be helpful. For advanced correlation analysis, the DBA can seek to identify correlations between instance-wide wait events and block-level waits. This is a critical way of combining human insight with the AWR and ASH information to isolate the exact file and object where the wait contention is occurring.

The ASH stores the history of a recent session's activity in *v$active_session_history* with the AWR history view *dba_hist_active_sess_history*. This data is designed as a rolling buffer in memory, and earlier information is overwritten when needed. To do this, the AWR *dba_hist_active_sess_history* view is needed. This view contains historical block-level contention statistics as shown in Table 11.3 below.

COLUMN	DESCRIPTION
snap_id	Unique snapshot ID
sample_time	Time of the sample
session_id	Session identifier
session_serial#	Session serial number. This is used to uniquely identify a session's objects.
user_id	Oracle user identifier
current_obj#	Object ID of the object that the session is currently referencing
current_file#	File number of the file containing the block that the session is currently referencing
current_block#	ID of the block that the session is currently referencing
wait_time	Total wait time for the event for which the session last waited (0 if currently waiting)
time_waited	Time that the current session actually spent waiting for the event. This column is set for waits that were in progress at the time the sample was taken.

Table 11.3: *Selected columns from the dba_hist_active_sess_history view*

The *wait_time_detail.sql* script below compares the wait event values from *dba_hist_waitstat* and *dba_hist_active_sess_history*. This script quickly allows the identification of the exact objects that are experiencing wait events.

💾 wait_time_detail_10g.sql

```
-- *****************************************************
-- Copyright © 2005 by Rampant TechPress
-- This script is free for non-commercial purposes
-- with no warranties.  Use at your own risk.
--
-- To license this script for a commercial purpose,
-- contact info@rampant.cc
-- *****************************************************

prompt
prompt  This will compare values from dba_hist_waitstat with
prompt  detail information from dba_hist_active_sess_history.
prompt

set pages 999
set lines 80

break on snap_time skip 2

col snap_time      heading 'Snap|Time'    format a20
col file_name      heading 'File|Name'    format a40
col object_type    heading 'Object|Type'  format a10
col object_name    heading 'Object|Name'  format a20
col wait_count     heading 'Wait|Count'   format 999,999
col time           heading 'Time'         format 999,999

select
   to_char(begin_interval_time,'yyyy-mm-dd hh24:mi') snap_time,
--   file_name,
   object_type,
   object_name,
   wait_count,
   time
from
   dba_hist_waitstat            wait,
   dba_hist_snapshot            snap,
   dba_hist_active_sess_history ash,
   dba_data_files               df,
   dba_objects                  obj
where
   wait.snap_id = snap.snap_id
and
   wait.snap_id = ash.snap_id
and
```

```
    df.file_id = ash.current_file#
and
    obj.object_id = ash.current_obj#
and
    wait_count > 50
order by
    to_char(begin_interval_time,'yyyy-mm-dd hh24:mi'),
    file_name
;
```

This script is also enabled to join into the *dba_data_files* view to get the file names associated with the wait event. This is a very powerful script that can be used to quickly drill-in to find the cause of specific waits. Below is sample output showing time-slices and the corresponding wait counts and times:

```
SQL> @wait_time_detail_10g

Copyright 2004 by Donald K. Burleson

This will compare values from dba_hist_waitstat with
detail information from dba_hist_active_sess_hist.


Snap                 Object       Object          Wait
Time                 Type         Name            Count      Time
------------------   ----------   ------------   -------   -------
2004-02-28 01:00     TABLE        ORDOR            4,273        67
                     INDEX        PK_CUST_ID      12,373       324
                     INDEX        FK_CUST_NAME     3,883        17
                     INDEX        PK_ITEM_ID       1,256       967


2004-02-29 03:00     TABLE        ITEM_DETAIL         83        69


2004-03-01 04:00     TABLE        ITEM_DETAIL      1,246        45


2004-03-01 21:00     TABLE        CUSTOMER_DET     4,381       354
                     TABLE        IND_PART           117        15


2004-03-04 01:00     TABLE        MARVIN          41,273        16
                     TABLE        FACTOTUM         2,827        43
                     TABLE        DOW_KNOB           853         6
                     TABLE        ITEM_DETAIL         57       331
                     TABLE        HIST_ORD         4,337       176
                     TABLE        TAB_HIST           127        66
```

This example demonstrates how the AWR and ASH data can be used to create an almost infinite number of sophisticated custom performance reports.

The AWR can also be used with the Oracle Data Mining (ODM) product to analyze trends. Using Oracle ODM, the AWR tables can be scanned for statistically significant correlations between metrics. Sophisticated multivariate Chi-Square techniques can also be applied to reveal hidden patterns within the AWR treasury of Oracle performance information.

The Oracle10g ODM uses sophisticated Support Vector Machines (SVM) algorithms for binary, multi-class classification models and has built-in linear regression functionality.

Conclusion

If the DBA takes the time to become familiar with the wealth of metrics within the AWR and ASH tables, it becomes easy to get detailed correlation information between any of the 500+ performance metrics captured by the AWR.

As the Oracle database evolves, Oracle will continue to enhance the mechanisms for analyzing the valuable performance information in AWR. At the present rate, future releases of Oracle may have true artificial intelligence built-in to detect and correct even the most challenging Oracle optimization issues.

The AWR provides the foundation for sophisticated performance analysis, including exception reporting, trend analysis, correlation analysis, hypothesis testing, data mining, and best of all the ability to anticipate future stress on the database.

The main points of this chapter include:

- The AWR *dba_hist* views are similar to well-known STATSPACK tables, making it easy to migrate existing performance reports to Oracle10g.

- The *dba_hist* views are fully documented and easy to use for writing custom scripts.

- The creation of AWR and ASH provides a complete repository for diagnosing and fixing any Oracle performance issue.

- The AWR and ASH are the most exciting performance optimization tools in Oracle's history and provide the foundation for the use of artificial intelligence techniques to be applied to Oracle performance monitoring and optimization.

- As Oracle evolves, the AWR and ASH will likely automate the tedious and time consuming task of Oracle tuning.

Now that the basic idea behind proactive time-series and correlation analysis has been revealed, the next step is to take a look at how the AWR and ASH data can be used to monitor external server conditions. Oracle10g shows that Oracle recognizes that the server hardware is critical to Oracle performance and offers many exciting tools to help the DBA with tuning.

Server & Network Tuning with AWR

"Mom! It's the server again!"

Oracle Server Tuning

Oracle became one of the world's leading databases because it is optimized to work on any database server from a mainframe to a Macintosh. However, Oracle does not run in a vacuum and the DBA must be careful to avoid server overload conditions.

Fortunately, the Oracle10g Automated Workload Repository (AWR) tracks server performance over time and allows the production of detailed management reports that show exactly when the server was overloaded.

AWR trend reports on RAM, disk I/O, and CPU can be generated to help isolate hardware stress and predict when new hardware is needed. Careful attention to server utilization is required to maintain good performace.

The first step in evaluation of server utilization is the examination of the influence of the external environment on server performance. The DBA can then employ specific monitoring techniques for evaluating the external environment. This will be examined more closely next.

Outside the Oracle Instance

While server overload conditions may indicate a sub-optimal Oracle component, overload on a pre-tuned database might indicate that more hardware resources are needed.

Is it legitimate to throw hardware at an atrocious database application loaded with sub-optimal SQL and inferior code? The answer has to do more with economics than with theory.

For example, there might be a database that has thousands of sub-optimal SQL statements and 100,000 lines of poor PL/SQL. This hypothetical database is heavily I/O bound with a large amount of unnecessary logical and physical I/O. Users might be presented with the following options:

- The code could be repaired for $50k in consulting, and it would take 8 weeks; or

- The tablespaces could be moved to a high-speed solid-state disk for $20k and be finished tomorrow. Of course, solid state disks will do nothing more than perform an equivalent of caching the entire database in memory, and the customer may eventually have to fix the code.

If a hardware fix is used to address a software issue, the code will still be inefficient, but it might run 20 times faster and present a cheaper and less risky solution to the IT manager. This approach is more common than one might think. Oracle has tools to address server tuning issues, and the following sections will provide details on these tools.

Oracle Server Bottlenecks

If SQL has not been completely optimized, the following server overload conditions are generally true:

I/O overload: This is sometimes evidenced by high *db file sequential read* and *db file scattered read* waits and can be detected in the Oracle10g *dba_hist_filestatxs* view. SQL that issues unnecessary table block access, possibly due to missing indexes or poor statistics, should be investigated. Assuming that the SQL is optimized, the only remaining solutions are the addition of RAM for the data buffers or a switch to solid-state disks.

CPU overhead: With the advent of 64-bit Oracle and large data block buffers such as *db_cache_size* and *db_keep_cache_size*, the main bottleneck for many databases has shifted from I/O to CPU. If CPU is listed in the top wait events, sub-optimal SQL that may be causing unnecessary logical I/O against the data buffers should be investigated. The library cache can also be investigated to see if excessive parsing might be causing the CPU consumption. Assuming that Oracle has been optimized, the options to relieve a CPU bottleneck are to add more CPUs or faster CPU processors. This is an extremely rare event. On most installations which have paid only minimal attention to sizing, CPU bottleneck is suffered only as a consequence of bad SQL. Bad sort or cached nested loop will do that. Typically, CPU set is never used more then 25%. Throwing hardware at a problem is typically not a good idea.

Network Overload: In many Oracle-based applications, the largest component of end-user response time is network latency. Oracle captures important metrics that will show if the Oracle database is network bound, specifically using the SQL*Net statistics from the

---

dba_hist_sysstat view. Due to the Oracle Transparent Network Substrate (TNS) isolation, there are only a few network tuning options, and most network issues, such as packet sizes, are usually external to the Oracle database.

RAM overload: The Oracle10g Automatic Memory Management (AMM) utility has facilities for re-sizing the *db_cache_size, shared_pool_size,* and *pga_aggregate_target* SGA regions, and Oracle Enterprise Manager for detecting SGA regions that are too small. RAM can be reallocated within these regions which will reduce *pga_aggregate_target* if there are no disk sorts or hash joins, reduce *shared_pool_size* if there is no library cache contention, and reduce *db_cache_size* if there is low disk I/O activity.

Historically, tiny data buffers meant that disk I/O was the most common wait event, but this has changed with the introduction of Solid State RAM disk and 64-bit Oracle where large RAM data buffer caches can be implemented to reduce disk reads. This has shifted many databases from I/O to CPU constraints, and it is one of the reasons that Oracle introduced CPU based costing into the SQL optimizer.

Disk I/O and Oracle

Oracle tuning techniques are continuously being modified to match changes in the hardware technology. Having current tuning tools is especially important with data intensive applications like Oracle. The cost and speed of disk devices have had a considerable impact on Oracle tuning activities.

In 1985, a 1.2 gigabyte disk sold for more than $250,000. Today, users can buy 100 gigabytes disks for $200 and 100 gigabytes of RAM-disk for $100,000. The following statements show how storage trends change over time:

- Disk storage improves tenfold every year.

- Storage media becomes obsolete every 25 years.

- RAM-SAN will replace disks by 2006.

In Oracle, physical disk I/O can be measured by querying STATSPACK and the AWR for the physical disk reads information that is captured inside the *stats$filestatxs* and *dba_hist_filestatxs* tables.

For example, the following Oracle10g script detects all files with physical reads over 10,000 during the snapshot period:

```
break on begin_interval_time skip 2

column phyrds format 999,999,999
column begin_interval_time format a25

select
   begin_interval_time,
   filename,
   phyrds
from
   dba_hist_filestatxs
natural join
   dba_hist_snapshot
where
   phyrds > 10000
;
```

The results yield a running total of Oracle physical reads. The snapshots are collected every hour in this example, and many DBAs will increase the default collection frequency of AWR snapshots. Starting from this script, users could easily add a WHERE clause criteria and create a unique time-series exception report.

```
SQL> @phys_reads

BEGIN_INTERVAL_TIME FILENAME PHYRDS
----------------------- ----------------------------------------- -------
24-FEB-04 11.00.32.000 PM E:\ORACLE\ORA92\FSDEV10G\SYSTEM01.DBF    164,700
                          E:\ORACLE\ORA92\FSDEV10G\UNDOTBS01.DBF     26,082
                          E:\ORACLE\ORA92\FSDEV10G\SYSAUX01.DBF     472,008
                          E:\ORACLE\ORA92\FSDEV10G\USERS01.DBF       21,794
                          E:\ORACLE\ORA92\FSDEV10G\T_FS_LSQ.ORA      12,123

24-FEB-04 12.00.32.000 PM E:\ORACLE\ORA92\FSDEV10G\SYSTEM01.DBF    164,700
                          E:\ORACLE\ORA92\FSDEV10G\UNDOTBS01.DBF     26,082
```

This concept is particularly true when considering Moore's Law, which essentially states that processor capacity increases steadily while hardware costs fall. While Moore's law does not apply to RAM chip characteristics, RAM is steadily falling in cost, but the speed has remained the same for more than 30 years, hovering at about 50 nanoseconds.

Moore's Law

Back in the mid-1960's, Gordon Moore, the director of the research and development labs at Fairchild Semiconductor, published a research paper titled *"Cramming More Components into Integrated Circuits."* In his paper, Moore performed a linear regression on the rate of change in server processing speed and costs and noted an exponential growth in processing power and an exponential reduction of processing costs. This landmark paper gave birth to "Moore's Law," which postulated that CPU power will get four times faster every three years as illustrated in Figure 12.1.

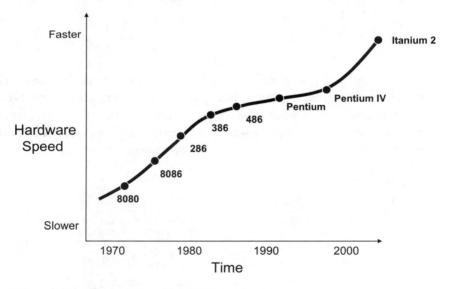

Figure 12.1: *Moore's Law for CPU speed*

In the 1970's, a 4-way Symmetric Multiprocessing (SMP) processor cost over three million dollars. Yet today, the same CPU can be purchased for less than three thousand dollars. CPUs will increase in speed four times every three years and only increase in cost by 50%.

While Moore's Law is generally correct, the curve is not linear. The formerly marginal rate of advances in CPU speed has increased dramatically in the past decade, most notably with the introduction of the Itanium2 processors.

The large RAM data buffers enabled by 64-bit operating systems have shifted the bottleneck for many Oracle databases from I/O to CPU. Oracle10g accommodates this shift to CPU consumption by providing a new *cpu_cost* feature that allows Oracle's cost-based SQL optimizer to evaluate SQL execution plan costs based on predicted CPU costs as well as I/O costs. This is an adjustable feature in Oracle10g, and it is controlled by the *_optimizer_cost_model* hidden parameter.

Even though it is true that a CPU bottleneck exists when the run queue exceeds the number of processors on the server, this condition does not always mean that the best solution is to add processors. Excessive CPU load can be caused by many internal Oracle conditions including inefficient SQL statements that perform excessive logical I/O, non-reentrant SQL inside the library cache, and many other conditions. Fortunately, Oracle 10g Enterprise Manager allows users to look back in time and find these conditions, even though the immediate run queue issue has passed.

While Moore's law is quite correct for processor speed and cost, many have over-generalized this principle as it applies to disks and RAM. It is true that costs are continually falling for RAM and disk, but the speed assumptions do not apply.

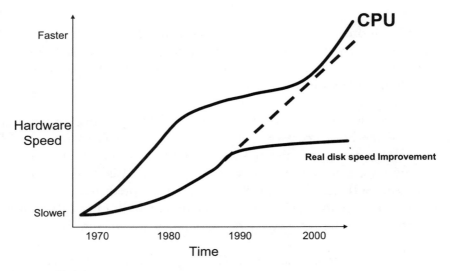

Figure 12.2: *Moore's Law for Disk speed*

The old-fashioned spinning platters of magnetic-coated metal disks have an upper limit of spin speed, and the read/write head movement speed is limited. In the early 1990's, it became apparent that the 1950's disk technology had reached the limits of its physical capabilities. It became necessary for disk manufacturers to add on-board RAM caches to disk arrays and include asynchronous writing mechanisms to continue to improve disk speed.

One glaring exception to Moore's law is RAM speed as shown in Figure 12.3 below.

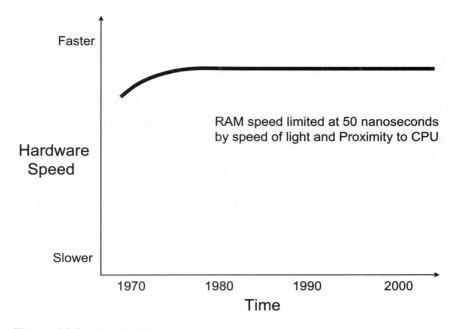

Figure 12.3: *Moore's Law for RAM speed*

RAM has not made many significant gains in speed since the mid 1970's. This is due to the limitations of silicon and the fact that access speed in nanoseconds approaches the speed of light. The only way to further improve the speed of RAM would be to employ a radical new medium such as Gallium Arsenide.

This flat speed curve for RAM has important ramifications for Oracle processing. Since CPU speed continues to outpace RAM speed, RAM sub-systems must be localized to keep the CPUs running at full capacity. This type of approach is evident in the new Itanium2 servers where the RAM is placed as close to the CPU as possible as shown in Figure 12.4.

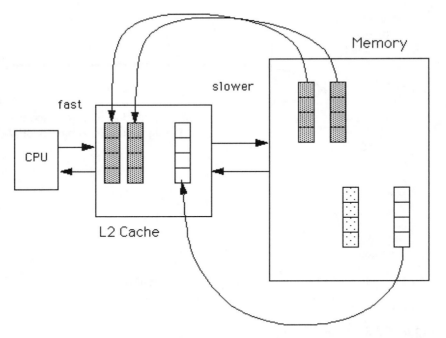

Figure 12.4: *Localizing RAM in Itanium2 Servers*

This represents the Oracle servers of the 21st century (e.g. the UNISYS ES7000 series) which have a special L2 RAM that is placed near the processors for fast RAM access. Low-cost RAM technology has dramatically changed the way that Oracle databases are tuned.

Server RAM and Oracle

Today, 100 gigabytes of RAM-disk can be purchased for as little as $100,000 and can deliver access times 6,000 times faster than traditional disk devices. By 2013, a gigabyte of RAM is projected to cost the same as a gigabyte of disk today, which is approximately $200.

RAM I/O bandwidth is projected to grow one bit every 18 months, making 128 bit architecture due in about 2010 according to the data in Table 12.1.

8 bit	1970's
16 bit	1980's
32 bit	1990's
64 bit	2000's
128 bit	2010's

Table 12.1: *RAM bandwidth evolution*

The fact that RAM does not get faster means that CPU speed continues to outpace memory speed. This means that RAM subsystems must be localized close to the processors to keep the CPUs running at full capacity, and this architecture impacts Oracle performance.

Traditionally, the Oracle DBA measured RAM page-in operations to judge RAM utilization on the database server as shown in Figure 12.5. All virtual memory servers (VM) anticipate RAM shortages and asynchronously page-out RAM frames in case the RAM is required for an upcoming task.

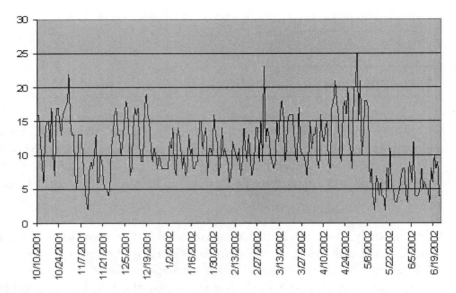

Oracle Server RAM page-in's

Figure 12.5: *Long-term measurements of Oracle server RAM page-in operations*

When the real RAM on the server is exceeded, the OS will overlay the RAM and must then page-in the saved memory frames from the swap disk on the Oracle server. However, measuring RAM usage based solely on page-ins is a mistake, because the page-ins are a normal part of program start-up.

For an Oracle metric to be effective, the page-in operations from *vmstat* or *glance,* for instance, must be correlated with the OS scan rate. When an Oracle server begins to run low on RAM, the page-stealing daemon process awakens and UNIX begins to treat the RAM memory as a sharable resource by moving memory frames to the swap disk with paging operations.

In most UNIX and Linux implementations, the page-stealing daemon operates in two modes. When the real RAM capacity is exceeded, the page-stealing daemon will steal small chunks of least recently used RAM memory from a program. If RAM resource demands continue to increase beyond the real capacity of the Oracle server, the daemon escalates and begins to page-out entire programs' RAM regions. Unfortunately, on Linux kernel 2.6 users have no control over this. Every parameter available for tuning the kernel has been taken away from the system administrators.

Because of this, it is not always clear if the page-in operations are normal housekeeping or a serious memory shortage unless the activity of the page-stealing daemon is correlated with the page-in output. Paging occurs in kernel mode. Generally speaking, if the system exhibits more than 10% of kernel mode CPU usage for a prolonged period of time, there is a problem with paging.

To aid in measuring real page-ins, the UNIX and Linux *vmstat* utility yields the scan rate *(sr)* column which designates the memory page scan rate. If the scan rate rises steadily, the page-stealing daemon's first threshold will be identified, indicating that that particular program's entire RAM memory regions are being paged-out to the swap disk. This behavior can then be correlated with the *vmstat* page-in *(pi)* metric.

The following is an example from a *vmstat* output. The spike in the scan rate immediately precedes an increase in page-in operations.

```
oracle > vmstat 2
```

procs			memory				page				
r	b	w	avm	free	re	at	pi	po	fr	de	sr
3	0	0	144020	12778	17	9	0	14	29	0	3
3	0	0	144020	12737	15	0	1	34	4	0	8
3	0	0	144020	12360	9	0	1	46	2	0	13
1	0	0	142084	12360	5	0	3	17	0	0	21
1	0	0	142084	12360	3	0	18	0	0	0	8
1	0	0	140900	12360	1	0	34	0	0	0	0
1	0	0	140900	12360	0	0	39	0	0	0	0
1	0	0	140900	12204	0	0	3	0	0	0	0
1	0	0	137654	12204	0	0	0	0	0	0	0

Fortunately, the AWR can be used to track these important external server metrics.

Tracking External Server Metrics with AWR

Oracle sets several important initialization parameters based on the number of CPUs on the Oracle sever and is now more mindful of the costs of CPU cycles and I/O operations. Indeed, with each new release of Oracle, the database becomes more in tune to its external environment.

Further, 64-bit Oracle servers have changed Oracle server metric tuning activities for the DBA.

Oracle and the 64-bit server technology

The advent of 64-bit CPUs has lead to a dramatic change in the way that Oracle databases are managed and tuned. To understand the issues, one must understand the advantages of a 64-bit server, especially the ability to have large data buffer caches. The following are the architectural benefits of the 64-bit processors listed in order of importance to Oracle shops:

Improved RAM addressing: A 32-bit word size can only address approximately four gigabytes of RAM (2 to the 32nd power). All 64-bit servers have a larger word size that allows for up to 18 billion gigabytes (2 to the 64th power or 18 exabytes). These servers allow for huge scalability as the processing demand grows.

Faster Processors: Intel's 64-bit Itanium2 architecture is more powerful than the older 32-bit chipsets. While faster chips are not a direct result of the 64-bit architecture, they are an important consideration for shops with computationally-intensive databases.

High parallelism: Multiple CPU and SMP support allows large scale parallel processing. For example, the Unisys 64-bit ES7000 servers support up to 32 processors which yields large parallel benefits.

Cluster architecture: The 64-bit servers, such as the Unisys 64-bit ES7000 servers, are generally cluster-ready.

While having a 64-bit processor might be an attractive option, a large number of Oracle shops continued to run 32-bit versions of the Oracle database on their servers.

The new Intel Itanium2 processor architecture now rivals the proprietary UNIX systems with the ability to house CPUs and over 20 gigabytes of RAM capacity as shown in Figure 12.6. This architecture can support thousands of users while providing sub-second response time.

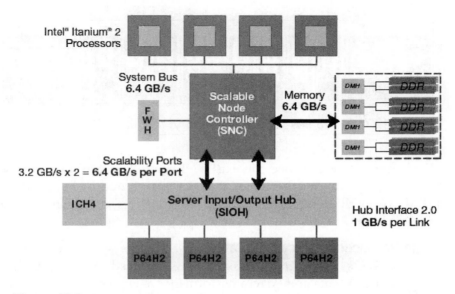

Figure 12.6: *The Intel E8870 Chipset supporting the Itanium 2 processor*

Intel also allows architecture to be scaled to a 16-way SMP configuration as shown in Figure 12.7, and it is apparent that Intel will continue to pursue the hardware-level expansion of this architecture.

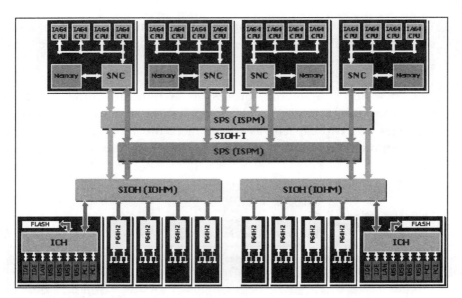

Figure 12.7: *The 16-way Itanium 2 architecture (Courtesy UNISYS)*

With the 16-way processors using Itanium2, there exists server architecture reminiscent of the larger servers offered by Sun, HP, and IBM. As all the vendors are offering 64-bit servers, the greatest benefit to Oracle shops occurs in these areas:

High transactions processing rates: For systems with more than 200 disk I/Os per second, disk I/O is reduced by caching large amounts of data and system performance skyrockets.

Declining performance: The 32-bit limitations prevent continued growth beyond a certain point. The 64-bit architecture raises the ceiling on that growth.

Anticipating rapid growth: For systems that require uninterrupted growth and scalability, the 64-bit architecture allows almost infinite scalability. Many large enterprise resource planning (ERP) systems have been able to scale successfully on Windows 64 platforms.

Computationally intensive system – If an Oracle database is CPU-bound or if it performs multiple parallel full-table scans, the faster processors in a 64-bit architecture are very appealing.

What does this mean to the Oracle professional? Larry Ellison, CEO of Oracle, noted at OracleWorld in 2003 that:

> "If you want the world's faster processors then you will be forced to pay less."

He was referring to the Intel Itanium2 chips which appear to be making strong advances in the displacement of the proprietary UNIX environments, especially HP/UX and Solaris. The major operating environments for Itanium2 servers are Linux and Microsoft Windows:

- **Linux**: Offers large scale uptake but is hindered by non-open source costs and lackluster support.

- **Windows**: Increasing in popularity but suffering from unreliable past performance.

These large inexpensive servers provide the ultimate in resource sharing. With many Oracle instances on a single server, processes that need more CPU will automatically be allocated cycles from the server run queue. Likewise, an instance that requires additional RAM for the SA or PGA can easily get the resources without cumbersome manual intervention.

In summary, 16-way and 32-way SMP servers are leading the way into a new age of Oracle database consolidation.

The New Age of Oracle Server Consolidation

It is ironic that the old mainframe architectures of the 1970's and 1980's are now brand new again. Back in the days of data processing, it was not uncommon for a single server to host a dozen databases.

The advent of the inexpensive Itanium2 servers is leading the way back to server consolidation. There was nothing inherently wrong with a centralized server environment, and in many ways it was superior to the distributed client-server architectures of the 1990's.

When companies first started to leave the mainframe environment, it was not because there were particular benefits to having a number of tiny servers. Instead, it was a pure economic decision based on the low cost of the UNIX-based minicomputers of the day.

These minicomputers of the 1980's could be purchased for as little as $30k which was a bargain when compared to the three million dollar cost of a mainframe. As minicomputers evolved into the UNIX-centric Oracle servers of the 1990's, some shops found themselves with hundreds of servers, one for each Oracle database.

In fact, the break down of the mainframe was a nightmare for the Oracle DBA. Instead of a single server to manage, the DBA had dozens or even hundreds of servers, each with its own copy of the Oracle software.

The 1990's was the age of client/server computing, where multi-tiered applications were constructed with dozens of small servers. Systems might have been comprised of a Web server layer, an application server layer, and a database layer, each with dozens of individual servers as shown in Figure 12.8.

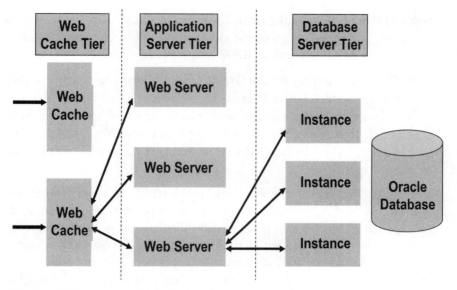

Figure 12.8: *The multi-server Oracle architectures of the 1990's*

The example in Figure 12.8 shows a multi-server architecture that employs Oracle Real Application Clusters (RAC) which is a processing architecture that allows multiple Oracle instances on separate servers that access a common Oracle database.

One of the issues associated with single server Oracle systems was the deliberate over-allocation of computing resources. Each system would experience periodic processing spikes, and each server had to be equipped with additional resources to accommodate the irregular frequency of the demands of various applications. This led to a condition in which Oracle servers had unused CPU and RAM resources that could not be easily shared.

The client/server Oracle paradigm had many serious problems:

High Expense: In large enterprise data centers with many servers and many instances, hardware resources must be deliberately over-allocated in order to accommodate the sporadic peaks in CPU and RAM resources.

High Waste: Since each Oracle instance resides on a separate single server, there is a significant duplication of work which results in sub-optimal utilization of RAM and CPU resources.

Very Time Consuming for the Oracle DBA: In many large Oracle shops, a shuffle occurs when a database outgrows its server. When a new server is purchased the Oracle database is moved to the new server, leaving the older server to accept yet another smaller Oracle database. This shuffling consumes considerable time and attention from the DBA.

This waste and high DBA overhead has lead IT managers to recognize the benefits of a centralized server environment, and there is now resurgence in popularity of large monolithic servers for bigger Oracle shops. There is also a rapid depreciation rate for servers, which has also contributed to the movement towards server consolidation. For example, three year-old Oracle servers that cost over $100k brand new are now worth less than five thousand dollars.

These new mainframes may contain 16, 32, or even 64 CPUs and have processing capabilities that dwarf the traditional mainframe ancestors of the 1980s. These new super-servers are capable of blistering performance, and a recent UNISYS benchmark exceeded 250,000 transactions per minute (TPM) on a Windows based server using Oracle10g and nearly a million TPM on large Linux servers. The new Oracle10g benchmarks of server performance make use of many of the new features of Oracle including:

- Multiple blocksizes

- 115 gigabyte total data buffer cache

- 78 gigabyte KEEP pool

- 16 CPU Server - Each a 64-bit Itanium 2 Processor

There are those who argue that it is not a good idea to throw everything onto a single server because it introduces a single point of failure. Even Oracle Corporation says that it's not a good idea to place all of the proverbial eggs in one basket; therefore, they advocate the grid approach in Oracle10g.

Many of these concerns are unfounded. In reality, these large systems have redundant everything, and with the use of Oracle Streams for replication at different geographical locations, they are virtually unstoppable.

In the new server architectures, everything from disk, CPU, RAM, and internal busses are fully fault tolerant and redundant which makes the monolithic approach appealing to large corporations for the following reasons:

Lower costs - Monolithic servers are extremely good at sharing computing resources between applications, making grid computing unnecessary.

Lower Oracle DBA maintenance - Instead of maintaining 30 copies or more of Oracle and the OS, DBAs only need to manage a single copy.

Cost savings aside, there are other compelling reasons to consolidate Oracle instances onto a single server:

Oracle server consolidation: Server consolidation technology can greatly reduce the number of Oracle database servers.

Centralized management: A single server means a single copy of the Oracle software. Plus, the operating system controls resource allocation and the server will automatically balance the demands of many Oracle instances for processing cycles and RAM resources. Of course, the Oracle DBA still maintains control and can dedicate Oracle instances to a single CPU thereby utilizing processor affinity or adjust the CPU dispatching priority using the UNIX *nice* command.

Transparent high availability: If any server component fails, the monolithic server can re-assign the processing without interruption. This is a more affordable and far simpler solution than Real Applications Clusters or Oracle9i DataGuard, either of which requires duplicate servers.

Scalability: Using a single large server, additional CPU and RAM can be added seamlessly for increased performance.

Reduced DBA workload: By consolidating server resources, the DBA has fewer servers to manage and need not be concerned with outgrowing server capacity.

So, what does this mean to the Oracle DBA? Clearly, less time will be spent installing and maintaining multiple copies of Oracle. This will free time for the DBA to pursue more advanced tasks such as SQL tuning and database performance optimization.

Following this information on the impact of the new server environments for Oracle, it is logical to look at the overhauled Oracle10g Enterprise Manager and see how it now displays AWR server-side metrics.

Enterprise Manager for Server & Environment

Using the new Oracle 10g Enterprise Manager (OEM) interface, the Oracle professional can now get access to external information that has never before been available in a single interface. This is important because it removes the need for the DBA to have any experience with the cumbersome OS command syntax that is required to display server-side information.

In UNIX for example, the DBA would need to know the command-line syntax of various UNIX utilities such as SAR, GLANCE, TOP, LSATTR, and PRTCONF to display server metrics. The Oracle10g OEM screens allow seamless access server-side performance metrics including:

- Oracle server-side file contents such as ALERT LOG and TRACE DUMPS

- Oracle archives redo log file performance

- Server OS kernel performance parameter values

- Server OS characteristics such as the number of CPUs, the amount of RAM, and the network.

- Historical capture of CPU and RAM activity

A quick look at the Oracle 10g OEM display screens for external information reveals how the DBA is relieved of the burden of having to know and recall hundreds of server-side commands.

Oracle 10g OEM allows DBAs to quickly see the status of Oracle server-side file performance and error messages, including the alert log file, archived redo log status and file system status as shown in Figure 12.9.

ORACLE
Enterprise Manager

Database: FSDEV10G > All Metrics
All Metrics

Expand All | Collapse All

Metrics	Thresholds	Collection Stat
▼ FSDEV10G		
▼ Alert Log	Some	Not Collected
Alert Log Error Trace File	Not Set	Not Collected
Alert Log Name	Not Set	Not Collected
Archiver Hung Alert Log Error	Set	Not Collected
Data Block Corruption Alert Log Error	Set	Not Collected
Generic Alert Log Error	Set	Not Collected
Session Terminated Alert Log Error	Set	Not Collected
▼ Alert Log Content	None	Not Collected
Content	Not Set	Not Collected
▼ Alert Log Error Status	All	Last Collected
Archiver Hung Alert Log Error Status	Set	Last Collected
Data Block Corruption Alert Log Error Status	Set	Last Collected
Generic Alert Log Error Status	Set	Last Collected
Session Terminated Alert Log Error Status	Set	Last Collected
▼ Archive Area	Some	Last Collected
Archive Area Used (%)	Set	Last Collected
Archive Area Used (KB)	Not Set	Last Collected
Free Archive Area (KB)	Not Set	Last Collected

Figure 12.9: *A partial listing of the AWR metrics from inside Oracle 10g Enterprise Manager*

The ability of Oracle10g OEM to monitor server-side metrics makes it a one stop tool for monitoring both Oracle and the server. In addition, a Systems Administrator may no longer be required to buy separate, expensive tools to monitor the server and the data files. Best of all, the Oracle professional does not have to worry about a server-side problem (i.e. file-system full) causing an Oracle interruption.

From these Oracle10g OEM interfaces, server-side Oracle components can be displayed and managed without having to sign on to the server. This is an advantage for those Oracle professionals running UNIX servers who may not be fluent in UNIX commands and the complex *vi* editor. Figure 12.10 shows the display of server OS details including all of the OS kernel parameters.

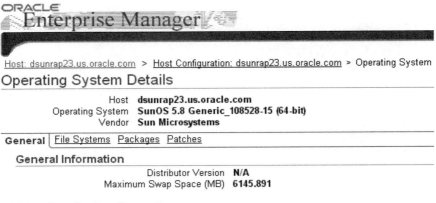

Figure 12.10: *The Oracle 10g OEM display of server-side performance parameters*

Users can also throw away existing checklists of cumbersome OS commands required to display server hardware characteristics. For example, the following are some of the cryptic commands the Oracle UNIX professional would have to know in order to display the number of CPUs on the Oracle server:

Linux command:

```
cat /proc/cpuinfo|grep processor|wc -l
```

Solaris command:

```
psrinfo -v|grep "Status of processor"|wc -l
```

AIX command:

```
lsdev -C|grep Process|wc -l
```

HP/UX command:

```
ioscan -C processor | grep processor | wc -l
```

The Oracle10g OEM issues these commands and displays all hardware characteristics in an easy-to-read display as shown in Figure 12.11.

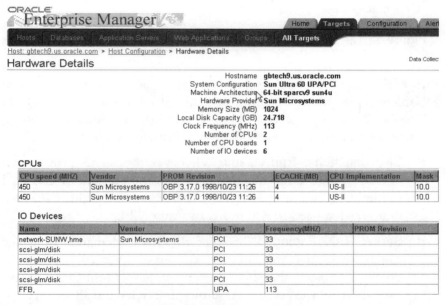

Figure 12.11: *The Oracle 10g OEM display of server-side hardware configuration*

Oracle10g OEM does much more than simply display the server parameters and configuration information. A shortage of server resources may cause slow performance, and the OEM now quickly

---

displays the relevant CPU and RAM metrics. The main performance display screen in the OEM now displays a current summary of the CPU Run Queue and RAM paging as shown in Figure 12.12.

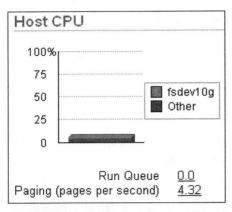

Figure 12.12: *The HOST CPU section of the main OEM performance screen*

If a shortage of Oracle server resources is causing a performance bottleneck, it quickly becomes evident. If the instance and SQL have already been optimized, this server-side information can give immediate insight into server resource shortages such as:

- **CPU dispatcher Run Queue***:* Whenever the server processors are overstressed, the run queue will exceed the number of CPUs. For example, a run queue value of nine on an eight CPU server indicates the need to add more, or faster, CPUs.

- **Server RAM Paging***:* Whenever the RAM demands of a server exceed the real RAM capacity, the server's Virtual Memory (VM) utility will page, thereby transferring RAM frames to a special swap-disk on the server. Assuming the SGA and PGA regions are optimized, paging indicates the need to add RAM resources to the server.

The Oracle10g OEM also tracks server usage over time, allowing quick access to information regarding those times when a hardware-related constraint occurs as shown in Figure 12.13. This figure displays the historical CPU usage as well as user defined threshold alert status which is defined by setting a threshold alert for the *Average CPU (%)* Oracle10g OEM Metric.

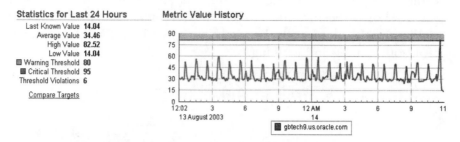

Figure 12.13: *The Oracle 10g OEM historical tracking of CPU consumption*

The OEM also tracks server run queue waits over time and combines the CPU and Paging display into a single screen. This allows users to determine when there are server-side waits on hardware resources as shown in Figure 12.14. This is important because Oracle performance issues are often transient in nature as evidenced by short spikes indicating excessive CPU demands.

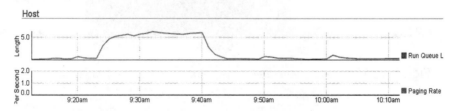

Figure 12.14: *Server CPU run queue and RAM paging values over time*

Due the fast nature of CPU dispatching, a database might be CPU constrained for a few minutes at a time at different times of the day. The time series OEM display can give a quick visual clue about those times when the system is experiencing a CPU or RAM bottleneck.

Further detailed information can be obtained by using the OEM drill-down function and clicking on any area of the graph.

Due to Oracle's commitment to extending the OEM beyond the boundaries of the Oracle instance, virtually all areas of server utilization can be tracked over time as shown in Figure 12.15. The chart shows specific times when the server exceeded the maximum CPU capacity along with the total time spent by active Oracle sessions for both waiting and working.

Active Sessions: Waiting and Working

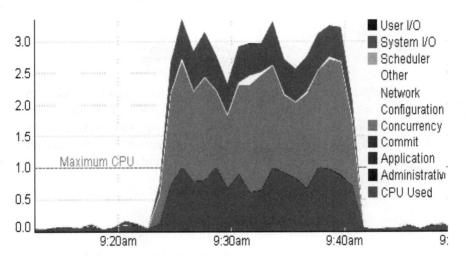

Figure 12.15: *Oracle server time-series resource component utilization*

The legend indicates the components of Oracle wait times including CPU time, concurrency management overhead in the form of locks and latches, and I/O. This display also shows the times when CPU usage exceeds the server capacity.

The same AWR data that is rendered within OEM can also be used as input to more sophisticated scripts for covariate analysis and trending of server-side AWR and ASH data. New server-side abilities of AWR clearly influence the execution of SQL within Oracle.

Server Metrics and SQL Execution

When determining the best execution plan for an SQL query, the newly enhanced cost-based optimizer (CBO) considers external influences. Since the Oracle database does not run in a vacuum, the CBO must have the ability to factor in the costs of external disk I/O as well as the cost of CPU cycles for each SQL operation. This is a significant step forward in making the CBO one of the most sophisticated software packages in the world. Choosing the best execution plan for any SQL statement is always the job of the CBO and is no small challenge.

In accordance with Oracle documentation, the I/O and CPU costs are estimated as shown below:

```
Cost =   (#SRds * sreadtim + #MRds * mreadtim + #CPUCycles
         -----------------------------------------------
                         cpuspeed )
         -----------------------------------------------
                         sreadtim
```

where:

- **#SRDs:** number of single block reads
- **#MRDs:** number of multi block reads
- **#CPUCycles:** number of CPU Cycles
- **sreadtim:** single block read time
- **mreadtim:** multi block read time
- **cpuspeed:** CPU cycles per second

The external costing is markedly influenced by the calculated cost of disk reads as measured by the *v$* tables and the estimated CPU costs associated with each internal operation. By storing the details regarding the costs of many components of SQL execution, Oracle can use these average costs to influence the choices made by the cost-based SQL optimizer. Here are some examples:

Hash join costs: Oracle records the average amount of RAM memory consumed by a hash join.

Sort costs: Oracle tracks the RAM necessary for sorting and aggregation operations.

Table scan costs: Oracle keeps information about the amount of time that is essential to performing a multiblock read such as *db file scatter reads*.

Index block access costs: Oracle stores the average time required to fetch a single block such as *db file sequential reads*.

Depending on the *optimizer_mode* choice, Oracle costs are weighed differently. If the *all_rows* optimizer mode is utilized for a data warehouse, the CBO will be heavily influenced by external factors due to the fact that the *all_rows* mode is designed to minimize resource consumption. On the other hand, if there is an OLTP system with the *first_rows* optimizer mode, the CBO deems it more imperative to return rows quickly than to minimize resource costs.

CPU Based Optimizer Costing

The new CPU Costing feature, controlled by the *_optimizer_cost_model* = hidden parameter, enhances the CBO's capabilities by allowing it to estimate the number of machine cycles necessary for an operation. This cost subsequently counts in the execution plan calculation. The CPU costs affiliated with servicing an Oracle query hinge on the current server load, which Oracle cannot see. Generally, CPU costs are not considered significant unless the entire Oracle instance is using excessive CPU resources.

I/O Costing

While the CBO is now enhanced to figure the number of physical block reads required for an operation, it has not yet been quite perfected. For example, the CBO is not yet aware of the percentage of a table's blocks that reside in the data buffer.

The I/O cost is proportional to the number of physical data blocks read by the operation. However, the CBO has no prior information on the data buffer contents and cannot distinguish between a logical read (in-buffer) and a physical read. Due to this shortcoming, the CBO cannot know if the data blocks are already in the RAM data buffers.

The best environment for using CPU costing is for *all_rows* execution plans, where cost is more noteworthy than with *first_rows* optimization.

External costing does not take into account the number of data blocks residing in the RAM data buffers; however, a future release of the CBO is likely to incorporate this element. Additionally, costs are a function of the number of reads and the relative read times plus the CPU cost estimate for the query.

In evaluating the execution plan, Oracle uses both the CPU and I/O cost estimations. This equation becomes even more complex when parallel querying is factored in when several concurrent processes are servicing the query.

Oracle Network affects Oracle performance and the AWR data can help users detect and fix data transmission issues.

Network Tuning

Oracle databases are often shared across dispersed geographical locations, so it is imperative that the Oracle professional comprehend how database performance is affected by network communications. In response to this, Oracle provides the Transparent Network Substrate (TNS), which allows distributed communications between databases.

As a distributed protocol, the TNS allows for transparent database communications between remote systems. The TNS serves the physical communications between the remote servers and acts as an insulator between Oracle's logical data requests. This allows the network administrator to control much of the network performance tuning; however, it also subsequently leaves the Oracle administrator little control over the network settings that can affect overall database performance as shown in Figure 12.16.

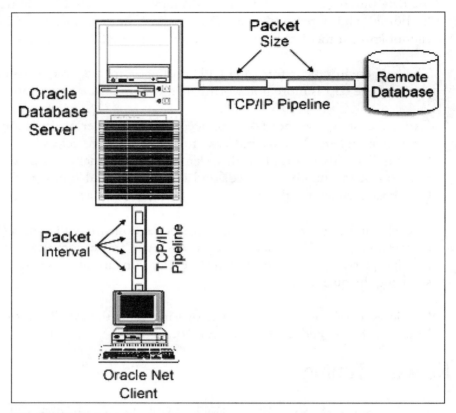

Figure 12.16: *The Oracle*Net architecture*

By using some network parameter settings, several of which are presented in this chapter, the performance of distributed transactions can be improved. This review of the network tuning parameters should indicate that the *init.ora* parameters relate to distributed communications, while the TCP parameters, such as *tcp.nodelay*, can be used to change the packet shipping mechanisms such as size and frequency of packet transmission.

The parameters within the *sqlnet.ora, tnsnames.ora,* and *protocol.ora* files can also be used to change the configuration and size of TCP packets. The setting for these parameters can have a profound impact on the underlying network transport layer's ability to improve the throughput of all Oracle transactions.

Oracle*Net is a layer in the OSI model that resides above the network specific protocol stack. Oracle*Net prohibits the Oracle administrator from tuning Oracle network parameters to improve network performance.

Oracle*Net takes the data and gives it to the protocol stack for transmission in response to a data request. The protocol stack then creates a packet from this data and transmits it over the network. Passing data to the protocol stack is Oracle*Net's sole task so there is little allowance for the DBA to improve network performance.

The DBA does have the ability to control the frequency and size of network packets. Oracle offers a number of tools that are used to change packet frequency and size. Changing the refresh interval for a snapshot to ship larger amounts of data at less frequent intervals is a simple example.

Using several parameters, Oracle*Net connections between servers can be tuned; however, network tuning is outside the scope of Oracle and a qualified network administrator should be consulted for tuning the network. By using settings contained in the following parameter files, the frequency and size of packets shipping across the network can be impacted:

FILE	PARAMETER
protocol.ora	*tcp.nodelay*
sqlnet.ora	*automatic_ipc*
sqlnet.ora	*break_poll_skip*
tnsnames.ora	*SDU and TDU*
listener.ora	*SDU, TDU, and queuesize*

Table 12.2: *Oracle network parameter locations*

While limited in power, the settings for these parameters can still make a huge difference in the performance of distributed Oracle databases. A closer look at these parameters is warranted.

The *tcp.nodelay* parameter

By default, Oracle*Net waits until the buffer is full before transmitting data; therefore, requests are not always sent immediately to their destinations. This is most commonly found when large amounts of data are streamed from one location to another, and Oracle*Net does not transmit the packet until the buffer is full. Adding a *protocol.ora* file and specifying a *tcp.nodelay* to stop buffer flushing delays can sometimes remedy this problem. The parameter can be used both on the client and server. The *protocol.ora* statement is:

```
tcp.nodelay = YES
```

When this parameter is specified, TCP buffering is skipped so that every request is sent immediately. Slowdowns in the network may be caused by an increase in network traffic due to smaller and more frequent packet transmission.

The *automatic_ipc* parameter

Speeding local connections to the database occurs when the *automatic_ipc* parameter bypasses the network layer. When *automatic_ipc* is set to ON, Oracle*Net checks to see if a local database is defined by the same alias.

```
automatic_ipc=ON
```

Only when an Oracle*Net connection must be made to the local database should the *automatic_ipc* parameter be used on the database server. Set this parameter to OFF if local connections are not needed or required. This will improve the performance of all Oracle*Net clients.

The SDU and TDU parameters

The session data unit (SDU) specifies the size of the packets to send over the network. The maximum transmission unit (MTU) is a fixed value that depends on the actual network implementation used. Ideally, SDU should not surpass the size of the MTU. Oracle recommends that SDU be set equal to the MTU. The *tnsnames.ora* and *listener.ora* files house the SDU and TDU parameters.

To group data together, the TDU value is the default packet size used within Oracle*Net. The default value for both SDU and TDU is 2,048 bytes and the maximum value is 32,767 bytes. The TDU parameter should ideally be a multiple of the SDU parameter. For SDU and TDU, the following guidelines apply:

- On fast network connections such as T1 or T3 lines, SDU and TDU should be set equal to the MTU for the network. On standard Ethernet networks, the default MTU size should be set to 1,514 bytes. On standard token ring networks, the default MTU size is 4,202 bytes.

- If the users are connecting via dial-up modem lines, it may be desirable to set SDU and TDU to smaller values in consideration of the frequent resends that occur over modem connections.

- The *mts_dispatchers* must also be set with the proper MTU- TDU configuration, if a Multi-Threaded Server (MTS) is used.

- As a rule, SDU should not be set greater than the TDU because network resources will be wasted by shipping wasted space in each packet.

This brief review of network-related parameters was intended provide an introduction to the scope and complexity of network tuning. It is important to understand that Oracle*Net is simply a layer in the OSI model that is above the network-specific protocol stack, and therefore, virtually all network tuning is external to Oracle.

Conclusion

The future of Oracle database administration is constantly changing. These changes will forever alter the way that Oracle DBAs perform their work. The following are examples of some expected changes:

- **Fully-cached databases**: Just as the UNISYS benchmark used 115 gigabyte data buffers, many Oracle systems will become fully cached. This is largely a result of decreasing RAM costs and the advent of 64-bit Oracle servers.

- **Solid-state Oracle**: The advent of Solid-State Disk (SSD) will produce a faster replacement for the archaic spinning platters of magnetic coated media and will someday relieve the need for data buffers.

- **Back to the mainframe**: The Oracle system of the future will run an entire corporate enterprise on a two server system consisting of a main server and a geographically distant failover server, which provides both failover and disaster recovery.

- **Changing role of the DBA**: A single DBA will be able to manage dozens of Oracle instances in a consolidated environment. This is reminiscent of the 1980s, when the DBA for a large corporation was required to have credentials, including advanced degrees and skills far exceeding those of the typical Oracle DBA of the late 1990s.

Having experienced the huge wave of demand for Oracle DBAs in the early 1990s as the direct result of server deconsolidation, many DBAs would welcome the return to the old days where they could manage dozens of Oracle instances within a single server environment.

The next step is to take a look at disk tuning issues with Oracle and see how the new AWR and ASH views can help.

Disk Tuning with Oracle

"Yeah, It looks like a hot disk problem".

Monitoring Disk Performance

Monitoring disk performance is getting more and more difficult with each improvement to disk technology. In the days when DBAs ran single disks and spread their files across them, it was easy to pinpoint the location of the hot drives needing to be fixed.

Now with striping, plaiding, and other even more esoteric technologies, it can be nearly impossible to track a single hot disk without resorting to the vendor supplied tools.

In this chapter, the use of the *dba_hist* tables for locating disk I/O-related problems will be presented. The use of AWR for time-based tracking of disk I/O will be explored as well as how the AWR can be used to infer the cause of I/O-related issues.

A logical starting place is with an overview of the basic disk I/O mechanisms followed by a look at the use of the *dba_hist* tables for tracking disk I/O.

Inside Oracle Disk Architecture

Nearly all databases were I/O-bound back in the days of Oracle7. Since most applications are data intensive, the database industry developed all types of elaborate methods for load balancing the I/O subsystem to relieve disk contention

On the IBM mainframes, the DBA could specify the absolute track number for any data file with the absolute track (ABSTR) JCL argument, allowing the mainframe DBA to control placement of the data files on their IBM 3380 disks. Prior to the advent of RAID and the Oracle10g SAME (Stripe and Mirror Everywhere) architecture, the data file placement rules were quite different.

Today's disks still have three sources of delay, and there can be wide variations in disk access speed even though the average disk latency is 8-15 milliseconds. Internally, disks have changed little in the past 40 years. They remain physical mechanisms with spinning platters and mechanical read-write heads. The following list details how disk I/O works at the device level:

Read-write head delay (seek delay): The time required to position the read-write head under the appropriate disk cylinder can consist of 90 percent of disk access time. Be aware that it is especially unwise to place competing files in outermost cylinders. Back in the days of 3350 disks, the DBA could load an ISAM file into a 3350 and literally watch the device shake as the read-write heads swung back and forth.

Data transmission Delay: A huge source of delay for distributed databases and databases on the Internet. For instance, many worldwide Oracle shops use replication techniques and place systems staggered across the world to reduce data transmission time.

Rotational delay: The rotational delay is the speed of rotation divided by two, assuming that a platter will have to spin a half-revolution to access any given track header. Once on the proper cylinder, the read-write heads must wait until the track header passes beneath them.

Indeed, even now these three components of disk access latency exist. Before large data buffer caches and RAID, the DBA had to manually place data files on the disk and monitor I/O patterns to ensure there was no disk contention.

If RAID striping is not in use, the manual disk placement rules remain important. The rules include:

File Placement: On disks greater than 100 gigabytes where the data cannot be cached in the data buffers, the DBA might consider placing high I/O data files in the middle absolute track number to minimize read-write head movement. This is a situation in which the low access data files reside on the inner and outer cylinders of the disk. As shown below, high impact data files should be placed to minimize read-write head movement:

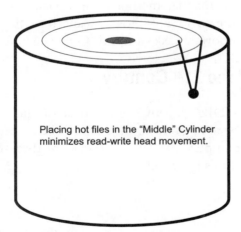

Placing hot files in the "Middle" Cylinder minimizes read-write head movement.

File Striping: High impact data files should extend across many disk drives to spread the load and relieve disk and channel contention:

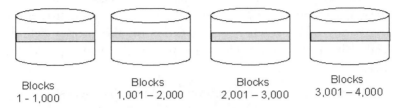

Blocks
1 - 1,000

Blocks
1,001 – 2,000

Blocks
2,001 – 3,000

Blocks
3,001 – 4,000

File Segregation: To relieve contention, the redo files and data files should be placed on separate disk spindles. This is also true for the archived redo log file directory and the undo log files.

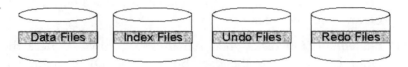

Data Files   Index Files   Undo Files   Redo Files

All of these disk I/O rules still apply even if hardware or software RAID, Solid-state Disk (SSD), or 100 percent data caching are not in use.

With that introduction to the manual methods for Oracle data file management, it is a good time to look at how advances of the past decade have simplified this important task of disk I/O management.

Disk Architectures of the 21st Century

During the 1980s, countless DBAs spent a great deal of their time managing the disk I/O sub-system. Indeed, the manual file placement rules are cumbersome and complex. However, there are three main technologies that have altered this approach:

Solid State Disk

At a cost of about $10k (USD) per gigabyte, the new solid state disks retrieve data hundreds of time faster than traditional disks. Many Oracle shops are using RAM SAN technology for their TEMP tablespace, undo files, and redo log files.

Large RAM Caching

In 64-bit Oracle, the *db_cache_size* is only limited by the server, allowing many shops to run fully cached databases. Prices of RAM should fall in the next five years, such that most systems can be fully cached, thereby making disk management obsolete.

Oracle has a utility called *v$db_cache_advice* that allows the DBA to predict the benefit of adding RAM buffers. This same concept has been incorporated into the Oracle10g Automatic Memory Management (AMM) as shown in Figure 13.1.

P	Size for Estimate (M)	Size Factr	Buffers for Estimate	Est Physical Read Factor	Estimated Physical Reads	
D	88	.1	11,011	1.17	303,724,926	
D	176	.2	22,022	1.08	279,266,295	
D	264	.3	33,033	1.04	269,705,297	
D	352	.4	44,044	1.03	267,659,834	
D	440	.5	55,055	1.03	265,832,346	← 50%
D	528	.6	66,066	1.02	264,201,407	
D	616	.7	77,077	1.02	263,383,442	
D	704	.8	88,088	1.01	262,127,570	
D	792	.9	99,099	1.01	260,556,789	
D	**856**	**1.0**	**107,107**	**1.00**	**258,904,392**	**←100%**
D	880	1.0	110,110	1.00	258,519,097	
D	968	1.1	121,121	0.99	257,297,933	
D	1,056	1.2	132,132	0.99	255,607,306	
D	1,144	1.3	143,143	0.98	254,234,319	
D	1,232	1.4	154,154	0.98	252,440,731	
D	1,320	1.5	165,165	0.97	251,822,046	
D	1,408	1.6	176,176	0.97	251,074,320	
D	1,496	1.7	187,187	0.97	249,856,517	
D	1,584	1.9	198,198	0.96	249,110,957	
D	1,672	2.0	209,209	0.70	182,328,040	←200%
D	1,760	2.1	220,220	0.37	94,912,876	

Figure 13.1: *Output from the v$db_cache_advice utility.*

Oracle estimates the physical reads for different sizes of the *db_cache_size*. In Figure 13.1, it is clear that doubling the *db_cache_size* from 856 to 1,672 will cut disk I/O by more than 80 million disk reads. However, as full-caching is approached, less frequently referenced data becomes cached, and the marginal benefit of caching decreases as shown in Figure 13.2.

The marginal increase in data buffer blocks is asymptotic to disk I/O.

This is a y = 1/x function where:

$$\text{RAM buffers} = \frac{1}{\text{physical reads}}$$

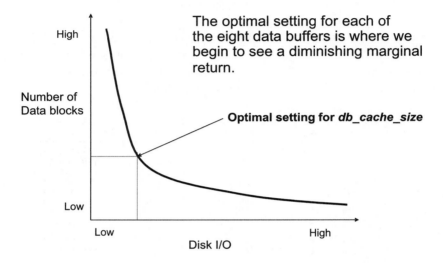

Figure 13.2: *The marginal gains from large RAM caches.*

In Figure 13.2, as full data caching is approached, the marginal advantage of blocks to *db_cache_size* decreases. With the Automatic Memory Management (AMM) feature in Oracle10g, Oracle can be used to track the usage of RAM within the *shared_pool_size, pga_aggregate_target* and *db_cache_size*. In addition, Oracle10g will automatically adjust the sizes of these SGA regions based on current usage.

Full details on tuning the RAM data buffers are available in the chapter on Instance Tuning with AWR. Now, it is time to take a look at the influence of RAID on Oracle databases.

RAID Technology

The need for the DBA to manually stripe data files across multiple disk spindles has been lessened with the advent of hardware and software RAID. The two most common levels of RAID are RAID 10 (mirroring and striping) and RAID 5.

For all systems experiencing significant updates, Oracle recommends using SAME (Stripe and Mirror Everywhere, a.k.a., RAID 1+0) due to the update penalty with RAID 5 architectures. The SAME approach is the foundation of the Oracle10g Automatic Storage Management (ASM) approach.

The Horrors of RAID 5

Many disk vendors persist in pushing RAID 5 as a viable solution for highly updated systems even though using RAID 5 for an Oracle system with a high update rate can be disastrous to performance.

In short, it is clearly troublesome for any company with high volumes of updates to use RAID 5, and the goal of Oracle10g with Automatic Storage Management (ASM) is to urge Oracle customers to use RAID 1+0.

The Oracle DBA will nevertheless be concerned about their most critical performance area, the disk I/O sub-system, until such time that solid-state disks are cheap enough to fully cache large databases. The main points of this section include the following:

- The old-fashion file placement rules still apply if RAID is not being used, and Oracle data files must be manually placed across the disk spindles to relieve I/O contention.

- RAID 5 is not recommended for high update Oracle systems. The performance penalty from the parity checking will greatly diminish Oracle performance.

- Using a RAID 10 approach (striping and mirroring) distributes data blocks across all of the disk spindles, making hot disks a random and transient event.

- Oracle10g continues to expand support for very large RAM data buffers and buffer monitoring with the *v$db_cache_advice* utility and Oracle10g Automatic Memory Management (AMM).

- Improving disk access speed will not help if disk is not the source of the bottleneck. The top-5 STATSPACK wait events should be checked to ensure that disk I/O is the bottleneck prior to undergoing expensive changes to the disk I/O subsystem.

- Many Oracle customers are using solid-state disk for high I/O data files such as TEMP, UNDO, and REDO files. Solid-state disk is becoming less expensive and may soon replace traditional disk devices.

In sum, Oracle DBAs must be steadfast in attempting to understand their disk I/O sub-system and making sure that disk I/O does not impede the high performance of their systems.

RAID 5 can be deadly for high-update databases!

Even with lots of caching, the goal of almost all Oracle tuning activities is to reduce I/O. Tuning the instance parameters, sizing the library cache, tuning SQL statements all have the common focus of reducing I/O. Even when physical disk I/O (POI) is minimized, logical I/O (LIO) is still a major contributor to response time. Even fully cached databases will run slowly if sub-optimal SQL statements force thousands of unnecessary LIOs against the buffer cache.

Time and time again, DBAs spend time and energy tuning a component of their database that is not a top wait event, and they are surprised to find that their change did not make a huge difference in performance. For example, a faster CPU does not help an I/O-bound system, and moving to faster disk does not help a CPU-bound system.

All Oracle databases have some physical constraint, and it is not always disk. The best way to find the constraints for the system is to examine the top five wait events on the STATSPACK report.

The system is disk I/O bound if the majority of the wait time is spent accessing data blocks. This can be *db file sequential read* waits, usually index access, and *db file scattered read* waits, usually full-table scans:

```
Top 5 Timed Events

                                                 % Total
Event                          Waits          Ela Time
----------------------------   ------------   -----------  --------
db file sequential read           2,598          48.54
db file scattered read           25,519          22.04
library cache load lock             673           9.26
CPU time                             44           7.83
log file parallel write          19,157           5.68
```

Once the determination has been made that the Oracle database is I/O-bound, the DBA should get a full grasp on the internals of disk devices, layers of caching, and the configuration of disk controllers and physical disk spindles.

An I/O bottleneck may also manifest itself with high CPU run queue values combined with high idle times.

```
SERVER_NAME     date       hour   runq   pg_in pg_ot   usr   sys   idl
-------------   -------    -----   ----   ----- ----    ----- ----- ----
CSS-HP1         04/06/15    22     10     4     0       11    2     87
CSS-HP1         04/06/15    09      9     4     0       11    2     87
CSS-HP1         04/06/14    22     10     2     0       46    6     50
CSS-HP1         04/06/14    07      9     4     0       10    2     88
```

Normally, a high *vmstat* run queue, where the run queue values exceed the number of CPUs on the server, indicates CPU overload. However, when combined with high CPU idle times, the run queue values indicate that the CPU is backed up waiting for I/O to complete.

Oracle and Direct I/O

Many Oracle shops are plagued with slow I/O intensive databases, and this tip is for anyone whose top 5 timed events shows disk I/O as a major event:

```
Top 5 Timed Events
                                                % Total
Event                          Waits            Ela Time
----------------------------  -----------      -----------  -----------
db file sequential read         2,598             48.54
db file scattered read         25,519             22.04
library cache load lock           673              9.26
CPU time                        2,154              7.83
log file parallel write        19,157              5.68
```

This tip is important if there are reads waits in the top-5 timed events. If disk I/O is not the bottleneck, then making it faster will not improve performance.

Direct I/O is an OS-level solution, and often I/O-bound Oracle databases can be fixed by tuning the SQL to reduce unnecessary large-table full-table scans. File I/O can be monitored using the AWR *dba_hist_filestatxs* table or the STATSPACK *stats$filestatxs* table.

For optimal disk performance, Oracle should always use direct I/O to its data files, bypassing any caching at the OS layer. Direct I/O must be enabled both in Oracle and in the operating system.

Oracle controls direct I/O with a parameter named *filesystemio_options*. According to the Oracle documentation, the *filesystemio_options* parameter must be set to TRUE or DIRECTIO in order for Oracle to read data blocks directly from disk:

Using DIRECTIO allows the enhancement of I/O through the bypassing of the redundant OS block buffers, reading the data block directly into the Oracle SGA. Using direct I/O also allows the creation of multiple blocksized tablespaces to improve I/O performance.

Checking the Server Direct I/O Option

Methods for configuring the OS will vary depending on the operating system and file system in use. The following sections contain some examples of quick checks that anyone can perform to ensure that direct I/O is in use.

Enabling Direct I/O with Kernel Parameters

Oracle recommends that all database files use Direct I/O, which is a disk access method that bypasses the additional overhead on the OS buffer. One important exception to this rule is the archived redo log filesystem which should use OS buffer caching. The following information details the method for ensuring that the OS uses Direct I/O:

Direct I/O for Windows

The Windows OS requires no special configuration to ensure that the database files use Direct I/O.

Direct I/O for IBM AIX

The *filesystemio_options* initialization parameter should be set to configure a database to use either direct I/O or concurrent I/O when accessing datafiles, depending on the file system that is used to store them.

Specification of the value SETALL for this parameter ensures that:

- Datafiles on a JFS file system are accessed using direct I/O

- Datafiles on a JFS2 file system are accessed using concurrent I/O

In Oracle 9i Server Release 2, *filesystemio_options* was a hidden parameter. Starting with 10g, the parameter is externally available.

filesystemio_options can be set to any of the following values:

- ASYNCH: Set by default. This allows asynchronous I/O to be used where supported by the OS.

- DIRECTIO: This allows direct I/O to be used where supported by the OS. Direct I/O bypasses any UNIX buffer cache.

- SETALL: Enables both ASYNC and DIRECT I/O.

- NONE: This disables ASYNC I/O and DIRECT I/O so that Oracle uses normal synchronous writes, without any direct I/O options.

Direct I/O for Linux

Direct I/O support is not available and is not supported on Red Hat Enterprise Linux 2.1 and UnitedLinux. It is available and is supported on Red Hat Enterprise Linux 3 also over NFS, if the driver being used on the system supports *varyio*. To enable direct I/O support:

- Set the *filesystemio_options* parameter in the parameter file to DIRECTIO (*filesystemio_options* = DIRECTIO)

- If the asynchronous I/O option is in use, the *filesystemio_options* parameter in the parameter file should be set to SETALL.

Also with 10g, this feature is already working which means that is does not require any patch. For Oracle9i, the DBA will need to download <patch:2448994> - Abstract: DIRECT IO SUPPORT OVER NFS

Direct I/O for Sun Solaris

The focus should be the FORCEDIRECTIO option. Oracle DBAs claim this option makes a tremendous difference in I/O speed for Sun servers.

Direct I/O for Veritas

For Veritas VxFS, including HP-UX, Solaris, and AIX Veritas, for the following setting should be used: *convosync*=direct. It is also possible to enable direct I/O on a per file basis using Veritas QIO. Refer to the QIOSTAT command and corresponding manual page for hints.

Oracle Blocksize and Disk I/O

By now, the importance of multiple block sizes and multiple RAM caches should be clear. Understanding the salient issues associated with block sizes enables the DBA to intelligently assign block sizes to tables and indexes.

The DBA should also realize that tuning changes are never permanent, and he or she can experiment with different block sizes and with moving tables from one tablespace to another. For example, if the I/O increases after a table is moved into a 2K tablespace, it can simply be moved into a larger sized tablespace. In the final analysis, minimizing I/O by adjusting block sizes is a long, iterative process.

The list below is a summary of rules for sizing objects into tablespaces of multiple block sizes:

Some index access likes large block sizes: B-tree indexes with frequent index range scans perform best in the largest supported block size. This facilitates retrieval of as many index nodes as possible with a single I/O, especially for SQL during index range scans. Some indexes do not perform range scans, so the DBA should make sure to identify the right indexes.

Use average row length: A tablespace should always have a larger block size than the average row length of the tables that reside in the tablespace as noted by the *avg_row_len column* in the *dba_tables* view. Excessive I/O is incurred when the block size is smaller than the average row length due to row chaining.

Use large blocks for data sorting: In some cases, the TEMP tablespace will also benefit from the largest supported block size. Large blocks allow disk sorting with a minimum of disk I/O.

The blocksize is especially important for Oracle indexes because the blocksize affects the b-tree structure and the amount of physical I/O required to fetch a *rowid*.

Oracle Blocksize & Index I/O

Within the Oracle index, each data block serves as a node in the index tree, with the bottom nodes or leaf blocks containing pairs of symbolic keys and *rowid* values. Oracle controls the allocation of pointers within each data block to properly manage the blocks. As an Oracle tree grows by inserting rows into the table, Oracle fills the block. When the block is full, it splits, creating new index nodes or data blocks to manage the symbolic keys within the index. Therefore, an Oracle index block may contain two types of pointers:

- *rowid* pointers to specific table rows

- Pointers to other index nodes

The freelist relink threshold for indexes, the *pctused* value, cannot be specified because Oracle manages the allocation of pointers within index blocks. By studying an index block structure, it is possible to see that the number of entries within each index node is a function of two values:

- The blocksize for the index tablespace

- The length of the symbolic key

The blocksize affects the number of keys within each index block, hence the blocksize will have an effect on the structure of the index tree. All else being equal, large 32K blocksizes will have more index keys resulting in a flatter index structure.

In any event, there appears to be evidence that block size affects the tree structure, which supports the argument that the size of the data blocks affects the structure of the Oracle index tree.

Do large index blocks actually help performance? A small but enlightening test can reveal the answer to that question. The following query for the test will be used against a 9i database that has a database block size of 8K, but also has the 16K cache enabled along with a 16K tablespace:

```
select
    count(*)
from
    scott.hospital
where
    patient_id between 1 and 40000;
```

The SCOTT.HOSPITAL table has 150,000 rows and has an index built on the *patient_id* column. An EXPLAIN of the query shows it uses an index fast full scan to manifest the desired end result:

```
Execution Plan
----------------------------------------------------------
0      SELECT STATEMENT Optimizer=CHOOSE
1      (Cost=41 Card=1 Bytes=4)
   1    0    SORT (AGGREGATE)
   2    1       INDEX (FAST FULL SCAN) OF 'HOSPITAL_PATIENT_ID'
               (NON-UNIQUE) (Cost=41 Card=120002 Bytes=480008)
```

Executing the query twice, to eliminate parse activity and to cache any data with the index residing in a standard 8K tablespace produces these runtime statistics:

```
Statistics
----------------------------------------------------
        0   recursive calls
        0   db block gets
      421   consistent gets
        0   physical reads
        0   redo size
      371   bytes sent via SQL*Net to client
      430   bytes received via SQL*Net from client
        2   SQL*Net roundtrips to/from client
        0   sorts (memory)
        0   sorts (disk)
        1   rows processed
```

To quiz the competency of the new 16K cache and 16K tablespace, the index used by the query will be rebuilt into the 16K tablespace, which has the exact same aspects as the original 8K tablespace, except for the larger blocksize:

```
alter index
    scott.hospital_patient_id
    rebuild nologging noreverse tablespace indx_16k;
```

When the index is lodged firmly into the 16K tablespace, the query is re-executed, again twice, with the following runtime statistics being produced:

```
Statistics
----------------------------------------------------
        0   recursive calls
        0   db block gets
      211   consistent gets
        0   physical reads
        0   redo size
      371   bytes sent via SQL*Net to client
      430   bytes received via SQL*Net from client
        2   SQL*Net roundtrips to/from client
        0   sorts (memory)
        0   sorts (disk)
        1   rows processed
```

Simply by using the new 16K tablespace and accompanying 16K data cache, the amount of logical reads has been reduced by half. Most assuredly, the benefits of properly using the new data caches and multi-block tablespace feature of Oracle9i and later, are worth examination and trials in a database.

Not all Indexes are used in Range Scans

When deciding to segregate indexes into larger blocksizes it is important to understand that those indexes that are subject to frequent index range scans and fast-full scans will benefit the most from a larger blocksize.

When Oracle joins two tables together with a nested loop, only one of the indexes may be accessed as a range. The optimizer always performs an index range scan on one index, gathers the *rowid* values, and does fetch by *rowid* on the matching rows in the other table. For example:

```
select
   customer_name,
   order_date
from
   customer
   orders
where
   customer.cust_key = orders.cust_key;
```

The Oracle documentation notes *"In a nested loop join, for every row in the outer row set, the inner row set is accessed to find all the matching rows to join. Therefore, in a nested loop join, the inner row set is accessed as many times as the number of rows in the outer row set."*

Oracle will only scan one index, build a set of keys, and then probe the rows from the other table. Refer to Figure 13.3.

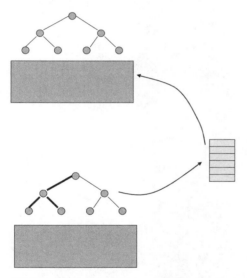

Figure 13.3: *Table joins include index range scans and index unique scans*

So, if this nested loop never uses the customer index, why is it there? The answer is, for index unique scans. In an index unique scan, a single row is accessed within the index, as seen in this query:

```
select
   customer_last_name,
   customer_address
from
   customer
where
   cust_key = 123;
```

In sum, the DBA must find out how their indexes are being used by the SQL. An index that never experiences range scans would not benefit from a larger blocksize. The question becomes one of finding those indexes that experience lots of range scans, and AWR can help.

It is possible to identify those indexes with the most index range scans with the following simple AWR script.

```
col c1 heading 'Object|Name'         format a30
col c2 heading 'Option'              format a15
col c3 heading 'Index|Usage|Count'   format 999,999

select
  p.object_name c1,
  p.options      c2,
  count(1)       c3
from
   dba_hist_sql_plan p,
   dba_hist_sqlstat  s
where
   p.object_owner <> 'SYS'
and
   p.options like '%RANGE SCAN%'
and

   p.operation like '%INDEX%'
and
   p.sql_id = s.sql_id
group by
   p.object_name,
   p.operation,
   p.options
order by
  1,2,3;
```

The following is the output showing overall total counts for each object and table access method.

```
                                           Index
Object                                     Usage
Name                       Option          Count
-------------------------  --------------  --------
CUSTOMER_CHECK             RANGE SCAN        4,232
AVAILABILITY_PRIMARY_KEY   RANGE SCAN        1,783
CON_UK                     RANGE SCAN          473
CURRENT_SEVERITY           RANGE SCAN          323
CWM$CUBEDIMENSIONUSE_IDX   RANGE SCAN           72
ORDERS_FK                  RANGE SCAN           20
```

This will quickly identify indexes that will benefit the most from a 32k blocksize.

This index list can be double verified by using the AWR to identify indexes with high disk reads during each AWR snapshot period. The sample script below exposes the top five tables accessed mostly heavily by physical disk reads for every snapshot interval:

```
col c0 heading 'Begin|Interval|time'  format a8
col c1 heading 'Table|Name'           format a20
col c2 heading 'Disk|Reads'           format 99,999,999
col c3 heading 'Rows|Processed'       format 99,999,999

select
*
from (
select
     to_char(s.begin_interval_time,'mm-dd hh24') c0,
     p.object_name c1,
     sum(t.disk_reads_total) c2,
     sum(t.rows_processed_total) c3,
     DENSE_RANK() OVER (PARTITION BY
to_char(s.begin_interval_time,'mm-dd hh24') ORDER BY
SUM(t.disk_reads_total) desc) AS rnk
from
  dba_hist_sql_plan p,
  dba_hist_sqlstat t,
  dba_hist_snapshot s
where
   p.sql_id = t.sql_id
and
   t.snap_id = s.snap_id
and
   p.object_type like '%TABLE%'
group by
   to_char(s.begin_interval_time,'mm-dd hh24'),
   p.object_name
order by
c0 desc, rnk
)
where rnk <= 5
;
```

The following is the sample output from the above script:

```
Begin
Interval  Table                    Disk        Rows
time      Name                     Reads   Processed        RNK
--------  --------------------  ----------  ----------  ----------
10-29 15  CUSTOMER_CHECK            55,732     498,056           1
10-29 15  CON_UK                   18,368     166,172           2
10-29 15  CURRENT_SEVERITY         11,727     102,545           3
10-29 15  ORDERS_FK                 5,876      86,671           4
10-29 15  SYN$                      2,624      23,674           5

10-29 14  CUSTOMER_CHECK           47,756     427,762           1
10-29 14  CON_UK                   15,939     142,878           2
10-29 14  CURRENT_SEVERITY          6,976     113,649           3
10-29 14  X$KZSRO                   4,772     119,417           4
10-29 14  ORDERS_FK                 2,274      20,292           5

10-29 13  CUSTOMER_CHECK           25,704     213,786           1
10-29 13  CON_UK                    8,568      71,382           2
10-29 13  OBJ$                      3,672      30,474           3
10-29 13  X$KZSRO                   2,448      20,328           4
10-29 13  SYN$                      1,224      10,146           5
```

This report shows the tables with the highest disk reads which is very important information for disk tuning.

The *dba_hist_sql_plan* table can also be used to gather counts about the frequency of participation of objects inside queries. This is a great query to quickly see what's going on between the tables and the SQL that accesses them.

```
col c1  heading 'Object|Name'        format a30
col c2  heading 'Operation'          format a15
col c3  heading 'Option'             format a15
col c4  heading 'Object|Count'       format 999,999

break on c1 skip 2
break on c2 skip 2

select
  p.object_name c1,
  p.operation   c2,
  p.options     c3,
  count(1)      c4
from
  dba_hist_sql_plan p,
  dba_hist_sqlstat  s
where
  p.object_owner <> 'SYS'
```

```
and
    p.sql_id = s.sql_id
group by
    p.object_name,
    p.operation,
    p.options
order by
    1,2,3;
```

The following output shows overall total counts for each object and table access method.

```
Object                                                                   Object
Name                          Operation        Option              Count
----------------------------- ---------------  ---------------   --------
CUSTOMER                      TABLE ACCESS     FULL                   305

CUSTOMER _CHECK               INDEX            RANGE SCAN               2

CUSTOMER_ORDERS               TABLE ACCESS     BY INDEX ROWID         311
CUSTOMER_ORDERS                                FULL                     1

CUSTOMER_ORDERS_PRIMARY       INDEX            FULL SCAN                2
CUSTOMER_ORDERS_PRIMARY                        UNIQUE SCAN            311
AVAILABILITY_PRIMARY_KEY                       RANGE SCAN               4
CON_UK                                         RANGE SCAN               3
CURRENT_SEVERITY_PRIMARY_KEY                   RANGE SCAN               1

CWM$CUBE                      TABLE ACCESS     BY INDEX ROWID           2
CWM$CUBEDIMENSIONUSE                           BY INDEX ROWID           2

CWM$CUBEDIMENSIONUSE_IDX      INDEX            RANGE SCAN               2
CWM$CUBE_PK                                    UNIQUE SCAN              2
CWM$DIMENSION_PK                               FULL SCAN                2

MGMT_INV_VERSIONED_PATCH      TABLE ACCESS     BY INDEX ROWID           3
MGMT_JOB                                       BY INDEX ROWID         458
MGMT_JOB_EMD_STATUS_QUEUE                      FULL                   181
MGMT_JOB_EXECUTION                             BY INDEX ROWID         456

MGMT_JOB_EXEC_IDX01           INDEX            RANGE SCAN             456

MGMT_JOB_EXEC_SUMMARY         TABLE ACCESS     BY INDEX ROWID         180

MGMT_JOB_EXEC_SUMM_IDX04      INDEX            RANGE SCAN             180

MGMT_JOB_HISTORY              TABLE ACCESS     BY INDEX ROWID           1

MGMT_JOB_HIST_IDX01           INDEX            RANGE SCAN               1
MGMT_JOB_PK                                    UNIQUE SCAN            458

MGMT_METRICS                  TABLE ACCESS     BY INDEX ROWID         180
```

Using the output above, it is easy to monitor object participation, especially indexes, in the SQL queries and the mode with which an object was accessed by Oracle.

Why is it important to know how tables and indexes are accessed? Objects that experience multi-block reads may perform faster in a larger blocksize and also reduce SGA overhead.

Using Oracle Multiple Blocksizes

Databases with multiple blocksizes have been around for more than 20 years and were first introduced in the 1980's as a method to segregate and partition data buffers. Once Oracle adopted multiple blocksizes in Oracle9i in 2001, the database foundation for using multiple blocksizes was already a well tested and proven approach. Non-relational databases such as the CA IDMS/R network database have been using multiple blocksizes for nearly two decades.

Originally implemented to support transportable tablespaces, Oracle DBA's quickly realized the huge benefit of multiple blocksizes for improving the utilization and performance of Oracle systems. These benefits fall into several general areas, which are detailed in the following sections.

Reducing data buffer waste

By performing block reads of an appropriate size, the DBA can significantly increase the efficiency of the data buffers. For example, consider an OLTP database that randomly reads 80 byte customer rows. If there is a 16k *db_block_size*, Oracle must read all of the 16k into the data buffer to get the 80 bytes, which is a waste of data buffer resources. If this customer table is migrated into a 2k blocksize, only 2k needs to be read in to get the row data. This results in eight times more available space for random block fetches as shown in Figure 13.4.

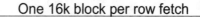

One 16k block per row fetch

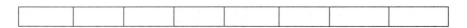

Eight 2k blocks – Same storage area, better utilization

Figure 13.4: *Improvements in data buffer utilization*

Reducing logical I/O

As more and more Oracle databases become CPU-bound as a result of solid-state disks and 64-bit systems with large data buffer caches, minimizing logical I/O consistent gets from the data buffer has become an important way to reduce CPU consumption.

This can be illustrated with indexes. Oracle performs index range scans during many types of operations such as nested loop joins and enforcing row order for result sets with an ORDER BY clause. In these cases, moving Oracle indexes into large blocksizes can reduce both the physical I/O (disk reads) and the logical I/O (buffer gets).

Robin Schumacher has proven in his book *Oracle Performance Troubleshooting* (2003, Rampant TechPress) that Oracle b-tree indexes are built in flatter structures in 32k blocksizes. There is also evidence that bitmap indexes will perform faster in a 32k blocksize.

There is also a huge reduction in logical I/O during index range scans and sorting within the TEMP tablespace because adjacent rows are located inside the same data block as shown in Figure 13.5.

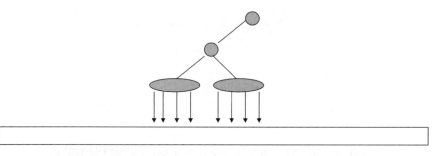

Index Range scan on 32k block – One consistent get

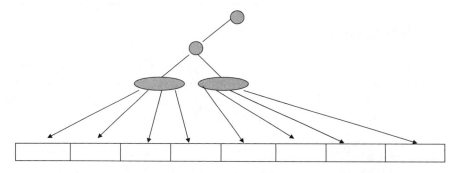

Index Range scan on 2k blocks – Eight consistent gets

Figure 13.5: *Improvements Logical I/O*

Improving data buffer efficiency

One of the greatest problems with very large data buffers is the overhead of Oracle in cleaning out direct blocks that result from truncate operations and high activity DML. This overhead can drive up CPU consumption of databases that have large data buffers as shown in Figure 13.6.

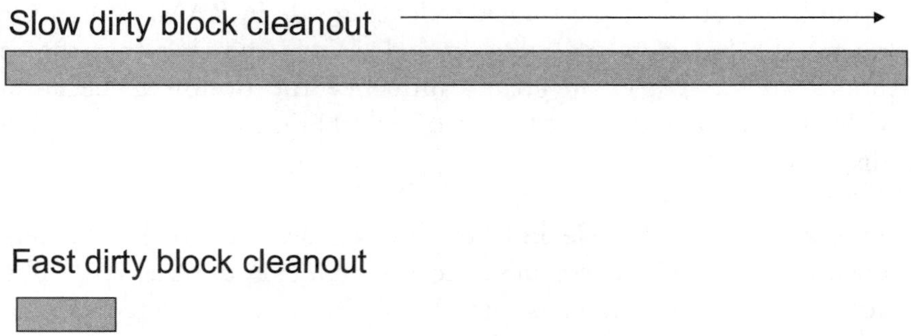

Slow dirty block cleanout ⟶

Fast dirty block cleanout

Figure 13.6: *Dirty Block cleanup in a large vs. small data buffer*

By segregating high activity tables into a separate, smaller data buffer, Oracle has far less RAM frames to scan for dirty block, improving the throughput and also reducing CPU consumption. This is especially important for high update tables with more than 100 row changes per second.

Improving SQL execution plans

Intelligent buffer segregation improves overall execution speed by reducing buffer gets, but there are also some other important reasons to use multiple blocksizes.

In general, the Oracle CBO is unaware of buffer details, except when the *optimizer_index_caching* parameter is set where using multiple data buffers will not impact SQL execution plans. When data using the new *cpu_cost* parameter in Oracle10g, the Oracle SQL optimizer builds the SQL plan decision tree based on the execution plan that will have the lowest estimated CPU cost. For example, if a 32k data buffer is implemented for the index tablespaces, the DBA can ensure that the indexes are cached for optimal performance and minimal logical I/O in range scans.

For example, if a database has 50 gigabytes of index space, a 60 gigabyte *db_32k_cache_size* can be defined and then the *optimizer_index_caching* parameter can be set to 100, telling the SQL optimizer that all of the Oracle indexes reside in RAM. When Oracle makes the index versus table scan decision, knowing that the index nodes are in RAM will greatly influence the optimizer because the CBO knows that a logical I/O is often 100 times faster than a physical disk read.

In sum, moving Oracle indexes into a fully cached 32k buffer will ensure that Oracle favors index access, reducing unnecessary full table scans and greatly reducing logical I/O because adjacent index nodes will reside within the larger, 32k block.

Real World Applications of multiple blocksizes

The use of multiple blocksizes is the most important for very large databases with thousands of updates per second and thousands of concurrent users accessing terabytes of data. In these super large databases, multiple blocksizes have proven to make a huge difference in response time.

The largest benefit of multiple blocksizes can be seen in the following types of databases:

Large OLTP databases: Databases with a large amount of index access (*first_rows optimizer_mode*) and databases with random fetches of small rows are ideal for buffer pool segregation.

64-bit Oracle databases: Oracle databases with 64-bit software can support very large data buffer caches and these are ideal for caching frequently-referenced tables and indexes.

High-update databases: In databases where a small subset of the database receives large update activity (i.e. a single partition within a table) there will be a large reduction in CPU consumption when the high update objects are moved into a smaller buffer cache.

On the other hand, there are specific types of databases that may not benefit from the use of multiple blocksizes:

Small node Oracle10g Grid systems: Since each data blade in an Oracle10g grid node has only two to four gigabytes of RAM, data blade grid applications do not show a noticeable benefit from multiple block sizes.

Solid-state databases: Oracle databases using solid-state disks (RAM-SAN) perform fastest with super small data buffers that are just large enough to hold the Oracle serialization locks and latches.

Decision Support Systems: Large Oracle data warehouses with parallel large table full-table scans do not benefit from multiple blocksizes. Parallel full table scans bypass the data buffers and store the intermediate rows sets in the PGA region. As a general rule, databases with the *all_rows optimizer_mode* may not benefit from multiple blocksizes.

Even though Oracle introduced multiple blocksizes for an innocuous reason, their power has become obvious in very large database systems. The same divide and conquer approach that Oracle has used to support very large databases can also be used to divide and conquer Oracle data buffers.

Setting the *db_block_size* with multiple block sizes

When multiple blocksizes are implemented, the *db_block_size* should be set based on the size of the tablespace where the large object full scans will be occurring. The *db_file_multiblock_read_count* parameter is only applicable for tables/indexes that are full scanned.

With the implementation of multiple blocksizes, Oracle MetaLink notes that the *db_file_multiblock_read_count* should always be set to a value that sums to the largest supported blocksize of 32k:

db_block_size	db_file_multiblock_read_count
2k	16
4k	8
8k	4
16k	2

Table 13.1: *Oracle block size and corresponding read count*

One issue with Oracle multiple block sizes is the setting for *db_file_multiblock_read_count*. This value influences the SQL optimizer about the costs of a full table scan.

 Objects that experience full scans and indexes with frequent range scans might benefit from being placed in a larger block size, with *db_file_multiblock_read_count* set to the block size of that tablespace.

According to Oracle, the following formula can be used for setting *db_file_multiblock_read_count*:

```
                                max I/O chunk size
db_file_multiblock_read_count = -------------------
                                   db_block_size
```

But what is the maximum I/O chunk size? The maximum effective setting for *db_file_multiblock_read_count* is OS and disk dependant. Steve Adams, an independent Oracle performance consultant (www.ixora.com.au), has published a helpful script to assist in setting an appropriate level

💾 multiblock_read_test.sql

```
-------------------------------------------------------------------
--
-- Script:  multiblock_read_test.sql
-- Purpose: find largest actual multiblock read size
--
-- Copyright:      (c) Ixora Pty Ltd
-- Author:  Steve Adams
--
-- Description:This script prompts the user to enter the name of a
-- table to scan, and then does so with a large multiblock read
-- count, and with event 10046 enabled at level 8.  The trace file
-- is then examined to find the largest multiblock
-- read actually performed.
--
-------------------------------------------------------------------

@save_sqlplus_settings

alter session set db_file_multiblock_read_count = 32768;
/
```

```
column value heading "Maximum possible multiblock read count"
select
  value
from
  sys.v_$parameter
where
  name = 'db_file_multiblock_read_count'
/


prompt
@accept Table "Table to scan" SYS.SOURCE$
prompt Scanning ...
set termout off
alter session set events '10046 trace name context forever, level 8'
/
select /*+ full(t) noparallel(t) nocache(t) */ count(*) from &Table
t
/
alter session set events '10046 trace name context off'
/

set termout on


@trace_file_name


prompt
prompt Maximum effective multiblock read count
prompt ----------------------------------------

host sed -n '/scattered/s/.*p3=//p' &Trace_Name | sort -n | tail -1

@restore_sqlplus_settings
```

For more details on using multiple blocksizes, see the book *Creating a Self Tuning Oracle Database* (2004, Rampant TechPress). Here is a handy a script to display the data blocks associated with the data buffers, using the *x$* fixed tables:

```
select
  decode(
   pd.bp_id,
    1,'KEEP',
    2,'RECYCLE',
    3,'DEFAULT',
    4,'2K SUBCACHE',
    5,'4K SUBCACHE',
    6,'8K SUBCACHE',
    7,'16K SUBCACHE',
    8,'32K SUBCACHE',
   'UNKNOWN') subcache,
```

```
    bh.object_name,
    bh.blocks
from
    x$kcbwds ds,
    x$kcbwbpd pd,
    (select /*+ use_hash(x) */
        set_ds,
        o.name object_name,
        count(*) BLOCKS
    from
        obj$ o,
        x$bh x
    where
        o.dataobj# = x.obj
    and
        x.state !=0
    and
        o.owner# !=0
    group by
        set_ds,o.name) bh
where
    ds.set_id >= pd.bp_lo_sid
and
    ds.set_id <= pd.bp_hi_sid
and
    pd.bp_size != 0 and ds.addr=bh.set_ds;
```

The following section will introduce how the new high speed RAM disk (solid-state disk) helps improve disk I/O throughput.

Reducing disk I/O with SSD

As RAM storage becomes cheaper than ever, many companies are exploring the issue of fully cached Oracle databases. As noted in an earlier Oracle tip, solid-state disk is changing the way that Oracle professionals manage and tune their databases.

One of the issues is the relatively high cost of fetching an Oracle data block from disk. In theory, RAM is 10,000 times faster than disk with speeds in the milliseconds versus nanoseconds; however, when the overhead of lock serialization and latches is added in, a logical I/O might be less than a thousand times faster than a physical disk I/O.

SSD is especially useful for Oracle undo logs, redo logs and the TEMP tablespace, but it can be used with any Oracle data file for high-speed access. In a real world setting, SSD has been used to set a new record for table load rates, using SQL*Loader to get over 500,000 rows per second into a table! Yes, that is 30 million rows per minute!

Oracle speeds are very high with SSD, and SSD is cheap too at only $1k/gig USD. The existing TPC-C benchmark is always under challenge in hopes of setting the new world record by exceeding one million transactions per minute using Oracle9i with SSD.

Companies such as Texas Memory Systems are offering solid-state disk replacement for the Oracle data buffer cache to speed up I/O at the physical level. Companies such as UNISYS are getting blistering performance from Oracle using 100 gigabyte *db_cache_size* and *db_keep_cache_size*.

The following section will provide scripts for real time Oracle disk monitoring and then move on into information on the AWR and ASH tables as they relate to Oracle disk I/O.

Oracle Disk Monitoring

Everyone has better things to do than sit around and run disk performance scripts. The process can be automated using scripts and the *cron tab* in UNIX and Linux. A simple web search using any search tool of choice, one can find any number of shell, perl and other scripts to monitor using *iostat, vmstat* and *sar*.

Rather than recreating the wheel, the web can be used to find examples of scripts. Mike Ault's book, *Oracle Disk I/O Tuning* (2004, Rampant TechPress), also provides a plethora of scripts and examples.

Tuning professionals have noted that the primary bottleneck is disk I/O for the vast majority of non-scientific systems. Back in the days before RAID and giant *db_cache_size*, the DBA had to manually load balance the disk I/O subsystem to relieve contention on the disks and the disk controllers.

However, is it really important to find a hot disk? Unless the system is running in single disk sets (*jbod* technology), specific knowledge about a hot disk is not quite as important. However, the DBA should still be interested in disk performance and tracking data file and other I/O involved in databases. The database administrator and system manager must still monitor I/O, either through Oracle, through the OS, or via performance monitoring tools provided by the disk array or storage system software vendors such as Veritas.

Many DBAs would like to believe that this disk technology has changed. Unfortunately, the only major changes to disk technology since the 1970s are these hardware and software changes:

Large data buffers: Today the DBA can cache large portions of the data blocks in the *db_cache_size* reducing disk I/O.

Disks with on-board cache: Many of the newer disks have an on-board RAM cache to hold the most frequently referenced data blocks.

RAID: The randomizing of data blocks with RAID 1+0 and RAID 5 for low-write systems has removed the need for disk load balancing by scrambling the data blocks across many disk spindles. In Oracle10g, the Automatic Storage Management (ASM) feature requires Stripe and Mirror Everywhere (SAME) which is essentially RAID 1+0 and RAID-10.

Other than these advances, basic disk technology has not changed since the 1970s. The Oracle DBA must remember that disk I/O remains an important issue and understand the internals of disk management to maximize the performance of their I/O-bound systems.

When Oracle monitoring is used, at least in 9i and lower versions, DBAs were somewhat limited in what monitoring could be performed. Total I/O since startup and I/O/second since startup can be captured. This information could be acquired on a per datafile or tempfile basis. The *v$filestat* and *v$tempstat* dynamic performance views provide the I/O statistics from Oracle's point of view.

Examining Real-time Disk Statistics

The following scripts can be run anytime against the dynamic *v$* performance views to get a summary of instance wide activity for the database. Knowing the locations of the databases' storage level hot spots is beneficial for a several reasons:

- By viewing I/O statistics at the tablespace and datafile levels, the DBA can get a feel for overworked physical disks. Should a particular disk or set of disks be under too much strain, the tablespaces can be relocated to less used devices or create new tablespaces on different disks and move hot objects into them, if extra disks are available.

- The I/O statistics can be viewed for that tablespace to see if the indexes are actually being used if the users have followed standard DBA practice and placed indexes in their own tablespace.

To get a feel for physical I/O at the tablespace and datafile level, the following query can be used with Oracle 7.3.4 through 8.0:

```
select
   d.name file_name,
   c.name tablespace_name,
   b.phyrds,
   b.phywrts,
   b.phyblkrd,
   b.phyblkwrt,
   b.readtim,
   b.writetim
from
   sys.v_$datafile a,
   sys.v_$filestat b,
   sys.ts$ c,
   sys.v_$dbfile d,
   sys.file$ e
where
   a.file# = b.file#
and
   a.file# = d.file#
and
   e.ts# = c.ts#
 and
   e.file# = d.file#
 order by
   b.phyrds desc;
```

When using Oracle 8i or higher, this query can be used since these versions of Oracle have temp files in addition to regular datafiles:

```
select
   d.name file_name,
   c.name tablespace_name,
   b.phyrds,
   b.phywrts,
   b.phyblkrd,
   b.phyblkwrt,
   b.readtim,
   b.writetim
from
   sys.v_$datafile a,
   sys.v_$filestat b,
   sys.ts$ c,
   sys.v_$dbfile d,
   sys.file$ e
 where
   a.file# = b.file#
 and
   a.file# = d.file#
 and
   e.ts# = c.ts#
 and
   e.file# = d.file#
union all
select
   v.fnnam file_name,
   c.name tablespace_name,
   b.phyrds,
   b.phywrts,
   b.phyblkrd,
   b.phyblkwrt,
   b.readtim,
   b.writetim
from
   sys.v_$tempfile a,
   sys.v_$tempstat b,
   sys.ts$ c,
   sys.x$kccfn v,
   sys.x$ktfthc hc
where
   a.file# = b.file#
and
   a.file# = hc.ktfthctfno
and
   hc.ktfthctsn = c.ts#
and
   v.fntyp = 7
and
   v.fnnam is not null
and
   v.fnfno = hc.ktfthctfno
and
```

```
  hc.ktfthctsn = c.ts#
order by
  3 desc;
```

Output from the queries above might look like the WISE screens represented in Figure 13.7:

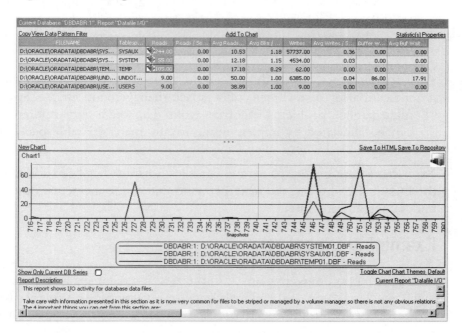

Figure 13.7: *Datafile and tablespace I/O details*

The following are a few areas to consider when examining the output of these queries:

- When temporary tablespaces devoted to sort activity show higher volumes of physical I/O, it could indicate a problem with excessive disk activity.

- If there are underutilized disk drives with their own controllers, consideration should be given to relocating some tablespaces that exhibit high I/O characteristics to those drives. The physical I/O for each drive/file system should be quickly reviewed in order to get a feel for the overworked disks on the server.

- Too much activity in the SYSTEM tablespace and datafiles may indicate a lot of recursive calls (space management, etc.). Space management problems incurred from data dictionary references can be alleviated by implementing locally managed tablespaces in Oracle8i and higher.

Now that locating tablespaces and datafiles hotspots has been added to the DBA's list of tools, the next step is to determine the actual objects under constant pressure.

Examining Global I/O

The first step in unraveling any I/O puzzles in a database is to make a quick check of some of the global database I/O metrics. A query such as the script that follows can be used to get a bird's eye view of a database's I/O:

```
select
   name,
   value
from
   sys.v_$sysstat
where
   name in
     ('consistent changes',
      'consistent gets',
      'db block changes',
      'db block gets',
      'physical reads',
      'physical writes',
      'sorts (disk)',
      'user commits',
      'user rollbacks'
     )
  order by
1;
```

The script queries the *sys.v_$sysstat* view and output from the query might look like the following:

```
NAME                        VALUE
---------------------------  -----
consistent changes              1
consistent gets             70983
db block changes              243
db block gets                 612
physical reads              11591
physical writes                52
sorts (disk)                    0
user commits                   26
user rollbacks                  1
```

Although there are some database experts who do not believe the buffer cache hit ratio is of much value anymore, a cursory check can still be performed to get an idea of overall disk I/O activity by using this script:

```
select
    100 -
    100 *
       (round ((sum (decode (name, 'physical reads',
       value, 0))
          -
       sum (decode (name, 'physical reads direct',
       value, 0)) -
          sum (decode (name,
       'physical reads direct (lob)',
          value, 0))) /
          (sum (decode (name, 'session logical reads',
          value, 1))
          ),3)) hit_ratio
 from
    sys.v_$sysstat
where
    name in
    ('session logical reads',
    'physical reads direct (lob)',
    'physical reads',
    'physical reads direct');
```

This script also queries the *sys.v_$sysstat* view and some quick items to look for in the statistics include:

- Increasing numbers of physical reads and a low hit ratio may indicate insufficient settings for *db_block_buffers* or *db_cache_size*.

The hit ratio reading, in particular, should be observed over a time period sufficient to see if the ratio is representative of the database's personality. Readings below the normal rule of thumb of 90% can be OK.

- High volumes of disk sorts could be indicative of a too low setting for *sort_area_size* (Oracle8i and below) or unnecessary sort activities. Large numbers of user rollbacks can be undesirable, since it indicates that user transactions are not completing for one reason or another.

The *fileio.sql* script listed below shows an example select statement to generate both regular and temporary file IO.

🖫 fileio.sql

```
--  ****************************************************
--  Copyright © 2005 by Rampant TechPress
--  This script is free for non-commercial purposes
--  with no warranties.  Use at your own risk.
--
--  To license this script for a commercial purpose,
--  contact info@rampant.cc
--  ****************************************************

rem
rem NAME: fileio.sql
rem
rem FUNCTION: Reports on the file io status of all of the
rem FUNCTION: datafiles in the database.

rem
column sum_io1 new_value st1 noprint
column sum_io2 new_value st2 noprint
column sum_io new_value divide_by noprint
column Percent format 999.999 heading 'Percent|Of IO'
column brratio format 999.99 heading 'Block|Read|Ratio'
column bwratio format 999.99 heading 'Block|Write|Ratio'
column phyrds heading 'Physical | Reads'
column phywrts heading 'Physical | Writes'
column phyblkrd heading 'Physical|Block|Reads'
column phyblkwrt heading 'Physical|Block|Writes'
column name format a45 heading 'File|Name'
column file# format 9999 heading 'File'
column dt new_value today noprint
select to_char(sysdate,'ddmonyyyyhh24miss') dt from dual;
set feedback off verify off lines 132 pages 60 sqlbl on trims on
rem
select
    nvl(sum(a.phyrds+a.phywrts),0) sum_io1
```

```
from
    sys.v_$filestat a;
select nvl(sum(b.phyrds+b.phywrts),0) sum_io2
from
      sys.v_$tempstat b;
select &st1+&st2 sum_io from dual;
rem
@title132 'File I/O Statistics Report'
spool rep_out\&db\fileio&&today
select
    a.file#,b.name, a.phyrds, a.phywrts,
    (100*(a.phyrds+a.phywrts)/&divide_by) Percent,
    a.phyblkrd, a.phyblkwrt, (a.phyblkrd/greatest(a.phyrds,1))
brratio,
      (a.phyblkwrt/greatest(a.phywrts,1)) bwratio
from
    sys.v_$filestat a, sys.v_$dbfile b
where
    a.file#=b.file#
union
select
    c.file#,d.name, c.phyrds, c.phywrts,
    (100*(c.phyrds+c.phywrts)/&divide_by) Percent,
    c.phyblkrd, c.phyblkwrt,(c.phyblkrd/greatest(c.phyrds,1))
brratio,
      (c.phyblkwrt/greatest(c.phywrts,1)) bwratio
from
    sys.v_$tempstat c, sys.v_$tempfile d
where
    c.file#=d.file#
order by
    1
/
spool off
pause Press enter to continue
set feedback on verify on lines 80 pages 22
clear columns
ttitle off
```

The output from the above script is shown below. This report is important because it shows the percent of total I/O for each datafile.

```
Date: 11/09/03
Page:   1
Time: 01:24 PM                                          File I/O Statistics Report
PERFSTAT
                                                          testdb database


Physical   Physical   Block   Block
    File                                       Physical   Physical   Percent
Block     Block     Read    Write
 File Name                                     Reads      Writes     Of I/O
Reads     Writes   Ratio   Ratio
-----   ------------------------------------------------  ----------  ----------  --------  --------
--  ----------  -------  -------
    1  /data001/oradata/testdb/system01.dbf        27396       2992    53.526
55735      2992    2.03    1.00
```

```
        1 /data001/oradata/testdb/temp01.dbf          1703      1357     5.390
7184       7177    4.22     5.29
        2 /data001/oradata/testdb/undotbs01.dbf        151     18034    32.032
151       18034    1.00     1.00
        3 /data001/oradata/testdb/drsys01.dbf          116       107      .393
116         107    1.00     1.00
        4 /data001/oradata/testdb/indx01.dbf           117       107      .395
117         107    1.00     1.00
        5 /data001/oradata/testdb/tools01.dbf          890      1403     4.039
1137       1403    1.28     1.00
        6 /data001/oradata/testdb/users01.dbf          115       107      .391
115         107    1.00     1.00
        7 /data001/oradata/testdb/xdb01.dbf            183       107      .511
194         107    1.06     1.00
        8 /data001/oradata/testdb/olof_data01.dbf     1045       620     2.933
1242        620    1.19     1.00
        9 /data001/oradata/testdb/olof_idx01.dbf       116       107      .393
116         107    1.00     1.00
```

Another important measurement is the actual timing. On some systems and some disk subsystems, the I/O timing data can be bad, so it should always be compared against actual *iostat* numbers. An example I/O timing report is shown below.

```
Date: 11/21/03
Page:   1
Time: 09:56 AM                              I/O Timing Analysis
PERFSTAT
                                              testdb database

      FILE# NAME                                                        PHYRDS     PHYWRTS
READTIM/PHYRDS WRITETIM/PHYWRTS
---------- ------------------------------------------------------ ---------- ----------
-------------- ----------------
          5 /oracle/oradata/testdb/tools01_01.dbf                       318        153
.377358491         .150326797
          1 /oracle/oradata/testdb/system01.dbf                        3749        806
.332622033        2.3101737
          9 /oracle/oradata/testdb/tcmd_data01_03.dbf                442389       1575
.058064283        6.90095238
          8 /oracle/oradata/testdb/tcmd_data01_02.dbf                540596       2508
.057647485        5.11961722
          7 /oracle/oradata/testdb/tcmd_data01_01.dbf              14446868       1177
.036516842        2.62531861
         10 /oracle/oradata/testdb/tcmd_idx01_02.dbf                 15694       5342
.035746145        6.50074878
          3 /oracle/oradata/testdb/rbs01_01.dbf                         757      25451
.034346103       10.7960002
         11 /oracle/oradata/testdb/tcmd_data01_04.dbf                  1391        606
.023005032        6.66336634
          6 /oracle/oradata/testdb/tcmd_idx01_01.dbf               1148402      10220
.015289942        6.35831703
          2 /oracle/oradata/testdb/temp01_01.dbf                     34961       8835
0                 0
          4 /oracle/oradata/testdb/users01_01.dbf                       78         76
0                 0

11 rows selected.
```

The output in listing above shows that all of the I/O timing is at or below 10 milliseconds. Normally, this would be considered to be good performance for disks; however, most modern arrays can give sub-millisecond response times by use of caching and by spreading I/O across multiple platters. While many experts say anything less than 10-

20 milliseconds is good, that was based on old disk technology. If the disk system is not giving response times that are at five milliseconds or less, one should consider tuning the I/O subsystems.

Another interesting statistic is the overall I/O rate for the system as it relates to Oracle. This is easily calculated using PL/SQL as shown in the *get_io.sql* script below.

🖫   **get_io.sql**

```
--   ****************************************************
--   Copyright © 2005 by Rampant TechPress
--   This script is free for non-commercial purposes
--   with no warranties.  Use at your own risk.
--
--   To license this script for a commercial purpose,
--   contact info@rampant.cc
--   ****************************************************

set serveroutput on
declare
cursor get_io is select
       nvl(sum(a.phyrds+a.phywrts),0) sum_io1,to_number(null)
sum_io2
from sys.gv_$filestat a
union
select
        to_number(null) sum_io1, nvl(sum(b.phyrds+b.phywrts),0)
sum_io2
from
        sys.gv_$tempstat b;
now date;
elapsed_seconds number;
sum_io1 number;
sum_io2 number;
sum_io12 number;
sum_io22 number;
tot_io number;
tot_io_per_sec number;
fixed_io_per_sec number;
temp_io_per_sec number;
begin
open get_io;
for i in 1..2 loop
fetch get_io into sum_io1, sum_io2;
if i = 1 then sum_io12:=sum_io1;
else
sum_io22:=sum_io2;
end if;
end loop;

select sum_io12+sum_io22 into tot_io from dual;
```

```
select sysdate into now from dual;
select ceil((now-max(startup_time))*(60*60*24)) into elapsed_seconds
from gv$instance;
fixed_io_per_sec:=sum_io12/elapsed_seconds;
temp_io_per_sec:=sum_io22/elapsed_seconds;
tot_io_per_sec:=tot_io/elapsed_seconds;
dbms_output.put_line('Elapsed Sec :'||to_char(elapsed_seconds,
'9,999,999.99'));
dbms_output.put_line('Fixed
IO/SEC:'||to_char(fixed_io_per_sec,'9,999,999.99'));
dbms_output.put_line('Temp IO/SEC :'||to_char(temp_io_per_sec,
'9,999,999.99'));
dbms_output.put_line('Total IO/SEC:'||to_char(tot_io_Per_Sec,
'9,999,999.99'));
end;
/
```

An example of the output from this report is shown below.

```
SQL> @io_sec

Elapsed Sec :     43,492.00
Fixed IO/SEC:        588.33
Temp IO/SEC :         95.01
Total IO/SEC:        683.34

PL/SQL procedure successfully executed
```

By examining the total average IO/SEC for the database, one can determine if the I/O subsystem is capable of handling the load. For example, if the above listing was for a RAID 10 system with 10 disks, in a five-way stripe in a two-way mirror array, then the DBA will know that they don't have any problems with I/O rate:

```
(10 DISKS * 110 IO/SEC/DISK = ~1100 IO/SEC max rate)
```

However, if there are only 6 disks in a RAID5, then there are probably periods when I/O is saturated (5 DISKS * 90 IO/SEC/DISK = ~ 450 IO/SEC max rate). The above I/O rate is an average, which means that if there is an equal distribution about the mean, then 50% of the time the I/O rate was higher than this reported value of 683 IO/SEC.

The other indications of possible I/O related problems with Oracle are examination of I/O related wait events from the wait interface of the Oracle kernel. If the STATSPACK reports or home-grown reports

---

show that any of the following waits are the majority wait on the system, look at tuning the I/O system in relationship to Oracle:

- *db file sequential read:* An event generated during index and other short term read events.

- *db file scattered read:* An event generated during full-table and index scans.

- *db file parallel write:* An event generated during writes to multiple extents across multiple datafiles.

- Log file or control file writes: Events generated during waits to write to a log or control file.

- Direct path read or write: Events generated during hash, sort, global temporary table I/O or other direct operations.

- LGWR waits: Events generated during writes to the redo logs.

These events must be reviewed in relationship to their overall contribution to the total service time. The following is an example Wait Report in Comparison to CPU Time.

```
Date: 02/03/04                                                         Page:    1
Time: 08:31 AM                    System Events Percent                   MAULT
                                    testdb database

                                                          Percent    Percent
                             Total     Average                 Of   of Total
Event Name                   Waits       Waits Time Waited Non-Idle Waits   Uptime
---------------------------- --------- ----------- ------------ --------------- ---------
CPU used when call started           0           0    3,580,091          52.659    3.8499
db file sequential read      9,434,983           0    1,278,929          18.811    1.3753
enqueue                            302       2,899      875,552          12.878     .9415
wait for stopper event to be     1,526         194      295,860           4.352     .3182
increased

db file scattered read         430,041           1      261,103           3.841     .2808
log file parallel write            339         590      199,881           2.940     .2149
db file parallel write          32,240           5      170,070           2.502     .1829
...                                                 ------------
sum                                                    6,798,684
```

So, even if all I/O related wait times in the above report are eliminated, the service time would only be reduced by about 27%. It cannot always be assumed that fixing I/O will give large performance returns. If there are CPU usage issues, adding the fastest disks in the world may not help performance that much. This directs the focus to the major tuning point for any Oracle or other database system: Tune the code first! Make the SQL as optimized as possible for both Logical and Physical IO, then tackle other issues.

The Wait Report shown above was generated using the following script.

💾 wait_report.sql

```
-- *************************************************
-- Copyright © 2005 by Rampant TechPress
-- This script is free for non-commercial purposes
-- with no warranties.  Use at your own risk.
--
-- To license this script for a commercial purpose,
-- contact info@rampant.cc
-- *************************************************

col event          format a30          heading 'Event Name'
col waits          format 999,999,999 heading 'Total|Waits'
col average_wait format 999,999,999 heading 'Average|Waits'
col time_waited  format 999,999,999 heading 'Time Waited'
col total_time new_value divide_by noprint
col value new_value val noprint
col percent format 999.990 heading 'Percent|Of|Non-Idle Waits'
col duration new_value millisec noprint
col p_of_total heading 'Percent|of Total|Uptime' format 999.9999

set lines 132 feedback off verify off pages 50

select to_number(sysdate-startup_time)*86400*1000 duration from
v$instance;

select
sum(time_waited) total_time
from v$system_event
where total_waits-total_timeouts>0
     and event not like 'SQL*Net%'
     and event not like 'smon%'
     and event not like 'pmon%'
     and event not like 'rdbms%'
         and event not like 'PX%'
         and event not like 'sbt%'
         and event not in ('gcs remote message','ges remote
message','virtual circuit status','dispatcher timer') ;

select value from v$sysstat where name ='CPU used when call
started';

@title132 'System Events Percent'

break on report
compute sum of time_waited on report
spool rep_out/&db/sys_events
```

```
select name event,
         0 waits,
   0 average_wait,
   value time_waited,
   value/(&&divide_by+&&val)*100 Percent,
   value/&&millisec*100 p_of_total
from v$sysstat
where name ='CPU used when call started'
union
select event,
       total_waits-total_timeouts waits,
       time_waited/(total_waits-total_timeouts) average_wait,
       time_waited,
       time_waited/(&&divide_by+&&val)*100 Percent,
       time_waited/&&millisec*100 P_of_total
from v$system_event
where total_waits-total_timeouts>0
    and event not like 'SQL*Net%'
    and event not like 'smon%'
    and event not like 'pmon%'
    and event not like 'rdbms%'
        and event not like 'PX%'
        and event not like 'sbt%'
        and event not in ('gcs remote message','ges remote
message','virtual circuit status','dispatcher timer')
        and time_waited>0
order by percent desc
/
spool off
clear columns
ttitle off
clear computes
clear breaks
```

The following section shows how one can track down disk I/O against specific tables and indexes. This can give great insight into the internal operations of the Oracle database application.

Locating Hot I/O Objects

Once the hotspots in the database have been located in relation to storage structures, it is time to drill further down and find the objects that are most in demand. The hub tables in a system will undoubtedly cause a major I/O bottleneck if they are not correctly designed and implemented.

Tracking I/O for specific Tables

If STATSPACK on Oracle9i release 2 or beyond is in use, I/O can be tracked for specific Oracle tables and indexes. This allows the DBA to see the specific sources of physical I/O. In Oracle9i release 2, the most notable enhancements to Oracle STATSPACK are:

- Track reads or writes for specific segments

- Track buffer busy waits by table or index

- Collect historical SQL execution plans using the level 8 snapshot

Using the level 7 STATSPACK collection, it is now possible to track I/O at the individual segment level, showing disk I/O for any Oracle table or index.

```
SQL> execute statspack.snap (i_snap_level=>7,
i_modify_parameter=>'true');
```

A level 7 STATSPACK snapshot collects all segment level statistics, including logical and physical reads, row lock, and buffer busy waits. The ability to track buffer busy waits at the table and index level is especially important for removing segment header contention.

To get an idea of which objects have been the favorite of a database's SQL calls, the following *toptables.sql* query, which retrieves the top 100 objects as determined by SQL statement execution can be run:

🖫 toptables.sql

```
-- ***************************************************
-- Copyright © 2005 by Rampant TechPress
-- This script is free for non-commercial purposes
-- with no warranties.  Use at your own risk.
--
-- To license this script for a commercial purpose,
-- contact info@rampant.cc
-- ***************************************************

select
   table_owner "table owner",
   table_name "table name",
   command "command issued",
   0 - executions    "executions",
```

```
    disk_reads "disk reads",
    gets "buffer gets",
    rows_processed "rows processed"
from
(select
        distinct executions,
                 command,
                 table_owner,
                 table_name,
                 gets,
                 rows_processed,
                 disk_reads
 from
(select
        decode (a.command_type ,
                2, 'insert ' ,
                3, 'select ',
                6, 'update   ' ,
                7, 'delete ' ,
                26,'table lock  ') command ,
                c.owner table_owner,
                c.name table_name ,
                sum(a.disk_reads) disk_reads  ,
                sum(0 - a.executions) executions ,
                sum(a.buffer_gets) gets  ,
                sum(a.rows_processed) rows_processed
 from
        sys.v_$sql                  a ,
        sys.v_$object_dependency b ,
        sys.v_$db_object_cache    c
where
        a.command_type in (2,3,6,7,26)and
        b.from_address = a.address and
        b.to_owner = c.owner and
        b.to_name= c.name and
        c.type = 'table' and
        c.owner not in ('SYS','SYSTEM')
 group by
        a.command_type , c.owner  , c.name )  )
where
        rownum <= 100;
```

Output from the above query might look like this:

	TABLE OWNER	TABLE NAME	COMMAND ISSUED	EXECUTIONS	DISK READS	BUFFER GETS	ROWS PROCESSED
1	ERADMIN	TESTXML_927	SELECT	13	2	131	0
2	ERADMIN	ADMISSION	SELECT	7	13	184	2508
3	ERADMIN	TESTXML_927NEW2	SELECT	4	0	94	0
4	ERADMIN	TESTLOB_NEW	SELECT	2	5	127	2
5	ERADMIN	ADMISSION_TEST	SELECT	1	1	111	0
6	ERADMIN	MEDICATION_DISP	SELECT	1	1	32	0
7	ERADMIN	PATIENT_PROCEDURE	SELECT	1	5	23	0
8	ERADMIN	TESTXML_927NEW	SELECT	1	0	53	3
9	WMSYS	WM$ENV_VARS	SELECT	1	8	403	1
10	WMSYS	WM$VERSIONED_TABLES	SELECT	1	8	403	1
11	WMSYS	WM$VERSION_HIERARCHY_TABLE	SELECT	1	8	403	1

One way to uncover a potential bottleneck for any system is to observe a single table with a lot of DML activity. Other things to consider when reviewing output from this query include:

- Small, regularly-accessed tables should be reviewed as candidates for the Oracle KEEP buffer pool in Oracle8i and higher or be set to CACHE for Oracle7 and higher.

- To determine if they can be partitioned, large tables that are often accessed and scanned should be reviewed. Partitioning can reduce scan times but only one or a handful of partitions can be scanned instead of the entire table.

If the DBA suspects that there are unnecessary large-table full-table scans, suspicions can be validated by making use of the new *v_$sql_plan* view. The following query uses this new view to reveal which large tables, defined in the query as tables over 1MB, are being scanned in the database:

```
select
   table_owner,
   table_name,
   table_type,
   size_kb,
   statement_count,
   reference_count,
   executions,
   executions * reference_count total_scans
from
   (select
       a.object_owner table_owner,
       a.object_name table_name,
       b.segment_type table_type,
       b.bytes / 1024 size_kb,
       sum(c.executions ) executions,
       count( distinct a.hash_value ) statement_count,
```

```
      count ( * ) reference_count
   from
      sys.v_$sql_plan a,
      sys.dba_segments b,
      sys.v_$sql c
   where
      a.object_owner (+) = b.owner
   and
         a.object_name (+) = b.segment_name
and
         b.segment_type IN ('TABLE', 'TABLE PARTITION')
and
         a.operation LIKE '%TABLE%'
and
         a.options = 'FULL'
and
         a.hash_value = c.hash_value
and
         b.bytes / 1024 > 1024
group by
   a.object_owner,
   a.object_name,
   a.operation,
   b.bytes / 1024,
   b.segment_type
order by
   4 desc, 1, 2 );
```

The following is sample output:

	TABLE_OWNER	TABLE_NAME	TABLE_TYPE	SIZE_KB	STATEMENT_COUNT	REFERENCE_COUNT	EXECUTIONS	TOTAL_SCANS
1	ERADMIN	EMP	TABLE	19456	2	2	2	4
2	SYS	DEPENDENCY$	TABLE	3496	1	1	1	1
3	SYS	OBJ$	TABLE	3136	4	7	25	175

Once one uncovers what is being accessed the most, one can then attempt to reveal who is causing all the activity.

Collecting Real-Time Wait Events

While tuning disk I/O waits is an important task, it should not be considered as a comprehensive approach to Oracle tuning.

The DBA must start by learning about the specific tables and indexes that are associated with the waits. Since the *v$* views are accumulators, one can only see the sum the total number of waits since the instance started.

The *v$session_wait* view is a great place to start. As disk read waits occur within the Oracle database, they appear in the *v$session_wait* view for a very short period of time.

Prior to the Automated Session History (ASH) table in Oracle10g, it was impossible to catch all of the run time waits because of the transient appearance of read waits. Regardless, it is possible to take a frequent sample of the *v$session_wait* view and catch a representative sample of the system-waits details at the exact moment that the events occur.

Determining the exact table or index where the wait occurred, when the file and block number are available, is also credible. Therefore, the enticing thing about the *v$session_wait* view is that the exact time the wait occurred can be captured as well as the file and block number that was being waited upon.

This view, shown below, provides the name of the wait event, the total number of waits and timeouts, the total time waited, and the average wait time per event.

```
select *
from
    v$system_event
where
    event like '%wait%';
```

EVENT	TOTAL_WAITS	TOTAL_TIMEOUTS	TIME_WAITED	AVERAGE_WAIT
buffer busy waits	636528	1557	549700	.863591232
write complete waits	1193	0	14799	12.4048617
free buffer waits	1601	0	622	.388507183

The type of buffer that causes the wait can be queried using the *v$waitstat* view. This view lists the waits per buffer type for buffer busy waits, where *count* is the sum of all waits for the class of block, and *time* is the sum of all wait times for that class:

```
select * from v$waitstat;

CLASS                  COUNT       TIME
------------------  ----------  ----------
  data block         1961113     1870278
  segment header       34535      159082
  undo header         233632       86239
  undo block            1886        1706
```

Buffer busy waits occur when an Oracle session needs to access a block in the buffer cache, but cannot because the buffer copy of the data block is locked. This *buffer busy wait* condition can happen for either of the following reasons:

The block is being read into the buffer by another session, so the waiting session must wait for the block read to complete.

Another session has the buffer block locked in a mode that is incompatible with the waiting session's request.

Since *buffer busy waits* are due to contention between particular blocks, there's nothing that can be done until the DBA knows which blocks are in conflict and why the conflicts are occurring. Tuning, therefore, involves identifying and eliminating the cause of the block contention.

```
SQL> desc v$session_wait

 Name                                      Null?    Type
 ----------------------------------------- -------- ----------------
 SID                                                NUMBER
 SEQ#                                               NUMBER
 EVENT                                              VARCHAR2(64)
 P1TEXT                                             VARCHAR2(64)
 P1                                                 NUMBER
 P1RAW                                              RAW(4)
 P2TEXT                                             VARCHAR2(64)
 P2                                                 NUMBER
 P2RAW                                              RAW(4)
 P3TEXT                                             VARCHAR2(64)
 P3                                                 NUMBER
 P3RAW                                              RAW(4)
 WAIT_TIME                                          NUMBER
 SECONDS_IN_WAIT                                    NUMBER
 STATE                                              VARCHAR2(19)
```

The columns of the *v$session_wait* view that are of particular interest for a *buffer busy wait* event are:

- P1: The absolute file number for the data file involved in the wait.

- P2: The block number within the data file referenced in P1 that is being waited upon.

- P3: The reason code describing why the wait is occurring.

The following is an Oracle data dictionary query for these values:

```
select
   p1 "File #".
   p2 "Block #",
   p3 "Reason Code"
from
   v$session_wait
where
   event = 'buffer busy waits';
```

If the output from repeatedly running the above query shows that a block or range of blocks is experiencing waits, the following query should be used to show the name and type of the segment:

```
select
   owner,
   segment_name,
   segment_type
from
   dba_extents
where
   file_id = &P1
and
  &P2 between block_id and block_id + blocks -1;
```

Once the segment is identified, the *v$segment_statistics* performance view facilitates real time monitoring of segment level statistics. This enables a DBA to identify performance problems associated with individual tables or indexes, as shown below.

```
select
   object_name,
   statistic_name,
   value
from
   V$SEGMENT_STATISTICS
where
   object_name = 'SOURCE$';
```

The output looks like the following:

```
OBJECT_NAME     STATISTIC_NAME                      VALUE
-----------     -----------------------         ----------
SOURCE$         logical reads                        11216
SOURCE$         buffer busy waits                      210
SOURCE$         db block changes                        32
SOURCE$         physical reads                       10365
SOURCE$         physical writes                          0
SOURCE$         physical reads direct                    0
SOURCE$         physical writes direct                   0
SOURCE$         ITL waits                                0
SOURCE$         row lock waits


select event,
       total_waits,
       round(100 * (total_waits / sum_waits),2) pct_waits,
       time_wait_sec,
       round(100 * (time_wait_sec / greatest(sum_time_waited,1)),2)
       pct_time_waited,
       total_timeouts,
       round(100 * (total_timeouts / greatest(sum_timeouts,1)),2)
       pct_timeouts,
       average_wait_sec
from
(select event,
       total_waits,
       round((time_waited / 100),2) time_wait_sec,
       total_timeouts,
       round((average_wait / 100),2) average_wait_sec
from sys.v_$system_event
where event not in
('lock element cleanup',
 'pmon timer',
 'rdbms ipc message',
 'rdbms ipc reply',
 'smon timer',
 'SQL*Net message from client',
 'SQL*Net break/reset to client',
 'SQL*Net message to client',
 'SQL*Net more data from client',
 'dispatcher timer',
 'Null event',
 'parallel query dequeue wait',
 'parallel query idle wait - Slaves',
 'pipe get',
 'PL/SQL lock timer',
 'slave wait',
 'virtual circuit status',
 'WMON goes to sleep',
 'jobq slave wait',
 'Queue Monitor Wait',
 'wakeup time manager',
 'PX Idle Wait') AND
 event not like 'DFS%' AND
 event not like 'KXFX%'),
(select sum(total_waits) sum_waits,
        sum(total_timeouts) sum_timeouts,
```

```
       sum(round((time_waited / 100),2)) sum_time_waited
from sys.v_$system_event
where event not in
('lock element cleanup',
'pmon timer',
'rdbms ipc message',
'rdbms ipc reply',
'smon timer',
'SQL*Net message from client',
'SQL*Net break/reset to client',
'SQL*Net message to client',
'SQL*Net more data from client',
'dispatcher timer',
'Null event',
'parallel query dequeue wait',
'parallel query idle wait - Slaves',
'pipe get',
'PL/SQL lock timer',
'slave wait',
'virtual circuit status',
'WMON goes to sleep',
'jobq slave wait',
'Queue Monitor Wait',
'wakeup time manager',
'PX Idle Wait') AND
 event not like 'DFS%' AND
 event not like 'KXFX%')
order by 4 desc, 1 asc;
```

The output of this script, in the WISE tool, looks like the following:

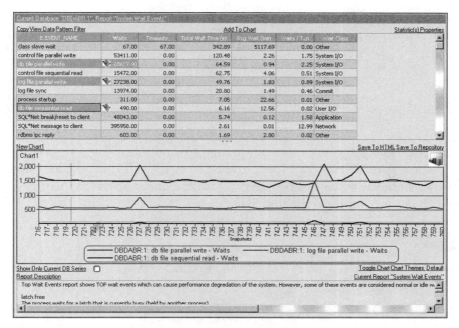

Figure 13.8: *Output of system_waits.sql from WISE tool*

The main wait class within ASH that relates to user I/O can be determined with the following script.

```
select  A.SID,
        B.USERNAME,
        A.WAIT_CLASS,
        A.TOTAL_WAITS,
        A.TIME_WAITED
from    V$SESSION_WAIT_CLASS A,
        V$SESSION B
where   B.SID = A.SID
and
        B.USERNAME IS NOT NULL
and
            A.WAIT_CLASS like '%I/O%'
order by 1,2,3;
```

Its output looks like this:

```
    SID USERNAME             WAIT_CLASS           TOTAL_WAITS TIME_WAITED
---------- -------------------- -------------------- ----------- -----------
    131 SYSMAN               User I/O                      11           5
    132 SYSMAN               User I/O                       3           2
    133 SYSMAN               User I/O                      13           7
```

```
        134 SYSMAN                    User I/O                          173        97
        138 SPV                       User I/O                           10         3
        140 SYSMAN                    User I/O                          387       413
        141 DBSNMP                    User I/O                          201       433
        142 SYSMAN                    User I/O                           36        71
        144 SYSMAN                    User I/O                            6         7
        146 SYSMAN                    User I/O                           35        28
        149 SYSMAN                    User I/O                           46        42
        154 DBSNMP                    System I/O                         84        68
        160 SYS                       System I/O                          5         3
        162 SYSMAN                    User I/O                           16        10
```

The ASH tables can also be queried to find all of the wait conditions for a specific session. Once the Session ID (SID) is acquired for the session, the value can be plugged into the query below to identify all of the wait conditions for that SID.

```
select  A.SID,
        B.USERNAME,
        A.STAT_NAME,
        ROUND((A.VALUE / 1000000),3) TIME_SECS
from    V$SESS_TIME_MODEL A,
        V$SESSION B
where   A.SID = B.SID and
        B.SID = < input SID here >
order by 4 DESC;
```

The result is shown below.

```
SID USERNAME    STAT_NAME                                         TIME_SECS
---- ---------- ------------------------------------------------- ----------
 160 SYS        DB time                                              18,592
 160 SYS        sql execute elapsed time                             18,168
 160 SYS        DB CPU                                               17,139
 160 SYS        parse time elapsed                                      456
 160 SYS        PL/SQL compilation elapsed time                        447
 160 SYS        hard parse elapsed time                                317
 160 SYS        PL/SQL execution elapsed time                           93
 160 SYS        connection management call elapsed time                 66
 160 SYS        background elapsed time                                  0
 160 SYS        Java execution elapsed time                             0
 160 SYS        inbound PL/SQL rpc elapsed time                         0
 160 SYS        hard parse (bind mismatch) elapsed time                 0
 160 SYS        background cpu time                                     0
 160 SYS        failed parse elapsed time                              0
 160 SYS        hard parse (sharing criteria) elapsed time             0
 160 SYS        failed parse (out of shared memory) elapsed time       0
 160 SYS        sequence load elapsed time                             0
```

The following section shows how to track I/O wait events for specific database objects.

Tracking I/O Waits on Specific Tables and Indexes

It should be clear that the DBA still must be able to translate the file number and block number into a specific table or index name. This can be accomplished by using the *dba_extents* view to determine the start block and end block for every extent in every table. Using *dba_extents* to identify the object and its data block boundaries, it becomes a trivial matter to read through the new table and identify those specific objects experiencing read waits or buffer busy waits. The next step is to add the segment name by joining into the *dba_extents* view.

The following is the output from this script. Here, one can see all of the segments that have experienced more than 10 disk read wait events:

Wait Event	Segment Name	Segment Type	Wait Count
SEQ_READ	SYSPRD.S_EVT_ACT_F51	INDEX	72
SEQ_READ	SYSPRD.S_ACCNT_POSTN_M1	INDEX	41
SEQ_READ	SYSPRD.S_ASSET_M3	INDEX	24
SEQ_READ	SYSPRD.S_ASSET_M51	INDEX	19
SEQ_READ	SYSPRD.S_COMM_REQ_U1	INDEX	11

This shows the exact indexes that are experiencing sequential read waits, and now there is an important clue for SQL tuning or object redistribution strategy.

The next step is to identify all hot blocks to complete the analysis. This can be accomplished by examining the *dba_hist_waitstat* table for any data blocks that have experienced multiple waits. In this sample output, each segment, the exact block where the wait occurred, and the number of wait events can be seen:

Wait Event	Segment Name	Segment Type	Block Number	Multiple Block Wait Count
SEQ_READ	SYSPRD.S_EVT_ACT_F51	INDEX	205,680	7
SEQ_READ	SYSPRD.S_EVT_ACT	TABLE	401,481	5
SEQ_READ	SYSPRD.S_EVT_ACT_F51	INDEX	471,767	5
SEQ_READ	SYSPRD.S_EVT_ACT	TABLE	3,056	4
SEQ_READ	SYSPRD.S_EVT_ACT_F51	INDEX	496,315	4
SEQ_READ	SYSPRD.S_DOC_ORDER_U1	INDEX	35,337	3

Since it identifies those data blocks that have experienced multiple block waits, this report is critical. It is then possible to go to each data block and see the contention on a segment header.

Find the Current I/O Session Bandits

To see which users are impacting the system in undesirable ways, the first thing to check is the connected sessions, especially if there are current complaints of poor performance. In this case, there are a few different avenues that can be taken.

Getting an idea of the percentage that each session has taken up with respect to I/O is one of the first steps.

If any session consumes 50% or more of the total I/O, that session and its SQL should be investigated further to determine the activities in which it is engaged. If the DBA is just concerned with physical I/O, the *physpctio.sql* query will provide the information needed:

💾 **physpctio.sql**

```
--  ***********************************************
--  Copyright © 2005 by Rampant TechPress
--  This script is free for non-commercial purposes
--  with no warranties.  Use at your own risk.
--
--  To license this script for a commercial purpose,
--  contact info@rampant.cc
--  ***********************************************

select
   sid,
   username,
   round(100 * total_user_io/total_io,2) tot_io_pct
from
(select
    b.sid sid,
    nvl(b.username,p.name) username,
    sum(value) total_user_io
 from
    sys.v_$statname c,
    sys.v_$sesstat a,
    sys.v_$session b,
```

```
     sys.v_$bgprocess p
 where
     a.statistic#=c.statistic# and
     p.paddr (+) = b.paddr and
     b.sid=a.sid and
     c.name in ('physical reads',
                'physical writes',
                'physical writes direct',
                'physical reads direct',
                'physical writes direct (lob)',
                'physical reads direct (lob)')
group by
     b.sid, nvl(b.username,p.name)),
(select
     sum(value) total_io
 from
     sys.v_$statname c,
     sys.v_$sesstat a
 where
     a.statistic#=c.statistic# and
     c.name in ('physical reads',
                'physical writes',
                'physical writes direct',
                'physical reads direct',
                'physical writes direct (lob)',
                'physical reads direct (lob)'))
order by
     3 desc;
```

If the DBA wants to see the total I/O picture, the *totpctio.sql* query should be used instead:

💾 **totpctio.sql**

```
-- *****************************************************
-- Copyright © 2005 by Rampant TechPress
-- This script is free for non-commercial purposes
-- with no warranties.  Use at your own risk.
--
-- To license this script for a commercial purpose,
-- contact info@rampant.cc
-- *****************************************************

SELECT
     SID,
     USERNAME,
     ROUND(100 * TOTAL_USER_IO/TOTAL_IO,2) TOT_IO_PCT
FROM
(SELECT
     b.SID SID,
     nvl(b.USERNAME,p.NAME) USERNAME,
     SUM(VALUE) TOTAL_USER_IO
FROM
```

```
     sys.V_$STATNAME c,
     sys.V_$SESSTAT a,
     sys.V_$SESSION b,
     sys.v_$bgprocess p
WHERE
     a.STATISTIC#=c.STATISTIC# and
     p.paddr (+) = b.paddr and
     b.SID=a.SID and
     c.NAME in ('physical reads','physical writes',
                'consistent changes','consistent gets',
                'db block gets','db block changes',
                'physical writes direct',
                'physical reads direct',
                'physical writes direct (lob)',
                'physical reads direct (lob)')
GROUP BY
     b.SID, nvl(b.USERNAME,p.name)),
(select
       sum(value) TOTAL_IO
from
       sys.V_$STATNAME c,
       sys.V_$SESSTAT a
WHERE
       a.STATISTIC#=c.STATISTIC# and
       c.NAME in ('physical reads','physical writes',
                  'consistent changes',
                  'consistent gets','db block gets',
                  'db block changes',
                  'physical writes direct',
                  'physical reads direct',
                  'physical writes direct (lob)',
                  'physical reads direct (lob)'))
ORDER BY
       3 DESC;
```

The output might resemble the following, regardless of which query is used:

```
SID  USERNAME      TOT_IO_PCT
--------------------------------
9    USR1              71.26
20   SYS               15.76
5    SMON               7.11
2    DBWR               4.28
12   SYS                1.42
6    RECO                .12
7    SNP0                .01
10   SNP3                .01
11   SNP4                .01
8    SNP1                .01
1    PMON                  0
3    ARCH                  0
4    LGWR                  0
```

Following the above example, a DBA would indeed be wise to study the USR1 session to see what SQL calls were made. The above queries are excellent resources that can be used to quickly pinpoint problem I/O sessions.

To see all the actual I/O numbers, the rather large *topiousers.sql* query can be used if the goal is to gather more detail with respect to the top I/O session in a database:

🖫 topiousers.sql

```
-- *************************************************
-- Copyright © 2005 by Rampant TechPress
-- This script is free for non-commercial purposes
-- with no warranties.  Use at your own risk.
--
-- To license this script for a commercial purpose,
-- contact info@rampant.cc
-- *************************************************
select
     b.sid sid,
     decode (b.username,null,e.name,b.username)
     user_name,
     d.spid os_id,
     b.machine machine_name,
     to_char(logon_time,'mm/dd/yy hh:mi:ss pm')
     logon_time,
     (sum(decode(c.name,'physical reads',value,0))
     +
     sum(decode(c.name,'physical writes',value,0))
     +
     sum(decode(c.name,
     'physical writes direct',value,0)) +
     sum(decode(c.name,
     'physical writes direct (lob)',value,0)) +
     sum(decode(c.name,
     'physical reads direct (lob)',value,0)) +
     sum(decode(c.name,
     'physical reads direct',value,0)))
     total_physical_io,
     (sum(decode(c.name,'db block gets',value,0))
     +
     sum(decode(c.name,
     'db block changes',value,0))   +
     sum(decode(c.name,'consistent changes',value,0)) +
     sum(decode(c.name,'consistent gets',value,0)) )
     total_logical_io,
     100 - 100 *(round ((sum (decode
     (c.name, 'physical reads', value, 0)) -
     sum (decode (c.name,
```

```
      'physical reads direct', value, 0))) /
      (sum (decode (c.name, 'db block gets',
   value, 1)) +
   sum (decode (c.name, 'consistent gets',
    value, 0))),3)) hit_ratio,
   sum(decode(c.name,'sorts (disk)',value,0))
   disk_sorts,
   sum(decode(c.name,'sorts (memory)',value,0))
   memory_sorts,
   sum(decode(c.name,'sorts (rows)',value,0))
   rows_sorted,
   sum(decode(c.name,'user commits',value,0))
   commits,
   sum(decode(c.name,'user rollbacks',value,0))
   rollbacks,
   sum(decode(c.name,'execute count',value,0))
   executions,
   sum(decode(c.name,'physical reads',value,0))
   physical_reads,
   sum(decode(c.name,'db block gets',value,0))
   db_block_gets,
   sum(decode(c.name,'consistent gets',value,0))
   consistent_gets,
   sum(decode(c.name,'consistent changes',value,0))
   consistent_changes
from
   sys.v_$sesstat a,
   sys.v_$session b,
   sys.v_$statname c,
   sys.v_$process d,
   sys.v_$bgprocess e
where
   a.statistic#=c.statistic#
and
   b.sid=a.sid
and
   d.addr = b.paddr
and
   e.paddr (+) = b.paddr
and
   c.name in
   ('physical reads',
   'physical writes',
   'physical writes direct',
   'physical reads direct',
   'physical writes direct (lob)',
   'physical reads direct (lob)',
   'db block gets',
   'db block changes',
   'consistent changes',
   'consistent gets',
   'sorts (disk)',
   'sorts (memory)',
   'sorts (rows)',
   'user commits',
   'user rollbacks',
```

```
     'execute count'
)
group by
   b.sid,
   d.spid,
   decode (b.username,null,e.name,b.username),
        b.machine,
        to_char(logon_time,'mm/dd/yy hh:mi:ss pm')
order by
   6 desc;
```

Output from the query above could look like the following:

	SID	USER_NAME	OS_ID	MACHINE_NAME	LOGON_TIME	TOTAL_PHYSICAL_IO	TOTAL_LOGICAL_IO	HIT_RATIO	DISK_SORTS	MEMORY_SORTS	ROWS_SORTED	COMMIT
1	2	DBW0	1064	EBT2K11	12/05/02 03:12:10 PM	9982	0	100	0	0	0	
2	12	ORA_MONITOR	2488	EBT2K\EBT2K08	12/12/02 05:28:18 PM	8527	59015775	100	0	289379	126302548	
3	5	SMON	296	EBT2K11	12/05/02 03:12:11 PM	2657	465527	99.4	0	78	175	
4	3	LGWR	980	EBT2K11	12/05/02 03:12:10 PM	34	0	100	0	0	0	
5	6	RECO	1220	EBT2K11	12/05/02 03:12:11 PM	1	1753	99.9	0	8	48	
6	1	PMON	1032	EBT2K11	12/05/02 03:12:09 PM	0	0	100	0	0	0	
7	4	CKPT	1144	EBT2K11	12/05/02 03:12:10 PM	0	0	100	0	0	0	
8	16	SYS	3956	EBT2K\ROBINWS	12/17/02 04:55:29 PM	0	4	100	0	0	0	
9	11	SYS	3096	EBT2K\ROBINWS	12/17/02 05:26:31 PM	0	235	100	0	66	27449	

A query such as this reveals details about the actual raw I/O numbers for each connected session. Armed with this information, it is then possible to drill down into each heavy-hitting I/O session to evaluate what SQL calls are made and which sets of SQL are the I/O hogs.

Even though troubleshooting I/O from a user standpoint has been explained, one should not forget about all the system activity caused by Oracle itself.

A cursory, global check of the system level wait events should be performed to get an idea of the I/O bottlenecks that may be occurring. A script like the *syswaits.sql* script can be used to perform such a check:

🖫 syswaits.sql

```
--  ******************************************************
--  Copyright © 2005 by Rampant TechPress
--  This script is free for non-commercial purposes
--  with no warranties.  Use at your own risk.
--
--  To license this script for a commercial purpose,
--  contact info@rampant.cc
--  ******************************************************

select
```

```
      event,
      total_waits,
      round(100 * (total_waits / sum_waits),2) pct_tot_waits,
      time_wait_sec,
      round(100 * (time_wait_sec / sum_secs),2) pct_secs_waits,
      total_timeouts,
      avg_wait_sec
from
(select
      event,
      total_waits,
      round((time_waited / 100),2) time_wait_sec,
      total_timeouts,
      round((average_wait / 100),2) avg_wait_sec
from
      sys.v_$system_event
where
      event not in
      ('lock element cleanup ',
      'pmon timer ',
      'rdbms ipc message ',
      'smon timer ',
      'SQL*Net message from client ',
      'SQL*Net break/reset to client ',
      'SQL*Net message to client ',
      'SQL*Net more data to client ',
      'dispatcher timer ',
      'Null event ',
      'parallel query dequeue wait ',
      'parallel query idle wait - Slaves ',
      'pipe get ',
      'PL/SQL lock timer ',
      'slave wait ',
      'virtual circuit status ',
      'WMON goes to sleep') and
      event not like 'DFS%' and
      event not like 'KXFX%'),
(select
      sum(total_waits) sum_waits,
      sum(round((time_waited / 100),2)) sum_secs
 from
      sys.v_$system_event
 where
      event not in
      ('lock element cleanup ',
      'pmon timer ',
      'rdbms ipc message ',
      'smon timer ',
      'SQL*Net message from client ',
      'SQL*Net break/reset to client ',
      'SQL*Net message to client ',
      'SQL*Net more data to client ',
      'dispatcher timer ',
      'Null event ',
      'parallel query dequeue wait ',
      'parallel query idle wait - Slaves ',
```

```
        'pipe get ',
        'PL/SQL lock timer ',
        'slave wait ',
        'virtual circuit status ',
        'WMON goes to sleep') and
        event not like 'DFS%' and
        event not like 'KXFX%')
order by
   2 desc;
```

The script queries the *sys.v_$system_event* view and here are a few quick things to note about the output from the waits SQL script:

- Numerous waits for the *db file scattered read* event may indicate a problem with table scans.

- Many waits for the latch free event could indicate excessive amounts of logical I/O activity.

- High wait times for the enqueue event pinpoints a problem with lock contention.

Once the DBA has a feel for the I/O numbers at a global level, it is possible to begin working further down into what is really going on below the surface.

Measuring Disk I/O Speed

The relative cost of physical disk access is an important topic since all Oracle databases retrieve and store data.

A significant factor in weighing these costs is physical disk speed. Quicker disk access speeds can diminish the costs of a full table scan versus single block reads to a negligible level.

In a solid-state disk environment, disk I/O is far more rapid and multiblock reads become far cheaper compared to traditional disks. The new solid-state disks provide up to 100,000 I/Os per second, six times faster than traditional disk devices.

The standard STATSPACK report can be generated when the database is processing a peak load, and it is also possible to get a

---

detailed report of all elapsed time metrics. The STATSPACK top-five timed event report is the most important of these metrics. The report is critical for it displays the database events that constitute the bottleneck for the system. The listing below from a STATSPACK report shows that the system is clearly constrained by disk I/O.

```
Top 5 Timed Events
                                                            % Total
Event                         Waits         Time (s)      Ela Time
--------------------------- ------------   -----------    --------
db file sequential read       2,598          7,146          48.54
db file scattered read       25,519          3,246          22.04
library cache load lock         673          1,363           9.26
CPU time                                     1,154           7.83
log file parallel write      19,157            837           5.68
```

Reads and writes constitute the majority of the total database time as shown above. In such a case, the RAM size of the *db_cache_size* should be increased in order to reduce disk I/O, the SQL tuned to reduce disk I/O, or a faster disk I/O subsystem should be invested in.

Not only do the ideal optimizer settings rely on the environment, they are heavily swayed by the system's costs for *scattered disk reads* versus *sequential disk reads*. A great script to measure these I/O costs on the database is shown below.

```
col c1 heading 'Average Waits|forFull| Scan Read I/O'      format 9999.999
col c2 heading 'Average Waits|for Index|Read I/O'         format 9999.999
col c3 heading 'Percent of| I/O Waits|for Full Scans'     format 9.99
col c4 heading 'Percent of| I/O Waits|for Index Scans'    format 9.99
col c5 heading 'Starting|Value|for|optimizer|index|cost|adj' format 999

select
   a.average_wait                              c1,
   b.average_wait                              c2,
   a.total_waits /(a.total_waits + b.total_waits)  c3,
   b.total_waits /(a.total_waits + b.total_waits)  c4,
   (b.average_wait / a.average_wait)*100       c5
from
  v$system_event  a,
  v$system_event  b
where
   a.event = 'db file scattered read'
and
   b.event = 'db file sequential read'
;
```

While there are varied opinions regarding full-table scans, they are not necessarily a detriment to performance. Indeed they are often the quickest way to access the table rows. The CBO option of performing a full table scan depends on many factors, some being the settings for Oracle Parallel Query, the *db_block_size,* the *clustering_factor,* and the estimated percentage of rows returned by the query according to the CBO statistics.

Once Oracle selects a full-table scan, the speed of performing a full-table scan (SOFTS) rests with internal and external factors:

- Table partitioning

- The number of CPUs on the system

- The setting for Oracle Parallel Query (parallel hints, alter table)

- The speed of the disk I/O subsystem (e.g., hardware-cached I/O, solid-state disk RAM 3)

When factoring in all these elements, it may be impossible to decide the exact best setting for the weight in *optimizer_index_cost_adj.* In reality, the decision to petition a full-table scan is heavily influenced by run-time factors such as:

- The present demands on the CPUs

- The attainability of free blocks in the data buffers

- The amount of TEMP tablespace, if the FTS has an *order by* clause

No two database systems are the same and good DBAs must adjust *optimizer_index_cost_adj* according to database configuration and data access patterns.

The encompassing amount of time performing full-table scans is equal to the percentage of *db file sequential read* waits as a percentage of total I/O waits from *v$system_event.*

The following section will introduce how to measure system I/O wait events in real-time.

Analyzing real time I/O waits

The majority of activity in a database involves reading data. Therefore the ability to analyze and correct Oracle Database physical read wait events is critical in any tuning project. This type of tuning can have a huge, positive impact on performance.

Since it can show those wait events that are the primary bottleneck for the system, system wait tuning has become very popular. Certain expert techniques like the 10046 wait event (level 8 and higher) analysis and Oracle MetaLink now have an analysis tool called *trcanlzr.sql* written by Carlos Sierra to interpret bottlenecks via 10046 trace dumps. Details are available in MetaLink note 224270.1.

In theory, any Oracle database will run faster if access to hardware resources associated with waits is increased. It is critical to remember all Oracle databases experience wait events, and the presence of waits does not always indicate a problem. In reality, every well tuned database experiences some bottleneck. For example, a computationally intensive database may be CPU-bound and a data warehouse may be bound by disk-read waits.

While this section explores a small subset of wait analysis, it also illustrates the critical concept of Oracle tuning that every task waits on specific events. It is the DBA's job to find out whether the Oracle database is I/O bound, CPU bound, memory bound, or bound waiting on latches or locks. Once the source of the bottleneck has been identified, ASH data can be used to determine the causes of these events and attempt to remove them.

The Oracle Database provides numerous views such as *v$system_event* and *v$session_wait* to give insight into the wait events and to aid in their identification. The *v$system_event* dictionary views provides information regarding the total number of I/O-related waits within the Oracle database, but it does not identify the specific object involved. In Oracle9*i* Release 2, the *v$segment_statistics* view gives this information.

The *v$session_wait* view offers detailed file and block data, from which the object can be extracted from the block number.

Oracle event waits occur quite swiftly, and it is difficult to get data unless the query is run at the exact moment the database is experiencing the wait. For this reason, a method for using the *v$session_wait* view must be created so a sample of the transient physical I/O waits can be captured.

If the *v$system_event* view is used, there are over 300 specific wait events. There are two critical I/O read waits within any Oracle database:

- *db file scattered read waits:* Scattered read waits happen whenever multiblock (full scan) I/O is invoked by an SQL statement. When the Oracle Database performs a full-table scan or sort operation, multiblock block read is automatically invoked.

- *db file sequential read waits:* A *db file sequential read* wait occurs within an Oracle database when a single block is requested, usually via index access. A single read is most commonly an index probe by *rowid* into an individual table or the access of an index block. Sequential reads are single block reads, as opposed to multiblock (scattered) reads.

First, those objects that experience physical read waits and when they do so must be identified in order to tune these wait events. The issue would then be addressed with tuning techniques. The following section starts by studying the solutions, and then looks at ways to identify wait conditions.

Solutions to Physical Read Waits

Once the objects that experience the physical read waits have been identified, STATSPACK can be used to extract the SQL associated with the waits. The following actions can then be taken to correct the problem. These corrective actions are presented in the order in which they are most likely to be effective. Some may not apply to a particular environment:

Tune the SQL statement: Tuning the SQL is the single most important factor in reducing disk I/O contention. If an SQL statement can be tuned to reduce disk I/O by using an index to remove an unnecessary large-table full-table scan, the amount of disk I/O and associated waits are dramatically reduced. Other SQL tuning might include:

Change table join order: For sequential read waits, the SQL may be tuned to change the order that the tables are joined, often using the ORDERED hint.

Change indexes: The SQL can be tuned by adding function-based indexes or using an INDEX hint to make the SQL less I/O-intensive by using a more selective index.

Change table join methods: Often, nested loop joins have fewer I/O waits than hash joins, especially for sequential reads. Table join methods can be changed with SQL hints (*use_nl*, for example). Prior to Oracle9*i* with *pga_aggregate_target*, the propensity for hash join must be changed by adjusting the *hash_area_size* parameter.

The database can also be tuned at the instance level with these techniques:

Get better CBO statistics: Stale or non-representative statistics can cause suboptimal SQL execution plans, resulting in unnecessary disk waits. The solution is to use the *dbms_stats* package to analyze the schema. Also, it should be noted if column data values are skewed, the addition of histograms may also be necessary.

Distribute disk I/O across more spindles: Disk channel contention is often responsible for physical read waits, and they will show up in the ASH data. If the system experiences disk waits as a result of hardware contention and RAID is not in use, the DBA may consider segregating the table of index into a separate tablespace with many data files and striping the offending data file across multiple disk spindles by reorganizing the object and using the *minextents* and *next* parameters.

Use the KEEP pool: Many experts recommend implementing the KEEP pool for reducing scattered reads. In the Oracle Magazine article *Advanced Tuning with STATSPACK* (Jan/Feb. 2003), the author notes that small table full-table scans should be placed in the KEEP pool to reduce scattered read waits.

Increase the *db_cache_size*: - The more data blocks in the RAM buffer, the smaller the probability of physical read wait events.

The *dba_hist_sqltext* table keeps a record of historical SQL source statements, and it is easy to extract the SQL that was executing at the time of the read waits. From there, the execution plans for the SQL statements can be gathered. The DBA can then verify they are using an optimal execution plan.

The next section will explore how the data needed to fix the causes of the physical read waits can be acquired now that the solutions have been identified.

Time series I/O Wait Analysis

Every database will have "signatures," which are typically caused by regularly scheduled processing. When these signatures are identified, STATSPACK must be used to extract the SQL and ensure that it is properly optimized. When the detailed event waits data has been acquired, it is a trivial task to roll up the data and create trend reports.

If the read waits persist, the next step is to manipulate the schedule to execute the colliding SQL at different times. Some of the workload can be moved to a different time window if there is not sufficient I/O bandwidth to run the full workload all at once. To display a trend by day, a similar query may be run that will average the number of sequential read waits by day of the week.

More importantly, there is the detailed wait information in the *dba_hist_waitstat* table, so the exact table or index that is experiencing the real time wait can be investigated. By doing that in conjunction with AWR, the SQL may also be collected in the AWR table such that it is clear what SQL is precipitating the disk wait events.

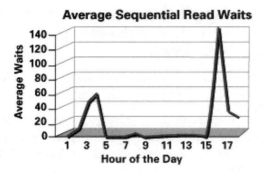

Figure 13.9: *Plotting real-time waits averages by hour of the day*

Figure 13.9 shows a high number of real time *db file sequential read* waits between 2:00AM and 3:00AM with another spike between 9:00PM and midnight. This information can go to STATSPACK for use in extracting the SQL that was running during this period.

One can also average to read waits by day of the week as shown in Figure 13.10. The figure shows that there is an obvious increase in scattered read waits every Tuesday and Thursday and the SQL can be extracted during these periods.

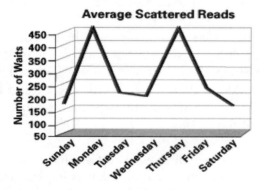

Figure 13.10: *Plotting real-time waits averages by day of the week*

Ordinarily, this insight would be ineffective because the source of the waits would not be obvious. Of course, with Oracle9*i* release 2 and beyond, the *v$segment_statistics* view can be used to see some of this information if the *statistics_level* parameter is set to a value of seven or higher.

Now, the DBA can drill in and see those specific table and indexes that were experiencing the sequential read waits.

```
Block
                      Segment                           Segment      Wait
Date            Hr.   Name                              Type         Count
--------------- ----  --------------------------------  ----------   ----
23-jan-2003 21        SYSPRD.S_COMM_REQ_SRC_U1          INDEX        23
23-jan-2003 21        SYSPRD.S_EVT_ACT                  TABLE        44
23-jan-2003 21        SYSPRD.S_EVT_ACT_F51              INDEX        16
23-jan-2003 22        SYSPRD.S_EVT_ACT                  TABLE        32
```

The specific object that experiences the physical read wait must be identified since the goal may be to distribute the object over additional disk spindles.

The details about the objects that experience physical read waits can be easily captured using a real time wait sampling method. Once they are recognized, STATSPACK can be used to find the problematic SQL and begin the tuning. The tuning of physical read waits involves SQL tuning, object striping across multiple disks, employing the KEEP pool for small objects, rescheduling the SQL to relieve the contention, or increasing the data buffer cache size.

A simple query can be used to plot the user I/O wait time statistic for each AWR snapshot. Using the following script the physical read counts can be extracted from the AWR.

```
break on begin_interval_time skip 2

column phyrds              format 999,999,999
column begin_interval_time format a25

select
   begin_interval_time,
   filename,
   phyrds
from
   dba_hist_filestatxs
```

```
natural join
   dba_hist_snapshot
;
```

The output below shows a running total of Oracle physical reads. The snapshots are collected every half-hour. Starting from this script, a *where* clause criteria could easily be added to create a unique time series exception report.

```
SQL> @phys_reads

BEGIN_INTERVAL_TIME        FILENAME                                       PHYRDS
-------------------------- -------------------------------------------- --------
24-FEB-04 11.00.32.000 PM  E:\ORACLE\ORA92\FSDEV10G\SYSTEM01.DBF         164,700
                           E:\ORACLE\ORA92\FSDEV10G\UNDOTBS01.DBF         26,082
                           E:\ORACLE\ORA92\FSDEV10G\SYSAUX01.DBF         472,008
                           E:\ORACLE\ORA92\FSDEV10G\USERS01.DBF            1,794
                           E:\ORACLE\ORA92\FSDEV10G\T_FS_LSQ.ORA           2,123
```

The next step is to take a look at how these simple scripts can be enhanced to produce powerful exception reports.

In the simple report generated with the following script, the *dba_hist_filestatxs* is queried to identify hot write datafiles where the file consumed more than 25% of the total physical writes for the instance. The query compares the physical writes in the *phywrts* column of *dba_hist_filestatxs* with the instance-wide physical writes on *statistic# = 55* from *dba_hist_sysstat*.

This simple yet powerful script allows the Oracle professional to track hot-write datafiles over time, thereby gaining important insights into the status of the I/O sub-system over time.

```
prompt
prompt   This will identify any single file who's write I/O
prompt   is more than 25% of the total write I/O of the database.
prompt

set pages 999

break on snap_time skip 2

col filename      format a40
col phywrts       format 999,999,999
col snap_time     format a20

select
   to_char(begin_interval_time,'yyyy-mm-dd hh24:mi') snap_time,
```

```
    filename,
    phywrts
from
    dba_hist_filestatxs
natural join
    dba_hist_snapshot
where
    phywrts > 0
and
    phywrts * 4 >
(
select
    avg(value)              all_phys_writes
from
    dba_hist_sysstat
  natural join
    dba_hist_snapshot
where
    stat_name = 'physical writes'
and
  value > 0
)
order by
    to_char(begin_interval_time,'yyyy-mm-dd hh24:mi'),
    phywrts desc
;
```

The following is sample output. This is a very useful report because the high write datafiles as well as those times when they are hot are revealed.

```
SQL> @hot_write_files

This will identify any single file who's write I/O
is more than 25% of the total write I/O of the database.

SNAP_TIME            FILENAME                                         PHYWRTS
------------------- ---------------------------------------- ----------
2004-02-20 23:30    E:\ORACLE\ORA92\FSDEV10G\SYSAUX01.DBF            85,540

2004-02-21 01:00    E:\ORACLE\ORA92\FSDEV10G\SYSAUX01.DBF            88,843

2004-02-21 08:31    E:\ORACLE\ORA92\FSDEV10G\SYSAUX01.DBF            89,463

2004-02-22 02:00    E:\ORACLE\ORA92\FSDEV10G\SYSAUX01.DBF            90,168

2004-02-22 16:30    E:\ORACLE\ORA92\FSDEV10G\SYSAUX01.DBF           143,974
                    E:\ORACLE\ORA92\FSDEV10G\UNDOTBS01.DBF           88,973
```

Time series exception reporting is extremely useful for detecting those times when an Oracle10g database is experiencing stress. Many Oracle professionals will schedule these types of exception reports for automatic e-mailing every day.

Time series I/O Wait Analysis

Time Series Monitoring of the Data Buffers

Before one can self-tune the data buffers, there needs to be a mechanism for monitoring the data buffer hit ratio (BHR) for all pools that have been defined. All seven data buffers can be monitored with this script, but remember, unless objects are segreated into separate buffers, aggregate BHR values are largely meaningless.

```
select
   name,
   block_size,
   (1-(physical_reads/ decode(db_block_gets+consistent_gets, 0, .001,
db_block_gets+consistent_gets)))*100   cache_hit_ratio
from
   v$buffer_pool_statistics;
```

The following is a sample output from this script. The names of the sized block buffers remain DEFAULT, and the *block_size* column must be selected to differentiate between the buffers. The sample output shows all 7 data buffers.

NAME	BLOCK_SIZE	CACHE_HIT_RATIO
DEFAULT	32,767	.97
RECYCLE	16,384	.61
KEEP	16,384	1.00
DEFAULT	16,384	.92
DEFAULT	4,096	.99
DEFAULT	8,192	.98
DEFAULT	2,048	.86

Of course, this report is not extremely useful because the *v$sysstat* view only shows averages since the instance was started. To perform self-tuning of the data buffers, Oracle's AWR views can be used to measure the data buffer hit ratios every hour.

To do this, an AWR data buffer exception report table can be used. Figure 13.11 shows the output from a time based data buffer hit ratio report.

```
yr.   mo dy Hr.    Name     bhr
-------------    --------   -----
2001-01-27  09  DEFAULT    45
2001-01-28  09  RECYCLE    41
2001-01-29  10  DEFAULT    36
2001-01-30  09  DEFAULT    28
2001-02-02  10  DEFAULT    83
```

Between 8:00-10:00 AM   BHR is too low

Figure 13.11: *Time-based proactive problem detection*

In Figure 13.11, it appears that the database regularly experiences a decline in the data buffer hit ratio between 9:00 and 11:00 AM. Once it has been confirmed that this is a signature and repeats on a regular basis, action can be taken to correct the deficiency as follows:

- Review and tune all SQL between 9:00-11:00 AM, using the SQL source captured in the *stats$sql_summary* table.

- Schedule a job (*dbms_job* or *dbms_scheduler*) to increase the *db_cache_size* during this period.

The following section provides a look at time series disk monitoring and analysis using the powerful AWR tables.

Monitoring Disk I/O with AWR

One of the great features of AWR is that it can directly monitor disk input and output (I/O). The following is a great technique that can be used for extending the capabilities of Oracle's STATSPACK performance utility to report statistics on I/O activity at the disk and file level in a UNIX environment.

Statistics ordinarily captured by an AWR snapshot are related only to the read and write activity at the Oracle data file level. Normally, AWR cannot show I/O at the disk or mount point level, which can be valuable information in determining hyperactivity on particular files or disks.

Instead of using standard utilities to generate a report for a single time period, utilities can be modified to collect I/O data over consistent intervals, storing the results in Oracle tables for easy access and reporting. The following is an outline of requirements.

The *dba_hist_filestatxs* table contains I/O data collected by snapshots taken at consistent intervals. I/O data captured includes the actual number of physical reads, physical writes, block reads, block writes, and the time required for each operation. Disk activity over time is represented in Figure 13.12.

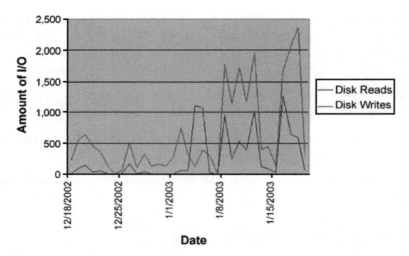

Figure 13.12: *Disk activity over time*

Holistic data, which yields the status internal to Oracle and external with the various UNIX and Linux commands, can be gathered and analyzed using just STATSPACK and system utilities.

The data collected by STATSPACK can be accessed with normal scripts such as the *snapfileio_10g.sql* listed below:

💾 **snapfileio_10g.sql**

```
-- ****************************************************
-- Copyright © 2005 by Rampant TechPress
```

```
-- This script is free for non-commercial purposes
-- with no warranties.  Use at your own risk.
--
-- To license this script for a commercial purpose,
-- contact info@rampant.cc
-- *************************************************

rem
rem NAME: snapfileio.sql

rem FUNCTION: Reports on the file io status of all of the
rem FUNCTION: datafiles in the database for a single snapshot.


column sum_io1 new_value st1 noprint
column sum_io2 new_value st2 noprint
column sum_io new_value divide_by noprint
column Percent format 999.999 heading 'Percent|Of IO'
column brratio format 999.99 heading 'Block|Read|Ratio'
column bwratio format 999.99 heading 'Block|Write|Ratio'
column phyrds heading 'Physical | Reads'
column phywrts heading 'Physical | Writes'
column phyblkrd heading 'Physical|Block|Reads'
column phyblkwrt heading 'Physical|Block|Writes'
column filename format a45 heading 'File|Name'
column file# format 9999 heading 'File'

set feedback off verify off lines 132 pages 60 sqlbl on trims on

select
    nvl(sum(a.phyrds+a.phywrts),0) sum_io1
from
    dba_hist_filestatxs a where snap_id=&&snap;

select nvl(sum(b.phyrds+b.phywrts),0) sum_io2
from
        dba_hist_tempstatxs b where snap_id=&&snap;

select &st1+&st2 sum_io from dual;

rem
@title132 'Snap&&snap File I/O Statistics Report'

spool rep_out\&db\fileio&&snap

select
    a.filename, a.phyrds, a.phywrts,
    (100*(a.phyrds+a.phywrts)/&divide_by) Percent,
    a.phyblkrd, a.phyblkwrt, (a.phyblkrd/greatest(a.phyrds,1))
brratio,
      (a.phyblkwrt/greatest(a.phywrts,1)) bwratio
from
    dba_hist_filestatxs a
where
    a.snap_id=&&snap
union
```

```
select
    c.filename, c.phyrds, c.phywrts,
    (100*(c.phyrds+c.phywrts)/&divide_by) Percent,
    c.phyblkrd, c.phyblkwrt,(c.phyblkrd/greatest(c.phyrds,1))
brratio,
      (c.phyblkwrt/greatest(c.phywrts,1)) bwratio
from
    dba_hist_tempstatxs c
where
    c.snap_id=&&snap
order by
    1
/

spool off
pause Press enter to continue
set feedback on verify on lines 80 pages 22
clear columns
ttitle off
undef snap
```

Of course, a single AWR reading suffers from the same limitations that a single read of the *v$* or *gv$* dynamic performance views. It only gives the cumulative data from when the database was started to the time that the snapshot was taken. A better methodology is shown in *snapdeltafileio_awr.sql*.

🖫 snapdeltafileio_awr.sql

```
-- ****************************************************
-- Copyright © 2005 by Rampant TechPress
-- This script is free for non-commercial purposes
-- with no warranties.  Use at your own risk.
--
-- To license this script for a commercial purpose,
-- contact info@rampant.cc
-- ****************************************************

rem
rem NAME: snapdeltafileio.sql
rem
rem FUNCTION: Reports on the file io status of all of
rem FUNCTION: the datafiles in the database across
rem FUNCTION: two snapshots.
rem HISTORY:
rem WHO             WHAT           WHEN
rem Mike Ault            Created       11/19/03
rem

column sum_io1 new_value st1 noprint
column sum_io2 new_value st2 noprint
column sum_io new_value divide_by noprint
```

```
column Percent format 999.999 heading 'Percent|Of IO'
column brratio format 999.99 heading 'Block|Read|Ratio'
column bwratio format 999.99 heading 'Block|Write|Ratio'
column phyrds heading 'Physical | Reads'
column phywrts heading 'Physical | Writes'
column phyblkrd heading 'Physical|Block|Reads'
column phyblkwrt heading 'Physical|Block|Writes'
column filename format a45 heading 'File|Name'
column file# format 9999 heading 'File'
set feedback off verify off lines 132 pages 60 sqlbl on trims on

select
    nvl(sum((b.phyrds-a.phyrds)+(b.phywrts-a.phywrts)),0) sum_io1
from
    dba_hist_filestatxs a, dba_hist_filestatxs b
where
        a.snap_id=&&first_snap_id and b.snap_id=&&sec_snap_id
        and a.filename=b.filename;

select
    nvl(sum((b.phyrds-a.phyrds)+(b.phywrts-a.phywrts)),0) sum_io2
from
    dba_hist_tempstatxs a, dba_hist_tempstatxs b
where
        a.snap_id=&&first_snap_id and b.snap_id=&&sec_snap_id
        and a.filename=b.filename;

select &st1+&st2 sum_io from dual;

rem
@title132 'Snap &&first_snap_id to &&sec_snap_id File I/O Statistics
Report'
spool rep_out\&db\fileio'&&first_snap_id'_to_'&&sec_snap_id'

select
    a.filename, b.phyrds -a.phyrds phyrds, b.phywrts-a.phywrts
phywrts,
    (100*((b.phyrds-a.phyrds)+(b.phywrts-a.phywrts))/&divide_by)
Percent,
    b.phyblkrd- a.phyblkrd phyblkrd, b.phyblkwrt-a.phyblkwrt
phyblgwrt,
        ((b.phyblkrd-a.phyblkrd)/greatest((b.phyrds-a.phyrds),1))
brratio,
        ((b.phyblkwrt-a.phyblkwrt)/greatest((b.phywrts-
a.phywrts),1)) bwratio
from
    dba_hist_filestatxs a, dba_hist_filestatxs b
where
        a.snap_id=&&first_snap_id and b.snap_id=&&sec_snap_id
        and a.filename=b.filename
union
select
    c.filename, d.phyrds-c.phyrds phyrds, d.phywrts-c.phywrts
phywrts,
    (100*((d.phyrds-c.phyrds)+(d.phywrts-c.phywrts))/&divide_by)
Percent,
```

```
      d.phyblkrd-c.phyblkrd phyblkrd, d.phyblkwrt-c.phyblkwrt
phyblgwrt,
        ((d.phyblkrd-c.phyblkrd)/greatest((d.phyrds-c.phyrds),1))
brratio,
        ((d.phyblkwrt-c.phyblkwrt)/greatest((d.phywrts-
c.phywrts),1)) bwratio
from
    dba_hist_tempstatxs c, dba_hist_tempstatxs d
where
        c.snap_id=&&first_snap_id and d.snap_id=&&sec_snap_id
        and c.filename=d.filename
order by
    1
/
spool off
pause Press enter to continue
set feedback on verify on lines 80 pages 22
clear columns
ttitle off
undef first_snap_id
undef sec_snap_id
```

Figure 13.13 below shows a representation of a daily disk delta report.

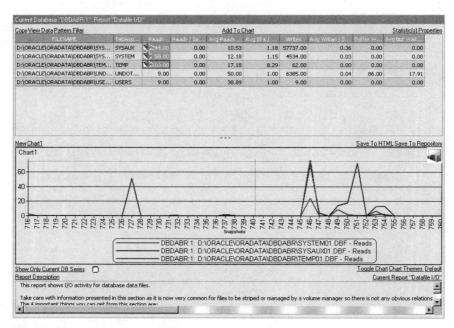

Figure 13.13: *A daily disk delta report in WISE*

The report accepts two snapshot IDs and uses them to calculate the delta between the I/O readings. This I/O delta information is vital to help pinpoint real I/O problems for a given time period.

Combined with *iostat* and *vmstat* readings from the same time period, one can get a complete picture of the I/O profile of the database. A similar technique can be used for I/O timing and other useful delta statistics. These scripts and many others are available from <u>oracle-script.com</u>.

Scripts can be written to show the signature for any Oracle system statistic, averaged by hour of the day. This information is great for plotting disk activity. The following shows an average for every hour of the day. This information can then be easily pasted into an MS Excel spreadsheet and plotted with the chart wizard as shown in Figure 13.14 below.

```
SQL> @rpt_10g_sysstat_hr
```

This will query the dba_hist_sysstat view to display average values by hour of the day

Enter Statistics Name: physical reads

SNAP_TIME	AVG_VALUE
00	120,861
01	132,492
02	134,136
03	137,460
04	138,944
05	140,496
06	141,937
07	143,191
08	145,313
09	135,881
10	137,031
11	138,331
12	139,388
13	140,753
14	128,621
15	101,683
16	116,985
17	118,386
18	119,463
19	120,868
20	121,976
21	112,906
22	114,708
23	116,340

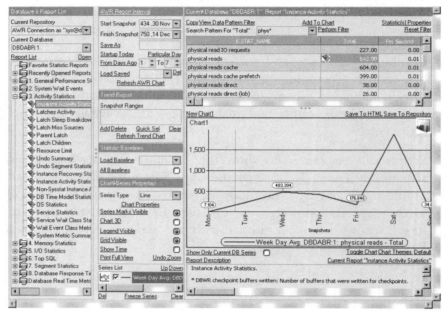

Figure 13.14: *An hourly disk read I/O trend signature*

The following script will generate results aggregated by day of the week instead of hour of the day.

```
prompt   Copyright 2004 by Donald K. Burleson
prompt
prompt
prompt   This will query the dba_hist_sysstat view to
prompt   display average values by hour of the day
prompt

set pages 999

break on snap_time skip 2

accept stat_name char prompt 'Enter Statistics Name:   ';


col snap_time    format a19
col avg_value    format 999,999,999
```

```
select

decode(snap_time1,1,'Monday',2,'Tuesday',3,'Wednesday',4,'Thursday',
5,'Friday',6,'Saturday',7,'Sunday') snap_time,
   avg_value
from (
select
   to_char(begin_interval_time,'d') snap_time1,
   avg(value)                              avg_value
from
   dba_hist_sysstat
  natural join
   dba_hist_snapshot
where
   stat_name = 'physical reads'
group by
   to_char(begin_interval_time,'d')
order by
   to_char(begin_interval_time,'d')
)
;
```

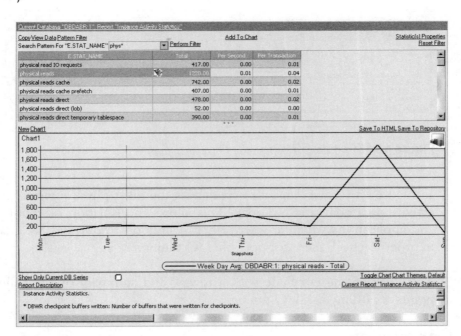

Figure 13.15: *A daily disk reads I/O trend signature*

In Figure 13.15, the daily aggregation of disk read I/O shows that the database experiences the most physical read I/O activity on Saturday.

This allows the isolation of routines and applications which are performed mainly on Saturday in order to check them for possible I/O tuning.

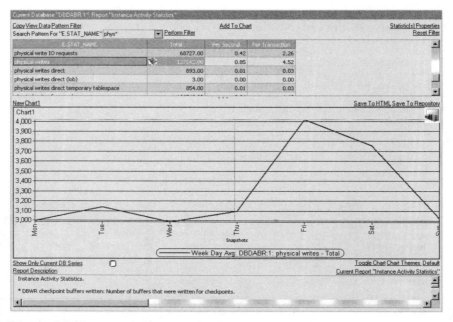

Figure 13.16: *A daily disk write I/O trend signature*

In Figure 13.16, the database experiences the most physical write I/O activity on Friday and Saturday. This allows the isolation of routines and applications which are performed mainly on Friday and Saturday in order to check them for possible I/O tuning.

This chapter will conclude with a review and summary of the major points regarding disk I/O tuning.

Conclusion

Disks have evolved over the past 40 years but remain an archaic component of Oracle. Disk array manufacturers are now homogenizing disk arrays to the point where they can get I/O rates to match the disk capacity. This results in the spread of the I/O across many more platters than ever before, but it makes tracking Oracle I/O problems more difficult.

The main points of this chapter include:

- Databases used to be largely I/O bound, but this is changing as a result of large data buffer caches. Many databases in Oracle10g have shifted to being CPU bound.

- Solid-state disk is making inroads with Oracle and many systems are now using SSD instead of disk.

- Verify that the database is I/O bound before undertaking the tuning of the I/O sub-system. Check the top 5 wait events for the database.

- Oracle *v$* views and the AWR tables provide time series I/O tracking information so that read and write I/O signatures can be plotted, aggregated by hour of the day and day of the week.

The next step is to dive into the Oracle instance and look at how the AWR and ASH tables can give insight into the data for sizing the main SGA regions.

Oracle Instance Tuning

Semper Vigilans

The increasing sophistication and flexibility of Oracle10g offers new challenges to the database administrator with regard to determining the optimal size of each System Global Area (SGA) region. Making the proper decisions required to efficiently utilize RAM resources can mean the savings of millions of dollars.

This chapter will address the following areas of Oracle instance tuning:

- **Operating System configuration:** There are many settings on the server that affect the performance of the Oracle database.

- **Oracle instance para**meters: Oracle has over 250 documented and over one hundred undocumented instance configuration parameters.

- **Oracle data caching:** Properly defining data buffer caches (KEEP pool, multiple data buffers) has a tremendous impact on reducing disk I/O.

Instance Tuning comes first!

Some beginners advocate tuning individual SQL statements before optimizing the instance parameters. This can be a huge waste of effort. Changing instance parameters after SQL tuning can undo a lot of hard work.

Instance tuning is the process of determining the optimal settings for over 250 instance initialization parameters. Some instance parameters (*optimizer_mode*, *optimizer_index_caching*) control how Oracle configures itself to process and optimize SQL statements. These parameters must be pre-set to optimize the bulk of the SQL statements before any individual SQL tuning takes place. If individual SQL statements were tuned prior to determining the instance parameter settings, much of that hard would have to be redone.

For example, v$bh can be sampled AWR and STATSPACK tables can be used to determine the average amount of index segments in the data buffers. The parameter *optimizer_index_caching* can be reset from its default value of 0. From the Oracle 10g performance tuning guide the following advice can be found on setting *optimizer_index_caching*:

> "OPTIMIZER_INDEX_CACHING - This parameter controls the costing of an index probe in conjunction with a nested loop. The range of values 0 to 100 for OPTIMIZER_INDEX_CACHING indicates percentage of index blocks in the buffer cache, which modifies the optimizer's assumptions about index caching for nested loops and IN-list iterators. A value of 100 infers that 100% of the index blocks are likely to be found in the buffer cache and the optimizer adjusts the cost of an index probe or nested loop accordingly. Use caution when using this parameter because execution plans can change in favor of index caching."

Here, the Oracle 10g Reference suggests that the DBA should set this instance parameter according to average system load:

> "The cost of executing an index using an IN-list iterator or of executing a nested loops join when an index is used to access the inner table depends on the caching of that index in the buffer cache. The amount of caching depends on factors that the optimizer cannot predict, such as the load on the system and the block access patterns of different users.
>
> You can modify the optimizer's assumptions about index caching for nested loops joins and IN-list iterators by setting this parameter to a value between 0 and 100 to indicate the percentage of the index blocks the optimizer should assume are in the cache."

Consider the following scenario. The default value for *optimizer_index_caching* was left unchanged and 10 weeks were spent tuning 5,000 SQL statements using hints, adding histograms, etc. Later on, it comes to light that *optimizer_index_caching* is set at the default value of zero. This means that the CBO assumes that there are no index data blocks in the cache. Inspections of *x$bh* confirm that an average of 80% of all indexes are in the data buffer. This factor will greatly influence the CBO's decision about the speed of index vs. table scan access. So, *optimizer_index_caching* is reset to a more real-world value. Suddenly thousands of SQL execution plans change, undoing all of that hard tuning work.

The moral: Always set good baseline values for instance parameters BEFORE tuning any individual SQL statements.

Instance Configuration for High Performance

With the introduction of Oracle10g, there are benchmarks using multi-million dollar servers with up to 64 CPUs and over a half-terabyte of SGA RAM. The vendors want to dazzle, so they hire the best experts to hypercharge benchmarks using Oracle high performance techniques. There are many Oracle parameters that can have a profound impact on database performance.

One of the most common mistakes made by the Oracle tuning professional is diving into specific tuning issues before tuning the instance. The instance is always changing, but the proper configuration of initialization parameters can make a tremendous difference in overall database performance. These all-important parameters include OS kernel parameters and Oracle initialization parameters.

Oracle10g introduced Automatic Memory Management (AMM), but this feature is reactive, only reallocating the memory regions as problems are detected. The single most important region for purposes of Oracle tuning is the data buffer cache, and the data buffers can easily be automated using scripts and the *dbms_scheduler* utility. To briefly review, the Oracle data buffers use RAM to cache incoming data blocks from disk. The data can then be retrieved from RAM thousands of times faster than a disk access. Managing these RAM buffers intelligently will have a huge positive impact on Oracle performance.

OS kernel parameters

Oracle's OS specific installation instructions provide guidelines for the OS configuration, but the settings for the OS parameters can make an enormous difference in Oracle performance.

Because Oracle runs on over 60 different operating systems from a mainframe to a Macintosh, it is impossible to cover every single platform. However, the common configuration issues for UNIX and Microsoft Windows platforms will be presented.

Server Settings for Windows Servers

Windows servers for Oracle are relatively simple when compared to UNIX-based servers. There are only a few major points to cover to ensure that the Windows server is optimized for an Oracle database. The larger Windows servers (e.g. the UNISYS ES7000 servers) can have up to 32 CPUs and hundreds of gigabytes of RAM. They can support dozens of Oracle instances, but many third party applications can hog server resources, causing Oracle performance issues.

Kernel setting for UNIX and Linux servers

In UNIX and Linux, there is much more flexibility in configuration and hundreds of kernel setting that can benefit database performance. Table 14.1 lists some of the most common kernel parameters that influence Oracle:

PARAMETER NAME	DESCRIPTION	DEFAULT VALUE	SET BY THE DBA
shmmax	The maximum size, in bytes, of a single shared memory segment. For best performance, it should be large enough to hold the entire SGA.	1048576	YES
shmmin	The minimum size, in bytes, of a single shared memory segment.	1	YES
shmseg	The maximum number of shared memory segments that can be attached (i.e. used) by a single process.	6	YES
shmmni	This determines how many shared memory segments can be on the system.	100	YES
shmmns	The amount of shared memory that can be allocated system-wide.	N/A	NO

Table 14.1: *OS Parameters*

For details, the OS specific Oracle installation guide should be consulted for details. One of the most common problems with Oracle server configuration is sub-optimal I/O. For example, the most important thing with Linux is enabling direct I/O on the underlying file system. Without that being enabled, Linux will cache files both in the system buffer cache and in SGA. That double caching is unnecessary and will deprive the server of RAM resources. The following section provides a closer look by outlining some of the important Oracle parameters for performance.

Oracle Parameter Tuning

Oracle10g has more than 250 initialization parameters, and these parameters govern the overall behavior of the Oracle instance. When set to suboptimal values, Oracle parameters can cause serious performance problems. This is especially true for the parameters that govern the SQL optimizer.

The following is a list of some of the most important parameters for Oracle10g SQL tuning:

- *optimizer_mode*
- *optimizer_index_cost_adj*
- *optimizer_index_caching*
- *optimizer_percent_parallel*

There are parameters that control the sizes of the SGA regions and the proper configuration and settings for these parameters can have a profound impact on database performance. These parameters include:

- *db_cache_size*
- *db_keep_cache_size*
- *shared_pool_size*
- *pga_aggregate_target*
- *log_buffer*
- *query_rewrite_enabled*
- *cursor_sharing*
- *db_file_multiblock_read_count*
- *hash_multiblock_io_count*

If the Oracle Automatic Memory Management (AMM) is utilized, Oracle will automatically change the relative sizes of the SGA regions, such as *db_cache_size*, *pga_aggregate_target* and *shared_pool_size*, based on current demands; however, the overall parameters for the instance must be set.

Oracle Hidden Parameters

There are also a number of hidden parameters that greatly impact Oracle performance. For example, a recent Linux world record benchmark used the following hidden Oracle parameters:

```
_in_memory_undo=false
_cursor_cache_frame_bind_memory = true
_db_cache_pre_warm = false
_in_memory_undo=false
_check_block_after_checksum = false
_lm_file_affinity
```

WARNING!

These are unsupported parameters and they should not be used unless an iTar has been opened and their behavior has been tested on your own database and you are willing to accept full responsibility for any issues.

Oracle will not provide support if any of these values are modified, so DBAs must do careful research in a test database before making any production database changes.

Hidden Latch Parameters

- *_db_block_hash_buckets:* Defaults to two times *db_block_buffers* but should be the nearest prime number to the value of 2 times *db_block_buffers*

- *_db_block_hash_latches:* Defaults to 1024, but 32768 is sometimes a better value.

- *_kgl_latch_count:* This defaults to zero and lock contention can often be reduced by resetting this value to 2*CPUs +1.

- *_latch_spin_count:* This parameter shows how often a latch request will be taken.

- *_db_block_write_batch:* Formerly documented, this parameter is now undocumented. It is the number of blocks that the database writers will write in each batch. It defaults to 512 or *db_files*db_file_simultaneous_writes/2* up to a limit of one-fourth the value of *db_cache_size*.

Hidden Parallel Parameters

The most important of the hidden parallel parameters is the *_parallelism_cost_fudge_factor*. This parameter governs the invocation of Oracle Parallel Query (OPQ) by the cost-based SQL optimizer when *parallel_automatic_tuning=TRUE*. By adjusting this parameter, the threshold for invoking parallel queries can be controlled.

```
NAME                              VALUE
---------------------------------- --------
_parallel_adaptive_max_users      1
_parallel_default_max_instances   1
_parallel_execution_message_align FALSE
_parallel_fake_class_pct          0
_parallel_load_bal_unit           0
_parallel_load_balancing          TRUE
_parallel_min_message_pool        64560
_parallel_recovery_stopat         32767
_parallel_server_idle_time        5
_parallel_server_sleep_time       10
_parallel_txn_global              FALSE
_parallelism_cost_fudge_factor    350
```

While the Oracle hidden parameters are wonderful for the high level DBA, all others need to make sure they thoroughly test any changes to hidden parameters before using them in the production environment. The Oracle benchmarks are a great way to see Oracle hidden parameters in action, as hardware vendors often know secrets for optimizing their servers. The following section will examine some Oracle SQL parameters.

SQL Optimizer Parameters

Despite the name Oracle, the Cost Based Optimizer (CBO) is not psychic, and it can never know the exact load on the system in advance. Hence, the Oracle professional must adjust the CBO behavior, and most Oracle professionals adjust the CBO with two parameters: *optimizer_index_cost_adj* and *optimizer_index_caching*.

The parameter named *optimizer_index_cost_adj* controls the CBO's propensity to favor index scans over full-table scans. In a dynamic system, the ideal value for *optimizer_index_cost_adj* may change radically in just a few minutes, as the type of SQL and load on the database changes.

SQL Optimizer undocumented parameters

These parameters control the internal behavior of the cost-based SQL optimizer.

- *_fast_full_scan_enabled:* This enables or disables fast full index scans, if only indexes are required to resolve the queries.

- *_always_star_transformation*: This parameter helps tune data warehouse queries, provided that the warehouse is designed properly.

- *_small_table_threshold*: - This sets the size definition of a small table. A small table is automatically pinned into the buffers when queried. In Oracle 9i, this parameter defaults to two percent.

Data Buffer Cache Hidden Parameters

For the brave DBA, the caching and aging rules within the Oracle *db_cache_size* can be changed. This will modify the way that Oracle keeps data blocks in RAM memory. While modifying these parameters is somewhat dangerous, some savvy DBAs have been able to get more efficient data caching by adjusting these values:

WARNING!

These parameters determine the dynamics of the buffer aging and are dynamically generated. It influences Oracle's LRU approximation and should never be touched without the direction from Oracle Support.

- *_db_aging_cool_count:* Touch count set when buffer cooled.

- *_db_aging_freeze_cr:* Make consistent read buffers always be FALSE; too cold to keep in cache.

- *_db_aging_hot_criteria*: Adjust aging for the touch count which sends a buffer to the head of the replacement list.

- *_db_aging_stay_count*: Adjust aging stay count for touch count.

- *_db_aging_touch_time*: Touch time that sends a buffer to the head of LRU.

- *_db_block_cache_clone:* Always clone data blocks on get, for debugging.

- *_db_block_cache_map:* Map/unmap and track reference counts on blocks, for debugging.

- *_db_block_cache_protect:* Protect database blocks. This is true only when debugging.

- *_db_block_hash_buckets:* Number of database block hash buckets.

- *_db_block_hi_priority_batch_size:* Fraction of writes for high priority reasons.

- *_db_block_max_cr_dba:* Maximum Allowed Number of CR buffers per DBA.

- *_db_block_max_scan_cnt:* Maximum number of buffers to inspect when looking for free space.

- *_db_block_med_priority_batch_size:* Fraction of writes for medium priority reasons.

Oracle does not support changing the hidden parameters, and any change should be carefully tested prior to employing them in any production database.

After this introduction to the importance of setting instance wide parameters, it is time to look at a general approach to Oracle instance tuning.

Instance Wait Tuning

The use of the Active Session History (ASH) data collection within Oracle 10g provides a wealth of excellent instance tuning opportunities. The *dba_hist_sys_time_model* table can be queried to locate aggregate information on where Oracle sessions are spending most of their time.

The *v$active_session_history* table can be used to view specific events with the highest resource waits.

```
select
   ash.event,
   sum(ash.wait_time +
   ash.time_waited) ttl_wait_time
from
   v$active_session_history ash
where
   ash.sample_time between sysdate - 60/2880 and sysdate
group by
   ash.event
order by 2;
```

The following is sample output from this script:

```
EVENT                                    TTL_WAIT_TIME
---------------------------------------- -------------
SQL*Net message from client                        218
db file sequential read                          37080
control file parallel write                     156462
jobq slave wait                                3078166
Queue Monitor Task Wait                        5107697
rdbms ipc message                             44100787
class slave wait                             271136729
```

The *v$active_session_history* table can be used to view users, and see which users are waiting the most time for database resources:

```
col wait_time format 999,999,999
select
   sess.sid,
   sess.username,
   sum(ash.wait_time + ash.time_waited) wait_time
from
   v$active_session_history ash,
   v$session sess
where
   ash.sample_time > sysdate-1
and
   ash.session_id = sess.sid
group by
   sess.sid,
   sess.username
order by 3;
```

The following is sample output from this script:

```
 SID USERNAME                           WAIT_TIME
---------- ------------------------------ ----------
 140 OPUS                                  30,055
 165                                       30,504
 169                                    9,234,463
 167                                   27,089,994
 160                                   34,145,401
 168                                   40,033,486
 152                                   45,162,031
 159                                   81,921,987
 144 OPUS                             129,249,875
 150 SYS                              134,263,687
 142                                  163,752,689
 166                                  170,700,889
 149 OPUS                             195,664,013
 163                                  199,860,105
 170                                  383,992,930
```

For a given session, an Oracle user may issue multiple SQL statements and it is the interaction between the SQL and the database that determines the wait conditions. The *v$active_session_history* table can be joined into the *v$sqlarea* and *dba_users* to quickly see the top SQL waits as well as the impacted user and session with which they are associated:

```
select
   ash.user_id,
   u.username,
```

Instance Wait Tuning   **477**

```
      sqla.sql_text,
      sum(ash.wait_time + ash.time_waited) wait_time
from
      v$active_session_history ash,
      v$sqlarea                sqla,
      dba_users                u
where
      ash.sample_time > sysdate-1
and
      ash.sql_id = sqla.sql_id
and
      ash.user_id = u.user_id
group by
      ash.user_id,
      sqla.sql_text,
      u.username
order by 4;
```

The following is sample output from this script:

```
   USER_ID USERNAME
---------- -----------------------------
SQL_TEXT
--------------------------------------------------------------------------------
WAIT_TIME
----------
        54 SYSMAN
DECLARE job BINARY_INTEGER := :job; next_date DATE := :mydate;  broken BOOLEAN :
= FALSE; BEGIN EMD_MAINTENANCE.EXECUTE_EM_DBMS_JOB_PROCS(); :mydate := next_date
; IF broken THEN :b := 1; ELSE :b := 0; END IF; END;
        0

        58 DABR
select tbsp       , reads "Reads"        , rps  "Reads / Second"       , atpr   "Avg
 Reads (ms)"      , bpr  "Avg Blks / Read"       , writes  "Writes"       , wps
"Avg Writes / Second"      , waits  "Buffer Waits"        , atpwt"Avg Buf Wait (m
s)" From ( select e.tsname tbsp      , sum (e.phyrds - nvl(b.phyrds,0))
       reads      , Round(sum (e.phyrds - nvl(b.phyrds,0))/awr101.getEla( :
pDbId,:pInstNum,:pBgnSnap,:pEndSnap,'NO' ),3)    rps     , Round(decode( sum(e.p
hyrds - nvl(b.phyrds,0))          , 0, 0             , (sum(e.readtim - nvl
(b.readtim,0)) /          sum(e.phyrds  - nvl(b.phyrds,0)))*10),3)
atpr      , Round(decode( sum(e.phyrds - nvl(b.phyrds,0))        , 0, to_n
umber(NULL)          , sum(e.phyblkrd - nvl(b.phyblkrd,0)) /
sum(e.phyrds   - nvl(b.phyrds,0)) ),3)     bpr     , sum (e.phywrts    - n
vl(b.phywrts,0))            writes     , Round(sum (e.phywrts    - nvl(b.ph
ywrts,0))/awr101.getEla( :pDbId,:pInstNu
        174

        58 DABR
select e.stat_name                     "E.STAT_NAME"       , (e.value - b.value
)/1000000        "Time (s)"       , decode( e.stat_name,'DB time'         ,
to_number(null)          , 100*(e.value - b.value)              )/awr101.get
DBTime(:pDbId,:pInstNum,:pBgnSnap,:pEndSnap) "Percent of Total DB Time"   from d
ba_hist_sys_time_model e       , dba_hist_sys_time_model b  where b.snap_id
      = :pBgnSnap    and e.snap_id              = :pEndSnap    and b.dbid
      = :pDbId    and e.dbid              = :pDbId     and b.ins
tance_number       = :pInstNum   and e.instance_number       = :pInstNum    a
nd b.stat_id            = e.stat_id    and e.value - b.value > 0  order by 2
 desc
```

Once the SQL details have been identified, the DBA can drill down deeper by joining *v$active_session_history* with *dba_objects* and find important information about the interaction between the SQL and specific tables and indexes. What follows is an ASH script that can be used to show the specific events that are causing the highest resource waits. Some contention is NOT caused by SQL but by faulty network, slow disk, or some other external causes. Also, frequent deadlocks may be caused by improperly indexed foreign keys.

```
select
   obj.object_name,
   obj.object_type,
   ash.event,
   sum(ash.wait_time + ash.time_waited) wait_time
from
   v$active_session_history ash,
   dba_objects              obj
where
   ash.sample_time > sysdate -1
and
   ash.current_obj# = obj.object_id
group by
   obj.object_name,
   obj.object_type,
   ash.event
order by 4 desc;
```

The following is sample output from this script:

```
OBJECT_NAME            OBJECT_TYPE    EVENT                          WAIT_TIME
--------------------   -------------  ----------------------------   -------
SCHEDULER$_CLASS       TABLE          rdbms ipc message              199,853,456
USER$                  TABLE          rdbms ipc message               33,857,135
USER$                  TABLE          control file sequential read      288,266
WRI$_ALERT_HISTORY     TABLE          db file sequential read            26,002
OL_SCP_PK              INDEX          db file sequential read            19,638
C_OBJ#                 CLUSTER        db file sequential read            17,966
STATS$SYS_TIME_MODEL   TABLE          db file scattered read             16,085
WRI$_ADV_DEFINITIONS   INDEX          db file sequential read            15,995
```

It is apparent that table *wri$_alert_history* experiences a high wait time on *db file sequential read* wait event. Based on this fact, the DBA can further investigate causes of such behavior in order to find the primary problem. It could be, for example, a non-optimal SQL query that performs large full table scans on this table.

Now that it's been shown how ASH information can enlighten DBAs about specific wait events for active session, it is time to return to the detailed information on instance wide tuning and see how to optimize the Oracle data buffer pools.

Tuning the Oracle10g Data Buffer Pools

There were many new features in the Oracle10g database that were announced with fanfare in the publicity that accompanied its introduction, but Oracle's ability to support multiple block sizes received comparatively little attention. As a result, the important role that multiple block sizes play in the reduction of disk I/O was less appreciated than it might have been. For the Oracle administrator, multiple block sizes are extremely significant and exciting. For the first time, data buffer sizes can be customized to fit the specific needs of the database.

Prior to the introduction of multiple block sizes, the entire Oracle database had a single block size, and this size was determined at the time the database was created. Historically, Oracle8i allowed tables and index blocks to be segregated into three separate data buffers, but the buffer caches had to be the same size. The KEEP pool stored table blocks that were referenced frequently, the RECYCLE pool held blocks from large-table full-table scans, and the DEFAULT pool contained miscellaneous object blocks.

Oracle10g opened up a whole new world of disk I/O management with its ability to configure multiple block sizes. Tablespaces can be defined with block sizes of 2K, 4K, 8K, 16K, and 32K. These tablespaces can be matched with similar sized tables and indexes, thus minimizing disk I/O and efficiently minimizing wasted space in the data buffers. In Oracle10g, there are a total of seven separate and distinct data buffers that are used to segregate incoming table and index rows.

Many Oracle professionals still fail to appreciate the benefits of multiple block sizes and do not understand that the marginal cost of I/O for large blocks is negligible. A 32K block fetch costs only one percent more than a 2K block fetch because 99 percent of the disk

I/O is involved with the read-write head and rotational delay in getting to the cylinder and track. It also depends on the file system, since some file systems cannot handle multi-block I/O well.

This is an important concept for Oracle indexes because indexes perform better when stored in large block size tablespaces. The indexes perform better because the b-trees may have a lower height and mode entries per index node, resulting in less overall disk overhead with sequential index node access. The exploration of this important new feature begins with a review of data caching in Oracle10g.

The Problem of Duplicitous RAM Caches

As hardware evolved though the 1990's, independent components of database systems started to employ their own RAM caching tools as shown in Figure 14.1.

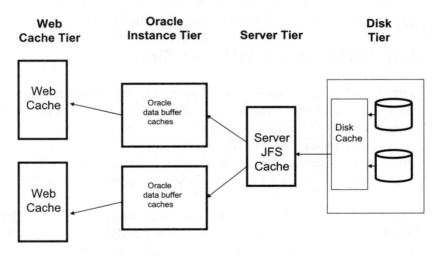

Figure 14.1: *Multiple RAM caches in an Oracle enterprise*

In this figure, the Oracle database is not the only component to utilize RAM caching. The disk array employs a RAM cache, the servers have a Journal File System (JFS) RAM cache, and the front-end web server also serves to cache Oracle data.

This concept is important because many enterprises may inadvertently double cache Oracle data. Even more problematic are the fake statistics reported by Oracle when multiple level caches are employed:

- **Fake Physical I/O times**: If a disk array with a built-in RAM cache is in use, the disk I/O subsystem may acknowledge ("ack") a physical write to Oracle, when in reality the data has not yet been written to the physical disk spindle. This false "ack" can skew timing of disk read/write speeds.

- **Wasted Oracle Data Buffer RAM**: In system that employs web servers, the Apache front end may cache frequently used data. Thus, significant Oracle resources may be wasted by caching data blocks that are already cached on the web server tier.

The next step is to take a look at the best way to use SSD in an Oracle environment. First is the examination of the relationship between physical disk I/O (PIO) and Oracle Logical I/O (LIO).

Why is Oracle Logical I/O so Slow?

Disk latency is generally measured in milliseconds while RAM access is expressed in nanoseconds. In theory, RAM is four orders of magnitude, 10,000 times, faster than disk; however, this is not true when using Oracle. In practice, logical I/O is seldom more than 1,000 times faster than disk I/O. Most Oracle experts say that logical disk I/O is only 15 times to 100 times faster than a physical disk I/O.

Oracle has internal data protection mechanisms that cause a RAM data block access, a consistent get, to be far slower due to internal locks and latch serialization mechanisms. This overhead is required in order to maintain read consistency and data concurrency.

If Oracle logical I/O is expensive, can this expense be avoided by reading directly from disk? The answer to this question is important to the discussion about the most appropriate placement for SSD in an Oracle environment.

There are also issues associated with super large disks. With 144 gigabyte disks becoming commonplace, I/O intensive databases will often see disk latency because many tasks are competing to read blocks on different parts of the super large disk.

An Oracle physical read must read the disk data block and then transfer it into the Oracle RAM buffer before the data is passed to the requesting program as shown in Figure 14.2.

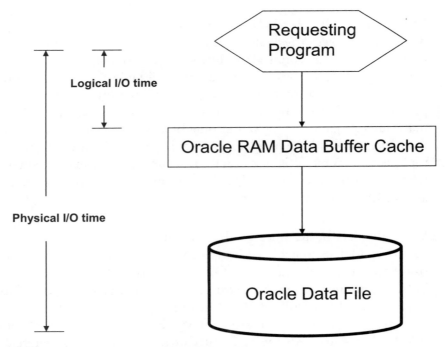

Figure 14.2: *Physical reads include logical I/O latency*

So if the DBA accepts that LIO expense is going to happen regardless of whether or not a PIO is performed, valuable insight can be gained into the proper placement for SSD in an Oracle environment:

In the next section, information will be presented on the KEEP and RECYCLE data buffers and how objects are selected for inclusion.

Data Block Caching in the SGA

When an SQL statement makes a row request, Oracle first checks the internal memory to see if the data is already in a data buffer, thereby avoiding unnecessary disk I/O. Now that very large SGAs are available with 64-bit versions of Oracle, small databases can be entirely cached, and one data RAM buffer can be defined for each database block.

For databases that are too large to be stored in data buffers, Oracle has developed a *Touch Count* algorithm to retain the most popular RAM blocks. The touch count algorithm is an approximation of the LRU algorithm. Certain types of uses, like the full table scan, do not add to the touch count, so that blocks keep loosing the touch count and the probability of them being replaced increases significantly. Blocks maintain so called *touch count* and only blocks with touch counts lower than prescribed by an undocumented parameter are eligible for replacement. While it is not exactly a queue structure, as was the case with the proper LRU method, latch contention is significantly reduced as no LRU queue latches are needed.

When the data buffer does not have enough room to cache the whole database, Oracle utilizes a least recently used algorithm that selects pages to flush from memory. Oracle assigns each block in the data buffer an in-memory control structure, and each incoming data block is placed in the middle of the data buffer. Every time the block is requested, it moves to the front of the buffer list, shifting all other RAM blocks toward the age out area. Data blocks referenced infrequently will eventually reach the end of the data buffer, where they will be erased thereby making room for new data blocks, as shown in Figure 14.3.

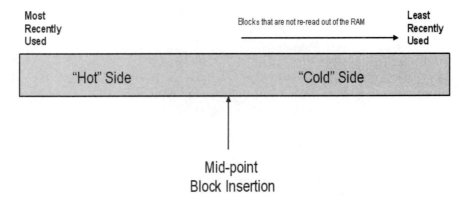

Figure 14.3: *Aging data blocks from the RAM block buffer*

Oracle 7 always placed incoming blocks at the most recently used end of the buffer. Beginning with Oracle8, Oracle provided three separate pools of RAM, the KEEP, RECYCLE, and DEFAULT pools, in the *db_cache_size* region to hold incoming data blocks. With Oracle8i, Oracle dramatically changed the way data blocks were handled within the buffers by inserting them into the midpoint of the block and dividing the block into HOT and COLD areas.

With Oracle10g, the highly efficient technique of prioritizing data blocks within the buffers has been combined with the additional flexibility of multiple block sizes.

To view the current database buffer parameters, SQL*Plus can be used to issue the *show parameters buffer* command. A list of parameters from an Oracle8i database is shown below.

```
SQL> show parameters buffer

NAME                                TYPE    VALUE
----------------------------------- ------- ----------------------
buffer_pool_keep                    string  500
buffer_pool_recycle                 string
db_block_buffers                    integer 6000
log_archive_buffer_size             integer 64
log_archive_buffers                 integer 4
log_buffer                          integer 2048000
sort_write_buffer_size              integer 32768
```

```
sort_write_buffers                      integer 2
use_indirect_data_buffers               boolean FALSE
```

This output shows the KEEP pool (*buffer_pool_keep*), the RECYCLE pool (*buffer_pool_recycle*) and the DEFAULT pool (*db_cache_size*). The same listing for an Oracle10g database is shown below. Note the re-naming of *db_block_buffers* to *db_cache_size*.

```
SQL> show parameters buffer

NAME                                    TYPE    VALUE
------------------------------------    ------- ------
buffer_pool_keep                        string
buffer_pool_recycle                     string
db_block_buffers                        integer 0
log_buffer                              integer 524288
use_indirect_data_buffers               boolean FALSE
```

Full Table Caching in Oracle10g

The large RAM region within Oracle8i made it possible to fully cache an entire database. Before Oracle introduced 64-bit versions, the maximum size of the SGA was 1.7 gigabytes on many UNIX platforms. With the introduction of 64-bit addressing, there is no practical limitation on the size of an Oracle SGA, and there are enough data buffers for the DBA to cache the whole database.

The benefits of full data caching become clear when the savvy DBA recalls that retrieving data from RAM is an order of magnitude faster than reading it from disk. Access time from disks is expressed in milliseconds, while RAM speed is expressed in nanoseconds. In Oracle10g, RAM cache access is at least 100 times faster than disk access.

If the DBA intends to fully cache an Oracle database, there must be careful planning. The multiple data buffer pools are not needed, and most DBAs cache all the data blocks in the DEFAULT pool. In general, any database that is less than 20 gigabytes is fully cached, while larger databases still require partial data buffer caches. The DBA can issue the following simple command to calculate the number of allocated data blocks:

```
SQL> select
  2      sum(blocks)
  3  from
  4      dba_data_files;

SUM(BLOCKS)
-----------
     217360

SQL> select
  2      sum(blocks)
  3  from
  4*     dba_extents

SUM(BLOCKS)
-----------
     127723
```

As the database grows, the DBA must carefully monitor the buffers in order to increase the *db_cache_size* to match the database size. Another common approach is to use solid-state disks (RAM-SAN) and use a small data buffer.

This technique insures that all data blocks are cached for reads, but write activity still requires disk I/O. With RAM becoming cheaper each year, the trend of fully caching smaller databases will continue.

Oracle Data Buffer Metrics

The *data buffer hit ratio* (DBHR) measures the propensity for a data block to be cached in the buffer pool. The goal of the DBA must be to keep as many of the frequently used Oracle blocks in buffer memory as possible. However, this goal is clouded by the use of Solid-state disk (SSD) and the on-board RAM caches of the newer disk arrays. Oracle may appear to be performing a disk I/O, when in reality; the data block is already in RAM on the disk subsystem cache.

Hence, the DBHR has become a largely meaningless number except in cases of predicting changes in system processing patterns and the initial sizing of the *db_cache_size*.

As the hit ratio approaches 100 percent, more data blocks are found in memory which normally results in fewer I/O's and faster overall database performance.

On the other hand, if the DBHR falls below 50 percent, fewer data blocks are resident in memory which requires Oracle to perform additional, often expensive disk, I/O to move the data blocks into the data buffer. The formula for calculating the DBHR in Oracle8 is:

```
1 - (Physical Reads - Physical Reads Direct)
--------------------------------------------
             (session logical reads)
```

The formula for calculating the hit ratio in Oracle7 and Oracle8 does not include direct block reads. Direct block reads became a separate statistic in Oracle8i.

The hit ratio for Oracle8i can be gathered from the *v$* views, as shown below. However, this particular value is not very useful because it shows the total buffer hit ratio since the beginning of the instance.

```
select
   1 - ((a.value - (b.value))/d.value) "Cache Hit Ratio"
from
   v$sysstat a,
   v$sysstat b,
   v$sysstat d
where
   a.name='physical reads'
and
   b.name='physical reads direct'
and
   d.name='session logical reads';
```

Many novice DBAs make the mistake of using the DBHR from the *v$* views. The *v$buffer_pool_statistics* view does contain the accumulated values for data buffer pool usage, but computing the *data buffer hit ratio* from the *v$* tables only provides the average since the database was started.

The next section explains how the AWR can provide a wealth of information for tracking buffer pool utilization and computing the *data buffer hit ratio*.

Using AWR for buffer pool statistics

AWR uses the *dba_hist$buffer_pool_statistics* table for monitoring buffer pool statistics. This table contains the following useful columns:

- *name:* This column shows the name of the data buffer; KEEP, RECYCLE, or DEFAULT.

- *free_buffer_wait:* This is a count of the number of waits on free buffers.

- *buffer_busy_wait:* This is the number of times a requested block was in the data buffer but was unavailable because of a conflict.

- *db_block_gets:* This is the number of database block gets which are either logical or physical.

- *consistent_gets:* This is the number of logical reads.

- *physical_reads:* This is the number of disk block fetch requests issued by Oracle. This is not always a real read because of disk array caching.

- *physical_writes:* This is the number of physical disk write requests from Oracle. If there is a disk array, the actual writes are performed asynchronously.

These AWR columns provide information that can be used to measure several important metrics, including the most important, the DBHR.

Data Buffer Monitoring with STATSPACK and AWR

There are two ways to use the AWR to compute the DBHR. In Oracle10g, there is the *dba_hist_buffer_pool_stat* table. In Oracle9i and Oracle8i, the DBA can use the *stats$buffer_pool_statistics* table, and for Oracle 8.0, the *stats$sesstat* table should be used.

The *rpt_bhr_all.sql* script listed below is used for Oracle 8.1 through Oracle9i:

💾 **rpt_bhr_all.sql**

```
-- ***************************************************
-- Copyright © 2005 by Rampant TechPress
-- This script is free for non-commercial purposes
-- with no warranties.  Use at your own risk.
--
-- To license this script for a commercial purpose,
-- contact info@rampant.cc
-- ***************************************************

column bhr format 9.99
column mydate heading 'yr.  mo dy Hr.'

select
   to_char(snap_time,'yyyy-mm-dd HH24')       mydate,
   new.name                                   buffer_pool_name,
   (((new.consistent_gets-old.consistent_gets)+
   (new.db_block_gets-old.db_block_gets))-
   (new.physical_reads-old.physical_reads))
   /
   ((new.consistent_gets-old.consistent_gets)+
   (new.db_block_gets-old.db_block_gets))     bhr
from
   dba_hist_buffer_pool_stat old,
   dba_hist_buffer_pool_statnew,
   dba_hist_sgasn
where
   (((new.consistent_gets-old.consistent_gets)+
   (new.db_block_gets-old.db_block_gets))-
   (new.physical_reads-old.physical_reads))
   /
   ((new.consistent_gets-old.consistent_gets)+
   (new.db_block_gets-old.db_block_gets)) < .90
and
   new.name = old.name
and
   new.snap_id = sn.snap_id
and
   old.snap_id = sn.snap_id-1
;
```

If Oracle8 is in use, the following version will work:

💾 **rpt_bhr_oracle8.sql**

```
-- ***************************************************
-- Copyright © 2005 by Rampant TechPress
```

```
-- This script is free for non-commercial purposes
-- with no warranties.  Use at your own risk.
--
-- To license this script for a commercial purpose,
-- contact info@rampant.cc
-- ***************************************************

set pages 9999;

column logical_reads   format 999,999,999
column phys_reads      format 999,999,999
column phys_writes     format 999,999,999
column "BUFFER HIT RATIO" format 999

select
   to_char(snap_time,'yyyy-mm-dd HH24'),
   a.value + b.value   "logical_reads",
   c.value             "phys_reads",
   d.value             "phys_writes",
   round(100 * (((a.value-e.value)+(b.value-f.value))-(c.value-
g.value)) /
(a.value-e.value)+(b.value-f.v
value)))
        "BUFFER HIT RATIO"
from
   perfstat.stats$sysstat a,
   perfstat.stats$sysstat b,
   perfstat.stats$sysstat c,
   perfstat.stats$sysstat d,
   perfstat.stats$sysstat e,
   perfstat.stats$sysstat f,
   perfstat.stats$sysstat g,
   perfstat.stats$snapshot   sn
where
   a.snap_id = sn.snap_id
and
   b.snap_id = sn.snap_id
and
   c.snap_id = sn.snap_id
and
   d.snap_id = sn.snap_id
and
   e.snap_id = sn.snap_id-1
and
   f.snap_id = sn.snap_id-1
and
   g.snap_id = sn.snap_id-1
and
   a.statistic# = 39
and
   e.statistic# = 39
and
   b.statistic# = 38
and
   f.statistic# = 38
and
```

```
   c.statistic# = 40
and
   g.statistic# = 40
and
   d.statistic# = 41
;
```

The following is the Oracle10g method using the AWR tables:

🖫 rpt_bhr_all_awr.sql

```
-- **********************************************
-- Copyright © 2005 by Rampant TechPress
-- This script is free for non-commercial purposes
-- with no warranties.  Use at your own risk.
--
-- To license this script for a commercial purpose,
-- contact info@rampant.cc
-- **********************************************

column bhr format 9.99
column mydate heading 'yr.  mo dy Hr.'

select
   to_char(end_interval_time,'yyyy-mm-dd HH24')       mydate,
   new.name                              buffer_pool_name,
   (((new.consistent_gets-old.consistent_gets)+
   (new.db_block_gets-old.db_block_gets))-
   (new.physical_reads-old.physical_reads))
   /
   ((new.consistent_gets-old.consistent_gets)+
   (new.db_block_gets-old.db_block_gets))    bhr
from
   dba_hist_buffer_pool_stat old,
   dba_hist_buffer_pool_stat new,
   dba_hist_snapshot sn
where
   (((new.consistent_gets-old.consistent_gets)+
   (new.db_block_gets-old.db_block_gets))-
   (new.physical_reads-old.physical_reads))
   /
   ((new.consistent_gets-old.consistent_gets)+
   (new.db_block_gets-old.db_block_gets)) < .90
and
   new.name = old.name
and
   new.snap_id = sn.snap_id
and
   old.snap_id = sn.snap_id-1
;
```

Sample output from this script is shown below:

```
yr.  mo dy Hr      BUFFER_POOL_NAME       BHR
------------       --------------------   -
2001-12-12 15      DEFAULT                .92
2001-12-12 15      KEEP                   .99
2001-12-12 15      RECYCLE                .75

2001-12-12 16      DEFAULT                .94
2001-12-12 16      KEEP                   .99
2001-12-12 16      RECYCLE                .65
```

This script provides the *data buffer hit ratio* for each of the buffer pools at one hour intervals. It is important that the KEEP pool always have a 99-100 percent DBHR. If this is not the case, data blocks should be added to the KEEP pool to make it the same size as the sum of all object data blocks that are assigned to the KEEP pool. It is easy to size the KEEP pool, and the DBA should add up all of the data blocks that are assigned, such as BUFFER-POOL=KEEP, adding a 20% overhead in case of growth.

 The Data Buffer Hit ratio may be meaningless for Data Warehouse and Decision Support systems that perform frequent large-table full-table scans (i.e. databases that use the *all_rows optimizer_mode*).

This DBHR is also of little value in databases that perform parallel large-table full-table scans, which bypass the data buffer, storing the retrieved rows in their PGA region.

The DBA will notice that, in practice, variation in the DBHR will increase with the frequency of measured intervals, such as the snapshot collection interval. For example, the AWR may report a DBHR of 92% at hourly intervals, but there may be a wide variation in DBHR values when the ratio is sampled in two minute intervals, as shown in Figure 14.4.

Oracle Data Buffer Metrics

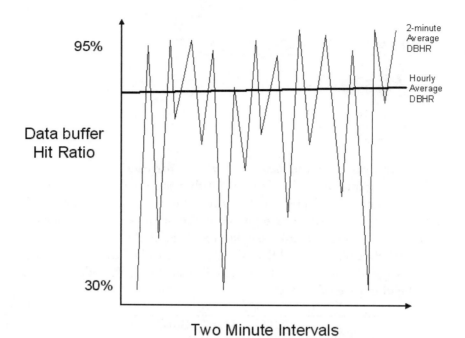

Figure 14.4: *Sampling the data buffer hit ratio over two-minute intervals*

This variation can be illustrated with a simple example. In this case, a database instance is started, and the first ten tasks read ten separate blocks. At this point, the *data buffer hit ratio* is zero because all the requested blocks had to be retrieved via a physical disk I/O. Also, the Oracle 10g Automatic Memory Manager (AMM) will continuously change the sizes of the data buffer pools to accommodate existing processing needs.

In general, data warehouses will have lower buffer hit ratios because they are exposed to large-table full-table scans, while Online Transaction Processing (OLTP) databases will have higher buffer hit ratios because the indexes used most frequently are cached in the data buffer.

A good guiding principle for the Oracle DBA is that as much RAM as possible should be allocated to the data buffers without causing the server to page-in RAM.

Oracle's Seven Data Buffer Hit Ratios

The DBHR is a common metric used by Oracle tuning experts to measure the propensity of a row to be in the data buffer. For example, a hit ratio of 95 percent means that 95 percent of row requests were already present in the data buffer, thereby avoiding an expensive disk I/O. In general, as the size of the data buffers increases, the DBHR will also increase and approach 100 percent.

Oracle10g has a separate DBHR for all seven data buffer caches. For optimum performance, the Oracle DBA might consider a manual approach, such as turning off AMM, and monitor all seven data buffers and adjust their sizes based on each DBHR. Oracle10g provides the exciting feature of allowing the number of RAM buffers within any of the data buffer caches to be changed dynamically.

This is done through ALTER SYSTEM commands that allow the size of the buffers to be changed while Oracle remains available. This means that the DBA can maximize performance in response to current statistics by manually de-allocating RAM from one data buffer and shifting it to another buffer cache.

The general rule is that the more data that can be retrieved from a single I/O, the better the overall hit ratio. However, it is important to delve a little deeper to get a more complete understanding of how multiple data buffers operate.

Allocating Oracle10g Data Buffer Caches

It is important to know how multiple data buffers actually work. As an example, the following buffer cache allocations might be defined in the initialization parameters.

```
db_block_size=32768          -- This is the system-wide
                             -- default block size

db_cache_size=3G             -- This allocates a total of 3
                             -- gigabytes for all of the 32K
                             -- data buffers

db_keep_cache_size=1G        -- Use 1 gigabyte for the KEEP pool

db_recycle_cache_size=500M   -- Here is 500 meg for the RECYCLE pool
                             -- Hence, the DEFAULT pool is 1,500 meg

-- ************************************************************
-- The caches below are all additional RAM memory (total=3.1 gig)
-- that are above and beyond the allocation from db_cache_size
-- ************************************************************

db_2k_cache_size=200M        -- This cache is reserved for random
                             -- block retrieval on tables that
                             -- have small rows.

db_4k_cache_size=500M        -- This 4K buffer will be reserved
                             -- exclusively for tables with a small
                             -- average row length and random access

db_8k_cache_size=800M        -- This is a separate cache for
                             -- segregating I/O for specific tables

db_16k_cache_size=1600M      -- This is a separate cache for
                             -- segregating I/O for specific tables
```

What is the total RAM allocated to the data buffer caches in the example above? The total RAM is the sum of all the named buffer caches plus *db_cache_size*. Hence, the total RAM in the example is 6,100 megabytes, or 6.1 gigabytes.

Before Oracle9i, these were subsets of the DEFAULT pool, and the *db_keep_cache_size* and *db_recycle_cache_size* are subtracted from the *db_cache_size*. After subtracting the allocation for the KEEP and RECYCLE pools, the DEFAULT pool in the example is 1.5 gigabytes. Of course, the total size must be less than the value of *sga_max_size*. In Oracle9i and beyond, the KEEP and RECYCLE became separate RAM areas.

At this point, the basic concepts behind the data buffers should be a little clearer, so it is an appropriate time to go deeper into the internals and see how AWR data can allow the monitoring and self-tuning of the data buffers. Remember, AMM is reactive and only changes the pool sizes after performance has degraded. By identifying trends in buffer utilization, the DBA can use the *dbms_scheduler* package to anticipate and self-tune the data buffers, thereby supplementing and improving AMM.

Viewing Information about SGA Performance

The following Oracle Database10g views provide information about the SGA components and their dynamic resizing:

VIEW	DESCRIPTION
v$sga	Displays summary information about the system global area (SGA).
v$sgainfo	Displays size information about the SGA, including the sizes of different SGA components, the granule size, and free memory.
v$sgastat	Displays detailed information about the SGA.
v$sga_dynamic_components	Displays information about the dynamic SGA components. This view summarizes information based on all completed SGA resize operations since instance startup.
v$sga_dynamic_free_memory	Displays information about the amount of SGA memory available for future dynamic SGA resize operations.
v$sga_resize_ops	Displays information about the last 100 completed SGA resize operations.
v$sga_current_resize_ops	Displays information about SGA resize operations which are currently in progress. An operation can be a grow or a shrink of a dynamic SGA component.

Table 14.2: *Oracle Database 10g Views*

Determining the optimal size for the data buffers is a critical task for very large databases. It is economically prohibitive to cache an entire database in RAM as databases grow ever larger, perhaps reaching sizes in the hundreds of billions of bytes. The difficulty Oracle professionals face is finding the point of diminishing marginal returns as additional RAM resources are allocated to the database.

Successfully determining the point of diminishing marginal return and effectively optimizing RAM can save a company hundreds of thousands, if not millions, of dollars in RAM expenses.

Among the features that Oracle10g has automated within AMM is the *v$db_cache_advice* view. This view can help predict the benefit of adding buffers to the data buffer cache. It estimates the miss rate for twenty potential buffer cache sizes, ranging from 10 percent of the current size to 200 percent of the current size. This tool allows the Oracle DBA to accurately predict the optimal size for each RAM data buffer. A few examples will help illustrate the process.

In order to use the new view, RAM memory must be pre-allocated to the data buffers, just as it was in the Oracle7 *x$kcbcbh* utility. Setting the *init.ora* parameter, *db_cache_advice,* to the value of ON or READY enables the cache advice feature. The DBA can set these values while the database is running by using the ALTER SYSTEM command, taking advantage of the predictive feature dynamically.

However, since the additional RAM buffers must be allocated before the *db_cache_size* can use *v$db_cache_advice*, the DBA may wish to use the utility only once to determine the optimal size.

The *v$db_cache_advice* view is similar to an Oracle7 utility that also predicted the benefit of adding data buffers. The Oracle7 utility used the *x$kcbrbh* view to track buffer hits and the *x$kcbcbh* view to track buffer misses. Also, there is no way to get cache advice on Oracle8 since *db_block_lru_statistics* was made obsolete.

The *data buffer hit ratio* can provide data similar to *v$db_cache_advice,* and most Oracle tuning professionals use both tools to monitor the effectiveness of data buffers and monitor how AMM adjusts the sizes of the buffer pools.

The following query can be used to perform the cache advice function, once the *db_cache_advice* has been enabled and the database has run long enough to give representative results.

```
column c1    heading 'Cache Size (m)'          format 999,999,999,999
column c2    heading 'Buffers'                 format 999,999,999
column c3    heading 'Estd Phys|Read Factor' format 999.90
column c4    heading 'Estd Phys| Reads'        format 999,999,999

select
   size_for_estimate            c1,
   buffers_for_estimate         c2,
   estd_physical_read_factor   c3,
   estd_physical_reads          c4
from
   v$db_cache_advice
where
   name = 'DEFAULT'
and
   block_size  = (SELECT value FROM V$PARAMETER
                    WHERE name = 'db_block_size')
and
   advice_status = 'ON';
```

The output from the script is shown below. The values range from 10 percent of the current size to double the current size of the *db_cache_size*.

Cache Size (MB)	Buffers	Estd Phys Read Factor	Estd Phys Reads	
30	3,802	18.70	192,317,943	← 10% size
60	7,604	12.83	131,949,536	
91	11,406	7.38	75,865,861	
121	15,208	4.97	51,111,658	
152	19,010	3.64	37,460,786	
182	22,812	2.50	25,668,196	
212	26,614	1.74	17,850,847	
243	30,416	1.33	13,720,149	
273	34,218	1.13	11,583,180	
304	38,020	1.00	10,282,475	Current Size
334	41,822	.93	9,515,878	
364	45,624	.87	8,909,026	
395	49,426	.83	8,495,039	
424	53,228	.79	8,116,496	
456	57,030	.76	7,824,764	
486	60,832	.74	7,563,180	
517	64,634	.71	7,311,729	
547	68,436	.69	7,104,280	
577	72,238	.67	6,895,122	
608	76,040	.66	6,739,731	← 2x size

The output shows neither a peak in total disk I/O nor a marginal trend with additional buffer RAM. This result is typical of a data warehouse database that reads large tables with full-table scans. In this case, there is no specific optimal setting for the *db_cache_size* parameter. Oracle will devour as much data buffer RAM as is fed to it, and disk I/O will continue to decline. However, there is no tangential line that indicates a point of diminishing returns for this application.

This predictive model is the basis for Oracle10g AMM. When the data from Oracle's buffer caching advisory is plotted, the tradeoff is clearly visible as shown in Figure 14.5.

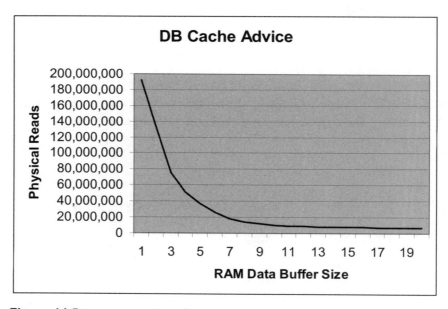

Figure 14.5: *A plot from the output of v$db_cache_advice*

The *v$db_cache_advice* view is now run dynamically in the *sysaux_xxx* views. It is similar to an Oracle7 utility that also predicted the benefit of adding data buffers. The Oracle7 utility used the *x$kcbrbh* view to track buffer hits and the *x$kcbcbh* view to track buffer misses.

The DBHR can provide data similar to *v$db_cache_advice*, and most Oracle tuning professionals use both tools to monitor the effectiveness of data buffers.

If the advisory output shows neither a peak in total disk I/O nor a marginal trend with additional buffer RAM, the advisory utility may not apply, and the DBA might consider disabling AMM. Taking the above into account, Oracle10*g* will apply this simple rule: *db_cache_size* should be increased if spare memory is available and marginal gains can be achieved by adding buffers.

The main point of this relationship between RAM buffering and physical reads is that all Oracle databases have data that is accessed with differing popularity. In sum, the larger the working set of frequently referenced data blocks, the greater the benefit from speeding up block access.

The next section provides insight into the internal mechanism of Oracle AMM and how it reacts to changes in buffer demands.

AMM and Oracle Instance Tuning

To fully understand AMM, the DBA needs to look at what happens at a detailed level within the buffers. Figure 14.4 shows that a marginal increase in data buffer blocks is asymptotic to disk I/O.

In databases with a very small *db_cache_size*, a large reduction in disk I/O is achieved with a small increase in the size of a small RAM buffer, as shown in the following diagram.

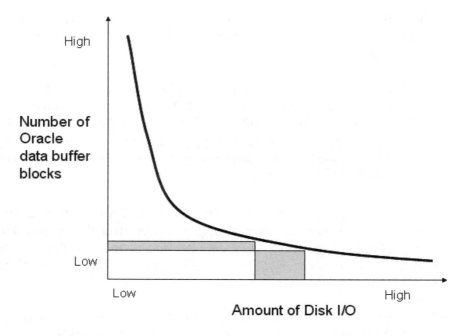

Figure 14.6: *Reduction in disk I/O from an increase to RAM data buffer.*

This shows that a small increase in the size of *db_cache_size* results in a large reduction in actual disk I/O. This happens because the cache is now larger and frequently referenced data blocks can now stay resident in the RAM data buffer.

However, the impressive reduction in disk I/O does not continue indefinitely. As the total RAM size begins to approach the database size, the marginal reduction in disk I/O begins to decline as shown in Figure 14.7.

This low marginal cost is due to the fact that all databases have data that is accessed infrequently. Infrequently accessed data does not normally have a bearing on the repeated reads performed by traditional OLTP applications, and this is why there is a marked decline in the marginal benefit as the database approaches full RAM caching.

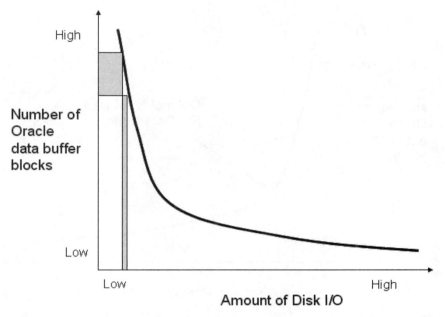

Figure 14.7: *Large buffers changes result in small I/O gains*

As a general guideline, all memory available on the host should be tuned, and the *db_cache_size* should be allocating RAM resources up to the point of diminishing returns as shown in Figure 14.8.

This is the point where additional buffer blocks do not significantly improve the buffer hit ratio.

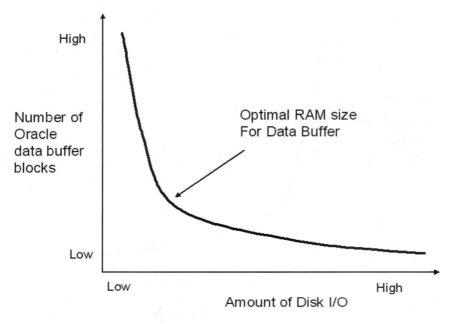

Figure 14.8: *The optimal size of the RAM data buffer*

Taking the above into account, the thrifty DBA will apply this simple rule: *db_cache_size* should be increased if spare memory is available and marginal gains can be achieved by adding buffers. Of course, increasing the buffer blocks increases the amount of RAM running on the database.

Hence, the database management system may place more demands on the processor than it can handle. The administrator must carefully juggle the amount of available memory with the limitations of the hardware in determining the optimal size of buffer blocks.

In Oracle9i and earlier, the DBA should prepare a strategy for enabling cache advice. Setting the *dba_cache_advice=on* while the database is running will cause Oracle to grab RAM pages from the shared pool RAM area, with potentially disastrous consequences for the objects in the library cache.

For complex databases that can benefit from Oracle's sophistication, the DBA controls not only the size of each data buffer, but also the block size of each individual buffer. For example, suppose the database tends to cluster records on a single database block, while the other data blocks remain small. Realizing that the I/O for a 32K block is virtually the same as the I/O for a 4K block, the database designer might choose to make some of the buffers larger to minimize I/O contention.

With the cache advice utility, Oracle10g provides the DBA with another tool to streamline database performance by predicting the optimal size of the RAM buffer pools.

The following sections will plot the average DBHR for an Oracle database over different intervals.

Plotting the Data Buffer Usage by Hour of the Day

The AWR can easily compute the average DBHR by the hour of the day. The *rpt_bhr_awr_hr.sql* script below performs this function. The script references the *stats$buffer_pool_statistics* table. This table contains the values used for computing the DBHR. These values are time specific and are only indicative of conditions at the time of the AWR snapshot. However, a technique that will yield that an elapsed time measure of the hit ratio is needed.

To convert the values into elapsed time data, the *stats$buffer_pool_statistics* table can be joined against itself, and the original snapshot can be compared with each successive one. Since the desired collection interval is hourly, the script presented below will compute each hourly buffer hit ratio. The hourly DBHR for each day can be derived by selecting the *snap_time* column with a mask of HH24.

⊞ rpt_bhr_awr_hr.sql

```
-- ******************************************************
-- Copyright © 2005 by Rampant TechPress
-- This script is free for non-commercial purposes
-- with no warranties.  Use at your own risk.
```

```
--
-- To license this script for a commercial purpose,
-- contact info@rampant.cc
-- *************************************************

set pages 999;

column bhr format 9.99
column mydate heading 'yr.  mo dy Hr.'

select
   to_char(snap_time,'HH24')        mydate,
   avg(
   (((new.consistent_gets-old.consistent_gets)+
   (new.db_block_gets-old.db_block_gets))-
   (new.physical_reads-old.physical_reads))
   /
   ((new.consistent_gets-old.consistent_gets)+
   (new.db_block_gets-old.db_block_gets))
   ) bhr
from
   dba_hist_buffer_pool_stat old,
   dba_hist_buffer_pool_stat new,
   dba_hist_sga              sn
where
   new.name in ('DEFAULT','FAKE VIEW')
and
   new.name = old.name
and
   new.snap_id = sn.snap_id
and
   old.snap_id = sn.snap_id-1
and
   new.consistent_gets > 0
and
   old.consistent_gets > 0
having
   avg(
   (((new.consistent_gets-old.consistent_gets)+
   (new.db_block_gets-old.db_block_gets))-
   (new.physical_reads-old.physical_reads))
   /
   ((new.consistent_gets-old.consistent_gets)+
   (new.db_block_gets-old.db_block_gets))
   ) < 1
group by
   to_char(snap_time,'HH24')
;
```

The output from the DBHR hourly average script from the WISE tool
is shown in Figure 14.9. The report displays the average hit ratio for
each day. The report provides insight, but the signature of the
database becomes much more obvious if it is plotted with WISE.

Oracle professionals use the AWR to extract the signatures for all of the important metrics and then plot the metrics to reveal the trend-based patterns. The signatures are typically gathered by hour of the day and day of the week.

Signatures become more evident over longer periods of time. Nevertheless, the plot of this database already presents some interesting trends.

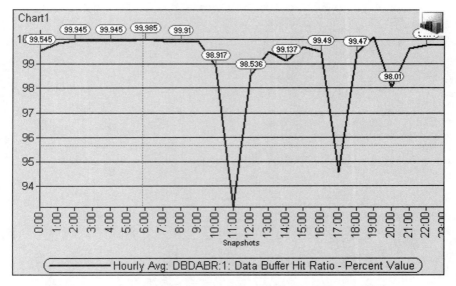

Figure 14.9: A plot of buffer hit ratio averages by hour of day

Once the signature has been visualized, the DBA will know exactly when to take a closer look at the database performance.

Plotting the Data Buffer Hit Ratio by Day of the Week

A similar analysis will yield the average DBHR by day of the week. This is achieved by changing the script snap_time format mask from HH24 to DAY.

```
set pages 999;

column bhr format 9.99
column mydate heading 'yr.  mo dy Hr.'

select
   to_char(end_interval_time,'day')        mydate,
   avg(
   (((new.consistent_gets-old.consistent_gets)+
   (new.db_block_gets-old.db_block_gets))-
   (new.physical_reads-old.physical_reads))
   /
   ((new.consistent_gets-old.consistent_gets)+
   (new.db_block_gets-old.db_block_gets))
   ) bhr
from
   dba_hist_buffer_pool_stat old,
   dba_hist_buffer_pool_stat           new,
   dba_hist_snapshot sn
where
   new.name in ('DEFAULT','FAKE VIEW')
and
   new.name = old.name
and
   new.snap_id = sn.snap_id
and
   old.snap_id = sn.snap_id-1
and
   new.consistent_gets > 0
and
   old.consistent_gets > 0
having
   avg(
   (((new.consistent_gets-old.consistent_gets)+
   (new.db_block_gets-old.db_block_gets))-
   (new.physical_reads-old.physical_reads))
   /
   ((new.consistent_gets-old.consistent_gets)+
   (new.db_block_gets-old.db_block_gets))
   ) < 1
group by
   to_char(end_interval_time,'day')
;
```

The output from the script is below. The days must be manually re-sequenced because they are given in alphabetical order. This can be done after pasting the output into a spreadsheet for graphing.

```
Day        BHR
--------- -----
friday     .89
monday     .98
saturday   .92
sunday     .91
```

```
thursday     .96
tuesday      .93
wednesday    .91
```

The following is another example of output from this script when run under WISE on a different database. The resulting graph is plotted with WISE as shown in Figure 14.10. The WISE tool can be downloaded for free with the purchase of this book, and it can be used to run this report on any Oracle database.

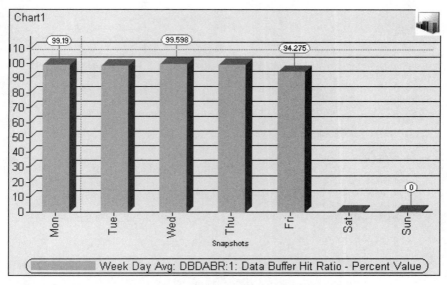

Figure 14.10: Average data buffer hit ratio by day of the week

This is all the DBA needs to know in order to plot and interpret data buffer hit ratios. It is also important to understand the value of trend analysis for indicating pattern signatures. The next step in the learning process is look at some more AWR script for tuning the structure of the SGA, and the place to start is with an exploration of the library cache.

A script similar to the preceding DBHR scripts, applied to the library cache, can reveal deficiencies within the shared pool. The utility takes time-based Oracle tuning information, such as the library cache miss ratio, and stores it within Oracle tables.

Once the DBA is familiar with the structure of the tables and columns within these tables, simple Oracle queries, like the one shown below that will display trend-based information can be devised. The trend-based data can then be applied to predictive models that inform the DBA of the appropriate times to change the internal structure of the SGA.

```
set lines 80;
set pages 999;

column mydate heading 'Yr.  Mo Dy  Hr.'       format a16
column c1       heading "execs"               format 9,999,999
column c2       heading "Cache Misses|While Executing" format
9,999,999
column c3       heading "Library Cache|Miss Ratio" format 999.99999

break on mydate skip 2;

select
   to_char(snap_time,'yyyy-mm-dd HH24')   mydate,
   sum(new.pins-old.pins)                 c1,
   sum(new.reloads-old.reloads)           c2,
   sum(new.reloads-old.reloads)/
   sum(new.pins-old.pins)                 library_cache_miss_ratio
from
   stats$librarycache old,
   stats$librarycache new,
   stats$snapshot      sn
where
   new.snap_id = sn.snap_id
and
   old.snap_id = new.snap_id-1
and
   old.namespace = new.namespace
group by
   to_char(snap_time,'yyyy-mm-dd HH24');
```

The output below indicates a RAM shortage in the shared pool between 9:00 and 10:00 a.m.

Yr. Mo Dy Hr.	execs	Cache Misses While Executing	Library Cache Miss Ratio
2001-12-11 10	10,338	6,443	.64
2001-12-12 10	182,477	88,136	.43
2001-12-14 10	190,707	101,832	.56
2001-12-16 10	72,803	45,932	.62

The DBA merely needs to schedule additional RAM for the *shared_pool_size* during the deficient period.

From the example above, it is apparent that a high number of library cache misses indicate that the shared pool is too small. To further summarize, a DBHR of less than 90 percent for any of the seven Oracle data buffer pools indicates that memory should be moved from other database regions and reallocated to the data buffer area.

Also, whenever the percentage of optimal executions within the Program Global Area (PGA) is less than 95, the value of the PGA aggregate target parameter should be increased. The next step is to evaluate those times at which the DBA should trigger a dynamic reconfiguration of Oracle.

Once the DBA understands the basics of buffer block size allocation, time can be spent taking a closer look at the internal mechanisms of the data buffers.

Internals of the Oracle Data Buffers

This section is a little more advanced and provides information about the internal mechanisms of the Oracle data buffers.

Oracle has always had RAM buffers with the goal of preventing expensive data block rereads from disk; however, the way the buffers internally handle the incoming data has evolved radically. Prior to Oracle8i, an incoming data block was placed at the front of the list in the buffer, and subsequent to the release of Oracle8i, the incoming block is placed in the middle of the buffer chain. New blocks are inserted into the middle of the buffer and their positions are adjusted according to access activity.

This scheme effectively partitions each data buffer into two sections: a hot section that contains the data used most recently; and a cold section containing the data used least recently.

This is a tremendous advance over the performance of earlier buffers. The midpoint insertion method essentially creates two subregions within the KEEP, RECYCLE, and DEFAULT pools. Each buffer pool has a hot and cold area, and only the data blocks that are requested repeatedly will migrate into the hot area of each pool. This method greatly improves the efficiency of the data buffers.

The size of the hot regions is internally configured by three hidden parameters:

- *_db_percent_hot_default*
- *_db_percent_hot_keep*
- *_db_percent_hot_recycle*

Oracle Corporation does not recommend changing these parameters. These parameters should only be altered by advanced DBAs who thoroughly understand the internal mechanisms of data buffers and wish to alter the performance of the buffers.

Finding Hot Blocks inside the Oracle Data Buffers

The relative performance of the data buffer pools is shown in Oracle8i by the internal x$bh view. This view shows the following columns:

- *tim* – The *tim* column governs the amount of time between touches and is related to the new *db_aging_touch_time* parameter.

- *tch* – The *tch* column gives the number of times a buffer is touched by user accesses. This is the count that directly relates to the promotion of buffers from the cold region into the hot, based on having been touched the number of times specified by the *db_aging_hot_criteria* parameter.

Since the tch column gives the number of touches for a specific data block, the hot blocks within the buffer can be displayed with a simple dictionary query like the one shown below:

```
SELECT
   obj       object,
   dbarfil   file#,
   dbablk    block#,
   tch       touches
FROM
   x$bh
WHERE
   tch > 10
ORDER BY
   tch desc;
```

This advanced query is especially useful for tracking objects in the
DEFAULT pool. It was pointed out earlier that there should be
enough data blocks in the KEEP pool to fully cache the table or index.
If the DBA finds hot blocks in the DEFAULT pool, they should be
moved into the KEEP pool.

The next section presents a technique for viewing the actual objects
inside the data buffers and the scripts that will show their contents.

Viewing the Data Buffer Contents

The Oracle v$bh view shows the contents of the data buffers as well as
the number of blocks for each type of segment in the buffer. This
view is primarily useful for indicating the amount of table and index
caching in multiple data blocks. Combining the *v$bh* view with
dba_objects and *dba_segments* provides a block-by-block listing of the data
buffer contents and indicates how well the buffers are caching tables
and indexes. This is very important in Oracle10g since the data buffer
sizes can be altered dynamically.

There are several data dictionary tricks that can be used when writing a
script for mapping data objects to RAM buffers:

- Duplicate object names: When joining *dba_objects* to *dba_segments*,
  the name, type, and owner are all required to distinguish the object
  sufficiently.

- Multiple blocksizes: To show objects in the separate instantiated
  buffers such as *db_2k_cache_size*, etc., the block size for the object

must be displayed. This is achieved by computing the block size from *dba_segments*, dividing bytes by blocks.

- Partitions: With a standard equi-join, every object partition joins to every segment partition for a particular object. Hence, the following qualification is required to handle partitions:

```
and nvl(t1.subobject_name,'*') = nvl(s.partition_name,'*')
```

- Clusters: Clusters present a challenge when joining the *v$bh* row with its corresponding database object. Instead of joining the *bh.objd* to *object_id*, it needs to be joined into *data_object_id*.

- Multiple caches: There are situations where a particular block may be cached more than once in the buffer cache. This is a mystifying concept, but it is easily overcome by creating the following in-line view:

```
(select distinct objd, file#, block# from v$bh where status !=
'free')
```

Many thanks to Randy Cunningham for developing this great script that can be used to watch the data buffers. His *buf_blocks.sql* script which is listed below only works with Oracle9i and beyond.

🖫 buf_blocks.sql

```
-- ***************************************************
-- Copyright © 2005 by Rampant TechPress
-- This script is free for non-commercial purposes
-- with no warranties.  Use at your own risk.
--
-- To license this script for a commercial purpose,
-- contact info@rampant.cc
-- ***************************************************

set pages 999
set lines 92

ttitle 'Contents of Data Buffers'

drop table t1;

create table t1 as
select
   o.owner          owner,
   o.object_name    object_name,
   o.subobject_name subobject_name,
   o.object_type    object_type,
```

```
      count(distinct file# || block#)            num_blocks
from
   dba_objects   o,
   v$bh          bh
where
   o.data_object_id  = bh.objd
and
   o.owner not in ('SYS','SYSTEM')
and
   bh.status != 'free'
group by
   o.owner,
   o.object_name,
   o.subobject_name,
   o.object_type
order by
   count(distinct file# || block#) desc
;

column c0 heading "Owner"                        format a12
column c1 heading "Object|Name"                  format a30
column c2 heading "Object|Type"                  format a8
column c3 heading "Number of|Blocks in|Buffer|Cache" format
99,999,999
column c4 heading "Percentage|of object|blocks in|Buffer" format 999
column c5 heading "Buffer|Pool"                  format a7
column c6 heading "Block|Size"                   format 99,999

select
   t1.owner                                      c0,
   object_name                                   c1,
   case when object_type = 'TABLE PARTITION' then 'TAB PART'
        when object_type = 'INDEX PARTITION' then 'IDX PART'
        else object_type end c2,
   sum(num_blocks)                               c3,
   (sum(num_blocks)/greatest(sum(blocks), .001))*100 c4,
   buffer_pool                                   c5,
   sum(bytes)/sum(blocks)                        c6
from
   t1,
   dba_segments s
where
   s.segment_name = t1.object_name
and
   s.owner = t1.owner
and
   s.segment_type = t1.object_type
and
   nvl(s.partition_name,'-') = nvl(t1.subobject_name,'-')
group by
   t1.owner,
   object_name,
   object_type,
   buffer_pool
having
   sum(num_blocks) > 10
```

```
order by
   sum(num_blocks) desc
;
```

A sample listing from this exciting report is shown below. The report lists the tables and indexes that reside inside the data buffer at the exact moment that the script was executed. This is important information for the Oracle professional who needs to know how many blocks for each object reside in the RAM buffer. To effectively manage the limited RAM resources, the Oracle DBA must be able to know the ramifications of decreasing the size of the data buffer caches.

The following is the report from *buf_blocks.sql* when run against a large Oracle data warehouse.

```
                          Contents of Data Buffers

                                    Number of Percentage
                                    Blocks   in of object
                   Object   Object  Buffer   Buffer  Buffer    Block
Owner              Name     Type    Cache    Blocks  Pool      Size
------------       ------   ------  -------  ------  -------   ------
```

Owner	Object Name	Object Type	Number of Blocks in Buffer Cache	Percentage of object Buffer Blocks	Buffer Pool	Block Size
DW01	WORKORDER	TAB PART	94,856	6	DEFAULT	8,192
DW01	HOUSE	TAB PART	50,674	7	DEFAULT	16,384
ODSA	WORKORDER	TABLE	28,481	2	DEFAULT	16,384
DW01	SUBSCRIBER	TAB PART	23,237	3	DEFAULT	4,096
ODS	WORKORDER	TABLE	19,926	1	DEFAULT	8,192
DW01	WRKR_ACCT_IDX	INDEX	8,525	5	DEFAULT	16,384
DW01	SUSC_SVCC_IDX	INDEX	8,453	38	KEEP	32,768
DW02	WRKR_DTEN_IDX	IDX PART	6,035	6	KEEP	32,768
DW02	SUSC_SVCC_IDX	INDEX	5,485	25	DEFAULT	16,384
DW02	WRKR_LCDT_IDX	IDX PART	5,149	5	DEFAULT	16,384
DW01	WORKORDER_CODE	TABLE	5,000	0	RECYCLE	32,768
DW01	WRKR_LCDT_IDX	IDX PART	4,929	4	KEEP	32,768
DW02	WOSC_SCDE_IDX	INDEX	4,479	6	KEEP	32,768
DW01	SBSC_ACCT_IDX	INDEX	4,439	8	DEFAULT	32,768
DW02	WRKR_WKTP_IDX	IDX PART	3,825	7	KEEP	32,768
DB_AUDIT	CUSTOMER_AUDIT	TABLE	3,301	99	DEFAULT	4,096
DW01	WRKR_CLSS_IDX	IDX PART	2,984	5	KEEP	32,768
DW01	WRKR_AHWO_IDX	INDEX	2,838	2	DEFAULT	32,768
DW01	WRKR_DTEN_IDX	IDX PART	2,801	5	KEEP	32,768

This is an interesting report because there are three object types: tables; indexes; and partitions. The subsets of the DEFAULT pool for KEEP and RECYCLE are also evident. Also, all indexes are defined in the largest supported block size (*db_32k_cache_size*), and multiple buffer pools of 4K, 8K, 16K and 32K sizes are defined.

The output of this script can be somewhat confusing due to the repeated DEFAULT buffer pool name. In earlier releases of Oracle, the KEEP and RECYCLE buffer pools are subsets of *db_cache_size* and can ONLY accommodate objects with the DEFAULT *db_block_size*. In later releases, the KEEP and RECYCLE pools become independent pools.

Conversely, any block sizes that are NOT the default *db_block_size*, go into the buffer pool named DEFAULT. The output listing shows that there are really six mutually exclusive and independently sized buffer pools and four of them are called DEFAULT.

Gathering v$bh status for multiple buffer pools

When using multiple blocksizes, standard *v$bh* scripts would report large amounts of free buffers even when the default pool was full and needed more when the optional areas had free. So, here is a first cut at finding the status of the blocks by blocksize in the buffer.

🖫 **all_vbh_status.sql**

```
-- *************************************************
-- Copyright © 2005 by Rampant TechPress
-- This script is free for non-commercial purposes
-- with no warranties.  Use at your own risk.
--
-- To license this script for a commercial purpose,
-- contact info@rampant.cc
-- *************************************************

set pages 50
@title80 'All Buffers Status'
spool rep_out\&&db\all_vbh_status
select
  '32k '||status as status,
  count(*) as num
from
 v$bh
where file# in(
   select file_id
     from dba_data_files
     where tablespace_name in (
       select tablespace_name
        from dba_tablespaces
        where block_size=32768))
group by '32k '||status
```

```
union
select
  '16k '||status as status,
  count(*) as num
from
 v$bh
where
  file# in(
   select file_id
    from dba_data_files
    where tablespace_name in (
     select tablespace_name
      from dba_tablespaces
      where block_size=16384))
group by '16k '||status
union
select
  '8k '||status as status,
  count(*) as num
from
 v$bh
where
  file# in(
   select file_id
    from dba_data_files
    where tablespace_name in (
     select tablespace_name
      from dba_tablespaces
      where block_size=8192))
group by '8k '||status
union
select
  '4k '||status as status,
  count(*) as num
from
 v$bh
where
 file# in(
  select file_id
   from dba_data_files
   where tablespace_name in (
    select tablespace_name
     from dba_tablespaces
     where block_size=4096))
group by '4k '||status
union
select
  '2k '||status as status,
  count(*) as num
from
 v$bh
where
 file# in(
  select file_id
   from dba_data_files
   where tablespace_name in (
```

```
    select tablespace_name
    from dba_tablespaces
    where block_size=2048))
group by '2k '||status
union
select
  status,
  count(*) as num
from
  v$bh
where status='free'
group by status
order by 1
/
spool off
ttitle off
```

Here is a sample of the *v$bh* output for a database with multiple blocksizes:

```
STATUS      NUM
--------- ----------
32k cr       1456
32k xcur   30569
8k  cr     32452
8k  free        6
8k  xcur  340742
free        15829
```

It is interesting to run this report repeatedly because the Oracle data buffers are so dynamic. Running the script frequently allows the DBA to view the blocks entering and leaving the data buffer. The midpoint insertion method can be seen in action and the hot and cold regions can be seen as they update.

The *v$segment_statistics* view is a goldmine for funding wait events that are associated with a specific Oracle table. The following script was written to show run-time details about a segment, usually a table or an index. This powerful script interrogates the *v$segment_statistics* view by use of a CASE statement. Examination of the script will yield how the v$segment_statistics view is grouped by *object_name*. For each object, counts of the major object wait events are displayed, as seen in the CASE expression. The most important of these object-level wait events will provide clues into the source of the contention.

Internals of the Oracle Data Buffers

For example, buffer busy waits and ITL waits all have a clear set of causes. Knowing this information is critical to understanding the root cause of the contention.

When reviewing objects for possible tuning issues, it is handy to have statistics such as the number of internal transaction list (ITL) waits, buffer busy waits, and row lock waits that the object has experienced. Combined with the number of logical and physical reads the object has experienced, the above statistics give a complete picture of the usage of the object in question.

The *v$segment_statistics* provides a *statistic_name* and value column for each table. Unfortunately, this format does not lend itself to easy use. By utilizing the crosstab technique a report can easily be created to show these vital tuning statistics for the system. An example of this type of cross tab report is shown below.

💾 obj_xtab.sql

```
-- ***************************************************
-- Copyright © 2005 by Rampant TechPress
-- This script is free for non-commercial purposes
-- with no warranties.  Use at your own risk.
--
-- To license this script for a commercial purpose,
-- contact info@rampant.cc
-- ***************************************************

-- Crosstab of object and statistic for an owner
-- by Mike Ault www.oracle-script.com

col "Object" format a20
set numwidth 12
set lines 132
set pages 50
@title132 'Object Wait Statistics'
spool rep_out\&&db\obj_stat_xtab

select * from
(
   select
      DECODE
      (GROUPING(a.object_name), 1, 'All Objects', a.object_name)
   AS "Object",
sum(case when
   a.statistic_name = 'ITL waits'
then
```

```
    a.value else null end) "ITL Waits",
sum(case when
    a.statistic_name = 'buffer busy waits'
then
    a.value else null end) "Buffer Busy Waits",
sum(case when
    a.statistic_name = 'row lock waits'
then
    a.value else null end) "Row Lock Waits",
sum(case when
    a.statistic_name = 'physical reads'
then
    a.value else null end) "Physical Reads",
sum(case when
    a.statistic_name = 'logical reads'
then
    a.value else null end) "Logical Reads"
from
    v$segment_statistics a
where
    a.owner like upper('&owner')
group by
    rollup(a.object_name)) b
where (b."ITL Waits">0 or b."Buffer Busy Waits">0)
/
spool off
clear columns
ttitle off
```

The cross tab report generates a listing showing the statistics of concern as headers across the page rather than listings going down the page and summarizes them by object. This allows the easy comparison of total buffer busy waits to the number of ITL or row lock waits. This ability to compare the ITL and row lock waits to buffer busy waits allows for determination of what objects may be experiencing contention for ITL lists, which may be experiencing excessive locking activity and through comparisons, which are highly contended for without the row lock or ITL waits. AN example of the output of the report, edited for length, is shown below.

```
Object        ITL Waits Buffer Busy Waits Row Lock Waits Physical Reads Logical Reads
------------- --------- ----------------- -------------- -------------- -------------
BILLING            0              63636          38267        1316055     410219712
BILLING_INDX1      1              16510             55         151085      21776800
...
DELIVER_INDX1   1963              36096          32962        1952600      60809744
DELIVER_INDX2     88              16250           9029       18839481     342857488
DELIVER_PK      2676              99748          29293       15256214     416206384
...
All Objects    12613           20348859        1253057     1139977207   20947864752
```

Internals of the Oracle Data Buffers

In the above report, the BILLING_INDX1 index has a large amount of buffer busy waits but can not be accounted for from the ITL or Row Lock waits. This indicates that the index is being constantly read and the blocks then aged out of memory forcing waits as they are re-read for the next process. On the other hand, almost all of the buffer busy waits for the DELIVER_INDX1 index can be attributed to ITL and Row Lock waits. In situations where there are large numbers of ITL waits the DBA needs to consider the increase of the INITRANS setting for the table to remove this source of contention.

If the predominant wait is row lock waits then the DBA needs to determine if the proper use of locking and cursors is being utilized in the application. For example, the SELECT...FOR UPDATE type code may be overused. If, on the other hand, all the waits are un-accounted for buffer busy waits, then consideration needs to be given to increasing the amount of database block buffers in the SGA. This object wait cross tab report can be a powerful addition to the tuning arsenal.

The *buf_blocks.sql* script, shown previously in this Chapter, is even more important when considering a decrease in a cache size. When an ALTER SYSTEM command is issued to decrease the cache size, Oracle will grab pages from the least recently used (LRU) end of the buffer. Depending on the amount of RAM removed, an ALTER SYSTEM command will un-cache data blocks that may be needed by upcoming SQL statements.

The Downside of Mega Data Buffers

The 64-bit Oracle database now allows for far larger SGA regions. Unfortunately, a 32-bit word size can only address 2 to the 32nd power, or about 4 gigabytes of RAM. All 64-bit servers have a larger word size of 2 to the 64th power that allows for up to 18 billion gigabytes. That's 18 exabytes! Hence, many Oracle DBAs are running SGAs larger than 20 gigabytes with most of it dedicated to the data buffer caches.

There are downsides to having a large *db_cache_size*. While direct access to data is done with hashing, there are times when Oracle performance might slow down with a large cache. In these cases, objects may be segregated into a distinct, smaller buffer cache.

- **Objects with High Invalidations:** Whenever a program issues a truncate table, uses non-Global temporary tables, or runs a large data purge, Oracle performance might suffer.

- **High Update Objects:** Tables and indexes that experience high Data Manipulation Lock (DML) activity may perform better if mapped into a separate buffer cache.

- **RAC systems:** Systems using Oracle10g RAC may experience high cross-instance calls when using a large *db_cache_size* in multiple RAC instances. This inter-instance pinging can cause excessive overhead, and that is why RAC DBA's try to segregate RAC instances to access specific areas of the database.

If a DBA has a system that has any of these characteristics, special operations to reduce the stress on the RAM will need to be performed.

In these types of systems, the data buffer caches can be downsized prior to these operations, the buffer can be flushed if Oracle10g is in use, and then the data buffer region can be resized using a script like the following:

```ksh
#!/bin/ksh

# First, we must set the environment . . . .
ORACLE_SID=$1
export ORACLE_SID
ORACLE_HOME=`cat /etc/oratab|grep ^$ORACLE_SID:|cut -f2 -d':'`
#ORACLE_HOME=`cat /var/opt/oracle/oratab|grep ^$ORACLE_SID:|cut -f2
-d':'`
export ORACLE_HOME
PATH=$ORACLE_HOME/bin:$PATH
export PATH

# ************************************************************
#
# This will reduce the size of the data buffer
# immediately preceding a large truncate or data purge
#
# ************************************************************
```

```
$ORACLE_HOME/bin/sqlplus -s /nologin<<!
connect system/manager as sysdba;
alter system set db_cache_size=10m;
alter system flush buffer_cache;
exit
!

# ************************************************************
# Now we can invoke the specialty task.
# ************************************************************

nohup purge_job.ksh > /tmp/purge.lst 2>&1 &

$ORACLE_HOME/bin/sqlplus -s /nologin<<!
connect system/manager as sysdba;
alter system set db_cache_size=1500m;
exit
!
```

DBA's must remember that the AMM does not yet analyze detailed workloads. Oracle has provided the KEEP and RECYCLE pools so that the DBA can add intelligence to the database and assign appropriate objects to the right buffer pool. The next section covers the allocation process.

Allocating Oracle Objects into Multiple RAM data Buffers

Since very few Oracle databases can afford the cost of full RAM caching, many rules have been developed for the segregation and isolation of cached objects. Some of these rules of thumb will yield clues about the best way to utilize Solid State Disk (SSD) in a solid-state Oracle environment:

- Segregate large-table full-table scans: Tables that experience large-table full-table scans will benefit from the largest supported block size and should be placed in a tablespace with the largest block size.

- Use the RECYCLE Pool: If the *db_cache_size* is not set to the largest supported block size for the server, the *db_recycle_cache_size* parameter should not be used. Instead, use a *db_32k_cache_size*, or whatever the maximum size for the system is, and assign all tables that experience frequent large-table full-table scans to the largest buffer cache in the database.

- Segregate Indexes: In many cases, Oracle SQL statements will retrieve index information via an index range scan, scanning the b-tree or bitmap index for ranges of values that match the SQL search criteria. Hence, it is beneficial to have as much of an index residing in RAM as possible. One of the first things the Oracle9i DBA should do is to migrate all of their Oracle indexes into a large blocksize tablespace. Indexes will always favor the largest supported blocksize.

- Segregate random access reads: For those databases that fetch small rows randomly from the disk, the Oracle DBA can segregate these types of tables into 2K Tablespaces. While disk is becoming cheaper every day, no one wants to waste any available RAM by reading in more information to RAM than is actually going be used by the query. Hence, many Oracle DBAs will use small block sizes in cases of tiny, random access record retrieval.

- Segregate Locator Object (LOB) column tables: For those Oracle tables that contain raw, long raw, or in-line LOBs, moving the table rows to large block size will have an extremely beneficial effect on disk I/O. Experienced DBAs will check *dba_tables.avg_row_len* to make sure that the blocksize is larger than the average size. Row chaining will be reduced while at the same time the entire LOB can be read within a single disk I/O, thereby avoiding the additional overhead of having Oracle to go out to read multiple blocks.

- Segregate large-table full-table scan rows: When the RECYCLE pool was first introduced in Oracle8i, the idea was that the full table scan data blocks, which are not likely to be reread by other transactions, could be quickly flushed through the Oracle SGA thereby reserving critical RAM for those data blocks which are likely to be reread by another transaction. In Oracle9i, the RECYCLE pool can be configured to use a smaller block size.

- Check the average row length: The block size for a tables' tablespace should always be greater than the average row length for the table (*dba_tables.avg_row_len*). If the block size is smaller than the average row length, rows chaining occurs and excessive disk I/O is incurred.

- Use large blocks for data sorting: The TEMP tablespace will benefit from the largest supported blocksize. This allows disk sorting to happen in large blocks with a minimum of disk I/O.

Recent TPC-C benchmarks make it clear that very large RAM regions are a central component in high performance Oracle databases. The 2004 UNISYS Oracle Windows benchmark exceeded 300,000 transactions per minute using a Windows-based 16-CPU server with 115 gigabytes of Oracle data buffer cache. The following are the actual Oracle parameters that were used in the benchmark, and the benefit of large scale RAM caching becomes more evident:

```
db_16k_cache_size  = 15010M
db_8k_cache_size   = 1024M
db_cache_size      = 8096M
db_keep_cache_size = 78000M
```

At this point, it should be clear that RAM resources are an important factor in maintaining the performance of I/O intensive Oracle systems.

Automatically Generate KEEP Syntax

A DBA can easily write a script that automatically identifies candidates for the KEEP pool and generates the syntax to move the tables into the pool. The placement criteria for tables and indexes into the KEEP buffer are straightforward:

- Frequently accessed tables: The threshold for access can be adjusted in the script.

- High buffer residency: Any table that has more than 80% of its blocks in the data buffer should be cached in the KEEP pool.

The approach to identifying tables for the KEEP pool is simple. All objects that have more than 80% of their data blocks in the buffer should be assigned to the KEEP pool. The following section contains scripts for each of these methods.

Automating the Assignment of KEEP Pool Contents

Another method for identifying tables and indexes for the KEEP pool involves the examination of the current blocks in the data buffer. For the *buf_keep_pool.sql* query, the rules are simple.

- Use the KEEP pool if the object consumes more than 10% of the total size of the data buffer.

- Use the KEEP pool if more than 50% of the objects blocks already resides in the data buffer, according to an *x$bh* query.

It is highly unlikely that an undeserving table or index would meet this criterion. Of course, this script would need to be run at numerous times during the day because the buffer contents change very rapidly.

The following script can be run every hour via *dbms_job* and will automate the monitoring of KEEP pool candidates. Every time it finds a candidate, the DBA will execute the syntax and adjust the total KEEP pool size to accommodate the new object.

🖫 buf_keep_pool.sql

```
-- ***************************************************
-- Copyright © 2005 by Rampant TechPress
-- This script is free for non-commercial purposes
-- with no warranties.  Use at your own risk.
--
-- To license this script for a commercial purpose,
-- contact info@rampant.cc
-- ***************************************************

set pages 999

set lines 92


spool keep_syn.lst

drop table t1;

create table t1 as
select
   o.owner          owner,
   o.object_name    object_name,
   o.subobject_name subobject_name,
   o.object_type    object_type,
   count(distinct file# || block#)      num_blocks
```

```
from
   dba_objects   o,
   v$bh          bh
where
   o.data_object_id  = bh.objd
and
   o.owner not in ('SYS','SYSTEM')
and
   bh.status != 'free'
group by
   o.owner,
   o.object_name,
   o.subobject_name,
   o.object_type
order by
   count(distinct file# || block#) desc
;

select
   'alter '||s.segment_type||' '||t1.owner||'.'||s.segment_name||'
storage (buffer_pool keep);'
from
   t1,
   dba_segments s
where
   s.segment_name = t1.object_name
and
   s.owner = t1.owner
and
   s.segment_type = t1.object_type
and
   nvl(s.partition_name,'-') = nvl(t1.subobject_name,'-')
and
   buffer_pool <> 'KEEP'
and
   object_type in ('TABLE','INDEX')
group by
   s.segment_type,
   t1.owner,
   s.segment_name
having
   (sum(num_blocks)/greatest(sum(blocks), .001))*100 > 80
;


spool off;
```

The following is sample of the output from this script.

```
alter TABLE BOM.BOM_DELETE_SUB_ENTITIES storage (buffer_pool keep);
alter TABLE BOM.BOM_OPERATIONAL_ROUTINGS storage (buffer_pool keep);
alter INDEX BOM.CST_ITEM_COSTS_U1 storage (buffer_pool keep);
alter TABLE APPLSYS.FND_CONCURRENT_PROGRAMS storage (buffer_pool keep);
alter TABLE APPLSYS.FND_CONCURRENT_REQUESTS storage (buffer_pool keep);
alter TABLE GL.GL_JE_BATCHES storage (buffer_pool keep);
alter INDEX GL.GL_JE_BATCHES_U2 storage (buffer_pool keep);
```

```
alter TABLE GL.GL_JE_HEADERS storage (buffer_pool keep);
alter TABLE INV.MTL_DEMAND_INTERFACE storage (buffer_pool keep);
alter INDEX INV.MTL_DEMAND_INTERFACE_N10 storage (buffer_pool keep);
alter TABLE INV.MTL_ITEM_CATEGORIES storage (buffer_pool keep);
alter TABLE INV.MTL_ONHAND_QUANTITIES storage (buffer_pool keep);
alter TABLE INV.MTL_SUPPLY_DEMAND_TEMP storage (buffer_pool keep);
alter TABLE PO.PO_REQUISITION_LINES_ALL storage (buffer_pool keep);
alter TABLE AR.RA_CUSTOMER_TRX_ALL storage (buffer_pool keep);
alter TABLE AR.RA_CUSTOMER_TRX_LINES_ALL storage (buffer_pool keep);
alter INDEX WIP.WIP_REQUIREMENT_OPERATIONS_N3 storage (buffer_pool keep);
```

In sum, there are two ways to identify tables and indexes for full caching in the KEEP pool. The first step is to explain all of the SQL in the databases that are looking for small-table, full-table scans. Next, the data buffer cache should be examined repeatedly in order to identify any objects that have more than 80% of their blocks in RAM. The next section covers how the job is finished and how the KEEP pool can be resized to accommodate the new objects.

Sizing the KEEP Pool

Once the tables and indexes have been loaded into the KEEP buffer pool, the *buffer_pool_keep* parameter must be increased by the total number of blocks in the migrated tables.

The following script will total the number of blocks that the KEEP pool requires, insuring 100 percent data caching. The script adds 20 percent to the total to allow for growth in the cached objects. The DBA should run this script frequently to make sure the KEEP pool always has a DBHR of 100 percent.

```
prompt The following will size your init.ora KEEP POOL,
prompt based on Oracle8 KEEP Pool assignment values
prompt

select
'BUFFER_POOL_KEEP = ('||trunc(sum(s.blocks)*1.2)||',2)'
from
   dba_segments s
where
   s.buffer_pool = 'KEEP';
;
```

This script outputs the Oracle parameter that resizes the KEEP pool for the next restart of the Oracle instance. The parameter is placed in the *init.ora* file. Oracle10g deprecates *buffer_pool_keep* and it cannot be modified with an ALTER SYSTEM command.

```
BUFFER_POOL_KEEP=(1456, 3)
```

Now, the database can be bounced and the parameter change will take effect.

Advanced KEEP Pool Candidate Identification

The KEEP pool is an excellent storage location for small-table, full-table scans. It can also be a good place to store data blocks from frequently used segments that consume a lot of block space in the data buffers. These blocks are usually found within small reference tables that are accessed through an index and do not appear in the full-table scan report.

The *x$bh* internal view is the only window into the internals of the Oracle database buffers. The view contains much detailed information about the internal operations of the data buffer pools. Both the number of objects in a specific type and the number of touches for that object type can be counted in the *x$bh* table. It can even be used to create a snapshot of all the data blocks in the buffer.

The query shown below utilizes the *x$bh* view to identify all the objects that reside in blocks averaging over five touches and occupying over twenty blocks in the cache. It finds tables and indexes that are referenced frequently and are good candidates for inclusion in the KEEP pool.

```
-- You MUST connect as SYS to run this script
connect sys/manager;

set lines 80;
set pages 999;

column avg_touches           format 999
column myname heading 'Name' format a30
column mytype heading 'Type' format a10
column buffers               format 999,999

SELECT
   object_type   mytype,
```

```
   object_name    myname,
   blocks,
   COUNT(1) buffers,
   AVG(tch) avg_touches
FROM
   sys.x$bh      a,
   dba_objects b,
   dba_segments s
WHERE
   a.obj = b.object_id
and
   b.object_name = s.segment_name
and
   b.owner not in ('SYS','SYSTEM')
GROUP BY
   object_name,
   object_type,
   blocks,
   obj
HAVING
   AVG(tch) > 5
AND
   COUNT(1) > 20;
```

The script will only run on Oracle8i and subsequent versions. This is because the *tch* column was not added until Oracle 8.1.6.

The output from the script is shown next. It identifies the active objects within the data buffers based on the number of data blocks and the number of touches.

Type	Name	BLOCKS	BUFFERS	AVG_TOUCHES
TABLE	PAGE	104	107	44
TABLE	SUBSCRIPTION	192	22	52
INDEX	SEQ_KEY_IDX	40	34	47
TABLE	SEC_SESSIONS	80	172	70
TABLE	SEC_BROWSER_PROPERTIES	80	81	58
TABLE	EC_USER_SESSIONS	96	97	77
INDEX	SYS_C008245	32	29	270

The DBA must now decide whether the hot objects are to be segregated into the KEEP pool. In general, there should be enough RAM available to store the entire table or index. Using the example, if consideration is given to adding the page table to the KEEP pool, 104 blocks would have to be added to the Oracle *buffer_pool_keep* parameter.

The results from this script will differ every time it is executed because the data buffers are dynamic, and data storage is transient. Some DBAs schedule this script as often as every minute, if they need to see exactly what is occurring inside the data buffers.

Automating KEEP Pool Assignment

The Oracle documentation states:

> A good candidate for a segment to put into the KEEP pool is a segment that is smaller than 10% of the size of the DEFAULT buffer pool and has incurred at least 1% of the total I/Os in the system.

It is easy to locate segments that are less than 10% of the size of their data buffer, but Oracle does not have a mechanism to track I/O at the segment level. To get around this issue, some DBAs place each segment into an isolated tablespace, so that the AWR can show the total I/O. However, this is not a practical solution for complex schemas with hundreds of segments.

Since the idea of the KEEP is to fully cache the object, the goal is to locate those objects that are small and experience a disproportional amount of I/O activity. Using this guideline, there are two approaches. Unlike the recommendation from the Oracle documentation, these approaches can be completely automated:

- Cache tables & indexes where the table is small (<50 blocks) and the table experiences frequent full-table scans.

- Cache any objects that consume more than 10% of the size of their data buffer.

The first method that uses *v$sql_plan* to examine all execution plans, searching for small-table, full-table scans, is found in *get_keep_pool.sql*. This can automatically generate the KEEP syntax for any small table, with the DBA adjusting the table size threshold, for tables that have many full-table scans.

🖫 get_keep_pool.sql

```
--  **************************************************
-- Copyright © 2005 by Rampant TechPress
-- This script is free for non-commercial purposes
-- with no warranties.  Use at your own risk.
--
-- To license this script for a commercial purpose,
-- contact info@rampant.cc
--  **************************************************

select
   'alter table '||p.owner||'.'||p.name||' storage (buffer_pool
keep);'
from
   dba_tables   t,
   dba_segments s,
   dba_hist_sqlstat a,
   (select distinct
     pl.sql_id,
     pl.object_owner owner,
     pl.object_name name
   from
     dba_hist_sql_plan pl
   where
     pl.operation = 'TABLE ACCESS'
     and
     pl.options = 'FULL') p
where
   a.sql_id = p.sql_id
   and
   t.owner = s.owner
   and
   t.table_name = s.segment_name
   and
   t.table_name = p.name
   and
   t.owner = p.owner
   and
   t.owner not in ('SYS','SYSTEM')
   and
   t.buffer_pool <> 'KEEP'
having
   s.blocks < 50
group by
   p.owner, p.name, t.num_rows, s.blocks
UNION
--  *********************************************************

-- Next, get the index names

--  *********************************************************
select
   'alter index '||owner||'.'||index_name||' storage (buffer_pool
keep);'
```

```
from
   dba_indexes
where
   owner||'.'||table_name in
(
select
   p.owner||'.'||p.name
from
   dba_tables        t,
   dba_segments      s,
   dba_hist_sqlstat  a,
   (select distinct
     p1.sql_id,
     p1.object_owner owner,
     p1.object_name name
   from
     dba_hist_sql_plan p1
   where
     p1.operation = 'TABLE ACCESS'
     and
     p1.options = 'FULL') p
where
   a.sql_id = p.sql_id
   and
   t.owner = s.owner
   and
   t.table_name = s.segment_name
   and
   t.table_name = p.name
   and
   t.owner = p.owner
   and
   t.owner not in ('SYS','SYSTEM')
   and
   t.buffer_pool <> 'KEEP'
having
   s.blocks < 50
group by
   p.owner, p.name, t.num_rows, s.blocks
)
```

By running this script, the Oracle10g *v$* views can be used to generate suggestions for the KEEP syntax, based on the number of blocks in the object.

```
alter index DING.PK_BOOK storage (buffer_pool keep);
alter table DING.BOOK storage (buffer_pool keep);
alter table DING.BOOK_AUTHOR storage (buffer_pool keep);
alter table DING.PUBLISHER storage (buffer_pool keep);
alter table DING.SALES storage (buffer_pool keep);
```

Another method for identifying tables and indexes for the KEEP pool examines the current blocks in the data buffer. For this query, the rules are simple. Any object that has more than 80% of its data blocks in the data buffer should probably be fully cached.

It is highly unlikely that an undeserving table or index would meet this criterion. Of course, this script would need to be run numerous times during the day because the buffer contents change very rapidly.

The script in *keep_syn.sql* can be run every hour via *dbms_job*, and automate the monitoring of KEEP pool candidates. Every time it finds a candidate, the DBA will execute the syntax and adjust the total KEEP pool size to accommodate the new object.

🖫 keep_syn.sql

```
-- ****************************************************
-- Copyright © 2005 by Rampant TechPress
-- This script is free for non-commercial purposes
-- with no warranties.  Use at your own risk.
--
-- To license this script for a commercial purpose,
-- contact info@rampant.cc
-- ****************************************************

set pages 999
set lines 92


spool keep_syn.lst

drop table t1;

create table t1 as
select
   o.owner          owner,
   o.object_name    object_name,
   o.subobject_name subobject_name,
   o.object_type    object_type,
   count(distinct file# || block#)          num_blocks
from
   dba_objects  o,
   v$bh         bh
where
   o.data_object_id  = bh.objd
and
   o.owner not in ('SYS','SYSTEM')
and
   bh.status != 'free'
```

```
group by
   o.owner,
   o.object_name,
   o.subobject_name,
   o.object_type
order by
   count(distinct file# || block#) desc
;

select
   'alter '||s.segment_type||' '||t1.owner||'.'||s.segment_name||'
storage (buffer_pool keep);'
from
   t1,
   dba_segments s
where
   s.segment_name = t1.object_name
and

   s.owner = t1.owner
and
   s.segment_type = t1.object_type
and
   nvl(s.partition_name,'-') = nvl(t1.subobject_name,'-')
and
   buffer_pool <> 'KEEP'
and
   object_type in ('TABLE','INDEX')
group by
   s.segment_type,
   t1.owner,
   s.segment_name
having
   (sum(num_blocks)/greatest(sum(blocks), .001))*100 > 80
;
```

The following is a sample of the output from this script:

```
alter TABLE IS.GL_JE_BATCHES storage (buffer_pool keep);
alter INDEX IS.GL_JE_BATCHES_U2 storage (buffer_pool keep);
alter TABLE IS.GL_JE_HEADERS storage (buffer_pool keep);
```

Once the segments for assignment to the KEEP pool have been identified, the DBA will need to adjust the *db_keep_cache_size* parameter to ensure that it has enough blocks to fully cache all of the segments that are assigned to the pool.

Of course, there are many exceptions to this automated approach. For example, these scripts do not handle table partitions and other object types. Hence, these scripts should be used as a framework for a KEEP pool caching strategy, and should not be run as is.

The next section provides information on scripts that can be used to automate the identification of objects for the RECYCLE pool. The identification of candidates for the RECYCLE pool is very similar to the KEEP pool process.

Tuning the RECYCLE Pool

Oracle8 introduced the RECYCLE pool as a reusable data buffer for transient data blocks. Transient data blocks are blocks that are read as parts of large-table full-table scans and are not likely to be needed again soon. The goal is to use the RECYCLE pool for segregating large tables involved in frequent full-table scans.

To locate these large-table full-table scans, the *plan9i.sql* script which can be obtained from the code depot can be used once again:

```
                     full table scans and counts

OWNER      NAME                     NUM_ROWS C K   BLOCKS  NBR_FTS
---------- ------------------------ -------- - - -------- -------
APPLSYS    FND_CONC_RELEASE_DISJS         39 N K        2   98,864
APPLSYS    FND_CONC_RELEASE_PERIODS       39 N K        2   98,864
APPLSYS    FND_CONC_RELEASE_STATES         1 N K        2   98,864
SYS        DUAL                              N K        2   63,466
APPLSYS    FND_CONC_PP_ACTIONS         7,021 N      1,262   52,036
APPLSYS    FND_CONC_REL_CONJ_MEMBER        0 N K       22   50,174
```

One table in the listing is a clear candidate for inclusion in the RECYCLE pool. The *fnd_conc_pp_actions* table contains 1,262 blocks and experienced 52,036 full-table scans.

After candidates for the RECYCLE pool have been identified, a script that reads the plan table generated from plan9i.sql can be run. This query will search for large tables of over 10,000 blocks that are subject to full-table scans and are not already in the RECYCLE pool.

 CAUTION: The prudent DBA should verify that the large-table full-table scan is legitimate before blindly assigning a table to the RECYCLE pool.

Many queries are structured to perform full-table scans on tables, even though far less than 40 percent of the table rows will be referenced. A better designed query will only perform large-table full-table scans in systems such as data warehouses that require frequent SUM or AVG queries that touch most or all of the table rows.

9i_recycle_syntax.sql

```
-- ************************************************
-- Copyright © 2005 by Rampant TechPress
-- This script is free for non-commercial purposes
-- with no warranties.  Use at your own risk.
--
-- To license this script for a commercial purpose,
-- contact info@rampant.cc
-- ************************************************

set pages 999;
set heading off;
set feedback off;

ttitle off;

spool keep_syntax.sql

-- *********************************************************
-- First, get the table list
-- *********************************************************
select
   'alter table '||p.owner||'.'||p.name||' storage (buffer_pool
recycle);'
from
   dba_tables    t,
   dba_segments s,
   v$sqlarea     a,
   (select distinct
    address,
    object_owner owner,
    object_name name
   from
    v$sql_plan
   where
    operation = 'TABLE ACCESS'
```

```
          and
          options = 'FULL') p
where
   a.address = p.address
   and
   t.owner = s.owner
   and
   t.table_name = s.segment_name
   and
   t.table_name = p.name
   and
   t.owner = p.owner
   and
   t.owner not in ('SYS','SYSTEM')
   and
   t.buffer_pool <> 'RECYCLE'
having
   s.blocks > 10000
group by
   p.owner, p.name, t.num_rows, s.blocks
UNION
-- ************************************************************
-- Next, get the index names
-- ************************************************************
select
   'alter index '||owner||'.'||index_name||' storage (buffer_pool
recycle);'
from
   dba_indexes
where
   owner||'.'||table_name in
(
select
   p.owner||'.'||p.name
from
   dba_tables     t,
   dba_segments s,
   v$sqlarea      a,
   (select distinct
     address,
     object_owner owner,
     object_name name
   from
     v$sql_plan
   where
     operation = 'TABLE ACCESS'
     and
     options = 'FULL') p
where
   a.address = p.address
   and
   t.owner = s.owner
   and
   t.table_name = s.segment_name
   and
   t.table_name = p.name
```

```
   and
   t.owner = p.owner
   and
   t.owner not in ('SYS','SYSTEM')
   and
   t.buffer_pool <> 'RECYCLE'
having
   s.blocks > 10000
group by
   p.owner, p.name, t.num_rows, s.blocks
)
;

spool off;
```

The output from this script is shown below:

```
SQL> @9i_recycle_syntax

alter table APPLSYS.FND_CONC_PP_ACTIONS storage (buffer_pool
recycle);
```

As a general rule, the DBA should check the SQL source to verify that a full-table query is retrieving over 40 percent of the table rows before adding any table to the RECYCLE pool.

The *x$bh* view can be used as another approach for finding RECYCLE candidates, similar to what was done for the KEEP pool. This topic is addressed in the next section.

Advanced RECYCLE Pool Tuning

The query below uses *x$bh.tch* to identify objects in the buffer cache that are larger than five percent of the total cache and have single touch buffer counts.

A significant amount of cache space is filled with these blocks that have only been used once. They are good candidates for inclusion in the RECYCLE buffer pool. Upon careful examination, DBAs will find that the script below will identify the percentage of an object's block in the buffer.

```
set lines 80;
set pages 999;
```

```
column avg_touches format 999
column myname heading 'Name' format a30
column mytype heading 'Type' format a10
column buffers format 999,999

SELECT
   object_type  mytype,
   object_name    myname,
   blocks,
   COUNT(1) buffers,
   100*(COUNT(1)/totsize) pct_cache
FROM
   sys.x$bh     a,
   dba_objects b,
   dba_segments s,
   (select value totsize from v$parameter
        where name = 'db_cache_size')
WHERE
   a.obj = b.object_id
and
   tch=1  -- This line only works in 8.1.6 and above
and
   b.object_name = s.segment_name
and
   b.owner not in ('SYS','SYSTEM')
GROUP BY
   object_type,
   object_name,
   blocks,
   totsize
HAVING
   100*(COUNT(1)/totsize) > 5
;
```

DBAs must remember that Oracle releases prior to 8.1.6 do not support the reference to the touch (*tch*) column. The report can still be useful with releases prior to 8.1.6, but there is no way of knowing how many times the objects have been touched since their entry into the data pool.

A sample report from this script is shown below. These tables and indexes occupy over five percent of the data buffer space and have only been touched once. This behavior is characteristic of large-table, full-table scans.

```
Type       Name                            BLOCKS   BUFFERS PCT_CACHE
---------  --------------------------  ----------  -------- ---------
INDEX      WIP_REQUIREMENT_OPERATIONS_U1     1042       334      5.57
TABLE      MTL_DEMAND_INTERFACE               847       818     13.63
TABLE      MTL_SYSTEM_ITEMS                  4227       493      8.22
```

The DBA must take into consideration both the number of blocks in the table and how often the table appears in the query output when determining whether or not to add objects to the RECYCLE pool.

Selecting candidates for the RECYCLE pool is an iterative process, just as it is for the KEEP pool. Data buffers are constantly changing, and the DBA may choose to run this script every minute over a period of several hours to get as complete a picture as possible of block activity within the data buffer.

This information covered how to monitor and tune the data buffer pools, now it is time to return to a more general consideration of large block sizes and their behavior inside the Oracle data buffers.

Large Blocks and Oracle Instance Caching

When an SQL query retrieves a result set from an Oracle table, it is probably gathering the table rows through an index. Many Oracle tuning experts have recommended that databases created prior to Oracle10g be redefined with large block sizes. The performance gains realized from switching a 2K block size database to an 8K block size have perplexed many DBAs.

Resistance to increasing the block size was typically expressed as "Why will moving to a large block size improve a database that only randomly fetches small rows?" The answer to this question is not so simple, but it involves indexes.

Many DBAs fail to consider index trees and the index range scan process of sequential retrieval of the index when choosing a block size. Nested loop joins usually indicate an index range scan, and the vast majority of rows are accessed using indexes.

Locating indexes in larger size blocks reduces I/O and further improves throughput for the entire database because index range scans gather index nodes sequentially. If this is the case, why not just create the database with large block sizes and forget about multiple block sizes?

The answer to this question is also complex. RAM buffer memory cannot be utilized with maximum efficiency unless the tables are segregated according to the distribution of related data between them. In allocating block sizes, the same general rules can be applied, with some modification in understanding.

Small block size

Tables containing small rows that are accessed randomly should be placed into tablespaces with smaller block sizes. This way, more of the buffer RAM remains available to store rows from other tables that are referenced frequently.

Larger block size

Larger block sizes are suitable for indexes, row ordered tables, single-table clusters, and tables with frequent full-table scans. In this way, a single I/O will retrieve many related rows, and future requests for related rows will already be available in the data buffer.

Some objects that may benefit from a larger blocksize, such as 16K or 32K, include:

- Some indexes, such as those that experience index range scans
- Large tables that are the target of full table scans
- Tables with large object, such as BLOB, CLOB, etc., data
- Tables with large row sizes that might blossom into chained/migrated rows
- Temporary tablespaces used for sorting

The simple goal is to maximize the amount of RAM available to the data buffers by setting the block size according to the amount of I/O the table or index sees. Smaller block sizes are appropriate for randomly accessed small rows while larger blocks are more suitable for rows that are sequentially accessed.

To illustrate, suppose a query retrieves 100 random 80 byte rows from Oracle. Since the rows are randomly accessed, it is safe to assume that no two rows exist on the same block, implying that it is necessary to read 100 blocks to fulfill the task.

If the blocks are sized at 16K, the *db_16k_cache_size* buffer will need 16 MB (16K * 100) of RAM. If the blocks are sized at 2K instead, only 2 MB of RAM is needed in the buffer for the 100 I/Os. Using the smaller block size would save 14 MB of RAM for this query alone. This is RAM that will be available elsewhere to hold other data.

Maximizing Oracle10g Block Space Usage

The RAM that is allocated to the data buffers will have to be carefully managed until memory becomes cheap enough to cache the entire database. Properly allocating tables and indexes according to block size is a balancing act. If the data blocks are set too large, valuable buffer space is wasted holding row data that will never be referenced. If the blocks are set too small, Oracle is forced to perform more disk I/O to satisfy a query.

The following are some further general guidelines that can be used for allocating data block sizes:

- Segregate large-table full-table scans. Tables subject to large-table, full-table scans will benefit from the largest supported block size. They should be placed in a tablespace with the largest block size.

- Set *db_recycle_cache_size* carefully. If *db_cache_size* is not set to the largest supported block size, the *db_recycle_cache_size* parameter should be used. Instead, a *db_32k_cache_size*, or whatever the max size is, should be created, and then assign all tables and indexes subject to large-table, full-table scans to the largest data buffer in the database.

The data dictionary will use the default block size. Make sure that the dictionary, the SYSTEM tablespace for example, is always fully cached in a data buffer pool. The block size, per se, of the dictionary is less important than having enough RAM in the SYSTEM tablespace buffer to fully cache all of the dictionary blocks.

Finding Baselines

Oracle databases are always changing, and the databases that are examined at 10:00 AM may be completely different than the databases that exist at 3:00 PM. Does this mean that a broad brush application of SSD is not valid?

When the performance of Oracle disk I/O is examined over different time periods, regular signatures appear when the I/O information is aggregated by hours of the day and day of the week as shown in Figure 14.11.

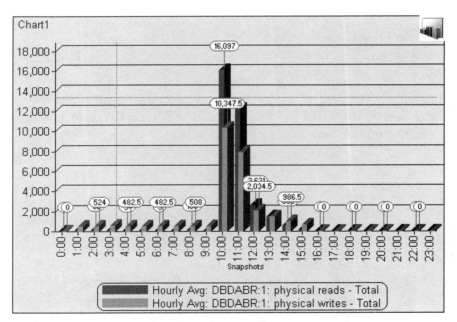

Figure 14.11: *Average disk reads and writes by hour of the day*

Most Oracle professionals will use Oracle9i STATSPACK or Oracle10g AWR information to gather these baselines. Once the repeating I/O trends have been identified, the DBA will be able to apply a broad brush to the use of SSD, placing the fast I/O devices where they will do the most good.

I/O information can be captured at the file level and this can give insight into the best data files to place on super fast SSD. The following script extracts the physical read information from the Oracle 10g *dba_hist_filestatxs* view:

```
break on begin_interval_time skip 2

column phyrds   format 999,999,999
column begin_interval_time format a25

select
   begin_interval_time,
   filename,
   phyrds
from
   dba_hist_filestatxs
  natural join
   dba_hist_snapshot
;
```

The sample output below shows a running total of physical reads by datafile. The snapshots are collected every half-hour. Starting from this script, the DBA could easily add a WHERE clause criteria and create a unique time-series exception report.

```
SQL> @reads

BEGIN_INTERVAL_TIME        FILENAME                                   PHYRDS
-------------------------  -------------------------------------    --------
24-FEB-04 11.00.32.000 PM  E:\ORACLE\ORA92\FSDEV10G\SYSTEM01.DBF     164,700
                           E:\ORACLE\ORA92\FSDEV10G\UNDOTBS01.DBF     26,082
                           E:\ORACLE\ORA92\FSDEV10G\SYSAUX01.DBF     472,008
                           E:\ORACLE\ORA92\FSDEV10G\USERS01.DBF        1,794
                           E:\ORACLE\ORA92\FSDEV10G\T_FS_LSQ.ORA       2,123


24-FEB-04 11.30.18.296 PM  E:\ORACLE\ORA92\FSDEV10G\SYSTEM01.DBF     167,809
                           E:\ORACLE\ORA92\FSDEV10G\UNDOTBS01.DBF     26,248
                           E:\ORACLE\ORA92\FSDEV10G\SYSAUX01.DBF     476,616
                           E:\ORACLE\ORA92\FSDEV10G\USERS01.DBF        1,795
                           E:\ORACLE\ORA92\FSDEV10G\T_FS_LSQ.ORA       2,244


25-FEB-04 12.01.06.562 AM  E:\ORACLE\ORA92\FSDEV10G\SYSTEM01.DBF     169,940
                           E:\ORACLE\ORA92\FSDEV10G\UNDOTBS01.DBF     26,946
                           E:\ORACLE\ORA92\FSDEV10G\SYSAUX01.DBF     483,550
                           E:\ORACLE\ORA92\FSDEV10G\USERS01.DBF        1,799
                           E:\ORACLE\ORA92\FSDEV10G\T_FS_LSQ.ORA       2,248
```

A little tweaking to the reads.sql script and the DBA could report on physical writes, read time, write time, single block reads, and a host of other interesting metrics from the *dba_hist_filestatxs* view.

Learning Instance Tuning from Performance Benchmarks

A close look at the benchmark methodology leads to the conclusion that blistering transaction speed cannot be attributed solely to high-speed hardware platforms. In order to appreciate the nature of these benchmarks, a closer look at how the Oracle professionals designed the database to accommodate high-speed data retrieval is needed.

Oracle 10g Windows Benchmark

The benchmark where UNISYS set the world record for price-performance, achieving over a quarter of a million transactions per minute using Oracle10g on Windows has already been mentioned in this text. The $1,400,000 server had 16 Intel Itanium 2 processors running at 1.5GHz, each with 6MB of Level 3 (iL3) cache and 128GB of memory. The techniques used by the Oracle DBA in this benchmark included:

- Oracle Multiple blocksizes

- 115 gigabyte total SGA data buffer cache (*db_cache_size*, *db_32k_cache_size*)

- 78 gigabyte KEEP pool (*db_keep_cache_size*)

HP Linux Benchmark

This world record benchmark used a $6,000,000 HP server with 64-Intel Itanium2 processors and 768 gigabytes of RAM and achieved over one million transactions per minute.

This voluminous benchmark disclosure report numbered 206 pages and offered some interesting clues into the way that the Oracle DBA configured Oracle10g for this world record benchmark:

- Real Application Clusters: The benchmark used 16 Oracle instances, each mapping to four processors.

- Multiple blocksizes: This world record used four separate blocksizes (2k, 4k, 8k, 16k) to isolate RAM data buffers and place objects within the most appropriate block sizes.

- Oracle Hidden Parameters: The benchmark DBA employed several Oracle hidden parameters to boost performance. Like most vendors, they take advantage of hardware specific performance features:

```
_in_memory_undo=false
_cursor_cache_frame_bind_memory = true
_db_cache_pre_warm = false
_in_memory_undo=false
_check_block_after_checksum = false
_lm_file_affinity
```

- Large RAM data buffers: For each of the 16 RAC nodes, this benchmark used about 44 gigabytes of RAM data buffers each, distributed into five separate RAM data block buffers. The total RAM data block buffer storage was over 700 billion bytes. The following are the data block buffer parameters for each RAC node:

```
db_cache_size = 4000M
db_recycle_cache_size = 500M
db_8k_cache_size = 200M
db_16k_cache_size = 4056M
db_2k_cache_size = 35430M
```

- Single table hash cluster: The benchmark used single-table hash clusters to speed access to specific rows, bypassing index access with faster hash access to rows. Their hash cluster used of the RECYCLE pool because single-table hash cluster access is random by nature and another task is unlikely to need the block in the buffer.

There are some important lessons in these benchmarks for the Oracle professional desiring to hypercharge their application:

- Multiple blocksizes: Using multiple blocksizes allows the DBA to segregate data blocks in the SGA data buffer cache. Multiple blocksizes are also beneficial for improving the speed of sequential access tablespaces, indexes and temp tablespace, by using the db_32k_cache_size parameter.

- Large data buffers: Both of these benchmarks had over 100 gigabytes of data buffer cache (*db_cache_size*, *db_keep_cache_size*, *db_32k_cache_size*). Caching of data can improve the rate of logical I/O to physical disk I/Os and experts say that logical I/O is 20 to 200 times faster than disk access.

- Hash clusters: Oracle hash cluster tables can improve random row access speed by up to four times because the hash can get the row location far faster than index access. Also multiple table hash clusters can store logically related rows on a single data block, allowing the DBA to access a whole unit of data in a single physical I/O.

The importance of instance configuration should be clear.

Conclusion

The proper settings for the Oracle instance parameters are the single most important aspect of Oracle tuning. Oracle parameters control the sizes of the SGA regions, the SQL optimization process, and the ability of Oracle to invoke automatic tuning activities such as cursor sharing, automatic query rewrite and automatic memory management.

The main points of this chapter include:

- Oracle instance tuning involves adjusting important *init.ora* parameters, configuring the SGA regions and adjusting the disk I/O block sizes.

- Oracle server kernel parameter, especially I/O configuration, has a huge influence on Oracle instance performance.

- The most important Oracle parameters are those that govern the SQL optimizer and the sizes of the SGA regions.

- Oracle provides hidden instance parameters and these can be very helpful on specific hardware. The TPC Oracle benchmarks (www.tpc.org) should be consulted to see the hidden Oracle parameters used by hardware vendors to see how they are used.

- Oracle has created a special KEEP pool to ensure that frequently references data blocks stay inside the SGA. It is the job of the DBA to identify and cache all high impact tables and indexes in the KEEP pool.

- Benchmarks show that multiple blocksizes should be defined so that the DBA can map Oracle objects to the most beneficial blocksize.

- Any tablespaces whose objects experience full-scans should be placed into a large blocksize. This includes certain indexes, the TEMP tablespace, and data warehouse tables.

- Objects that experience high invalidations, such as truncate table or high DML, should be segregated into a separate data buffer, sometimes with a small size.

This chapter has been extensive, but it lays the foundation for a look at proactive SQL Tuning which is a very complex an important component of Oracle tuning.

SQL Tuning

"I think we need to tune your SQL"

Understanding SQL Tuning

Before relational databases were introduced, database queries required knowledge of the internal structures and developers needed to build in the tuning as a part of writing the database query. However, the SQL standard imposed a declarative solution to database queries where the database optimizer determines important data access methods such as what indexes to use and the optimal sequence to join multiple tables together.

Today, it is not enough for a developer to write an SQL statement that provides the correct answer. SQL is declarative, so there are many ways to formulate a query, each with identical results but with far different execution times.

Oracle SQL tuning is a phenomenally complex subject. Entire books have been devoted to the nuances of Oracle SQL tuning, most notably the Kimberly Floss book *Oracle SQL & CBO Internals* by Rampant TechPress.

This chapter provides a review the following areas of SQL tuning:

- The goals of SQL tuning
- Simplifying complex SQL
- SQL Optimization instance parameters
- Statistics and SQL optimization
- Oracle10g and CBO statistics
- Oracle tuning with hints
- Oracle10g SQL profiles
- AWR and SQL tuning
- ADDM and SQL tuning

The first three sections will be an overview of general Oracle10g tuning concepts, so that the basic tools and techniques for tuning SQL optimization are clearly introduced. The focus will then shift to an exploration of the new Oracle10g SQL Profiles, and will eventually delve into the internals of AWR and explore how the SQLTuning and SQLAccess advisor use time-series metadata.

Optimizing Oracle SQL Execution

The key to success with the Oracle Cost-based Optimizer (CBO) is stability. Ensuring success with the CBO involves the consideration of several important infrastructure issues.

- Ensure static execution plans: Whenever an object is re-analyzed, the execution plan for thousands of SQL statements may be changed. Most successful Oracle sites will choose to lock down their SQL execution plans by carefully controlling CBO statistics, using stored outlines (optimizer plan stability), adding detailed hints to their SQL, or by using Oracle10g SQL Profiles. Again, there are exceptions to this rule such as LIMS databases, and for these databases, the DBA will choose to use dynamic sampling and allow the SQL execution plans to change as the data changes.

- Reanalyze statistics only when necessary: One of the most common mistakes made by Oracle DBAs is to frequently re-analyze the schema. The sole purpose of doing that is to change the execution plans for its SQL, and if it isn't broken, don't fix it. If the DBA is satisfied with current SQL performance, re-analyzing a schema could cause significant performance problems and undo the tuning efforts of the development staff. In practice, very few shops are sufficiently dynamic to require periodic schema re-analysis.

- Pre-tune the SQL before deploying: Many Oracle systems developers assume that their sole goal is to write SQL statements that deliver the correct data from Oracle. In reality, writing the SQL is only half their job. Successful Oracle sites require all developers to ensure that their SQL accesses Oracle in an optimal fashion. Many DBAs will export their production CBO statistics into their test databases so that their developers can see how their SQL will execute when it is placed into the production system. DBAs and staff should be trained to use the AUTOTRACE and TKPROF utilities and to interpret SQL execution results.

- Manage schema statistics: All Oracle DBAs should carefully manage the CBO statistics to ensure that the CBO works the same in their test and production environments. A savvy DBA knows how to collect high quality statistics and migrate their production statistics into their test environments. This approach ensures that all SQL migrating into production has the same execution plan as it did in the test database.

- Tune the overall system first: The CBO parameters are very powerful because a single parameter change could improve the performance of thousands of SQL statements. Changes to critical

CBO parameters such as optimizer_mode, *optimizer_index_cost_adj*, and *optimizer_index_caching* should be done before tuning individual SQL statements. This reduces the number of suboptimal statements that require manual tuning.

Prior to Oracle10g, it was an important job of the Oracle DBA to properly gather and distribute statistics for the CBO. The goal of the DBA was to keep the most accurate production statistics for the current processing. In some cases, there may be more than one set of optimal statistics.

For example, the best statistics for OLTP processing may not be the best statistics for the data warehouse processing that occurs each evening. In this case, the DBA will keep two sets of statistics and import them into the schema when processing modes change.

The following section provides a quick, simple review of the goals of SQL tuning.

Goals of SQL Tuning

There are many approaches to SQL tuning and this section describes a fast, holistic method of SQL tuning where the SGA and the all-important optimizer parameters are fine-tuned and the CBO statistics are adjusted, all based on current system load. Once the best overall optimization is achieved, specific cases of sub-optimal SQL can be reviewed, and execution plans can be changed with SQL profiles, specialized CBO stats, or hints.

Despite the inherent complexity of tuning SQL, there are general guidelines that every Oracle DBA follows in order to improve the overall performance of their Oracle systems. The goals of SQL tuning are simple:

- Replace unnecessary large-table full-table scans with index scans

- Cache small-table full table scans

- Verify optimal index usage

- Verify optimal JOIN techniques

- Tune complex subqueries to remove redundant access

These goals may seem deceptively simple, but these tasks comprise 90 percent of SQL tuning. They do not require a thorough understanding of the internals of Oracle SQL. This venture will begin with an overview of the Oracle SQL optimizers.

Of course, the SQL can be tuned to one's heart's content, but if the optimizer is not fed with the correct statistics, the optimizer may not make the correct decisions. Before tuning, it is important to ensure that statistics are available and that they are current.

The following section will provide a closer look at the goals listed above as well as how they simplify SQL tuning.

Remove unnecessary large-table full table scans

Unnecessary full table scans (FTS) are an important symptom of sub-optimal SQL and cause unnecessary I/O that can drag down an entire database. The tuning expert first evaluates the SQL based on the number of rows returned by the query. Oracle says that if the query returns less than 40 percent of the table rows in an ordered table or seven percent of the rows in an unordered table, based on the index key value described by clustering_factor in dba_indexes, the query can be tuned to use an index in lieu of the full-table scan. However, it's not that simple. The speed of a FTS versus an index scan depends on many factors:

- Missing indexes, especially function-based indexes

- Bad/stale CBO statistics

- Missing CBO Histograms

- Clustering of the table rows to the used index

- System ability to optimize multiblock I/O, for example, *db_file_multiblock_read_count*

The most common tuning tool for addressing unnecessary full table scans is the addition of indexes, especially function-based indexes. The decision about removing a full-table scan should be based on a careful examination of the amount of logical I/O (consistent gets) of the index scan versus the costs of the full table scan. This decision should be made while factoring in the multiblock reads and possible parallel full-table scan execution. In some cases, an unnecessary full-table scan can be forced to use an index by adding an index hint to the SQL statement.

Cache small-table full table scans

For cases in which a full table scan is the fastest access method, the tuning professional should ensure that a dedicated data buffer is available for the rows. In Oracle7, an *alter table xxx cache* command can be issued. In Oracle8 and beyond, the small-table can be cached by forcing it into the KEEP pool.

Logical reads (consistent gets) are often 100x faster than a disk read and small, frequently referenced objects such as tables, clusters and indexes should be fully cached in the KEEP pool. Most DBA's check *x$bh* periodically and move any table that has 80% or more of its blocks in the buffer into the KEEP pool. In addition, *dba_hist_sqlstat* should be checked for tables that experience frequent small-table full-table scans.

Verify optimal index usage

Determining the index usage is especially important for improving the speed of queries with multiple WHERE clause predicates. Oracle sometimes has a choice of indexes, and the tuning professional must examine each index and ensure that Oracle is using the best index, meaning the one that returns the result with the least consistent gets.

Verify optimal JOIN techniques

Some queries will perform faster with NESTED LOOP joins, some with HASH joins, while others favor sort-merge joins. It is difficult to predict what join technique will be fastest, so many Oracle tuning experts will test run the SQL with each different table join method.

Tuning by Simplifying SQL Syntax

There are several methods for simplifying complex SQL statements, and Oracle10g will sometimes automatically rewrite SQL to make it more efficient.

- Rewrite the query into a more efficient form
- Use the WITH clause
- Use Global Temporary Tables
- Use Materialized Views

The following example shows how SQL can be rewritten. For a simple example of SQL syntax and execution speed, the following queries can be used. All of these SQL statements produce the same results, but they have widely varying execution plans and execution performance.

```
-- A non-correlated sub-query

select
  book_title
from
  book
where
  book_key not in (select book_key from sales);

Execution Plan
----------------------------------------------------------
   0      SELECT STATEMENT Optimizer=CHOOSE (Cost=1 Card=1 Bytes=64)
   1    0   FILTER
   2    1     TABLE ACCESS (FULL) OF 'BOOK' (Cost=1 Card=1 Bytes=64)
   3    1     TABLE ACCESS (FULL) OF 'SALES' (Cost=1 Card=5 Bytes=25)


-- An outer join
```

```
select
  book_title
from
  book    b,
  sales   s
where
  b.book_key = s.book_key(+)
and
  quantity is null;


Execution Plan
-----------------------------------------------------------
0    SELECT STATEMENT Optimizer=CHOOSE (Cost=3 Card=100 Bytes=8200)

1  0 FILTER
2  1   FILTER
3  2     HASH JOIN (OUTER)
4  3       TABLE ACCESS (FULL) OF 'BOOK' (Cost=1 Card=20 Bytes=1280)
5  3       TABLE ACCESS (FULL) OF 'SALES' (Cost=1 Card=100 Bytes=1800)


-- A Correlated sub-query

select
  book_title
from
  book
where
  book_title not in (
                select
                distinct
                  book_title
                from
                  book,
                  sales
                where
                  book.book_key = sales.book_key
                and
                  quantity > 0);


Execution Plan
-----------------------------------------------------------
0    SELECT STATEMENT Optimizer=CHOOSE (Cost=1 Card=1 Bytes=59)
1  0 FILTER
2  1   TABLE ACCESS (FULL) OF 'BOOK' (Cost=1 Card=1 Bytes=59)
3  1   FILTER
4  3     NESTED LOOPS (Cost=6 Card=1 Bytes=82)
5  4       TABLE ACCESS (FULL) OF 'SALES' (Cost=1 Card=5 Bytes=90)
6  4       TABLE ACCESS (BY INDEX ROWID) OF 'BOOK' (Cost=1 Card=1)
7  6         INDEX (UNIQUE SCAN) OF 'PK_BOOK' (UNIQUE)
```

The formulation of the SQL query has a dramatic impact on the execution plan for the SQL, and the order of the WHERE clause predicates can make a difference. Savvy Oracle developers know the most efficient way to code Oracle SQL for optimal execution plans, and savvy Oracle shops train their developers to formulate efficient SQL.

The following section will show how the WITH clause can help simplify complex queries.

Using the WITH clause to simplify complex SQL

Oracle SQL can run faster when complex subqueries are replaced with global temporary tables. Starting in Oracle9i release 2, there was an incorporation of a subquery factoring utility implemented the SQL-99 WITH clause. The WITH clause is a tool for materializing subqueries to save Oracle from having to recompute them multiple times.

Use of the SQL WITH clause is very similar to the use of Global Temporary Tables (GTT), a technique that is often employed to improve query speed for complex subqueries. The following are some important notes about the Oracle WITH clause:

- The SQL WITH clause only works on Oracle 9i release 2 and beyond.

- Formally, the WITH clause was called subquery factoring.

- The SQL WITH clause is used when a subquery is executed multiple times.

- The ANSI WITH clause is also useful for recursive queries, but this feature has not yet been implemented in Oracle SQL.

The following example shows how the Oracle SQL WITH clause works and see how the WITH clause and Global temporary tables can be used to speed up Oracle queries.

All Stores with above average sales

To keep it simple, the following example only references the aggregations once, where the SQL WITH clause is normally used when an aggregation is referenced multiple times in a query.

The following is an example of a request to see the names of all stores with above average sales. For each store, the average sales must be compared to the average sales for all stores as shown in Figure 15.1.

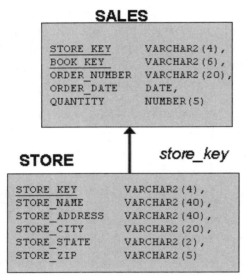

Figure 15.1: *The relationship between STORE and SALES*

Essentially, the query below accesses the STORE and SALES tables, comparing the sales for each store with the average sales for all stores. To answer this query, the following information must be available:

- The total sales for all stores.

- The number of stores.

- The sum of sales for each store.

To answer this in a single SQL statement, inline views will be employed along with a subquery inside a HAVING clause:

```
select
   store_name,
   sum(quantity)
store_sales,
   (select sum(quantity) from sales)/(select count(*) from store)
avg_sales
from
   store   s,
   sales   sl
where
   s.store_key = sl.store_key
having
   sum(quantity) > (select sum(quantity) from sales)/(select
count(*) from store)
group by
   store_name
;
```

While this query provides the correct answer, it is difficult to read and complex to execute as it is recomputing the sum of sales multiple times.

To prevent the unnecessary re-execution of the aggregation (sum(sales)), temporary tables could be created and used to simplify the query. The following steps should be followed:

- Create a table named T1 to hold the total sales for all stores.

- Create a table named T2 to hold the number of stores.

- Create a table named T3 to hold the store name and the sum of sales for each store.

A fourth SQL statement that uses tables T1, T2, and T3 to replicate the output from the original query should then be written. The final result will look like this:

```
create table t1 as
select sum(quantity) all_sales from stores;

create table t2 as
select count(*) nbr_stores from stores;

create table t3 as
select store_name, sum(quantity) store_sales from store natural join
sales;
```

```
select
   store_name
from
   t1,
   t2,
   t3
where
   store_sales > (all_sales / nbr_stores)
;
```

While this is a very elegant solution and easy to understand and has a faster execution time, the SQL-99 WITH clause can be used instead of temporary tables. The Oracle SQL WITH clause will compute the aggregation once, give it a name, and allow it to be referenced, perhaps multiple times, later in the query.

The SQL-99 WITH clause is very confusing at first because the SQL statement does not begin with the word SELECT. Instead, the WITH clause is used to start the SQL query, defining the aggregations, which can then be named in the main query as if they were real tables:

```
WITH
   subquery_name
AS
   (the aggregation SQL statement)
SELECT
   (query naming subquery_name);
```

Retuning to the oversimplified example, the temporary tables should be replaced with the SQL WITH clause:

```
WITH
   sum_sales      AS
      select /*+ materialize */
      sum(quantity) all_sales from stores
   number_stores  AS
      select /*+ materialize */
      count(*) nbr_stores from stores;
   sales_by_store AS
      select /*+ materialize */
      store_name, sum(quantity) store_sales from
      store natural join sales
SELECT
   store_name
FROM
   store,
   sum_sales,
   number_stores,
   sales_by_store
```

```
WHERE
   store_sales > (all_sales / nbr_stores)
;
```

Note the use of the Oracle undocumented materialize hint in the WITH clause. The Oracle materialize hint is used to ensure that the Oracle CBO materializes the temporary tables that are created inside the WITH clause, and its opposite is the undocumented inline hint. This is not necessary in Oracle10g, but it helps ensure that the tables are only created one time.

Tip!

Depending on the release of Oracle in use, the global temporary tables (GTT) might be a better solution than the WITH clause because indexes can be created on the GTT for faster performance.

Future enhancement to the WITH clause

Even though it is part of the ANSI SQL standard, as of Oracle 10g, it should be noted that the WITH clause is not yet fully functional within Oracle SQL, and it does not yet support the use of WITH clause replacement for CONNECT BY when performing recursive queries.

To show how the WITH clause is used in ANSI SQL-99 syntax, the following is an excerpt from Jonathan Gennick's work Understanding the WITH Clause showing the use of the SQL-99 WITH clause to traverse a recursive bill of materials hierarchy.

NOTE: This ANSI SQL syntax does NOT work (yet) with Oracle SQL

```
WITH recursiveBOM
   (assembly_id, assembly_name, parent_assembly) AS
(SELECT parent.assembly_id,
       parent.assembly_name,
       parent.parent_assembly
FROM bill_of_materials parent
WHERE parent.assembly_id=100
UNION ALL
SELECT child.assembly_id,
```

```
        child.assembly_name,
        child.parent_assembly
FROM recursiveBOM parent, bill_of_materials child
WHERE child.parent_assembly = parent.assembly_id)
SELECT assembly_id, parent_assembly, assembly_name
FROM recursiveBOM;
```

The WITH clause allows one to pre-materialize components of a complex query, making the entire query run faster. This same technique can also be used with Global temporary tables.

Tuning SQL with Temporary Tables

It has long been understood that materializing a subquery component can greatly improve SQL performance. Oracle global temporary tables are a great way to accomplish this.

With global temporary tables Oracle can allow hundreds of end-users to create their own copies of intermediate SQL result sets, independent of other users in the system. A silver bullet has been included at the end of this chapter with more details on tuning SQL with temporary tables.

Before delving into the tuning of individual SQL statements, it will be useful to examine how global Oracle parameters and features influence SQL execution. When tuning SQL, it is critical to optimize the instance as a whole before tuning individual SQL statements. This is especially important for proactive SQL tuning where the SQL may change execution plans based on changes in object statistics.

Oracle SQL Performance Parameters

Making the cost-based SQL optimizer (CBO) one of the most sophisticated tools ever created has cost Oracle Corporation millions of dollars. While the job of the CBO is to always choose the most optimal execution plan for any SQL statement, there are some things that the CBO cannot detect. This is when the DBA's expertise is needed.

The best execution plan for an SQL statement is affected by the types of SQL statements, the speed of the disks, and the load on the CPUs. For instance, the best execution plan resulting from a query run at 4:00 a.m. when 16 CPUs are idle may be quite different from the same query at 3:00 p.m. when the system is 90 percent utilized.

The CBO is not psychic, despite the literal definition of Oracle. Oracle can never know, the exact load on the Oracle system; therefore, the Oracle professional must adjust the CBO behavior periodically.

Most Oracle professionals make these behavior adjustments using the instance wide CBO behavior parameters such as *optimizer_index_cost_adj* and *optimizer_index_caching*. However, Oracle does not advise altering the default values for many of these CBO settings because the changes can affect the execution plans for thousands of SQL statements.

Some major adjustable parameters that influence the behavior of the CBO are shown below:

- *parallel_automatic_tuning*: Full-table scans are parallelized when set to ON. Since parallel full-table scans are extremely quick, the CBO will give a higher cost to index access and will be friendlier to full-table scans.

- *hash_area_size* (if not using *pga_aggregate_target*): The setting for the *hash_area_size* parameter governs the propensity of the CBO to favor hash joins over nested loops and sort merge table joins.

- *db_file_multiblock_read_count*: The CBO, when set to a high value, recognizes that scattered (multi-block) reads may be less expensive than sequential reads. This makes the CBO friendlier to full-table scans.

- *optimizer_index_cost_adj*: This parameter changes the costing algorithm for access paths involving indexes. The smaller the value, the cheaper the cost of index access.

- *optimizer_index_caching*: This is parameter tells Oracle the amount the index is likely to be in the RAM data buffer cache. The setting for optimizer_index_caching affects the CBO's decision to use an index for a table join (nested loops) or to favor a full-table scan.

- *optimizer_max_permutations*: This controls the maximum number of table join permutations allowed before the CBO is forced to pick a table join order. For a six-way table join, Oracle must evaluate six factorial (6!), or 720 possible join orders for the tables. This parameter has been deprecated in Oracle10g.

- *sort_area_size* (if not using *pga_aggregate_target*): The *sort_area_size* influences the CBO when deciding whether to perform an index access or a sort of the result set. The higher the value for *sort_area_size*, the more likely a sort will be performed in RAM, and the more likely that the CBO will favor a sort over pre-sorted index retrieval. Note that *sort_area_size* is ignored when *pga_aggregate_target* is set and when *workarea_size_policy* =*auto*, unless you are using a specialized feature such as the MTS (shared servers). If dedicated server connections are used, the *sort_area_size* parameter is ignored.

Note: Oracle10g release 2 has a new sorting algorithm which claims to use less server resources, specifically CPU and RAM resources. A hidden parameter called _newsort_enabled, which can be set to TRUE or FALSE, is used to turn-on the new sorting method.

The *optimizer_index_cost_adj* parameter controls the CBO's propensity to favor index scans over full-table scans. In a dynamic system, as the type of SQL and load on the database changes, the ideal value for *optimizer_index_cost_adj* may change radically in just a few minutes.

Using *optimizer_index_cost_adj*

The most important parameter is the *optimizer_index_cost_adj*, and the default setting of 100 is incorrect for most Oracle systems. For OLTP systems, resetting this parameter to a smaller value (between 10 and 30) may result in huge performance gains as SQL statements change from large-table full-table scans to index range scans. The Oracle environment can be queried so that the optimal setting for *optimizer_index_cost_adj* can be intelligently estimated.

The *optimizer_index_cost_adj* parameter defaults to a value of 100, but it can range in value from one to 10,000. A value of 100 means that equal weight is given to index versus multiblock reads. In other words, *optimizer_index_cost_adj* can be thought of as a "how much do I like full-table scans?" parameter.

With a value of 100, the CBO likes full-table scans and index scans equally, and a number lower than 100 tells the CBO index scans are faster than full-table scans. Although, with a super low setting such as *optimizer_index_cost_adj*=1, the CBO will still choose full-table scans for no-brainers such as tiny tables that reside on two blocks.

The following script illustrates the suggested initial setting for the *optimizer_index_cost_adj*.

```
col c1 heading 'Average Waits for|Full Scan Read I/O' format
9999.999
col c2 heading 'Average Waits for|Index Read I/O'      format
9999.999
col c3 heading 'Percent of| I/O Waits|for Full Scans' format 9.99
col c4 heading 'Percent of| I/O Waits|for Index Scans' format 9.99
col c5 heading 'Starting|Value|for|optimizer|index|cost|adj' format
999

select
   a.average_wait                                   c1,
   b.average_wait                                   c2,
   a.total_waits /(a.total_waits + b.total_waits)   c3,
   b.total_waits /(a.total_waits + b.total_waits)   c4,
   (b.average_wait / a.average_wait)*100            c5
from
   v$system_event   a,
   v$system_event   b
where
   a.event = 'db file scattered read'
and
   b.event = 'db file sequential read'
;
```

The following is the output from the script.

```
Starting
                                                               Value
                                                                 for
                                                           optimizer
                                         Percent of    Percent of    index
Average waits for   Average waits for    I/O waits       I/O waits     cost
full scan read I/O  index read I/O     for full scans  for index scans  adj
------------------  ------------------  --------------  ---------------  -----
         1.473               .289            .02              .98          20
```

In this example, the suggested starting value of 20 for *optimizer_index_cost_adj* may be too high because 98 percent of the data waits are on index (sequential) block access. Weighting this starting value for *optimizer_index_cost_adj* to reflect the reality that this system has only two percent waits on full-table scan reads, a typical OLTP system with few full-table scans, is a practical matter. It is not desirable to have an automated value for *optimizer_index_cost_adj* to be less than one or more than 100.

This same script may give a very different result at a different time of the day because these values change constantly, as the I/O waits accumulate and access patterns change. Oracle10g now has the *dba_hist_sysmetric_summary* table for time-series analysis of this behavior.

Setting the SQL Optimizer Cost Model

Starting with Oracle9i, DBAs have the ability to view the estimated CPU, TEMP and I/O costs for every SQL execution plan step. Oracle Corporation has noted that typical OLTP databases are becomingly increasingly CPU-bound and has provided the ability for the DBA to make the optimizer consider the CPU costs associated with each SQL execution step.

The developers of Oracle10g recognized this trend toward CPU-based optimization by providing the ability to choose CPU-based or I/O-based costing during SQL optimization with the 10g default being CPU-costing. In Oracle10g, system stats are gathered by default, and in Oracle9i the DBA must manually execute the *dbms_stat.gather_system_stats* package to get CBO statistics.

```
alter session set "_optimizer_cost_model"=choose;
alter session set "_optimizer_cost_model"=io;
alter session set "_optimizer_cost_model"=cpu;
```

This parameter can be used to choose the best optimizer costing model for a particular database, based on the I/O and CPU load.

The choice of relative weighting for these factors depends upon the existing state of the database. Databases using 32-bit technology and the corresponding 1.7 gigabyte limit on SGA RAM size tend to be I/O-bound with the top timed events being those performing disk reads:

```
Top 5 Timed Events
~~~~~~~~~~~~~~~~~                                      % Total
Event                               Waits    Time (s) Ela Time
----------------------------------- -------- -------- --------
db file sequential read             xxxx     xxxx        30
db file scattered read              xxxx     xxxx        40
```

Once 64-bit became popular, Oracle SGA sizes increased, more frequently referenced data was cached, and databases became increasingly CPU-bound. Also, solid-state disk (RAM SAN) has removed disk I/O as a source of waits:

```
Top 5 Timed Events
~~~~~~~~~~~~~~~~~                                      % Total
Event                               Waits    Time (s) Ela Time
----------------------------------- -------- -------- --------
CPU time                            xxxx     xxxx       55.76
db file sequential read             xxxx     xxxx       27.55
```

The gathered statistics are captured via the *dbms_stats* package in 9.2 and above, and the following CPU statistics are captured automatically in 10g and stored in the *sys.aux_stat$* view.

- single block disk read time, in microseconds

- multiblock disk read-time, in microseconds)

- CPU speed in mhz

- average *multiblock_read_count* in number of blocks

A database where CPU is the top timed event may benefit from a change in the SQL optimizer to consider the CPU costs associated with each execution plan.

Using CPU costing may not be good for databases that are I/O-bound. Also, changing to CPU-based optimizer costing will change the predicate evaluation order of the query. MetaLink bulletin 276877.1 provides additional information on this.

Turning on CPU Costing

The default setting for the optimizer cost model is CHOOSE, meaning that the presence of CBO statistics will influence whether or not CPU costs are considered. According to the documentation, CPU costs are considered when SQL optimizer schema statistics are gathered with the *dbms_stat.gather_system_stats* package, which is the default behavior in Oracle10g, and CPU costs will be considered in all SQL optimization.

It gets tricky because of Bug 2820066 where CPU cost is computed whenever *optimizer_index_cost_adj* is set to a non-default value. Unless the 9.2.0.6 server patch set has been applied, the Oracle9i database may be generating CPU statistics, regardless of the CBO stats collection method.

To ensure that CPU costing is in use:

- In Oracle9i, use *dbms_stats.gather_system_stats* to collect statistics

- Set the undocumented parameter *_optimizer_cost_model*=cpu;

Turning on I/O Costing

I/O-bound databases, especially 32-bit databases, may want to utilize I/O-based SQL costing. The default optimizer costing in Oracle10g is CPU, and it can be changed to IO costing by using these techniques:

- Ensure that *optimizer_index_cost_adj* is set to the default value (Oracle9i bug 2820066)

- Add a *no_cpu_costing* hint in the SQL

- alter session set "*_optimizer_cost_model*"=io;

- Set *init.ora* hidden parameter *_optimizer_cost_model*=io

Notes on Bug 2820066:

CPU cost is computed when *optimizer_index_cost_adj* is set to a non-default value. If *optimizer_index_cost_adj* is set to a non-default value, CPU costs are calculated regardless of the optimizer cost model used. If *optimizer_index_cost_adj* is set and the optimizer CPU cost model is not in use, but the explain plan shows that for queries not using domain indexes CPU costs are being calculated, this bug is likely in play.

In sum, CPU cost is always computed regardless of optimizer mode when *optimizer_index_cost_adj* is set in unpatched Oracle versions less than 10.1.0.2.

The following section shows how to change from CPU-based to I/O-based SQL optimization when the processing characteristics of the database change on a regular basis.

Bi-modal system configuration

It is not uncommon for databases to be bi-modal, operating OLTP during the day (CPU-intensive) and doing aggregations and rollups (I/O-intensive) at night.

The CPU and I/O statistics can now be captured using *dbms_stats* and then swapping them in as the processing mode changes. Most shops do this with the *dbms_scheduler* (*dbms_job*) package so that the statistics are swapped at the proper time.

With that introduction to the influence of parameters, it is time to examine other Oracle features that influence SQL execution. The most important system level factor is the schema statistics which have a huge influence on SQL execution.

Statistics and SQL Optimization

The new features in Oracle10g that indicate when statistics are old and need to be recalculated are extremely helpful. Gone are the days when statistics were calculated weekly, or on whatever schedule, just in case the data changed. It is now possible to know, for certain, one way or the other. Of course, some will still believe that new statistics should only be calculated if there is a problem, and once a decent access path exists, it should be left alone.

Some believe in the practice of running statistics by schedule such as weekly. Some believe in just calculating statistics when the data changes. Still others believe that statistics are only needed to fix a poor access path, and once things are good; they should not be touched. It is difficult to say who is correct.

Oracle10g automatically reanalyzes schema statistics based on the number of changes to row in the table, but it may be sub-optimal, and many senior Oracle DBAs use more sophisticated methods for determining when to re-analyze CBO statistics.

Although the Oracle CBO is one of the world's most sophisticated software achievements, it is still the job of the Oracle professional to provide valid statistics for the schema and understand how Oracle parameters affect the overall performance of the SQL optimizer.

Keep in mind, suboptimal SQL execution plans are a major reason for poorly performing Oracle databases, and because the CBO determines the execution plans, it is a critical component in Oracle optimization.

The *dbms_stats* utility is a great way to improve SQL execution speed. By using *dbms_stats* to collect top quality statistics, the CBO will usually make an intelligent decision about the fastest way to execute any SQL query. The *dbms_stats* utility continues to improve and the exciting new features of automatic sample size and automatic histogram generation greatly simplify the job of the Oracle professional.

Managing Schema Statistics with *dbms_stats*

Most experts agree that the majority of common SQL problems can be avoided if statistics are carefully defined and managed. In order for the CBO to make an intelligent decision about the best execution plan for SQL, the CBO must have information about the table and indexes that participate in the query. This information includes:

- The size of the tables

- The indexes on the tables

- The distribution of column values

- The cardinality of intermediate result sets

Given this information, the CBO can make an informed decision and almost always generates the best execution plan. The following section will cover how to gather top quality statistics for the CBO, as well as how to create an appropriate CBO environment for the database.

Getting top quality statistics with *dbms_stats*

The choice of execution plans is only as good as the optimizer statistics available to the query. *dbms_stats* package is the best ways to get statistics, superceding the old-fashioned analyze table and *dbms_utility* methods.

The *dbms_stats* utility does a far better job in estimating statistics, especially for large partitioned tables, and the better statistics result in faster SQL execution plans. The following is a sample execution of *dbms_stats* with the OPTIONS clause:

```
exec dbms_stats.gather_schema_stats( -
   ownname          => 'SCOTT', -
   options          => 'GATHER AUTO', -
   estimate_percent => dbms_stats.auto_sample_size, -
   method_opt       => 'for all columns size repeat', -
   degree           => 34 -
   )
```

There are several values for the *options* parameter:

- **GATHER:** This option re-analyzes the whole schema.

- **GATHER EMPTY:** This option only analyzes objects that have no statistics,

- **GATHER STALE:** This option is used with the monitoring feature and only re-analyzes tables with more than 10 percent modifications (INSERTS, UPDATES, DELETES).

- **GATHER AUTO:** This option will re-analyze objects that currently have no statistics and objects with stale statistics (objects with more than 10% row changes). Using the GATHER AUTO option is like combining GATHER STALE and GATHER EMPTY options.

Both GATHER STALE and GATHER AUTO *dbms_stats* options require monitoring. In Oracle9i, table monitoring can be implemented with the *alter table xxx monitoring* command. In Oracle10g, table monitoring is automatic. Oracle tracks changed tables with the *dba_tab_modifications* view and compares the number of modifications with the *num_rows* column in the *dba_tables* based on on the *sys.tab$* fixed view. The modifications are kept in *sys.mon_mos$* table.

The *dba_tab_modifications* contains the cumulative number of INSERTS, UPDATES, and DELETES that are tracked since the last analysis of statistics:

```
SQL> desc dba_tab_modifications;

Name                  Type
------------------------------------
TABLE_OWNER           VARCHAR2(30)
TABLE_NAME            VARCHAR2(30)
PARTITION_NAME        VARCHAR2(30)
SUBPARTITION_NAME     VARCHAR2(30)
INSERTS               NUMBER
UPDATES               NUMBER
DELETES               NUMBER
TIMESTAMP             DATE
TRUNCATED             VARCHAR2(3)
```

The most interesting of these options is the GATHER STALE option. Since all statistics will become stale quickly in a robust OLTP database, it is important to remember that the rule for GATHER STYLE is > 10% row change based on *num_rows* at statistics collection time.

As a result, almost every table except read-only tables will be reanalyzed with the GATHER STYLE option, making the GATHER STYLE option best for systems that are largely read-only. For example, if only five percent of the database tables get significant updates, then only five percent of the tables will be reanalyzed with the GATHER STYLE option.

To aid in intelligent histogram generation, Oracle uses the *method_opt* parameter of *dbms_stats*. There are also important new options within the *method_opt* clause, namely SKEWONLY, REPEAT and AUTO:

```
method_opt=>'for all columns size skewonly'

method_opt=>'for all columns size repeat'

method_opt=>'for all columns size auto'
```

The SKEWONLY option is very time intensive because it examines the distribution of values for every column within every index.

If *dbms_stats* finds an index whose columns are unevenly distributed, it will create a histogram for that index to aid the cost-based SQL optimizer in making a decision about index versus full-table scan access. For example, if an index has one column that is in 50 percent of the rows, a full-table scan is faster than an index scan to retrieve these rows.

```
--*************************************************************
-- SKEWONLY option—Detailed analysis
--
-- Use this method for a first-time analysis for skewed indexes
-- This runs a long time because all indexes are examined
--*************************************************************

begin
  dbms_stats.gather_schema_stats(
      ownname          => 'SCOTT',
      estimate_percent => dbms_stats.auto_sample_size,
      method_opt       => 'for all columns size skewonly',
       degree           => 7
    );
end;
```

If the statistics need to be reanalyzed, the reanalyze task will be less resource intensive with the REPEAT option. Using the REPEAT option, Oracle will only reanalyze indexes with existing histograms and will not search for other histogram opportunities. This is statistics should be reanalyzed on a regular basis.

```
--***************************************************************
-- REPEAT OPTION - Only reanalyze histograms for indexes
-- that have histograms
--
-- Following the initial analysis, the weekly analysis
-- job will use the "repeat" option. The repeat option
-- tells dbms_stats that no indexes have changed, and
-- it will only reanalyze histograms for
-- indexes that have histograms.
--***************************************************************
begin
   dbms_stats.gather_schema_stats(
      ownname          => 'SCOTT',
      estimate_percent => dbms_stats.auto_sample_size,
      method_opt       => 'for all columns size repeat',
      degree           => 7
   );
end;
```

The *dbms_stats* procedure can be made to analyze schema statistics very quickly on SMP servers with multiple CPU's. Oracle allows for parallelism when collecting CBO statistics, which can greatly speed up the time required to collect statistics. A parallel statistics collection requires an SMP server with multiple CPUs.

The following section will introduce the importance of estimating the optimal sample size when gathering schema statistics.

Automating Statistics Sample Size with *dbms_stats*

The higher the quality of the schema statistics will result in higher probability that CBO will choose the optimal execution plan. Unfortunately, doing a complete analysis of every rows of every table in a schema could take days and most shops must sample their database to get CBO statistics.

The goal of estimating the sample size is to take a large enough sample of the database to provide top quality data for the CBO while not adversely impacting server resources. Now that how the *dbms_stats* option works has been introduced, it will be useful see how to specify an adequate sample size for *dbms_stats*.

In earlier releases, the DBA had to guess what percentage of the database provided the best sample size and sometimes under analyzed the schema. Starting with Oracle9i Database, the *estimate_percent* argument was added to *dbms_stats* to allow Oracle to automatically estimate the best percentage of a segment to sample when gathering statistics. A sample invocation follows below:

```
estimate_percent => dbms_stats.auto_sample_size
```

After collecting statistics with an automatic sample size, the accuracy of the automatic statistics sampling can be verified by looking at the *sample_size* column on any of these data dictionary views:

- *dba_object_tables*
- *dba_tab_col_statistics*
- *dba_tab_partitions*
- *dba_tab_subpartitions*
- *dba_part_col_statistics*
- *dba_subpart_col_statistics*
- *dba_tables*
- *dba_tab_cols*
- *dba_tab_columns*
- *dba_all_tables*
- *dba_indexes*
- *dba_ind_partitions*
- *dba_ind_subpartitions*

In practice, the *auto_sample_size* option of dbms_stats generally chooses a *sample_size* from five to 20 percent when using automatic sampling, depending on the size of the tables and the distribution of column values.

Too small a sample can impact the CBO, so one should always make sure to take a statistically significant sample size for every object in the schema. The next section will introduce some methods DBA's use to ensure that their SQL optimizer always has great schema statistics.

Schema Statistics Management

Many infrastructure issues must be addressed in order to avoid surprises with SQL optimization. Shops that do not create this infrastructure are plagued by constantly changing SQL execution plans and poor database performance.

It is very rare for the fundamental nature of a schema to change. Large tables remain large, and index columns rarely change distribution, cardinality, and skew. The DBA should only consider periodically re-analyzing the total schema statistics if the database matches the following criteria:

- CPU-intensive databases: Many scientific systems load a small set of experimental data, analyze the data, produce reports, and then truncate and reload a new set of experiments. There are also Oracle databases with super large data buffer caches, with reduce physical I/O at the expense of higher CPU consumption. For these types of systems, it may be necessary to re-analyze the schema each time the database is reloaded.

- Highly volatile databases: In these rare cases, the size of tables and the characteristics of index column data changes radically. For example, Laboratory Information Management Systems (LIMS) load, analyze, and purge experimental data so frequently that it is very difficult to always have optimal CBO statistics. If a database has a table that has 100 rows one week and 10,000 rows the next week, the DBA may want to consider using Oracle10g dynamic sampling or a periodic reanalysis of statistics.

The following section will show how Oracle SQL optimization can be adjusted to evaluate I/O costs of CPU costs.

External Costing with the Optimizer

Over the past decade, Oracle has been enhanced to consider external influences when determining the best execution plan. Because the Oracle Database does not run in a vacuum, the optimizer must be able to factor in the costs of external disk I/O and the cost of CPU cycles for each SQL operation. This process is especially critical for queries running *all_rows* optimization, where minimizing server resources is a primary goal.

- *cpu_cost:* The Oracle10g SQL optimizer can now estimate the number of machine cycles required for an operation and factors this cost into the execution plan calculation. The CPU costs associated with servicing an Oracle query depends upon the current server configuration, which Oracle cannot see.

- *io_cost:* The CBO had been enhanced to estimate the number of physical block reads required for an operation. The I/O cost is proportional to the number of physical data blocks read by the operation.

Internally, Oracle uses both the CPU and I/O cost estimations in evaluating the execution plans, but these factors can be weighted according to the stress on the server. If the top 5 timed events include CPU, then the SQL may need to be optimized to minimize CPU resources. This equation becomes even more complex when parallel query is factored in, where many concurrent processes are servicing the query.

The best benefit for using CPU costing is for *all_rows* execution plans where cost is more important than with *first_rows* optimization.

The following section will provide a look at column histograms and how they help SQL execute faster.

Tuning SQL with Histograms

Histograms are an add-on feature to the *dbms_stats* procedure that stores the distribution of column values in either height-balanced or weight-balanced buckets. Histograms may help the Oracle optimizer in two ways:

- Skewed index – Histograms are important when the column value requires the CBO to decide whether to use an index vs. a full-table scan.

- Table join order – Histograms can reveal the expected number of rows returned from a table query, i.e. *select * from customer where state = 'NC';*, thereby helping the optimizer determine the fastest table join order.

Optimal table join order

When large tables are joined and the resukt set is small, it's critical that Oracle know the number of rows in each table after the queries WHERE clause is considered. Histograms can help. If the cardinality of the table is too-high, meaning the intermediate row sizes are larger than they have to be, then histograms on the most selective column in the WHERE clause will tip-off the optimizer and change the table join order.

Histograms are also used to predict cardinality and the number of rows returned is an important factor in determining the fastest table join order. In a situation where there is a *vehicle_type* index and 65 percent of the values are for the CAR type, when a query with WHERE *vehicle_type* = 'CAR' is specified, a full-table scan would be the fastest execution plan. However, a query with WHERE *vehicle_type* = 'TRUCK' would be faster when using access via an index.

For manually determining the best table join order, i.e. to add an ordered or leading hint, the WHERE clause of the query can be inspected along with the execution plan for the original query. The problem with forcing the sequence of table joins with the ordered hint is that it is not dynamic. Careful application of histograms can do the same job and apply to all queries.

Index skew

The distribution of values within an index will often affect the cost-based optimizer's (CBO's) decision whether to perform a full-table scan to satisfy a query or to use an index. This can happen whenever the column referenced within a SQL query WHERE clause has a non-uniform distribution of values, making a full-table scan faster than index access.

Since they affect performance, histograms should only be used when they are required for a faster CBO execution plan. Histograms incur additional overhead during the parsing phase of an SQL query and can be used effectively only when:

- A column's values cause the CBO to make an incorrect guess: If the CBO makes a wrong assumption about the size of an intermediate result set, it may choose a sub-optimal execution plan. A histogram added to the column often provides the additional information required for the CBO to choose the best plan.

- Significant skewing exists in the distribution of a column's data values: The skew must be important enough to make the CBO choose another execution plan.

- A table column is referenced in one or more queries: Never create histograms if queries do not reference the column. Novice DBAs may mistakenly create histograms on a skewed column, even if it is not referenced in a query.

The ability to seek columns that should have histograms, and then automatically create the histograms is a new Oracle9i feature of the *dbms_stats* package.

Before Oracle9i, the DBA had to manually detect those data columns that needed histograms and manually create them using these guidelines:

- Create a histogram whenever a column is referenced by many SQL WHERE clauses and when the data is heavily skewed, such that the optimal execution plan would change depending on the value in the WHERE clause.

- Create histograms when the optimizer cannot accurately predict the size of intermediate result sets in n-way table joins.

Figure 15.2 below shows an example of skewed and non-skewed data columns.

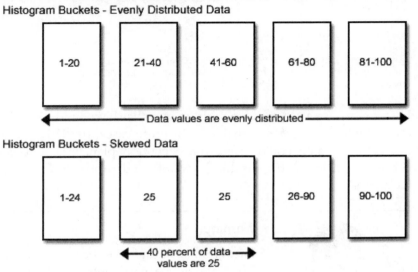

Figure 15.2: *Skewed data distribution vs. evenly distributed data.*

By using the REPEAT option, histograms are collected only on the columns that already have histograms. Like any other CBO statistic, histograms are static and need to be refreshed when column value distributions change. When refreshing statistics, the REPEAT option would be used as in the example below:

```
execute dbms_stats.gather_schema_stats(
  ownname         => 'SCOTT',
  estimate_percent => DBMS_STATS.AUTO_SAMPLE_SIZE,
  method_opt      => 'for all columns size repeat',
  degree          => DBMS_STATS.DEFAULT_DEGREE);
```

Since it examines the data distribution of values for every column within every index, the SKEWONLY option introduces a very time consuming build process. The *dbms_stats* package creates histograms to help the CBO make a table access decision; i.e., index versus a full-table scan when it finds an index whose column values are distributed unevenly. From the earlier *vehicle_type* example, if an index has one column value (e.g., CAR) that exists in 65 percent of the rows, a full-table scan will be faster than an index scan to access those rows, as in this example:

```
execute dbms_stats.gather_schema_stats(
  ownname          => 'SCOTT',
  estimate_percent => DBMS_STATS.AUTO_SAMPLE_SIZE,
  method_opt       => 'for all columns size skewonly',
  degree           => DBMS_STATS.DEFAULT_DEGREE);
```

Histograms are also effective with queries that have bind variables and queries with *cursor_sharing* enabled. In these cases, the CBO decides if the column value could affect the execution plan, and if it does, it substitutes a literal for the bind variable and proceeds to perform a hard parse.

Warning!

Histograms should not be used arbitrarily. They should be used only when they allow the CBO to significantly improve query speed.

The following section will provide an introductory look at another exciting new SQL optimization feature, Dynamic Sampling.

Inside Oracle10g Dynamic Sampling

One of the greatest problems with the Oracle CBO was the failure of the Oracle DBA to gather accurate schema statistics. Even with the *dbms_stats* package, the schema statistics were often stale and the DBA did not always create histograms for skewed data columns and data columns that are used to estimate the size of SQL intermediate result sets.

This resulted in a bum rap for Oracle's CBO, and beginner DBAs often falsely accused the CBO of failing to generate optimal execution plans when the real cause of the suboptimal execution plan was the DBA's failure to collect complete schema statistics.

Oracle has automated the collection and refreshing of schema statistics in Oracle10g. This automates the DBA's task and ensures that Oracle will always gather good statistics and choose the best execution plan for any query. Using the enhanced *dbms_stats* package, Oracle will automatically estimate the sample size, detect skewed columns that would benefit from histograms, and refresh the schema statistics when they become stale. This automates a very important DBA task and ensures that Oracle always has the statistics that it needs to make good execution plan choices.

The following is an example of using the *dbms_stats* package:

```
begin
   dbms_stats.gather_schema_stats(
      ownname           => 'SCOTT',
      estimate_percent => dbms_stats.auto_sample_size,
      method_opt => 'for all columns size repeat',
      degree            => 7
   );
end;
/
```

However, there was always a nagging problem with the CBO. Even with good statistics, the CBO would sometimes determine a suboptimal table join order, causing unnecessarily large intermediate result sets. For example, consider the complex WHERE clause in the query below.

Even with the best schema statistics it can be impossible to predict the optimal table join order. The table join order that has the smallest intermediate baggage. As one might expect, reducing the size of the intermediate row sets can greatly improve the speed of the query.

```
select
   stuff
from
   customer
natural join
   orders
natural join
   item
natural join
   product
```

```
where
   credit_rating * extended_credit > .07
and
   (qty_in_stock * velocity) /.075 < 30
or
   (sku_price / 47) * (qty_in_stock / velocity) > 47;
```

In this example, the SQL invokes a 4-way table join that only returns 18 rows, but the query carries 9,000 rows in intermediate result sets, which slows the overall SQL execution speed. This phenomenon is illustrated in Figure 15.3 below.

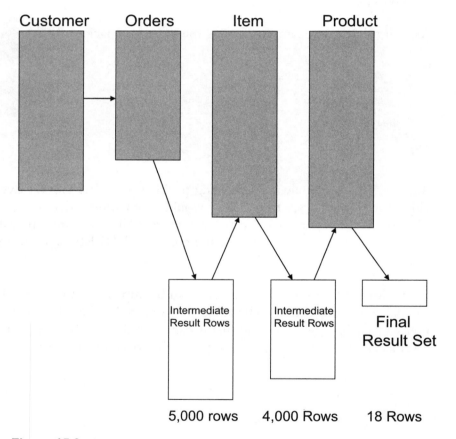

Figure 15.3: *Suboptimal intermediate row sets*

If there was a way to somehow predict the sizes of the intermediate results, the table join order can be resequenced to carry less intermediate baggage during the 4-way table join. The result for this particular example would yield carrying only 3,000 intermediate rows between the table joins. This phenomenon is illustrated in Figure 15.4.

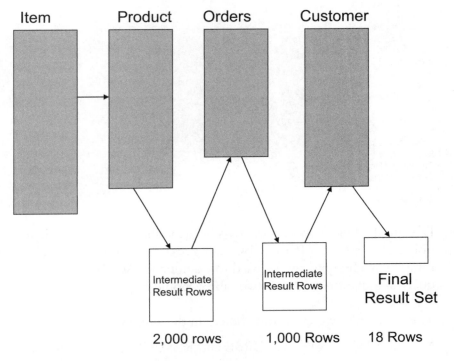

Figure 15.4: *Optimal intermediate row sets*

For the following example, one must assume there is a three-way table join against tables that all contain over 10,000 rows each. This database has 50,000 student rows, 10,000 course rows and 5,000 professor rows.

If the number of rows in the table determined the best table join order, one would expect that any 3-way table join would start by joining the PROFESSOR and COURSE tables, and then join the RESULT set to the STUDENT table.

However, whenever there is a WHERE clause, the total number of rows in each table does not matter if index access is being used. The following is a sample query:

```
select
   student_name
from
   professor
natural join
   course
natural join
   student
where
   professor = 'jones'
and
   course = 'anthropology 610';

Stan Nowakowski
Bob Crane
James Bakke
Patty O'Furniture

4 Rows selected.
```

Despite the huge numbers of rows in each table, the final result set will only be four rows. If the CBO can guess the size of the final result, sampling techniques can be used to examine the WHERE clause of the query and determine which two tables should be joined together first.

There are only two table join choices in the simplified example:

- Join STUDENT to COURSE and RESULT to PROFESSOR

- Join PROFESSOR to COURSE and RESULT to STUDENT

Which is better? The best solution will be the one where RESULT is smallest. Because the query is filtered with a WHERE clause, the number of rows in each table is incidental, and the real concern is the number of rows where professor = 'jones' and "where course = 'Anthropology 610'.

If the specific output goal is known, the best table join order becomes obvious. One might assume that Professor Jones is very popular and teaches 50 courses, and that Anthropology 610 has a total of eight students. With this knowledge, it is clear that the size of the intermediate row baggage is very different as shown in Figure 15.5.

Figure 15.5 shows the following: Join PROFESSOR to COURSE and RESULT to STUDENT.

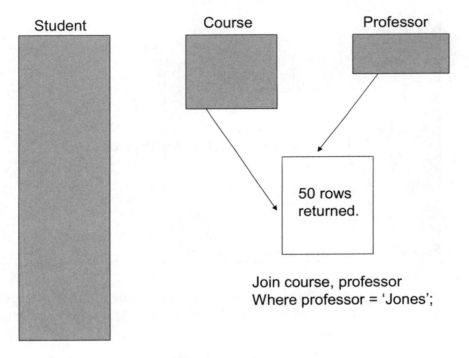

Figure 15.5: *A suboptimal intermediate row size*

If the CBO were to join the STUDENT table to the COURSE table first, the intermediate result set would only be eight rows, far less baggage to carry over to the final join as shown in Figure 15.6 which demonstrates the following: Join STUDENT to COURSE and RESULT to PROFESSOR.

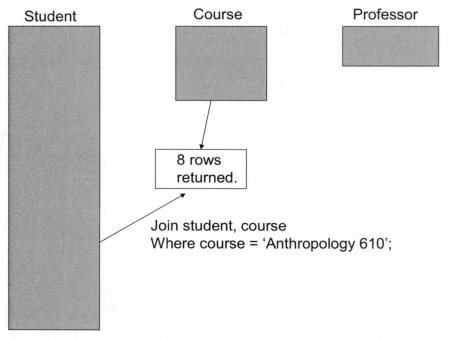

Figure 15.6: *An optimal intermediate row size*

Now that there are only eight rows returned from the first query, it easy to join the tiny eight row result set into the PROFESSOR table to get the final answer.

How is join cardinality estimated?

In the absence of column histograms, the Oracle CBO must be able to guess on information, and sometimes the guess is wrong. This is one reason why the ORDERED hint is one of the most popular SQL tuning hints, because using the ORDERED hint allows the DBA to specify that the tables be joined together in the same order that they appear in the FROM clause, like this:

```
select /+ ORDERED */
   student_name
from
   student
```

```
natural join
   course
natural join
   professor
where
   professor = 'jones'
and
   course = 'anthropology 610';
```

If the values for the PROFESSOR and COURSE table columns are not skewed, it is unlikely that the 10g automatic statistics would have created histograms buckets in the *dba_histograms* view for these columns.

The Oracle CBO needs to be able to accurately estimate the final number of rows returned by each step of the query and then use schema metadata from running *dbms_stats* to choose the table join order that results in the least amount of baggage, in the form of intermediate rows, from each of the table join operations.

This is a daunting task. When an SQL query has a complex WHERE clause, it can be very difficult to estimate the size of the intermediate result sets, especially when the WHERE clause transforms column values with mathematical functions. Oracle has made a commitment to making the CBO infallible, even when incomplete information exists.

Oracle9i introduced the new dynamic sampling method for gathering run-time schema statistics, and it is now enabled by default in Oracle10g.

However, dynamic sampling is not for every database. The following section will reveal why this is the case.

Enabling Dynamic Sampling

The main objective of dynamic sampling is to create more accurate selectivity and cardinality estimates, which in turn helps the CBO generate faster execution plans. Dynamic sampling is normally used to estimate single-table predicate selectivity when collected statistics cannot be used or are likely to lead to significant errors in estimation. It is also used to estimate table cardinality for tables without statistics or for tables whose statistics are too out of date to trust.

The *optimizer_dynamic_sampling* initialization parameter controls the number of blocks read by the dynamic sampling query. The parameter can be set to a value from zero to ten. In 10g, the default for this parameter is set to two, automatically enabling dynamic sampling. The *optimizer_features_enable* parameter will turn OFF dynamic sampling if it is set to a version earlier than 9.2.0.

A value of zero means dynamic sampling will not be performed. Increasing the value of the parameter results in more aggressive dynamic sampling in terms of both the type of tables sampled, analyzed, or unanalyzed, and the amount of I/O spent on sampling.

By default, Oracle will sample 32 random blocks. It is also important to know that dynamic sampling does not occur on tables that contain less than 32 blocks.

There is also a new dynamic sampling hint, *dynamic_sampling*(tablename level), where tablename is the name of the table to be dynamically sampled and level is the same setting from zero to ten. The default value for the level is two, which will only sample tables that have not been analyzed with *dbms_stats*.

```
select /*+ dynamic_sampling (customer 4) */
   customer_name, . . . .
```

The following are the level descriptions. The higher the level, the deeper the sampling. The sampling levels are cumulative and each level contains all of the sampling of the prior level:

- Level 1: Samples tables that appear in join or subquery conditions that have no indexes and have more blocks than 32, the default for dynamic sampling.

- Level 2 (default): Samples all unanalyzed tables that have more than 32 blocks.

- Level 3: Samples tables using a single column that applies selectivity to the table being sampled.

- Level 4: Samples tables using two or more columns that apply selectivity to the table being sampled.

- Level 5: Doubles the dynamic sample size and samples 64 blocks on tables.

- Level 6: Quadruples the dynamic sample size and samples 128 blocks on tables.

- Level 7: Samples 256 blocks on tables.

- Level 8: Samples 1,024 blocks on tables.

- Level 9: Samples 4,096 blocks on tables.

- Level 10: Samples all of the block in the tables.

 Dynamic sampling is not for everyone!

When *dynamic_sampling* was first introduced in Oracle9i, it was used primarily for data warehouse system with complex queries. Because it is enabled by default in Oracle10g, the DBA may want to turn off dynamic_sampling to remove unnecessary overhead if any of the following are true:

- The system utilizes an online transaction processing (OLTP) database with small, single-table queries.

- Queries are not frequently re-executed as determined by the executions column in *v$sql* and *executions_delta* in *dba_hist_sqlstat*.

- Multi-table joins have simple WHERE clause predicates with single-column values and no built-in or mathematical functions.

Dynamic sampling is ideal whenever a query is going to execute multiple times, because the sample time is small compared to the overall query execution time.

By sampling data from the table at runtime, Oracle10g can quickly evaluate complex WHERE clause predicates and determine the selectivity of each predicate, using this information to determine the optimal table join order. The following section will introduce the Oracle SQL SAMPLE clause and show how it works.

Sampling Table Scans

A sample table scan retrieves a random sample of data of a selected size. The sample can be from a simple table or a complex SELECT statement, such as a statement involving multiple joins and complex views.

To peek inside dynamic sampling, some simple SQL queries can be run. The following SQL statement uses a sample block and sample rows scan on the CUSTOMER table. There are 50,000 rows in this table. The first statement shows a sample BLOCK SCAN and the last SQL statement shows a sample ROW SCAN.

```
select
   count(*)
from
   customer
   sample block(20);


  COUNT(*)
----------
     12268


select
   pol_no,
   sales_id,
   sum_assured,
   premium
from
   customer
   sample (0.02) ;
```

```
    POL_NO   SALES_ID SUM_ASSURED    PREMIUM
---------- ---------- ----------- ---------- --
      2895         10        2525          2
      3176         10        2525          2
      9228         10        2525          2
     11294         11        2535          4
     19846         11        2535          4
     25547         12        2545          6
     29583         12        2545          6
     40042         13        2555          8
     47331         14        2565         10
     45283         14        2565         10
```

10 rows selected.

Just as the data can be sampled with SQL, the Oracle10g CBO can sample the data prior to formulating the execution plan. For example, the new *dynamic_sampling* SQL hint can be used to sample rows from the table:

```
select /*+ dynamic_sampling (customer 10) */
   pol_no,
   sales_id,
   sum_assured,
   premium
from
   customer;
```

```
    POL_NO   SALES_ID SUM_ASSURED    PREMIUM
---------- ---------- ----------- ---------- --
      2895         10        2525          2
      3176         10        2525          2
      9228         10        2525          2
     11294         11        2535          4
     19846         11        2535          4
     25547         12        2545          6
     29583         12        2545          6
     40042         13        2555          8
     47331         14        2565         10
     45283         14        2565         10
```

10 rows selected.

Dynamic sampling addresses an innate problem in SQL, and this issue is common to all relational databases. Estimating the optimal join order involves guessing the sequence that results in the smallest amount of intermediate row sets, and it is impossible to collect every possible combination of WHERE clauses.

Dynamic sampling is almost a miracle for databases that have large n-way table joins that execute frequently. By sampling a tiny subset of the data, the Oracle10g CBO gleans clues as to the fastest table join order.

dynamic_sampling does not take a long time to execute, but it can cause unnecessary overhead for all Oracle10g databases. Dynamic sampling is just another example of Oracle's commitment to making Oracle10g an intelligent, self-optimizing database.

The next section will provide an introduction to an important tool for tuning SQL, the *clustering_factor* column in the *dba_indexes* view.

Tuning SQL access with *clustering_factor*

With each new release of Oracle, the CBO improves. The most current enhancement with Oracle9i, when formulating an execution plan, is the consideration of external influences such as CPU cost and I/O cost. As Oracle evolved into release Oracle10g, there have been even more improvements in the ability of the CBO to get the optimal execution plan for a query, but it is still important to understand this mechanism.

Rules for Oracle Indexing

In order to understand how Oracle decides on an execution plan for a query, one first needs to learn the rules Oracle uses when it determines whether to use an index.

The most important characteristics of column data are the clustering factor for the column and the selectivity of column values, even though other important characteristics within tables are available to the CBO. A column called *clustering_factor* in the *dba_indexes* view offers information on how the table rows are synchronized with the index. When the clustering factor is close to the number of data blocks and the column value is not row ordered when the *clustering_factor* approaches the number of rows in the table, the table rows are synchronized with the index.

To illustrate this, the following query will filter the result set using a column value:

```
select
   customer_name
from
   customer
where
   customer_state = 'New Mexico';
```

An index scan is faster for this query if the percentage of customers in New Mexico is small and the values are clustered on the data blocks. The decision to use an index versus a full-table scan is at least partially determined by the percentage of customers in New Mexico.

So, why would a CBO choose to perform a full-table scan when only a small number of rows are retrieved?

Four factors synchronize to help the CBO choose whether to use an index or a full-table scan: the selectivity of a column value; the *db_block_size*; the *avg_row_len*; and the *cardinality*. An index scan is usually faster if a data column has high selectivity and a low *clustering_factor* as shown in Figure 15.7.

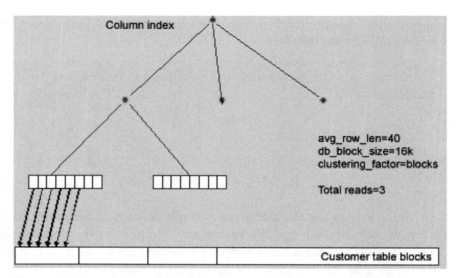

Figure 15.7: *This column has a low clustering factor, small rows and large blocks.*

If there is a frequent query that performs large index range scans, the table can be forced to be in the same order as the index. By maintaining row order and thereby removing suboptimal full-table scans, placing all adjacent rows in the same data block may allow some queries to run far faster.

Table row order can be forced with a single-table table cluster or by reorganizing the table with the CREATE TABLE AS SELECT syntax, using the SQL ORDER BY clause to force the row order. This is especially important when a majority of the SQL references a column with a high *clustering_factor*, a large *db_block_size*, and a small *avg_row_len*.

Even when a column has high selectivity, a high *clustering_factor*, and a small *avg_row_len*, there is still an indication that column values are randomly distributed in the table, and that an additional I/O will be required to obtain the rows.

On the other hand, as the *clustering_factor* nears the number of rows in the table, the rows fall out of sync with the index. This high *clustering_factor*, in which the value is close to the number of rows in the table (*num_rows*), indicates that the rows are out of sequence with the index and an additional I/O may be required for index range scans.

An index range scan would cause a huge amount of unnecessary I/O as shown in Figure 15.8, thus making a full-table scan more efficient.

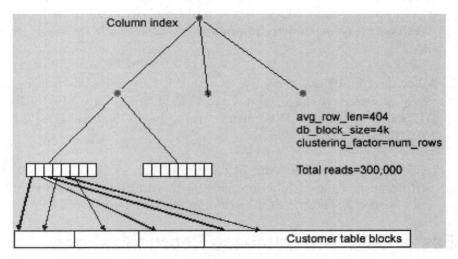

Figure 15.8: *This column has a high clustering factor small blocks and large rows.*

The CBO's choice to execute a full-table scan versus an index range scan is influenced by the *clustering_factor*, *db_block_size*, and *avg_row_len*.

Oracle developers have recognized that certain types of queries will run thousands of times faster when related data is placed together on disk. Oracle provides several tools for keeping an optimal *clustering_factor* for important queries:

- Multi-table table clusters: If the system always accesses related data together, using a multi-table cluster can greatly improve query performance. For example, if the system always displays customer row data with data from the orders table, the customer row and all of the orders can be placed on a single data block, requiring only a single consistent get to acquire all of the required data.

- Single-table table clusters: This technique allows Oracle to guarantee that data blocks are stored in column value order, allowing index range scans to run very quickly.

However, Oracle cluster tables have overhead, namely wasted disk space that must be reserved, using PCTFREE, for new rows to be placed on the proper block. There is also the overhead of maintaining overflow areas when it is impossible to store rows on their target block.

Many Oracle DBAs will choose to manually reorganize tables using the *dbms_redefinition* package, the CREATE TABLE AS SELECT or ALTER TABLE MOVE syntax using an ORDER BY and a PARALLEL clause.

Since it is apparent that the placement of data on disk effects SQL performance, a closer look at changing the organization of the tables and indexes to speed up SQL execution speed is a good next step.

Faster SQL with Database Reorganizations

Ever since the earliest days of data processing, database experts have known that the physical layout of the data on disk can make queries run faster. Despite the reduced costs of RAM and disk, clustering data together can reduce logical I/O (consistent gets) and disk reads (physical reads) thereby making queries run far faster. Oracle also offers cluster tables to allow related row data to be clustered together in the same data blocks.

Oracle10g provides table and index maintenance tools that allow the DBA to re-optimize data while the database continues to accept updates with the Oracle *dbms_redefinition* package. To keep the databases running super fast, Oracle chose not to incur the overhead of coalescing table rows and restructuring indexes during peak update times. That is why the DBA maintenance utilities exist. The trick is understanding when a table or index will benefit from reorganization.

Oracle10g has offered some huge improvements in indexing, especially related to the detection of missing indexes and materialized views and the automation of index histogram detection for the SQL optimizer. There are also improvements to table maintenance in Oracle10g. Oracle Database 10g includes the following online data reorganization enhancements:

- Online table redefinition enhancements

- Easy cloning of indexes, grants, constraints, etc.

- Conversion from LONG to LOB online

- Allowing unique index instead of primary key

- Changing tables without recompiling stored procedures

- Online segment shrink

Despite all of the great automated tools, the Oracle DBA must still perform routine table and index maintenance to keep highly active databases performing at peak levels.

It has been shown through experience that rebuilding tables and indexes improves the speed of queries, and there has been a great debate about the benefits of rebuilding Oracle indexes. There are two schools of thought on this important issue, and both sides make strong opposing arguments, sometimes leaving the DBA confused about the real benefit of table and index reorganization:

- Oracle Index Rebuilding is a waste of time: Some claim that indexes are always self-balancing and rarely need re-building. Even after an Oracle index rebuild, they say that SQL query performance is rarely any faster.

- Index Rebuilds improve performance: Others note that indexes on tables with high DML, such as SQL INSERTs, UPDATEs and DELETEs, will be heavily fragmented, with many empty blocks and a suboptimal access structure. They claim to see huge performance improvements after rebuilding a busy Oracle index.

On the surface, both stances sound like good arguments, but one must dig deeper to fully understand index maintenance. The following is a logical approach to the issue of Oracle index rebuilding, and it starts with these assertions:

- It's about I/O: If SQL performance is faster after an index rebuild, it is because the query does fewer index block reads. This should be evident in the consistent gets, logical reads from the data buffer, and physical reads, which are calls to the disk spindle that may or may not result in a physical disk read depending on whether or not there is a RAM buffer on the disk.

- Only some index access methods will benefit: Index Fast Full scans and some Index Range Scans will run faster after a rebuild. Just like a full-table scan takes a long time when it reads a table with many empty blocks, reading a range of a sparse index will result in excessive logical reads, as empty index nodes are accessed by the SQL query execution. Index unique scans will not improve after a rebuild, since they only read their participating nodes.

- Oracle Indexes can get clogged with empty and near empty index blocks: As massive DELETEs take place, large chunks of an index are logically deleted, meaning that they are passed over by the pointers but still remain in the structure. Because the empty blocks remain, block-by-block scans, such as any scan effected by *db_file_multiblock_read_count*, and some index range scans will perform less reads; hence, the result is less I/O and faster performance.

The following section looks at the age-old debate about whether Oracle indexes will benefit from periodic rebuilding.

Oracle Indexes – Is Maintenance Required?

The question about whether Oracle indexes are self-balancing is largely a matter of semantics. As rows are added to an empty table, Oracle controls the addition of same level blocks, called splitting, until the higher level index node is unable to hold any more key pointer pairs. When the index can no longer split because the owner block is full, Oracle will spawn a whole new index level, keeping the index tree in perfect logical and physical balance.

However, DELETEs are a different story. Physically, Oracle indexes are always balanced because empty blocks stay inside the tree structure after a massive DELETE. Logically, Oracle indexes are not self-balancing because Oracle does not remove the dead blocks as they become empty. For example, Figure 15.9 shows an Oracle index before a massive delete.

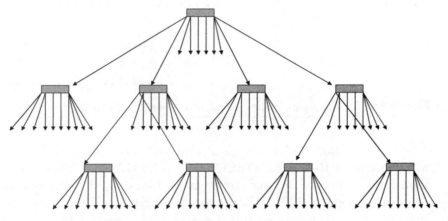

Figure 15.9: *A physical index before a massive row delete*

Now, after a massive delete, the physical representation of the index is exactly the same because the empty data blocks remain as illustrated in Figure 15.10. However, the logical internal pointer structure is quite unbalanced, because Oracle has routed around the deleted leaf nodes and has placed the empty index blocks back on the freelist, where they can be reused anywhere in the index tree structure

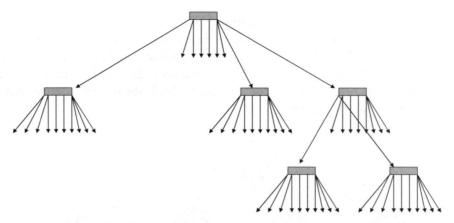

Figure 15.10: *The logical pointer structure of an index after a massive row delete*

This type of sparse index is typical of an index on highly active tables with large scale INSERTs, DELETEs and UPDATEs. There may be thousands of empty or near empty index blocks, and the sparse data can cause excessive I/O. There are several types of Oracle execution steps that will run longer on this type of sparse index:

- Index Range Scans: Index range scans that must access many near empty blocks will have excessive I/O compared to a rebuilt index.

- Index Fast Full Scans: Because 70% of an index can be deleted and the index will still have the same number of data blocks, a full index scan might run many times slower before it is rebuilt.

Since the SQL must visit the sparse blocks, the task will take longer to execute.

When Should Indexes be rebuilt?

From a software engineering perspective, it is impossible to make a database with physically self-balancing blocks. For example, a database has a bulk delete that removes 250,000 rows from a table, and each index block contains 1,000 pointers. Each index block may contain hundreds of pointers to other index nodes depending on the symbolic key size and the blocksize.

If the index software was written to rebalance the physical tree whenever an index block became empty, the bulk delete operation could take hundreds of time longer to execute. Oracle has made a deliberate decision not to coalesce near empty blocks and rebalance physical blocks solely for performance reasons.

In the example, to be physically self-balancing, the physical tree would have to be rebalanced 250 times during the bulk delete, and there would also be huge overhead when coalescing nearly empty blocks, shifting their pointers to nearly-full blocks. It is much more efficient to rebuild the index once, after the bulk delete. In fact, many shops that perform massive bulk operations in indexes tables will REMOVE the indexes first, DELETE and UPDATE the rows and rebuild the indexes afterward.

When Oracle rebuilds an index, the index nodes in LOGICAL orders are swept, chasing the pointer chains and placing the new index into the designated tablespace as temporary segments. The DBA controls the free space for node inserts with the *pctfree* parameter, which dictates how much room in the index block is reserved for future updates. For example, if the table will have 50% more rows added at a later time, *pctfree* could be set to 50 and half of each index would be left free to accept new entries without splitting or spawning.

The shape of the index tree can be controlled with two techniques:

- *pctfree*: Setting pctfree to a low value will leave space within each index block, creating a more vertical index tree as shown in Figure 15.11:

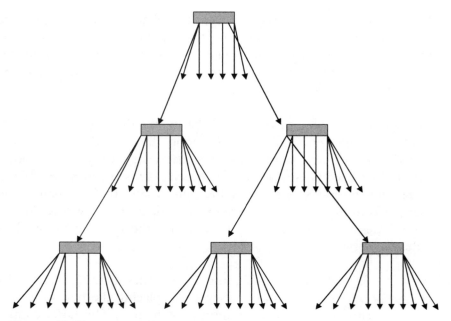

Figure 15.11: *A vertical Oracle index*

- Index Blocksize: Because index splitting and spawning are controlled at the block level, a larger blocksize will result in a flatter index tree structure. This was demonstrated by Robin Schumacher in his book *Oracle Performance Troubleshooting* (2004, Rampant TechPress):

> "As you can see, the amount of logical reads has been reduced in half simply by using the new 16K tablespace and accompanying 16K data cache. Clearly, the benefits of properly using the new data caches and multi-block tablespace feature of Oracle9i and above are worth your investigation and trials in your own database."

Schumacher suggests using multiple blocksizes and putting all indexes and tables that experience full-table scans because of the requirements of *db_file_multiblock_read_count* into a 32k blocksize. This results in a flatter index tree with fewer levels as illustrated in Figure 15.12.

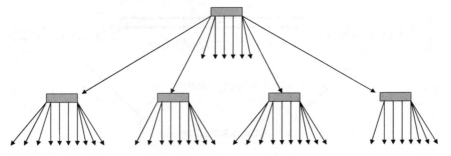

Figure 15.12: *An index with a large blocksize*

Detractors of scheduled index rebuilding say that indexes should only be rebuilt when there is a clear test case that the rebuild will reduce logical I/O and/or physical I/O for SQL queries. However, many shops with downtime maintenance windows will schedule periodic rebuilding because it is a low risk operation such as the index will not be replaced unless it is successfully rebuilt.

All DBA's acknowledge that database maintenance of a part of the job and they use tools such as the Oracle online redefinition utility, *dbms_redefinition* package, to periodically rebuild Oracle tables and indexes online, while the database continues to receive updates.

But how does the DBA perform maintenance on a 24x7 database? Oracle10g has the exciting online redefinition utility that uses Oracle replication techniques to allow the DBA to reorganize a table and its indexes while the database continues to accept updates. This structure is shown in Figure 15.13.

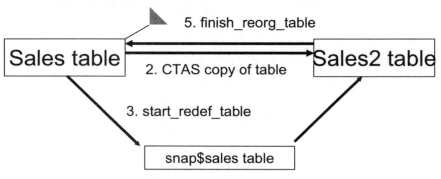

Figure 15.13: *Oracle10g online redefinition utility*

Even as Oracle10g improves the tools, it is still up to the subjective judgment of the DBA to decide when it is necessary to reorganize Oracle tables and indexes.

The following section will provide a look at techniques for locating indexes for the Oracle KEEP pool.

Locating Tables and Indexes for the KEEP Pool

From the chapter on Instance tuning:

> "A good candidate for a segment to put into the KEEP pool is a segment that is smaller than 10% of the size of the DEFAULT buffer pool and has incurred at least 1% of the total I/Os in the system."

More concisely, a small table that is in high demand is a good candidate for KEEP caching.

Internally, it is critical to cache small-table full-table scans because the Oracle data buffer does not increase the touch count when blocks from full-table scans are referenced. Hence, small-table full-table scan blocks will age out of the data buffers very quickly, causing unnecessary disk I/O.

For details on caching in the KEEP pool, see the chapter on Oracle Instance Tuning.

Interrogating SQL execution Plans

The script below examines the execution plans of *plan9i.sql* and reports on the frequency of every type of table and index access including full-table scans, index range scans, index unique scans and index full scans. The script goes to the appropriate view, *v$sql_plan* in *plan9i.sql* and *dba_hist_sqlplan* in *plan10g.sql*, and parses the output, counting the frequency of execution for each type of access.

The following *plan9i.sql* script will show the SQL that is currently inside the library cache.

🖫 **plan9i.sql**

```
-- ***************************************************
-- Copyright © 2005 by Rampant TechPress
-- This script is free for non-commercial purposes
-- with no warranties.  Use at your own risk.
--
-- To license this script for a commercial purpose,
-- contact info@rampant.cc
-- ***************************************************

set echo off;
set feedback on

set pages 999;
column nbr_FTS   format 999,999
column num_rows  format 999,999,999
column blocks    format 999,999
column owner     format a14;
column name      format a24;
column ch        format a1;

column object_owner heading "Owner"              format a12;
column ct           heading "# of SQL selects" format 999,999;

select
   object_owner,
   count(*)   ct
from
   v$sql_plan
where
```

```
   object_owner is not null
group by
   object_owner
order by
   ct desc
;
--spool access.lst;

set heading off;
set feedback off;

set heading on;
set feedback on;
ttitle 'full table scans and counts|  |The "K" indicates that the
table is in the KEEP Pool (Oracle8).'
select
   p.owner,
   p.name,
   t.num_rows,
--    ltrim(t.cache) ch,
   decode(t.buffer_pool,'KEEP','Y','DEFAULT','N') K,
   s.blocks blocks,
   sum(a.executions) nbr_FTS
from
   dba_tables    t,
   dba_segments s,
   v$sqlarea     a,
   (select distinct
     address,
     object_owner owner,
     object_name name
   from
     v$sql_plan
   where
     operation = 'TABLE ACCESS'
     and
     options = 'FULL') p
where
   a.address = p.address
   and
   t.owner = s.owner
   and
   t.table_name = s.segment_name
   and
   t.table_name = p.name
   and
   t.owner = p.owner
   and
   t.owner not in ('SYS','SYSTEM')
having
   sum(a.executions) > 9
group by
   p.owner, p.name, t.num_rows, t.cache, t.buffer_pool, s.blocks
order by
   sum(a.executions) desc;
```

```
column nbr_RID   format 999,999,999
column num_rows  format 999,999,999
column owner     format a15;
column name      format a25;

ttitle 'Table access by ROWID and counts'
select
   p.owner,
   p.name,
   t.num_rows,
   sum(s.executions) nbr_RID
from
   dba_tables t,
   v$sqlarea s,
   (select distinct
      address,
      object_owner owner,
      object_name name
   from
      v$sql_plan
   where
      operation = 'TABLE ACCESS'
      and
      options = 'BY ROWID') p
where
   s.address = p.address
   and
   t.table_name = p.name
   and
   t.owner = p.owner
having
   sum(s.executions) > 9
group by
   p.owner, p.name, t.num_rows
order by
   sum(s.executions) desc;

--*************************************************
--   Index Report Section
--*************************************************

column nbr_scans  format 999,999,999
column num_rows   format 999,999,999
column tbl_blocks format 999,999,999
column owner      format a9;
column table_name format a20;
column index_name format a20;

ttitle 'Index full scans and counts'
select
   p.owner,
   d.table_name,
   p.name index_name,
   seg.blocks tbl_blocks,
   sum(s.executions) nbr_scans
from
```

```
      dba_segments seg,
      v$sqlarea s,
      dba_indexes d,
     (select distinct
         address,
         object_owner owner,
         object_name name
      from
         v$sql_plan
      where
         operation = 'INDEX'
         and
         options = 'FULL SCAN') p
where
      d.index_name = p.name
      and
      s.address = p.address
      and
      d.table_name = seg.segment_name
      and
      seg.owner = p.owner
having
      sum(s.executions) > 9
group by
      p.owner, d.table_name, p.name, seg.blocks
order by
      sum(s.executions) desc;


ttitle 'Index range scans and counts'
select
      p.owner,
      d.table_name,
      p.name index_name,
      seg.blocks tbl_blocks,
      sum(s.executions) nbr_scans
from
      dba_segments seg,
      v$sqlarea s,
      dba_indexes d,
     (select distinct
         address,
         object_owner owner,
         object_name name
      from
         v$sql_plan

      where
         operation = 'INDEX'
         and
         options = 'RANGE SCAN') p
where
      d.index_name = p.name
      and
      s.address = p.address
      and
```

```
   d.table_name = seg.segment_name
   and
   seg.owner = p.owner
having
   sum(s.executions) > 9
group by
   p.owner, d.table_name, p.name, seg.blocks
order by
   sum(s.executions) desc;


ttitle 'Index unique scans and counts'
select
   p.owner,
   d.table_name,
   p.name index_name,
   sum(s.executions) nbr_scans
from
   v$sqlarea s,
   dba_indexes d,
  (select distinct
     address,
     object_owner owner,
     object_name name
   from
     v$sql_plan
   where
     operation = 'INDEX'
     and
     options = 'UNIQUE SCAN') p
where
   d.index_name = p.name
   and
   s.address = p.address
having
   sum(s.executions) > 9
group by
   p.owner, d.table_name, p.name
order by
   sum(s.executions) desc;
```

Below is the AWR version of the SQL execution plan script. Unlike the *plan9i.sql* script that only extracts current SQL from the library cache, the *plan10g.sql* script accesses the AWR *dba_hist_sqlplan* table and yields a time-series view of the ways that Oracle is accessing tables and indexes.

💾 plan10g.sql

```
-- with no warranties.  Use at your own risk.
--
-- To license this script for a commercial purpose,
-- contact info@rampant.cc
-- ************************************************


spool plan.lst

set echo off
set feedback on

set pages 999;
column nbr_FTS  format 99,999
column num_rows format 999,999
column blocks   format 9,999
column owner    format a10;
column name     format a30;
column ch       format a1;
column time     heading "Snapshot Time"         format a15

column object_owner heading "Owner"             format a12;
column ct           heading "# of SQL selects" format 999,999;

break on time

select
   object_owner,
   count(*)   ct
from
   dba_hist_sql_plan
where
   object_owner is not null
group by
   object_owner
order by
   ct desc
;


--spool access.lst;

set heading on;
set feedback on;

ttitle 'full table scans and counts|  |The "K" indicates that the
table is in the KEEP Pool (Oracle8).'
select
   to_char(sn.end_interval_time,'mm/dd/rr hh24') time,
   p.owner,
   p.name,
   t.num_rows,
--   ltrim(t.cache) ch,
   decode(t.buffer_pool,'KEEP','Y','DEFAULT','N') K,
   s.blocks blocks,
   sum(a.executions_delta) nbr_FTS
```

```
from
   dba_tables    t,
   dba_segments s,
   dba_hist_sqlstat     a,
   dba_hist_snapshot sn,
   (select distinct
     pl.sql_id,
     object_owner owner,
     object_name name
   from
     dba_hist_sql_plan pl
   where
     operation = 'TABLE ACCESS'
     and
     options = 'FULL') p
where
   a.snap_id = sn.snap_id
   and
   a.sql_id = p.sql_id
   and
   t.owner = s.owner
   and
   t.table_name = s.segment_name
   and
   t.table_name = p.name
   and
   t.owner = p.owner
   and
   t.owner not in ('SYS','SYSTEM')
having
   sum(a.executions_delta) > 1
group by
   to_char(sn.end_interval_time,'mm/dd/rr hh24'),p.owner, p.name,
t.num_rows, t.cache, t.buffer_pool, s.blocks
order by
   1 asc;


column nbr_RID  format 999,999,999
column num_rows format 999,999,999
column owner      format a15;
column name       format a25;

ttitle 'Table access by ROWID and counts'
select
   to_char(sn.end_interval_time,'mm/dd/rr hh24') time,
   p.owner,
   p.name,
   t.num_rows,
   sum(a.executions_delta) nbr_RID
from
   dba_tables t,
   dba_hist_sqlstat     a,
   dba_hist_snapshot sn,
   (select distinct
     pl.sql_id,
```

```
       object_owner owner,
       object_name name
    from
       dba_hist_sql_plan pl
    where
       operation = 'TABLE ACCESS'
       and
       options = 'BY USER ROWID') p
where
   a.snap_id = sn.snap_id
   and
   a.sql_id = p.sql_id
   and
   t.table_name = p.name
   and
   t.owner = p.owner
having
   sum(a.executions_delta) > 9
group by
   to_char(sn.end_interval_time,'mm/dd/rr hh24'),p.owner, p.name,
t.num_rows
order by
   1 asc;

--****************************************************
--   Index Report Section
--****************************************************

column nbr_scans  format 999,999,999
column num_rows   format 999,999,999
column tbl_blocks format 999,999,999
column owner      format a9;
column table_name format a20;
column index_name format a20;

ttitle 'Index full scans and counts'
select
   to_char(sn.end_interval_time,'mm/dd/rr hh24') time,
   p.owner,
   d.table_name,
   p.name index_name,
   seg.blocks tbl_blocks,
   sum(s.executions_delta) nbr_scans
from
   dba_segments seg,
   dba_indexes d,
   dba_hist_sqlstat    s,
   dba_hist_snapshot sn,
   (select distinct
      pl.sql_id,
      object_owner owner,
      object_name name
    from
       dba_hist_sql_plan pl
    where
       operation = 'INDEX'
```

```
      and
      options = 'FULL SCAN') p
where
   d.index_name = p.name
   and
   s.snap_id = sn.snap_id
   and
   s.sql_id = p.sql_id
   and
   d.table_name = seg.segment_name
   and
   seg.owner = p.owner
having
   sum(s.executions_delta) > 9
group by
   to_char(sn.end_interval_time,'mm/dd/rr hh24'),p.owner,
d.table_name, p.name, seg.blocks
order by
   1 asc;


ttitle 'Index range scans and counts'
select
   to_char(sn.end_interval_time,'mm/dd/rr hh24') time,
   p.owner,
   d.table_name,
   p.name index_name,
   seg.blocks tbl_blocks,
   sum(s.executions_delta) nbr_scans
from
   dba_segments seg,
   dba_hist_sqlstat    s,
   dba_hist_snapshot sn,
   dba_indexes d,
   (select distinct
     pl.sql_id,
     object_owner owner,
     object_name name
   from
     dba_hist_sql_plan pl
   where
     operation = 'INDEX'
     and
     options = 'RANGE SCAN') p
where
   d.index_name = p.name
   and
   s.snap_id = sn.snap_id
   and
   s.sql_id = p.sql_id
   and
   d.table_name = seg.segment_name
   and
   seg.owner = p.owner
having
   sum(s.executions_delta) > 9
```

```
group by
   to_char(sn.end_interval_time,'mm/dd/rr hh24'),p.owner,
d.table_name, p.name, seg.blocks
order by
   1 asc;

ttitle 'Index unique scans and counts'
select
   to_char(sn.end_interval_time,'mm/dd/rr hh24') time,
   p.owner,
   d.table_name,
   p.name index_name,
   sum(s.executions_delta) nbr_scans
from
   dba_hist_sqlstat      s,
   dba_hist_snapshot sn,
   dba_indexes d,
  (select distinct
     pl.sql_id,
     object_owner owner,
     object_name name
   from
      dba_hist_sql_plan pl
   where
     operation = 'INDEX'
     and
     options = 'UNIQUE SCAN') p
where
   d.index_name = p.name
   and
   s.snap_id = sn.snap_id
   and
   s.sql_id = p.sql_id
having
   sum(s.executions_delta) > 9
group by
   to_char(sn.end_interval_time,'mm/dd/rr hh24'),p.owner,
d.table_name, p.name
order by
   1 asc;

spool off
```

The output is shown below, and it is the same in 9i and 10g. A good way to start the review of the results is by looking at the counts of full-table scans for each AWR snapshot period. This report gives all the information needed to select candidate tables for the KEEP pool. The database will benefit from placing small tables, less than two percent of *db_cache_size*, that are subject to frequent full-table scans in the KEEP pool. The report from an Oracle Applications database below shows full-table scans on both large and small tables.

The goal is to use the RECYCLE pool for segregating large tables involved in frequent full-table scans. To locate these large-table full-table scans, the plan9i.sql full-table scan report for a 9i database:

```
                    full table scans and counts
Snapshot Time   OWNER       NAME                     NUM_ROWS C K   BLOCKS  NBR_FTS
-------------   ----------  ------------------------ -------- - -  -------- -----
12/08/04 14     APPLSYS     FND_CONC_RELEASE_DISJS         39 N K        2  98,864
                APPLSYS     FND_CONC_RELEASE_PERIODS       39 N K        2  98,864
                APPLSYS     FND_CONC_RELEASE_STATES         1 N K        2  98,864
                SYS         DUAL                              N K        2  63,466
                APPLSYS     FND_CONC_PP_ACTIONS         7,021 N       1,262  52,036
                APPLSYS     FND_CONC_REL_CONJ_MEMBER        0 N K       22  50,174

12/08/04 15     APPLSYS     FND_CONC_RELEASE_DISJS         39 N K        2  33,811
                APPLSYS     FND_CONC_RELEASE_PERIODS       39 N K        2   2,864
                APPLSYS     FND_CONC_RELEASE_STATES         1 N K        2  32,864
                SYS         DUAL                              N K        2  63,466
                APPLSYS     FND_CONC_PP_ACTIONS         7,021 N       1,262  12,033
                APPLSYS     FND_CONC_REL_CONJ_MEMBER        0 N K       22  50,174
```

One table in the listing is a clear candidate for inclusion in the RECYCLE pool. The *fnd_conc_pp_actions* table contains 1,262 blocks and has experienced many full-table scans.

Examining this report, one can quickly identify three files that should be moved to the KEEP pool by selecting the tables with less than 50 blocks that have no "K" designation.

Oracle developed the KEEP pool to fully cache blocks from frequently accessed tables and indexes in a separate buffer. When determining the size of the KEEP pool, the number of bytes comprising all tables that will reside in the KEEP area must be summed. This will insure that the KEEP buffer is large enough to fully cache all the tables that have been assigned to it.

Oracle10g requires that a table only reside in a tablespace of the same blocksize as the buffer assigned to the table. For example, if the DEFAULT buffer is set at 32K, the alter command below would not work if the customer table resides in a 16K tablespace. The DEFAULT, KEEP, and RECYCLE designations only apply to the default blocksize; KEEP and RECYCLE buffers cannot be assigned different sizes than that of the default *db_block_size*.

```
alter table CUSTOMER storage (buffer_pool KEEP);
```

The whole reason for the existence of the KEEP pool is to always have a data buffer hit ratio of 100 percent. The blocksize of the KEEP pool is not important because all blocks, once loaded, will remain in RAM memory. A KEEP pool might be defined as a 32K blocksize because a large RECYCLE buffer was needed to improve the performance of full-table scans.

CAUTION!

Selecting tables for the KEEP pool requires inspecting the data cache over time. These reports include only SQL that happens to be in the library cache at the time the report is run.

Since the goal for the data buffer hit ratio of the KEEP pool is 100 percent, each time a table is added to KEEP, the number of blocks in that table must also be added to the KEEP pool parameter in the Oracle file.

These scripts also show counts for indexes that are accessed via rowid, indicative of non-range scan access. The result is shown below.

```
Table access by ROWID and counts
Wed Dec 22
```

Snapshot	Time	OWNER	NAME	NUM_ROWS	NBR_RID
12/16/04	19	SYSMAN	MGMT_TARGET_ROLLUP_TIMES	110	10
12/17/04	06	SYSMAN	MGMT_TARGET_ROLLUP_TIMES	110	10
12/17/04	07	SYSMAN	MGMT_TARGET_ROLLUP_TIMES	110	10
12/17/04	08	SYSMAN	MGMT_TARGET_ROLLUP_TIMES	110	10
12/17/04	12	SYSMAN	MGMT_TARGET_ROLLUP_TIMES	110	10
12/17/04	13	SYSMAN	MGMT_TARGET_ROLLUP_TIMES	110	10
12/17/04	14	SYS	VIEW$	2,583	84
		SYSMAN	MGMT_TARGET_ROLLUP_TIMES	110	10
12/17/04	17	SYS	VIEW$	2,583	82
12/17/04	18	SYSMAN	MGMT_TARGET_ROLLUP_TIMES	110	10
12/17/04	20	SYSMAN	MGMT_TARGET_ROLLUP_TIMES	110	10
12/17/04	21	SYSMAN	MGMT_TARGET_ROLLUP_TIMES	110	10
12/17/04	22	SYSMAN	MGMT_TARGET_ROLLUP_TIMES	110	10
12/17/04	23	SYSMAN	MGMT_TARGET_ROLLUP_TIMES	110	10
12/18/04	00	SYSMAN	MGMT_TARGET_ROLLUP_TIMES	110	10
12/18/04	01	SYSMAN	MGMT_TARGET_ROLLUP_TIMES	110	20
12/18/04	02	SYSMAN	MGMT_TARGET_ROLLUP_TIMES	110	10
12/18/04	03	SYSMAN	MGMT_TARGET_ROLLUP_TIMES	110	10

```
12/18/04 04    SYSMAN    MGMT_TARGET_ROLLUP_TIMES          110        10
12/18/04 05    SYSMAN    MGMT_TARGET_ROLLUP_TIMES          110        10
12/18/04 09    SYSMAN    MGMT_TARGET_ROLLUP_TIMES          110        20
12/18/04 11    SYSMAN    MGMT_TARGET_ROLLUP_TIMES          110        20
```

Counts of index full scans and index range scans can also be acquired, and this data is very useful for locating those indexes that might benefit from segregation onto a larger blocksize.

```
Index full scans and counts

Snapshot Time  OWNER     TABLE_NAME              INDEX_NAME           TBL_BLOCKS  NBR_SCANS
-------------- --------- ---------------------- -------------------- ----------  ---------
12/08/04 14    SYSMAN    MGMT_FAILOVER_TABLE     PK_MGMT_FAILOVER          8         59
12/08/04 15    SYSMAN    MGMT_FAILOVER_TABLE     PK_MGMT_FAILOVER          8         58
12/08/04 16    SYS       WRH$_TEMPFILE           WRH$_TEMPFILE_PK          8         16
               SYSMAN    MGMT_FAILOVER_TABLE     PK_MGMT_FAILOVER          8         59
12/08/04 17    SYS       WRH$_STAT_NAME          WRH$_STAT_NAME_P          8        483
               SYSMAN    MGMT_FAILOVER_TABLE     PK_MGMT_FAILOVER          8         58
12/08/04 18    SYSMAN    MGMT_FAILOVER_TABLE     PK_MGMT_FAILOVER          8         59
12/08/04 19    SYSMAN    MGMT_FAILOVER_TABLE     PK_MGMT_FAILOVER          8         58
12/08/04 20    SYSMAN    MGMT_FAILOVER_TABLE     PK_MGMT_FAILOVER          8         59
12/08/04 21    SYSMAN    MGMT_FAILOVER_TABLE     PK_MGMT_FAILOVER          8         58
12/08/04 22    SYSMAN    MGMT_FAILOVER_TABLE     PK_MGMT_FAILOVER          8         58
12/08/04 23    SYSMAN    MGMT_FAILOVER_TABLE     PK_MGMT_FAILOVER          8         59
12/09/04 00    SYSMAN    MGMT_FAILOVER_TABLE     PK_MGMT_FAILOVER          8         58
12/09/04 01    SYSMAN    MGMT_FAILOVER_TABLE     PK_MGMT_FAILOVER          8         59
12/09/04 02    SYSMAN    MGMT_FAILOVER_TABLE     PK_MGMT_FAILOVER          8         59
12/09/04 03    SYSMAN    MGMT_FAILOVER_TABLE     PK_MGMT_FAILOVER          8         59
12/09/04 04    SYSMAN    MGMT_FAILOVER_TABLE     PK_MGMT_FAILOVER          8         58
12/09/04 05    SYSMAN    MGMT_FAILOVER_TABLE     PK_MGMT_FAILOVER          8         59
12/09/04 06    SYSMAN    MGMT_FAILOVER_TABLE     PK_MGMT_FAILOVER          8         58
12/09/04 07    SYSMAN    MGMT_FAILOVER_TABLE     PK_MGMT_FAILOVER          8         59
12/09/04 08    SYSMAN    MGMT_FAILOVER_TABLE     PK_MGMT_FAILOVER          8         58
12/09/04 09    SYSMAN    MGMT_FAILOVER_TABLE     PK_MGMT_FAILOVER          8         59

Index range scans and counts

Snapshot Time  OWNER     TABLE_NAME              INDEX_NAME                TBL_BLOCKS  NBR_SCANS
-------------- --------- ---------------------- ------------------------- ----------  ---------
12/08/04 14    SYS       SYSAUTH$                I_SYSAUTH1                     8        345
               SYSMAN    MGMT_JOB_EXECUTION      MGMT_JOB_EXEC_IDX01            8       1373
               SYSMAN    MGMT_JOB_EXEC_SUMMARY   MGMT_JOB_EXEC_SUMM_IDX04       8         59
               SYSMAN    MGMT_METRICS            MGMT_METRICS_IDX_01           80         59
               SYSMAN    MGMT_PARAMETERS         MGMT_PARAMETERS_IDX_01         8        179
               SYSMAN    MGMT_TARGETS            MGMT_TARGETS_IDX_02            8         61
12/08/04 15    SYS       SYSAUTH$                I_SYSAUTH1                     8        273
               SYSMAN    MGMT_JOB_EXECUTION      MGMT_JOB_EXEC_IDX01            8       1423
               SYSMAN    MGMT_JOB_EXEC_SUMMARY   MGMT_JOB_EXEC_SUMM_IDX04       8         58
```

Now that the use of the *v$sql_plan* view to see how tables and indexes are used by our SQL has been introduced, it is time to investigate techniques for finding the most resource intensive SQL for tuning.

Identifying Problem SQL

One short path to identifying performance problems in an Oracle database includes the following steps:

- Find the sessions responsible for hogging the most resources (I/O, CPU, etc.).

- Identify the code these sessions are running.

- Peel away the bad code these sessions have executed from the good and acceptable code.

- Highlight the worst SQL and then work to tune it for better performance.

This process has been made much easier in Oracle9i and Oracle10g, especially with respect to identifying problem SQL that gets run in a production database. The following sections work through these four steps and see how several performance views can assist in this process.

Find the Problem Sessions

Even if there is no database monitor that offers a top sessions view, it is easy to pinpoint the sessions that are giving the database grief. Different database professionals have their own ideas about what constitutes a top session. Some feel that the sum total of physical I/O alone tells the story, while others look at CPU, and still others use a combination of physical and logical I/O.

Whatever the preference, the script in *top_20_sessions.sql* can be used to quickly bubble to the top twenty sessions in an Oracle database. The initial sort is on physical I/O, but this can be changed to any other column desired.

🖫 top_20_sessions.sql

```
-- ************************************************
-- Copyright © 2005 by Rampant TechPress
-- This script is free for non-commercial purposes
-- with no warranties.  Use at your own risk.
--
-- To license this script for a commercial purpose,
-- contact info@rampant.cc
-- ************************************************


select * from
(select b.sid sid,
```

```
        decode (b.username,null,e.name,b.username) user_name,
        d.spid os_id,
        b.machine machine_name,
        to_char(logon_time,'dd-mon-yy hh:mi:ss pm') logon_time,
        (sum(decode(c.name,'physical reads',value,0)) +
        sum(decode(c.name,'physical writes',value,0)) +
        sum(decode(c.name,'physical writes direct',value,0)) +
        sum(decode(c.name,'physical writes direct (lob)',value,0))+
        sum(decode(c.name,'physical reads direct (lob)',value,0)) +
        sum(decode(c.name,'physical reads direct',value,0)))
        total_physical_io,
        (sum(decode(c.name,'db block gets',value,0)) +
        sum(decode(c.name,'db block changes',value,0)) +
        sum(decode(c.name,'consistent changes',value,0)) +
        sum(decode(c.name,'consistent gets
        total_logical_io,
        (sum(decode(c.name,'session pga memory',value,0))+
        sum(decode(c.name,'session uga memory',value,0)) )
        total_memory_usage,
        sum(decode(c.name,'parse count (total)',value,0)) parses,
        sum(decode(c.name,'cpu used by this session',value,0))
        total_cpu,
        sum(decode(c.name,'parse time cpu',value,0)) parse_cpu,
        sum(decode(c.name,'recursive cpu usage',value,0))
          recursive_cpu,
        sum(decode(c.name,'cpu used by this session',value,0)) -
        sum(decode(c.name,'parse time cpu',value,0)) -
        sum(decode(c.name,'recursive cpu usage',value,0))
          other_cpu,
        sum(decode(c.name,'sorts (disk)',value,0)) disk_sorts,
        sum(decode(c.name,'sorts (memory)',value,0)) memory_sorts,
        sum(decode(c.name,'sorts (rows)',value,0)) rows_sorted,
        sum(decode(c.name,'user commits',value,0)) commits,
        sum(decode(c.name,'user rollbacks',value,0)) rollbacks,
        sum(decode(c.name,'execute count',value,0)) executions
from sys.v_$sesstat a,
        sys.v_$session b,
        sys.v_$statname c,
        sys.v_$process d,
        sys.v_$bgprocess e
where a.statistic#=c.statistic# and
        b.sid=a.sid and
        d.addr = b.paddr and
        e.paddr (+) = b.paddr and
        c.NAME in ('physical reads',
                   'physical writes',
                   'physical writes direct',
                   'physical reads direct',
                   'physical writes direct (lob)',
                   'physical reads direct (lob)',
                   'db block gets',
                   'db block changes',
                   'consistent changes',
                   'consistent gets',
                   'session pga memory',
                   'session uga memory',
```

```
                    'parse count (total)',
                    'CPU used by this session',
                    'parse time cpu',
                    'recursive cpu usage',
                    'sorts (disk)',
                    'sorts (memory)',
                    'sorts (rows)',
                    'user commits',
                    'user rollbacks',
                    'execute count'
)
group by b.sid,
        d.spid,
        decode (b.username,null,e.name,b.username),
        b.machine,
        to_char(logon_time,'dd-mon-yy hh:mi:ss pm')
order by 6 desc)
where rownum < 21
```

The above query can also be modified to exclude Oracle background processes, the SYS and SYSTEM user, etc. The end result should be a current list of top offending sessions in the database as ranked by various performance metrics, which is the normal way to rank problem user accounts. Figure 15.14 shows a sample output of this query:

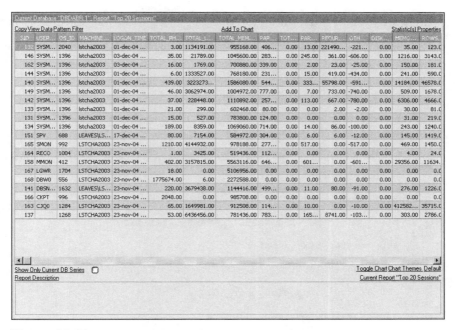

Figure 15.14: *The sample top_20_sessions.sql query output*

Some DBAs feel that this method, while useful, lacks depth. Specifically, because DBAs know that a user's resource consumption is almost always tied to inefficient SQL, they would like to cut to the chase and find the problem sessions in a database that have, for example, caused most of the large table scans on the system or have submitted queries containing Cartesian joins.

Such a thing was difficult to determine in earlier versions of Oracle, but fortunately, 9i provides a new performance view that can be used to derive such data. The *v$sql_plan* view contains execution plan data for all submitted SQL statements. Such a view provides a wealth of information regarding the performance and efficiency of SQL statements and the sessions that submitted them.

For example, if a DBA wants to know what sessions have parsed SQL statements that caused large table scans, with large defined as being

---

anything over 1 MB, on a system along with the total number of large scans by session, the following query could be submitted:

```
select
    c.username username,
    count(a.hash_value) scan_count
from
    sys.v_$sql_plan a,
    sys.dba_segments b,
    sys.dba_users c,
    sys.v_$sql d
where
    a.object_owner (+) = b.owner
and
    a.object_name (+) = b.segment_name
and
    b.segment_type IN ('TABLE', 'TABLE PARTITION')
and
    a.operation like '%TABLE%'
and
    a.options = 'FULL'
and
    c.user_id = d.parsing_user_id
and
    d.hash_value = a.hash_value
and
    b.bytes / 1024 > 1024
group by
    c.username
order by
    2 desc
;
```

The output from the above query might look something like the following:

```
USERNAME    SCAN_COUNT
---------- ----------
SYSTEM             14
SYS                11
ERADMIN             6
ORA_MONITOR         3
```

In like fashion, if a DBA wants to uncover what sessions have parsed SQL statements containing Cartesian joins along with the number of SQL statements that contain such joins, the following query could be used:

```
select
    username,
    count(distinct c.hash_value) nbr_stmts
from
    sys.v_$sql a,
    sys.dba_users b,
    sys.v_$sql_plan c
where
    a.parsing_user_id = b.user_id
and
    options = 'CARTESIAN'
and
    operation like '%JOIN%'
and
    a.hash_value = c.hash_value
group by
    username
order by
    2 desc
;
```

A result set from this query could look similar to the following:

```
USERNAME    NBR_STMTS
---------   ---------
SYS                 2
SYSMAN              2
ORA_MONITOR         1
```

The *v$sql_plan* view adds more meat to the process of identifying problem sessions in a database. When combined with the standard performance metrics query, DBAs can really begin to pinpoint the sessions that are wreaking havoc inside their critical systems.

Identify the Resource-Intensive SQL

After identifying the top resource hogging sessions in a database, the DBA's attention can then be turned to the code they and others are executing that is likely causing system bottlenecks. As with top session monitors, many decent database monitors have a top SQL feature that can help ferret out bad SQL code. Without access to such tools, a script like the one shown in *awr_high_resource_sql.sql* can be used.

💾 **awr_high_resource_sql.sql**

```
-- ************************************************
-- Copyright © 2005 by Rampant TechPress
```

```
-- This script is free for non-commercial purposes
-- with no warranties.  Use at your own risk.
--
-- To license this script for a commercial purpose,
-- contact info@rampant.cc
-- ************************************************

select sql_text,
       username,
       disk_reads_per_exec,
       buffer_gets,
       disk_reads,
       parse_calls,
       sorts,
       executions,
       rows_processed,
       hit_ratio,
       first_load_time,
       sharable_mem,
       persistent_mem,
       runtime_mem,
       cpu_time,
       elapsed_time,
       address,
       hash_value
from
(select sql_text ,
        b.username ,
 round((a.disk_reads/decode(a.executions,0,1,
 a.executions)),2)
       disk_reads_per_exec,
       a.disk_reads ,
       a.buffer_gets ,
       a.parse_calls ,
       a.sorts ,
       a.executions ,
       a.rows_processed ,
       100 - round(100 *
       a.disk_reads/greatest(a.buffer_gets,1),2) hit_ratio,
       a.first_load_time ,
       sharable_mem ,
       persistent_mem ,
       runtime_mem,
       cpu_time,
       elapsed_time,
       address,
       hash_value
from
   sys.v_$sqlarea a,
   sys.all_users b
where
   a.parsing_user_id=b.user_id and
   b.username not in ('sys','system')
order by 3 desc)
where rownum < 21
```

The code above will pull the top twenty SQL statements as ranked by disk reads per execution. The rownum filter at the end can be changed to show more or all SQL that has executed in a database. WHERE predicates can be added that only show the SQL for one or more of the previously identified top sessions.

In Oracle9i, the cpu_time and elapsed_time columns have been added, which provide more data that can be used to determine the overall efficiency of an SQL statement. Figure 15.15 shows a sample output of this query:

	SQL_TEXT	USERI	DISK_REA	BUFFER_GETS	DISK_READS	PARS	SORTS	EXEC	ROWS	HIT_RAT
1	update lob$ set retention = :1 where retention >= 0	SYS	791	1005	791	1	0	1	511	
2	delete from sys.wri$_optstat_histgrm_history where s	SYS	759	846	759	1	0	1	0	
3	delete from WRH$_SYSMETRIC_SUMMARY tab w	SYS	691	7172	691	1	0	1	5831	
4	delete from WRH$_WAITCLASSMETRIC_HISTOR	SYS	630	11132	630	1	0	1	9633	
5	delete from WRH$_SQL_PLAN tab where (:beg_sn	SYS	533	3743	533	1	0	1	993	
6	delete from wrh$_sqltext tab where (tab.dbid = :dbid	SYS	522	1196	522	1	0	1	99	
7	BEGIN prvt_advisor.delete_expired_tasks; END;	SYS	454	1424	454	1	0	1	1	
8	begin dbms_feature_usage_internal.exec_db_usage	SYS	453	433868	453	1	0	1	1	
9	delete from WRH$_ENQUEUE_STAT tab where (:b	SYS	427	10306	427	1	0	1	3137	
10	SELECT T.ID FROM WRI$_ADV_TASKS T, WRI$_	SYS	421	1133	421	1	0	1	0	
11	select s.synonym_name object_name, o.object_type	SYS	397.5	434481	1590	4	0	4	13536	
12	select o.owner#,o.obj#,decode(o.linkname,null, dec	SYS	362.5	6051	725	2	0	2	0	
13	select atc + ix, NULL, NULL from (select count(*) atc	SYS	296	293988	296	1	0	1	1	
14	delete from sys.wri$_optstat_histhead_history where	SYS	231	292	231	1	0	1	0	
15	delete from WRH$_BG_EVENT_SUMMARY tab w	SYS	207	6695	207	1	0	1	2057	
16	delete from WRI$_ALERT_HISTORY where time_su	SYS	188	2071	188	1	0	1	582	
17	begin "SYS"."DBMS_REPCAT_UTL"."DROP_USE	SYS	163	4048	163	1	0	1	1	
18	BEGIN ECM_CT.POSTLOAD_CALLBACK(:1, :2); EN	SYSM/	154	7904	308	2	0	2	2	
19	begin "CTXSYS"."CTX_ADM"."DROP_USER_OBJ	SYS	118	2395	118	1	0	1	1	
20	select table_objno, primary_instance, secondary_inst	SYS	111	688	111	1	0	1	0	

Figure 15.15: *The sample high_resource_sql.sql query output*

The new Oracle9i *v$sql_plan* view can also help with identification of problem SQL. For example, a DBA may want to know how many total SQL statements are causing Cartesian joins on a system. The following query can answer that question:

```
select
   count(distinct hash_value)  carteisan_statements,
   count(*)                     total_cartesian_joins
from
   sys.v_$sql_plan
where
   options = 'CARTESIAN'
and
   operation like '%JOIN%'
```

Output from this query will resemble the following, noting that it is possible for a single SQL statement to contain more than one Cartesian join:

```
CARTESIAN_STATEMENTS    TOTAL_CARTESIAN_JOINS
----------------------  ---------------------
                     3                      3
```

A DBA can then view the actual SQL statements containing the Cartesian joins, along with their performance metrics by using a query like the following:

```
select *
from
   sys.v_$sql
where
   hash_value in
      (select hash_value
       from
          sys.v_$sql_plan
       where
          options = 'CARTESIAN'
          and
          operation LIKE '%JOIN%' )
order by hash_value;
```

Another area of interest for DBAs is table scan activity. Most DBAs don't worry about small-table scans because Oracle can many times access small tables more efficiency through a full scan than through index access. Large table scans, however, are another matter. Most DBAs prefer to avoid those where possible through smart index placement or intelligent partitioning.

Using the *v$sql_plan* view, a DBA can quickly identify any SQL statement that contains one or more large table scans. The following query shows any SQL statement containing a large table scan, defined as a table over 1 MB, along with a count of how many large scans it causes for each execution, the total number of times the statement has been executed, and the sum total of all scans it has caused on the system:

```
select
    sql_text,
    total_large_scans,
```

```
      executions,
      executions * total_large_scans sum_large_scans
from
(select
      sql_text,
      count(*) total_large_scans,
      executions
 from
      sys.v_$sql_plan a,
      sys.dba_segments b,
      sys.v_$sql c
 where
      a.object_owner (+) = b.owner
   and
      a.object_name (+) = b.segment_name
   and
      b.segment_type IN ('TABLE', 'TABLE PARTITION')
   and
      a.operation LIKE '%TABLE%'
   and
      a.options = 'FULL'
   and
      c.hash_value = a.hash_value
   and
      b.bytes / 1024 > 1024
   group by
      sql_text, executions)
order by
   4 desc
;
```

This query produces output like that shown in Figure 15.16. Should a DBA worry more about a SQL statement that causes only one large table scan but has been executed 1000 times, or should they care more about an SQL statement that has ten large scans in it but has only been executed a handful of times?

SQL_TEXT	TOTAL_L	EXECUTIONS	SUM_LARGE_SCANS
1 select name,type#,obj#,remoteowner,linkname,namespace, subname from obj$ v	1	71	71
2 select o.name,o.type#,o.obj#,o.remoteowner,o.linkname,o.namespace, o.subnan	1	16	16
3 select object_name, object_type from sys.user_objects o where o.object_type in	2	3	6
4 select s.synonym_name object_name, o.object_type from sys.all_synonyms s,	1	4	4
5 select name, type#, obj#, remoteowner, linkname, namespace, subname from ob	1	3	3
6 select object_name, object_type from sys.user_objects o where o.object_type in	2	1	2
7 SELECT NUM("IIDX_OR_TAB)"."IPTYPE)"."ISUBPTYPE)"."IPCNT)"."ISUBPCN1	2	1	2
8 SELECT /"+ full(o) "/ U.NAME, COUNT(DECODE(0.TYPE#, 7,1, 8,1, 9,1, 11,1,	1	1	1
9 delete from WRH$_SQL_PLAN tab where (:beg_snap <= tab.snap_id and	1	1	1
10 delete from WRH$_BG_EVENT_SUMMARY tab where (:beg_snap <= tab.snap	1	1	1
11 select name,type#,obj#,remoteowner,linkname,namespace, subname from obj$ v	1	1	1
12 select name, type#, obj#, remoteowner, linkname, namespace, subname from ob	1	1	1
13 select name, type#, obj#, remoteowner, linkname, namespace, subname from ob	1	1	1
14 delete from wrh$_sqltext tab where (tab.dbid = :dbid and :beg_snap <= tab.	1	1	1
15 select grantor#,ta.obj#,o.type# from objauth$ ta, obj$ o where grantee#=:1 and t	1	1	1
16 select name, type#, obj#, remoteowner, linkname, namespace, subname from ob	1	1	1
17 select name, type#, obj#, remoteowner, linkname, namespace, subname from ob	1	1	1
18 delete from WRH$_WAITCLASSMETRIC_HISTORY tab where (:beg_snap <= t	1	1	1
19 delete from WRH$_SYSMETRIC_SUMMARY tab where (:beg_snap <= tab.snap	1	1	1
20 delete from WRH$_ENQUEUE_STAT tab where (:beg_snap <= tab.snap_id anc	1	1	1
21 delete from WRI$_ALERT_HISTORY where time_suggested < :1	1	1	1
22 select max(bytes) from dba_segments	1	1	1

Figure 15.16: *The sample large_scan_count.sql query output*

Each DBA will likely have an opinion on this, but regardless, it is apparent how such a query can assist in identifying SQL statements that have the potential to cause system slowdowns.

Now that a way to find suboptimal SQL execution has been introduced, it would be useful to have a way to change the SQL execution plans with special optimizer directives called hints. After the tuning hints have been introduced, readers will be able to appreciate how SQL Profiles improve the SQL tuning process.

Oracle tuning with hints

Oracle ensures that the cost-based SQL optimizer becomes more sophisticated with each release. With each new release, Oracle provides an increasing number of methods for changing the execution plans for SQL statements. While hints are used for tuning as well as documentation, the most common use for Oracle hints is as a debugging tool. The hints can be used to determine the optimal execution plan, and then work backward, adjusting the statistics to make the vanilla SQL simulate the hinted query.

Using Oracle hints can be very complicated, and Oracle developers only use hints as a last resort, preferring to alter the statistics to change the execution plan. Oracle contains more than 124 hints, and many of them are not found in the Oracle documentation. Table 15.1 contains a detailed list of these hints.

all_rows	index_ss_asc	parallel
and_equal	index_ss	parallel_index
antijoin	index	piv_gb
append	leading	piv_ssf
bitmap	like_expand	pq_distribute
buffer	local_indexesmaterialize	pq_map
bypass_recursive_check	merge	pq_nomap
bypass_ujvc	merge_aj	push_pred
cache	merge_sj	push_subq
cache_cb	mv_merge	remote_mapped
cache_temp_table	nested_table_get_refs	restore_as_intervals
cardinality	nested_table_set_refs	rewrite
choose	nested_table_set_setid	rule
civ_gb	nl_aj	save_as_intervals
collections_get_refs	nl_sj	scn_ascending
cpu_costing	no_access	selectivity
cube_gb	no_buffer	semijoin
cursor_sharing_exact	no_expand	semijoin_driver
defref_no_rewrite	no_expand_gset_to_union	skip_ext_optimizer
dml_update	no_fact	sqlldr
domain_index_no_sort	no_filtering	star
domain_index_sort	no_index	star_transformation
driving_site	no_merge	swap_join_inputs
dynamic_sampling	no_monitoring	sys_dl_cursor
dynamic_sampling_est_cdn	no_order_rollups	sys_parallel_txn
expand_gset_to_union	no_prune_gsets	sys_rid_order
fact	no_push_pred	tiv_gb
first_rows	no_push_subq	tiv_ssf
force_sample_block	no_qkn_buff	unnest
full	no_semijoin	use_anti
gby_conc_rollup	no_stats_gsets	use_concat
global_table_hints	no_unnest	use_hash
hash	noappend	use_merge
hash_aj	nocache	use_nl
hash_sj	nocpu_costing	use_semi
hwm_brokered	noparallel	use_ttt_for_gsets
ignore_on_clause	noparallel_index	

ignore_where_clause	norewrite	
index_asc	or_expand	
index_combine	ordered	
index_desc	ordered_predicates	
index_ffs	overflow_nomove	
index_join		
index_rrs		
index_ss		

Table 15.1: *Documented Oracle Hints*

Undocumented Hints:

bypass_recursive_check	ignore_on_clause	overflow_nomove
bypass_ujvc	ignore_where_clause	piv_gb
cache_cb	index_rrs	piv_ssf
cache_temp_table	index_ss	pq_map
civ_gb	index_ss_asc	pq_nomap
collections_get_refs	index_ss_desc	remote_mapped
cube_gb	like_expand	restore_as_intervals
cursor_sharing_exact	local_indexes	save_as_intervals
deref_no_rewrite	mv_merge	scn_ascending
dml_update	nested_table_get_refs	skip_ext_optimizer
domain_index_no_sort	nested_table_set_refs	sqlldr
domain_index_sort	nested_table_setid	sys_dl_cursor
dynamic_sampling	no_expand_gset_to_union	sys_parallel_txn
dynamic_sampling_est_cdn	no_fact	sys_rid_order
expand_gset_to_union	no_filtering	tiv_gb
force_sample_block	no_order_rollups	tiv_ssf
gby_conc_rollup	no_prune_gsets	unnest
global_table_hints	no_stats_gsets	use_ttt_for_gsets
hwm_brokered	no_unnest	
	nocpu_costing	

Table 15.2: *Undocumented Oracle Hints*

Hints can be used to alter optimizer execution plans. Remember, an optimizer hint is a directive that is placed inside comments inside the SQL statement and used in those rare cases where the optimizer makes an incorrect decision about the execution plan. Since hints are inside comments, it is important to ensure that the hint name is spelled correctly and that the hint is appropriate to the query.

For example, the following hint is invalid because first_rows access and parallel access are mutually exclusive. That is because parallel access always assumes a full-table scan and *first_rows* favors index access.

```
-- An invalid hint
select /*+ first_rows parallel(emp,8)*/
   emp_name
from
   emp
order by
   ename;
```

Some Oracle professionals will place hints together to reinforce their wishes. For example, if there is a SMP server with eight or more CPUs, one may want to use Oracle Parallel Query to speed up legitimate full-table scans.

When using parallel query, one should seldom turn on parallelism at the table level, alter table customer parallel 35, because the setting of parallelism for a table influences the optimizer. This causes the optimizer to see that the full-table scan is inexpensive. Hence, most Oracle professionals specify parallel query on a query-by-query basis, combining the full hint with the parallel hint to ensure a fast parallel full-table scan:

```
-- A valid hint
select /*+ full parallel(emp,35)*/
   emp_name
from
   emp
order by
   ename;
```

Now that the general concept of hints has been introduced, it is an appropriate to look at one of the most important hints for optimizer tuning.

The ordered hint determines the driving table for the query execution and also specifies the order that tables are joined together. The ordered hint requests that the tables should be joined in the order that they are specified in the FROM clause, with the first table in the FROM clause specifying the driving table. Using the ordered hint can save a huge amount of parse time and speed SQL execution because the optimizer is given the best order to join the tables.

For example, the following query uses the ordered hint to join the tables in their specified order in the FROM clause. In this example, the execution plan is further refined by specifying that the emp to dept join use a hash join and the sal to bonus join uses a nested loop join:

```
select
/*+ ordered use_hash (emp, dept) use_nl (sal, bon) */
from
    emp,
    dept,
    sal,
    bon
where . . .
```

Of course, the ordered hint is most commonly used in data warehouse queries or in SQL that joins more than five tables.

SQL execution is dynamic, and tuning an SQL statement for the current data may not be optimal at a future date. The following section provides a brief tour of the Oracle10g Automated Workload Repository (AWR) and how it can be used to perform proactive SQL tuning.

AWR and SQL Tuning

Just as the *v$sql_plan* view revolutionized Oracle9i tuning, the new Oracle10g AWR tables have revolutionized SQL tuning. Most Oracle experts note that SQL optimization is one of the most important factors in database tuning, yet the transient nature of SQL execution has made it difficult to see the impact of SQL execution over time. All of this changed with Oracle10g.

The AWR tables contain useful information about the time-series execution plans for SQL statements. This repository can be used to display details about the frequency of usage for table and indexes.

The following basic relationships between database objects and SQL statements are important:

- Each SQL statement may generate many access plans: From the information on dynamic sampling and dbms_stats, the execution plans for SQL statements will change over time to accommodate changes in the data they access. It is important to understand how and when a frequently executed SQL statement changes its access plan.

- Each object is access by many access plans: In most OLTP systems, tables and indexes show repeating patterns of usage and clear patterns can be detected when averaging object access of day-of-the-week and hour-of-the-day.

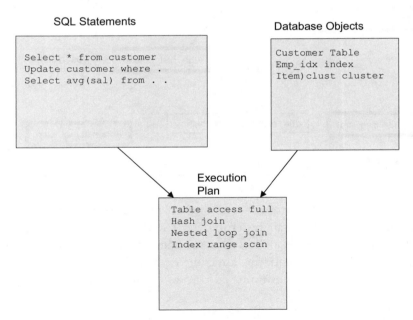

Figure 15.17: *Time-series relationships between SQL and database objects*

Figure 15.17 shows that there is a many-to-many relationship between any given SQL statement and the tables they access. Once this fundamental relationship is clear, the AWR tables can be used to perform time-based SQL tuning. The following AWR tables are available for SQL tuning as shown in 15.18:

- *dba_hist_sqlstat*
- *dba_hist_sql_summary*
- *dba_hist_sql_workarea*
- *dba_hist_sql_plan*
- *dba_hist_sql_workarea_histogram*

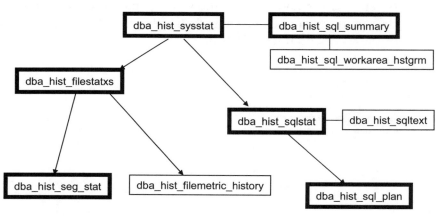

Figure 15.18: *The dba_hist views for SQL tuning*

These simple tables represent a revolution in Oracle SQL tuning, and time-series techniques can be employed to optimize SQL with better results than ever before. The following section provides a closer look at these AWR tables and the amazing details that they can provide about SQL execution over time.

The *dba_hist_sqlstat* Table

This view is very similar to the *v$sql* view, but it contains important SQL metrics for each snapshot. These include important change information on disk reads and buffer gets, as well as time-series delta information on application, I/O and concurrency wait times.

```
col c1 heading 'Begin|Interval|time'       format a8
col c2 heading 'SQL|ID'                     format a13
col c3 heading 'Exec|Delta'                 format 9,999
col c4 heading 'Buffer|Gets|Delta'          format 9,999
col c5 heading 'Disk|Reads|Delta'           format 9,999
col c6 heading 'IO Wait|Delta'              format 9,999
col c7 heading 'Application|Wait|Delta'     format 9,999
col c8 heading 'Concurrency|Wait|Delta'     format 9,999


break on c1

select
  to_char(s.begin_interval_time,'mm-dd hh24')  c1,
  sql.sql_id               c2,
  sql.executions_delta     c3,
  sql.buffer_gets_delta    c4,
  sql.disk_reads_delta     c5,
  sql.iowait_delta         c6,
  sql.apwait_delta         c7,
  sql.ccwait_delta         c8
from
   dba_hist_sqlstat         sql,
   dba_hist_snapshot          s
where
   s.snap_id = sql.snap_id
order by
   c1,
   c2
;
```

The following is a sample of the output. This is very important because the changes in SQL execution over time periods can be visualized. For each snapshot period, it is possible to see the change in the number of times that the SQL was executed as well as important performance information about the performance of the statement.

Begin Interval time	SQL ID	Exec Delta	Buffer Gets Delta	Disk Reads Delta	IO Wait Delta	Application Wait Delta	Concurrency Wait Delta
10-10 16	0sfgqjz5cs52w	24	72	12	0	3	0
	1784a4705pt01	1	685	6	0	17	0

```
           19rkm1wsf9axx      10       61      4      0          0          0
           1d5d88cnwxcw4      52      193      4      6          0          0
           1fvsn5j51ugz3       4        0      0      0          0          0
           1uym1vta995yb       1      102      0      0          0          0
           23yu0nncnp8m9      24       72      0      0          6          0
           298ppdduqr7wm       1        3      0      0          0          0
           2cpffmjm98pcm       4       12      0      0          0          0
           2prbzh4qfms7u       1    4,956     19      1         34          5

10-10 17   0sfgqjz5cs52w      30       90      1      0          0          0
           19rkm1wsf9axx      14       88      0      0          0          0
           1fvsn5j51ugz3       4        0      0      0          0          0
           1zcdwkknwdpgh       4        4      0      0          0          0
           23yu0nncnp8m9      30       91      0      0          0          5
           298ppdduqr7wm       1        3      0      0          0          0
           2cpffmjm98pcm       4       12      0      0          0          0
           2prbzh4qfms7u       1    4,940     20      0          0          0
           2ysccdanw72pv      30       60      0      0          0          0
           3505vtqmvvf40       2      321      5      1          0          0
```

This report is especially useful because it is possible to track the logical I/O (buffer gets) versus. Physical I/O for each statement over time, thereby yielding important information about the behavior of the SQL statement.

This output gives a quick overview of the top SQL during any AWR snapshot period and shows how their behavior has changed since the last snapshot period. Detecting changes in the behavior of commonly executed SQL statements is the key to time-series SQL tuning.

A WHERE clause can easily be added to the above script and the I/O changes plotted over time:

```
col c1  heading  'Begin|Interval|time'      format a8
col c2  heading  'Exec|Delta'               format 999,999
col c3  heading  'Buffer|Gets|Delta'        format 999,999
col c4  heading  'Disk|Reads|Delta'         format 9,999
col c5  heading  'IO Wait|Delta'            format 9,999
col c6  heading  'App|Wait|Delta'           format 9,999
col c7  heading  'Cncr|Wait|Delta'          format 9,999
col c8  heading  'CPU|Time|Delta'           format 999,999
col c9  heading  'Elpsd|Time|Delta'         format 999,999

accept sqlid prompt 'Enter SQL ID: '

ttitle 'time series execution for|&sqlid'

break on c1

select
  to_char(s.begin_interval_time,'mm-dd hh24')   c1,
  sql.executions_delta        c2,
```

```
    sql.buffer_gets_delta      c3,
    sql.disk_reads_delta       c4,
    sql.iowait_delta           c5,
    sql.apwait_delta           c6,
    sql.ccwait_delta           c7,
    sql.cpu_time_delta         c8,
    sql.elapsed_time_delta     c9
from
    dba_hist_sqlstat           sql,
    dba_hist_snapshot          s
where
    s.snap_id = sql.snap_id
and
    sql_id = '&sqlid'
order by
    c1
;
```

The following output shows changes to the execution of a frequently used SQL statement and how its behavior changes over time:

Begin Interval time	Exec Delta	Buffer Gets Delta	Disk Reads Delta	IO Wait Delta	App Wait Delta	Cncr Wait Delta	CPU Time Delta	Elpsd Time Delta
10-14 10	709	2,127	0	0	0	0	398,899	423,014
10-14 11	696	2,088	0	0	0	0	374,502	437,614
10-14 12	710	2,130	0	0	0	0	384,579	385,388
10-14 13	693	2,079	0	0	0	0	363,648	378,252
10-14 14	708	2,124	0	0	0	0	373,902	373,902
10-14 15	697	2,091	0	0	0	0	388,047	410,605
10-14 16	707	2,121	0	0	0	0	386,542	491,830
10-14 17	698	2,094	0	0	0	0	378,087	587,544
10-14 18	708	2,124	0	0	0	0	376,491	385,816
10-14 19	695	2,085	0	0	0	0	361,850	361,850
10-14 20	708	2,124	0	0	0	0	368,889	368,889
10-14 21	696	2,088	0	0	0	0	363,111	412,521
10-14 22	709	2,127	0	0	0	0	369,015	369,015
10-14 23	695	2,085	0	0	0	0	362,480	362,480
10-15 00	709	2,127	0	0	0	0	368,554	368,554
10-15 01	697	2,091	0	0	0	0	362,987	362,987
10-15 02	696	2,088	0	0	0	2	361,445	380,944
10-15 03	708	2,124	0	0	0	0	367,292	367,292
10-15 04	697	2,091	0	0	0	0	362,279	362,279
10-15 05	708	2,124	0	0	0	0	367,697	367,697
10-15 06	696	2,088	0	0	0	0	361,423	361,423
10-15 07	709	2,127	0	0	0	0	374,766	577,559
10-15 08	697	2,091	0	0	0	0	364,879	410,328

In the listing above, it is possible to see how the number of executions varies over time.

In Figure 15.19 below, the WISE tool allows one to plot time-series charts for particular *sql_id* of interest:

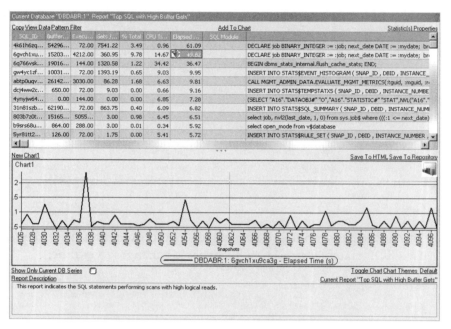

Figure 15.19: *The time-series plot for particular SQL statement*

The above example shows the average elapsed time for the SQL statement over time. Of course, the execution speed may change due to any number of factors:

- Different bind variables

- Database resource shortage

- High physical reads from data buffer shortage

With this information, it is possible to drill down into those specific times when SQL statements performed badly and see exactly why its execution time was slow.

For example, one can chart the average executions by day-of-the-week as shown in Figure 15.20.

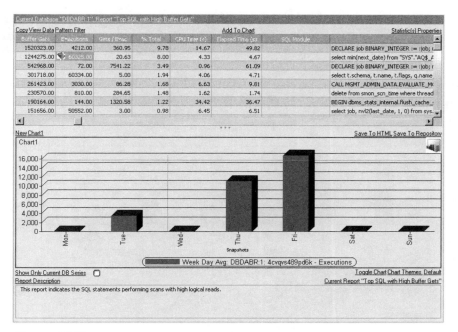

Figure 15.20: *Signature for a specific SQL statement in WISE tool*

The above script can be changed slightly in order to examine logical I/O (consistent gets) versus physical I/O (disk reads) averages for any given SQL statement as shown in Figure 15.21.

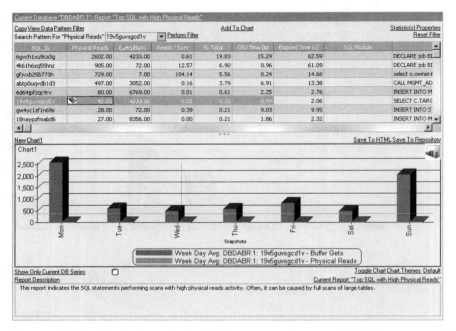

Figure 15.21: *Logical vs. physical I/O averages for a specific SQL statement in WISE tool.*

The plot above shows that the ratio of logical to physical reads changes depending on the day of the week. If execution speed for this SQL query is critical, the DBA would want to examine those times when it has high physical disk reads and consider segregating the tables that participate in this query into the KEEP pool.

The following section provides a look at another exciting new table, the *dba_hist_sql_plan* table, which stores time-series execution details.

The *dba_hist_sql_plan* Table

The *dba_hist_sql_plan* table contains time-series data about each object, table, index, or view, involved in the query. The important columns include the cost, cardinality, *cpu_cost*, *io_cost* and *temp_space* required for the object.

The sample query below retrieves SQL statements which have high query execution cost identified by Oracle optimizer.

```
col c1 heading 'SQL|ID'      format a13
col c2 heading 'Cost'        format 9,999,999
col c3 heading 'SQL Text'    format a200


select
  p.sql_id              c1,
  p.cost                c2,
  to_char(s.sql_text)   c3
from
  dba_hist_sql_plan      p,
  dba_hist_sqltext       s
where
     p.id = 0
  and
     p.sql_id = s.sql_id
  and
     p.cost is not null
order by
  p.cost desc
;
```

The output of the above query might look like this, showing the high cost SQL statements over time:

```
SQL
ID            Cost  SQL Text
------------- ----- -------------------------------------------
847ahztscj4xw 358,456 select
                        s.begin_interval_time   c1,
                        p1.sql_id               c2,
                        p1.object_name          c3,
                        p1.search_columns       c4,
                        p1.cardinality          c5,
                        p1.access_predicates    c6,
                        p1.filter_predicates    c7
                      from
                        dba_hist_sql_plan p1,
                        dba_hist_snapshot s
                      order by
                        c1, c2

58du2p8phcznu 5,110 select
                        begin_interval_time     c1,
                        search_columns          c2,
                        count(*)                c3
                      from
                        dba_hist_sqltext
                      natural join
                        dba_hist_snapshot
```

```
                    natural join
                       dba_hist_sql_plan
                    where
                       lower(sql_text) like lower('%idx%')
                    group by
                       begin_interval_time,search_columns
```

There is much more information in *dba_hist_sql_plan* that is useful. The query below will extract important costing information for all objects involved in each query. SYS objects are not counted.

```
col c1 heading 'Owner'              format a13
col c2 heading 'Object|Type'        format a15

col c3 heading 'Object|Name'        format a25
col c4 heading 'Average|CPU|Cost'   format 9,999,999
col c5 heading 'Average|IO|Cost'    format 9,999,999

break on c1 skip 2
break on c2 skip 2

select
  p.object_owner    c1,
  p.object_type     c2,
  p.object_name     c3,
  avg(p.cpu_cost)   c4,
  avg(p.io_cost)    c5
from
  dba_hist_sql_plan p
where
       p.object_name is not null
   and
       p.object_owner <> 'SYS'
group by
  p.object_owner,
  p.object_type,
  p.object_name
order by
  1,2,4 desc
;
```

The following is a sample of the output. The results show the average CPU and I/O costs for all objects that participate in queries, over time periods.

Owner	Object Type	Object Name	Average CPU Cost	Average IO Cost
OLAPSYS	INDEX	CWM$CUBEDIMENSIONUSE_IDX	200	0
OLAPSYS	INDEX (UNIQUE)	CWM$DIMENSION_PK		
OLAPSYS		CWM$CUBE_PK	7,321	0
OLAPSYS		CWM$MODEL_PK	7,321	0

OLAPSYS	TABLE	CWM$CUBE	7,911	0
OLAPSYS		CWM$MODEL	7,321	0
OLAPSYS		CWM2$CUBE	7,121	2
OLAPSYS		CWM$CUBEDIMENSIONUSE	730	0
MYSCHEMA		CUSTOMER_DETS_PK	21,564	2
MYSCHEMA		STATS$SGASTAT_U	21,442	2
MYSCHEMA		STATS$SQL_SUMMARY_PK	16,842	2
MYSCHEMA		STATS$SQLTEXT_PK	14,442	1
MYSCHEMA		STATS$IDLE_EVENT_PK	8,171	0
SPV	INDEX (UNIQUE)	WSPV_REP_PK	7,321	0
SPV		SPV_ALERT_DEF_PK	7,321	0
SPV	TABLE	WSPV_REPORTS	789,052	28
SPV		SPV_MONITOR	54,092	3
SPV		SPV_SAVED_CHARTS	38,337	3
SPV		SPV_DB_LIST	37,487	3
SPV		SPV_SCHED	35,607	3
SPV		SPV_FV_STAT	35,607	3

This script can now be changed to allow the user to enter a table name and see changes in access details over time:

```
accept tabname prompt 'Enter Table Name:'

col c0 heading 'Begin|Interval|time' format a8
col c1 heading 'Owner'               format a10
col c2 heading 'Object|Type'         format a10
col c3 heading 'Object|Name'         format a15
col c4 heading 'Average|CPU|Cost'    format 9,999,999
col c5 heading 'Average|IO|Cost'     format 9,999,999


break on c1 skip 2
break on c2 skip 2

select
  to_char(sn.begin_interval_time,'mm-dd hh24') c0,
  p.object_owner                               c1,
  p.object_type                                c2,
  p.object_name                                c3,
  avg(p.cpu_cost)                              c4,
  avg(p.io_cost)                               c5
from
  dba_hist_sql_plan p,
  dba_hist_sqlstat  st,
  dba_hist_snapshot sn
where
  p.object_name is not null
and
   p.object_owner <> 'SYS'
and
```

AWR and SQL Tuning

```
  p.object_name = 'CUSTOMER_DETS'
and
  p.sql_id = st.sql_id
and
  st.snap_id = sn.snap_id
group by
  to_char(sn.begin_interval_time,'mm-dd hh24'),
  p.object_owner,
  p.object_type,
  p.object_name
order by
  1,2,3 desc
;
```

This script is great because it is possible to see changes to the table's access patterns over time, which is a very useful feature:

Begin Interval time	Owner	Object Type	Object Name	Average CPU Cost	Average IO Cost
10-25 17	MYSCHEMA	TABLE	CUSTOMER_DETS	28,935	3
10-26 15	MYSCHEMA		CUSTOMER_DETS	28,935	3
10-27 18	MYSCHEMA		CUSTOMER_DETS	5,571,375	24
10-28 12	MYSCHEMA		CUSTOMER_DETS	28,935	3

Figure 15.22 below shows a time-series plot for table access pattern produced by WISE tool

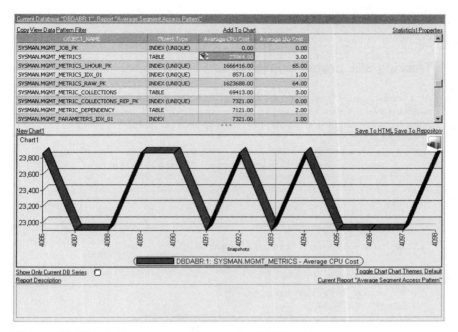

Figure 15.22: *Table access signature in the WISE tool.*

Now that the DBA has access to the important table structures, it would be appropriate to examine how spectacular reports can be retrieved from the AWR data to reveal hidden bottlenecks and show exactly how the database is performing.

Viewing table and index access with AWR

One of the problems in Oracle9i was the single bit-flag that was used to monitor index usage. The flag can be set with the *alter index xxx monitoring usage* command, and see if the index was accessed by querying *the v$object_usage* view.

The goal of any index access is to use the most selective index for a query. This would be the one that produces the smallest number of rows. The Oracle data dictionary is usually quite good at this, but it is up to the DBA to define the index. Missing function-based indexes are a common source of suboptimal SQL execution because Oracle

---

AWR and SQL Tuning

will not use an indexed column unless the WHERE clause matches the index column exactly.

Tracking SQL nested loop joins

As a review, nested loop joins are the most common method for Oracle to match rows in multiple tables. Nested loop joins always invoke an index and they are never parallelized. The following script can be used to count nested loop joins per hour:

```
col c1 heading 'Date'                  format a20
col c2 heading 'Nested|Loops|Count'    format 99,999,999
col c3 heading 'Rows|Processed'        format 99,999,999
col c4 heading 'Disk|Reads'            format 99,999,999
col c5 heading 'CPU|Time'              format 99,999,999

accept nested_thr char prompt 'Enter Nested Join Threshold: '

ttitle 'Nested Join Threshold|&nested_thr'

select
  to_char(
    sn.begin_interval_time,
    'yy-mm-dd hh24'
  )                                    snap_time,
  count(*)                             ct,
  sum(st.rows_processed_delta)         row_ct,
  sum(st.disk_reads_delta)             disk,
  sum(st.cpu_time_delta)               cpu
from
  dba_hist_snapshot    sn,
  dba_hist_sqlstat     st,
  dba_hist_sql_plan    sp
where
  st.snap_id = sn.snap_id
and
  st.dbid = sn.dbid
and
  st.instance_number = sn.instance_number
and
  sp.sql_id = st.sql_id
and
  sp.dbid = st.dbid
and
  sp.plan_hash_value = st.plan_hash_value
and
  sp.operation = 'NESTED LOOPS'
group by
  to_char(sn.begin_interval_time,'yy-mm-dd hh24')
having
      count(*) > &nested_thr;
```

The output below shows the number of total nested loop joins during the snapshot period along with a count of the rows processed and the associated disk I/O. This report is useful where the DBA wants to know if increasing *pga_aggregate_target* will improve performance.

Date	Nested Loops Count	Rows Processed	Disk Reads	CPU Time
04-10-10 16	22	750	796	4,017,301
04-10-10 17	25	846	6	3,903,560
04-10-10 19	26	751	1,430	4,165,270
04-10-10 20	24	920	3	3,940,002
04-10-10 21	25	782	5	3,816,152
04-10-11 02	26	905	0	3,935,547
04-10-11 03	22	1,001	0	3,918,891
04-10-11 04	29	757	8	3,939,071
04-10-11 05	28	757	745	4,395,197
04-10-11 06	24	839	4	4,010,775

In the report above, nested loops are favored by SQL that returns a small number of *rows_processed* than hash joins, which tend to return largest result sets.

The following script exposes the cumulative usage of database indexes:

```
col c0 heading 'Begin|Interval|time'  format a8
col c1 heading 'Index|Name'           format a20
col c2 heading 'Disk|Reads'           format 99,999,999
col c3 heading 'Rows|Processed'       format 99,999,999
select
   to_char(s.begin_interval_time,'mm-dd hh24')  c0,
   p.object_name                c1,
   sum(t.disk_reads_total)      c2,
   sum(t.rows_processed_total)  c3
from
      dba_hist_sql_plan  p,
      dba_hist_sqlstat   t,
      dba_hist_snapshot  s
where
      p.sql_id = t.sql_id
   and
      t.snap_id = s.snap_id
   and
      p.object_type like '%INDEX%'
group by
      to_char(s.begin_interval_time,'mm-dd hh24'),
      p.object_name
order by
      c0,c1,c2 desc
;
```

The following is a sample of the output where the stress on every important index is shown over time. This information is important for placing index blocks into the KEEP pool to reduce disk reads and for determining the optimal setting for the important *optimizer_index_caching* parameter.

```
Begin
Interval  Index                        Disk         Rows
time      Name                        Reads    Processed
--------  --------------------    ---------  -----------
10-14 12  I_CACHE_STATS_1                            114
10-14 12  I_COL_USAGE$                  201        8,984
10-14 12  I_FILE1                         2            0
10-14 12  I_IND1                         93          604
10-14 12  I_JOB_NEXT                      1      247,816
10-14 11  I_KOPM1                         4        2,935
10-14 11  I_MON_MODS$_OBJ                12       28,498
10-14 11  I_OBJ1                     72,852          604
10-14 11  I_PARTOBJ$                     93          604
10-14 11  I_SCHEDULER_JOB2                4            0
10-14 11  SYS_C002433                   302        4,629
10-14 11  SYS_IOT_TOP_8540                0       75,544
10-14 11  SYS_IOT_TOP_8542                1        4,629
10-14 11  WRH$_DATAFILE_PK                2            0
10-14 10  WRH$_SEG_STAT_OBJ_PK           93          604
10-14 10  WRH$_TEMPFILE_PK                             0
10-14 10  WRI$_ADV_ACTIONS_PK            38        1,760
```

The above report shows the highest impact tables.

The following script will summarize index access by snapshot period.

🖫 awr_sql_index_access.sql

```
-- *****************************************************
-- Copyright © 2005 by Rampant TechPress
-- This script is free for non-commercial purposes
-- with no warranties.  Use at your own risk.
--
-- To license this script for a commercial purpose,
-- contact info@rampant.cc
-- *****************************************************

col c1 heading 'Begin|Interval|Time'   format a20
col c2 heading 'Index|Range|Scans' format 999,999
col c3 heading 'Index|Unique|Scans' format 999,999
col c4 heading 'Index|Full|Scans' format 999,999

select
  r.c1   c1,
  r.c2   c2,
  u.c2   c3,
  f.c2   c4
```

```
from
(
select
  to_char(sn.begin_interval_time,'yy-mm-dd hh24')  c1,
  count(1)                                          c2
from
   dba_hist_sql_plan p,
   dba_hist_sqlstat  s,
   dba_hist_snapshot sn
where
   p.object_owner <> 'SYS'
and
   p.operation like '%INDEX%'
and
   p.options like '%RANGE%'
and
   p.sql_id = s.sql_id
and
   s.snap_id = sn.snap_id
group by
  to_char(sn.begin_interval_time,'yy-mm-dd hh24')
order by
1 ) r,
(
select
  to_char(sn.begin_interval_time,'yy-mm-dd hh24')  c1,
  count(1)                                          c2
from
   dba_hist_sql_plan p,
   dba_hist_sqlstat  s,
   dba_hist_snapshot sn
where
   p.object_owner <> 'SYS'
and
   p.operation like '%INDEX%'
and
   p.options like '%UNIQUE%'
and
   p.sql_id = s.sql_id
and
   s.snap_id = sn.snap_id
group by
  to_char(sn.begin_interval_time,'yy-mm-dd hh24')
order by
1 ) u,
(
select
  to_char(sn.begin_interval_time,'yy-mm-dd hh24')  c1,
  count(1)                                          c2
from
   dba_hist_sql_plan p,
   dba_hist_sqlstat  s,
   dba_hist_snapshot sn
where
   p.object_owner <> 'SYS'
and
```

```
    p.operation like '%INDEX%'
and
    p.options like '%FULL%'
and
    p.sql_id = s.sql_id
and
    s.snap_id = sn.snap_id
group by
   to_char(sn.begin_interval_time,'yy-mm-dd hh24')
order by
1 ) f
where
        r.c1 = u.c1
    and
        r.c1 = f.c1
;
```

The sample output below shows those specific times when the database performs unique scans, index range scans and index fast full scans:

```
Begin                       Index     Index     Index
Interval                    Range     Unique    Full
Time                        Scans     Scans     Scans
--------------------       -------   -------   -------
04-10-21 15                     36        35         2
04-10-21 19                     10         8         2
04-10-21 20                                8         2
04-10-21 21                                8         2
04-10-21 22                     11         8         3
04-10-21 23                     16        11         3
04-10-22 00                     10         9         1
04-10-22 01                     11         8         3
04-10-22 02                     12         8         1
04-10-22 03                     10         8         3
04-10-22 04                     11         8         2
04-10-22 05                                8         3
04-10-22 06                                8         2
04-10-22 07                     10         8         3
04-10-22 08                                8         2
04-10-22 09                                8         2
```

SQL object usage can also be summarized by day-of-the-week:

```
col c1 heading 'Object|Name'        format a30
col c2 heading 'Week Day'           format a15
col c3 heading 'Invocation|Count'   format 99,999,999

break on c1 skip 2
break on c2 skip 2
```

```
select

decode(c2,1,'Monday',2,'Tuesday',3,'Wednesday',4,'Thursday',5,'Frida
y',6,'Saturday',7,'Sunday') c2,
   c1,
   c3
from
(
select
   p.object_name                       c1,
   to_char(sn.end_interval_time,'d')   c2,
   count(1)                            c3
from
   dba_hist_sql_plan    p,
   dba_hist_sqlstat     s,
   dba_hist_snapshot    sn
where
   p.object_owner <> 'SYS'
and
   p.sql_id = s.sql_id
and
   s.snap_id = sn.snap_id
group by
   p.object_name,
   to_char(sn.end_interval_time,'d')
order by
   c2,c1
)
;
```

The output below shows the top objects within the database during each snapshot period.

Week Day	Object Name	Invocation Count
Monday	CUSTOMER	44
	CUSTOMER_ORDERS	44
	CUSTOMER_ORDERS_PRIMARY	44
	MGMT_CURRENT_METRICS_PK	43
	MGMT_FAILOVER_TABLE	47
	MGMT_JOB	235
	MGMT_JOB_EMD_STATUS_QUEUE	91
	MGMT_JOB_EXECUTION	235
	MGMT_JOB_EXEC_IDX01	235
	MGMT_JOB_EXEC_SUMMARY	94
	MGMT_JOB_EXEC_SUMM_IDX04	94
	MGMT_JOB_PK	235
	MGMT_METRICS	65
	MGMT_METRICS_1HOUR_PK	43
Tuesday	CUSTOMER	40
	CUSTOMER _CHECK	2
	CUSTOMER _PRIMARY	1

```
                          CUSTOMER_ORDERS                               46
                          CUSTOMER_ORDERS_PRIMARY                       46
                          LOGMNR_LOG$                                    3
                          LOGMNR_LOG$_PK                                 3
                          LOGSTDBY$PARAMETERS                            2
                          MGMT_CURRENT_METRICS_PK                       31
                          MGMT_FAILOVER_TABLE                           42
                          MGMT_JOB                                     200
                          MGMT_JOB_EMD_STATUS_QUEUE                     78
                          MGMT_JOB_EXECUTION                           200
                          MGMT_JOB_EXEC_IDX01                          200
                          MGMT_JOB_EXEC_SUMMARY                         80
                          MGMT_JOB_EXEC_SUMM_IDX04                      80
                          MGMT_JOB_PK                                  200
                          MGMT_METRICS                                  48

Wednesday                 CURRENT_SEVERITY_PRIMARY_KEY                   1
                          MGMT_CURRENT_METRICS_PK                       17
                          MGMT_CURRENT_SEVERITY                          1
                          MGMT_FAILOVER_TABLE                           24
                          MGMT_JOB                                     120
                          MGMT_JOB_EMD_STATUS_QUEUE                     46
                          MGMT_JOB_EXECUTION                           120
                          MGMT_JOB_EXEC_IDX01                          120
                          MGMT_JOB_EXEC_SUMMARY                         48
                          MGMT_JOB_EXEC_SUMM_IDX04                      48
                          MGMT_JOB_PK                                  120
                          MGMT_METRICS                                  36
                          MGMT_METRICS_1HOUR_PK                         14
                          MGMT_METRICS_IDX_01                           24
                          MGMT_METRICS_IDX_03                            1
                          MGMT_METRICS_PK                               11
...
```

When these results are posted, the result is a well-defined signature that emerges for particular tables, access plans and SQL statements. Most Oracle databases are remarkably predictable, with the exception of DSS and ad-hoc query systems, and the DBA can quickly track the usage of all SQL components.

Understanding the SQL signature can be extremely useful for determining what objects to place in the KEEP pool, and to determining the most active tables and indexes in the database.

Once a particular SQL statement for which details are desired has been identified, it is possible to view its execution plan used by optimizer to actually execute the statement. The query below retrieves an execution plan for a particular SQL statement of interest:

```
accept sqlid prompt 'Please enter SQL ID: '

col c1 heading 'Operation'          format a20
col c2 heading 'Options'            format a20
col c3 heading 'Object|Name'        format a25
col c4 heading 'Search Columns'     format 999,999
col c5 heading 'Cardinality'        format 999,999

select
   operation           c1,
   options             c2,
   object_name         c3,
   search_columns      c4,
   cardinality         c5
from
   dba_hist_sql_plan p
where
      p.sql_id = '&sqlid'
order by
   p.id;
```

This is one of the most important of all of the SQL tuning tools. Here is a sample of the output from this script:

```
                                            Search
Operation         Options       Name        Cols Cardinality
----------------  ------------- ----------------------  --- -----------
SELECT STATEMENT                            0
VIEW                                        3              4
SORT              ORDER BY                  4              4
VIEW                                        2              4
UNION-ALL                                   0
FILTER                                      6
NESTED LOOPS      OUTER                     0              3
NESTED LOOPS      ANTI                      0              3
TABLE ACCESS      BY INDEX ROWID STATS$SYSTEM_EVENT     0    70
INDEX             RANGE SCAN    STATS$SYSTEM_EVENT_PK   3    70
INDEX             UNIQUE SCAN   STATS$IDLE_EVENT_PK     1    46
TABLE ACCESS      BY INDEX ROWID STATS$SYSTEM_EVENT     0     1
INDEX             UNIQUE SCAN   STATS$SYSTEM_EVENT_PK   4     1
FILTER                                      0
FAST DUAL                                   1              1
```

The following section will show how one can count the frequency that indexes are used within Oracle.

Counting index usage inside SQL

Prior to Oracle9i, it was very difficult to see if an index was being used by the SQL in the database. It required explaining all of the SQL in the library cache into a holding area and then parsing through the execution plans for the index name. Things were simplified slightly in Oracle9i when the primitive ALTER INDEX XXX MONITORING command and the ability to see if the index was invoked were introduced.

One problem has always been that it is very difficult to know what indexes are the most popular. In Oracle10g, it is easy to see what indexes are used, when they are used and the context in which they are used. The following is a simple AWR query that can be used to plot index usage:

```
col c1 heading 'Begin|Interval|time'  format a20
col c2 heading 'Search Columns'       format 999
col c3 heading 'Invocation|Count'     format 99,999,999


break on c1 skip 2

accept idxname char prompt 'Enter Index Name: '

ttitle 'Invocation Counts for index|&idxname'

select
   to_char(sn.begin_interval_time,'yy-mm-dd hh24')  c1,
   p.search_columns                                 c2,
   count(*)                                         c3
from
   dba_hist_snapshot   sn,
   dba_hist_sql_plan   p,
   dba_hist_sqlstat    st
where
   st.sql_id = p.sql_id
and
   sn.snap_id = st.snap_id
and
   p.object_name = '&idxname'
group by
   begin_interval_time,search_columns;
```

The query will produce an output showing a summary count of the index specified during the snapshot interval. This can be compared to the number of times that a table was invoked from SQL. Here is a sample of the output from the script:

```
Invocation Counts for cust_index

Begin
Interval                          Invocation
time                Search Columns    Count
------------------- -------------- -----------
04-10-21 15                      1           3
```

```
04-10-10 16                    0           1
04-10-10 19                    1           1
04-10-11 02                    0           2
04-10-11 04                    2           1
04-10-11 06                    3           1
04-10-11 11                    0           1
04-10-11 12                    0           2
04-10-11 13                    2           1
04-10-11 15                    0           3
04-10-11 17                    0          14
04-10-11 18                    4           1
04-10-11 19                    0           1
04-10-11 20                    3           7
04-10-11 21                    0           1
```

Figure 15.23 shows a sample screenshot of a time-series plot produced by WISE tool for index access.

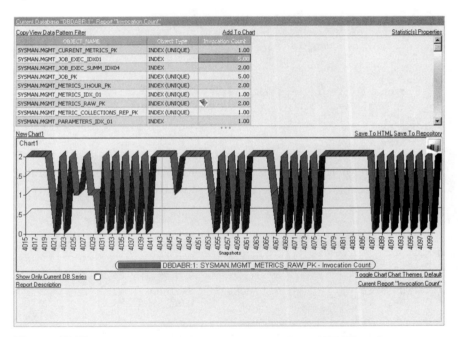

Figure 15.23: *Index invocation count time-series plot in WISE tool.*

The AWR SQL tuning tables offer a wealth of important time metrics. This data can also be summed up by snapshot period giving an overall view of how Oracle is accessing the table data.

```
ttile 'Table Access|Operation Counts|Per Snapshot Period'

col c1 heading 'Begin|Interval|time'   format a20
col c2 heading 'Operation'             format a15
col c3 heading 'Option'                format a15
col c4 heading 'Object|Count'          format 999,999

break on c1 skip 2
break on c2 skip 2

select
  to_char(sn.begin_interval_time,'yy-mm-dd hh24')   c1,
  p.operation   c2,
  p.options     c3,
  count(1)      c4
from
  dba_hist_sql_plan p,
  dba_hist_sqlstat  s,
  dba_hist_snapshot sn
where
  p.object_owner <> 'SYS'
and
  p.sql_id = s.sql_id
and
  s.snap_id = sn.snap_id
group by
  to_char(sn.begin_interval_time,'yy-mm-dd hh24'),
  p.operation,
  p.options
order by
  1,2,3;
```

The output of the query is shown below, and it includes overall total counts for each object and table access method.

```
Begin
Interval                                          Object
time                Operation        Option        Count
----------------    ---------------  ---------------  --------
04-10-15 16         INDEX            UNIQUE SCAN           1

04-10-15 16         TABLE ACCESS     BY INDEX ROWID        1
04-10-15 16                          FULL                  2

04-10-15 17         INDEX            UNIQUE SCAN           1

04-10-15 17         TABLE ACCESS     BY INDEX ROWID        1
04-10-15 17                          FULL                  2

04-10-15 18         INDEX            UNIQUE SCAN           1

04-10-15 18         TABLE ACCESS     BY INDEX ROWID        1
04-10-15 18                          FULL                  2

04-10-15 19         INDEX            UNIQUE SCAN           1
```

```
04-10-15 19          TABLE ACCESS     BY INDEX ROWID     1
04-10-15 19                           FULL               2

04-10-15 20          INDEX            UNIQUE SCAN         1

04-10-15 20          TABLE ACCESS     BY INDEX ROWID     1
04-10-15 20                           FULL               2

04-10-15 21          INDEX            UNIQUE SCAN         1

04-10-15 21          TABLE ACCESS     BY INDEX ROWID     1
04-10-15 21                           FULL               2
```

If the DBA has a non-OLTP database that regularly performs large full-table and full-index scans, it is helpful to know those times when the full scan activity is high. The following query will yield that information:

🖫 awr_sql_full_scans.sql

```
-- ***************************************************
-- Copyright © 2005 by Rampant TechPress
-- This script is free for non-commercial purposes
-- with no warranties.  Use at your own risk.
--
-- To license this script for a commercial purpose,
-- contact info@rampant.cc
-- ***************************************************
col c1 heading 'Begin|Interval|Time'    format a20
col c2 heading 'Index|Table|Scans' format 999,999
col c3 heading 'Full|Table|Scans' format 999,999

select
  i.c1   c1,
  i.c2   c2,
  f.c2   c3
from
(
select
  to_char(sn.begin_interval_time,'yy-mm-dd hh24')  c1,
  count(1)                          c2
from
  dba_hist_sql_plan p,
  dba_hist_sqlstat  s,
  dba_hist_snapshot sn
where
  p.object_owner <> 'SYS'
and
```

```
   p.operation like '%TABLE ACCESS%'
and
   p.options like '%INDEX%'
and
   p.sql_id = s.sql_id
and
   s.snap_id = sn.snap_id
group by
  to_char(sn.begin_interval_time,'yy-mm-dd hh24')
order by
1 ) i,
(
select
  to_char(sn.begin_interval_time,'yy-mm-dd hh24')  c1,
  count(1)                                  c2
from
   dba_hist_sql_plan p,
   dba_hist_sqlstat  s,
   dba_hist_snapshot sn
where
   p.object_owner <> 'SYS'
and
   p.operation like '%TABLE ACCESS%'
and
   p.options = 'FULL'
and
   p.sql_id = s.sql_id
and
   s.snap_id = sn.snap_id
group by
  to_char(sn.begin_interval_time,'yy-mm-dd hh24')
order by
1 ) f
where
     i.c1 = f.c1
;
```

The output below shows a comparison of index-full scans versus full-table scans.

Begin Interval Time	Index Table Scans	Full Table Scans
04-10-21 15	53	18
04-10-21 17	3	3
04-10-21 18	1	2
04-10-21 19	15	6
04-10-21 20		6
04-10-21 21		6
04-10-21 22	16	6
04-10-21 23	21	9
04-10-22 00	16	6
04-10-22 01		6

```
04-10-22 02                    17        6
04-10-22 03                    15        6
```

Knowing the signature for large-table full-table scans can help in both SQL tuning and instance tuning. For SQL tuning, this report will tell when to drill down to verify that all of the large-table full-table scans are legitimate. Once verified, this same data can be used to dynamically reconfigure the Oracle instance to accommodate the large scans.

With that introduction to the indexing component, it will be useful to learn how to use the AWR data to track full-scan behavior over time.

Tracking full scan access with AWR

All of the specific SQL access methods can be counted and their behavior tracked over time. This is especially important for large-table full-table scans (LTFTS) because they are a common symptom of suboptimal execution plans (i.e. missing indexes).

Once it has been determined that the large-table full-table scans are legitimate, the DBA must know those times when they are executed so that a selective parallel query can be implemented, depending on the existing CPU consumption on the server. Oracle Parallel Query (OPQ) drives up CPU consumption, and should be invoked when the server can handle the additional load.

```
ttile 'Large Full-table scans|Per Snapshot Period'

col c1 heading 'Begin|Interval|time' format a20
col c4 heading 'FTS|Count'           format 999,999

break on c1 skip 2
break on c2 skip 2

select
  to_char(sn.begin_interval_time,'yy-mm-dd hh24')  c1,
  count(1)                                          c4
from
  dba_hist_sql_plan p,
  dba_hist_sqlstat  s,
  dba_hist_snapshot sn,
  dba_segments      o
where
```

```
    p.object_owner <> 'SYS'
and
    p.object_owner = o.owner
and
    p.object_name = o.segment_name
and
    o.blocks > 1000
and
    p.operation like '%TABLE ACCESS%'
and
    p.options like '%FULL%'
and
    p.sql_id = s.sql_id
and
    s.snap_id = sn.snap_id
group by
  to_char(sn.begin_interval_time,'yy-mm-dd hh24')
order by
  1;
```

The output below shows the overall total counts for tables that experience large-table full-table scans because the scans may be due to a missing index.

```
        Large Full-table scans
        Per Snapshot Period

Begin
Interval                    FTS
time                        Count
-------------------    --------
04-10-18 11                   4
04-10-21 17                   1
04-10-21 23                   2
04-10-22 15                   2
04-10-22 16                   2
04-10-22 23                   2
04-10-24 00                   2
04-10-25 00                   2
04-10-25 10                   2
04-10-25 17                   9
04-10-25 18                   1
04-10-25 21                   1
04-10-26 12                   1
04-10-26 13                   3
04-10-26 14                   3
04-10-26 15                  11
04-10-26 16                   4
04-10-26 17                   4
04-10-26 18                   3
04-10-26 23                   2
04-10-27 13                   2
04-10-27 14                   3
04-10-27 15                   4
```

```
04-10-27 16              4
04-10-27 17              3
04-10-27 18             17
04-10-27 19              1
04-10-28 12             22
04-10-28 13              2
04-10-29 13              9
```

This data can be easily plotted to see the trend for a database as shown in Figure 15.24:

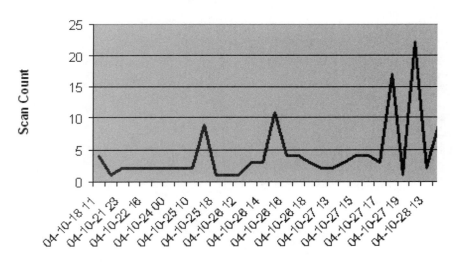

Figure 15.24: *Trends of large-table full-table scans*

Search for Symptoms!

One of the most common manifestations of suboptimal SQL execution is a large-table full-table scan. Whenever an index is missing, Oracle may be forced to read every row in the table when an index might be faster.

If the large-table full-table scans are legitimate, the DBA will want to know the periods that they are invoked, so Oracle Parallel Query (OPQ) can be invoked to speed up the scans as shown in the script that follows:

```
ttile 'Large Table Full-table scans|Averages per Hour'

col c1 heading 'Day|Hour'             format a20
col c2 heading 'FTS|Count'            format 999,999

break on c1 skip 2
break on c2 skip 2
select
  to_char(sn.begin_interval_time,'hh24')  c1,
  count(1)                            c2
from
  dba_hist_sql_plan p,
  dba_hist_sqlstat  s,
  dba_hist_snapshot sn,
  dba_segments      o
where
  p.object_owner <> 'SYS'
and
  p.object_owner = o.owner
and
  p.object_name = o.segment_name
and
  o.blocks > 1000
and
  p.operation like '%TABLE ACCESS%'
and
  p.options like '%FULL%'
and
  p.sql_id = s.sql_id
and
  s.snap_id = sn.snap_id
group by
  to_char(sn.begin_interval_time,'hh24')
order by
  1;
```

The following output shows the average number of large-table full-table scans per hour.

```
Large Table Full-table scans
Averages per Hour

Day                          FTS
Hour                         Count
--------------------    --------
00                              4
```

```
10                        2
11                        4
12                       23
13                       16
14                        6
15                       17
16                       10
17                       17
18                       21
19                        1
23                        6
```

The script below shows the same data for day of the week:

```
ttile 'Large Table Full-table scans|Averages per Week Day'

col c1 heading 'Week|Day'              format a20
col c2 heading 'FTS|Count'             format 999,999

break on c1 skip 2
break on c2 skip 2

select
  to_char(sn.begin_interval_time,'day')  c1,
  count(1)                          c2
from
   dba_hist_sql_plan p,
   dba_hist_sqlstat  s,
   dba_hist_snapshot sn,
   dba_segments      o
where
   p.object_owner <> 'SYS'
and
   p.object_owner = o.owner
and
   p.object_name = o.segment_name
and
   o.blocks > 1000
and
   p.operation like '%TABLE ACCESS%'
and
   p.options like '%FULL%'
and
   p.sql_id = s.sql_id
and
   s.snap_id = sn.snap_id
group by
  to_char(sn.begin_interval_time,'day')
order by
1;
```

The following sample query output shows specific times the database experienced large table scans.

```
Large Table Full-table scans
Averages per Week Day


Week                        FTS
Day                       Count
-------------------    --------
sunday                        2
monday                       19
tuesday                      31
wednesday                    34
thursday                     27
friday                       15
Saturday                      2
```

The *awr_sql_scan_sums.sql* script will show the access patterns of usage over time. If a DBA is really driven to know their system, all they need to do is understand how SQL accesses the tables and indexes in the database to provide amazing insight. The optimal instance configuration for large-table full-table scans is quite different than the configuration for an OLTP databases, and the report generated by the *awr_sql_scan_sums.sql* script will quickly identify changes in table access patterns.

🖫 awr_sql_scan_sums.sql

```
--  ***************************************************
--  Copyright © 2005 by Rampant TechPress
--  This script is free for non-commercial purposes
--  with no warranties.  Use at your own risk.
--
--  To license this script for a commercial purpose,
--  contact info@rampant.cc
--  ***************************************************

col c1 heading 'Begin|Interval|Time'           format a20
col c2 heading 'Large|Table|Full Table|Scans'  format 999,999
col c3 heading 'Small|Table|Full Table|Scans'  format 999,999
col c4 heading 'Total|Index|Scans'             format 999,999


select
   f.c1  c1,
   f.c2  c2,
   s.c2  c3,
   i.c2  c4
from
(
select
```

```
   to_char(sn.begin_interval_time,'yy-mm-dd hh24')   c1,
   count(1)                                 c2
from
   dba_hist_sql_plan p,
   dba_hist_sqlstat  s,
   dba_hist_snapshot sn,
   dba_segments      o
where
   p.object_owner <> 'SYS'
and
   p.object_owner = o.owner
and
   p.object_name = o.segment_name
and
   o.blocks > 1000
and
   p.operation like '%TABLE ACCESS%'
and
   p.options like '%FULL%'
and
   p.sql_id = s.sql_id
and
   s.snap_id = sn.snap_id
group by
   to_char(sn.begin_interval_time,'yy-mm-dd hh24')
order by
1 ) f,
(
select
   to_char(sn.begin_interval_time,'yy-mm-dd hh24')   c1,
   count(1)                                 c2
from
   dba_hist_sql_plan p,
   dba_hist_sqlstat  s,
   dba_hist_snapshot sn,
   dba_segments      o
where
   p.object_owner <> 'SYS'
and
   p.object_owner = o.owner
and
   p.object_name = o.segment_name
and
   o.blocks < 1000
and
   p.operation like '%INDEX%'
and
   p.sql_id = s.sql_id
and
   s.snap_id = sn.snap_id
group by
   to_char(sn.begin_interval_time,'yy-mm-dd hh24')
order by
1 ) s,
(
select
```

```
   to_char(sn.begin_interval_time,'yy-mm-dd hh24')  c1,
   count(1)                                   c2
from
   dba_hist_sql_plan p,
   dba_hist_sqlstat  s,
   dba_hist_snapshot sn
where
   p.object_owner <> 'SYS'
and
   p.operation like '%INDEX%'
and
   p.sql_id = s.sql_id
and
   s.snap_id = sn.snap_id
group by
   to_char(sn.begin_interval_time,'yy-mm-dd hh24')
order by
1 ) i
where
      f.c1 = s.c1
  and
      f.c1 = i.c1
;
```

The sample output looks like the following, where there is a comparison of index versus table scan access. This is a very important signature for any database because it shows, at a glance, the balance between index (OLTP) and data warehouse type access.

Begin Interval Time	Large Table Full Table Scans	Small Table Full Table Scans	Total Index Scans
04-10-22 15	2	19	21
04-10-22 16		1	1
04-10-25 10		18	20
04-10-25 17	9	15	17
04-10-25 18	1	19	22
04-10-25 21		19	24
04-10-26 12		23	28
04-10-26 13	3	17	19
04-10-26 14		18	19
04-10-26 15	11	4	7
04-10-26 16	4	18	18
04-10-26 17		17	19
04-10-26 18	3	17	17
04-10-27 13	2	17	19
04-10-27 14	3	17	19
04-10-27 15	4	17	18
04-10-27 16		17	17
04-10-27 17	3	17	20
04-10-27 18	17	20	22

```
04-10-27 19                  1          20          26
04-10-28 12                  22          17          20
04-10-28 13                  2          17          17
04-10-29 13                  9          18          19
```

This is a very important report because it shows the method with which Oracle is accessing data over time periods. This is especially important because it shows when the database processing modality shifts between OLTP (first_rows index access) to a batch reporting mode (*all_rows* full scans) as shown in Figure 15.25.

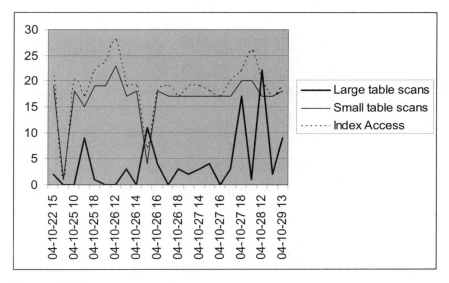

Figure 15.25: *Plot of full scans vs. index access*

The example in Figure 15.25 is typical of an OLTP database with the majority of access being via small-table full-table scans and index access. In this case, the large-table full-table scans must be carefully checked, their legitimacy verified for such things as missing indexes, and then they should be adjusted to maximize their throughput.

Of course, in a really busy database, there may be concurrent OLTP index access and full-table scans for reports and it is the DBA's job to know the specific times when the system shifts table access modes as well as the identity of those tables that experience the changes.

The following *awr_sql_full_scans_avg_dy.sql* script can be used to roll-up average scans into daily averages.

💾 awr_sql_full_scans_avg_dy.sql

```
-- *******************************************************
-- Copyright © 2005 by Rampant TechPress
-- This script is free for non-commercial purposes
-- with no warranties.  Use at your own risk.
--
-- To license this script for a commercial purpose,
-- contact info@rampant.cc
-- *******************************************************

col c1 heading 'Begin|Interval|Time'   format a20
col c2 heading 'Index|Table|Scans' format 999,999
col c3 heading 'Full|Table|Scans' format 999,999

select
  i.c1   c1,
  i.c2   c2,
  f.c2   c3
from
(
select
  to_char(sn.begin_interval_time,'day')  c1,
  count(1)                               c2
from
  dba_hist_sql_plan p,
  dba_hist_sqlstat  s,
  dba_hist_snapshot sn
where
  p.object_owner <> 'SYS'
and
  p.operation like '%TABLE ACCESS%'
and
  p.options like '%INDEX%'
and
  p.sql_id = s.sql_id
and
  s.snap_id = sn.snap_id
group by
  to_char(sn.begin_interval_time,'day')
order by
1 ) i,
(
select
  to_char(sn.begin_interval_time,'day')  c1,
  count(1)                               c2
from
  dba_hist_sql_plan p,
  dba_hist_sqlstat  s,
```

```
    dba_hist_snapshot sn
where
   p.object_owner <> 'SYS'
and
   p.operation like '%TABLE ACCESS%'
and
   p.options = 'FULL'
and
   p.sql_id = s.sql_id
and
   s.snap_id = sn.snap_id
group by
  to_char(sn.begin_interval_time,'day')
order by
1 ) f
where
     i.c1 = f.c1
;
```

The sample output is shown below:

Begin Interval Time	Index Table Scans	Full Table Scans
sunday	393	189
monday	383	216
tuesday	353	206
wednesday	357	178
thursday	488	219
friday	618	285
saturday	400	189

For example, the signature shown in Figure 15.26 below indicates that Fridays are very high in full-table scans, probably as the result of weekly reporting.

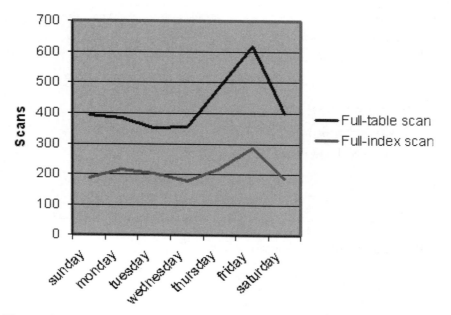

Figure 15.26: *Plot of full scans*

With this knowledge, the DBA can anticipate the changes in processing from index access to large-table full-table scans (LTFTS) access by adjusting instance configurations.

Whenever the database changes into a mode dominated by LTFTS, the data buffer sizes, such as *db_cache_size* and *db_nk_cache_size*, can be decreased. Since parallel LTFTS bypass the data buffers, the intermediate rows are kept in the *pga_aggregate_target* region. Hence, it may be desirable to use *dbms_scheduler* to anticipate this change and resize the SGA just in time to accommodate the regularly repeating change in access patterns.

One important use for the AWR tables is tracking table join methods over time.

Interrogating table join methods

The choice between a hash join and a nested loop join depends on several factors:

- The relative number of rows in each table

- The presence of indexes on the key values

- The settings for static parameters such as *index_caching* and *cpu_costing*

- The current setting and available memory in *pga_aggregate_target*

Hash joins do not use indexes and perform full-table scans often using parallel query. Consequently, the use of hash joins with parallel full-table scans tend to drive-up CPU consumption.

Also, PGA memory consumption becomes higher when hash joins are used, but if AMM is enabled, it is not usually a problem.

The following query produces a report alerting an Oracle DBA when hash join operations count exceeds some threshold:

```
col c1 heading 'Date'              format a20
col c2 heading 'Hash|Join|Count'   format 99,999,999
col c3 heading 'Rows|Processed'    format 99,999,999
col c4 heading 'Disk|Reads'        format 99,999,999
col c5 heading 'CPU|Time'          format 99,999,999

accept hash_thr char prompt 'Enter Hash Join Threshold: '

ttitle 'Hash Join Threshold|&hash_thr'

select
  to_char(
    sn.begin_interval_time,
    'yy-mm-dd hh24'
  )                                snap_time,
  count(*)                         ct,
  sum(st.rows_processed_delta)     row_ct,
  sum(st.disk_reads_delta)         disk,
  sum(st.cpu_time_delta)           cpu
from
   dba_hist_snapshot    sn,
   dba_hist_sqlstat     st,
   dba_hist_sql_plan    sp
where
```

```
   st.snap_id = sn.snap_id
and
   st.dbid = sn.dbid
and
   st.instance_number = sn.instance_number
and
   sp.sql_id = st.sql_id
and
   sp.dbid = st.dbid
and
   sp.plan_hash_value = st.plan_hash_value
and
   sp.operation = 'HASH JOIN'
group by
   to_char(sn.begin_interval_time,'yy-mm-dd hh24')
having
      count(*) > &hash_thr;
```

The sample output might look the following, showing the number of hash joins during the snapshot period along with the relative I/O and CPU associated with the processing. The values for *rows_processed* are generally higher for hash joins which do full-table scans as opposed to nested loop joins with generally involved a very small set of returned rows.

Hash Join Thresholds

Date	Hash Join Count	Rows Processed	Disk Reads	CPU Time
04-10-12 17	22	4,646	887	39,990,515
04-10-13 16	25	2,128	827	54,746,653
04-10-14 11	21	17,368	3,049	77,297,578
04-10-21 15	60	2,805	3,299	5,041,064
04-10-22 10	25	6,864	941	4,077,524
04-10-22 13	31	11,261	2,950	46,207,733
04-10-25 16	35	46,269	1,504	6,364,414

Hash Join Tuning is tricky!

The sorting default is that no single task may consume more than 5% of the *pga_aggregate_target* region before the sort pages out to the TEMP tablespace for a disk sort.

Supersizing the PGA for large sorts and hash joins

Almost every Oracle professional agrees that the old-fashioned *sort_area_size* and *hash_area_size* parameters imposed a cumbersome one-size-fits-all approach to sorting and hash joins. Different tasks require different RAM areas, and the trick has been to allow "enough"

PGA RAM for sorting and hash joins without having any high-resource task "hog" all of the PGA, to the exclusion of other users.

Oracle9i introduced the *pga_aggregate_target* parameters to fix this resource issue, and by-and-large, *pga_aggregate_target* works very well for most systems. Overall PGA usage can be checked with the *v$pga_target_advice* advisory utility or a STATSPACK or AWR report. High values for multi-pass executions, high disk sorts, or low hash join invocation might indicate a low resource usage for PGA regions.

There are important limitations of pga_aggregate_target:

- The total work area cannot exceed 200 megabytes of RAM because of the default setting for *_pga_max_size*.

- No RAM sort may use more than 5% of *pga_aggregate_target* or *_pga_max_size*, whichever is smaller. This means that no task may use more than 200 megabytes for sorting or hash joins. The algorithm further reduces this to (200/2) for sorts so the actual limit for pure sorts will be 100 megabytes.

These restrictions were made to ensure that no large sorts or hash joins hog the PGA RAM area. There are some secrets to optimize the PGA. For example, the following set of parameters may be mutually-exclusive:

- *sort_area_size=1048576* <-- *sort_area_size* is ignored when *pga_aggregate_target* is set and when *workarea_size_policy =auto,* unless a specialized feature such as the MTS is being used. If dedicated server connections are used, the *sort_area_size* parameter is ignored.

- *pga_aggregate_target = 500m* <-- The maximum default allowed value is 200 megabytes, this limits sorts to 25 megabytes (5% of 500m).

- *mts_servers<>0* <-- If Multi-threaded server is being used, the *pga_aggregate_target* setting would be ignored in all versions except Oracle10g.

Note: there may be some cases where *sort_area_size* is used in Oracle utilities, but these have not been documented, even with *pga_aggregate_target*.

The next section looks at some expert tricks for advanced PGA management.

Hidden parameters for Oracle PGA regions

With proper guidance and keeping in mind that these undocumented parameters are not supported by Oracle, PGA regions can be adjusted to allow for system-specific sorting and hash joins.

- *_pga_max_size* – this hidden parameter defaults to 200 megabytes, regardless of the setting for *pga_aggregate_target*.

- *_smm_px_max_size* – This parameter is used for Oracle parallel query. It defaults to 30% of the *pga_aggregate_target* setting divided by degree of parallelism, as set by a PARALLEL hint, *alter table xxx parallel* command, or the *parallel_automatic_tuning* initialization parameter. For example, by default a DEGREE=4 parallel query would have a maximum sort area value of 15 megabytes per session with a 200 megabyte *pga_aggregate_target* setting. Remember, parallel full-table scans bypass the data buffers and store the incoming data rows in the PGA region and not inside the data buffers (as defined by the *db_cache_size* parameter).

There are also these additional undocumented parameters:

- *_smm_advice_enabled*: If TRUE, enable *v$pga_advice*

- *_smm_advice_log_size*: This overwrites default size of the PGA advice workarea history log

- *_smm_auto_cost_enabled*: If TRUE, use the AUTO size policy cost functions

- *_smm_auto_max_io_size*: The maximum I/O size (in KB) used by sort/hash-join in auto mode

- *_smm_auto_min_io_size*: The minimum I/O size (in KB) used by sort/hash-join in auto mode

- *_smm_bound*: This overwrites memory manager automatically computed bound

- *_smm_control*: This provides controls on the memory manager

- *_smm_max_size*: This is the maximum work area size in auto mode (serial)

- *_smm_min_size*: The minimum work area size in auto mode

- *_smm_px_max_size*: The maximum work area size in auto mode (global)

- *_smm_trace*: The on/off tracing for SQL memory manager

WARNING!

These are unsupported parameters and they should not be used unless you have opened an iTar and tested their behavior on your own database and you are willing to accept full responsibility for any issues.

Super-sizing the PGA

For certain Oracle applications the Oracle professional will want to allow individual tasks to exceed the default limits imposed by Oracle. For example, PC-based, 64 bit Oracle servers (1 or 2 CPU's with 8 gigabytes of RAM) will often have unused RAM available. For example, a fully-cached 5 gigabyte database on an 8 gigabyte dedicated Oracle server will have approximately 1 gigabyte available for the PGA (allowing 20% for the OS and other SGA regions):

O/S	1.6 gig
SGA	5 gig
PGA Space	1 gig
Total	8 gig

The system has a *pga_aggregate_target* setting of 1 gigabyte and the undocumented parameters are at their default settings.

While it is unusual for an online system to require super-sized regions for sorting because the result sets for online screens are normally small,

---

there can be a benefit to having large RAM regions available for the Oracle optimizer.

The Oracle cost-based optimizer will determine whether a hash join would be beneficial over a nested-loop join. Consequently, making more PGA available for hash joins will not have any detrimental effect since the optimizer will only invoke a super-sized hash join if it is better than a nested-loop join. In a system like the example above, the following settings would increase the default sizes for large sorts and hash joins while limiting those for parallel sorts.

```
pga_aggregate_target = 4g
_pga_max_size = 400m
_smm_px_max_size = 333m
```

With these hidden parameters set there is a significant size increase for serial sorts and a throttling effect for parallel queries and sorts. However, bear in mind that it is only valid for a specific release of Oracle10g, on a specific hardware and OS environment, and not using any optional features such as the MTS.

A RAM sort or hash join may now have up to the full 200 megabytes (5% of *pga_aggregate_target*) a 400% increase over a 1 gigabyte *pga_aggregate_target* setting. With the default settings, only a 200% (100 megabyte size) increase would be possible.

Parallel queries are now limited to 333 megabytes of RAM (30% of *pga_aggregate_target* or *_smm_px_max_size*), such that a DEGREE=4 parallel query would have a maximum of 83 megabytes (333 meg/4) per slave which may actually be less due to internal sizing algorithms that set the memory increments used in setting sort areas. This throttling is to prevent one parallel query from using all available memory since *_smm_px_max_size* would default to 1.2 gigabytes with the setting for *pga_aggregate_target* at 4 gigabytes.

Be careful in setting the *pga_aggregate_target* to greater than the available memory. Calculate the maximum number of users who would be sorting/hashing and multiple that times the predicted size to get the actual limitations otherwise ORA-4030 errors or swapping may occur.

In conclusion, overriding the built-in safeguards of *pga_aggregate_target* can make more efficient use of RAM resources in cases where large RAM regions are available on the database server. When used with care (and the blessing of Oracle Technical Support) it can often make sense to over-ride these default values to make better use of expensive RAM resources. There is also lots of evidence that changing these parameters will have a positive effect on large, batch-oriented Oracle jobs, but be very careful to fully understand the limitations of the PGA parameters:

Important caveats in PGA management

- Do not adjust any hidden parameters without opening an iTar and getting the consent and advice of Oracle Technical Support. These are undocumented, hidden parameters and the DBA must be willing to accept full responsibility for any issues.

- Some hidden parameters have no effect when set at session level and alter system commands must be issued for them to take effect.

- These PGA rules no not apply to shared server environments using Oracle multi-threaded server (MTS). However, the vast majority of Oracle shops do not use the MTS.

- Each process (with one PGA area) may have multiple work areas. For example, a query might perform a parallel full-table scan followed by an ORDER BY sort, having one PGA and two workareas. The *_pga_max_size* controls the PGA size and *_smm_max_size* controls the size for each workarea.

Now that the basics of instance tuning have been presented, it is a good time to take a look at Oracle's new SQL tuning advisor functions.

Oracle10g SQL Tuning

Before Oracle10g, it was extremely difficult to track index usage and see how SQL statements behaved except when they were in the library cache. With Oracle10g, it is now possible to track SQL behavior over time and ensure that all SQL is using an optimal execution plan. Oracle10g provides the ability to track SQL execution metrics with new dba_hist tables, most notably *dba_hist_sqlstat* and *dba_hist_sql_plan*.

It is important to track the relationship between database objects, such as tables, indexes, and the SQL that accesses the objects. Oracle SQL execution plans for any given statement may change if the system statistics change, dynamic sampling is used, materialized views are created, or indexes are created or dropped.

The SQL Tuning Advisor

The SQL Tuning Advisor (STA) works with the Automatic Tuning Optimizer (ATO) to analyze historical SQL workload using data from the AWR. It generates recommendations for new indexes and materialized views that will reduce the disk I/O associated with troublesome SQL statements.

The STA is primarily designed to replace the manual tuning of SQL statements and speed up the overall SQL tuning process. The SQL Tuning Advisor studies poorly executing SQL statements and evaluates resource consumption in terms of CPU, I/O, and temporary space.

The advisor receives one or more SQL statements as input and provides advice on how to optimize their execution plans, gives the rationale for the advice, the estimated performance benefit, and the actual command to implement the advice.

The STA can be thought of as a container for conducting and analyzing many tuning tasks. It calls the optimizer internally and performs the analysis as follows:

- Executes the stale or missing statistics analysis and makes a recommendation to collect, if necessary.

- Plans the tuning analysis and creates an SQL Profile. The SQL Profile is a collection of the historical information of prior runs of the SQL statement, comparison details of the actual and estimated cardinality, and predicate selectivity, etc. SQL Profile is stored persistently in the data dictionary, so it does not require any application code changes.

- Performs the access path analysis. The Optimizer recommends new indexes that produce a significantly faster execution path.

- Restructure the SQL statement. Optimizer identifies SQL statements that have bad plans and makes relevant suggestions to restructure them.

The plan analysis mode, which creates the SQL Profiles, is a significant stage where additional information for the query is collected by the optimizer. This analysis is not possible in the normal mode.

Such an SQL profile helps generate a better execution plan than the normal optimization. Additional tasks like checking for advanced predicate selectivity, correlation between columns, join skews, and complex predicates such as functions, help in profiling the SQL statement. Once a statement is profiled and stored, it can be used at will.

Using SQL Tuning Advisor Session

This method has many stages. In the first stage, the SQL Advisor task can be created by taking SQL statement input from a variety of sources. They are as follows:

- High Load SQL statements, identified by ADDM.

- SQL statements that are currently in cursor cache from the *v$sql_plan* view.

- SQL statements based on the range of snapshot IDs from the Automatic Workload Repository (AWR). By default, the AWR maintains data for up to seven days.

- Simple SQL Statement Text. A user can define a custom workload consisting of statements of interest to the user. These may be statements that are either in cursor cache or high-load, to be captured by ADDM or AWR.

- SQL Tuning Set (STS). An SQL Tuning Set is a named set of SQL statements with their associated execution context and basic execution statistics.

The following is an example of an SQL Tuning session, using this new functionality:

Step 1: Create a tuning task

There is an SQL statement, perhaps from a packaged application, and the DBA may not be able to change the code.

```
create_tuning_task (
sql_text => 'select * from emp_history
where empid_id = :bnd_var',f
bind_list =>
sql_binds(anydata.ConvertNumber(100)),
usern_name => 'scott',
scope => 'comprehensive',
time_limit => 60,
task_name => 'bad_sql',
description => 'sql that performs poorly');
```

The time limit is set to 60, so the optimizer will spend up to 60 seconds analyzing this SQL statement. The comprehensive setting indicated that the optimizer should perform its additional analysis. Instead of using the above SQL, the *sql_id* out of OEM or other catalog tables such as *sql_advisor_%* can be used.

```
create_tuning_task (sql_id =>
'abc123456xyz');
```

Step 2: Execute the tuning task.

```
Execute_tuning_task (
Task_name => 'bad_sql');
```

The results of this execution have been put into the new catalog tables, and can be seen by querying *dba_advisor_%* views such as *dba_advisor_findings*, *dba_advisor_recommendations*, etc.

Step 3: See the results.

```
set long 10000;
select report_tuning_task (task_name => 'bad_sql') from dual;
```

This will return a complete report of the results, including findings and recommendations. This report can also be run via OEM.

Step 4: Determine what is to be implemented and execute accordingly.

```
accept_sql_profile (tastk_name => 'bad_sql',
name => 'use_this_profile');
```

This will store the profile in the catalog, which is similar to a stored outline in previous releases of Oracle. So, when using the optimizer in normal mode, when the bad SQL comes along, instead of using the original access path, this new profile will be used instead.

Following that introduction to the SQL Tuning Advisor, it will be helpful to investigate the Automatic Database Diagnostic Monitor (ADDM) in more detail.

Oracle10g Automatic Database Diagnostics Management

Oracle10g offers a number of new advisors to help tune SQL. Prior to Oracle10g, SQL tuning could not be automated and the DBA spent much of their time adding indexes, managing materialized views, changing *init.ora* parameters, testing hints, reading TKPROF output, examining explain plans, and so on.

Oracle10g offers more automatic mechanisms for rudimentary SQL tuning. The AWR tables allow Oracle10g to collect and maintain detailed SQL execution statistics, and this stored data is then used by the Advanced Database Diagnostic Monitor (ADDM, pronounced 'adam').

ADDM attempts to supply a root cause analysis along with recommendations on what to do to fix the problem. An ADDM output might contain information that there is read/write contention, a freelist problem, or the need to use locally managed tablespaces.

More information on how to use ADDM inside Oracle Enterprise Manager is included in Chapter 19 of this book.

The ADDM tool can be accessed either via the command line interface or through the Oracle Enterprise Manager (OEM), but most DBAs prefer the command line interface.

Oracle10g also has the new SQL Tuning Advisor to assist with tuning SQL. This use of this tool is based on changes to the optimizer. The optimizer now has a tuning mode that is used when tuning SQL. The tuning mode causes the optimizer to go through four checks:

- **Analyze SQL Statistics:** Check for missing or stale CBO statistics.

- **SQL Profiling:** Determine additional information that will make a statement run better and save it off for use later , similar to a stored outline.

- **SQL Access Analysis:** Verify that the access path is the most optimal or make recommendations for a better one.

- **SQL Structure Analysis:** Determine if tweaking the SQL will make it run better such as changing a NOT IN to a NOT EXISTS, for example.

ADDM can identify high load SQL statements, which can, in turn, be fed into the SQL Tuning Advisor below. ADDM automatically detects common performance problems, including:

- Excessive I/O

- CPU Bottlenecks

- Contention Issues

- High Parsing

- Lock Contention

- Buffer Sizing Issues

- RAC Tuning Issues

ADDM is invoked every 30 minutes or whenever the DBA specifies. The DBA can begin with ADDM by creating a new snapshot with information populated in *dba_hist_snapshot*:

```
exec dbms_workload_repository.create_snapshot();
```

The following script can be used to view the output of the snapshot, including recommendations:

```
set long 1000000
set pagesize 50000

column get_clob format a80

select dbms_advisor.get_task_report(task_name, 'TEXT', 'ALL') as
first_ADDM_report
from dba_advisor_tasks
where task_id=(
select max(t.task_id)
from dba_advisor_tasks t, dba_advisor_log l
where t.task_id = l.task_id
and t.advisor_name='ADDM'
and l.status= 'COMPLETED');
```

The following is an example of output that ADDM might generate. This result shows that the ADDM detected excessive physical reads and used the *v$db_cache_advice* method to determine that this instance would benefit from a larger data buffer cache::

```
FINDING 3: 5.2% impact (147 seconds)
------------------------------------
The buffer cache was undersized causing significant additional read
I/O.

RECOMMENDATION 1: DB Configuration, 5.2% benefit (147 seconds)
ACTION: Increase SGA target size by increasing the value of
parameter "sga_target" by 24 M.

SYMPTOMS THAT LED TO THE FINDING:
Wait class "User I/O" was consuming significant database time. (5.3%
impact [150 seconds])
```

The following section will reveal some real world SQL tuning Silver Bullets.

Oracle SQL Tuning Silver Bullets

A silver bullet is a SQL tuning technique whereby a single action may have a positive effect on many SQL statements.

The next section will delve into silver bullets as they relate to Oracle SQL tuning and show some techniques that can improve SQL performance.

Using Function-based Indexes (FBI)

In almost all cases, the use of a built-in function like *to_char*, decode, substr, etc. in an SQL query may cause a full-table scan of the target table. To avoid this problem, many Oracle DBAs will create corresponding indexes that make use of function-based indexes. If a corresponding function-based index matches the built-in function of the query, Oracle will be able to service the query with an index range scan thereby avoiding a potentially expensive full-table scan.

The following is a simple example. Suppose the DBA has identified an SQL statement with hundreds of full-table scans against a large table with a built-in function (BIF) in the WHERE clause of the query. After examining the SQL, it is simple to see that it is accessing a customer by converting the customer name to uppercase using the upper BIF.

```
select
   c.customer_name,
   o.order_date
from
   customer c,
   order    o
where
  upper(c.customer_name) = upper(:v1)
and
   c.cust_nbr = o.cust_nbr
;
```

Running the explain plan utility confirms the DBA's suspicion that the upper BIF is responsible for an unnecessary large-table full-table scan.

```
OPTIONS                        OBJECT_NAME                    POSITION
------------------------------ ------------------------------ ----------
SELECT STATEMENT
                                                                  4
  NESTED LOOPS
                                                                  1
    TABLE ACCESS
FULL                           CUSTOMER                           1
    TABLE ACCESS
BY INDEX ROWID                 ORDER                              2
      INDEX
RANGE SCAN                     CUST_NBR_IDX                       1
```

The table access full customer option confirms that this BIF not using the existing index on the customer_name column. Since a matching function-based index may change the execution plan, a function-based index can be added on upper(customer_name).

It can be risky to add indexes to a table because the execution plans of many queries may change as a result. This is not a problem with a function-based index because Oracle will only use this type of index when the query uses a matching BIF.

```
create index
   upper_cust_name_idx
on
   customer
     (upper(customer_name))
  tablespace customer
  pctfree 10
  storage
    (initial 128k next 128k maxextents 2147483645 pctincrease 0);
```

Now, the SQL can be re-explained to show that the full-table scan has been replaced by a index range scan on the new function-based index. For this query, the execution time has been decreased from 45 seconds to less than two seconds.

```
OPERATION
-------------------------------------------------------------------------
OPTIONS                        OBJECT_NAME                    POSITION
------------------------------ ------------------------------ ----------
SELECT STATEMENT
                                                                  5
  NESTED LOOPS
                                                                  1
    TABLE ACCESS
```

```
BY INDEX ROWID              CUSTOMER                          1
    INDEX
RANGE SCAN                  CUST_NBR_IDX                      1
    TABLE ACCESS
BY INDEX ROWID              ORDER                             2
    INDEX
RANGE SCAN                  UPPER_CUST_NAME_IDX               1
```

This simple example serves to illustrate the foremost SQL tuning rule for BIFs. Whenever a BIF is used in a SQL statement, a function-based index must be created.

Silver Bullet

Using Temporary Tables

The prudent use of temporary tables can dramatically improve Oracle SQL performance. The following example from the DBA world can be used to illustrate this concept. In the query that follows, the goal is to identify all users existing within Oracle who have not been granted a role. The query could be formulated as an anti-join with a noncorrelated subquery as shown here:

```
select
    username
from
    dba_users
where
    username NOT IN
        (select grantee from dba_role_privs);
```

This query runs in 18 seconds. These anti-joins can often be replaced with an outer join, but the use of temporary tables offers another option. Now, the same query is rewritten to utilize temporary tables by selecting the distinct values from each table.

```
drop table temp1;
drop table temp2;

create table
    temp1
as
  select
      username
```

```
   from
      dba_users;

create table
   temp2
as
  select distinct
     grantee
   from
     dba_role_privs;

select
   username
from
   temp1
where
   username not in
      (select grantee from temp2);
```

With the addition of temporary tables to hold the intermediate results, this query runs in less than three seconds, a 6x performance increase. Again, it is not easy to quantify the reason for this speed increase, since the DBA views do not map directly to Oracle tables; however, it is clear that temporary table show promise for improving the execution speed of certain types of Oracle SQL queries.

Fixing CBO Statistics

A client had just moved their system into production and was experiencing a serious performance problem. The emergency support DBA found that the *optimizer_mode*=choose, and there was only one table with statistics. The DBA was running cost-based but seemed completely unaware of the necessity to analyze the schema for CBO statistics.

The trouble began when the DBA wanted to know the average row length for a table. After using a Google search to determine that the location of that information was the *dba_tables.avg_row_len* column, it was determined that the values were NULL. The DBA then went to

MetaLink and learned that an analyze table command would fill in the *avg_row_len* column.

CBO will dynamically estimate statistics for all tables with missing statistics, and when using *optimizer_mode*=choose with only one table analyzed, any SQL that touches the table will be optimized as a cost-based query. In this case, a multi-step silver bullet did the trick:

```
alter table customer delete statistics;
exec dbms_stats (…);
```

When the system immediately returned to an acceptable performance level, the DBA realized the importance of providing complete and timely statistics for the CBO using the dbms_stats utility.

Changing CBO SQL Optimizer Parameters

An emergency involving an Oracle 9.0.2 client from Phoenix who was experiencing steadily degrading performance involved a large number of large-table full-table scans which were suspected to be unnecessary. This suspicious information was found by a quick look into *v$sql_plan* view using the plan9i.sql script that is found earlier in this chapter.

The top SQL was extracted from *v$sql* and timed as-is with an index hint. While it was unclear why the CBO was not choosing the index, the query with the index hint ran almost 20x faster. After acting fast and running a script against *v$bh* and *user_indexes*, the DBA discovered that approximately 65 percent of the indexes were currently inside the data buffer cache.

Based on similar systems, the next step was to lower *optimizer_index_cost_adj* to a value of 20 in hopes of forcing the CBO to lower the relative costs of index access.

```
optimizer_index_cost_adj=20
optimizer_index_caching=65
```

Some parameters can be dynamically altered in database versions Oracle9i and newer.

```
alter system set optimizer_index_cost_adj=20 scope = pfile;
```

As a result of these actions, the execution plans for over 350 SQL statements were changed, and the overall system response time was cut in half.

Repairing Obsolete CBO Statistics Gathering

A client called and expressed confusion as to why their system was grinding to a halt. There was a serious degradation in SQL performance after the implementation of partitioned tablespaces in a 16-CPU Solaris 64-bit Oracle 9.0.4 system. The changes in the development and QA instances had been thoroughly tested.

As it turned out, analyze table and analyze index commands had been used to gather the CBO statistics. The *dbms_stats* utility gathers partition-wise statistics. There was not time to pull a deep sample collection, so a *dbms_stats* was issued with a ten percent sample size. It is parallelized with 15 parallel processes to speed-up the statistics collection:

```
exec dbms_stats.gather_schema_stats( -
   ownname          => 'SAPR4', -
   options          => 'GATHER AUTO', -
   estimate_percent => 10, -
   method_opt       => 'for all columns size repeat', -
   degree           => 15 -
)
```

In less than 30 minutes, the improved CBO statistics tripled the performance of the entire database.

Removing full-table scans with Oracle Text

One serious SQL performance problem occurs when the SQL LIKE operator is used to find a string within a large Oracle table column such as VARCHAR(2000), CLOB, or BLOB:

```
select stuff from bigtab where text_column like '%ipod%';
select stuff from bigtab where full_name like '%JONES';
```

Since standard Oracle cannot index into a large column, their LIKE queries cause full-table scans, and Oracle must examine every row in the table, even when the result set is very small. The following problems can be caused by unnecessary full-table scans:

- Large-table full-table scans increase the load on the disk I/O subsystem

- Small-table full-table scans(in the data buffer cause high consistent gets and drive up CPU consumption

The Oracle*Text utility, also called Oracle ConText and Oracle Intermedia, allows parsing through a large text column and index on the words within the column. Unlike ordinary b-tree or bitmap indexes, Oracle context ctxcat and ctxrule indexes are not updated as content is changed. Since most standard Oracle databases will use the ctxcat index with standard relational tables, the DBA must decide on a refresh interval.

As a result, Oracle Text indexes are only useful for removing full-table scans when the tables are largely read-only and/or the end-users do not mind not having 100% search recall:

- The target table is relatively static (e.g. nightly batch updates)

- The end-users would not mind missing the latest row data

Oracle Text works with traditional data columns as well as with MS-Word docs and Adobe PDF files that are stored within Oracle. Oracle Text has several index types:

- CTXCAT Indexes: A CTXCAT index is best for smaller text fragments that must be indexed along with other standard relational data (VARCHAR2).

- WHERE CATSEARCH(text_column, 'ipod')> 0;

- CONTEXT Indexes: The CONTEXT index type is used to index large amounts of text such as Word, PDF, XML, HTML or plain text documents.

- WHERE CONTAINS(test_column, 'ipod', 1) > 0

- CTXRULE Indexes: A CTXRULE index can be used to build document classification applications.

These types of indexes allow users to replace the old-fashioned SQL LIKE syntax with CONTAINS or CATSEARCH SQL syntax.

When the query is executed with the new index, the full-table scan is replaced with an index scan, thereby greatly reducing execution speed and improving hardware stress:

```
Execution Plan
--------------------------------------------------------
   0        SELECT STATEMENT Optimizer=FIRST_ROWS
   1    0     SORT (ORDER BY)
   2    1       TABLE ACCESS (BY INDEX ROWID) OF 'BIGTAB'
   3    2         DOMAIN INDEX OF 'TEXT-COLUMN_IDX'
```

Oracle Text Index Re-synchronization

Since rebuilding an Oracle Text index with CONTEXT, CTXCAT, or CTXRULE requires a full-table scan and lots of internal parsing, it is not practical to use triggers for instantaneous index updates.

Updating Oracle Text indexes is easy, and they can be scheduled using *dbms_job* or the Oracle10g *dbms_scheduler* utility package: Oracle text provides a CTX_DDL package with the *sync_index and optimize_index* procedures:

```
SQL> EXEC CTX_DDL.SYNC_INDEX('text_column_idx');
SQL> EXEC CTX_DDL.OPTIMIZE_INDEX('text_column_idx','FULL');
```

For example, if a nightly *dbms_scheduler* job is created to call *sync_index*, the index will be refreshed, but the structure will become suboptimal over time. Oracle recommends that the *optimize_index* package be used periodically to rebuild the whole index from scratch. Index optimization can be performed in three modes: FAST; FULL; or TOKEN.

In sum, the Oracle Text indexes are great for removing unnecessary full-table scans for static Oracle tables, and they can reduce I/O by several orders of magnitude. This will greatly improving overall SQL performance.

The following conclusion section includes a summary of the most important techniques in time-series SQL tuning.

Conclusion

This chapter has provided an overview of SQL tuning in Oracle10g, with a focus on the new 10g SQL tuning features. The main points of this chapter include:

- The goals of SQL tuning involve verifying the best execution plan for any statements.

- The best execution plan is either the plan that starts returning rows the fastest or the plan that executes the query with the smallest resource consumption.

- Oracle10g now automatically collects and refreshes schema statistics using the *dbms_stats* package.

- Histogram collection can now be easily automated, and some of these databases choose to put histograms on all key columns to improve the accuracy of table join order.

- One common cause of suboptimal SQL is missing materialized view and indexes, especially function-based indexes.

- The SQLTuning Advisor and SQLAccess Advisor provide an easy method for identifying and tuning SQL with suboptimal execution plans.

- Oracle provides a wealth of hints to change the optimizer execution plans.

- SQL Profiles are a great improvement over the stored outlines of the Optimizer Plan Stability.

- The new dba_hist tables contain a wealth of historical information about historical SQL execution statistics.

- Time-series analysis of object usage within SQL can yield important insights into holistic tuning for SQL statements.

The next chapter will introduce the new Automated Session History (ASH) tables and show how ASH can be used to quickly identify and tune resource bottlenecks.

Oracle10g Wait Event Tuning with AWR and ASH

Fighting excessive waits requires dexterity and skill!

The Oracle Wait Event Model

The Oracle wait event model was originally introduced in Oracle7 and eventually became a popular tuning method despite the complex and cumbersome wait exposure interfaces.

The Oracle wait event interface evolves with every new version of Oracle database software and provides DBAs with valuable information or insights about where time is consumed by SQL statements, sessions, and the data base as a whole. Wait event information is gathered by the Oracle MMON background process, stored in intermediate *x$* structures in a circular SGA buffer, and later transferred to Oracle10g *dba_hist* tables.

Prior to Oracle10g, capturing wait event information was a cumbersome process involving the setting of special events like 10046 and the reading of complex trace dumps as shown below:

```
PARSING IN CURSOR #1 len=42 dep=0 uid=47 oct=3 lid=47
                       tim=2941832446 hv=1811837456 ad='69b05900'
select *
from sapr3.vbap
where vlelm < sysdate
END OF STMT
PARSE #1:c=0,e=870,p=0,cr=0,cu=0,mis=1,r=0,
        dep=0,og=0,tim=2941832432
BINDS #1:
 bind 0: dty=2 mxl=22(22) mal=00 scl=00 pre=00
         oacflg=03 oacfl2=0 size=24 offset=0
   bfp=04af96b8 bln=22 avl=01 flg=05
   value=0
EXEC #1:c=0,e=950,p=0,cr=0,cu=0,mis=0,r=0,dep=0,
        og=4,tim=2941835605
WAIT #1: nam='SQL*Net message to client' ela= 6
         p1=1111838976 p2=1 p3=0
FETCH #1:c=0,e=148,p=0,cr=3,cu=0,mis=0,r=1,dep=0,
         og=4,tim=2941836146
WAIT #1: nam='SQL*Net message from client' ela= 543
         p1=1111838976 p2=1 p3=0
WAIT #1: nam='SQL*Net message to client' ela= 4
         p1=1111838976 p2=1 p3=0
```

The new Automated Session History (ASH) tables revolutionized Oracle wait event tuning. Earlier versions of Oracle provided special views called *v$session_wait* and *v$system_event* that contained detailed information about the wait state for ongoing Oracle transactions. This chapter explores how Oracle waits can be analyzed to look for system-wide bottlenecks and individual objects that experience wait issues.

Get the proper ASH license!

The ASH, AWR, and ADDM are separate components of the Oracle Enterprise Manager Diagnostic Pack which must be licensed as a separate option.

Fortunately, Oracle10g has simplified the way that wait event information is captured and there are a wealth of new v$ and wrh$ views relating to Oracle wait events as shown in Figure 16.1.

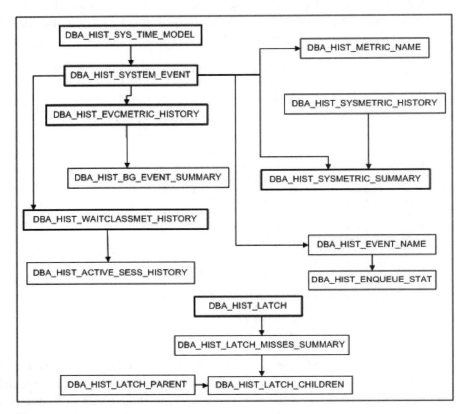

Figure 16.1: *Some common ASH dba_hist views of Oracle event data*

Oracle10g has introduced some new wait events, and the 10g database kernel now captures statistics on more than 800 specific wait events. These new wait events are the result of Oracle breaking out their latch waits into their individual components and breaking-out enqueue waits, or locks, into a finer level of granularity.

Don't lose wait data!

Whenever an AWR snapshot is taken, the current contents of the *x$* wait structures are transferred to the corresponding *dba_hist* tables. Since the wait information is collected in a circular SGA buffer, wait information may be lost if this buffer rolls over between the AWR snapshot interval.

After the *x$* structures are materialized in the *v$active_session_history* and *v$session_wait_history* views, a new AWR snapshot transfers and aggregates the events into corresponding *dba_hist_active_sess_history* and other dba_hist tables. Table 16.1 below shows some of the most important Oracle10g ASH wait event tables:

dba_hist_active_session_history	dba_hist_active_session_history_bl
dba_hist_bg_event_summary	dba_hist_event_name
dba_hist_metric_name	dba_hist_sessmetric_history
dba_hist_sys_time_model	dba_hist_sys_time_model_bl
dba_hist_sysmetric_history	dba_hist_sysmetric_summary
dba_hist_sysstat	dba_hist_sysstat_bl
dba_hist_system_event	dba_hist_system_event_bl
dba_hist_waitclassmetric_history	dba_hist_waitstat
dba_hist_waitstat_bl	

Table 16.1: *Oracle10g wait event dba_hist tables*

The following section begins with a quick review of Oracle wait events in order to assist users' understanding of how they can help identify and tune bottlenecks in the database.

Collecting ASH Wait Information

Oracle DBAs can use the ASH tables for both real time and historical trend analysis, but the real value is in time-series trend analysis. However, ASH views such as *v$active_session_history* and *v$session_wait_history* only report sessions' histories for a short, sliding period of time in a SGA buffer. The v$ views are good for real-time monitoring using OEM, but they are not as good for showing wait-related performance trends over a long time interval.

With Oracle10g database, the AWR that holds ASH history is sampled every second and stored inside x$ structures that are materialized by the *v$active_session_history* and *v$session_wait_history* views and stored inside a circular SGA buffer. When an AWR snapshot is taken, only the current session wait information that exists at that precise moment is transferred from the *v$active_session_history* in-memory view into the persistent *dba_hist_active_sess_history* table.

The default collection retention for AWR data is only seven days, but the retention period can be increased by using the new dbms package called *dbms_workload_repository.modify_snapshot_settings*. Many Oracle DBAs will increase the storage of detail information over longer time periods.

Once transferred to AWR tables, the data can be used for longer periods of time and the length of these time periods can be adjusted by the DBA, as needed. In order to track historical data longer than a few minutes or seconds in earlier Oracle versions, the DBA would have to increase the retention period for the ASH tables. This will change the retention period and collection frequency, thereby providing users with longer time periods of data:

```
BEGIN
  DBMS_WORKLOAD_REPOSITORY. modify_snapshot_settings (
    retention => 43200,        -- Minutes (= 30 Days).
    interval  => 30);          -- Minutes.
END;
/
```

In the above script, the retention period is indicated as 30 days (43200 min) while the interval between each snapshot is 30 min. Changes to these settings will be apparent if the *dba_hist_wr_control* view is queried after this procedure is executed.

Typically, the retention period should capture at least one complete workload cycle for the database. Some databases have hourly cycles, daily cycles and monthly processing cycles.

The retention argument of the *dbms_workload_repository. modify_snapshot_settings* procedure specifies how long all of the AWR data is retained, and many shops will keep at least two calendar years in order to capture repeating monthly workload cycles.

For wait event tuning, the *interval* parameter is the most important. If the interval is longer than the amount of real-time session wait information stored in the circular buffer for the *v$active_session_history* and *v$session_wait_history* views, some wait session data will be lost.

The next section will step back and explore why wait event tuning is a useful tool for Oracle tuning. As a reminder, there is no single Oracle tuning technique, SQL tuning, parameter tuning, ratio tuning, etc., that does it all, and wait event tuning is just another weapon in the Oracle10g tuning arsenal.

Why Wait Event Tuning for Oracle?

Wait event tuning has always been mysterious because the wait events happen so fast that it is often difficult to see what's happening without taking a detailed task dump. Now with ASH, not only can specific details about individual sessions, SQL statements, and users be seen, but wait information can be tracked over periods of time, revealing the all important signatures that help schedule just-in-time resources to relieve instance related wait bottlenecks.

Time-based wait tuning is especially useful for tracking changes to SQL execution over time as well as database-wide stress. The Oracle ASH tables can be used to show trends in wait event over long time periods, and fluctuations in waits can often provide useful information.

A top-down approach starts at a high level and shows scripts that can be used to track system wide events and show events for background processes. Time-based wait event analysis for Oracle can be broken down into several areas:

- External wait event analysis: The advent of the new mainframe-like SMP servers means that servers may share hardware resources with dozens of other applications and databases. These external resources demand server resources, such as RAM, CPU, and disk channels, which can affect Oracle waits, and the ASH tables provide insights into external network waits, such as SQL*Net waits, and disk waits such as db file sequential and scattered read waits.

- Internal wait event analysis: Oracle internal mechanisms, such as buffer busy waits and latch waits, can change over time, depending on the overall database load. Time-series analysis with the ASH tables allows the DBA to find the cause of internal bottlenecks, even after the transaction has completed.

- Session-level wait event analysis: Oracle resources associated with a session can be traced to the exact external or internal wait event.

- SQL event analysis: In most OLTP systems, the same SQL statements may execute thousands of times per hour. Because SQL is the interface between applications and Oracle, tracing waits on an SQL statement over time can be especially useful.

When running the system-wide time-based wait event scripts, the DBA will be able to identify areas where the database is spending most of its time waiting. Before custom ASH scripts are presented, the following section provides a quick tour of the Oracle10g OEM as well as information on how it materializes the information from the ASH component.

Active Session History in Enterprise Manager

Together, the AWR and ASH metrics form the foundation for a complete Oracle tuning framework, and the Enterprise Manager provides a great tool for visualizing the bottlenecks. Now that the underlying wait event collection mechanism has been explained, it is time to explore how OEM gives an intelligent window into this critical Oracle tuning information.

Before the use of OEM to identify a performance issue is examined, it must be noted that the AWR and ASH information can be used inside OEM to create customized exception alerts. Even when the DBA is not watching, OEM can send an e-mail warning about any impending performance issue. Figure 16.2 shows the ASH alert threshold screen:

▼ Wait Bottlenecks	None
Active Sessions	Not Set
Active Sessions Using CPU	Not Set
Active Sessions Using CPU (%)	Not Set
Active Sessions Waiting: I/O	Not Set
Active Sessions Waiting: I/O (%)	Not Set
Active Sessions Waiting: Other	Not Set
Active Sessions Waiting: Other (%)	Not Set
Average Instance CPU (%)	Not Set
CPU Time (sec)	Not Set
Wait Time (%)	Not Set
Wait Time (sec)	Not Set

Figure 16.2: *OEM ASH wait bottleneck metrics*

This is an especially important screen for customizing OEM alerts because thresholds can be set based on changes with either absolute of delta-based metrics. For example, it may be desirable to have OEM alert the DBA when the following session metrics are exceeded:

- Active Sessions Waiting: I/O: Alert when there are more than 500 Active sessions waiting on I/O

- Active Sessions Waiting: I/O (%): Alert when active sessions waiting on I/O increases by more than 10%

- Wait Time (sec): Alert when wait time exceeds two seconds

- Wait Time (%): Alert when wait time increases by more than 25%

The new OEM also allows the viewing of session wait information at the metric level. For example, if OEM informs the DBA that the major wait event in the database is related to concurrency, such as locks, latches, pins, etc. The DBA can drill down on the concurrency link to go to the OEM Active sessions waiting screen as shown in Figure 16.3.

Active Sessions Waiting: Concurrency

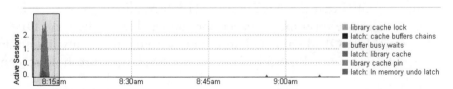

Figure 16.3: *The OEM display for active sessions waiting on concurrency*

This display is also a learning aid because OEM lists all of the sources of concurrency waits, including library cache lock, latch, and *buffer busy waits*, and it also displays the values associated with each concurrency component. When one double clicks on the chosen snapshot, OEM delivers a summary histogram of the response time components for the top ten SQL statements and top ten sessions that were identified during the AWR snapshot as shown in Figure 16.4 below.

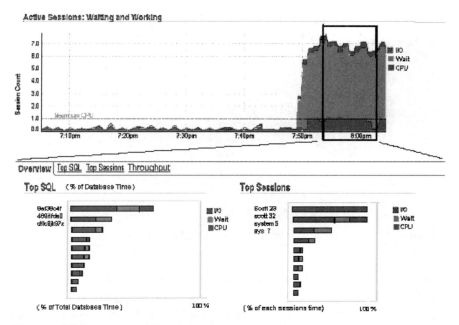

Figure 16.4: *The OEM top ten SQL and top ten session response time component display*

This visual display of summary information allows the quick identification of the most resource intensive tasks. In addition, one can instantly see if the main response time component is I/O, CPU, or Oracle internal wait events. Oracle performance investigations that used to take hours are now completed in a matter of seconds.

While this functionality of OEM is amazing in its own right, Oracle10g has taken the AWR model beyond the intelligent display of performance metrics. Using true Artificial Intelligence (AI), Oracle Enterprise Manager (OEM) now has a built-in interface to the Automatic Database Diagnostic Monitor (ADDM), and the intelligent SQL Tuning Advisor, both of which are explored in other chapters.

The main OEM performance screen displays a summary of session wait time server side components as shown in Figure 16.6. Understanding the components involved in total response time can give huge insight into the root cause of a performance bottleneck.

Active Sessions

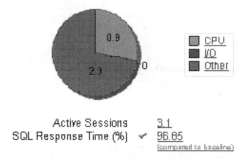

Active Sessions   3.1
SQL Response Time (%) ✓ 96.85
(compared to baseline)

Figure 16.5: *Active session response time OEM summary display*

In Figure 16.5, there are currently 3.1 active sessions with approximately one-third of the response time being consumed in CPU activities, which is a very common profile for 10g databases with large data caches. The figure also includes the important SQL Response Time (%) delta metric that displays marginal changes on overall SQL performance.

The OEM interface to ASH also allows the DBA to drill down and view details on any of the active Oracle session. Figure 16.6 shows the hyperlinks to detailed session statistics, wait events, open cursors and locks associated with the task.

Session Details: SID 42

Collected From Target

General | Statistics Wait Events Open Cursors Locks

Serial Number **52801**	Logged On Since **2003-08-13 08:22:58.0**
Current Status **INACTIVE**	Last Activity On **2003-08-13 09:09:57.0**
Wait Event **IDLE**	Connection Type **DEDICATED**
OS Server Process ID **2445**	SQL ID **No currently executing SQL**
DB User Name **OLAF**	
Resource Consumer Group **0**	

Application Information

Program **JDBC Thin Client**
Module **Oracle Enterprise Manager**
Command **UNKNOWN**

Client Information

OS Client Process ID **1234**
OS User Name **0**
Terminal **0**

Figure 16.6: *Session level detail display in OEM*

Active Session History in WISE

Oracle10g OEM has limited functionality, especially for plotting and trending of Oracle wait event information, and WISE can easily relieve this burden.

Figure 16.7 shows the WISE screen for trending and plotting Oracle wait events. WISE also allows the DBA to monitor, in real time, ASH wait statistics as shown in Figure 16.8 below:

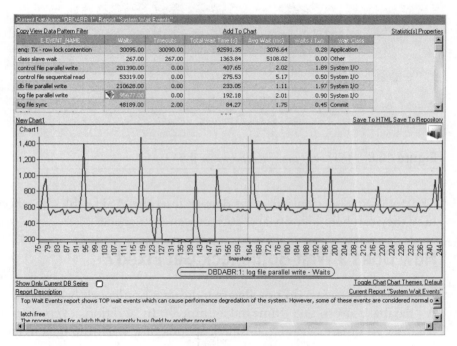

Figure 16.7: *AWR Wait Events plotting in WISE.*

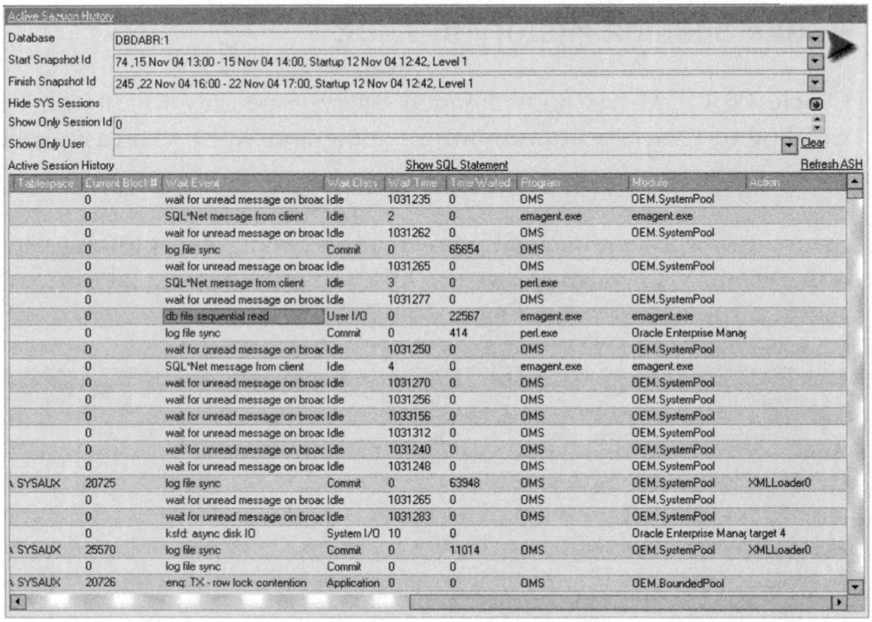

Figure 16.8: *ASH real time monitoring in WISE.*

The following section will dive deeper into the ASH tables to show how they can help identify and correct wait bottlenecks.

How Does a Wait Bottleneck Get Fixed?

High waits on events do not always indicate a bottleneck or a problem. As database users say: "time takes time." In addition, every Oracle database, no matter how well-tuned, spends time performing activities. High waits may indicate a bottleneck, but some waits are a normal part of database operations.

In general, the system wide wait events will show where the database spends most of its time. For example, high waits on *db file sequential reads* events may indicate a disk bottleneck, but the average disk queue length for each disk spindle must be checked to be sure that these waits are abnormal.

In one case, an Oracle shop ran the script for system-wide wait events and discovered that their RAID-5 configuration was causing a huge amount of disk enqueues. The shop reorganized their disk to RAID 0+1 and experienced a 3x performance improvement for the whole database. The following is just a small sample of some common wait bottlenecks:

- SQL*Net waits: High SQL*Net waits could be due to poor encapsulation of SQL statements within the application. For example, a screen may need data from six different tables, and there is much less network traffic and database overhead if all of the information for an online screen is captured in a single trip to the database. High SQL*Net waits can also signify an error in the application programming logic or a serious network problem.

- *parallel query dequeue waits*: The default degree of parallelism for database objects need to be checked, and parallelism at the system level should be turned off using specific *parallel* hints. The value of *parallel_threads_per_cpu* should be checked and adjusted to reduce automatic parallel query and its influence on the CBO.

- *db file scattered reads* waits: These are caused by competing demands for large-table full-table scans and are the most common in data warehouse and decision support systems.

- *db file sequential reads* waits: These are sometimes due to segment header contention on hot rows or indexes, but it could also be due to disk-level contention. The first step in this process is to increase the number of freelists on the indexes. If the waits persist, the offending index should be striped across multiple disk spindles. The DBA should check for segment header contention/waits on index headers or create multiple segment header blocks for stressed indexes using *alter index xxx storage(freelists 4)*. The DBA could also distribute heavy impact tables and indexes onto a faster disk or stripe the rows across more data b-locks by setting a high *pctfree* for a table and reorganizing the table.

These are very general wait conditions, but they can sometimes be fixed by changing parameters or object characteristics.

System-wide Wait Event Tuning

Sometimes, a major external problem such as bad disk RAID can cause the entire database to run slowly, so it is always a good idea to start with a listing of the AWR top five wait event listing. Detailed wait event tuning will not do much good until any database-wide issues have been fixed. Common database-wide wait bottleneck issues may include network, CPU, disk and instance bottlenecks. The following sections will provide a closer look at using the top five timed event list from the AWR report to search for global wait issues:

Network Bottleneck

A slow or untuned network can be a nightmare. Network overload can also be caused by Oracle TNS issues or by an inefficient application that makes too many trips to Oracle to fetch screen data.

Network bottlenecks are very common in distributed systems and those with high network traffic. They are manifested as SQL*Net wait events, like this example:

```
Top 5 Timed Events
~~~~~~~~~~~~~~~~~~~                                   % Total
Event                       Waits     Time (cs)  Wt Time
-------------------------  --------   --------   --------
SQL*Net more data to client 3,914,935 9,475,372    99.76
db file sequential read     1,367,659     6,129      .06
db file parallel write          7,582     5,001      .05
rdbms ipc reply                    26     4,612      .05
db file scattered read         16,886     2,446      .03
```

CPU Bottleneck

A CPU-bound database may be due to a real overload of the CPU banks, in which case the problem can be remedied with more or faster processors. High CPU consumption can also be due to untuned SQL causing excessive logical I/O in the form of consistent gets or by contention within the shared pool, such as the total lack of SQL bind variables. The following top 5 events list shows a CPU-bound database.

```
Top 5 Timed Events
~~~~~~~~~~~~~~~~~~                                 % Total
Event                       Waits    Time (s) Ela Time
------------------------- --------- ----------- --------
CPU time                    4,851      4,042     55.76
db file sequential read     1,968      1,997     27.55
log file sync             299,097        369      5.08
db file scattered read     53,031        330      4.55
log file parallel write   302,680        190      2.62
```

In this example, it is easy to see that this system is clearly CPU-bound, with 55% of the processing time being spent in the CPU. One can also infer from the wait time that this server is experiencing CPU enqueues, where multiple processes must queue up to be dispatched by the CPUs. As a general rule, a server is CPU-bound when the number of processes in the execution queue exceeds the number of CPUs on the server.

Disk Bottleneck

A suboptimal RAID configuration can make even a well-tuned Oracle database slow to a crawl. The following example shows an I/O bound database:

```
Top 5 Timed Events
~~~~~~~~~~~~~~~~~~                               % Total
Event                     Waits     Time (s)  Ela Time
------------------------- --------- ----------- --------
db file sequential read     2,598      7,146     48.54
db file scattered read     25,519      3,246     22.04
library cache load lock       673      1,363      9.26
CPU time                               1,154      7.83
log file parallel write    19,157        837      5.68
```

Excessive *db file sequential read* waits on an OLTP database might indicate a suboptimal disk subsystem or configuration issues with the disk array. High I/O waits on *db file scatter read* waits associated with large-table full-table scans may not always indicate a problem, but they are most commonly found on these kinds of databases:

- Data warehouse and Decision Support applications, even with materialized views

- 32-bit Oracle systems with SGAs of less than 1.5 gigabytes

- Databases that do not have enough buffer cache space to cache their working set of frequently referenced objects.

Instance Bottleneck

Suboptimal settings for *init.ora* parameters, such as *optimizer_mode*, *optimizer_index_cost_adj*, *cursor_sharing*, etc., can precipitate database-wide wait problems. It is also possible to see object-level waits caused by suboptimal settings for *freelists*, *freelist_groups*, and other object parameters.

Now that holistic wait exploration has been covered, it is time to explore the new Oracle10g dba_hist views that are used to create time-series performance reports, both manually and within Enterprise Manager.

Not All Events Are Created Equal

The information contained in the AWR is substantial and over 800 distinct wait events are tracked. To facilitate the use of these events, they have been grouped into 12 areas called Wait Classes. These classes are listed in Table 16.2.

ADMINISTRATIVE WAIT CLASS EVENTS	APPLICATION WAIT CLASS EVENTS
Cluster	Commit
Concurrency	Configuration
Idle	Network
Other	Scheduler
System I/O	User I/O

Table 16.2: *Oracle10g wait event classes*

More detailed ASH information on waits that are occurring in a specific wait class is available in other areas of the repository. The following script lists the specific wait events that are part of each wait class.

```
break on wait_class skip 1

column event_name format a40
column wait_class format a20

select
  wait_class,
  event_name
from
  dba_hist_event_name
order by
  wait_class,
  event_name;
```

With over 800 events, this could be a bit overwhelming, so it may be advisable to filter this query with a WHERE clause to restrict the output to the wait class that of the most interest to the DBA. Some of the events for the System I/O and User I/O are shown below as an example:

```
WAIT_CLASS      EVENT_NAME
----------      ------------------------------
System I/O      db file parallel write
                io done
                kfk: async disk IO
                ksfd: async disk IO
                log file parallel write
                log file sequential read
                log file single write
                recovery read

User I/O        BFILE read
                buffer read retry
                db file parallel read
                db file scattered read
                db file sequential read
                db file single write
```

The listing above is useful if the AWR top five timed events report indicates a significant amount of time spent on I/O related waits.

One also has to filter out wait events that are not helpful to the tuning effort. In practice, idle events can be filtered out by adding where *wait_class* <> 'Idle' in the ASH queries. Table 16.3 below shows all system idle wait events that usually have no meaningful information in Oracle bottleneck analysis. One exception might be a batch program where idle events may indicate that the program is doing something

---

large which makes RDBMS wait. SQL*Net message to client waits almost always indicates network contention.

dispatcher timer	lock element cleanup
Null event	parallel query dequeue wait
parallel query idle wait - Slaves	pipe get
PL/SQL lock timer	pmon timer
rdbms ipc message	slave wait
smon timer	SQL*Net break/reset to client
SQL*Net message from client	SQL*Net message to client
SQL*Net more data to client	virtual circuit status

Table 16.3: *Oracle Idle events*

The next section will provide a look inside the most useful ASH tables for time-series wait event tuning.

Inside the Real-time *v$* Wait Events

The foundation concept of the ASH architecture is called the time model, and Oracle10g has introduced several important wait event v$ views. Table 16.4 below shows some v$ equivalents to dba_hist views.

v$ VIEW	dba_hist VIEW
v$active_sess_hist	dba_hist_active_sess_history
v$sys_time_model	dba_hist_sys_time_model
v$active_session_history	dba_hist_active_sess_history
v$event_histogram	No equivalent DBA view

Table 16.4: *Oracle v$ equivalents to ASH wait event tables*

The main components of OWE interface are the dynamic performance views: *v$session_wait*, and *v$session_event* as shown in Figure 16.9.

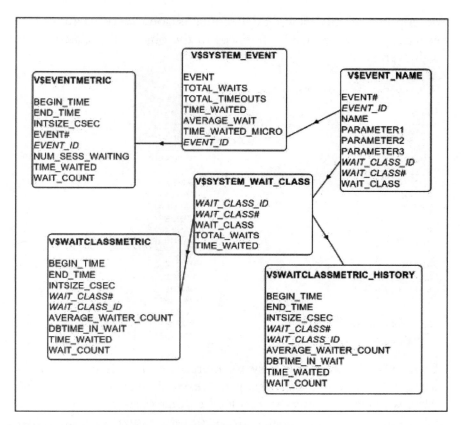

Figure 16.9: *The v$ event structures in Oracle10g*

These *v$* views are in-memory structures that feed data to the ASH tables which provide time-series wait event information.

The ASH samples for wait events every second and tracks the waits in the new *v$active_sess_hist* view. Before looking into the *wrh$* and ASH tables, it will be useful to take a quick tour of the important *v$* wait event views.

Inside *v$session_wait*

The *v$session_wait* view displays information about wait events for which active sessions are currently waiting. The following is the

---

description of this view, and it contains some very useful columns, especially the P1 and P2 references to the objects associated with the wait events.

```
SQL> desc v$session_wait

 Name                            Null?    Type
 ------------------------------- -------- ------------
 SID                                      NUMBER
 SEQ#                                     NUMBER
 EVENT                                    VARCHAR2(64)
 P1TEXT                                   VARCHAR2(64)
 P1                                       NUMBER
 P1RAW                                    RAW(4)
 P2TEXT                                   VARCHAR2(64)
 P2                                       NUMBER
 P2RAW                                    RAW(4)
 P3TEXT                                   VARCHAR2(64)
 P3                                       NUMBER
 P3RAW                                    RAW(4)
 WAIT_CLASS_ID                            NUMBER
 WAIT_CLASS#                              NUMBER
 WAIT_CLASS                               VARCHAR2(64)
 WAIT_TIME                                NUMBER
 SECONDS_IN_WAIT                          NUMBER
 STATE                                    VARCHAR2(19)
```

Using *v$session_wait*, it is easy to interpret each wait event parameter using the corresponding descriptive text columns for that parameter. Also, wait class columns were added so that various wait events could be grouped into the related areas of processing such as network, application, idle, concurrency, etc.

This view provides the DBA with a dynamic snapshot of the wait event picture for specific sessions. Each wait event contains other parameters that provide additional information about the event. For example, if a particular session waits for a *buffer busy waits* event, the database object causing this wait event can easily be determined:

```
select
   username,
   event,
   p1,
   p2
from
   v$session_wait
where
   sid = 74;
```

The output of this query for a particular session with SID 74 might look like this:

```
USERNAME    EVENT                SID   P1   P2
---------   -----------------    ---   --   ---
PCS         buffer busy waits     74    4   155
```

Columns P1 and P2 allow the DBA to determine file and block numbers that caused this wait event. The query below retrieves the object name that owns data block 155, the value of P2 above:

```
select
  segment_name,
  segment_type
from
  dba_extents
where
  file_id = 4
and
  155 between
  (block_id and block_id + blocks - 1);
```

```
SEGMENT_NAME                      SEGMENT_TYPE
------------------------------    ---------------
orders                            TABLE
```

The above output shows that the table named orders caused this wait event, a very useful clue when tuning the SQL within this session.

Inside *v$session_event*

The *v$session_event* view shows the cumulative time that each session has spent waiting for a particular event to complete. Unlike the *v$session_wait* view, the v$session_event view collects aggregate wait information, organized by System ID (SID) and a named event.

```
SQL> desc v$session_event
```

```
Name               Null?     Type
-----------------  --------  ------------
SID                          NUMBER
EVENT                        VARCHAR2(64)
TOTAL_WAITS                  NUMBER
TOTAL_TIMEOUTS               NUMBER
TIME_WAITED                  NUMBER
```

```
AVERAGE_WAIT              NUMBER
MAX_WAIT                  NUMBER
```

It will be useful to look at examples of how the *v$session_event* view might be used in real life. In this example, end users have started complaining about experiencing large delays when running a production application.

In some ERP applications (Oracle Applications, SAP), a single user account is used to connect to the database. In these cases, the DBA can issue the following statement to determine the particular event application for which the sessions are waiting:

```
select
   se.event,
   sum(se.total_waits),
   sum(se.total_timeouts),
   sum(se.time_waited/100) time_waited
from
   v$session_event se,
   v$session       sess
where
   sess.username = 'SAPR3'
and
   sess.sid = se.sid
group by
   se.event
order by 2 DESC;
```

The output of this script might look like the following:

```
                 Waits for user SAPR3

                             SUM   SUM              TIME
EVENT                       WAITS  TIMEOUTS        WAITED
-------------------------   -----  ---------       -----
SQL*Net message to client   7,824     0              .06
SQL*Net message from client 7,812     0       312,969.73
db file sequential read     3,199     0            16.23
SQL*Net more data to client   590     0              .08
SQL*Net break/reset to client 418     0               .2
direct path read              328     0              .01
SQL*Net more data from client  78     0             3.29
latch free                     62    10              .08
db file scattered read         56     0              .75
log file sync                  47     0              .96
direct path write              32     0               .4
file open                      32     0                0
library cache pin              13     0                0
log file switch completion      3     0              .53
```

From the listing above, the DBA can conclude that end users spend most of their wait time waiting on the event SQL*Net message from client. This may indicate that there is some network-related issue causing clients too much wait time to send data to the database server.

Unlike these old-fashioned *v$session* and *v$session_wait* accumulation views where waits can only be seen at the exact instant when they occurred, the new *v$session_wait_history* and *v$sys_time_model* views allow Oracle10g to capture system waits details in a time-series mode. The following section will provide a look at these new ASH table structures and see how time series wait event tuning gives unprecedented insights.

Using ASH for Time-series Wait Tuning

One of the most important areas of Oracle10g wait event tuning is the Oracle10g Active Session History (ASH). ASH data is visualized through the *v$active_sess_hist* view and the *wrh$active_session_history* tables.

At a basic level, the ASH stores the history of a recent session's activity and facilitates the analysis of the system performance at the current time. The ASH is designed as a rolling buffer in memory, and earlier information is overwritten when needed. The ASH uses the memory of the SGA.

Another innovation is the ability to use the new Oracle10g hash key for tracking session identification. This new hash key allows the tracking of common session processes and allows inter-call session tracking in cases such as OCI session bouncing where each call to Oracle has a different session ID.

The information presented in the following sections will begin with an overview of the *dba_hist* views, and then show examples of custom Oracle10g performance exception reports that can be easily generated from these views with SQL*Plus. More details on these ASH tables are available in the Oracle10g Database Reference Manual, where they are fully documented.

Once the AWR table data and inter-table relationships between AWR and performance metrics have been explained thoroughly, it will be important to understand how the wrh$ tables are used as input to the Automatic Memory Manager (AMM), the Automatic Database Diagnostic Monitor (ADDM), and the SQL Tuning Advisor.

The creation of the AWR and the ASH provides a complete repository for diagnosing and fixing any Oracle performance issue. The AWR provides the foundation for sophisticated performance analysis including exception reporting, trend analysis, correlation analysis, hypothesis testing and data mining. A good place to start is with time-series wait event analysis using the Oracle ASH tables.

Oracle's Graham Wood, inventor of ASH, notes in his presentation titled Sifting through the ASHes: Performance Analysis with the Oracle 10g Active Session History:

Internally, Oracle stores ASH data in ASH RAM buffers within the shared pool before writing the data to the ASH data files.

```
select * from v$sgastat where name like 'ASH buffers';

POOL          NAME                       BYTES
------------  -------------------------  ----------
shared pool   ASH buffers                  65011712
```

The ASH samples every 10 seconds and then writes every one of ten samples to the *dba_hist_active_sess_history* table.

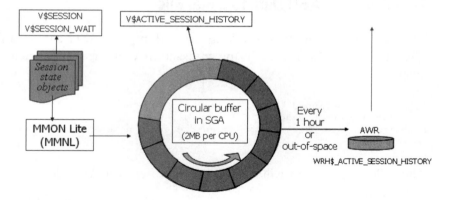

Figure 16.10: *Oracle's ASH process*

- Where is time being spent?

- What events were taking most time?

- What was a session doing?

- What does a SQL statement wait for?

ASH reports on active, non-idle sessions such as sessions waiting on a non-idle event, and this might be a small portion of the Oracle sessions. The design goal of ASH is to hold one hour of activity information in memory. The ASH component keeps this data:

- Wait event detail

- Session details

- SQL details such as the execution plan and step costs

- Tables and indexes like Object#, File#, and Block#

- Application information such as program, module, action, and client_id

Tip - Dumping ASH Data to a Flat File

The following commands are designed to dump the ASH data to a flat file. This is useful for analyzing transaction waits at a super-detailed level:

```
SQL>oradebug setmypid
SQL>oradebug dump ashdump 10
SQL>alter session set events 'immediate trace name ashdump level
10';
```

The following section will look at scripts to extract ASH details about current transactions.

Display SQL Wait Details

Before putting it all together, some of the ASH data will be examined to see how combining the scripts provides a complete picture. The following ASH script can be used to find details about the most active SQL in past 10 minutes:

```
col c1 heading "invocation|count"    format 9,999
col c2 heading "percentage|of|load" format 99

select
   sql_id, count(*)                          c1,
   round(count(*)/sum(count(*)) over (), 2) c2
from
   v$active_session_history
where
   sample_time > sysdate - 1/24/60
and
   session_type <> 'BACKGROUND'
group by
   sql_id
order by
   count(*) desc;


SQL_ID          COUNTS    PCTLOAD
-------------   ---------- ----------
25wtt4ycbtkyz      456      32.95
7umwqvcy7tusf      123       8.89
01vunx6d35khz      119       8.6
bdyq2uph07cmp      102       7.37
```

In this example, the script's output shows that the *sql_id* of 25wtt4ycbtkyz was the most active SQL during the past 10 minutes. This *sql_id* can be used to join into other ASH views to see more details about that specific SQL statement.

To display top I/O SQL, the script below joins *v$active_session_history to v$event_name* to display the SQL ID for all SQL statements that are wait on User I/O.

```
select
   ash.sql_id,
   count(*)
from
   v$active_session_history ash,
   v$event_name evt
where
   ash.sample_time > sysdate - 1/24/60
and
   ash.session_state = 'WAITING'
and
   ash.event_id = evt.event_id
and
   evt.wait_class = 'User I/O'
group by
   sql_id
order by
   count(*) desc;
```

The ASH Report is useful for finding the root causes of sudden spikes or transient performance problems lasting even a few minutes. The ASH Report has information that includes blocking session details, transaction ids, Top Sessions, SQL, wait events and other such information aggregated by different dimensions to help in narrowing down the cause of transient problems. Some highlights of the ASH report are presented in the next section.

Looks simple? Don't be fooled by the elegance of these small samples. There are many complexities buried in ASH so here are a few tips.

Although ASH provides innovative ways to collect and use information, it is not a perfect system. DBAs must be aware of the instances in which ASH might not yield the expected information. For example, the times in the *dba_hist_active_sess_history* are sampled times, and as such, they are not statistically valid for avg, min, or max.

Tip - *wait_time* vs. *time_waited*

These similar-sounding metrics sound the same, but are actually quite different. The differences between *wait_time* and *time_waited* are listed below:

- *wait_time*

  - Same as *v$session_wait*

  - Value of a zero (0) indicated WAITING

  - any other non-zero value means ON CPU

- *time_waited*

  - Actual time waited for that event

  - Updated later upon event completion

With this basic picture of ASH, the next step is to move deeper and see how to conduct a wait event analysis with ASH data.

Event Wait Analysis with ASH

With ASH tables, the DBA can get a snapshot of Oracle wait events every hour and plot changes in wait behavior over time. It is also possible to set thresholds and report only on wait events that exceed predefined threshold. The following script can be commonly used for exception reporting of wait events.

```
ttitle 'High waits on events|Rollup by hour'


column mydate heading 'Yr.  Mo Dy Hr'     format a13;
column event                              format a30;
column total_waits    heading 'tot waits' format 999,999;
column time_waited    heading 'time wait' format 999,999;
column total_timeouts heading 'timeouts'  format 9,999;

break on to_char(snap_time,'yyyy-mm-dd') skip 1;

 select
   to_char(e.sample_time,'yyyy-mm-dd HH24')     mydate,
   e.event,
   count(e.event)                               total_waits,
   sum(e.time_waited)                           time_waited
```

```
from
   v$active_session_history e
where
   e.event not like '%timer'
and
   e.event not like '%message%'
and
   e.event not like '%slave wait%'
having
   count(e.event) > 100
group by
   to_char(e.sample_time,'yyyy-mm-dd HH24'),
   e.event
order by 1
;
```

The output below is from this script. The result is a time-series, showing those days and hours when set thresholds are exceeded. From this listing, it appears that every evening between 10:00 PM and 11:00 PM, the system experiences high waits on the redo logs.

```
Wed Aug 21                                          page     1
                      High waits on events
                       Rollup by hour

Yr.  Mo Dy Hr EVENT                        tot waits time wait
------------ ---------------------------- --------- ---------
2002-08-18 22 LGWR wait for redo copy         9,326     1,109
2002-08-18 23 LGWR wait for redo copy         8,506       316
2002-08-18 23 buffer busy waits                 214    21,388
2002-08-19 00 LGWR wait for redo copy           498         5
2002-08-19 01 LGWR wait for redo copy           497        15
2002-08-19 22 LGWR wait for redo copy         9,207     1,433
2002-08-19 22 buffer busy waits                 529    53,412
2002-08-19 23 LGWR wait for redo copy         9,066       367
2002-08-19 23 buffer busy waits                 250    24,479
2002-08-20 00 LGWR wait for redo copy           771        16
2002-08-20 22 LGWR wait for redo copy         8,030     2,013
2002-08-20 22 buffer busy waits                 356    35,583
2002-08-20 23 LGWR wait for redo copy         8,021       579
2002-08-20 23 buffer busy waits                 441    44,677
2002-08-21 00 LGWR wait for redo copy         1,013        26
2002-08-21 00 rdbms ipc reply                   160    30,986
2002-08-21 01 LGWR wait for redo copy           541        17
```

The Oracle Wait Event Interface within Oracle10g OEM gives the DBA the ability to monitor database bottlenecks in real time. This tool becomes even more powerful when used together with the AWR tables.

Understanding Session Wait History

Prior to Oracle10g, there was no standard way to keep and analyze the history for a session's wait events into the Oracle database kernel. DBA's had to write custom code to vacuum wait information from the *v$* views and store them inside STATSPACK extension tables. This inability to capture information was critical to evaluating database performance because most wait events occurred in real time were not caught using manual queries.

This issue caused database specialists to develop custom tools to monitor wait events in an automated manner; however, this approach had a downside of placing additional overhead on the system. Oracle10g relieves the DBA from this problem through the introduction of a new feature known as the Active Session History (ASH). ASH dynamic performance views contain history for wait events that occurred during recent sessions.

The first component of ASH is *v$session_wait_history* view. This view contains the last ten wait events for every current database session.

```
SQL> desc v$session_wait_history

Name                      Null?     Type
----------------------    --------  ------------
SID                                 NUMBER
SEQ#                                NUMBER
EVENT#                              NUMBER
EVENT                               VARCHAR2(64)
P1TEXT                              VARCHAR2(64)
P1                                  NUMBER
P2TEXT                              VARCHAR2(64)
P2                                  NUMBER
P3TEXT                              VARCHAR2(64)
P3                                  NUMBER
WAIT_TIME                           NUMBER
WAIT_COUNT                          NUMBER
```

If this ASH dynamic view is queried for the particular session, number 74, mentioned in the preceding example that faced buffer busy waits event, it becomes apparent that this session waited for some additional latch events as shown by the following script:

```
select
   swh.seq#,
   sess.sid,
   sess.username username,
   swh.event      event,
   swh.p1,
   swh.p2
from
   v$session               sess,
   v$session_wait_history swh
where
   sess.sid = 74
and
   sess.sid = swh.sid
order by
   swh.seq#;

SEQ# SID USERNAME EVENT                             P1         P2
---- --- -------- -------------------------- ---------- ----------
   1  74 PCS      buffer busy waits                   3      21277
   2  74 PCS      latch: cache buffers chains 1556332118      172
   3  74 PCS      latch: cache buffers chains 1556332118      172
   4  74 PCS      buffer busy waits                   4        155
```

By querying the *v$session_wait_history* view, it becomes clear that users were faced with some additional waits including *buffer busy waits* for UNDO segment determined by P1=3 and P2=21277. Also, it appears that the session had many waits for cache buffer chain latch. This contention has two likely causes: very long buffer chains or very heavy access to the same data blocks.

The next step is to determine what SQL statements the session executed regarding the orders table that owns the hot block in order to identify statements that may cause such the contention.

Usually, this contention is caused by identical SQL queries being issued by numerous sessions, all of which retrieve rows from the same set of data blocks. The tuning options available in this situation are to either tune the SQL statement or application so that it will access the data blocks less often (i.e. cache the data inside the application).

Another approach is to spread the data across many data blocks by setting *pctused* to a high value such as 90, thereby allowing only a few rows in each data block before the block is taken off the freelist. This spreads the hot rows across more data blocks.

Another ASH dynamic performance view, *v$active_session_history*, comes to the DBA's rescue in this task. This view contains snapshots of sessions' activities taken once per second.

A database session is considered active when it waits on CPU or was waits for some event that is not idle. Idle events are indicated by the *wait_class* column for the corresponding wait event in the *v$event_name* view. This view reports one row per active session for every snapshot taken. Table 16.5 below shows the content of the description of this useful view:

snap_id	UNIQUE SNAPSHOT ID
dbid	Database ID for the snapshot
instance_number	Instance number for the snapshot
sample_id	ID of the sample
sample_time	Time of the sample
session_id	Session identifier
session_serial#	Session serial number
user_id	Oracle user identifier
sql_id	SQL identifier of the SQL statement *sql_child_number*. Child number of the SQL statement
sql_opcode	Indicates what phase of operation the SQL statement is in
current_obj#	Object ID of the object that the session is currently referencing
current_file#	File number of the file containing the block that the session is currently referencing
current_block#	ID of the block that the session is currently referencing
event_id	Identifier of the resource or event for which the session is waiting or for which the session last waited
wait_time	Total wait time for the event for which the session last waited
time_waited	Time that the current session actually spent waiting for the event.
program	Name of the operating system program
module	Name of the currently executing module
client_id	Client identifier of the session
snap_id	Unique snapshot ID

Table 16.5: *Contents of the v$event_name view*

From the listing, one can see that the *v$active_session_history* view allows the DBA to determine the real recent history for every database session without any additional overhead placed by third-party tools.

The information available in this view allows the determination of which SQL statement was executed at a given time, what wait event the sessions waited for, what database file, object, or data block was accessed. Thus, the information provided by the ASH *v$active_session_history* view fully replaces the functionality provided by the well known 10046 trace event.

At this point, it is probably appropriate to include some additional details about information contained in particular *v$active_session_history* columns.

If *wait_time* is zero, the session currently has a *session_state* of WAITING, and the EVENT listed is the event that is the last event waited for before this sample. The *time_waited* is the amount of time that the session waited for the event listed in the EVENT field.

If wait_time is greater than zero, the session currently has a *session_state* of ON CPU, and the EVENT listed is the event that was last waited for before this sample. The *time_waited* will be zero. *time_waited* will only contain a value when waits are occurring at the instant the sample is taken.

For clarity, this means that if *wait_time* in one row is two, the *session_state* will be ON CPU and the *time_waited* will be zero. The value of two in *wait_time* represents the time spent waiting the last time it waited before the current time on the CPU.

In order to use ASH, the DBA will need to understand the layout of the views. Figure 16.11 shows the connection between the *v$session* data, the key ASH view named *v$active_session_history*, and the Automated Workload Repository (AWR) structure named *wrh$_active_session_history*. The underlined fields can be used to join the other views to gather the specific information needed to diagnose performance problems.

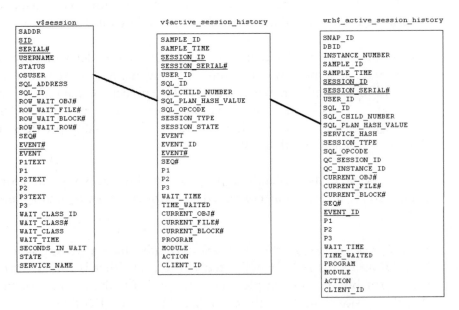

Figure 16.11: *Relationships among v$session and other structures*

Due to the volume of data that can be found in *v$active_session_history* during times of heavy activity, not all of the data is stored in the AWR tables. This is because of the dirty read mechanism which reads data even though it may belong to an in-process transaction. This allows the impact on the database to be negligible. In spite of this limitation, enough data is kept to allow the ASH information to be statistically accurate and useful for historical review.

For example, using the query below, the DBA is able to identify SQL statements that accessed the orders table for session number 74 on the current day:

```
select
   h.sql_id,
   s.sql_text
from
   dba_hist_active_sess_history h,
```

```
   v$sql                      s
where
   h.session_id = 74
AND
   h.sql_id = s.sql_id
AND
   TRUNC(h.sample_time) = TRUNC(SYSDATE)
AND
   s.sql_fulltext like '%orders%';
```

The output of this query shows the actual SQL statements executed against the orders table. This output is truncated to only one record that was retrieved due the large amount of data available:

```
SQL_ID       SQL_TEXT
------------ -----------------------------------------------------------------------------
4g5qdabvfumhc select c.c_day wrk_date, c.day_type, nvl(c.rl_day, 'N') rl_day, nvl(c.short_day,
              'N') short_day, c.week_day,        p.id ewp_id, p.emp_id, p.dep_id, p.flag_main,
              p.eca_id, p.emp_sal, p.sal_prc,        nvl(d.start_date, p.start_date) start_date,
              nvl(nvl(d.finish_date, p.finish_date), to_date('9999', 'yyyy')) finish_date,
              d.id wpd_id, d.wsc_id, d.team_num, d.ept_id,        (select decode(c.day_type, 'W',
```

The output above shows the SQL that was issued against the orders table. Since this application produces the same set of SQL statements against the database, the DBA can go further and determine what SQL statements issued against the orders table were issued most frequently in the recent past.

These SQL statements are the most likely candidates for further investigations in order to find an effective way to reduce buffer busy waits events. The following is the query that retrieves the most frequent SQL statements identifiers against the orders table:

Don't cause a performance problem!

Repeated querying of the *v$sql* view causes memory access against the library latch once for each retrieved row. This could cause a performance showdown. Be careful!

```
select
   h.sql_id,
   count(*)
from
   dba_hist_active_sess_history h,
   v$sql                      s
where
```

```
    h.sql_id = s.sql_id
and
    s.sql_fulltext like '%orders%'
having
    count(*) > 1
group by
    h.sql_id
order by
    2 DESC;
```

The output of the above query yields the following results:

```
SQL_ID              COUNT(*)
-------------       ----------
3ta4tz9xbn4gf          2,678
fxr47mpnpc2yx            740
```

The DBA can now retrieve actual SQL statements from the *v$sql* view using the SQL identifiers retrieved above and then conduct a deeper investigation of those suspect SQL statements.

The example above gives an idea of one possible usage of the ASH feature in a real tuning session.

Signature Analysis of Wait Events

There are many more benefits that can be achieved using information provided by the ASH as it is a useful tool for database activity analysis and performance tuning. The two sample analytical reports below make use of the ASH *v$active_session_history* view.

Signature analysis is an important area of Oracle tuning and one that especially applies to time-series wait event analysis. Just as Socrates said "Know Thy Self" the Oracle DBA must "Know thy Database". Signature analysis is ideal for wait event tuning particularly in the areas of:

- Spotting hidden trends

- Allowing holistic tuning

- Allowing just-in-time anticipation and self-tuning using the *dbms_scheduler* package

- Allowing adjustment of object characteristics such as freelists, file placement, caching, and block population

The following script compares the wait event values from *dba_hist_waitstat* and *dba_hist_active_sess_history*. This allows the identification of the exact objects that are experiencing wait events.

```
set pages 999
set lines 80

break on snap_time skip 2

col snap_time      heading 'Snap|Time'     format a20
col file_name      heading 'File|Name'     format a40
col object_type    heading 'Object|Type'   format a10
col object_name    heading 'Object|Name'   format a20
col wait_count     heading 'Wait|Count'    format 999,999
col time           heading 'Time'          format 999,999

select
   to_char(begin_interval_time,'yyyy-mm-dd hh24:mi') snap_time,
--    file_name,
   object_type,
   object_name,
   wait_count,
   time
from
   dba_hist_waitstat                wait,
   dba_hist_snapshot                snap,
   dba_hist_active_sess_history     ash,
   dba_data_files                   df,
   dba_objects                      obj
where
   wait.snap_id = snap.snap_id
and
   wait.snap_id = ash.snap_id
and
   df.file_id = ash.current_file#
and
   obj.object_id = ash.current_obj#
and
   wait_count > 50
order by
   to_char(begin_interval_time,'yyyy-mm-dd hh24:mi'),
   file_name
;
```

This script is enabled to join into the dba_data_files view to get the file names associated with the wait event. This is a very powerful script that can be used to quickly drill in to find the cause of specific waits. Below is a sample output:

```
SQL> @wait_time_detail
```

This will compare values from dba_hist_waitstat with
detail information from dba_hist_active_sess_history.

Snap Time	Object Type	Object Name	Wait Count	Time
2004-02-28 01:00	TABLE	ORDOR	4,273	67
	INDEX	PK_CUST_ID	12,373	324
	INDEX	FK_CUST_NAME	3,883	17
	INDEX	PK_ITEM_ID	1,256	967
2004-02-29 03:00	TABLE	ITEM_DETAIL	83	69
2004-03-01 04:00	TABLE	ITEM_DETAIL	1,246	45
2004-03-01 21:00	TABLE	CUSTOMER_DET	4,381	354
	TABLE	IND_PART	117	15
2004-03-04 01:00	TABLE	MARVIN	41,273	16
	TABLE	FACTOTUM	2,827	43
	TABLE	DOW_KNOB	853	6
	TABLE	ITEM_DETAIL	57	331
	TABLE	HIST_ORD	4,337	176
	TABLE	TAB_HIST	127	66

The first analytic trend report yields total wait times by the hour of a day. The following script shows when database sessions have to wait for resources that decrease response time:

```
select
   TO_CHAR(h.sample_time,'HH24')  "Hour",
   Sum(h.wait_time/100)           "Total Wait Time (Sec)"
from
   v$active_session_history    h,
   v$event_name                n
where
   h.session_state = 'ON CPU'
and
   h.session_type = 'FOREGROUND'
and
   h.event_id = n.EVENT_ID
and
   n.wait_class <> 'Idle'
group by
   TO_CHAR(h.sample_time,'HH24');
```

The output of this query might look like the results listed below, and it shows a distinct signature, or repeating wait event pattern within the database.

This signature will be valid for the entire range of ASH snapshots that the DBA chooses to retain. Many DBA's will retain several months' worth of ASH data so they can perform system-wide wait event tuning.

```
Hr Total Wait Time (Sec)
-- --------------------
1                   219
2               302,998
3                60,982
4               169,716
5                39,593
6               299,953
7               122,933
8                 5,147
```

From the above listing, it appears that the database had the most wait times at 12AM and 4PM as shown in the graph in Figure 16.12.

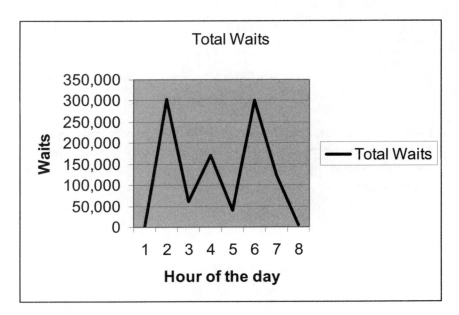

Figure 16.12: *Aggregate total waits by hour of the day*

Most Oracle databases also have daily signatures with regularly repeating trends in wait events. In the same manner, the following query that reports total wait times by the day of the week could be run:

```
select
   TO_CHAR(h.sample_time,'Day') "Hour",
   sum(h.wait_time/100) "Total Wait Time (Sec)"
from
   v$active_session_history      h,
   v$event_name                  n
where
   h.session_state = 'ON CPU'
and
   h.session_type = 'FOREGROUND'
and
   h.event_id = n.EVENT_ID
and
   n.wait_class <> 'Idle'
group by
   TO_CHAR(h.sample_time,'Day');
```

This query produces a listing that looks like the one shown below:

```
Hour        Total Wait Time (Sec)
---------   ---------------------
Monday                    679,089
Tuesday                   141,142
Wednesday                 181,226
Thursday                  241,711
Friday                    319,023
Saturday                   93,362
Sunday                     81,086
```

From this output, it is clear that the database is most stressed on Monday, and the numbers can be visualized by pasting them into a spreadsheet and plotting them with the chart wizard as shown in Figure 16.13.

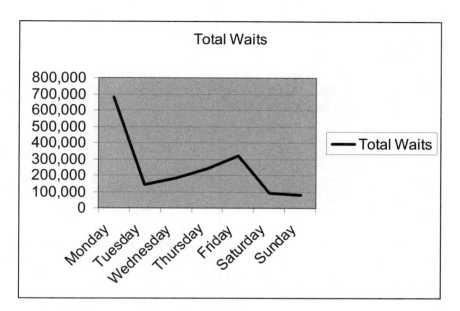

Figure 16.13: *Wait signature by day of the week*

The results from the two above trend reports allow the DBA to further investigate ASH data in order to get more detailed information. The query below retrieves a list of wait events that had high wait time from 12AM to 1PM.

A previous report on the same system showed that sessions experienced high wait times during this time period.

```
select
   h.event                "Wait Event",
   SUM(h.wait_time/100) "Wait Time (Sec)"
from
   v$active_session_history     h,
   v$event_name                 n
where
   h.session_state = 'ON CPU'
and
   h.session_type = 'FOREGROUND'
and
   h.event_id = n.EVENT_ID
and
   to_char(h.sample_time,'HH24') = '12'
and
   n.wait_class <> 'Idle'
```

```
group by
   h.event
order by
  2 DESC;
```

This query returns results that look like the following, showing aggregate totals for important wait events.

```
Wait Event                      Wait Time (Sec)
------------------------------- ---------------
buffer busy waits                       522,152
db file sequential read                 299,572
SQL*Net more data to client                 317
SQL*Net more data from client               201
SQL*Net message to client                    55
```

From the listing above, the DBA can conclude that between 12AM and 1PM the database sessions waited most for *buffer busy waits* and *db file sequential read* events indicating table access by index.

After these results are acquired, the DBA can determine what SQL statements were issued during this time period and probably find ones that may cause buffer cache contention or heavy disk read access.

The ASH provides the Oracle DBA with the ability to build different trend reports in order to observe database activity from various points of view.

The AWR repository stores snapshots for the ASH view called *v$active_session_history* in its internal table *wrh$_active_session_history*. This table is available to DBAs through the *dba_hist_active_sess_history* view. The AWR does not store snapshots of ASH activity on a continuous basis. This means that the *wrh$_active_session_history* table stores sessions' activity records that were in the SGA circular buffer at the time the AWR snapshot was taken.

This data archiving approach does not allow the DBA to monitor activity for particular sessions because the AWR misses all the activity that occurred in the session during the period of time between two AWR snapshots.

However, trend reports based on data exposed by *dba_hist_active_sess_history* view can be built. The following sections will present information on valuable trend analysis that can be performed against the AWR concerning ASH activity.

It is possible to identify hot datafiles or database objects that were accessed by sessions more frequently than others. These hot datafiles or database objects could be candidates for additional tuning investigations. The following query shows hot datafiles that caused the most wait times during access:

```
select
    f.file_name            "Data File",
    COUNT(*)               "Wait Number",
    SUM(h.time_waited) "Total Time Waited"
from
    v$active_session_history    h,
    dba_data_files              f
where
    h.current_file# = f.file_id
group by
    f.file_name
order by 3 DESC;
```

This query produces output like the following:

Data File	Wait Number	Total Time Waited
D:\ORACLE\ORADATA\DBDABR\SYSAUX01.DBF	153	11,169,771
D:\ORACLE\ORADATA\DBDABR\SYSTEM01.DBF	222	6,997,212
D:\ORACLE\ORADATA\DBDABR\UNDOTBS01.DBF	45	1,758,065

The datafile named d:\oracle\oradata\dbdabr\sysaux01.dbf had the highest wait time during access to its data. This might indicate the need to further investigate SQL statements that are accessing data within this datafile or the need to spread its content between several datafiles, thus eliminating a possible hot spot.

The Oracle multiple data buffers or the KEEP pool could also be used to reduce waits on these objects by caching them in the data buffers. If there are high waits on in-buffer reads, the SQL that accesses the hot object needs to be tuned to reduce the amount of logical I/O.

The next query against the *dba_hist_active_sess_history* view reports a list of resources that were in high demand in the last hour. This query does not reflect idle wait events.

```
select
    e.name                          "Wait Event",
    SUM(h.wait_time + h.time_waited) "Total Wait Time"
from
    v$active_session_history        h,
    v$event_name                    e
where
    h.event_id = e.event_id
and
    e.wait_class <> 'Idle'
group by
    e.name
order by 2 DESC;
```

This query produces a listing like the one below, showing aggregate wait time for each event:

```
Wait Event                      Total Wait Time
------------------------------  ---------------
log buffer space                      9,638,484
db file sequential read               8,442,918
log file switch completion            5,231,711
write complete waits                  5,200,368
db file scattered read                4452,153
process startup                       3623,464
rdbms ipc reply                         917,765
log file sync                           662,224
latch free                              550,241
latch: library cache                    370,696
db file parallel write                  364,641
free buffer waits                       319,151
latch: redo allocation                   64,984
LGWR wait for redo copy                  63,647
read by other session                    52,757
log file sequential read                 46,126
null event                               33,011
log file parallel write                  26,280
SQL*Net more data to client               8,894
latch: cache buffers chains               7,005
control file sequential read              3,966
direct path read temp                       395
direct path write temp                      229
SQL*Net message to client                    74
```

From the listing above, one can see that the DBA has an issue with the log buffer space wait event that may indicate the need to increase the

---

log_buffer parameter to increase the cache in order to minimize this possible bottleneck.

Using the AWR ASH view, the DBA can also retrieve a list of database users who have experienced high wait times during the time period between any two snapshots. The following query can be used to identify these target users:

```
select
   s.sid,
   s.username,
   sum(h.wait_time + h.time_waited) "total wait time"
from
   v$active_session_history     h,
   v$session                    s,
   v$event_name                 e
where
   h.session_id = s.sid
and
   e.event_id = h.event_id
and
   e.wait_class <> 'Idle'
and
   s.username IS NOT NULL
group by
   s.sid, s.username
order by 3;
```

This sample output shows the total wait time, both by process ID (SID) and by individual users.

SID	USERNAME	total wait time
261	SYS	1,537,288
259	SYS	12,247,007
254	SYS	18,640,736

The next sample query against the AWR ASH table shows a list of database objects that caused the most wait times during time interval stored in AWR. Idle wait times are not included in the output.

```
select
   o.owner,
   o.object_name,
   o.object_type,
   SUM(h.wait_time + h.time_waited) "total wait time"
from
   v$active_session_history     h,
```

```
    dba_objects                o,
    v$event_name               e
where
    h.current_obj# = o.object_id
and
    e.event_id = h.event_id
and
    e.wait_class <> 'Idle'
group by
    o.owner,
    o.object_name,
    o.object_type
order by 4 DESC;
```

This report produces a list of hot objects which might be candidates for further tuning investigations:

OWNER	Object Name	Object Type	total wait time
SYSMAN	MGMT_OMS_PARAMETERS	TABLE	1,1232E+10
SYS	SCHEDULER$_WINDOW_DE TAILS	TABLE	2989867
SYSMAN	MPVV_PK	INDEX	1333198
SYSMAN	MGMT_DELTA_ENTRY_SHO ULD_BE_UK	INDEX	835641
SYSMAN	MGMT_DB_LATEST_HDM_F INDINGS	TABLE	397504
SYS	CDEF$	TABLE	116853
SYS	I_LINK1	INDEX	46922
SYS	SYS_IOT_TOP_8542	INDEX	25469
SYS	I_COM1	INDEX	24908
SYS	I_CDEF3	INDEX	23125
SYSMAN	MGMT_DB_LATEST_HDM_F INDINGS	INDEX	11325
SYS	I_OBJ2	INDEX	5953
SYS	WRH$_ACTIVE_SESSION_ HISTORY_BL	TABLE	304
SYSTEM	SQLPLUS_PRODUCT_PROF ILE	TABLE	3

The *dba_hist_waitclassmet_history* table contains summary information for these categories. There are times when summary information may provide clues as to the nature of the performance problem. The following script provides one way to look at this summary level data grouped by the AWR snapshot and wait class.

```
break on begin_time skip 1

column wait_class format a15

select
  begin_time,
  wait_class,
  average_waiter_count,
  dbtime_in_wait
from
  dba_hist_waitclassmet_history
where
  dbtime_in_wait >10
order by
  begin_time,
  wait_class,
  average_waiter_count DESC;
```

The following is a sample output:

BEGIN_TIM	WAIT_CLASS	AVERAGE WAITER COUNT	DBTIME IN WAIT
12-NOV-04	Commit	0	18
	Other	0	100
	Commit	0	17
	Other	0	100
	Other	0	100
	Commit	0	17
	Commit	0	14
	Commit	0	18
	Other	0	100

The information in the AWR can provide valuable information about cumulative statistics such as file I/O. The following script demonstrates the physical read statistics gathered for each datafile.

```
break on begin_interval_time skip 1

column phyrds                format 999,999,999
column begin_interval_time   format a25
column file_name             format a45

select
  begin_interval_time,
  filename,
  phyrds
from
  dba_hist_filestatxs
  natural join
  dba_hist_snapshot
```

```
order by
  begin_interval_time
;
```

The sample output below shows a running total of physical reads for each datafile. The snapshots are collected every hour with additional ad-hoc snapshots at other times. Starting from this script, it would be easy to add a WHERE clause criteria and create a unique time-series exception report.

```
BEGIN_INTERVAL_TIME        FILENAME                          PHYRDS
------------------------    ------------------------------    ------
10-NOV-04 09.00.01.000 PM  /oradata/test10g/system01.dbf      3,982
                           /oradata/test10g/undotbs01.dbf        51
                           /oradata/test10g/users01.dbf           7
                           /oradata/test10g/example01.dbf        14
                           /oradata/test10g/sysaux01.dbf        551
                           /oradata/test10g/tbsalert.dbf          7

10-NOV-04 09.11.06.131 PM  /oradata/test10g/system01.dbf      6,120
                           /oradata/test10g/users01.dbf          21
                           /oradata/test10g/tbsalert.dbf         21
                           /oradata/test10g/example01.dbf        28
                           /oradata/test10g/sysaux01.dbf      4,786
                           /oradata/test10g/undotbs01.dbf       231

10-NOV-04 10.00.16.672 PM  /oradata/test10g/system01.dbf     10,950
                           /oradata/test10g/undotbs01.dbf       262
                           /oradata/test10g/users01.dbf          22
                           /oradata/test10g/tbsalert.dbf         22
                           /oradata/test10g/example01.dbf        40
                           /oradata/test10g/sysaux01.dbf      6,320
```

Latch contention can be a source of performance problems. When faced with latch issues, the following script can help to identify the biggest latch issues from this repository. Rather than transient data, this will allow the DBA to examine recent data and determine trend information as well as data from a point in the recent past. How far in the past depends on the settings that have been used for the database.

```
break on begin_interval_time skip 1

column begin_interval_time format a25
column latch_name          format a40

select
  begin_interval_time,
  latch_name,
  gets,
```

```
    misses,
    sleeps
from
    dba_hist_latch
natural join
    dba_hist_snapshot
where
    (misses + sleeps ) > 0
order by
    begin_interval_time,
    misses DESC,
    sleeps DESC
;
```

This script results in a very important listing, because now latch misses can be tracked over time. Since Oracle is very dynamic and latch related performance problems are often so sporadic, they often disappear before the DBA is even aware of them.

BEGIN	LATCH NAME	GETS	MISSES	SLEEPS
6 AM	library cache	4,451,177	856	943
	shared pool	3,510,651	482	611
	redo allocation	146,500	139	139
	cache buffers chains	13,050,732	52	104
	session allocation	8,176,366	43	43
	slave class create	2,534	41	41
	cache buffers lru chain	347,142	33	33
	row cache objects	2,556,877	24	26
	library cache pin	2,611,493	8	8
	messages	1,056,963	7	5
	library cache lock	1,483,983	4	4
	object queue header operation	1,386,809	3	3
	enqueue hash chains	2,915,290	3	3
	enqueues	2,693,816	2	2
	client/application info	11,578	1	3
	JOX SGA heap latch	43,033	1	2
	simulator lru latch	17,806	1	1
	JS slv state obj latch	85	1	1
7 AM	library cache	4,540,521	862	950
	shared pool	3,582,239	485	614
	redo allocation	149,434	140	140
	cache buffers chains	13,214,066	53	105
	session allocation	8,342,651	43	43
	slave class create	2,590	42	42
	cache buffers lru chain	352,002	33	33
	row cache objects	2,606,652	24	26
	library cache pin	2,663,535	8	8
	messages	1,079,305	7	5
	library cache lock	1,514,016	4	4
	object queue header operation	1,412,733		3

These trends can be expanded by examining the delta values between ASH statistics using the new *dba_hist_sys_time_model* table as shown in the following script:

```
break on begin_interval_time skip 0

column stat_name format a25

select
  begin_interval_time,
  new.stat_name,
  (new.value - old.value) "Difference"
from
   dba_hist_sys_time_model old,
   dba_hist_sys_time_model new,
   dba_hist_snapshot         ss
where
   new.stat_name = old.stat_name
and
   new.snap_id = ss.snap_id
and
   old.snap_id = ss.snap_id - 1
and
   new.stat_name like '%&stat_name%'
order by
   begin_interval_time;
```

This produces a report similar to the one below. This report was run for the event *hard parse elapsed time*. The output can be analyzed to detect repeating patterns of specific wait events.

There is a huge increase at 11 PM when the wait time delta nearly doubled from the previous hour. This gives an important clue for further investigation.

```
BEGIN_INTERVAL_TIME         STAT_NAME                  Difference
-------------------------   ------------------------   ----------
12-NOV-04 08.00.20.745 PM   hard parse elapsed time    10,605,028
12-NOV-04 09.00.48.205 PM   hard parse elapsed time    15,628,615
12-NOV-04 10.00.13.470 PM   hard parse elapsed time    54,707,455
12-NOV-04 11.00.41.412 PM   hard parse elapsed time    96,643,842
13-NOV-04 12.00.06.899 AM   hard parse elapsed time    16,890,047
```

Similarly, ASH information on enqueues is also maintained. This allows a query such as the one that follows to produce a report on enqueue waits.

```
column begin_interval_time format a10
column req_reason          format a25
column cum_wait_time       head CUM|WAIT|TIME
column total_req#          head TOTAL|REQ#
column total_wait#         head TOTAL|WAIT#
column failed_req#         head FAILED|REQ#

select
   begin_interval_time,
   eq_type,
   req_reason,
   total_req#,
   total_wait#,
   succ_req#,
   failed_req#,
   cum_wait_time
from
   dba_hist_enqueue_stat
 natural join
   dba_hist_snapshot
where
   cum_wait_time > 0
order by
    begin_interval_time,
    cum_wait_time;
```

The following sample results show top waits by time period:

TIME	EQ	REQ REASON	TOT REQUEST	TOT WT NUM	SUCCESS REQ NUM	FAILED REQ NUM	CUM WAIT TIME
1 PM	JS	slave enq get lock1	11	2	11	0	2,990
1 PM	RO	fast object reuse	1,960	31	1,960	0	1,940
1 PM	SQ	contention	244	4	244	0	550
1 PM	TM	contention	121,391	1	121,370	21	100
1 PM	TX	contention	66,793	1	66,793	0	60
1 PM	TX	index contention	1	1	1	0	50
2 PM	JS	slave enq get lock1	22	4	233	0	4,332
2 PM	RO	fast object reuse	1,960	31	1,960	0	5,730
2 PM	SQ	contention	244	4	244	0	950
2 PM	TX	row lock contention	1	1	1	0	870
2 PM	JS	queue lock	1151,724	1	1151,724	0	790
2 PM	SQ	contention	247	4	247	0	550
2 PM	TM	contention	122,513	1	122,492	21	450
2 PM	TX	contention	67,459	1	67,459	0	360
2 PM	TX	index contention	1	1	1	0	250
2 PM	TX	row lock contention	1	1	1	0	170

In the above samples, it is clear that the savvy DBA can use AWR and ASH together to get more precise time-series trend pictures of database performance.

Conclusion

The new Active Session History (ASH) and enhanced Oracle Wait Event Interface tools should definitely be added to the DBA's day-to-day tuning toolbox. The main points of this chapter include:

- The wait event interface has been completely overhauled in Oracle10g, and it is now easier than ever to identify and track database bottlenecks.

- Oracle has expanded on the v$ views and created Active Session History (ASH) tables to provide trend analysis of wait-related performance data.

- The ASH tables are useful for identifying wait event information at many levels including individual sessions, specific SQL statements, specific users, or the database as a whole.

- Ancillary tools such as WISE can quickly help plot and spot hidden wait event bottlenecks.

The next chapter will explore Oracle10g's use of Automatic Segment Space Management (ASSM) and how bitmap freelists can help relieve wait contention for Oracle objects.

Tablespace & Object Tuning

Poorly optimized objects cause poor response time

Introduction to Oracle Segment Management

Previous chapters of this book introduced the benefits of performance tuning efforts using the Automated Workload Repository (AWR) together with the Active Session History (ASH) tables. In this chapter, insights will be provided into a new approach for tuning the Input/Output (I/O) subsystem using the new Automatic Segment Space Management (ASSM) introduced in Oracle10g. This feature should not be confused with another new feature with a similar abbreviation: ASM – Automatic Storage Management.

Historically, space management was one of the most time consuming tasks for DBAs. According to surveys conducted by Oracle Corporation, Oracle DBAs spend about twenty percent of their work time performing space management activities. Oracle10g significantly reduces the burden of this type of administrative work.

Inside Oracle Tablespace Management

Over the past few years, Oracle has been automating and improving the internal administration of tables and indexes. Recently, Oracle has introduced two new tablespace parameters that automate storage management functions:

- Locally Managed Tablespaces (LMT): The LMT tablespace is implemented by adding EXTENT MANAGEMENT LOCAL clause to the tablespace definition. LMT tablespaces automate extent management and remove the ability to specify the *next* storage parameter. The only exception is when *next* is used with *minextents* at table creation time. The LMT is the default in Oracle10g.

- Automatic Segment Space Management (ASSM): ASSM replaces the old-fashioned one-way linked lists of free data blocks with bitmap structures. The ASSM tablespace is implemented by adding the SEGMENT SPACE MANAGEMENT AUTO clause to the tablespace definition. ASSM tablespaces automate *freelist* management and remove the ability to specify *pctused*, *freelists*, and *freelist groups* storage parameters. The ASSM cannot be used unless LMTs are also used on a tablespace.

LMT and ASSM are optional and are used in the same instance with traditional tablespaces. LMT and ASSM are implemented at the tablespace level, and each instance can have LMT, LMT and ASSM tablespaces, or traditional tablespaces.

Before the differences between *bitmap freelists* and traditional *freelist* management are introduced, one must understand more about how *bitmap freelists* are implemented. The process starts with the creation of a tablespace with the segment space management auto parameter.

ASSM is only valid for locally managed tablespaces with extent management local syntax.

```
create tablespace
   asm_test
datafile
   'c:\oracle\oradata\diogenes\asm_test.dbf'
size
   5m
EXTENT MANAGEMENT LOCAL
SEGMENT SPACE MANAGEMENT AUTO
;
```

Once a table or index is allocated in this tablespace, the values for *pctused* for individual objects will be ignored, and Oracle will automatically manage the freelists for the tables and indexes inside the tablespace. For objects created in this tablespace, the *next* extent clause is now obsolete because of the locally managed tablespace, except when a table is created with the *minextents* and *next* clauses. The initial parameter is still required because Oracle cannot know in advance the size of the initial table load. When using Automatic Segment Space Management, the minimum value for initial is three blocks.

There is some debate about whether a one-size-fits-all approach is best for Oracle. In large databases, individual object settings can make a huge difference in both performance and storage. The setting for *pctused* governs *freelist* relinking as space is freed by *update* and *delete* statements.

The Issue of *pctfree*

The *pctfree* parameter is used to specify the amount of free space on a data block to reserve for future row expansion. If *pctfree* is set improperly, SQL update statements can cause a huge amount of row fragmentation and chaining.

The setting for *pctfree* is especially important where a row is initially stored small and expanded at a later time. In such systems, it is not uncommon to set *pctfree* equal to 95, telling Oracle to reserve 95 percent of the data block space for subsequent row expansion.

The Issue of *pctused*

Improper settings for *pctused* can cause huge degradation in the performance of SQL *insert*s. If a data block is not largely empty, excessive I/O will happen during SQL *insert*s because the reused Oracle data blocks already contain rows, and the block will fill-up faster causing extra I/O. Taken to the extreme, improper settings for *pctused* can create a situation in which the free space on the data block is smaller than the average row length for the table. In these cases, Oracle will try five times to fetch a new block from the *freelist* chain. After five attempts, Oracle will raise the high water mark for the table and grab five completely empty data blocks for the *insert*.

With Automatic Segment Management, the *pctused* parameter no longer governs the relink threshold for a table data block, and the DBA must rely on the judgment of Oracle to determine when a block is empty enough to be placed back onto the freelist.

Unlike *pctfree*, in which Oracle cannot tell in advance how much row expansion will occur, Oracle does have information about the right time to relink a data block after the row space shrinks. Since Oracle knows the average row length for the table rows, *dba_tables.avg_row_len*. With that information, Oracle should be able to adjust *pctused* to ensure that the relinked data block will have room for the insertion of new rows.

A Summary of Object Tuning Rules

The following rules govern the settings for the *init.ora* parameters *freelists*, *freelist groups*, *pctfree*, and *pctused*. The value of *pctused* and *pctfree* can easily be changed at any time with the ALTER TABLE command, and the observant DBA should be able to develop a methodology for deciding the optimal settings for these parameters. There is a direct tradeoff between effective space utilization and high performance.

- For efficient space re-use: A high value for *pctused* will effectively reuse space on data blocks but at the expense of additional I/O. A high *pctused* means that relatively full blocks are placed on the freelist. Therefore, these blocks will be able to accept only a few rows before becoming full again, leading to more I/O.

- For high performance: A low value for *pctused* means that Oracle will not place a data block onto the free list until it is nearly empty. The block will be able to accept many rows until it becomes full, thereby reducing I/O at *insert* time. It is always faster for Oracle to extend into new blocks than to reuse existing blocks. It takes fewer resources for Oracle to extend a table than to manage *freelists* and freelist management can be turned off by setting *pctused* to a value of one. This will cause the *freelists* to be populated exclusively from empty blocks. Of course, this approach requires lots of extra disk space, and the table must be reorganized periodically to reclaim the wasted storage.

The *pctused* parameter should always be set large enough to allow enough room to accept a new row. The DBA never wants to have free blocks that do not have enough room to accept a row. If this happens, a slowdown will be the result since Oracle will attempt to read five dead free blocks before extending the table to get a completely empty block.

The presence of chained rows in a table means that *pctfree* is too low. In most cases within Oracle, RAW and LONG RAW columns make huge rows that exceed the maximum blocksize for Oracle, making row fragmentation unavoidable.

If a table has simultaneous *insert* dialog processes, it needs to have multiple *freelists* to reduce segment header contention, and the application should parallelize the *delete* processes to evenly repopulate each freelist. Running a single purge job will place all of the free blocks on only one freelist, and none of the other *freelists* will contain any free blocks from the purge job.

Multiple *freelists* can also waste disk. Tables with dozens of *freelists* may exhibit the sparse table phenomenon as the table grows and each *freelist* contains free blocks that are not known to the other *freelists*. If these tables consume too much space, the Oracle DBA faces a tough decision. To maximize space reuse, the data block should be placed onto a *freelist* as soon as it is capable of receiving more than two new rows. Therefore, a fairly high value for *pctused* is desired to maximize space reuse. On the other hand, this would result in slower runtime performance since Oracle will only be able to insert a few rows before having to perform an I/O to get another block.

Reducing Segment Header Contention and Buffer Busy Waits

One huge benefit of Automatic Segment Space Management is the number of bitmap freelists that are guaranteed to reduce buffer busy waits. The following section provides more information on this feature, first introduced in Oracle9i.

Prior to Oracle9i, *buffer busy waits* were a major issue for systems with high concurrent *insert*s. As a review, a buffer busy wait often occurs when a data block is inside the data buffer cache, but it is unavailable because it is locked by another DML transaction. Without multiple *freelists*, every Oracle table and index has a single data block at the head of the table to manage the free block for the object. Whenever any SQL *insert* ran, it had to go to this segment header block and get a free data block on which to place its row.

Oracle's ASSM feature claims to improve the performance of concurrent DML operations significantly since different parts of the bitmap can be used, simultaneously eliminating serialization for free block lookups.

According to Oracle benchmarks, using bitmap freelists removes all segment header contention and allows for fast concurrent *insert* operations as shown in Figure 17.1.

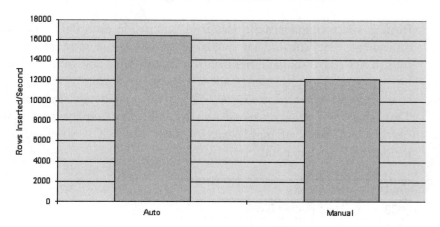

Figure 17.1: *Oracle Corp. benchmark on SQL insert speed with bitmap freelists*

The following section will introduce how the Oracle DBA can use these object management parameters to control every aspect of row storage on the data blocks.

Internal *freelist* Management

With ASSM, Oracle controls the number of bitmap freelists, providing up to 23 *freelists* per segment.

Internally within Oracle, a shortage of *freelists* is manifested by a buffer busy wait. In traditional non-bitmap freelists, Oracle has a manual mechanism for the DBA to use to allocate a new segment header block with another *freelist* whenever *buffer busy waits* are detected for the segment. Oracle first introduced dynamic *freelist* addition in Oracle8i.

The following section will provide information on how the bitmap freelists of ASSM control free blocks within a segment.

Characteristics of Bitmap Segment Management

Bitmap space management uses four bits inside each data block header to indicate the amount of available space in the data block. Unlike traditional space management with a fixed relink and unlink threshold, bitmap space managements allow Oracle to compare the actual row space for an *insert* with the actual available space on the data block. This enables better reuse of the available free space especially for objects with rows of highly varying size. Table 17.1 shows the values inside the four-bit space:

VALUE	MEANING
0000	Unformatted Block
0001	Block is logically full
0010	<25% free space
0011	>25% but <50% free space
0100	> 50% but <75% free space
0101	>75% free space

Table 17.1: *Bitmap value meanings*

The value column of this bitmap table indicates how much free space exists in a given data block. In traditional space management, each data block must be read from the *freelist* to see if it has enough space to accept a new row. In Oracle10g, the bitmap is constantly kept up to date with changes to the block and there is also a reduction of wasted space because blocks can be kept fuller because the overhead of *freelist* processing has been reduced.

Another benefit of ASSM is that concurrent DML operations improve significantly. This is because different parts of the bitmap can be used simultaneously, thereby eliminating the need to serialize free space lookups.

The bitmap segment control structures of ASSM are much larger than traditional one-way linked-list *freelist* management. Since each data block entry contains the four-byte data block address and the four-bit free space indicator, each data block entry in the space management bitmap will consume approximately six bytes of storage.

It is also important to note that the space management blocks are not required to be the first blocks in the segment. In Oracle8, the segment headers were required to be the first blocks in the segment. In Oracle8i this restriction was lifted, and the DBA could allocate additional *freelists* with the *alter table* command, causing additional non-contiguous segment headers. In Oracle10g, Oracle automatically allocates new space management blocks when a new extent is created and maintains internal pointers to the bitmap blocks as shown in Figure 17.2

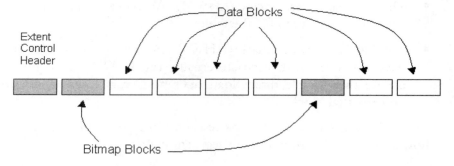

Figure 17.2: *Non-contiguous bitmap blocks within a segment*

Oracle Bitmap *freelist* Internals

Just like traditional *freelists*, the bitmap block (BMB) is stored in a separate data block within the table or index. Since Oracle does not publish the internals of space management, the structure must be inferred from block dumps. Therefore, this information may not be completely accurate, but it will give a general idea about the internal mechanisms of Oracle10g ASSM.

Unlike a linear-linked list in traditional *freelists*, bitmap blocks are stored in a b-tree structure, much the same as a bitmap. Since Oracle can use the *freelists* blocks much like a bitmap index, multiple transactions can simultaneously access free blocks without locking or concurrency problems.

The next section will provide a look inside the segment header and a closer look at bitmap space management techniques within ASSM.

New High Water Mark Pointers

The high water mark in the segment header has also changed in Oracle9i bitmap blocks. Instead of having a single pointer to the highest free block in an object, the b-tree index structure allows for a range of high water mark blocks. Therefore, two pointers for the high water mark can be seen.

- The low high water mark (LHWM): All blocks below this block have been formatted for the table.

- The high high water mark (HHWM): All blocks above this block have not been formatted. Internally, the HHWM is required to ensure that Oracle direct load operations can access contiguous unformatted blocks.

The following sections will explore each block in detail to understand how space is managed in bitmap segment control.

Extent Control Header Block

This block contains the high-high water mark, the low-high water mark, the extent map, and the data block addresses for each of the three levels of bitmap blocks.

The extent map lists all of the data block addresses for each block within each extent within the segment and shows the four-bit free space of each block within the extent. Since the extent size is controlled by Oracle locally managed tablespaces, each extent size within the tablespace is uniform, regardless of the *next* extent size for each object in the tablespace.

The first three blocks of the first extend list, blocks zero through two, are used for metadata and are not available for segment block addresses.

For each extent in the segment, Oracle keeps an entry pointing to the bitmap for that segment as shown in Figure 17.3.

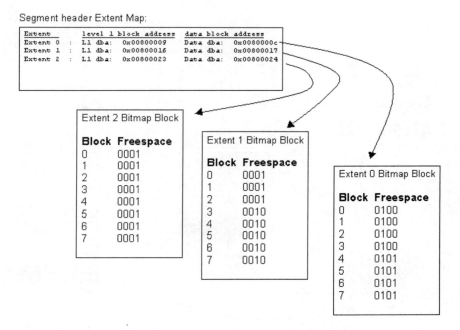

Segment header Extent Map:

Extent		level 1 block address	data block address
Extent 0	:	L1 dba: 0x00800009	Data dba: 0x0080000c
Extent 1	:	L1 dba: 0x00800016	Data dba: 0x00800017
Extent 2	:	L1 dba: 0x00800023	Data dba: 0x00800024

Figure 17.3: *Segment header extent map points to all extent bitmaps in segments*

Oracle10g also has pointers to the last bitmap block within each logical bitmap level as shown in Figure 17.4.

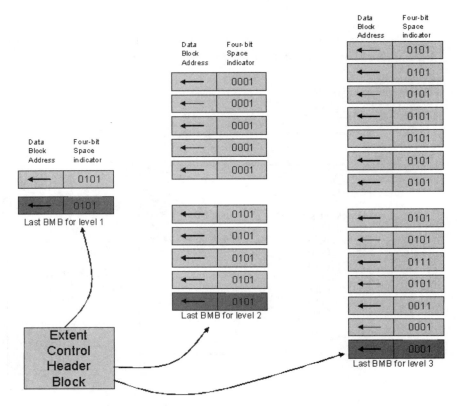

Figure 17.4: *Pointers to last bitmap block on each bitmap level*

This new pointer structure allows Oracle to quickly access multiple bitmaps to improve concurrency of high volume *insert*s.

Potential Performance Issues with ASSM

The Oracle community has mixed feelings about using ASSM tablespaces. Among the top points about ASSM, there are both pros and cons. The next two sections address these pros and cons.

Pros of ASSM:

- Varying row sizes: ASSM is better than a static *pctused*. The bitmaps make ASSM tablespaces better at handling rows with wide variations in row length.

- Reducing buffer busy waits: ASSM will remove buffer busy waits better than using multiple *freelists*. When a table has multiple *freelists*, all purges must be parallelized to reload the *freelists* evenly, and ASSM has no such limitation.

- Great for Real Application Clusters: The bitmap freelists remove the need to define multiple *freelists* groups for RAC and provide overall improved *freelist* management over traditional *freelists*.

Cons of ASSM:

- Slow for full-table scans: Several studies have shown that large-table full-table scans (FTS) will run longer with ASSM than standard bitmaps. ASSM FTS tablespaces are consistently slower than *freelist* FTS operations. This implies that ASSM may not be appropriate for decision support systems and warehouse applications unless partitioning is used with Oracle Parallel Query.

- Slower for high-volume concurrent *inserts*: Numerous experts have conducted studies that show that tables with high volume bulk loads perform faster with traditional multiple *freelists*.

- ASSM will influence index clustering: For row ordered tables, ASSM can adversely affect the *clustering_factor* for indexes. Bitmap *freelists* are less likely to place adjacent tows on physically adjacent data blocks, and this can lower the *clustering_factor* and the cost-based optimizer's propensity to favor an index range scan.

The combination of bitmap freelists, ASSM, and Locally Managed Tablespaces has greatly simplified and improved the internal management of data blocks within Oracle tablespaces. The use of bitmap freelists removes the need to define multiple *freelists* for tables and indexes that experience high volume concurrent DML and

---

provides a simple solution to the problem of segment header contention.

However, the savvy DBA recognizes the tradeoff between one-size-fits-all convenience and the power of being able to set individual object parameters for tables and indexes. The choice of LMT and ASSM for tablespace management depends heavily on the application, and real-world Oracle tablespaces will implement LMT and ASSM tablespaces only after careful consideration.

The following section examines proactive tablespace management techniques on Oracle10g.

Proactive Tablespace Management

The Proactive Tablespace Management (PTM) capability introduced in Oracle10g brings efficient and powerful space monitoring, notification, and space trending to the Oracle database. Prior to Oracle10g database, there were a number of third-party space management tools that queried the database on a regular basis to monitor its space usage. These queries placed additional overhead on production systems consuming CPU, I/O, and memory resources.

With PTM technology, Oracle10g introduces a light-weight and timely health check of space in the Oracle database. PTM is available by default and can operate on tablespaces of all available in Oracle10g types. Its functionality is available through both the Oracle Enterprise Manager and SQL interfaces.

Oracle10g database provides a convenient framework for working with tablespace alerts, which are built directly into the Oracle server kernel. Tablespace space alerts are automatically computed by the server, and notifications are sent to database administrators through e-mail service. Once a problem is fixed, alerts are cleared and moved to alert history.

Alert are pushed into the server side table that stores alerts. These alerts are available through the *dba_outstanding_alerts* data dictionary view. When the DBA clears an alert, it is archived to another history table available through the *dba_alert_history* view.

Alert notifications are implemented using a new Oracle10g technology known as server generated alerts. The alerts are triggered when a set space threshold is violated. By default, Oracle database has a predefined set of alert thresholds. DBA's may override default threshold values for a concrete tablespace. The same task can be performed using the PL/SQL *dbms_server_alert.set_threshold* procedure. To view the current threshold value, the procedure *dbms_server_alert.get_threshold* can be used.

In general, tablespace thresholds are defined in terms of percents of a tablespaces' space usage. There are two types of thresholds: critical and warning. When the tablespace space utilization becomes larger than any of these two thresholds, an appropriate alert is generated. When the cause of the alert is fixed, this alert is automatically cleared.

Reclaiming Segment Space

In an everyday production environment, Oracle DBAs face many challenges in tasks such as segment space management. For example, tables that are often updated may have very fragmented data segments or many chained rows. This may significantly affect the overall DML performance issued against such tables or introduce space wastage problems.

Until Oracle10g, there was no way to reclaim wasted space and compact data segments online without affecting end users. Figure 17.5 shows a data segment schema of a table. The small squares indicate rows stored in the segment.

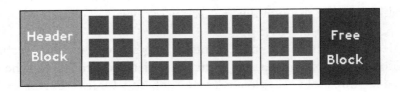

Figure 17.5: *The schema of table segment with stored rows within data blocks.*

When end users insert rows into the table, Oracle fills empty blocks allocated to the segment. Over the course of time, some rows might be deleted from the table, and at some point in time, the same segment could be presented by the schema in Figure 17.6.

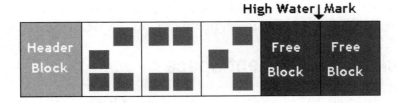

Figure 17.6: *After some rows have been deleted, the data segment wastes the space and HWM remains the same.*

The logical term High Water Mark (HWM) represents the highest space occupied by the segment. In Figure 17.7, it is clear that Oracle does not reclaim free space below the High Water Mark for other segments of the database or the free space within data blocks. This is because Oracle reserves that free space for future row inserts and possible row growth after updates. This method of space management within data segments has two weak spots. The first is that Oracle must scan all blocks below the HWM when performing full-table scans even though most of blocks are empty. This approach might significantly increase response time of full-table scans on tables which experience high data modification activity. The second thing that must be taken into account is when Oracle inserts rows through DIRECT PATH method such as an APPEND hint that is used in the *insert* statements, it always places new rows in data blocks above the HWM. Thus, the space below the HWM might be wasted.

In Oracle releases prior 10g, space could be reclaimed using such methods as exporting a table to the dump file, dropping it, and reloading data into the new table; or using the ALTER TABLE MOVE statement to move the table to another tablespace. The down side is that these methods prevent users from accessing their data during the table reorganization process. The online reorganization feature might also be used, but that process requires at least double space to perform the operation.

Online Segment Reorganization

An Oracle10g database can reclaim space within data segments online without affecting the ability of end users to access their data. The only thing that must be ensured before using online segment reorganization capability is that the tablespaces have the Automatic Segment Space Management (ASSM) and row movement features enabled. Oracle10g introduces the ability to reclaim space from a segment by shrinking of the segment. Shrinking a segment will make unused space available to other segments in the tablespace and may improve the performance of queries and DML operations.

With the introduction of the alter table xxx shrink space compact syntax, the DBA gets a powerful tool for effective and easy database space management. However, the DBA needs to know what data segments experience high space waste in order to reclaim free space to the database and shrink segments. The awr_list_seg_block_space.sql script below reports percentages of free space for data segments:

🖫 awr_list_seg_block_space.sql

```
-- ********************************************************
-- Copyright © 2005 by Rampant TechPress
-- This script is free for non-commercial purposes
-- with no warranties.  Use at your own risk.
--
```

```
-- To license this script for a commercial purpose,
-- contact info@rampant.cc
-- ****************************************************

drop type BlckFreeSpaceSet;
drop type BlckFreeSpace;

create type BlckFreeSpace as object
(
 seg_owner varchar2(30),
 seg_type varchar2(30),
 seg_name varchar2(100),
 fs1 number,
 fs2 number,
 fs3 number,
 fs4 number,
 fb  number
 );

create type BlckFreeSpaceSet as table of  BlckFreeSpace;

create or replace function BlckFreeSpaceFunc (seg_owner IN varchar2,
seg_type in varchar2 default null) return BlckFreeSpaceSet
pipelined
is
   outRec BlckFreeSpace :=
BlckFreeSpace(null,null,null,null,null,null,null,null);
   fs1_b number;
   fs2_b number;
   fs3_b number;
   fs4_b number;
   fs1_bl number;
   fs2_bl number;
   fs3_bl number;
   fs4_bl number;
   fulb number;
   fulbl number;
   u_b number;
   u_bl number;
begin
   for rec in (select s.owner,s.segment_name,s.segment_type from
dba_segments s where owner = seg_owner and segment_type =
nvl(seg_type,segment_type) )
   loop
     dbms_space.space_usage (
       segment_owner        => rec.owner,
       segment_name         => rec.segment_name,
       segment_type         => rec.segment_type,
       fs1_bytes            => fs1_b,
       fs1_blocks           => fs1_bl,
       fs2_bytes            => fs2_b,
       fs2_blocks           => fs2_bl,
       fs3_bytes            => fs3_b,
       fs3_blocks           => fs3_bl,
       fs4_bytes            => fs4_b,
       fs4_blocks           => fs4_bl,
```

```
       full_bytes          => fulb,
       full_blocks         => fulbl,
       unformatted_blocks => u_bl,
       unformatted_bytes  => u_b
   );

   outRec.seg_owner := rec.owner;
   outRec.seg_type := rec.segment_type;
   outRec.seg_name := rec.segment_name;

   outRec.fs1 := fs1_bl;
   outRec.fs2 := fs2_bl;
   outRec.fs3 := fs3_bl;
   outRec.fs4 := fs4_bl;
   outRec.fb  := fulbl;

   Pipe Row (outRec);

 end loop;
 return;
end;
/
```

The following script can be used to quickly generate a report showing which data segments are good candidates for segment shrinking, thus restoring the wasted space to the tablespace:

```
col seg_owner heading 'Segment|Owner' format a10
col seg_type heading 'Segment|Type'  format a10
col seg_name heading 'Segment|Name'  format a30

col fs1 heading '0-25%|Free Space'   format 9,999
col fs2 heading '25-50%|Free Space'  format 9,999
col fs3 heading '50-75%|Free Space'  format 9,999
col fs4 heading '75-100%|Free Space' format 9,999
col fb  heading 'Full|Blocks'        format 9,999

accept user_name prompt 'Enter Segment Owner: '

break on seg_owner

select
  *
from
  Table ( BlckFreeSpaceFunc ('&user_name', 'TABLE' ) )
order by
  fs4 desc
;
```

The following is the sample output of the above script for the PERFSTAT schema that owns STATSPACK utility:

Online Segment Reorganization

Segment Owner	Segment Type	Segment Name	0-25% Free Space	25-50% Free Space	50-75% Free Space	75-100% Free Space	Full Blocks
PERFSTAT	TABLE	STATS$EVENT_HISTOGRAM	0	0	2	47	321
	TABLE	STATS$LATCH	0	0	1	35	522
	TABLE	STATS$SQL_SUMMARY	0	1	0	28	1,285
	TABLE	STATS$SYSSTAT	1	0	1	13	355
	TABLE	STATS$LIBRARYCACHE	0	0	0	7	13
	TABLE	STATS$SQL_WORKAREA_HISTOGRAM	0	0	1	7	5
	TABLE	STATS$ROWCACHE_SUMMARY	0	0	1	6	43
	TABLE	STATS$ENQUEUE_STATISTICS	0	0	1	6	66
	TABLE	STATS$RESOURCE_LIMIT	1	0	1	6	5
	TABLE	STATS$TIME_MODEL_STATNAME	0	0	0	5	0
	TABLE	STATS$DATABASE_INSTANCE	0	0	0	5	0
	TABLE	STATS$LEVEL_DESCRIPTION	0	0	0	5	0
	TABLE	STATS$IDLE_EVENT	0	0	0	5	0
	TABLE	STATS$WAITSTAT	1	0	1	5	13
	TABLE	STATS$STATSPACK_PARAMETER	0	0	0	5	0
	TABLE	STATS$TEMP_HISTOGRAM	0	1	0	4	0
	TABLE	STATS$INSTANCE_RECOVERY	0	1	0	4	0
	TABLE	STATS$SQL_STATISTICS	0	0	1	4	0
	TABLE	STATS$SGASTAT	0	0	2	4	44
	TABLE	STATS$THREAD	0	0	1	4	0
	TABLE	STATS$ROLLSTAT	0	1	1	4	14
	TABLE	STATS$PARAMETER	1	0	0	4	301

Based on the 75-100% freespace numbers in the above output, one can see that tables *stats$event_histogram*, *stats$latch*, *stats$sql_summary*, and *stats$sysstat* are good candidates for segment shrinking. The following *alter table enable row movement* and *alter table shrink space compact* statements can be issued to shrink the segments mentioned:

```
SQL> alter table stats$event_histogram enable row movement;
Table altered.

SQL> alter table stats$event_histogram shrink space compact;
Table altered.

SQL> alter table stats$latch enable row movement;
Table altered.

SQL> alter table stats$latch shrink space compact;
Table altered.

SQL> alter table stats$sql_summary enable row movement;
Table altered.

SQL> alter table stats$sql_summary shrink space compact;
Table altered.

SQL> alter table stats$sysstat  enable row movement;
Table altered.

SQL> alter table stats$sysstat  shrink space compact;
Table altered.
```

In order to verify that Oracle reclaimed the space, the report script shown above should be issued again to yield the following result.

```
SQL> @ awr_report_seg_block_space.sql

Segment      Segment    Segment                            0-25%      25-50%      50-75%     75-100%     Full
Owner        Type       Name                          Free Space  Free Space  Free Space  Free Space   Blocks
----------   --------   ------------------------      ----------  ----------  ----------  ----------   -----
PERFSTAT     TABLE      STATS$LIBRARYCACHE                     0           0           0           7       13
             TABLE      STATS$SQL_WORKAREA_HISTOGRAM           0           0           1           7        5
             TABLE      STATS$ROWCACHE_SUMMARY                 0           0           1           6       43
             TABLE      STATS$RESOURCE_LIMIT                   1           0           1           6        5
             TABLE      STATS$ENQUEUE_STATISTICS               0           0           1           6       66
......
             TABLE      STATS$SHARED_POOL_ADVICE               1           0           0           2       17
             TABLE      STATS$BUFFER_POOL_STATISTICS           0           0           2           2        1
             TABLE      STATS$EVENT_HISTOGRAM                  0           1           0           1      320
             TABLE      STATS$SYSSTAT                          0           0           1           1      356
             TABLE      STATS$SGA                              0           1           1           1        2
             TABLE      STATS$BUFFERED_QUEUES                  0           1           2           1        1
             TABLE      STATS$PGASTAT                          1           1           1           1        9
             TABLE      STATS$SYS_TIME_MODEL                   0           1           1           1       10
....
             TABLE      STATS$PGA_TARGET_ADVICE                1           0           1           0       11
             TABLE      STATS$LATCH_PARENT                     0           0           0           0        0
             TABLE      STATS$LATCH_CHILDREN                   0           0           0           0        0
             TABLE      STATS$LATCH                            0           1           1           0      521
             TABLE      STATS$DB_CACHE_ADVICE                  0           1           0           0       27
             TABLE      STATS$SQL_SUMMARY                      1           0           0           0    1,284
             TABLE      STATS$SEG_STAT_OBJ                     0           0           0           0        0
             TABLE      STATS$SQL_PLAN                         0           0           0           0        0
             TABLE      STATS$SESS_TIME_MODEL                  0           0           0           0        0
             TABLE      STATS$DLM_MISC                         0           0           0           0        0
             TABLE      STATS$CR_BLOCK_SERVER                  0           0           0           0        0
             TABLE      STATS$CURRENT_BLOCK_SERVER             0           0           0           0        0
             TABLE      STATS$CLASS_CACHE_TRANSFER             0           0           0           0        0
```

From the listing above, it is apparent that the tables that underwent the shrink operation consume much less space than they did previously. The HWM for tables can be reset using a SQL statement like ALTER TABLE SHRINK SPACE. The shrink operation is performed completely online without affecting end users. If the CASCADE option is added to the SHRINK clause, Oracle will also compact indexes created on the target table.

How Can I Shrink Segments?

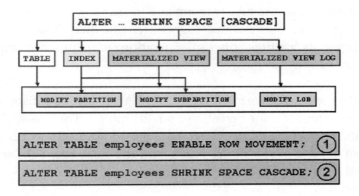

Figure 17.7: *Database objects that support the SHRINK SPACE operation.*

Figure 17.7 shows database objects that support the SHRINK SPACE operation. Oracle10g provides the ability to perform an in-place reorganization of data for optimal space utilization by shrinking it. This feature also provides the ability to both compact the space used in a segment and then deallocate it from the segment. The deallocated space is returned to the tablespace and is available to other objects in the tablespace. Sparsely populated tables may cause a performance problem for full-table scans. By performing SHRINK, data in the table is compacted and the high water mark of the segment is pushed down. This makes full-table scans read less blocks and hence, run faster. Also, during compaction, row chaining is eliminated whenever possible.

Segment shrink is an online operation where the table being shrunk is open to queries and DML while the segment is being shrunk. Additionally, segment shrink is performed in place. This is a key advantage over performing Online Table Redefinition for compaction and reclaiming space. The DBA may schedule segment shrink for one or all the objects in the database as nightly jobs without requiring any additional space to be provided to the database. Segment shrink works on heaps, IOTs, LOBs, Materialized Views and Indexes with row movement enabled in tablespaces with Automatic Segment Space Management.

When segment shrink is performed on tables with indexes on them, the indexes are automatically maintained when rows are moved around for compaction. User defined triggers are not fired, however, because compaction is a purely physical operation and does not impact the application.

The *dbms_space* package allows the DBA to also estimate sizes of indexes intended for creation on a table. The *create_index_cost* procedure from the dbms_space package allows users to get estimate for space usage of the future index, and the following SQL script can be used to accomplish this:

```
declare
   u_bytes number;
   a_bytes number;
```

```
begin
   dbms_space.create_index_cost (
      ddl => 'create index stats$sysstat_idx on stats$sysstat '||
        '(value) tablespace sysaux',
      used_bytes => u_bytes,
      alloc_bytes => a_bytes
   );
   dbms_output.put_line ('Used Bytes      = '|| u_bytes);
   dbms_output.put_line ('Allocated Bytes = '|| a_bytes);
end;
/
```

The result of this PL/SQL block looks like:

```
SQL>
   1   declare
   2      u_bytes number;
   3      a_bytes number;
   4   begin
   5      dbms_space.create_index_cost (
   6         ddl => 'create index stats$sysstat_idx on stats$sysstat
'||
   7            '(value) tablespace sysaux',
   8         used_bytes => u_bytes,
   9         alloc_bytes => a_bytes
  10      );
  11      dbms_output.put_line ('Used Bytes      = '|| u_bytes);
  12      dbms_output.put_line ('Allocated Bytes = '|| a_bytes);
  13*  end;
SQL> /
Used Bytes      = 392886
Allocated Bytes = 851968

PL/SQL procedure successfully completed.
```

This approach is useful because it allows the DBA to adjust some storage parameters before creating an index. The *create_table_cost* procedure for table space size estimates is also available within the *dbms_space* package.

Segment Space Growth Prediction

Most production databases grow over the course of time. Planning for growth is a very important task of every professional Oracle DBA. If resources are carefully planned out well in advance, such problems as the system being out of space are likely to be avoided. Of course, alerts will be generated when the space utilization crosses established alert thresholds. It is very good when the DBA proactively resolves such space related issues.

One of the most important features of Oracle10g is its ability to predict the growth of the segments. The *object_growth_trend* prediction mechanism is based on data collected and stored by the AWR, and the growth trend reporting is also built into the Oracle database kernel and is available by default. The active space monitoring of individual segments in the database gives the up-to-the-minute status of individual segments in the system available to the database. This provides sufficient information, over time, to perform growth trending of individual objects in the database as well as the database as a whole.

The query below allows the estimation of the segment growth trend for the *stats$sysstat* table:

```
SQL> select
*
from
table(dbms_space.OBJECT_GROWTH_TREND
('PERFSTAT','STATS$SYSSTAT','TABLE'));
```

The output of this query might look like this, showing the growth trend for the table. This is very useful for forecasting database growth and planning future disk storage needs:

TIMEPOINT	SPACE_USAGE	SPACE_ALLOC	QUALITY
02.10.04 15:58:04,218000	592359	1048576	INTERPOLATED
03.10.04 15:58:04,218000	592359	1048576	INTERPOLATED
04.10.04 15:58:04,218000	592359	1048576	INTERPOLATED
05.10.04 15:58:04,218000	592359	1048576	INTERPOLATED
06.10.04 15:58:04,218000	592359	1048576	INTERPOLATED
17.10.04 15:58:04,218000	592359	1048576	INTERPOLATED
18.10.04 15:58:04,218000	592359	1048576	INTERPOLATED
19.10.04 15:58:04,218000	592359	1048576	INTERPOLATED
20.10.04 15:58:04,218000	592359	1048576	INTERPOLATED
21.10.04 15:58:04,218000	592359	1048576	GOOD
22.10.04 15:58:04,218000	786887	1048576	INTERPOLATED
23.10.04 15:58:04,218000	826610	1048576	INTERPOLATED
24.10.04 15:58:04,218000	839843	1048576	INTERPOLATED
25.10.04 15:58:04,218000	846459	1048576	INTERPOLATED
26.10.04 15:58:04,218000	3072829	3145728	INTERPOLATED
27.10.04 15:58:04,218000	3072829	3145728	INTERPOLATED
28.10.04 15:58:04,218000	3072829	3145728	INTERPOLATED
29.10.04 15:58:04,218000	3072829	3145728	INTERPOLATED

```
30.10.04 15:58:04,218000          3072829      3145728  INTERPOLATED
31.10.04 15:58:04,218000          3072829      3145728  INTERPOLATED
01.11.04 15:58:04,218000          3072829      3145728  INTERPOLATED
02.11.04 15:58:04,218000          3678280      3678280  PROJECTED
03.11.04 15:58:04,218000          3764774      3764774  PROJECTED
04.11.04 15:58:04,218000          3851267      3851267  PROJECTED
05.11.04 15:58:04,218000          3937760      3937760  PROJECTED
06.11.04 15:58:04,218000          4024253      4024253  PROJECTED
```

The *space_usage* column shows how many bytes the *stats$sysstat* table actually consumes, and *space_alloc* reports the size, in bytes, of space used by the table.

ASSM and RAC Advantages

The performance and manageability gains provided by Oracle10g data management features are particularly noticeable in a Real Application Cluster (RAC) environment, especially the creation of multiple *freelist groups* for each node in the RAC cluster. The ASSM eliminates the need to alter the number of *freelists* and *freelist groups* when new instances are brought online, thereby saving the downtime associated with such table reorganizations. It also avoids the tuning effort previously required for multiple instance environments.

An Oracle internal benchmark comparing the performance of automatic and manual segment space management showed that the ASSM feature provided a 35% performance gain over an optimally tuned segment using the manual mode. This benchmark was conducted on a two node Real Application Cluster database by inserting about 3 million rows in a table. More details are available from Oracle Metalink Note 180608.1.

The new *dbms_space.space_usage* procedure can be used for reporting the space position in BMB segments. This procedure provides the space usage ratio within each block. The *block_count.sql* script below can be used to show how to get information about the blocks. It uses the dbms_space.space_usage procedure to examine the blocks within the specified table and count-up the free space ranges for all data blocks in the table. The block_count.sql script below can be used to show how to get information about the blocks:

🖫 block_count.sql

```
-- ****************************************************
-- Copyright © 2005 by Rampant TechPress
-- This script is free for non-commercial purposes
-- with no warranties.  Use at your own risk.
--
-- To license this script for a commercial purpose,
-- contact info@rampant.cc
-- ****************************************************

DECLARE
 v_unformatted_blocks number;
 v_unformatted_bytes number;
 v_fs1_blocks number;
 v_fs1_bytes number;
 v_fs2_blocks number;
 v_fs2_bytes number;
 v_fs3_blocks number;
 v_fs3_bytes number;
 v_fs4_blocks number;
 v_fs4_bytes number;
 v_full_blocks number;
 v_full_bytes number;

BEGIN
dbms_space.space_usage ('SYSTEM', 'TEST', 'TABLE',
v_unformatted_blocks, v_unformatted_bytes, v_fs1_blocks,
v_fs1_bytes, v_fs2_blocks, v_fs2_bytes, v_fs3_blocks, v_fs3_bytes,
v_fs4_blocks, v_fs4_bytes, v_full_blocks, v_full_bytes);
dbms_output.put_line('Unformatted Blocks = '||v_unformatted_blocks);
dbms_output.put_line('FS1 Blocks         = '||v_fs1_blocks);
dbms_output.put_line('FS2 Blocks         = '||v_fs2_blocks);
dbms_output.put_line('FS3 Blocks         = '||v_fs3_blocks);
dbms_output.put_line('FS4 Blocks         = '||v_fs4_blocks);
dbms_output.put_line('Full Blocks        = '||v_full_blocks);
end;

The script yields the following output:

  Unformatted Blocks = 0
  FS1 Blocks         = 0
  FS2 Blocks         = 0
  FS3 Blocks         = 0
  FS4 Blocks         = 1
  Full Blocks        = 9

Where:

  FS1 means 0-25%   free space within a block
  FS2 means 25-50%  free space within a block
  FS3 means 50-75%  free space within a block
  FS4 means 75-100% free space within a block
```

In summary, the Automatic Segment Space Management and the new online space management packages significantly facilitate space-related management tasks of Oracle DBAs in Oracle10g, especially in RAC environments.

Conclusion

The Automatic Segment Space Management (ASSM) functionality introduced in Oracle Database 10g is a powerful tool that can be used by the Oracle DBA to facilitate the automation of routine work and to make the database as self-managing as possible.

The key points of this chapter include:

- The bitmap freelists of ASSM greatly improve simultaneous *insert* concurrency.

- The DBA may need to manually control *freelist* un-linking and relinking to reduce row fragmentation and improve performance.

- ASSM removes the need to specify *freelist groups* in RAC.

- The new *dbms_space* procedures allow the DBA to see growth trends within specific objects.

The next chapter gives interesting insights into techniques and approaches of using AWR for tuning and management tasks of data warehouse systems.

References

The Self-Managing Database: Proactive Space & Schema Object Management

Oracle Data Warehouse Tuning

"We may need a hardware upgrade"

Oracle Data Warehouse Tuning

The intent of this chapter is to show the main tools and techniques that can be used by the Oracle10g data warehouse administrator for time-series warehouse tuning.

As corporate data warehouse systems grow from small scale applications into industry-wide systems, the IT manager must be postured to help the system grow without service interruption. Oracle10g fills this niche with their database that allows infinite scalability; however, the IT manager must also choose server hardware that allows seamless growth.

What Does a Data Warehouse Need?

Since the earliest days of Decision Support Systems (DSS) in the 1960's, database professionals have recognized that internal processing for data warehouse applications is very different than that of Online Transaction Processing Systems (OLTP).

Data warehouse applications tend to be very I/O intensive, since that type of database reads trillions of bytes of information. Data warehouse systems require specialized servers that can support the typical processing that is found in data warehouses. Most data warehouses are bi-modal and have batch windows, usually in the evenings, when new data is loaded, indexed, and summarized. The server must have on-demand CPU and RAM resources as well as a database management system that must be able to dynamically reconfigure its resources to accommodate these shifts in processing.

In the 1970's, Moore's law was introduced. Moore's law stated that processor costs were always falling while speed continued to improve. However, Moore's law does not apply to RAM.

While RAM costs continue to fall every year, the speed of RAM access is constrained by silicon technology and has not improved in the past three decades. These trends are shown in Figure 18.1.

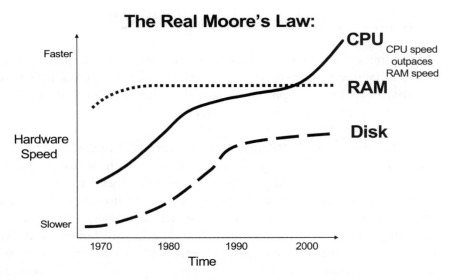

Figure 18.1: *Speed improvements of CPU versus RAM*

Because RAM speed has not improved like CPU speed, RAM must be localized near the CPUs to keep them running at full capacity, and this is a main feature of many of the new Intel-based servers. Non Uniform Memory Access (NUMA) has been available for years in high-end UNIX servers running Symmetric Multi-processor (SMP) configurations.

In order to process large volumes of data quickly, the server must be able to support parallel large-table full-table scans for data warehouse aggregation. One of the biggest improvements in multi-CPU servers is their ability to utilize Oracle parallel features for table summarization, aggregation, DBA maintenance and parallel data manipulation.

For example, this divide and conquer approach makes large-table full-table scans run seven times faster on an 8-CPU server and 15x faster on a 16-way SMP server. These relationships are illustrated in Figure 18.2.

- **Full-table scans can run 15x faster**
- **Parallel DML**
- **Parallel table reorganizations**

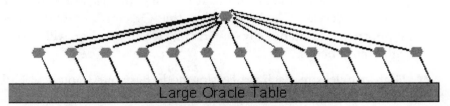

Figure 18.2: *Data Warehouse large-table full-table scans can be parallelized for super-fast response*

Historically, data warehouse applications have been constrained by I/O, but all of this is changing with the introduction of specialized data warehouse techniques, all with the goal of keeping the server CPUs running at full capacity. These techniques include:

- Partitioning: By having the database place data physically near other related data, excessive I/O is reduced.

- Materialized Views: By pre-summarizing data and pre-joining tables, server resources become less I/O intensive.

- Advanced indexing: Databases now offer specialized techniques such as bitmap join indexes and specialized internal table join techniques (STAR transformation schemes) that help shift the processing burden away from I/O.

All of these techniques have helped remove the I/O bottleneck and make data warehouse applications more CPU intensive. There are many server resources that are required for all large data warehouse applications. These features include:

- Large RAM Regions: All 64-bit servers have a larger word size, 2 to the 64th power, that allows for up to 18 billion GB. That is 18 exabytes! This allows for huge scalability as the processing demand grows and allows the database to have many gigabytes of data buffer storage.

- Fast CPU: Intel's 64-bit Itanium 2 architecture is far faster than the older 32-bit chipsets. The advanced features built into the Itanium 2 chipset allow much more real work to be done for each processor cycle. Combined with the Oracle10g NUMA RAM support, computationally intensive DSS queries will run at lightening speeds.

- High parallelism: Each processing node has four Itanium 2 CPUs interconnected to local memory modules and an inter-node crossbar interconnect controller via a high speed bus. Up to four of these processing nodes can be interconnected to create a highly scalable SMP system. This design allows large-scale parallel processing for Oracle full-table scans, which are the scattered reads that are the hallmark of Oracle warehouse systems. For example, the Unisys 64-bit ES7000 servers support up to 16 processors, allowing for large parallel benefits.

- High Performance I/O architecture: The I/O subsystem also influences scalability and performance. Enterprise systems must provide the channel capacity required to support large databases and networks. The Itanium 2 system architecture can support up to 64 peripheral component interconnect (PCI or PCI-X) 64-bit channels operating at speeds from 33 MHz to 100 MHz.

The advent of large RAM regions is also beneficial to the data warehouse. In most data warehouses, a giant central fact table exists, surrounded by smaller dimension tables. This schema is illustrated in Figure 18.3.

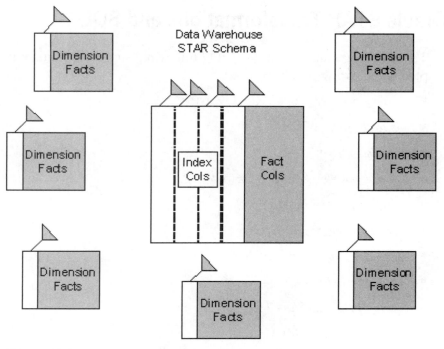

Figure 18.3: *A typical data warehouse schema*

In a typical STAR schema, the larger full-table scans can never be cached, but it is important to be able to control the caching of the dimension tables and indexes. When using a 64-bit server with fast RAM access, the Oracle KEEP pool and multiple buffer caches can be configured to guarantee that the smaller, frequently referenced objects always remain in the data buffers. This will shift the database bottleneck away from I/O. Once the bottleneck has been shifted from I/O to CPU, performance can be scaled by adding more processors.

These star_transformation joins can be successfully used to enable a data warehouse as explained below.

Oracle STAR Transformations and SQL

To enable a data warehouse, the following suggested initialization parameter settings might be used:

- *cursor_space_for_time=TRUE*

- *db_cache_size=XXX*

- *db_block_size=32*

- *db_file_multiblock_read_count=64*

- *filesystemio_options=ASYNC*

- *pga_aggregate_target=XXX*

- *optimizer_index_cost_adj=XXX*

- *optimizer_index_caching=XXX*

- *query_rewrite_enabled=TRUE*

- *shared_pool_size=150M*

- *star_transformation_enabled=TRUE*

- *workarea_size_policy=AUTO*

- *session_cached_cursors=100*

- *log_buffer=XXX*

- *bitmap_merge_area_size=XXX*

- *create_bitmap_area_size=XXX*

For *star_transformation* join plans, the following parameters must also be considered:

- * *star_transformation_enabled* = TRUE

- No hint STAR: So forcing a *star_query* excludes *star_transformation*

- No BIND VARIABLE in SELECT statement

- No CONNECT BY and start with

- For fact table columns involved in EQUIJOIN predicate, there must be bitmap index defined on them.

- More than 2 bitmap index on fact table

- Fact table must have more than 15,000 rows

- Fact table cannot be a view

- Fact table can not be a remote table

- No hint FULL on fact table

Failure to set proper parameters can result in a botched attempt to initiate a *star_transformation* join as shown by the following example.

Bad Star Transformation Plan

The following is an example of a failed attempt at a *star_transformation* join:

```
ALTER SESSION SET "_always_star_transformation"= TRUE;

select /*+ star_transformation */ wdate, hour, minute, sum(bytes)
from
network_fact nf,
date_dimension ddi,
hour_dimension hdi,
minute_dimension mdi
where
nf.date_key=ddi.date_key
and nf.hour_key=hdi.hour_key
and nf.minute_key=mdi.minute_key
and wdate>=to_date('2004/10/14 21', 'yyyy/mm/dd hh24')
and wdate<=to_date('2004/10/15 21', 'yyyy/mm/dd hh24')
group by wdate, hour, minute;

Execution Plan
-----------------------------------------------------------
    0        SELECT STATEMENT Optimizer=CHOOSE
    1     0   SORT (GROUP BY)
    2     1    HASH JOIN
    3     2     TABLE ACCESS (FULL) OF 'MINUTE_DIMENSION'
    4     2     HASH JOIN
    5     4      MERGE JOIN (CARTESIAN)
    6     5       TABLE ACCESS (FULL) OF 'DATE_DIMENSION'
    7     5       BUFFER (SORT)
    8     7        TABLE ACCESS (FULL) OF 'HOUR_DIMENSION'
    9     4      TABLE ACCESS (FULL) OF 'NETWORK_FACT'
```

Good Star Transformation Plan

The following is what a successful *star_transformation* join looks like:

```
Execution Plan
------------------------------------------------------------
    0       SELECT STATEMENT Optimizer=CHOOSE
    1    0  NESTED LOOPS
    2    1   HASH JOIN
    3    2    HASH JOIN
    4    2     TABLE ACCESS (FULL) OF 'MINUTE_DIMENSION'
    5    2    PARTITION CONCATENATED
    6    2     TABLE ACCESS BY ROWID
    7    2      BITMAP CONVERSION TO ROWIDS
    8    2     BITMAP AND
    9    2     BITMAP MERGE
   10    2     BITMAP KEY ITERATION
   11    2      SORT BUFFER
   12    2     TABLE ACCESS (FULL) OF 'MINUTE_DIMENSION'
              BITMAP INDEX RANGE SCAN I_C1
              BITMAP MERGE
              BITMAP KEY ITERATION
              SORT BUFFER
            TABLE ACCESS ... D2
              BITMAP INDEX RANGE SCAN I_C2
BITMAP MERGE
BITMAP KEY ITERATION
SORT BUFFER
TABLE ACCESS ... D3
BITMAP INDEX RANGE SCAN I_C3
TABLE ACCESS ... D2
TABLE ACCESS BY ... D3
```

The execution plan looks like:

```
SELECT STATEMENT C=301
NESTED LOOPS
HASH JOIN
HASH JOIN
TABLE ACCESS ... D1
PARTITION CONCATENATED
TABLE ACCESS BY ROWID F
BITMAP CONVERSION TO ROWIDS
BITMAP AND
BITMAP MERGE
BITMAP KEY ITERATION
SORT BUFFER
TABLE ACCESS ... D1
BITMAP INDEX RANGE SCAN I_C1
BITMAP MERGE
BITMAP KEY ITERATION
SORT BUFFER
TABLE ACCESS ... D2
```

```
BITMAP INDEX RANGE SCAN I_C2
BITMAP MERGE
BITMAP KEY ITERATION
SORT BUFFER
TABLE ACCESS ... D3
BITMAP INDEX RANGE SCAN I_C3
TABLE ACCESS ... D2
TABLE ACCESS BY ... D3
```

This means that with:

- (select C1_1 from D1 where D1.C1_2 op constant1), a bitmap B1 using I_C1 is generated.

- (select C2_1 from D2 where D1.C2_2 op constant2), a bitmap B2 using I_C2 is generated.

- (select C3_1 from D3 where D1.C3_2 op constant3), a bitmap B3 using I_C3 is generated.

Next, the DBA performs an AND between those bitmaps. At the end, those rows from F with rowid coming from bitmap merging are taken.

Why Oracle 10g for the Data Warehouse?

The large data buffer caches in most OLTP Oracle systems make them CPU-bound, but Oracle data warehouses are another story. With terabytes of information to aggregate and summarize, most Oracle data warehouses are I/O-bound and the DBA must choose a server that optimizes disk I/O throughput.

Oracle has always made very large database (VLDB) technology a priority as evidenced by their introduction of partitioned structures, advanced bitmap indexing, and materialized views. Oracle10g provides some features that are ideal for the data warehouse application:

- Read-only Tablespaces: If the DBA has a time-series warehouse where information eventually becomes static, using tablespace partitions and marking the older tablespaces as read only can greatly improve performance. When a tablespace is marked as read only, Oracle can bypass this read consistency mechanism, reducing overhead and resulting in faster throughput.

- Automatic Storage Management (ASM): The revolutionary new method for managing the disk I/O subsystem removes the tedious and time consuming chore of I/O load balancing and disk management. Oracle10g ASM allows all disks to be logically clustered together into disk groups and data files spread across all devices using the Oracle10g SAME (Stripe and Mirror Everywhere) standard. By making the disk backend a JBOD (Just a Bunch of Disks), Oracle10g manages this critical aspect of the data warehouse.

- Multi-level partitioning of tables and indexes: Oracle now has multi-level intelligent partitioning methods that allow Oracle to store data in a precise scheme. By controlling where data is stored on disk, Oracle10g SQL can reduce the disk I/O required to service any query.

- Advanced Data Buffer Management: Using the Oracle10g multiple block sizes and KEEP pool, the DBA can pre-assign warehouse objects to separate data buffers and ensure that the working set of frequently referenced data is always cached. Oracle10g also offers Automatic Memory Management (AMM) whereby Oracle10g will automatically re-assign RAM frames between the *db_cache_size* and the *pga_aggregate_target* region to maximize throughput of the data warehouse.

- Materialized Views: Oracle's materialized views (MV) use Oracle replication to allow the DBA to pre-summarize and pre-join tables. Best of all, Oracle MV's are integrated with the Oracle 10g query rewrite facility, so that any queries that might benefit from the pre-summarization will be automatically rewritten to reference the aggregate view. This will avoid a very expensive and unnecessary large-table full-table scan.

- Automated Workload Repository (AWR) analysis: The AWR provides a time-series component to warehouse tuning that is critical for the identification of materialized views and holistic warehouse tuning. The most important data warehouse tracking with AWR includes tracking large-table-full-table scans, hash joins which might be replaced with STAR joins, and tracking of RAM usage within the *pga_aggregate_target* region.

It is easy to identify when an Oracle warehouse is disk I/O bound. In the AWR report below, comparable to a STATSPACK report for Oracle9i and earlier, it is clear that this typical data warehouse system is clearly constrained by disk I/O, resulting from the high percentage of full-table and full-index scans.

```
Top 5 Timed Events
~~~~~~~~~~~~~~~~~~                                      % Total
Event                          Waits     Time (s)     Ela Time
-------------------------   ------------  -----------  --------
db file scattered read          2,598        7,146       58.54
db file sequential read        25,519        3,246       12.04
library cache load lock           673        1,363        9.26
CPU time                                      1,154        7.83
log file parallel write        19,157          837        5.68
```

This listing shows that scattered reads, as full-table scans, constitute the majority of the total database time. This is very typical of a data warehouse that performs aggregations via SQL. It is also common during the refresh period for Oracle materialized views. The problem is the I/O bottleneck that is introduced during these periods.

Due to the fact that the typical data warehouse is so data intensive, there is always a problem fully utilizing the CPU power. UNISYS has addressed this issue by leveraging on Non-Uniform Memory Access (NUMA), whereby Windows and Oracle10g are automatically configured to exploit NUMA to keep the CPUs busy. The data buffer hit ratio is not relevant for data warehouses, systems that commonly perform full-table scans, or those that use all_rows SQL optimization.

While a 30 GB *db_cache_size* might be appropriate for an OLTP shop or a shop that uses a large working set, a large SGA does not benefit data warehouse and decision support systems (DSS) where most data access is performed by a parallelized full-table scan. When Oracle performs a parallel full-table scan, the database blocks are read directly into the program global area (PGA), bypassing the data buffer RAM as illustrated in Figure 18.4.

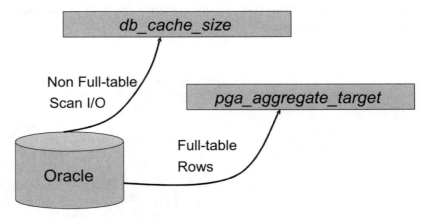

Figure 18.4: *Parallel Full Scans Bypass SGA data buffers*

The figure above shows that having a large *db_cache_size* does not benefit parallel large-table full-table scans, as this requires memory in the *pga_aggregate_target* region instead. With Oracle 10g, the multiple data buffer features can be used to segregate and cache dimension tables and indexes, all while providing sufficient RAM for the full scans. When the processing mode changes during evening Extract, Transform, and Load (ETL) and rollups, Oracle10g AMM will automatically detect the change in data access and re-allocate the RAM regions to accommodate the current processing.

All 64-bit servers have a larger word size (2 to the 64th power) that allows for up to 18 billion GB of addressable RAM. DBAs may be tempted to create a super large RAM data buffer. Data warehouse systems tend to bypass the data buffers because of parallel full-table scans, and maximizing disk I/O throughput is the single most critical bottleneck.

Most SMP servers have a specialized high speed RAM called a L2 cache that is localized near the CPUs as shown in Figure 18.5.

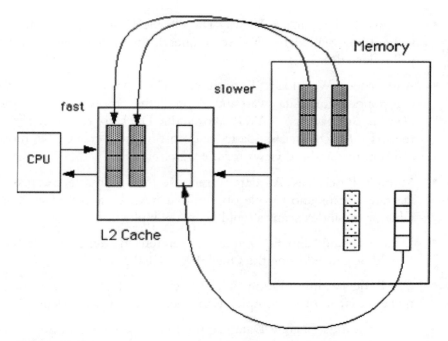

Figure 18.5: *The non-uniform memory access architecture*

Best of all, Oracle10g has been enhanced to recognize NUMA systems and adjust memory and scheduling operations accordingly. NUMA technology allows for faster communication between distributed memory in a multi-processor server. Better than the archaic UNIX implementations of the past decade, NUMA is fully supported by Linux and Windows Advanced Server 2003 and Oracle can now better exploit high end NUMA hardware in SMP servers.

Now that the use of Oracle10g has been justified for the warehouse, it is important to examine why many shops are moving from Linux to Windows for their mission critical warehouse applications.

Now, while the automated features of Oracle10g AMM, ASM and automatic query rewrite simplify the role of the Oracle DBA, savvy Oracle10g DBAs leverage other advanced Oracle10g features to get fast data warehouse performance:

- Extensive Materialized Views: The Oracle10g *dbms_advisor* utility will automatically detect and recommend, then a materialized view will reduce disk I/O.

- Automated Workload Repository: The AWR is a critical component for data warehouse predictive tools such as the *dbms_advisor* package. AWR allows the DBA to run time-series reports of SQL access paths and intelligently create the most efficient materialized views for the warehouse.

- Multiple Blocksizes: All data warehouse indexes that are accessed via range scans and Oracle objects that must be accessed via full-table or full-index scans should be in a 32k blocksize.

- Data Caching: Small, frequently referenced dimension tables should be cached using the Oracle10g KEEP pool.

- STAR query optimization: The Oracle10g STAR query features make it easy to make complex DSS queries run at fast speeds.

- Asynchronous Change Data Capture: Change data capture allows incremental extraction, which allows only changed data to be extracted easily. For example, if a data warehouse extracts data from an operational system on a weekly basis, the data warehouse requires only the data that has changed since the last extraction, which would be only the data that has been modified in the past 7 days.

- Oracle Streams: Streams based feed mechanisms can capture the necessary data changes from the operational database and send it to the destination data warehouse. The use of redo information by the Streams capture process avoids unnecessary overhead on the production database.

Oracle Database 10g is even more optimized for Itanium2 architecture than Oracle 9i was and many Oracle experts consider Intel-based servers as the best choice for running Oracle data warehouses. The following section explores this more closely.

Scaling the Oracle10g data warehouse

New generation Intel-based servers are pushing hard on the Oracle industry. Hardware vendors are calling out to Oracle professionals, each promising lower Total Cost of Ownership (TCO), faster performance, and easy scalability. With so many choices, migrating onto a 64-bit platform can be a confusing proposition. In general, the following are competing approaches to scaling the Oracle data warehouse:

- Scale Up: Vendors promise on-demand computing resources, lower TCO, and easy scalability. Their huge servers offer savings from CPU and RAM consolidation, far less human management costs, and seamless allocation of resources.

- Scale Out: Grid vendors offer solutions where server blades can be added to Oracle as processing demand increases. While Grid computing offers infinite scalability, no central point of failure, and the use of fast cheap server blades, it does have the same in-the-box parallelism that is found within a monolithic server. Unlike the scale up approach, Oracle10g Grid computing is not automatic and requires additional costs, additional training, as well as sophisticated monitoring and management software.

Most savvy Oracle data warehouse shops practice the scale up approach first. They only scale out when they reach the processing limits of their server, which is a very rare occurrence for today's data warehouses. Many Oracle warehouse professionals have learned that scaling out with Real Application Clusters (RAC) and Grid is not an optimal solution. Instead, they choose the scale up approach within a single server for many compelling reasons:

- High Parallelism: Complex data warehouse queries need easy parallel query capability and many on-board CPUs to maximize throughput. RAC nodes and Oracle Grid server blades rarely have more than 4 CPUs.

- Simplicity: Oracle clustering solutions are complex to configure and manage. For the Oracle data warehouse, a large monolithic server provides complete on demand resource allocation and scalability.

- Low Cost: Oracle RAC licenses are expensive, and the DBA staff needs expensive specialized training to master the complex inter-node communications.

- Seamless Scalability: Unlike the scale out approach, a scale up Oracle data warehouse will be instantly able to leverage new server resources without any changes to the environment.

There is also a common misconception that using a single server with scale up capabilities introduces a single point of failure problem. In reality, hardware redundancy, on servers, such as the Unisys ES7000 400 Series servers, offers further protection against failure including redundant cooling, power, and dual air conditioning with on-board power management, hot-pluggable components, automated failure diagnosis and recovery, and proactive failover mechanisms.

The scale up approach is the natural reaction to the rampant distribution of Oracle systems onto small, independent servers. This architecture saves money on hardware costs at the expense of having to hire a huge system administration and DBA staff. This is the appeal of consolidation: to avoid the high overhead and expense of such server farms.

Due to the advances in the UNISYS server technology, the concept of using a large SMP server for Oracle data warehousing has become very popular. The scale up approach provides on-demand resource allocation by sharing CPU and RAM between many resources, requiring less maintenance and human resources to manage fewer servers. More importantly, the scale up approach provides optimal utilization of RAM and CPU resources and gives the warehouse high availability through fault tolerant components. This approach provides a high degree of scalability and flexibility for high performance and also provides high availability and low cost of ownership (TCO).

The scale out approach is designed for super large Oracle databases that support many thousands of concurrent users. Unless the system has a need to support more than 10,000 transactions per second, it is likely that the system will benefit more from a scale up approach.

Conclusion

This chapter has made it clear that data warehouse tuning is all about minimizing disk I/O. Oracle data warehouses are disk intensive and require an architecture that helps to keep the CPUs running at full capacity. As server resources become like commodities, the savvy IT manager will choose the platform that offers reliability, scalability and, above all, the lowest total cost of ownership. In other words, go with the low TCO.

The main points of this chapter include:

- What a Data Warehouse Needs

- Oracle STAR Transformations and SQL

- Why Oracle 10g is suited for the Data Warehouse

- Methods for scaling the Oracle10g data warehouse

This chapter has shown the main tools and techniques that can be used by the Oracle10g data warehouse administrator for time-series warehouse tuning. With this information on Data Warehouse Tuning with AWR, the next chapter will delve into Oracle10g Tuning with the Oracle Enterprise Manager (OEM).

Oracle 10g Tuning with OEM

OEM can advise you about pending performance problems

Introduction to OEM

One of the reasons that Oracle achieved dominance in the early 1990's was their commitment to provide Oracle on over 60 hardware platforms running on everything from a mainframe to a Macintosh. In order to achieve this transparency between diverse hardware platforms, Oracle invested heavily in leveraging upon the strengths of each operating system while still providing a hardware independent look-and-feel.

Oracle's quest for platform-independent DBA management layer has gone though several incarnations over the past decade, from the archaic SQL*DBA command-line utility to the original Oracle Enterprise Manager (OEM).

The original OEM (circa 1996) was rejected by some experienced Oracle professionals as a simple SQL command generator, and seasoned DBAs preferred to enter the commands manually from SQL*Plus. Any DBA caught using OEM was immediately suspected of not knowing the Oracle command syntax.

The New OEM

Oracle recognized the need to improve the functionality of OEM for tuning activities and employed some of the world's leading Oracle experts including; Kyle Hailey, John Beresniewicz, Gaja Krishna Vaidyanatha and Graham Wood to help rebuild the OEM performance interface.

Bearing little resemblance to its OEM predecessor, the new OEM performance interfaces were designed by practicing Oracle tuning experts, and the new OEM offers an unparalleled performance management interface, worthy of the most seasoned Oracle DBA.

The OEM performance screens are straightforward and intuitive, making it easy to identify and correct performance issues. These new OEM tuning features include many powerful new elements:

- Automatic Display of Performance Information: The OEM performance screens enable a stunning visual display of important Oracle performance metrics. The monitoring and diagnostic abilities of Oracle10g are enabled by the AWR which collects and stores historical run-time performance data as an integral part of the Oracle10g database kernel.

- Incorporation of External Information: OEM samples server-side metrics and incorporates CPU consumption, run-queue length, physical I/O and RAM paging information. This enables a comprehensive picture of overall Oracle performance.

- Easy Exception Reporting Mechanism: OEM allows the customizing of alert thresholds to notify DBAs before their database experiences a performance problem. Since OEM is always watching, they are free to perform other important tasks, and customized thresholds can be set for hundreds of AWR metrics to guarantee that they will have the chance to address a pending problem before it affects their end-users.

- Automated Performance Diagnostics: Using the optional Database Diagnostic Pack and Database Tuning Pack components, OEM has a native interface to ADDM, allowing OEM to make intelligent performance recommendations.

- Improved Interface: OEM has a secure web-based HTML interface for remote access and the OEM2GO PDA interface, making it easy for the Oracle professional to manage their Oracle database anywhere in the world.

This chapter focuses on using the OEM performance screens to quickly locate performance bottlenecks. The core point of this chapter is OEMs use of intelligent time-series metric display to provide a framework for easy top-down time-series performance monitoring. This chapter covers the following topics:

- Navigating the OEM Tuning Architecture: This section explores the hierarchy of the OEM tuning screens and how they are organized. It also reviews the performance screen and the session details screens to show how the DBA can drill down to find even the most subtle tuning issue.

- Customizing OEM Alerts: The Oracle10g OEM allows for the easy creation of sophisticated notifications using hundreds of Oracle metrics. These custom alerts are deployed via e-mail, telephone, pager, or OEM2GO on a PDA.

- Using the OEM to Troubleshoot a Performance Issue: This section shows how to drill-down into the OEM performance display to reveal how easy it is to locate transient performance issues.

- A quick review of the OEM screen hierarchy showing how OEM interfaces with the Oracle data dictionary and kernel tables to provide a complete logical interface is merited.

At the most simplistic level, the OEM performance screens are a graphical user interface (GUI) for the display and manipulation of

Oracle performance information. Oracle10g has revolutionized the database industry by incorporating database performance information inside special built-in performance history tables.

Prior to Oracle10g Enterprise Manager, tuning a complex performance issue was extremely time-consuming. The Oracle professional had to manually collect time-series performance information, trace dumps, STATSPACK reports and wade through reams of complex data to find the root cause of the sub-optimal performance.

Everything changes with OEM which now filters through the AWR and ASH repository, quickly focusing on the important metrics. A brief tour of the OEM performance screens reveals how easy it is to spot and correct performance issues.

As previously noted, OEM was designed by practicing Oracle tuning professionals to provide a top-down, intuitive approach to Oracle monitoring. Using any web browser, secure access to the OEM performance screen can be acquired anywhere on the planet as shown in Figure 19.1.

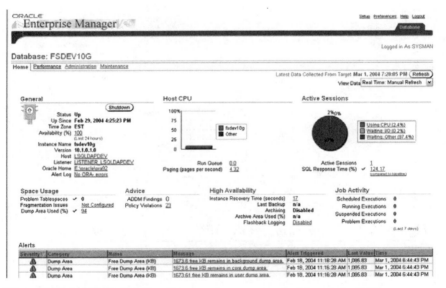

Figure 19.1: *The OEM performance home-screen for Enterprise Manager.*

This summary screen provides a complete overview of the current status of the database. All aspects of the database instance including tablespace and session summary information is shown. Exciting external metrics with hyperlinks to the listener, oracle_home, dump files and alert log directories are also shown.

Tuning with Metrics and Exceptions

From this main OEM performance screen the DBA can quickly drill-down and view all AWR metrics and scroll through the complete list of automatically captured statistics as shown in Figure 19.2.

Metrics	Thresholds	Collection Status
▼FSDEV10G		
▶Alert Log	Some	Not Collected
▶Alert Log Content	None	Not Collected
▶Alert Log Error Status	All	Last Collected Mar 1, 2004 6:47:07 PM
▶Archive Area	Some	Last Collected Feb 29, 2004 4:44:43 PM
▶Data Guard	Some	Last Collected Feb 29, 2004 4:59:57 PM
▶Database Files	None	Last Collected Mar 1, 2004 6:56:10 PM
▶Database Job Status	All	Last Collected Feb 29, 2004 5:03:53 PM
▶Database Limits	Some	Last Collected Mar 1, 2004 6:57:15 PM
▶Database Services	None	Last Collected Mar 1, 2004 6:56:10 PM
▶Deferred Transactions	All	Last Collected Feb 29, 2004 5:03:52 PM
▶Dump Area	Some	Last Collected Mar 1, 2004 6:44:43 PM
▶Efficiency	None	Last Collected Mar 1, 2004 6:57:15 PM
▶Invalid Objects	None	Not Collected
▶Invalid Objects by Schema	All	Last Collected Feb 29, 2004 4:47:51 PM
▶Num of Sessions Waiting (EvtCLs)	None	Last Collected Mar 1, 2004 6:56:10 PM
▶Recovery Area	None	Not Collected
▶Response	Some	Last Collected Feb 29, 2004 4:22:59 PM
▶SGA Pool Wastage	None	Last Collected Mar 1, 2004 6:55:29 PM
▶SQL Response Time	All	Last Collected Mar 1, 2004 6:53:52 PM
▶Session Suspended	None	Not Collected
▶Snap Shot Too Old	None	Not Collected
▶System Response Time Per Call	None	Last Collected Mar 1, 2004 6:56:10 PM
▶Tablespaces Full	All	Last Collected Mar 1, 2004 6:54:35 PM
▶Tablespaces With Problem Segments	Some	Not Collected
▶Throughput	None	Last Collected Mar 1, 2004 6:57:15 PM
▶User Audit	Some	Last Collected Mar 1, 2004 6:40:29 PM
▶User Block	Some	Not Collected
▶Wait Bottlenecks	None	Last Collected Mar 1, 2004 6:57:15 PM

Figure 19.2: *A partial listing of the AWR metrics from inside OEM.*

This feature allows the DBA to drill down into important Oracle performance areas including instance efficiency, SQL response time, SGA pool wastage, and wait bottlenecks.

There is more to the data collection than instance-wide metrics. OEM can be customized to send alerts for whatever combination of metric values desired.

For example, the OEM Grid controller is used to add an additional RAC node to the system during this period, just-in-time to meet the increased processing demands as shown in Figure 19.3.

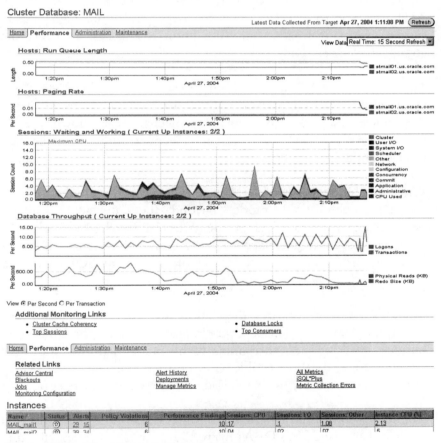

Figure 19.3: *The OEM Grid/RAC display screen.*

Now that it has been shown how OEM incorporates external metrics, the ways OEM makes it easy to view Active Session History (ASH) information will be revealed. The ASH component is brand new in Oracle10g and allows the DBA to quickly spotlight the important wait events associated with any Oracle task.

Active Session History in Enterprise Manager

Oracle10g now has an Active Session History (ASH) component that automatically collects detailed metrics on individual Oracle sessions. OEM also has an interface to the ASH component of AWR. The ASH uses special *dba_hist* views to collect and store highly detailed system event information allowing immediate access to every detail about Oracle execution.

Together, the AWR and ASH metrics form the foundation for a complete Oracle tuning framework, and Enterprise Manager provides the vehicle. Now that the underlying mechanism is shown, the DBA can explore how OEM gives an intelligent window into this critical Oracle tuning information.

While this functionality of OEM is amazing in its own right, Oracle10g has taken the AWR model beyond the intelligent display of performance metrics. Using true Artificial Intelligence (AI), OEM now has a built-in interface to the Automatic Database Diagnostic Monitor, pronounced "Adam", and the intelligent SQL Tuning and SQL Access advisors.

The next section explores the Automated Alert mechanism within Enterprise Manager. This is a very important feature for Oracle tuning because it allows alert thresholds to be predefined and notifications about pending database problems to be sent. This gives the DBA the critical time necessary to fix the issue before the end-users suffer.

The use of the Enterprise Manager with ADDM and the SQL Tuning advisor can save the DBA from the tedium of manually tuning hundreds of SQL statements. The new Oracle10g SQL profiles allow

DBAs to rapidly and reliably complete a complex tuning effort in just a few hours.

Easy Customization of OEM Alerts

The Oracle10g Enterprise Manager recognizes that no DBA has the time to constantly monitor all of the metrics in real-time and provides an easy to use exception reporting mechanism. Figure 19.4 shows the MANAGE METRICS screen in which the DBA can easily define a customized alert mechanism for a database.

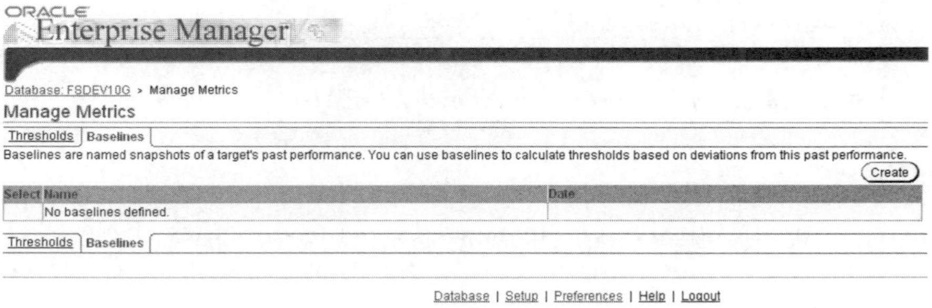

Figure 19.4: *The OEM Manage Metrics screen.*

When a drill down into the metric list occurs, OEM displays hundreds of individual tuning metrics and provides the ability to set personalized alert thresholds as shown in Figure 19.5. OEM allows the DBA to specify any scalar thresholds, such as greater than or less than, and has full pattern matching capabilities for text-based alerts such as alert log messages.

SQL Response Time (%)	>	500	
Scans on Long Tables (per second)	>		
Scans on Long Tables (per transaction)	>		
Segments Approaching Maximum Extents Count	>	0	
Segments Not Able to Extend Count	>	0	
Service CPU Time (per user call)	>		
Service Response Time (per user call)	>		
Session Limit Usage (%)	>	80	
Session Logical Reads (per second)	>		
Session Logical Reads (per transaction)	>		
Session Terminated Alert Log Error	Contains	ORA-	
Session Terminated Alert Log Error Status	>	0	
Shared Pool Free (%)	<		
Soft Parse (%)	<		
Sorts in Memory (%)	<		
Sorts to Disk (per second)	>		
Sorts to Disk (per transaction)	>		
System Response Time (centi-seconds)	>		
Tablespace Space Used (%)	>	85	97

Figure 19.5: *Setting alert thresholds within OEM.*

For example, DBAs can set an OEM threshold to send them a pager alert or use OEM2GO whenever their critical metrics change. There are several critical instance-wide performance metrics displayed in Figure 19.5:

- SQL Response Time (%)

- System Response Time (centi-seconds)

- Shared Pool Free (%)

Because of the time-series nature of AWR, it is easy to trigger an exception alert when the marginal values of any metrics change. All metrics denoted with the (%) are delta-based, meaning that OEM triggers an alert whenever any metric moves by more than a specified percentage, regardless of its current value. This delta-based mechanism is used to allow time to repair a pending performance issue before it cripples the end-users.

For automated notification, a SNMP interface can be easily configured to have OEM send the DBA a notification e-mail whenever the threshold value has been exceeded. This alert can be an e-mail, a telephone message or an alert on the OEM2GO PDA device.

Instance Efficiency Metrics

Oracle 10g OEM also allows the customization of important instance efficiency metrics as shown in Figure 19.6. These track overall SGA efficacy each time an AWR snapshot is collected. The AWR snapshot frequency is customizable and OEM displays the last snapshot collection date in the third column of the display.

▼ Efficiency	None	Last Collected Mar 1, 2004 7:07:15 PM
Buffer Cache Hit (%)	Not Set	Last Collected Mar 1, 2004 7:07:15 PM
CPU Usage (per second)	Not Set	Last Collected Mar 1, 2004 7:07:15 PM
CPU Usage (per transaction)	Not Set	Last Collected Mar 1, 2004 7:07:15 PM
Cursor Cache Hit (%)	Not Set	Last Collected Mar 1, 2004 7:07:15 PM
Data Dictionary Hit (%)	Not Set	Last Collected Mar 1, 2004 7:07:15 PM
Database CPU Time (%)	Not Set	Last Collected Mar 1, 2004 7:07:15 PM
Library Cache Hit (%)	Not Set	Last Collected Mar 1, 2004 7:07:15 PM
Library Cache Miss (%)	Not Set	Last Collected Mar 1, 2004 7:07:15 PM
PGA Cache Hit (%)	Not Set	Last Collected Mar 1, 2004 7:07:15 PM
Parallel Execution Downgraded 1 to 25% (per second)	Not Set	Last Collected Mar 1, 2004 7:07:15 PM

Figure 19.6: *Setting instance efficiency alert thresholds.*

Instance efficiency metrics are especially valuable when tracked over time. For example, the DBA can request a customized alert when the following changes occur:

- *PGA cache Hit (%)* drops by more than 10%.

- *PGA multi-pass executions* increase above 5%.

This custom alert might indicate a change in SQL processing on the server that may be experiencing excessive disk sorting. By alerting the DBA before the problem is fully manifested, OEM can be used to give the DBA an opportunity to adjust the resources just-in-time to address the issue before the end-users experience a response time delay.

Alerts Notification and Setup

Oracle Enterprise Manager can be used to send alert notifications to the DBA by pager or email. The following is an example of setting up an email notification for critical alerts using OEM.

From the Database Control page, click the Setup link visible in the header as well as footer areas.

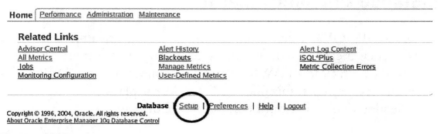

Figure 19.7: *Setting up Alerts.*

Click Notification Methods on the Setup page. See Figure 19.8 below.

Complete the information needed for the Mail Sever portion on this screen. Users should get help from the network administrator or refer online help to know more about the mail server names, as a discussion on it is beyond the scope of this book.

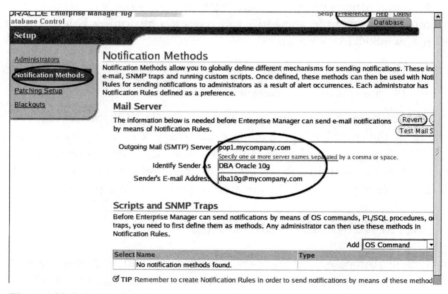

Figure 19.8: *Alert Notification*

From any Database Control page, click on the Preferences link visible in header or footer areas. See Figure 19.8 above.

Select General and enter an email address in the E-mail Address section. Select Notification Rules to modify any default notification rules. This page will show how to change the severity settings for receiving notification.

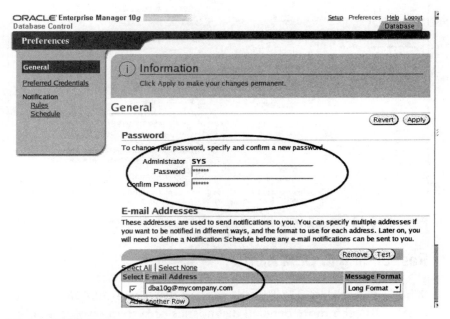

Figure 19.9: *OEM Alert Notification setup screen.*

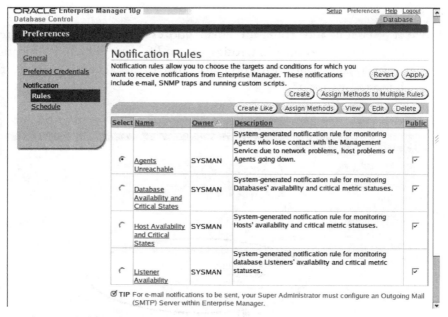

Figure 19.10: *Notification Rules.*

Responding to OEM Alerts

Whenever an alert is received, many DBA's run ADDM or another advisor to get a more detailed diagnostics of system or object behavior. The DBA can also opt to enable a corrective script to run on receiving an alert as mentioned in Managing Metric Thresholds section.

If a Tablespace Space Usage alert is received, remedial actions can be taken by running the Oracle10g Segment Advisor on the tablespace to identify objects for shrinking. Those objects can then be coalesced or extended.

All of the job details, including the schedule, job definition and the broken flag, can be edited within Enterprise Manager by double clicking on the job of interest. Figure 19.11 shows the edit job dialog.

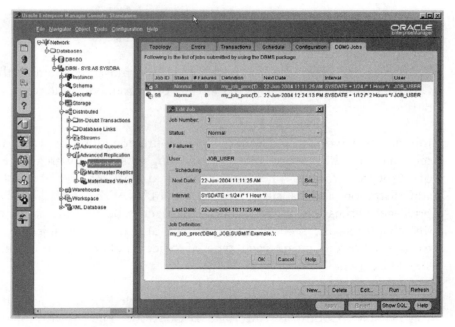

Figure 19.11: *OEM: Edit job.*

The run procedure on this screen allows the DBA to run a specified job immediately, with the *next_date* recalculated from that point. The force parameter indicates that the job queue affinity can be ignored allowing any instance to run the job.

Job information is also available from Oracle Enterprise Manager (OEM) (Network > Databases > Your-Instance > Distributed > Advanced Replication > Administration > DBMS Job Tab).

Overview of *dbms_scheduler* Functions

The *dbms_scheduler* package is the recommended way to schedule jobs in Oracle10g. The *dbms_job* package is still present, but only for backward compatibility. The jobs created using the *dbms_job* package are very much standalone in their nature in that they are defined with their own schedules and actions. In addition to this, the *dbms_scheduler* package allows the DBA to define standard programs and schedules which can be used by many jobs. Before creating jobs, the DBA should learn how to define these standard elements.

To access the *dbms_scheduler* package a user must be granted the CREATE JOB privilege. This has already been granted to the test user during the setup.

Job classes, windows, and window groups provide a link between the scheduler and the resource manager, allowing jobs to run with a variety of resource profiles. They are considered part of the scheduler administration and as such require the MANAGE SCHEDULER privilege. Discussion of the resource manager is beyond the scope of this chapter so the sections that deal with administration objects will focus on how to create each type of object, rather than how they should be used.

Support for the scheduler is built in to the Oracle Enterprise Manager 10g Database Control (OEM 10g DB Control). The majority of the scheduler objects can be managed via links from the administration page. Figure 19.12 shows the administration page with the scheduler links on the right hand side towards the bottom of the screen.

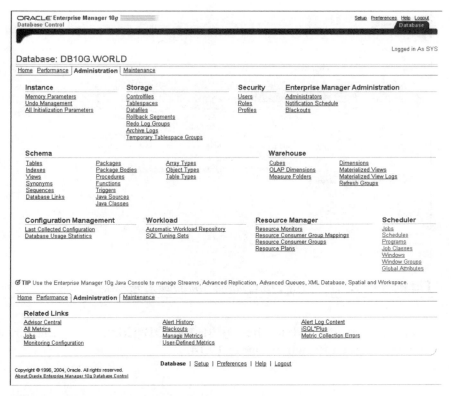

Figure 19.12: *OEM 10g DB Control: Administration.*

Program information is also available from the OEM 10g DB Control via the Scheduler Programs screen shown in Figure 19.13.

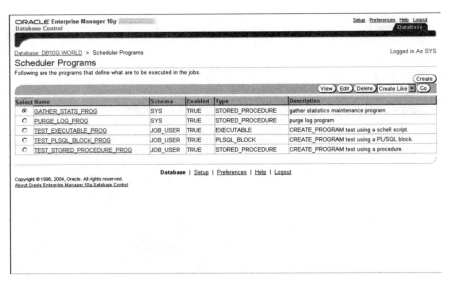

Figure 19.13: *OEM 10g DB Control: Scheduler Programs.*

Schedules are created in the OEM 10g DB Control via the Create Schedule screen shown in Figure 19.14.

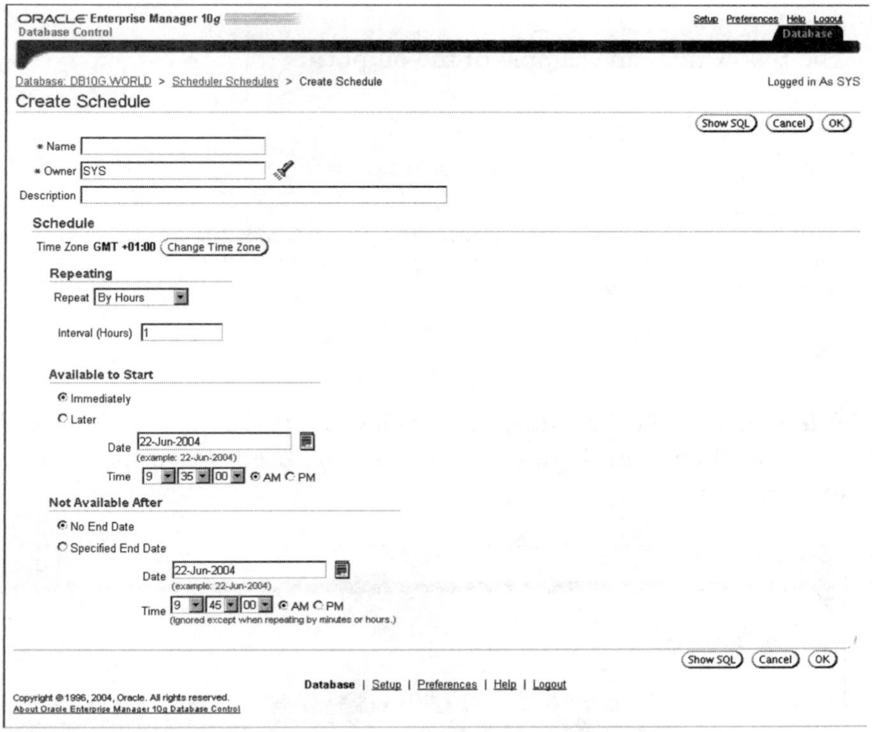

Figure 19.14: *OEM 10g DB Control: Create Schedule.*

Information about schedules can be displayed using the *dba_scheduler_schedules* view. The following script uses this view to display information about schedules for a specified user or all users.

```
-- Parameters:
--    1) Specific USERNAME or ALL which doesn't limit output.
-- ******************************************************************

set verify off

select
   owner,
   schedule_name,
   repeat_interval
from
   dba_scheduler_schedules
where
   owner = decode(upper('&1'), 'ALL', owner, upper('&1'))
;
```

The following is an example of the output.

```
SQL> @schedules job_user

OWNER                          SCHEDULE_NAME
------------------------------ ------------------------------
REPEAT_INTERVAL
-------------------------------------------------------------
JOB_USER                       TEST_HOURLY_SCHEDULE
freq=hourly; byminute=0


1 row selected.
```

Alternatively, the Scheduler Schedules screen of the OEM 10g DB Control shown in Figure 19.15, can be used to display schedule information.

Figure 19.15: *OEM 10g DB Control: Scheduler Schedules.*

The *dbms_job* screen can also be used for scheduling as shown in Figure 19.16.

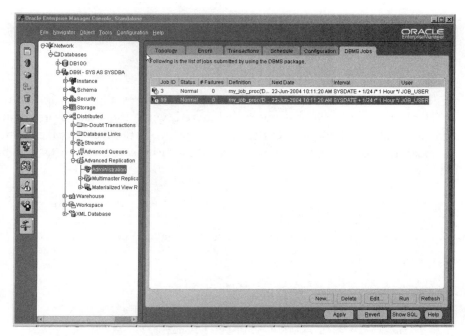

Figure 19.16: *OEM: DBMS Jobs.*

Once a job is scheduled, changes to some of its attributes can be achieved using the *what*, *next_date*, *instance*, *interval* and *change* procedures whose call specifications are displayed below.

```
PROCEDURE what (
   job       IN  BINARY_INTEGER,
   what      IN  VARCHAR2)

PROCEDURE next_date (
   job       IN  BINARY_INTEGER,
   next_date IN  DATE)

PROCEDURE instance (
   job       IN  BINARY_INTEGER,
   instance  IN  BINARY_INTEGER,
   force     IN  BOOLEAN DEFAULT FALSE)

PROCEDURE interval (
   job       IN  BINARY_INTEGER,
   interval  IN  VARCHAR2)

PROCEDURE change (
   job       IN  BINARY_INTEGER,
```

Overview of dbms_scheduler Functions **815**

```
what       IN  VARCHAR2,
next_date  IN  DATE,
interval   IN  VARCHAR2,
instance   IN  BINARY_INTEGER DEFAULT NULL,
force      IN  BOOLEAN DEFAULT FALSE)
```

The *what*, *next_date*, *instance* and *interval* procedures allow the individual attributes of the same name to be altered, while the change procedure allows all of them to be altered in one go, effectively replacing the existing job. The examples below show how the procedures can be used.

```
BEGIN
  DBMS_JOB.what (
    job  => 99,
    what => 'my_job_proc(''DBMS_JOB.ISUBMIT Example (WHAT).'');');

  DBMS_JOB.next_date (
    job       => 99,
    next_date => SYSDATE + 1/12);

  DBMS_JOB.interval (
    job      => 99,
    interval => 'SYSDATE + 1/12 /* 2 Hours */');

  COMMIT;
END;
/
```

The DBA can change the entire job definition back using the change procedure. If the what, next_date or interval parameters are NULL, the existing value is unchanged.

```
BEGIN
  DBMS_JOB.change (
    job       => 99,
    what      => 'my_job_proc(''DBMS_JOB.ISUBMIT Example.'');',
    next_date => TO_DATE('22-JUN-2004 10:11:20', 'DD-MON-YYYY
HH24:MI:SS'),
    interval  => 'SYSDATE + 1/24 /* 1 Hour */');

  COMMIT;
END;
/
```

Figures 19.17 and 19.18 show the Create Job (General) and Create Job (Schedule) screens respectively. These provide a web-based alternative to the *create_job* procedure.

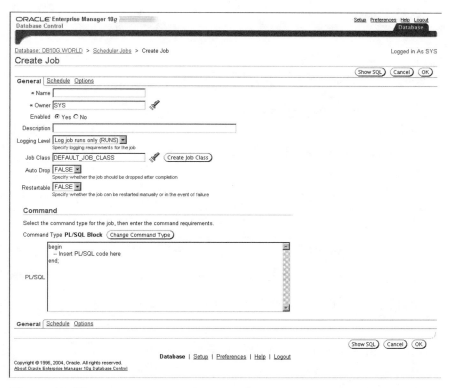

Figure 19.17: *OEM 10g DB Control: Create Job (General).*

Database DB10G.WORLD > Scheduler Jobs > Create Job

Create Job

General | **Schedule** | Options

Schedule Type | Standard

Time Zone **GMT +01:00** (Change Time Zone)

Repeating

Repeat | Do Not Repeat

Start

- Immediately
- Later

Date | 22-Jun-2004
(example: 22-Jun-2004)

Time | 9 | 30 | 00 | AM PM

Figure 19.18: *OEM 10g DB Control: Create Job (Schedule).*

Information about jobs is displayed using the *dba_scheduler_jobs* view. The following script uses this view to display information about currently defined jobs.

```
- Parameters:
--     1) Specific USERNAME or ALL which doesn't limit output.
-- ******************************************************************

set verify off

select
   owner,
   job_name,
   job_class,
   enabled,
   next_run_date,
   repeat_interval
from
   dba_scheduler_jobs
where
   owner = decode(upper('&1'), 'ALL', owner, upper('&1'))
;
```

The output of the script for the current user is displayed below.

```
SQL> @jobs_10g job_user

OWNER                               JOB_NAME
JOB_CLASS                           ENABL
-------------------------------- ------------------------------- ------
next_RUN_DATE
---------------------------------------------------------------------
REPEAT_INTERVAL
---------------------------------------------------------------------
JOB_USER                            TEST_FULL_JOB_DEFINITION
DEFAULT_JOB_CLASS                   TRUE
22-JUN-04 15.00.08.900000 +01:00
freq=hourly; byminute=0

JOB_USER                            TEST_PROG_SCHED_JOB_DEFINITION
DEFAULT_JOB_CLASS                   TRUE
22-JUN-04 15.00.16.200000 +01:00

JOB_USER                            TEST_PROG_JOB_DEFINITION
DEFAULT_JOB_CLASS                   TRUE
22-JUN-04 15.00.09.600000 +01:00
freq=hourly; byminute=0

JOB_USER                            TEST_SCHED_JOB_DEFINITION
DEFAULT_JOB_CLASS                   TRUE
22-JUN-04 15.00.16.200000 +01:00

4 rows selected.
```

Figure 19.19 shows the information displayed on the Scheduler Jobs screen in the OEM 10g DB Control.

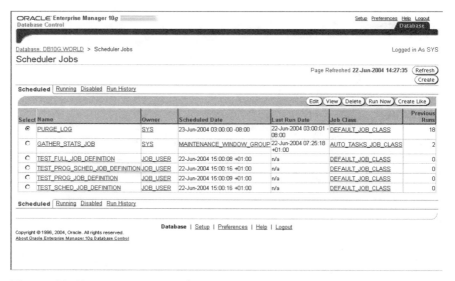

Figure 19.19: *OEM 10g DB Control: Scheduler Jobs.*

Jobs are normally run asynchronously under the control of the job coordinator, but they can be controlled manually using the *run_job* and *stop_job* procedures.

```
PROCEDURE run_job (
   job_name              IN VARCHAR2,
   use_current_session   IN BOOLEAN DEFAULT TRUE)

PROCEDURE stop_job (
   job_name              IN VARCHAR2,
   force                 IN BOOLEAN DEFAULT FALSE)
```

The parameters of these procedures and their usage are as follows.

- *job_name*: A name which identifies a single job, a job class, or a comma separated list of job names.

- *use_current_session*: When TRUE, the job is run in the user's current session; otherwise a job slave runs it in the background.

- *force*: When FALSE, a job is stopped using the equivalent of sending a ctrl-c to the job. When TRUE, a graceful shutdown is attempted but if this fails the slave process is killed. Using the *force* parameter requires the user to have the MANAGE SCHEDULER system privilege.

Figure 19.20 shows the Create Job Class screen in the OEM 10g DB Control.

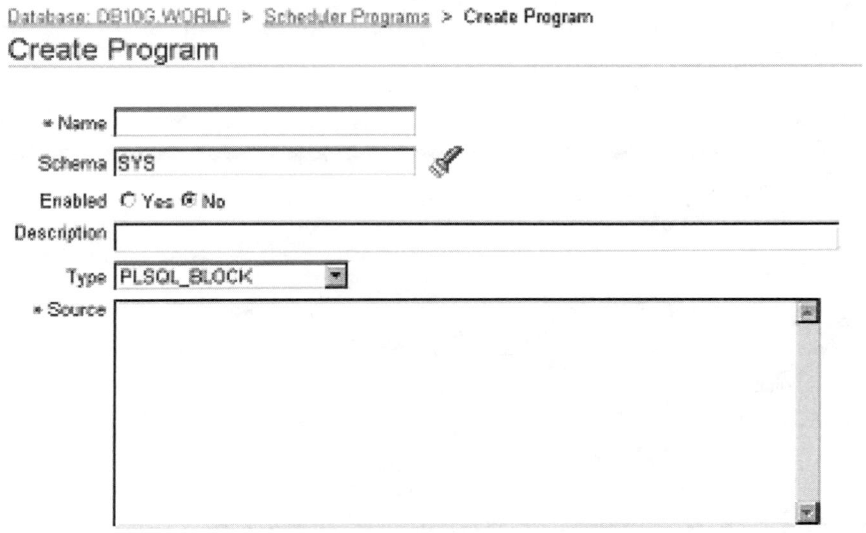

Figure 19.20: *OEM 10g DB Control: Create Job Class.*

Information about job classes can be displayed using the *dba_scheduler_job_classes* view. The following script uses this view.

```
select
   job_class_name,
   resource_consumer_group
from
   dba_scheduler_job_classes
;
```

The output from the script is displayed below.

```
SQL> @job_classes
```

```
JOB_CLASS_NAME                 RESOURCE_CONSUMER_GROUP
------------------------------ ------------------------------
DEFAULT_JOB_CLASS
AUTO_TASKS_JOB_CLASS           AUTO_TASK_CONSUMER_GROUP
TEST_JOB_CLASS                 DEFAULT_CONSUMER_GROUP

3 rows selected.
```

Figure 19.21 shows the Scheduler Job Classes screen in the OEM 10g DB Control.

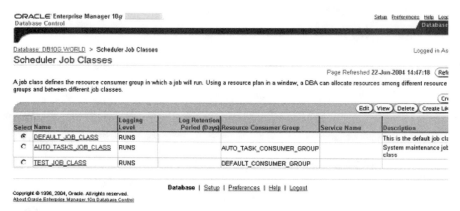

Figure 19.21: OEM 10g DB Control: Scheduler Job Classes.

Jobs can be assigned to a job class either during creation. It is also possible to assign a job to an alternative job class after creation using one of the *set_attribute* procedure overloads.

```
BEGIN
  -- Job defined and assigned to a job class.
  DBMS_SCHEDULER.create_job (
    job_name      => 'test_prog_sched_class_job_def',
    program_name  => 'test_plsql_block_prog',
    schedule_name => 'test_hourly_schedule',
    job_class     => 'test_job_class',
    enabled       => TRUE,
    comments      => 'Job defined and assigned to a job class ');
END;
/


BEGIN
  -- Assign an existing job to a job class.
  DBMS_SCHEDULER.set_attribute (
    name       => 'test_prog_sched_job_definition',
```

```
    attribute => 'job_class',
    value    => 'test_job_class');
END;
/
```

The output from the script shows that the job classes associated with these jobs have been set correctly.

```
job_user@db10g> @jobs_10g job_user

OWNER                          JOB_NAME
JOB_CLASS                      ENABL
------------------------------ ------------------------------ ------
next_RUN_DATE
--------------------------------------------------------------------
REPEAT_INTERVAL
--------------------------------------------------------------------
JOB_USER                       TEST_FULL_JOB_DEFINITION
DEFAULT_JOB_CLASS              TRUE
22-JUN-04 15.00.08.900000 +01:00
freq=hourly; byminute=0

JOB_USER                       TEST_PROG_SCHED_JOB_DEFINITION
TEST_JOB_CLASS                 TRUE
22-JUN-04 15.00.16.200000 +01:00

JOB_USER                       TEST_PROG_JOB_DEFINITION
DEFAULT_JOB_CLASS              TRUE
22-JUN-04 15.00.09.600000 +01:00
freq=hourly; byminute=0

JOB_USER                       TEST_SCHED_JOB_DEFINITION
DEFAULT_JOB_CLASS              TRUE
22-JUN-04 15.00.16.200000 +01:00

JOB_USER                       ARGUMENT_JOB_DEFINITION
DEFAULT_JOB_CLASS              TRUE
22-JUN-04 15.00.16.200000 +01:00

JOB_USER                       TEST_PROG_SCHED_CLASS_JOB_DEF
TEST_JOB_CLASS                 TRUE
22-JUN-04 15.00.16.200000 +01:00

6 rows selected.
```

Figure 19.22 shows the Create Window screen in the OEM 10g DB Control.

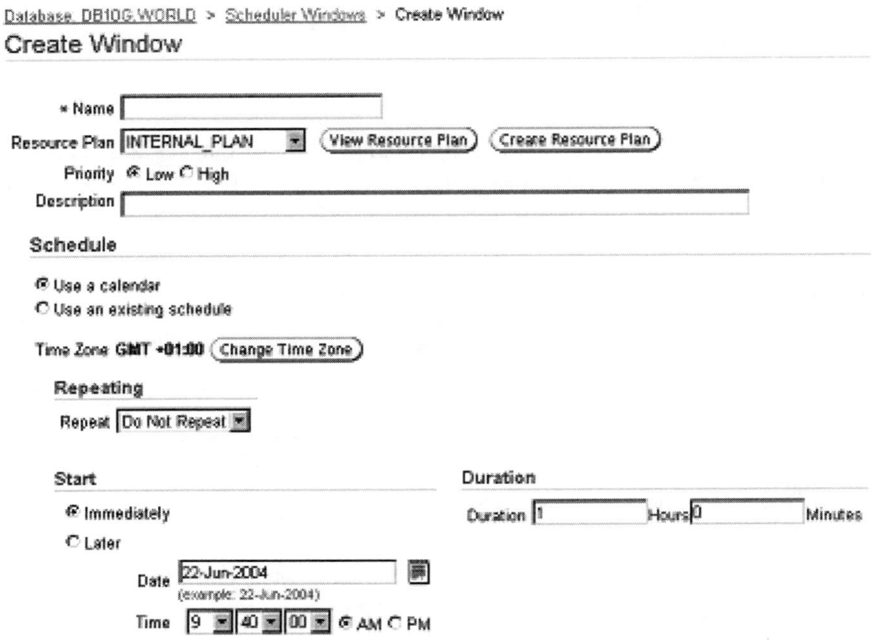

Create Window

```
        * Name  [                    ]
Resource Plan  [INTERNAL_PLAN   ▼]  ( View Resource Plan )  ( Create Resource Plan )
     Priority  ⦿ Low  ○ High
  Description  [                                              ]
```

Schedule

```
⦿ Use a calendar
○ Use an existing schedule

Time Zone  GMT +01:00  ( Change Time Zone )
```

Repeating

```
Repeat  [Do Not Repeat ▼]
```

```
Start                                    Duration
⦿ Immediately                            Duration [1        ] Hours [0        ] Minutes
○ Later
        Date  [22-Jun-2004        ]  📅
              (example: 22-Jun-2004)
        Time  [9 ▼][40 ▼][00 ▼] ⦿ AM ○ PM
```

Figure 19.22: *OEM 10g DB Control: Create Window.*

Information about windows can be displayed using the *dba_scheduler_windows* view. The following script uses this view.

```
select
   window_name,
   resource_plan,
   enabled,
   active
from
   dba_scheduler_windows
;
```

The output from the script is displayed below.

```
job_user@db10g> @windows.

WINDOW_NAME                 RESOURCE_PLAN                 ENABL ACTIV
------------------------    ----------------------------  ----- -----
TEST_WINDOW_1                                             TRUE  FALSE
TEST_WINDOW_2                                             TRUE  FALSE
WEEKEND_WINDOW                                            TRUE  TRUE
WEEKNIGHT_WINDOW                                          TRUE  FALSE

4 rows selected.
```

Figure 19.23 shows the Scheduler Windows screen in the OEM 10g DB Control.

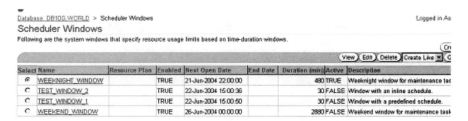

Scheduler Windows

Following are the system windows that specify resource usage limits based on time-duration windows.

Select	Name	Resource Plan	Enabled	Next Open Date	End Date	Duration (min)	Active	Description
⦿	WEEKNIGHT_WINDOW		TRUE	21-Jun-2004 22:00:00		480	TRUE	Weeknight window for maintenance tas
○	TEST_WINDOW_2		TRUE	22-Jun-2004 15:00:36		30	FALSE	Window with an inline schedule.
○	TEST_WINDOW_1		TRUE	22-Jun-2004 15:00:50		30	FALSE	Window with a predefined schedule.
○	WEEKEND_WINDOW		TRUE	26-Jun-2004 00:00:00		2880	FALSE	Weekend window for maintenance task

Figure 19.23: *OEM 10g DB Control: Scheduler Windows.*

The server normally controls the opening and closing of windows, but they can be opened and closed manually using the *open_window* and *close_window* procedures.

```
PROCEDURE open_window(
  window_name              IN VARCHAR2,
  duration                 IN INTERVAL DAY TO SECOND,
  force                    IN BOOLEAN DEFAULT FALSE)

PROCEDURE close_window(
  window_name              IN VARCHAR2)
```

The parameters of these procedures and their usage are as follows.

- *window_name*: A name which uniquely identifies the window.

- *duration*: The length of time in minutes the window should remain open.

- *force*: When FALSE, attempting to open a window when one is already open results in an error unless the currently open window is the one the DBA is attempting to open, in which case the close time is set to the current system time plus the specified duration.

Closing a window causes all jobs associated with that window to be stopped.

Figure 19.24 shows the Create Window Group screen in the OEM 10g DB Control.

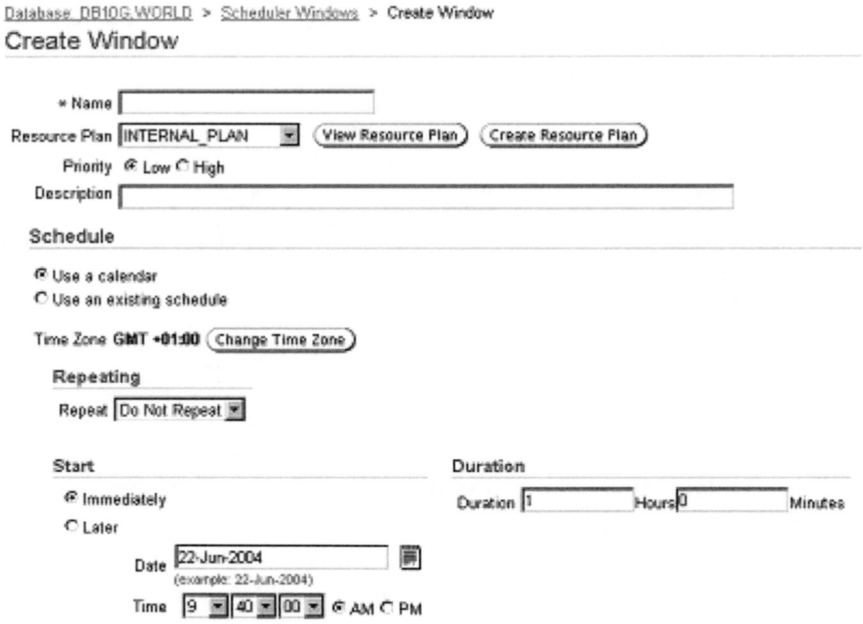

Create Window

```
       * Name [                          ]
Resource Plan [INTERNAL_PLAN    ▼]  (View Resource Plan)  (Create Resource Plan)
     Priority  ⊙ Low  ○ High
  Description [                                                              ]
```

Schedule

```
⊙ Use a calendar
○ Use an existing schedule

Time Zone  GMT +01:00  (Change Time Zone)
```

Repeating

```
Repeat [Do Not Repeat ▼]
```

Start	Duration
⊙ Immediately	Duration [1] Hours [0] Minutes
○ Later	
Date [22-Jun-2004] 🗓	
(example: 22-Jun-2004)	
Time [9 ▼][40 ▼][00 ▼] ⊙ AM ○ PM	

Figure 19.24: *OEM 10g DB Control: Create Window Group.*

Information about window groups can be displayed using the *dba_scheduler_window_groups* and *dba_scheduler_wingroup_members* views. The following script uses both views to display a summary of window group information.

```
prompt
prompt WINDOW GROUPS
prompt --------------

select
   window_group_name,
   enabled,
   number_of_windowS
from
   dba_scheduler_window_groups
;

prompt
prompt WINDOW GROUP MEMBERS
prompt --------------------
```

```
select
    window_group_name,
    window_name
from
    dba_scheduler_wingroup_members
;
```

The output from the script shows that the window group was created
successfully.

```
SQL> @window_groups

WINDOW GROUPS
-------------

WINDOW_GROUP_NAME                ENABL NUMBER_OF_WINDOWS
-------------------------------  ----- -----------------
MAINTENANCE_WINDOW_GROUP         TRUE                  2
TEST_WINDOW_GROUP                TRUE                  2

2 rows selected.

WINDOW GROUP MEMBERS
--------------------

WINDOW_GROUP_NAME                WINDOW_NAME
-------------------------------  ------------------------------
MAINTENANCE_WINDOW_GROUP         WEEKEND_WINDOW
MAINTENANCE_WINDOW_GROUP         WEEKNIGHT_WINDOW
TEST_WINDOW_GROUP                TEST_WINDOW_1
TEST_WINDOW_GROUP                TEST_WINDOW_2

4 rows selected.
```

Figure 19.25 shows the Scheduler Window Groups screen in the OEM
10g DB Control.

Figure 19.25: *OEM 10g DB Control: Scheduler Window Groups.*

Windows can be added and removed from a group using the *add_window_group_member* and *remove_window_group_member* procedures respectively.

```
PROCEDURE add_window_group_member (
  group_name              IN VARCHAR2,
  window_list             IN VARCHAR2)

PROCEDURE remove_window_group_member (
  group_name              IN VARCHAR2,
  window_list             IN VARCHAR2)
```

The parameters of these procedures and their usage are listed as follows:

- *group_name*: A name that uniquely identifies the window group.

- *window_list*: A comma separated list of windows to be added or removed from the window group.

Figure 19.26 shows the Edit Window Group screen in the OEM 10g DB Control. Windows can be added and removed from a window group using this screen.

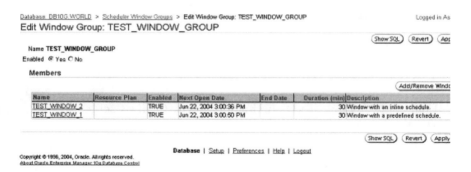

Figure 19.26: *OEM 10g DB Control: Edit Window Group.*

Windows groups are removed using the *drop_window_group procedure*.

```
PROCEDURE drop_window_group (
  group_name              IN VARCHAR2,
  force                   IN BOOLEAN DEFAULT FALSE)
```

The parameters of this procedure and their usage are listed as follows:

- *group_name*: A name that uniquely identifies the window group.

- *force*: When FALSE, an error is produced if any jobs reference the specified window group. When TRUE, any dependant jobs are disabled.

The following example shows how to drop a window group.

```
BEGIN
  DBMS_SCHEDULER.drop_window_group (
    group_name => 'test_window_group',
    force      => TRUE);
END;
/
```

The output from the script shows that the window group has been removed.

```
SQL> @window_groups

WINDOW GROUPS
-------------

WINDOW_GROUP_NAME               ENABL NUMBER_OF_WINDOWS
------------------------------- ----- -----------------
MAINTENANCE_WINDOW_GROUP        TRUE                  2

1 row selected.


WINDOW GROUP MEMBERS
--------------------

WINDOW_GROUP_NAME               WINDOW_NAME
------------------------------- ------------------------------
MAINTENANCE_WINDOW_GROUP        WEEKEND_WINDOW
MAINTENANCE_WINDOW_GROUP        WEEKNIGHT_WINDOW

2 rows selected.
```

Now that information on scheduling with OEM has been presented, the next step is to investigate to create custom OEM alerts with throughput metrics.

Throughput Metrics in OEM

Customized thresholds can be set for dozens of important Oracle throughput metrics as shown in Figure 19.27 below. These throughput metrics are critical for the senior Oracle professional because they can automate warning messages to allow time to fix an impending problem before end-users experience a performance slowdown. This is especially valuable when tuning a large OLTP database with high-volume I/O against many disk devices.

▼ Throughput	None	Last Collected Mar 1, 2004 7:07:15 PM
BG Checkpoints (per second)	Not Set	Last Collected Mar 1, 2004 7:07:15 PM
Branch Node Splits (per second)	Not Set	Last Collected Mar 1, 2004 7:07:15 PM
Branch Node Splits (per transaction)	Not Set	Last Collected Mar 1, 2004 7:07:15 PM
Consistent Read Changes (per second)	Not Set	Last Collected Mar 1, 2004 7:07:15 PM
Consistent Read Changes (per transaction)	Not Set	Last Collected Mar 1, 2004 7:07:15 PM
Consistent Read Gets (per second)	Not Set	Last Collected Mar 1, 2004 7:07:15 PM
Consistent Read Gets (per transaction)	Not Set	Last Collected Mar 1, 2004 7:07:15 PM
Cumulative Logons (per second)	Not Set	Last Collected Mar 1, 2004 7:07:15 PM
Cumulative Logons (per transaction)	Not Set	Last Collected Mar 1, 2004 7:07:15 PM
Cursor Blocks Created (per second)	Not Set	Last Collected Mar 1, 2004 7:07:15 PM
Cursor Blocks Created (per transaction)	Not Set	Last Collected Mar 1, 2004 7:07:15 PM
Cursor Undo Records Applied (per second)	Not Set	Last Collected Mar 1, 2004 7:07:15 PM
Cursor Undo Records Applied (per transaction)	Not Set	Last Collected Mar 1, 2004 7:07:15 PM
DBWR Checkpoints (per second)	Not Set	Last Collected Mar 1, 2004 7:07:15 PM
Database Block Changes (per second)	Not Set	Last Collected Mar 1, 2004 7:07:15 PM
Database Block Changes (per transaction)	Not Set	Last Collected Mar 1, 2004 7:07:15 PM
Database Block Gets (per second)	Not Set	Last Collected Mar 1, 2004 7:07:15 PM
Database Block Gets (per transaction)	Not Set	Last Collected Mar 1, 2004 7:07:15 PM
Enqueue Deadlocks (per second)	Not Set	Last Collected Mar 1, 2004 7:07:15 PM
Enqueue Deadlocks (per transaction)	Not Set	Last Collected Mar 1, 2004 7:07:15 PM
Enqueue Requests (per second)	Not Set	Last Collected Mar 1, 2004 7:07:15 PM
Enqueue Requests (per transaction)	Not Set	Last Collected Mar 1, 2004 7:07:15 PM
Enqueue Timeout (per second)	Not Set	Last Collected Mar 1, 2004 7:07:15 PM
Enqueue Timeout (per transaction)	Not Set	Last Collected Mar 1, 2004 7:07:15 PM
Enqueue Waits (per second)	Not Set	Last Collected Mar 1, 2004 7:07:15 PM

Figure 19.27: *OEM throughput metric thresholds*

For a typical OLTP system where the main bottleneck is I/O throughput, setting these OEM thresholds allow the detection of a pending problem and time to fix it before the database encounters a problem. For example, a threshold alert might be set whenever the following conditions are true:

- *Buffer Cache Hit (%)* falls by more than 20%.

- *Database block gets* (per second) exceeds 5000 block gets per second.

In this simple example, the condition might signal an increase in physical disk I/O, perhaps due to uncached small-table full-table scans. By detecting the condition early, OEM is used to re-allocate RAM to the *db_cache_size* or perhaps dynamically cache high-impact tables by placing them into the KEEP pool. Again, if OEM thresholds are used to alert the DBA at the first sign of the trend, time is available for the

DBA to use OEM2GO to correct the issue before it becomes a performance problem.

Even though OEM displays almost every conceivable internal metric, it does not stop there. The AWR architecture goes beyond the bounds of the Oracle instance and collects external environment information, providing OEM with invaluable information about the external server-side environment.

OEM Outside the Instance

Using OEM, the Oracle professional can now get access to external information that has never been available before in a single interface. This is very important because it removes the need for the DBA to have any experience with the cumbersome OS command syntax required to display server-side information.

For example, in UNIX the DBA needs to know the command-line syntax of various UNIX utilities, such as *SAR*, *glance*, *top*, *lsattr* and, *prtconf*, to display server metrics. The OEM screens now allow seamless access server-side performance metrics including:

- Oracle server-side file contents in the form of the alert log and trace dumps.

- Oracle archive redo log file performance.

- Server OS kernel performance parameter values.

- Server OS characteristics such as the number of CPUs, amount of RAM, and network.

- Historical capture of CPU and RAM activity.

A quick look at the OEM display screens for external information shows how this relieves the DBA of knowing hundreds of server-side commands.

Oracle10g OEM quickly reveals the status of Oracle server-side file performance and error messages, including the alert log file, archived redo log status and file system status as shown in Figure 19.28.

Database: FSDEV10G > All Metrics

All Metrics

Expand All | Collapse All

Metrics	Thresholds	Collection Stat
▼ FSDEV10G		
▼ Alert Log	Some	Not Collected
Alert Log Error Trace File	Not Set	Not Collected
Alert Log Name	Not Set	Not Collected
Archiver Hung Alert Log Error	Set	Not Collected
Data Block Corruption Alert Log Error	Set	Not Collected
Generic Alert Log Error	Set	Not Collected
Session Terminated Alert Log Error	Set	Not Collected
▼ Alert Log Content	None	Not Collected
Content	Not Set	Not Collected
▼ Alert Log Error Status	All	Last Collected
Archiver Hung Alert Log Error Status	Set	Last Collected
Data Block Corruption Alert Log Error Status	Set	Last Collected
Generic Alert Log Error Status	Set	Last Collected
Session Terminated Alert Log Error Status	Set	Last Collected
▼ Archive Area	Some	Last Collected
Archive Area Used (%)	Set	Last Collected
Archive Area Used (KB)	Not Set	Last Collected
Free Archive Area (KB)	Not Set	Last Collected

Figure 19.28: *A partial listing of the AWR metrics from inside OEM*

The ability of OEM to monitor server-side metrics makes it a one-stop tool for monitoring both Oracle and the server. A Systems Administrator may no longer be required to buy expensive tools to monitor the server and the data files. Best of all, the Oracle professional now does not have to worry about a server-side problem (i.e. file-system full) causing an Oracle interruption.

From these OEM interfaces, the DBA can display and manage all server-side Oracle components without having to sign on to the server. This is a blessing for those Oracle professionals running UNIX servers who may not be fluent in cryptic UNIX commands and the complex vi editor. In Figure 19.29, the display of server ODS details including all OS kernel parameters is shown.

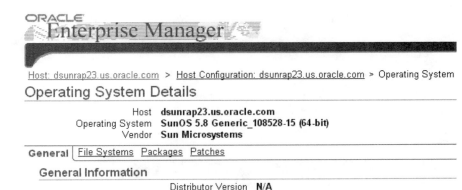

Operating System Details

Host	**dsunrap23.us.oracle.com**
Operating System	**SunOS 5.8 Generic_108528-15 (64-bit)**
Vendor	**Sun Microsystems**

General | File Systems Packages Patches

General Information

Distributor Version	**N/A**
Maximum Swap Space (MB)	**6145.891**

Operating System Properties

⊘ Previous | 1-25 of 148 ▾ | Next 25 ⊗

Name	Source	Value
OPEN_MAX	/bin/getconf	1024
defaultrouter	/etc/defaultrouter	144.25.32.1
nameserver 1	/etc/resolv.conf	list of DNS nameservers. NOTE: some OSs have trouble with > 3 entries
nameserver 2	/etc/resolv.conf	130.35.249.41 # dns1-us
nameserver 3	/etc/resolv.conf	130.35.249.52 # dns2-us
nameserver 4	/etc/resolv.conf	130.2.202.15 # dns4
autoup	/etc/system	240
bufhwm	/etc/system	7000

Figure 19.29: *The OEM display of server-side performance parameters*

The DBA can now throw away the checklist of cumbersome OS commands to display server hardware characteristics. For example, the following is a list of the cryptic commands the Oracle UNIX professional would have to know in order to display the number of CPUs on their Oracle server:

- Linux Command:

```
cat /proc/cpuinfo|grep processor|wc -l
```

- Solaris Command:

```
psrinfo -v|grep "Status of processor"|wc -l
```

- AIX Command:

```
lsdev -C|grep Process|wc -l
```

Throughput Metrics in OEM

- HP/UX Command:

```
ioscan -C processor | grep processor | wc -l
```

The Oracle10g OEM issues these commands on the DBA's behalf and displays all hardware characteristics in an easy-to-read display as shown in Figure 19.30.

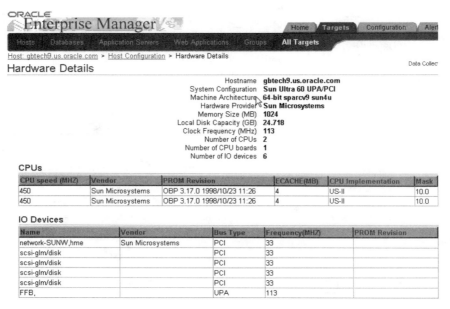

Figure 19.30: *The OEM display of server-side hardware configuration*

OEM does much more than display the server parameters and configuration information. Oracle tuning professionals know that a shortage of server resources may cause slow performance, and OEM now quickly displays the relevant CPU and RAM metrics. The main performance display screen in OEM now display a current summary of the CPU Run Queue and RAM paging as shown in Figure 19.31.

Host CPU

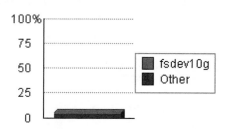

Run Queue   <u>0.0</u>
Paging (pages per second)   <u>4.32</u>

Figure 19.31: *The HOST CPU section of the main OEM performance screen.*

Here the DBA can quickly see if a shortage of Oracle server resources is causing a performance bottleneck. Assuming that the instance and SQL have already been optimized, this server-side information can give immediate insights to server resource shortages:

- CPU Dispatcher Run Queue: Whenever the server processors are overstressed, the run queue exceeds the number of CPUs. For example, a run queue value of nine on an 8-CPU server indicates the need to add more or faster CPUs.

- Server RAM Paging: Whenever the RAM demands of a server exceed the real RAM capacity, the servers Virtual Memory (VM) utility will page, transferring RAM frames to a special swap-disk on the server. Assuming the SGA and PGA regions are optimized, paging indicates the need to add RAM resources to the server.

The OEM also tracks server usage over time, allowing the DBA to quickly see those times when a hardware-related constraint is happening as shown in Figure 19.32. This display reveals the historical CPU usage, and a display of a self-defined threshold alert status, as defined by setting a threshold alert for the *Average CPU (%) OEM Metric*, is noted.

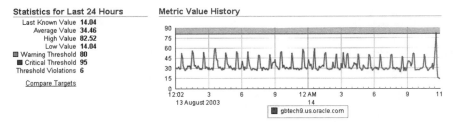

Figure 19.32: *The OEM historical tracking of CPU consumption.*

OEM also tracks server run queue waits over time, and combines the CPU and Paging display into a single OEM screen so the DBA can tell when server-side waits on hardware resources are being experienced as shown in Figure 19.33. This is important because Oracle performance issues are often transient in nature, with short spikes in excessive CPU demands. Because of the super-fast nature of CPU dispatching, a database might be CPU constrained for only a few minutes at a time during different times of the day. The time series OEM display can reveal a quick visual clue about those times when a CPU or RAM bottleneck is being experienced.

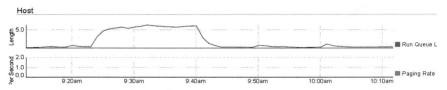

Figure 19.33: *Server CPU run queue and RAM paging values over time*

OEM has a drill down function which allows the DBA to easily click on any area of the graph to obtain detailed information.

Even though it is true that a CPU bottleneck exists when the run queue exceeds the number of processors, this condition does not always mean that the solution is to add processors.

Excessive CPU can be caused by many internal conditions including inefficient SQL statements that perform excessive logical I/O, non-reentrant SQL inside the library cache, and many other conditions.

Fortunately, OEM allows the DBA to go back in time and find these conditions, even though the immediate run queue issue has passed.

Because of Oracle's commitment to extending OEM beyond the boundaries of the Oracle instance, all areas of server utilization can be tracked over time as shown in Figure 19.34. Shown below are the specific times when the server exceeds the maximum CPU capacity, and the total time spent by active Oracle sessions, waiting and working.

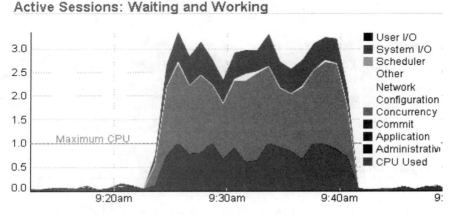

Figure 19.34: *Oracle server time-series resource component utilization*

Because of the clarity of the color OEM display, the total components of Oracle wait times including CPU time, concurrency management overhead (locks, latches), and I/O can be clearly seen. This display also shows the times when CPU usage exceeds the server capacity.

To fully understand how to customize OEM for maximum benefit, a brief tour of the OEM exception reporting mechanism and how it displays the predefined alerts will be provided.

Exception Tuning Inside Enterprise Manager

The Automatic Diagnostic component of the Oracle Performance OEM screen contains an alert area in which ADDM warns the DBA about historical performance exceptions. This exception-based reporting is very important to Oracle tuning because Oracle databases change rapidly, and transient performance issues are very difficult to detect without an exception-based mechanism.

Exception reports allow the Oracle professional to view specific times and conditions when Oracle processing demands have exceeded the server capacity. More important, these transient server exceptions give insight regarding repeating server trends.

Figure 19.35 is a representation of the OEM alert screen.

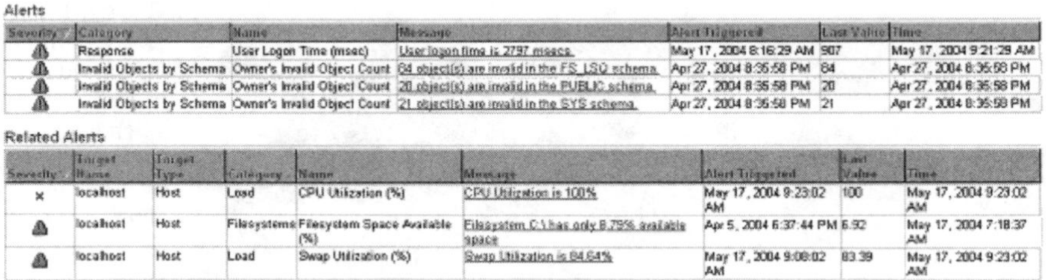

Alerts

Severity	Category	Name	Message	Alert Triggered	Last Value	Time
⚠	Response	User Logon Time (msec)	User logon time is 2797 msecs.	May 17, 2004 8:16:29 AM	907	May 17, 2004 9:21:29 AM
⚠	Invalid Objects by Schema	Owner's Invalid Object Count	64 object(s) are invalid in the FS_LSQ schema.	Apr 27, 2004 8:35:58 PM	64	Apr 27, 2004 8:35:58 PM
⚠	Invalid Objects by Schema	Owner's Invalid Object Count	20 object(s) are invalid in the PUBLIC schema.	Apr 27, 2004 8:35:58 PM	20	Apr 27, 2004 8:35:58 PM
⚠	Invalid Objects by Schema	Owner's Invalid Object Count	21 object(s) are invalid in the SYS schema.	Apr 27, 2004 8:35:58 PM	21	Apr 27, 2004 8:35:58 PM

Related Alerts

Severity	Target Name	Target Type	Category	Name	Message	Alert Triggered	Last Value	Time
✗	localhost	Host	Load	CPU Utilization (%)	CPU Utilization is 100%	May 17, 2004 9:23:02 AM	100	May 17, 2004 9:23:02 AM
⚠	localhost	Host	Filesystems	Filesystem Space Available (%)	Filesystem C:\ has only 8.75% available space	Apr 5, 2004 6:37:44 PM	6.92	May 17, 2004 7:18:37 AM
⚠	localhost	Host	Load	Swap Utilization (%)	Swap Utilization is 84.64%	May 17, 2004 9:08:02 AM	83.39	May 17, 2004 9:23:02 AM

Figure 19.35: *The OEM exception reporting screen*

In Figure 19.35, the Oracle alerts are located on the top-half of the screen and the external server alerts are located on the bottom half. The server-related alerts are critical to Oracle performance because Oracle10g allows the DBA to relieve server stress by adding additional servers. Common server-related alerts might include:

- CPU utilization: Whenever the CPU run queue exceeds the number of processors on the server, the database is CPU-bound. Actions might include tuning SQL to reduce logical I/O or adding more CPU resources.

- Filesystem Shortage: When using Oracle with autoextend datafiles, the only constraint to file growth is the limitation of the OS filesystem. Should a filesystem become unable to accommodate an automatic datafile expansion, Oracle halts the process until additional space is allocated. This monitoring task is critical to ensuring the continuous availability of the database.

- Swap Shortage: The swap disk is used on a virtual processor to store infrequently used RAM frames. When the swap disk becomes full, more disks should be added.

This ability to perform server-side alerts is extremely valuable to the Oracle professional who must monitor both internal and external Oracle environments.

The next section shows techniques for extending the OEM functionality for trend-based reporting, and explores the Automated Database Diagnostic Monitor (ADDM) as well as the SQL Tuning Advisor within OEM. A real world Oracle10g migration for an Oracle8i application using the obsolete rule-based SQL optimizer (RBO) is also shown.

A good understanding of the basic functionality of OEM performance monitoring and how OEM accesses the new AWR database is needed before exploring how Enterprise Manager interprets AWR and ASH information. This information is used to diagnose performance issues with the Automatic Database Diagnostic Monitor (pronounced "Adam").

The bottom of the following screen shows the Related Links, including the OEM Advisor Central link as shown in Figure 19.36:

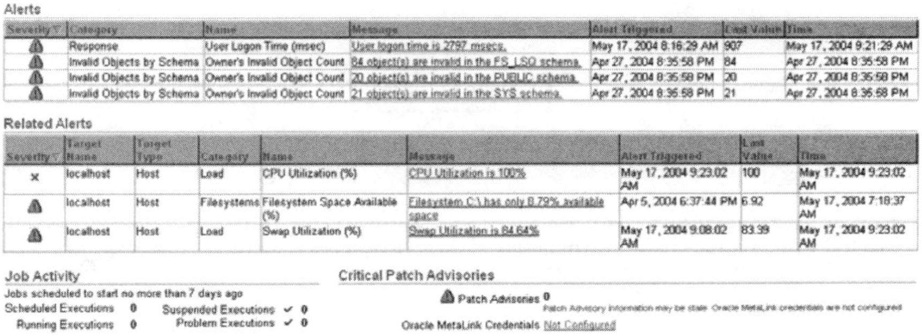

Figure 19.36: *The OEM alerts screen with link to Advisor Central.*

This link between the database and server exceptions provides a preview of the exceptional conditions and validates the recommendations from the Advisor Central area of OEM.

Next, attention can be focused on the examination of the OEM advisor area.

Advisor Central in OEM

The Advisor Central screen displays the three advisory areas of Enterprise Manager: ADDM, the SQL Tuning Advisor and the Segment Advisor as shown in Figure 19.37. This OEM information is externalized via the *dbms_advisor* package and the *dba_advisor_tasks* view.

Select	Advisory Type	Name	Description	User
⊙	SQL Tuning Advisor	SQL_TUNING_1084805982386	schedule new advisor run for post date sql statement	SYSMAN
○	ADDM	ADDM:2787970997_1_866	ADDM auto run: snapshots [865, 866], instance 1, database id 2787970997	SYS
○	Segment Advisor	SHRINK_4596553	Get shrink advice based on object growth trend	SYS

Figure 19.37: *The OEM Advisor Central Screen.*

Under the Advisors section of this screen, hyperlinks to the main Advisory areas are shown in Figure 19.38:

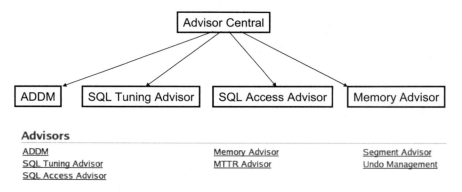

Figure 19.38: *The OEM Advisor Central Screen.*

Each of the hyperlinks provides important advisory functions, yet each one addresses very different areas of Oracle tuning noted as follows:

- **ADDM:** The Automatic Database Diagnostic Monitor provides intelligent recommendations regarding Oracle changes that improve performance and throughput.

- **SQL Tuning Advisor:** This component prepares SQL tuning sets and SQL profiles for tuning sub-optimal SQL statements.

- **SQL Access Advisor:** This component displays execution plans for SQL statements and recommends changes to the SQL data access paths.

- **Automatic Memory Manager:** This component implements the dynamic SGA features in Oracle10g in which any of the following SGA areas can be resized, depending on the database load. If the DBA is not using the Automatic Memory Management (AMM) features to automatically adjust the SGA pools, the Memory Advisor should be used to provide the necessary recommendations for resizing the following SGA pools:

  - Data Buffer Pool Advisory: This component implements the *v$db_cache_advice* view and the *dba_hist_db_cache_advice* view. Whenever Oracle detects a shortage of RAM data buffers, Oracle may borrow RAM frames from other regions to allocate to the data buffers.

  - Program Global Area (PGA) Advisory: This component implements the *v$pga_target_advice* utility and is externalized in the *dba_hist_pgastat* view. The PGA monitors disk sorts hash joins and determines the optimal setting for the PGA RAM region.

  - Shared Pool Advisory: This component adjusts the shared pool using *the* *v$shared_pool_advice* and the new *dba_hist_shared_pool_advice* view.

  - Automatic Segment Advisor (ASM): This component advises on segment conditions including changes to data file and tablespace characteristics.

These advisory functions are shown in detail later in this chapter, but it is important to note that OEM is an open-source tool, and all of the advisory information is externalized in a series of *dba_advisor* views, such as the following:

- *dba_advisor_actions*
- *dba_advisor_commands*
- *dba_advisor_definitions*
- *dba_advisor_def_parameters*
- *dba_advisor_directives*
- *dba_advisor_findings*
- *dba_advisor_journal*
- *dba_advisor_log*
- *dba_advisor_objects*
- *dba_advisor_object_types*
- *dba_advisor_parameters*
- *dba_advisor_rationale*
- *dba_advisor_recommendations*
- *dba_advisor_tasks*
- *dba_advisor_templates*
- *dba_advisor_usage*

To see the internals of the Automatic Segment Advisor, additional dictionary views are available. In the list below, sqla represents the Access advisor views, while sqlw represents the Workload tasks:

- *dba_advisor_sqla_rec_sum*
- *dba_advisor_sqla_wk_map*
- *dba_advisor_sqla_wk_stmts*
- *dba_advisor_sqlw_colvol*

- *dba_advisor_sqlw_journal*

- *dba_advisor_sqlw_parameters*

- *dba_advisor_sqlw_stmts*

- *dba_advisor_sqlw_sum*

- *dba_advisor_sqlw_tables*

- *dba_advisor_sqlw_tabvol*

- *dba_advisor_sqlw_templates*

Now, it is time to move on to an exploration of the ADDM. A review of the ADDM screens is started by clicking on the ADDM hyperlink. This reveals the ADDM Database Activity and ADDM Performance Analysis screens.

ADDM Main Screen

The ADDM hyperlink forwards the DBA to the main screen for ADDM. This screen is the heart of ADDM and shows the overview task bar for the main contributors to the response time.

The Database Activity chart on the top half of this screen provides vital Oracle tuning information because it reveals a time-based display of the main components of Oracle response time:

- Wait: This event is defined in the *dba_hist_waitclassmet_history* view and consists of all sources of waits on database processing including segment header waits, latch serialization, network and user I/O waits.

- I/O: This event is the physical disk I/O as captured in the *dba_hist_filestatxs* and *dba_hist_filemetric_history* views.

- CPU: High CPU consumption is typical for databases with large data buffer caches, sub-optimal logical I/O in the form of unnecessary consistent gets, or library cache contention. It can also be a legitimate condition requiring additional processor resources.

The database is constrained by physical disk I/O during the specified time period as shown in Figure 19.39.

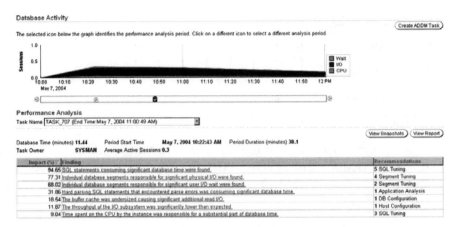

Figure 19.39: *The ADDM Database Activity and Performance Analysis screen.*

Under the performance analysis section, the DBA starts by choosing a specific task from the drop-down menu (TASK_707 on this screen). Figure 19.40 shows that for TASK_707, a host of diagnostic information is displayed.

Impact (%)	Finding	Recommendations
94.65	SQL statements consuming significant database time were found.	5 SQL Tuning
77.31	Individual database segments responsible for significant physical I/O were found.	4 Segment Tuning
68.02	Individual database segments responsible for significant user I/O wait were found.	2 Segment Tuning
31.86	Hard parsing SQL statements that encountered parse errors was consuming significant database time.	1 Application Analysis
18.54	The buffer cache was undersized causing significant additional read I/O.	1 DB Configuration
11.87	The throughput of the I/O subsystem was significantly lower than expected.	1 Host Configuration
9.04	Time spent on the CPU by the instance was responsible for a substantial part of database time.	3 SQL Tuning

Figure 19.40: *The drop down menu.*

The top finding on this screen is, "SQL Statements consuming significant database resources". When clicking on this hyperlink, the DBA drills-down into the ADDM Performance Details screen shown in Figure 19.41.

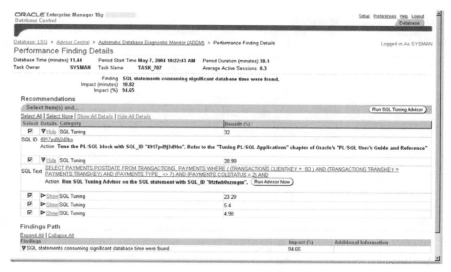

Figure 19.41: *The ADDM Performance Findings Details Screen.*

The Performance Findings Details screen reveals a list of hyperlinks for SQL tuning recommendations. If the DBA clicks the show hyperlink on any of the SQL in this list, the source for each suspect SQL statement is displayed as a hyperlink, and clicking on this hyperlink takes the DBA into the next area of the OEM, the SQL Tuning Advisor. But first, an exploration of the ADDM recommendations is merited.

ADDM Recommendations

The ADDM recommendations screen is the result of the AWR data analysis, and it shows recommendations for current changes based upon historical information. The following figure shows an ADDM recommendation to increase the size of the *sga_target* and the *db_cache_size* as shown in Figure 19.42.

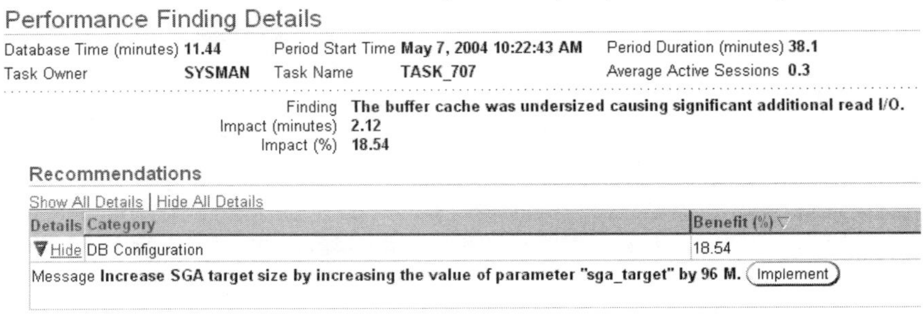

Performance Finding Details

Database Time (minutes) **11.44** Period Start Time **May 7, 2004 10:22:43 AM** Period Duration (minutes) **38.1**

Task Owner **SYSMAN** Task Name **TASK_707** Average Active Sessions **0.3**

Finding **The buffer cache was undersized causing significant additional read I/O.**

Impact (minutes) **2.12**

Impact (%) **18.54**

Recommendations

Show All Details | Hide All Details

Details	Category	Benefit (%) ▽
▼ Hide DB Configuration		18.54

Message **Increase SGA target size by increasing the value of parameter "sga_target" by 96 M.** (Implement)

Figure 19.42: *A ratio-based recommendation for increasing the data buffer cache.*

This advice is based on a predictive model similar to the *v$db_cache_advice* view from Oracle9i in which the marginal benefit of adding additional RAM blocks to the data buffers is seen. If the reduction in physical I/O is substantially more than the cost of the RAM blocks, a recommendation for increasing the size of the buffer is appropriate.

This ADDM function uses data from the AWR *dba_hist_db_cache_advice*, *dba_hist_pga_target_advice* and the *dba_hist_shared_pool_advice* views. This function continuously monitors the marginal benefits of changes to the shared pool, data cache size and PGA region, dynamically morphing the region sizes with the goal of achieving the optimal size for the pool.

Another ADDM recommendation for investigating an issue within the shared pool is shown in Figure 19.43. ADDM has detected excessive hard parses within the library cache. Rather than blindly adding resources, ADDM correctly recommends an investigation of the application logic to eliminate parse errors.

Database Time (minutes) **11.44**	Period Start Time **May 7, 2004 10:22:43 AM**	Period Duration (minutes) **38.1**	
Task Owner **SYSMAN**	Task Name **TASK_707**	Average Active Sessions **0.3**	

Finding **Hard parsing SQL statements that encountered parse errors was consuming significant database time.**
Impact (minutes) **3.64**
Impact (%) **31.86**

Recommendations

Show All Details | Hide All Details

Details	Category	Benefit (%)
▼ Hide	Application Analysis	31.86

Action **Investigate application logic to eliminate parse errors.**

Figure 19.43: *The ADDM recommendations for excessive hard parses in the library cache.*

Excessive hard parses occur when SQL is not reentrant. Non-reentrant code is sometimes associated with SQL that is never re-used because of the embedded literals values in the where clause. If the library cache is clogged with SQL that is identical except for the literal values in the where clause, using *cursor_sharing*=force replaces the literals with bind variables, making the SQL reusable and relieving the hard parsing problem.

The DBA must remember ADDM is not the only component that recommends changes. The SQL Tuning Advisor and the SQL Access Advisor also recommend changes to specific SQL statements. The following section presents a quick look at how OEM makes SQL tuning recommendations.

All these recommendations are stored in the SQL Access Advisor repository, a part of the Oracle database dictionary. The SQLA repository has many benefits such as being managed by the server and support of historical data etc.

Using the SQLAccess Advisor through OEM

The following steps can be used to access the SQLAccess Advisor through the Enterprise Manager. There are more details on the SQLAccess Advisor later in this chapter.

The first step is to go to *Advisor Central* and click the *SQL Access Advisor* link as shown in Figure 19.44.

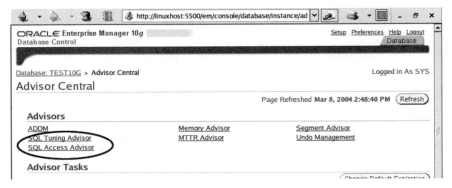

Figure 19.44: *SQL Access Advisor.*

This starts the wizard. It then asks for workload source as shown in Figure 19.45 and 19.46.

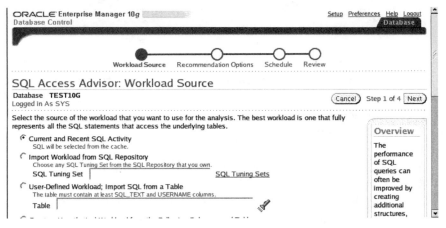

Figure 19.45: *SQL Access Advisor.*

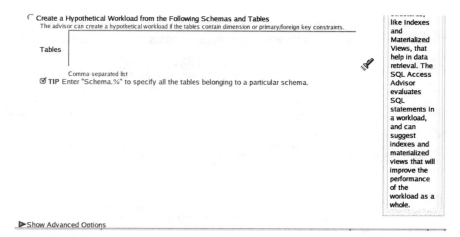

Figure 19.46: *SQL Access Advisor*.

The Advisor should be selected to run in Comprehensive or Limited mode as shown in Figure 19.47.

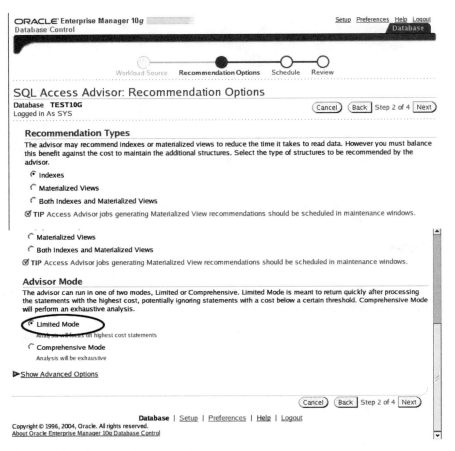

Figure 19.47: *SQL Access Advisor.*

Clicking on Show Advanced Options shows the following screen represented in Figure 19.48.

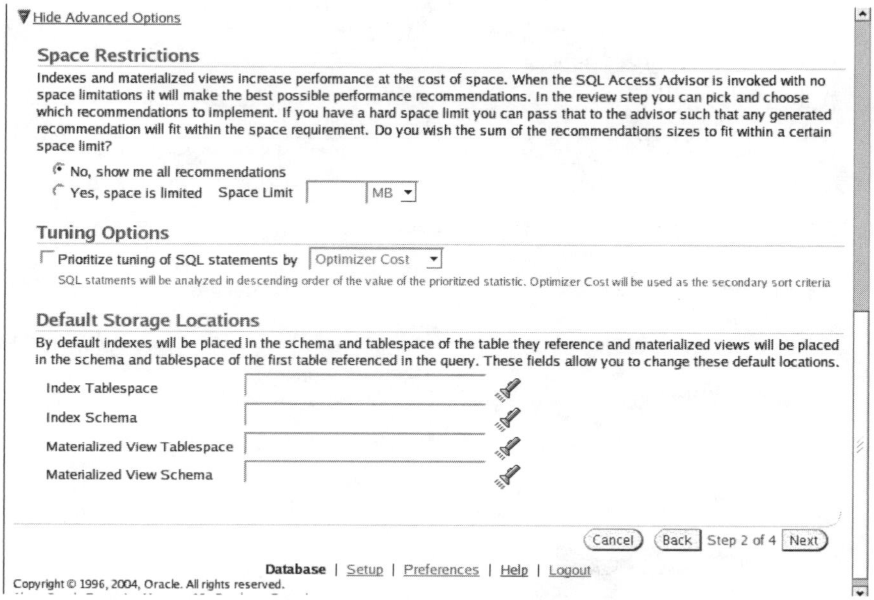

Figure 19.48: *SQL Access Advisor.*

The job should be scheduled and submitted as shown in Figures 19.49 and 19.50.

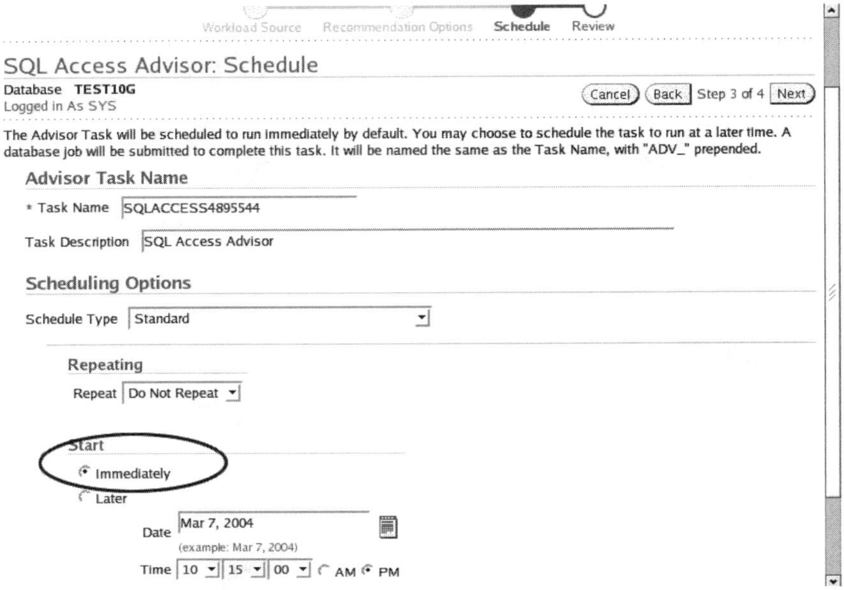

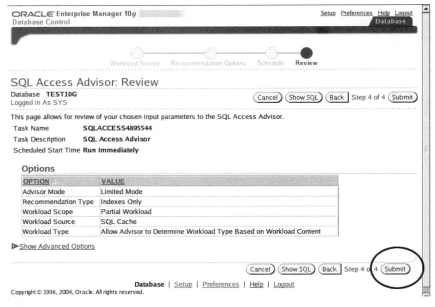

Figure 19.49: *SQL Access Advisor.*

Figure 19.50: *SQL Access Advisor.*

Results are available through the Advisor Central Page. Implement recommendations by clicking Schedule Implementation as shown in Figure 19.51.

Figure 19.51: *SQL Access Advisor.*

Understanding SQL Advisor Recommendations

The SQL Tuning Advisor and the SQL Access Advisor give specific recommendations regarding the best ways to tune the SQL execution. Figure 19.52 shows a sample screen from the SQL Access Advisor allowing the DBA to specify the types of SQL Access recommendations using indexes and materialized views.

Figure 19.52: *Using the SQL Access Advisor.*

The SQL Access Advisor allows the DBA to perform limited recommendations based on the top SQL or a comprehensive mode in which all important SQL is analyzed.

This was a quick tour through the powerful new ADDM features of Oracle10g Enterprise Manager, and the main points of this section include:

- The Advisor Central screen displays time-series performance summaries, showing the top areas for performance recommendations from ADDM, the SQL Tuning advisor the SQL Access advisor and the Memory advisor.

- Using the time-series information stored in the AWR and ASH tables, the OEM advisory functions provide excellent insights into the root causes of transient Oracle tuning problems.

- The OEM Advisor utilities now collect performance information from the server, including the all-important CPU and I/O costs associated with each Oracle task.

- ADDM analyzes system-wide performance metrics. Captures high-resource SQL and identifying those times when the database has exceeded pre-defined thresholds.

- ADDM will make intelligent recommendations regarding system-wide Oracle changes such as tablespace characteristics, sizes of the SGA pools, and changes to initialization parameters.

- ADDM is supplemented by the SQL advisor utilities. The SQL Access advisor makes specific recommendations about tuning opportunities, recommending new index and materialized views. The SQL Tuning advisor make recommendations for specific SQL statements, using SQL profiles to alter the execution plans for specific SQL statements.

Now, it is time to explore the SQL advisory utilities and take a closer look at the operation of the SQL Access and SQL Tuning advisors.

The SQL Tuning Advisor Links

At a high-level, the SQL Tuning Advisor samples historical SQL as captured in SQL Tuning Sets (STS) from the *dba_hist_sqlstat* and *dba_hist_sql_plan* views. The SQL Tuning Advisor can be launched from many places within Enterprise Manager:

- For high-load SQL statements identified by ADDM, SQL Tuning Advisor can be launched from the ADDM Finding Details screen.

- When selecting from the Top SQL statements, Advisor can be launched from the Top SQL Page.

- When the STS is the input for tuning, Advisor can be launched from the SQL Tuning Sets page.

The last input set for the SQL Tuning Advisor is user-input statements or the SQL Tuning Set. This could include untested SQL statements, or a set of SQL statements currently under development. For tuning a set of SQL statements, a SQL Tuning Set (STS) has to be constructed and stored, and fed to the SQL Tuning Advisor

The OEM display screen for the SQL Tuning Advisor has the menu options shown in Figure 19.53.

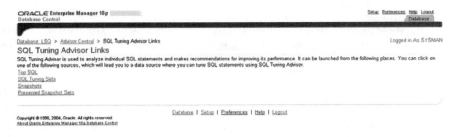

Figure 19.53: *The OEM SQL Tuning Advisor links screen.*

While each of these is explained in detail later in this chapter, it is important to understand that this is the main anchor screen for the SQL Tuning advisory functions. For more sophisticated DBA's, Oracle provides the *dbms_sqltune* DBMS package as an interface to this powerful analytical tool.

This series of screens are arranged in a hierarchy of screens, showing each of the sub-screens from the links screen shown in Figure 19.54.

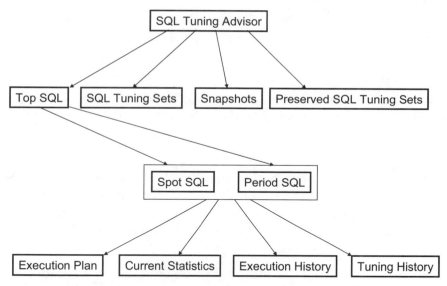

Figure 19.54: *The OEM hierarchy of screen for the SQL Tuning Advisor.*

In addition to using Enterprise Manager, the SQL Tuning Advisor is obtained by using the PL/SQL package *dbms_sqltune*. This is a new package introduced in 10g, and it has comprehensive procedures that help to conduct the full SQL Advisor session. Some of the useful procedures include:

- *create_tuning_task* - This procedure creates a tuning task for a given SQL statement or for a cached cursor.

- *execute_tuning_task* - This procedure executes the tuning task and generates the tuning data.

- *report_tuning_task* - This procedure generates a complete report of the results of a task.

- *report_plans* - This procedure shows the SQL plans.

Most Oracle professionals find the Enterprise Manager interface far easier to use than the *dbms_sqltune* package. Therefore, a closer look at these SQL Tuning functions is in order. The OEM SQL Tuning Advisor execution plan display is shown in Figure 19.56 below. From the top-level of the SQL Tuning advisor screen, hyperlinks to the following OEM areas are shown:

- Top SQL: This OEM screen displays the most resource intensive SQL for any time period that is specified. As the time-period changes, the top SQL is displayed along with the percentage of total elapsed time used by the statement, the CPU time consumed, the total wait time for the SQL and the average elapsed time per execution.

- SQL Tuning Sets: SQL tuning sets are encapsulations of SQL statements. They contain the source for the SQL statement; the host variables used during historical execution, performance metrics and allow a complete environment for testing the efficiency of a single SQL statement over time.

- Snapshots: SQL Snapshots are taken every hour and can be manipulated manually with the new *dbms_workload_repository* package.

- Preserved Snapshot Sets: A snapshot set, also known as a baseline, is a collection of multiple AWR snapshots. The preserved snapshot sets are then used to compare workload performance over specific periods.

Database: prod.tdslnx146.oracleads.com > Advisor Central > SQL Tuning Results:TASK_9819 >
Recommendations for SQL ID:7rch4vpva21hq > New Explain Plan

New Explain Plan

Expand All | Collapse All

Operation	Line ID	Order	Rows	KB	Cost	Time (seconds)	CPU Cost	IO Cost	Object
▼ SELECT STATEMENT	0	6	2	0.064	5	1	44468	5	
▼ NESTED LOOPS	1	5	2	0.064	5	1	44468	5	
▼ TABLE ACCESS BY GLOBAL INDEX ROWID	2	2	918843	18,843.461	4	1	28955	4	SH.SALES
INDEX FULL SCAN DESCENDING	3	1	1		3	1	21564	3	SH.SALES_TIME_IDX
▼ TABLE ACCESS BY INDEX ROWID	4	4	1	0.012	1	1	15512	1	SH.CUSTOMERS
INDEX UNIQUE SCAN	5	3	1		0	1	8171	0	SH.CUSTOMERS_PK

Database | Setup | Preferences | Help | Logout

Figure 19.55: *New OEM SQL Tuning Advisor execution plan display.*

Drilling down into the top SQL areas shows how it captures the most resource-intensive SQL allowing the DBA to explore the exact conditions leading to any Oracle performance bottleneck.

The Top SQL Screen

The Top SQL screen has two tabs, one for *Period SQL* and another for *Spot SQL* as shown in Figure 19.56. If the period tab is clicked, OEM presents a sliding time-series windows so that the DBA can examine the top SQL over time right next to a time-based summary of active session information.

The active session histogram allows the DBA to quickly zero in on the time period of interest, based on total waits, CPU or I/O during that period. This active session history data is stored inside the *dba_hist_active_session_history*, *dba_hist_waitclassmet_history* and *dba_hist_waitstat* views, so it is easy for Enterprise Manager to display the totals for these values in a colorful, easy-to-read fashion.

As the DBA moves the sliding right-hand bar, different sets of top SQL appear. The SQL for these statements are stored in the *dba_hist_sqltext*, *dba_hist_sql_plan* and *dba_hist_sqlstat* views, so it is easy for Enterprise Manager to access and display the top SQL as adjustments are made to the slide bar on the top SQL screen.

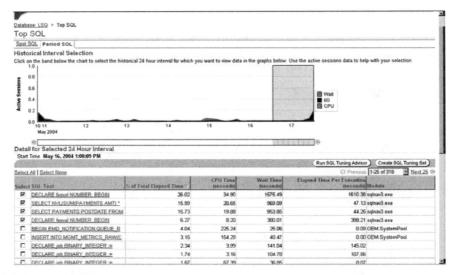

Figure 19.56: *The Period SQL screen showing top SQL and active session information.*

The following section presents the details for the Top SQL statements.

Viewing SQL Details in OEM

When the DBA clicks on any of the SQL statements, the SQL details screen, represented in Figure 19.57, is shown. The SQL detail screen reveals the source for the SQL statement plus the following informational tabs:

- **Execution Plan:** This displays the execution plan details including server CPU and I/O costs for each execution phase. It also includes hyperlinks to table details.

- **Current Statistics:** This shows important details for the execution statistics for the SQL statement during a specified time, including the number of executions, average response time and CPU resources consumed.

- **Execution History:** This screen shows a graphical depiction of the SQL statement over time, plotting the average CPU and response time for the SQL statement.

- **Tuning History:** This shows the historical SQL advisor tuning set tasks for the SQL statement.

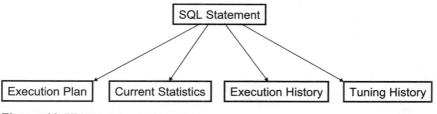

Figure 19.57: *The Top SQL sub-screens.*

The tour begins with a look at the execution plan details tab.

The Execution Plan Tab

The details in the execution plan have been greatly enhanced from previous releases of Oracle. This fantastic execution plan display shows the RAM used by each step, the computed cost for each step and best of all, the external server details, including the CPU and I/O costs for each phase of the SQL statement as shown in Figure 19.58.

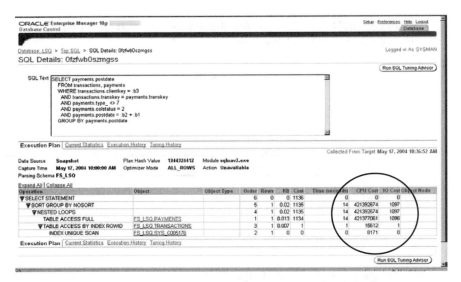

Figure 19.58: *SQL details with execution plans and external server CPU and I/O costs.*

Due to falling RAM prices, Solid-State Disk (SSD) and the ability of 64-bit architectures to support huge data caches, many Oracle databases have shifted from being I/O-bound to being CPU-bound. Rather than focusing on the minimization of physical disk I/O, Oracle10g tuning often focuses on the reduction of logical I/O's (consistent gets), often by tuning the SQL to reduce buffer touches and by addressing specific task wait events using the use Automated Session History (ASH) views.

Of course, Oracle has recognized this shifting bottleneck as evidenced by the new CPU and I/O costing for SQL statements execution steps in Oracle10g.

The table names for each table in the execution plan can be accessed to view details regarding the table column structure. The execution plan is only one of the areas in the detail display to view more details click on the Current Statistics.

Current Statistics Tab

The Current Statistics, shown in Figure 19.59, for the SQL statement are amazing. Unlike any earlier releases of Oracle, all resource components of the SQL can be seen, including important performance information from the *dba_hist_sys_time_model* view:

- Elapsed Time to Execute: This is includes all response time components including network time.

- CPU per Execution: This is the average CPU consumption per execution of the statement.

- Wait Ratio: This is a ration measuring the amount of wait events for the SQL statement.

- Sharable Memory: This shows the real RAM usage of the SQL for hash joins or sorting.

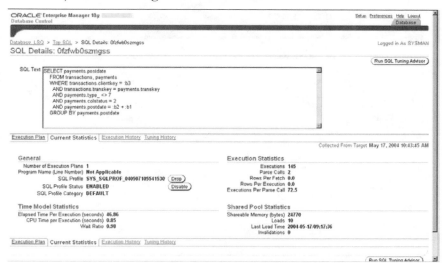

Figure 19.59: *Current Statistics for historical SQL execution.*

Viewing this screen reveals important tuning information including the SQL profile name, the number of executions, the average elapsed time per execution, average CPU time per execution, and the average number of rows returned by the SQL. This data gives important insights into the areas for tuning improvement for the SQL.

For even more details, the DBA can use the execution history tab.

Execution History Tab

The execution history tab presents an easy-to-read display of the historical behavior of the SQL statement as shown in Figure 19.60. This is especially important to visualize changes to SQL performance after a database change, such as a new index or adding a materialized view.

The display shows the average CPU and elapsed time per hour, and a radio button allows the DBA to choose between displaying the total CPU and elapsed execution time, in seconds, or the average CPU and execution time per execution.

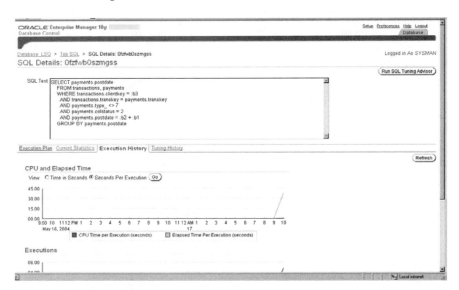

Figure 19.60: *Viewing historical SQL execution details.*

This screen also plots the number of executions over time so that those times when the SQL statement has the most impact on overall database performance can be viewed. Next, a look at the Tuning History tab is merited.

Tuning History Tab

The Tuning history screen shows a list of all previous advisor tasks and shows hyperlinks to the recommendations from both the SQL Tuning Advisor and the SQL Access Advisor shown in Figure 19.61.

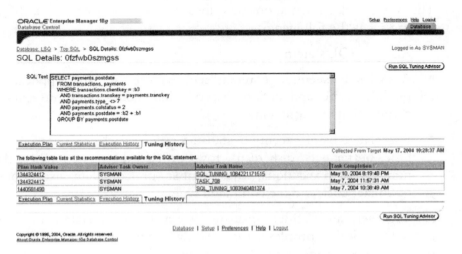

Figure 19.61: *Viewing historical SQL tuning recommendations.*

SQL workload tasks can be created to receive recommendations. However, as shown in the SQL tuning history screen, SQL Tuning advisor tasks are present and these are quite different from the SQL Tuning Advisor.

The SQL Tuning Advisor specifies the groupings of related SQL into SQL Tuning Sets, allowing Oracle to analyze them and to create SQL profiles that contain specific tuning recommendations for each statement. The following section presents a closer look at SQL Tuning sets.

Oracle SQL Tuning Sets

SQL Tuning sets are different from SQL Advisor tasks in several areas. While a SQL Access Advisor task analyzes for missing index and materialized views, the SQL Tuning advisor focuses on tuning the individual SQL by recommending changes to the execution plan via SQL Profiles.

The Oracle documentation describes the components of a SQL Tuning set as the following:

- A set of SQL statements.

- Associated execution context, such as user schema, application module name and action, list of bind values, and the cursor compilation environment.

- Associated basic execution statistics, such as elapsed time, CPU time, buffer gets, disk reads, rows processed, cursor fetches, the number of executions, the number of complete executions, optimizer cost, and the command type.

All together, an STS encapsulates a set of SQL statements and generates SQL profiles that allow implementation of any recommended changes to the SQL execution plan. The following section shows how to create a SQL tuning set.

Creating an SQL Tuning Set

An SQL Tuning set is usually created from the Top SQL screen by clicking the Create SQL Tuning Set hyperlink. This procedure presents a sub-screen that provides a name and description for the set, and includes all of the SQL from the Top SQL screen as shown in Figure 19.62.

Essentially, a SQL Tuning Set (STS) is a named set of SQL statements with their associated execution context and basic execution statistics.

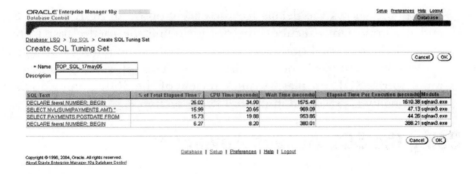

Figure 19.62: *Creating a SQL tuning set.*

Once created, the SQL Tuning advisor allows the DBA to schedule executions of the STS and view the specific recommendations from each execution. The following section explains how to view STS details.

Viewing SQL Tuning Set Details

Individual SQL Tuning sets are viewed by clicking on the Advisor Task name in the previous screen. Doing this presents a screen that displays a list of all SQL inside the SQL Tuning set as shown in Figure 19.63.

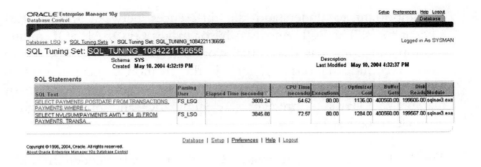

Figure 19.63: *Viewing SQL inside an SQL Tuning set.*

This figure shows the details for the execution of an SQL Tuning Set and the important execution metrics including the total elapsed time, total CPU time, total optimizer costs, as well as the number of logical I/Os (consistent gets) and total disk reads. This information is used as input to the SQL Profiles. A quick review of the SQL Tuning advisor functionality is explained in the following section.

Using the SQL Access Advisor

The previous section explained how ADDM makes specific system-wide recommendations. An exploration of the SQL Access Advisor will reveal how it makes system-wide SQL recommendations relating to SQL execution.

Figure 19.64 below shows the distinctions between the tools from the Advisor Central.

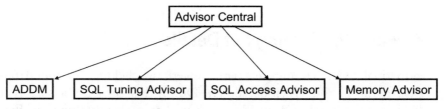

Figure 19.64: *The Advisor Central performance functional areas.*

It's important to understand the differences between these OEM advisor tools. The SQL Access Advisor makes GLOBAL SQL tuning recommendations based on the workload that is specified. These global recommendations may include the creation of new indexes to remove unnecessary large-table full-table scans and the creation of materialized views to pre-aggregate summaries and pre-join highly-normalized tables.

The SQL Access advisor makes GLOBAL recommendations on a workload while the SQL Tuning advisor makes SPECIFIC recommendations. The next section explores the important new features of the SQL advisors, and shows a real-world session with the SQL Access advisor.

New Features of the SQL Advisors

While there are many important enhancements in Oracle10g, the most important one is the integration and the at-your-fingertips access to all components of the task response time. The most important new features of the Oracle10g Enterprise Manager include:

- **Server Metrics:** This exciting feature is the ability of Oracle to step-out of the database areas and sample the server resources associated with every database operations.

- **Integration:** The Oracle10g Enterprise Manager allows the DBA to easily see all aspects of performance to relieve the tedium of running scripts and executing specialized routines.

The server metrics are especially important for SQL tuning because the server resources associated with every step within the execution plan for every SQL statement is shown in Figure 19.65.

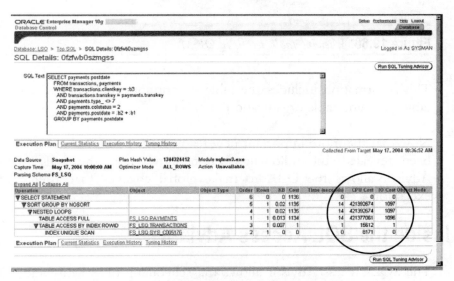

Figure 19.65: *SQL details with external server CPU and I/O costs.*

For any SQL statements, the components are displayed with hyperlinks for easy access.

By clicking on a table name in the execution plan in Figure 19.65, a detailed column representation of any table in the SQL query is easily viewed as shown in Figure 19.66.

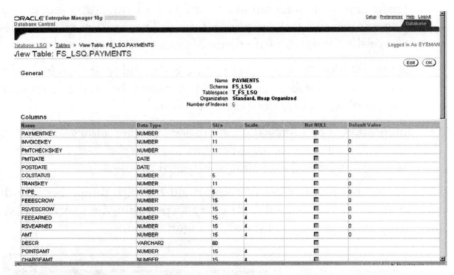

Figure 19.66: *Viewing table details in OEM.*

This information includes the table description, the schema, and the tablespace and table organization method.

Now that the more important new features of the SQL Advisors have been revealed, the following section shows how the SQL Access Advisor allows the DBA to make global changes that affect SQL execution.

Inside the SQL Access Advisor

The SQL Access Advisor allows the scheduling of system-wide SQL performance analysis and makes global recommendations to improve performance.

Unlike the SQL Tuning Advisor, which only tunes a single SQL statement, the SQL Access Advisor recommends changes that might improve the performance of hundreds of SQL statements.

Using the SQL Access Advisor requires the following steps:

- Workload Definition: This step allows the DBA to define the set of SQL statements to be used for the session.

- Definition Options: This step allows the DBA to choose the scope of the analysis (indexes, materialized views, or both) and the type of analysis (limited or comprehensive).

- Schedule Advisor: This step allows the DBA to schedule an analysis of the high-resource SQL defined in the workload.

- Review Recommendations: This step allows the DBA to see the recommendations and the justification for the recommendations.

The following section presents a closer look at each step of the process.

The SQL Access Advisor Workload Definition

The OEM workload screen allows the DBA to create a new workload or use a previously captured workload as shown in Figure 19.67. The source for the workload can be selected from the following four options:

- **Use Current and Recent SQL Activity:** This option uses the *dba_hist_sqlstat* and *dba_hist_sqltext* and *dba_hist_sql_plan* views to collect and analyze SQL statements.

- **Import a Workload:** This option is a pre-defined workload that has been stored in the new Oracle10g SQL repository.

- **User-Defined Workload:** This advanced feature allows the manual capture of SQL using a CTAS command and the result table as a workload. For example, here a *my_workload* table is created using personal criteria:

```
create table my_workload as
select
    sql_text,
    username
from
    dba_advisor_sqla_wk_stmts
where
    executions > 400
and
    buffer_gets > 10000;
```

- **Hypothetical Workload**: This advanced feature allows a comma-delimited list of tables to be entered and all SQL using these tables are included in the workload.

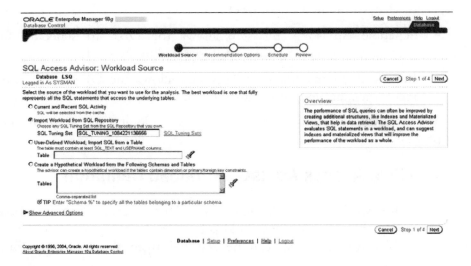

Figure 19.67: *The SQL Access advisor workload source definition screen.*

Once the workload is defined, the recommendation options can then be chosen.

The SQL Access Advisor Recommendation Options

The Recommendations Options screen in Figure 19.68 has two sections: the scope of the analysis and the type of analysis. This screen allows the workload to be analyzed for missing indexes and materialized view opportunities:

- Missing Indexes: Indexes, especially function-based indexes, can greatly reduce the amount of logical I/O required for an SQL statement to retrieve its result set.

- Materialized Views: If the target tables are not constantly changing, materialized views can be used to pre-join tables together or pre-summarize aggregate information. Materialized views can result in huge SQL performance improvements.

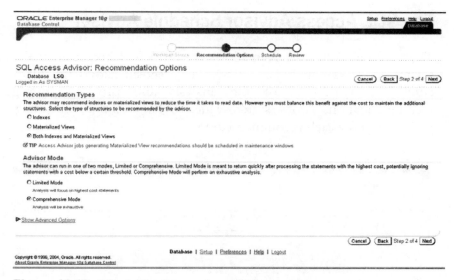

Figure 19.68: *The SQL Access advisor Recommendations options screen.*

The scope of the analysis can be limited, meaning that the SQL Access Advisor takes a quick look at the SQL and does not create SQL profiles; or comprehensive, meaning that detailed analysis is conducted and SQL profiles are created for the top SQL statements. Both the limited and comprehensive modes conduct the following activities against all SQL statements in the workload:

- **SQL Access**: The SQL *where* clause is interrogated and compared to the execution plan for each SQL statement to verify that the most efficient indexes are being used. If this step detects a missing index, it will be presented in the recommendations.

- **Statistics:** The statistics for all objects involved in each query are verified for quality and completeness.

- **Query Structure:** The structure of the SQL statement is checked to ensure the optimal syntax format of the query. Because SQL is a declarative language, a query can be formulated in many ways to achieve the same result, some more efficient than others.

The SQL Profiles can then be used by the SQL Tuning Advisor.

The SQL Access Advisor Schedule Advisor

The Schedule Advisor screen allows the DBA to schedule an analytical session as shown in Figure 19.69. This screen allows the DBA to control every aspect of the analysis and provides intelligent recommendations for system-wide SQL tuning, including a justification for each recommendation.

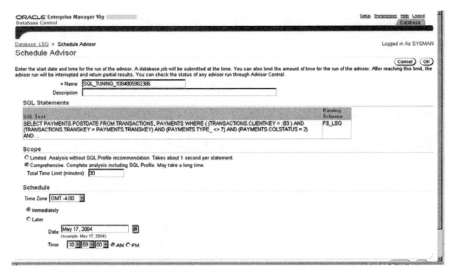

Figure 19.69: *The SQL Access advisor scheduling options.*

When an analytical schedule is created, the following metrics are specified:

- The Name for the Advisor Session: By specifying the name for the advisor session, multiple sessions are created and scheduled, each customized according to the type of database processing occurring at the specified time.

- Scope: The scope radio button allows the DBA to choose a limited analysis that only spends one wall-clock second on each SQL statement of the comprehensive option that analyzes each SQL statement and creates SQL profiles for all high-resource statements.

- Schedule: The scheduler option interfaces with the new Oracle10g scheduler, using the *dbms_scheduler* package, to allow for a scheduled execution, or an immediate execution of a tuning session can be chosen.

The final pre-processing step in this process is a review of the previous definitions.

The SQL Access Advisor Review

The final consolidation of the workload, options and scheduling screen is now displayed in Figure 19.70. This figure shows a summary of all the previous screens and presents the opportunity to make changes before running the tuning task.

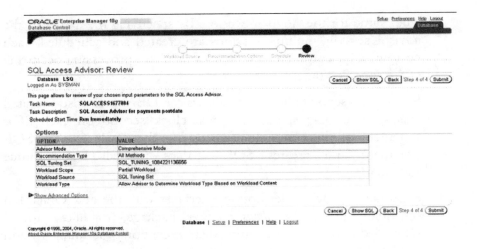

Figure 19.70: *The SQL Access advisor session review screen.*

Now that the workload is specified, the type and scope of the analysis that scheduled the execution is chosen and the plan reviewed, the output from the SQL Access Advisor session is now ready for examination.

SQL Access Advisor Recommendations

The output of a SQL Access Advisor session is shown in the recommendations screen as shown in Figure 19.71.

Figure 19.71: *The SQL Access advisor recommendations screen.*

This screen makes specific recommendations for the creation of indexes and materialized views. It includes the definitions for these new database entities.

The creation of a new index or materialized view may immediately cause thousands of SQL statements to change their execution plans, so special care is required before implementing the recommendations in a production environment.

This section has been a quick review of the SQL Access Advisor to show how it relates to the Enterprise Manager Advisor Central screen and how the SQL Access advisor makes recommendations about an entire pre-defined workload. The main points in this section were:

- The SQL Access Advisor allows the DBA to gather global recommendations for a workload. The SQL Tuning advisor is more granular, tuning a single statement.

- The DBA defines the SQL used in the SQL Access Advisor task, and can choose current SQL, a user-defined set of SQL, a historical workload, or a hypothetical workload.

- A hypothetical workload is very useful because the DBA need-only specify the tables that participate in the queries, and the SQL

Access advisor gathers the appropriate SQL statements to create the workload.

- The main functions of the SQL Access advisor is to recommend missing indexes and materialized views, but a comprehensive task analysis will also create SQL Profiles that can be used within the SQL Tuning advisor.

The following section presents the most powerful and intelligent of all of the OEM advisory utilities, the memory advisors.

Using the Memory Advisor through OEM

The Memory Advisor can be used only when the automatic memory management (AMM) feature is disabled. The Memory Advisor has three advisors that give recommendations on: the Shared Pool in the SGA, the Buffer Cache in the SGA, and the PGA.

The following steps can be used to access the Memory Advisor and tune its underlying structures.

The first step is to click on the Memory Advisor in the Advisor Central Page.

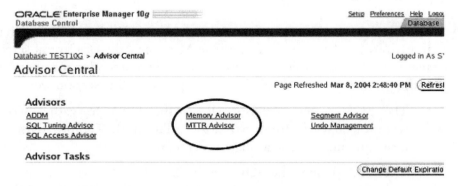

Figure 19.72: *Memory Advisor.*

The Memory Parameters: SGA page will appear as shown in Figure 19.73. This page has all the details on memory usage for the System

Global Area. The shared pool and the buffer cache are part of the SGA. Help can be clicked for more information on the structure shown here.

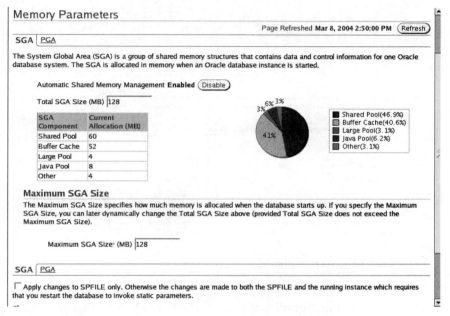

Figure 19.73: *Memory Parameters.*

The Automatic Shared Memory Management has to be disabled to run the advisor. To accomplish this, the shared pool or the buffer cache should be chosen and the Advice link next to it should be clicked.

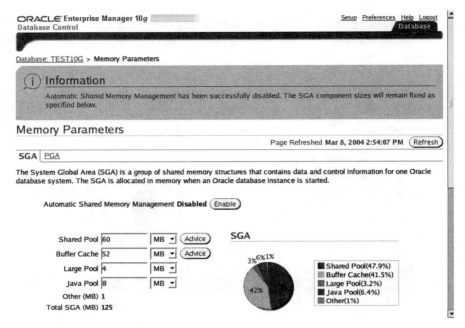

Figure 19.74: *Memory Advice.*

The corresponding graphs appear as shown below in Figures 19.75 and 19.76.

For Shared Pool size, the graph reveals that a shared pool size larger than 60 MB will not improve the performance much. So the recommended optimal shared pool size is 60 MB.

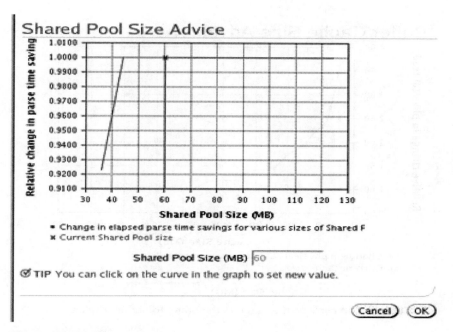

Figure 19.75: *Memory Advice.*

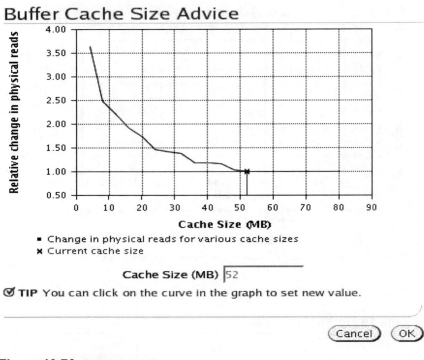

Buffer Cache Size Advice

- Change in physical reads for various cache sizes
- Current cache size

Cache Size (MB) | 52

☑ **TIP** You can click on the curve in the graph to set new value.

⟨ Cancel ⟩ ⟨ OK ⟩

Figure 19.76: *Memory Advice.*

For Buffer Cache, the graph reveals that a buffer cache size larger than 52MB does not improve the performance as much as in shared pool. A bigger cache prompts less disk reads and improves the performance.

The PGA Advisor is run by clicking on the PGA property page. This is similar to running the SGA advisors. The cache hit percentage is plotted against memory size. Higher hit ratios in the range of 75% to 100% indicate better cache performance.

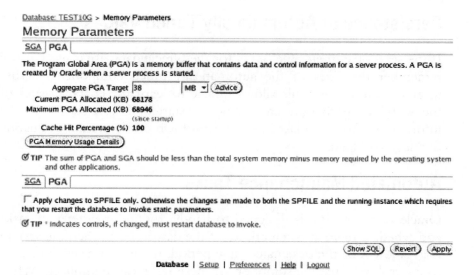

Figure 19.77: *PGA Memory.*

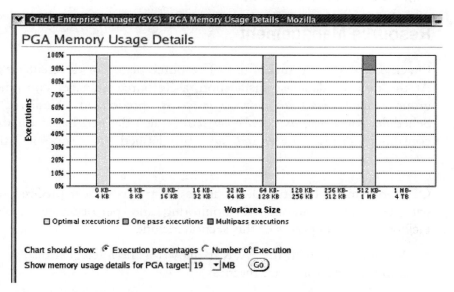

Figure 19.78: *PGA Memory.*

Persistence of Automatically Tuned Values

If the server parameter file (*spfile*) for the Oracle database is used, it will remember the sizes of the automatically tuned components across instance shutdowns. This allows Oracle to learn the characteristics of the workload each time an instance is started. It can start with the information from the last instance shutdown and continue evaluating the new workload.

Automated Maintenance Tasks

Oracle Database 10g is designed to handle routine maintenance tasks and schedule them at certain times of the day or week when the system load is low. For the designated time period, the use of a resource plan to control resource consumption of these tasks can be utilized. When the time elapses, the database can switch to a different resource plan with lower resource allocation.

Resource Management

Oracle Database 10g makes use of resource plans for different tasks. At the time of database installation, a Resource Manager consumer group called *auto_task_consumer_group* is predefined. Similarly a Scheduler job class, *auto_tasks_job_class* is also defined based on this consumer group. *gather_stats_job* is defined to run in the *auto_task_job_class* job class.

OEM has made quantum leaps in assisting the Oracle professional with creating an automated monitoring and performance display facility. The main points of this section include:

- EM interfaces with the AWR to allow for the intelligent display of important performance metrics.

- The OEM performance screens are design in an intuitive top-down fashion and require little training to use.

- The DBA can create customized exception reporting mechanisms allowing OEM to send a notification in time to correct an issue before it causes a performance problem.

- The ASH component of AWR allows to the DBA to view detailed Oracle session information within OEM.

The next section will present information on Oracle Tuning Techniques.

Introduction to Online Oracle Tuning Tools

Historically, Oracle tuning professionals used SQL*Plus scripts, and many Oracle Gurus wonder if any vendor will design a GUI that makes sense to the Oracle tuning DBA. Tuning Oracle is all about locating and fixing bottlenecks, and most DBAs pull out their native scripts rather than try to navigate their way through a convoluted interface.

Many DBA's will purchase a script collection such as the one at www.oracle-script.com. Oracle tuning experts are always skeptical of GUI tools that claim to assist with Oracle tuning, usually because the tool does not give them what they want to see.

For example, most Oracle tuning experts love the Automated Session History (ASH) cluster and the new ability to perform time-series tuning, but it only works on Oracle10g databases. The proliferation of third party tools, such as TOAD and WISE, that were developed to compete with the Oracle Enterprise Manager (OEM) speaks for itself; however, many Oracle professionals desire a time-series tool that would allow them to do advanced trending and predictive analysis. It appears that these new self-collecting ASH GUI tools may be the wave of the future.

This chapter provides an overview of how popular third-party Oracle tuning tools might assist in Oracle tuning efforts.

- Oracle Dictionary Scripts and Tools: The review will include a look at the Mike Ault Script collection from www.oracle-script.com.

- Trend-based tools: The review of trend-based tools will provide a quick look at WISE because it's the only tool outside OEM that will plot time-series data from the Automated Workload Repository (AWR) and ASH. It has capabilities that are move advanced than OEM because it allows users to view Oracle trends by day of the week and hour of the day. The WISE Enterprise Edition also allows the same interface to Oracle8i and Oracle 9i databases.

- Wait Event tuning tools: There are several online tools that focus on a wait event tuning methodology. The DBFlash product by Confio software was chosen for this review because it is built around a wait event tuning framework.

The following section provides a review of custom Oracle dictionary scripts.

Oracle Dictionary Scripts for Tuning

In the real world, most Oracle experts use custom data dictionary scripts to investigate Oracle performance problems. One of the reasons that third-party tools cannot replace native scripts is that the Oracle data dictionary is very sophisticated, and there are hundreds of thousands of ways that Oracle metrics can be combined and displayed.

Oracle tuning scripts can also be very sophisticated in structure, especially when performing advanced tuning activities such as hypothesis testing and multivariate analysis.

Even simple tasks can be far too complex for a GUI tool. For example, this simple script to display full-table scans would be nearly impossible to build from a GUI menu:

```
select
   to_char(sn.end_interval_time,'mm/dd/rr hh24') time,
   p.owner,
   p.name,
   t.num_rows,
   decode(t.buffer_pool,'KEEP','Y','DEFAULT','N') K,
   s.blocks blocks,
   sum(a.executions_delta) nbr_FTS
from
```

```
    dba_tables      t,
    dba_segments s,
    dba_hist_sqlstat      a,
    dba_hist_snapshot sn,
    (select distinct
      pl.sql_id,
      object_owner owner,
      object_name name
    from
       dba_hist_sql_plan pl
    where
       operation = 'TABLE ACCESS'
       and
       options = 'FULL') p
where
    a.snap_id = sn.snap_id
    and
    a.sql_id = p.sql_id
    and
    t.owner = s.owner
    and
    t.table_name = s.segment_name
    and
    t.table_name = p.name
    and
    t.owner = p.owner
    and
    t.owner not in ('SYS','SYSTEM')
having
    sum(a.executions_delta) > 1
group by
    to_char(sn.end_interval_time,'mm/dd/rr hh24'),p.owner, p.name,
t.num_rows, t.cache, t.buffer_pool, s.blocks
order by
    1 asc;
```

Native Oracle dictionary scripts also allow information to be displayed in novel ways and the creation of easy exception reports. To confound matters, every release of Oracle has changes to the underlying x$ tables and v$ views, and new scripts may need to be created for Oracle9i and Oracle10g.

With hundreds of thousands of possible tuning queries, how does the DBA manage to find the best possible solution? Most professional Oracle tuning professionals build collections of their top 500 scripts and organize them so that they can find the right script for desired outcome.

One extremely popular script collection is the Mike Ault collection available at www.oracle-script.com. This collection is organized with precise naming conventions to clue the DBA in about the functions of each script. Within each script, all possible column values are displayed and the DBA can comment out those that they are not interested in observing.

To a knowledgeable DBA, finding the right script is simple. For example, to find all scripts referencing physical disk reads, the following *grep* command can be issued:

```
grep -i "physical reads" *.sql
```

Most hardcore Oracle tuning professionals do not like being forced to tune within the confines of the tool, and they enjoy the flexibility of being able to get any metric that they want.

The exception to this rule is graphing time-series data. For visual plotting, many Oracle DBAs cut-and-paste output data into MS-Excel spreadsheets. The visualization of this data is one area where a third-party tool can assist the DBA.

The following section will provide a look at a third-party tool that is specifically designed to assist with this visualization problem.

Oracle Time Series Tuning Tools

The co-author of this book, Alexey Danchenkov, designed the WISE tool to supplement his extensive collection of Oracle dictionary tuning scripts, and a free copy of the standard edition is provided with the purchase of this book.

While scripts will give DBAs exactly what they want, the Oracle dictionary structure is very sophisticated and many Oracle professionals desire a framework in which to keep their hundreds of Oracle scripts. Danchenkov built into the WISE tool the ability to write new queries and add them directly into the WISE menu system, ensuring that they could easily be found. This process is illustrated in Figure 19.79.

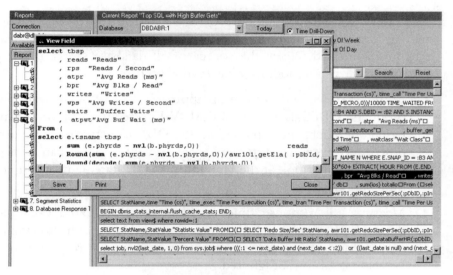

Figure 19.79: *A sample WISE interface*

With its sophisticated interface, WISE has been designed by senior DBAs for senior DBAs. Just like Oracle, the WISE interface is very complex, and it has every tuning area available including overall performance metrics, system wait events, instance activity and memory statistics, top sessions and SQL, plus detailed I/O metrics, aggregated by tablespace, segment and data file.

Third-party Wait Event Tuning Tools

Even though basic wait event tuning is available within OEM, DBFlash uses an expanded wait event methodology, similar to the ones codified by Cary Millsap and Gaja Krishna Vaidyanatha. Simply stated, this methodology proposes that performance issues can usually be solved by determining the major components of response time, where response time was broken down into service time and wait time. Service time is defined as CPU time and wait time is the summation of the various waits the individual SQL statements under go during their processing.

The online wait event methodology is a practical approach to Oracle tuning, primarily because it focuses on the direct causes of poor response time and targets the source of all database stress, the SQL statements. This methodology has several precepts:

- Both top-down and bottom-up approach: Unlike other drill-down products, DBFlash and the OEM ASH screens focus on a time-based approach. For any period, the DBA can start from the top-down and examine system-wide wait events. They can also go bottom-up and look at the high impact SQL statements during the time period.

- Measures all response time components: By default, each high impact SQL statement is shown as a stacked bar graph showing the contribution of each wait event to its overall response time. Nothing is left out or ignored.

- Focus on the SQL: Since the SQL and the resulting executions comprise all Oracle access, a tuning approach should include the source of the database load.

- Ignore the meaningless: The online wait even tools resist the temptation to include meaningless system-wide averages and event counters.

- Wait time matters: The wait time tuning approach recognizes that the wait events that comprise a tasks response time have the clues that are needed to resolve the problem.

Wait event tuning is a proactive, time-based solution with a five step methodology:

- Identify the SQL with the highest performance impact.

- Allocate impact of the SQL to the database customers, both users and programs.

- Quantify the real business impact, if any, of each bottleneck.

- Prioritize the most important actions for the organization.

- Assign the human resource best able to execute the identified actions.

All Oracle tuning experts, while their various implementations may differ, agree that utilization of a methodology based in wait interface monitoring of SQL is the best methodology for properly tuning the Oracle database system. For more information on wait event tuning, see the book Oracle Wait Event Tuning by Stephen Andert (2004, Rampant).

The next section will provide a closer look at a third-party wait event tuning tool. The top level view of DBFlash provides a two part window with the left side showing the monitored databases and the time frames over which they were monitored. The right side shows, for each monitored period of time, the performance issues associated with each time period. In each timeframe, a drill down into the menu tree shows Oracle events, Top SQL, Top OS users, Top DB usernames, Top Oracle Sessions, Top Machines and Top Programs by resource as shown in Figure 19.80 below.

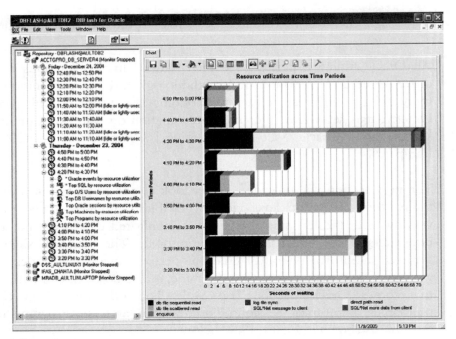

Figure 19.80: *DBFlash – Resource Utilization across Time Periods*

In this example the database can be seen as a whole, and the DBA can quickly see all resource events that contribute to overall response time. Oracle tuning professionals have long recognized that understanding the components of response time is the key to tuning any Oracle database.

External Bottlenecks

Oracle does not run in a vacuum, and any tool must be able to detect external bottlenecks from any area of the server environment:

- **Disk**: Both scattered reads, such as full-table scans, and sequential reads, such as index probes, are monitored.

- **Network**: The SQL*Net metrics are monitored and can easily spot when an application is network-bound.

- **CPU**: The display tracks processor consumption.

Internal Bottlenecks

Internally, the Oracle database has many shared resources and potential bottlenecks, and WISE OEM and DBFlash visualize the following metrics:

- *latch and lock waits*: These waits result from serialized access latches.

- *control file waits*: Oracle touches the control file very frequently.

- *buffer busy waits*: Segment header contention with the data buffers can cause bottlenecks.

- *enqueue waits*: This can indicate internal latch and lock contention.

- *log buffer waits*: Events such as redo log space requests can cripple Oracle performance.

- *undo segment waits*: Undo segments can cause serialization waits.

- *buffer deadlocks*: Internal locking and latching can cause contention.

By providing the experienced DBA with a detailed capability to slice and dice wait interface data by SQL, User, Process and other categories, these GUI tools provide unprecedented access to the wait data vital to proper tuning.

One nice feature of third-party tools is the ability to quickly find sub-optimal SQL statements. Any tuning tool must focus on the wait events that comprise the total response time, both for the system and for individual transactions.

Each submenu selection provides a graphical view of that cut across the performance picture for that time frame. Figure 19.81 shows an example slice for Oracle Events from the DBFlash tool for the 4:20 to 4:30 pm Time frame from Figure 19.80.

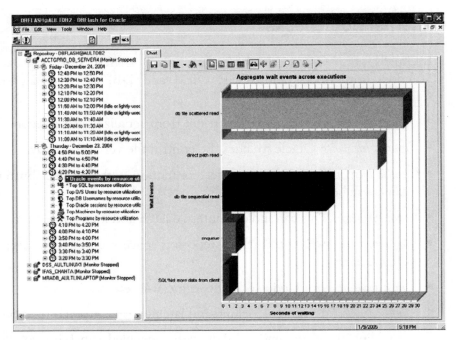

Figure 19.81: *A ten minute Time Slice for Oracle Event Waits*

From Figure 19.81, it is possible to identify the contribution of each event as it is clearly shown, in small, meaningful ten minute periods. By selecting the Top SQL by resource utilization for the same timeframe, as shown in Figure 19.82, it is simple to determine the SQL statements that need attention.

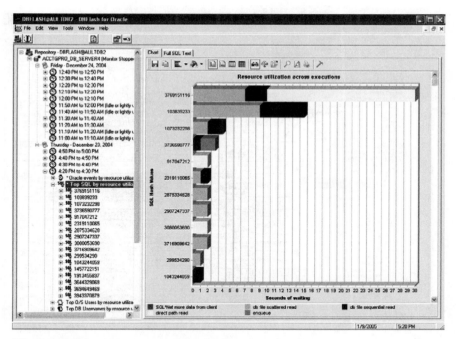

Figure 19.82: *Top SQL BY Resource Utilization*

As an alternative, the full SQL text can be displayed, as shown in Figure 19.83.

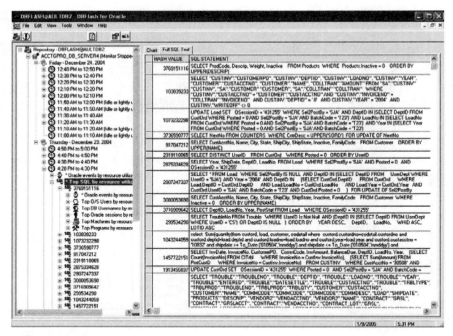

Figure 19.83: *SQL Text Display*

By clicking on any of the bar graphs or selecting the statement from the menu tree at the left, the user is quickly shown the offending SQL and given the opportunity to generate an explain plan. Additional tuning actions are represented in Figures 19.84 and 19.85.

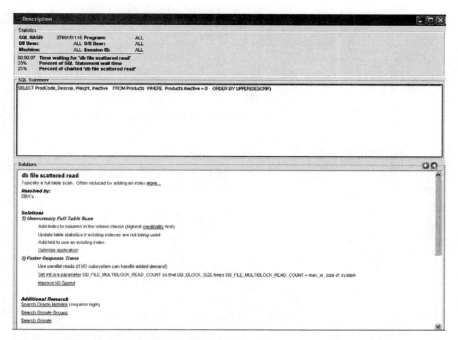

Figure 19.84: *Drill down on SQL statement*

These figures show some of the built-in intelligence of DBFlash. The DBFlash tool recognizes the common causes of a scattered read event and recommends some common solutions for the Oracle professional.

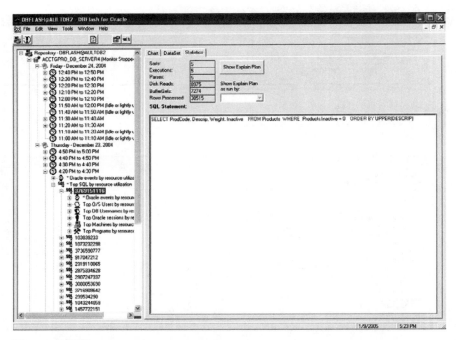

Figure 19.85: *DBFlash SQL View Screen*

The explain plan utility then provides the experienced DBA with the information needed to resolve the issue. The other menu options allow the DBA to isolate the offending SQL to a specific O/S or DB user or a program or machine.

In using the product with an actual client, it quickly allows a seasoned DBA to drill down to the problem SQL statements. Through its explain plan access, it can also find and fix the issues with the statements.

The following section will present information on the Oracle10g OEM.

Oracle10g OEM Review

In Oracle10g OEM, Oracle provides the performance monitor (ADDM) and SQL Analyzer. The two products are part of the performance pack and are a cost-plus add-on to OEM. Both ADDM and SQL Analyzer utilize the AWR series of tables and the MMON process to gather and store Oracle statistics. The AWR is nearly identical to earlier Oracle release's STATSPACK system of monitoring. In fact by simply changing the names of the applicable statistics storage tables to their new AWR version, many reports that were generated to run against the STATSPACK tables will run against their AWR counterparts.

Oracle recognized the need to improve the functionality of OEM for tuning activities and employed some of the world's leading Oracle experts, including Kyle Hailey, John Beresniewicz and Graham Wood, to rebuild the 10g OEM performance interface. Bearing little resemblance to its OEM predecessor, the new interface was dubbed Enterprise Manager (EM). Because it was designed by practicing Oracle tuning experts, the new OEM offers an unparalleled performance management interface, worthy of the most seasoned Oracle DBA.

- Comprehensive collection: The OEM performance screens enable a stunning visual display of important Oracle performance metrics. The monitoring and diagnostic abilities of Oracle10g are enabled by the AWR, which collects and stores historical run-time performance data as an integral part of the Oracle10g database kernel. The OEM now samples server side metrics and incorporates CPU consumption, run-queue length, physical I/O and RAM paging information. This enables a comprehensive picture of overall Oracle performance.

- Wait event Metrics: Oracle10g now has an Active Session History (ASH) component that automatically collects detailed metrics on individual Oracle sessions. OEM also has an interface to the ASH component of AWR using special *dba_hist* views to collect and store detailed system event information allowing immediate access to every detail about Oracle execution.

- Automated performance diagnostics: This is an extra cost feature available from Oracle Corporation. Using the optional Database Diagnostic Pack and Database Tuning Pack components, OEM has a native interface to ADDM, allowing OEM to make intelligent performance recommendations.

New Features of the SQL Advisors

While there are many important enhancements in Oracle10g, the most important is the integration and fingertip access to all components of task response time.

The server metrics are especially important for SQL tuning because now it is possible to see the server resources associated with every step within the execution plan for every SQL statement as shown in Figure 19.86.

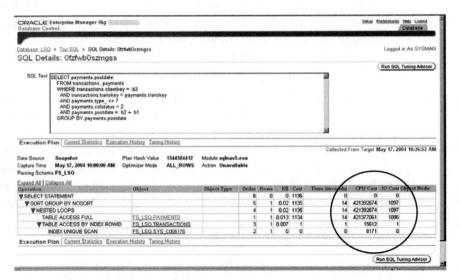

Figure 19.86: *SQL details with external server CPU and I/O costs*

Comprehensive Collection

When a user drills down into the metric list, OEM displays hundreds of individual tuning metrics and provides the ability to set personalized alert thresholds like those shown in Figure 19.87. OEM allows the DBA to specify numeric criteria, such as greater than and less than, and has full pattern matching capabilities for text-based metrics such as alert log messages.

SQL Response Time (%)	>	500	
Scans on Long Tables (per second)	>		
Scans on Long Tables (per transaction)	>		
Segments Approaching Maximum Extents Count	>	0	
Segments Not Able to Extend Count	>	0	
Service CPU Time (per user call)	>		
Service Response Time (per user call)	>		
Session Limit Usage (%)	>	80	
Session Logical Reads (per second)	>		
Session Logical Reads (per transaction)	>		
Session Terminated Alert Log Error	Contains	ORA-	
Session Terminated Alert Log Error Status	>	0	
Shared Pool Free (%)	<		
Soft Parse (%)	<		
Sorts in Memory (%)	<		
Sorts to Disk (per second)	>		
Sorts to Disk (per transaction)	>		
System Response Time (centi-seconds)	>		
Tablespace Space Used (%)	>	85	97

Figure 19.87: *Setting alert thresholds within OEM*

For example, an OEM threshold could be set to send a pager alert or use OEM2GO whenever a critical metric changed. There are several critical instance-wide performance metrics in the display in Figure 19.87:

- SQL response time (%)

- System Response Time (centi-seconds)

- Shared Pool Free (%)

Due to the time-series nature of the AWR, it is easy to trigger an exception alert when the marginal values of any metrics change. All of the metrics denoted with the (%) are delta-based, meaning that OEM will trigger an alert whenever any metric changes by more than a specified percentage, regardless of its current value. This delta-based mechanism to allows time to repair a pending performance issue before it cripples the end-users.

A SNMP interface can easily be configured to have OEM send a notification e-mail whenever the threshold value has been exceeded.

This alert can be an e-mail, a telephone message or an alert on an OEM2GO PDA device.

Customized thresholds can also be set for dozens of important Oracle Throughput metrics as shown in Figure 19.88. These throughput metrics are critical for the senior Oracle professional because they can automate warning messages to allow them to fix an impending problem before the end-users experience a performance slowdown. This is especially valuable when tuning a large OLTP database with high volume I/O against many disk devices.

▼ Throughput	None	Last Collected Mar 1, 2004 7:07:15 PM
BG Checkpoints (per second)	Not Set	Last Collected Mar 1, 2004 7:07:15 PM
Branch Node Splits (per second)	Not Set	Last Collected Mar 1, 2004 7:07:15 PM
Branch Node Splits (per transaction)	Not Set	Last Collected Mar 1, 2004 7:07:15 PM
Consistent Read Changes (per second)	Not Set	Last Collected Mar 1, 2004 7:07:15 PM
Consistent Read Changes (per transaction)	Not Set	Last Collected Mar 1, 2004 7:07:15 PM
Consistent Read Gets (per second)	Not Set	Last Collected Mar 1, 2004 7:07:15 PM
Consistent Read Gets (per transaction)	Not Set	Last Collected Mar 1, 2004 7:07:15 PM
Cumulative Logons (per second)	Not Set	Last Collected Mar 1, 2004 7:07:15 PM
Cumulative Logons (per transaction)	Not Set	Last Collected Mar 1, 2004 7:07:15 PM
Cursor Blocks Created (per second)	Not Set	Last Collected Mar 1, 2004 7:07:15 PM
Cursor Blocks Created (per transaction)	Not Set	Last Collected Mar 1, 2004 7:07:15 PM
Cursor Undo Records Applied (per second)	Not Set	Last Collected Mar 1, 2004 7:07:15 PM
Cursor Undo Records Applied (per transaction)	Not Set	Last Collected Mar 1, 2004 7:07:15 PM
DBWR Checkpoints (per second)	Not Set	Last Collected Mar 1, 2004 7:07:15 PM
Database Block Changes (per second)	Not Set	Last Collected Mar 1, 2004 7:07:15 PM
Database Block Changes (per transaction)	Not Set	Last Collected Mar 1, 2004 7:07:15 PM
Database Block Gets (per second)	Not Set	Last Collected Mar 1, 2004 7:07:15 PM
Database Block Gets (per transaction)	Not Set	Last Collected Mar 1, 2004 7:07:15 PM
Enqueue Deadlocks (per second)	Not Set	Last Collected Mar 1, 2004 7:07:15 PM
Enqueue Deadlocks (per transaction)	Not Set	Last Collected Mar 1, 2004 7:07:15 PM
Enqueue Requests (per second)	Not Set	Last Collected Mar 1, 2004 7:07:15 PM
Enqueue Requests (per transaction)	Not Set	Last Collected Mar 1, 2004 7:07:15 PM
Enqueue Timeout (per second)	Not Set	Last Collected Mar 1, 2004 7:07:15 PM
Enqueue Timeout (per transaction)	Not Set	Last Collected Mar 1, 2004 7:07:15 PM
Enqueue Waits (per second)	Not Set	Last Collected Mar 1, 2004 7:07:15 PM

Figure 19.88: *OEM throughput metric thresholds*

Oracle10g OEM allows the DBA to quickly see the status of Oracle server-side file performance and error messages, including the alert log file, archived redo log status and file system status as shown in Figure 19.89.

All Metrics

Expand All | Collapse All

Metrics	Thresholds	Collection Stat
▼FSDEV10G		
▼Alert Log	Some	Not Collected
Alert Log Error Trace File	Not Set	Not Collected
Alert Log Name	Not Set	Not Collected
Archiver Hung Alert Log Error	Set	Not Collected
Data Block Corruption Alert Log Error	Set	Not Collected
Generic Alert Log Error	Set	Not Collected
Session Terminated Alert Log Error	Set	Not Collected
▼Alert Log Content	None	Not Collected
Content	Not Set	Not Collected
▼Alert Log Error Status	All	Last Collected
Archiver Hung Alert Log Error Status	Set	Last Collected
Data Block Corruption Alert Log Error Status	Set	Last Collected
Generic Alert Log Error Status	Set	Last Collected
Session Terminated Alert Log Error Status	Set	Last Collected
▼Archive Area	Some	Last Collected
Archive Area Used (%)	Set	Last Collected
Archive Area Used (KB)	Not Set	Last Collected
Free Archive Area (KB)	Not Set	Last Collected

Figure 19.89: *A partial listing of the AWR metrics from inside OEM*

OEM Wait Event Metrics

Together, the AWR and ASH metrics form the foundation for a complete Oracle tuning framework and Enterprise Manager provides the vehicle. Now that the underlying mechanism has been introduced, it is possible to explore how OEM yields an intelligent window into this critical Oracle tuning information.

While this functionality of OEM is amazing in its own right, Oracle10g has taken the AWR model beyond the intelligent display of performance metrics. Using true Artificial Intelligence (AI), Oracle Enterprise Manager now has a built-in interface to the Automatic Database Diagnostic Monitor and the intelligent SQL Tuning advisor.

Using the Enterprise Manager with ADDM and the SQL Tuning advisor can save the manual tuning of hundreds of SQL statements. The new Oracle10g SQL profiles allow the DBA to rapidly and reliably complete a complex tuning effort in just a few hours.

Figure 19.90 below shows the specific times when the server exceeds the maximum CPU capacity and the total time spent by active Oracle sessions for both waiting and working.

Active Sessions: Waiting and Working

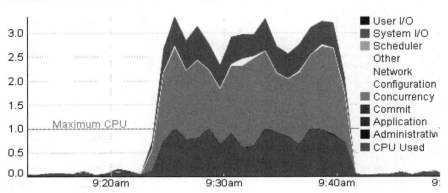

Figure 19.90: *OEM server time-series resource component utilization*

This is an especially important screen for customizing OEM alerts because thresholds can be set based on changes with either absolute of delta-based metrics. For example, the DBA might want to be alerted by OEM when the following session metrics are exceeded:

- Active Sessions Waiting: I/O - Alert when there are more than 500 active sessions waiting on I/O

- Active Sessions Waiting: I/O (%) – Alert when active sessions waiting on I/O increase by more than 10%

- Wait Time (sec) – Alert when wait time exceeds 2 seconds

- Wait Time (%) – Alert when wait time increases by more than 25%

The new OEM also allows the DBA to view session wait information at the metric level. For example, if OEM informs the DBA that the major wait event in the database is related to concurrency (locks, latches, pins), the DBA can drill down on the concurrency link to go to the OEM Active sessions waiting screen as shown in Figure 19.91.

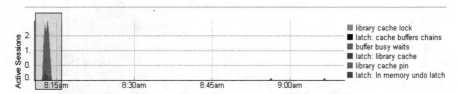

Figure 19.91: *The OEM display for active sessions waiting on concurrency*

This display is also a useful learning aid because OEM lists all of the sources of concurrency waits, such as library cache lock, latch, and *buffer busy waits*. It also displays the values associated with each concurrency component.

Double clicking on the chosen snapshot causes OEM to deliver a summary histogram of the response time components for the top 10 SQL statements and top 10 sessions that were identified during the AWR snapshot as shown in Figure 19.92.

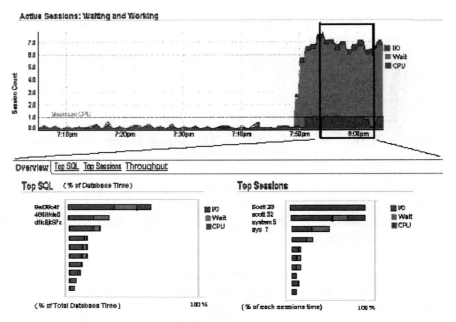

Figure 19.92: *The OEM top-10 SQL and top-10 session response time component display*

This visual display of summary information allows users to quickly find the most resource intensive tasks and instantly see if the main response time component is I/O, CPU, or Oracle internal wait events. Oracle performance investigations that used to take hours are now completed in a matter of seconds.

From this view, one can clearly see the total components of Oracle wait times including CPU time, concurrent management overhead (locks, latches), and I/O. This display also shows the times when CPU usage exceeds the server capacity.

The Automatic Diagnostic component of the Oracle Performance OEM screen contains an alert area where ADDM warns about historical performance exceptions. This exception-based reporting is very important to Oracle tuning because Oracle database change rapidly, and transient performance issues are very difficult to detect without an exception-based mechanism. The OEM alerts screen with the link to Advisor Central is shown in Figure 19.93.

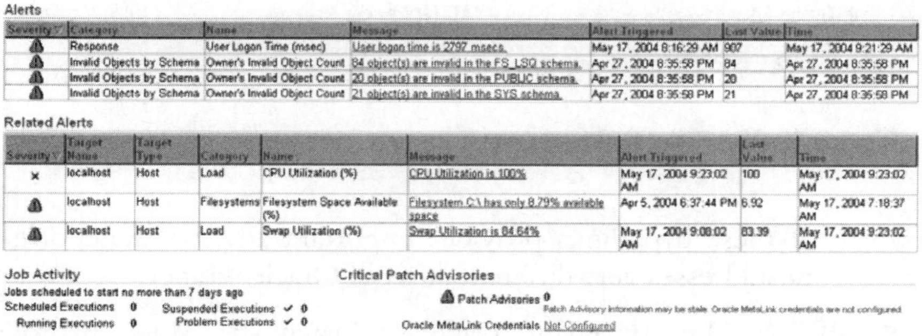
Alerts

Severity	Category	Name	Message	Alert Triggered	Last Value	Time
	Response	User Logon Time (msec)	User logon time is 2797 msecs.	May 17, 2004 8:16:29 AM	907	May 17, 2004 9:21:29 AM
	Invalid Objects by Schema	Owner's Invalid Object Count	84 object(s) are invalid in the FS_LSQ schema.	Apr 27, 2004 8:35:58 PM	84	Apr 27, 2004 8:35:58 PM
	Invalid Objects by Schema	Owner's Invalid Object Count	20 object(s) are invalid in the PUBLIC schema.	Apr 27, 2004 8:35:58 PM	20	Apr 27, 2004 8:35:58 PM
	Invalid Objects by Schema	Owner's Invalid Object Count	21 object(s) are invalid in the SYS schema.	Apr 27, 2004 8:35:58 PM	21	Apr 27, 2004 8:35:58 PM

Related Alerts

Severity	Target Name	Target Type	Category	Name	Message	Alert Triggered	Last Value	Time
×	localhost	Host	Load	CPU Utilization (%)	CPU Utilization is 100%	May 17, 2004 9:23:02 AM	100	May 17, 2004 9:23:02 AM
	localhost	Host	Filesystems	Filesystem Space Available (%)	Filesystem C:\ has only 8.79% available space	Apr 5, 2004 6:37:44 PM	6.92	May 17, 2004 7:18:37 AM
	localhost	Host	Load	Swap Utilization (%)	Swap Utilization is 84.64%	May 17, 2004 9:08:02 AM	83.39	May 17, 2004 9:23:02 AM

Job Activity

Jobs scheduled to start no more than 7 days ago

Scheduled Executions 0 Suspended Executions ✓ 0

Running Executions 0 Problem Executions ✓ 0

Critical Patch Advisories

Patch Advisories 0

Patch Advisory information may be stale. Oracle MetaLink credentials are not configured

Oracle MetaLink Credentials Not Configured

Figure 19.93: *The OEM alerts screen with link to Advisor Central*

This link between database and server exceptions gives a preview of the exceptional conditions and validates the recommendations from the Advisor Central area of OEM.

Automated Diagnostics in OEM

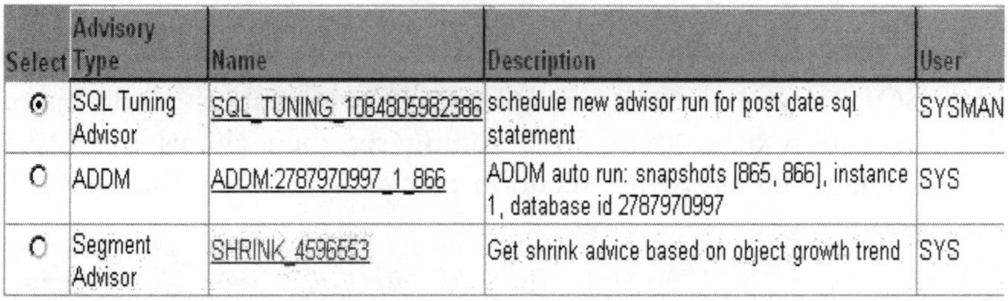

Select	Advisory Type	Name	Description	User
◉	SQL Tuning Advisor	SQL_TUNING_1084805982386	schedule new advisor run for post date sql statement	SYSMAN
○	ADDM	ADDM:2787970997_1_866	ADDM auto run: snapshots [865, 866], instance 1, database id 2787970997	SYS
○	Segment Advisor	SHRINK_4596553	Get shrink advice based on object growth trend	SYS

Figure 19.94: *The OEM Advisor Central Screen*

The Advisor Central screen which is shown in Figure 19.94 displays the three advisory areas of Enterprise Manager, ADDM, the SQL Tuning Advisor and the segment advisor. This OEM information is externalized via the *dbms_advisor* package and the *dba_advisor_tasks* view. The OEM Advisors are shown in Figure 19.95.

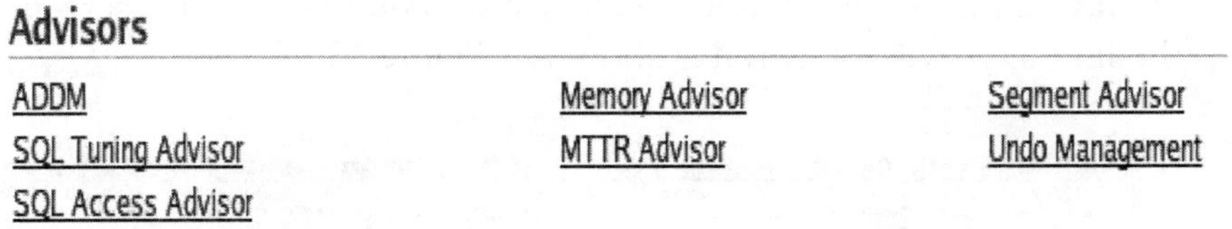

Advisors

ADDM	Memory Advisor	Segment Advisor
SQL Tuning Advisor	MTTR Advisor	Undo Management
SQL Access Advisor		

Figure 19.95: *The OEM advisors*

Each of these hyperlinks provides important advisory functions, but each one addresses very different areas of Oracle tuning:

- **ADDM:** The Automatic Database Diagnostic Monitor provides intelligent recommendations about Oracle changes that will improve performance ad throughput.

- **SQL Access advisor:** The SQL Access advisor makes GLOBAL SQL tuning recommendations based on the workload specified by the DBA. These global recommendations may include the creation of new indexes to remove unnecessary large-table full-table scans and the creation of materialized views to pre-aggregate summaries and prejoin highly normalized tables.

- **SQL Tuning Advisor:** The SQL Tuning advisor captures the top SQL over time and creates SQL Tuning Sets that encapsulate the SQL source, execution plans, host variables and historical execution data. The SQL tuning set then allows the DBA to intelligently alter the execution plan with the new Oracle10g SQL profiles.

A wait event is defined in the *dba_hist_waitclassmet_history* view and includes all sources of waits on database processing, including segment header waits, latch serialization, network and user I/O waits.

The SQL tuning advisor displays a list of tuning recommendations as shown in Figure 19.96.

Impact (%) ▽	Finding	Recommendations
94.65	SQL statements consuming significant database time were found.	5 SQL Tuning
77.31	Individual database segments responsible for significant physical I/O were found.	4 Segment Tuning
68.02	Individual database segments responsible for significant user I/O wait were found.	2 Segment Tuning
31.86	Hard parsing SQL statements that encountered parse errors was consuming significant database time.	1 Application Analysis
18.54	The buffer cache was undersized causing significant additional read I/O.	1 DB Configuration
11.87	The throughput of the I/O subsystem was significantly lower than expected.	1 Host Configuration
9.04	Time spent on the CPU by the instance was responsible for a substantial part of database time.	3 SQL Tuning

Figure 19.96: *Sample recommendations from OEM SQL Tuning Advisor*

- A single SQL statement is consuming a large amount of Oracle resources. (94%)

- A single segment, such as a table or index, is receiving a disproportional amount of I/O. (77%)

- This segment is experiencing wait conditions, such as possible segment header contention, etc. (68%)

- Hard parses caused by non-reentrant SQL with embedded literal values are causing stress on the library cache. (31%)

- The data buffer is too small, causing unnecessary physical disk I/0. (18%)

- The I/O subsystem throughput is slower than expected. This could be due to poor striping (RAID5), disk controller contention or multiple task enqueues on the disk device. (11%)

The SQL Tuning advisor and SQL Access advisor allow the generation of specific recommendations about the best ways to tune SQL execution.

The SQL Tuning Advisor architecture is illustrated in Figure 19.97. The last input set for the SQL Tuning Advisor is comprised of user input statements or SQL Tuning Set. This could include untested SQL statements or a set of SQL statements currently under development. For tuning a set of SQL statements, a SQL Tuning Set (STS) has to be constructed, stored, and fed to the SQL Tuning Advisor.

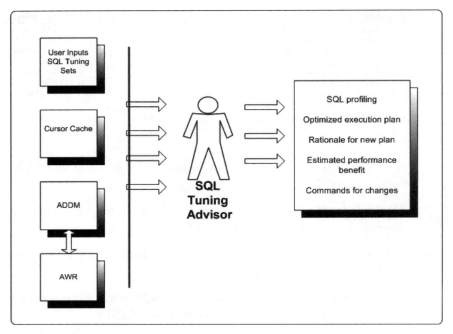

Figure 19.97: *SQL Tuning Advisor*

Most Oracle professionals will find the Enterprise Manager interface far easier to use than the *dbms_sqltune* package. This section will provide a closer look at these SQL Tuning functions. From the top level of the SQL Tuning advisor screen, hyperlinks to the following OEM areas are available:

- **Top SQL:** This OEM screen displays the most resource intensive SQL for any time period specified by the DBA. As the time period is changed, the top SQL is displayed along with the percentage of total elapsed time used by the statement, the CPU time consumed, the total wait time for the SQL and the average elapsed time per execution.

- **SQL Tuning Sets:** SQL tuning sets are encapsulations of SQL statements. They contain the source for the SQL statement, the host variables used during historical execution, and performance metrics. They allow a complete environment for testing the efficiency of a single SQL statement over time.

- **Snapshots:** SQL Snapshots are taken every hour and can be manipulated manually with the new dbms_workload_repository package.

- **Preserved Snapshot Sets:** A snapshot set, a.k.a. baseline, is a collection of multiple AWR snapshots. The preserved snapshot sets are then used to compare workload performance over specific periods.

The next section will drill down into the top SQL area, and show how it captures the most resource intensive SQL, allowing the DBA to explore the exact conditions leading to any Oracle performance bottleneck.

SQL Access Advisor

These recommendations are stored in the SQL Access Advisor repository, which is a part of the Oracle database dictionary. This repository has benefits like being managed by the server, support of historical data, etc.

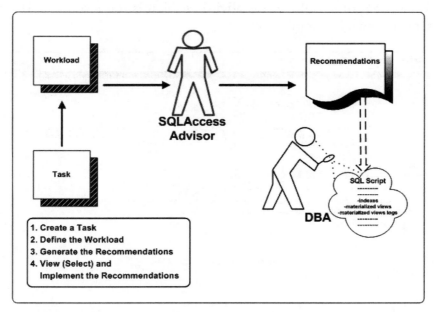

Figure 19.98: *The SQL Access Advisor Architecture*

The SQL Access advisor architecture, illustrated in Figure 19.98, allows the scheduling of system-wide SQL performance analysis and the development of global recommendations to improve performance. However, the utility of these recommendations can be limited:

- Missing indexes: Indexes, especially function-based indexes, can greatly reduce the amount of logical I/O required for an SQL statement to retrieve its result set.

- Materialized Views: If the target tables are not constantly changing, materialized views can be used to prejoin tables or presummarize aggregate information. Materialized views can result in huge SQL performance improvements.

The scope of the analysis can be limited, meaning that the SQL Access advisor will take a quick look at the SQL and not create SQL profiles, or the scope can be comprehensive, which means that detailed analysis will be conducted and SQL profiles may be created for the top SQL statements.

The output of a SQL Access advisor session is the recommendations screen shown in Figure 19.99.

Figure 19.99: *The SQL Access advisor recommendations screen*

This screen will offer specific recommendations for the creation of indexes and materialized views and include the definitions for these new database entities. As noted in earlier chapters, data dictionary scripts are often more powerful than any GUI tool.

Shortcomings of OEM

The OEM product is designed to be a comprehensive web-based interface for the DBA. In an attempt to do everything, it loses the direct focus and exception identification. For example, the top level OEM screen is shown in Figure 19.100.

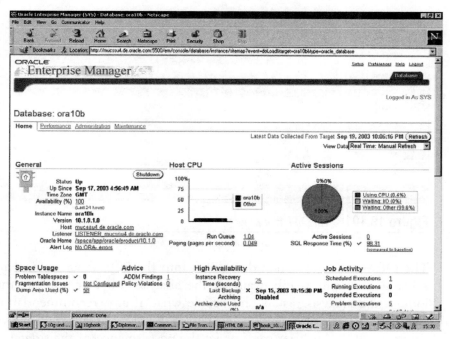

Figure 19.100: *Example OEM Top Level Screen*

This OEM screen is not focused directly on performance management. Rather, it is focused on the entire database, or databases, being monitored and their overall status. The user of OEM is presented with a sometimes bewildering array of options.

Another issue with OEM is that while the screen shows the ADDM findings and allows the user to view them as shown in Figure 19.101, the user must buy the additional license, or they could be found in default of their Oracle license agreement!

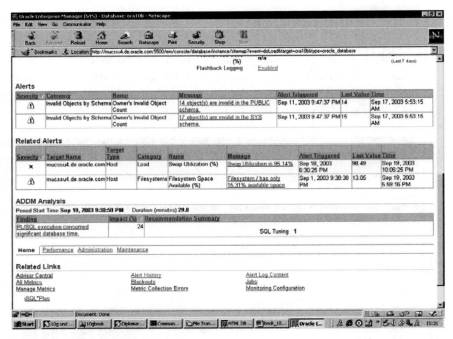

Figure 19.101: *ADDM Findings.*

The OEM user must then drill down into the SQL Analysis package, schedule an analysis job, wait for the analysis job to complete, then look at the analysis results and decide what, if any, recommendations to pursue. Oracle also cautions users that doing too detailed an analysis using the SQL Analyzer can impact the performance of their database and that it should be scheduled for off hours!

The ADDM addition to the OEM interface brings much needed depth to the Oracle product line and provides valuable input for the inexperienced DBA. With its distillation of Oracle experts' and consultants' tuning experience, it can provide the expertise lacking in many shops. However, this very strength can cause it to become a crutch, stifling the growth of key personnel and making them dependant on OEM. In addition, a more experienced DBA may recognize recommendations that would not be beneficial for their specific database, while an inexperienced DBA might take them as gospel and make decisions that could harm their database in the long run.

As shown in Figure 19.102, the SQL Detail screen is not forthcoming with wait event details specific to the problem SQL.

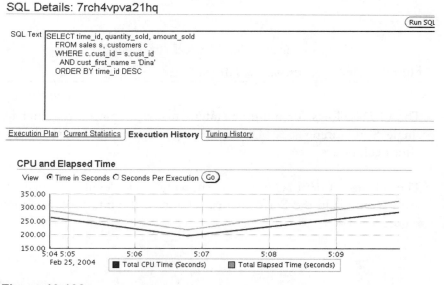

Figure 19.102: *SQL Detail Screen*

The SQL Analysis tool provides the user with a set of recommendations, weighted by expected percentage of improvement as shown in Figure 19.103.

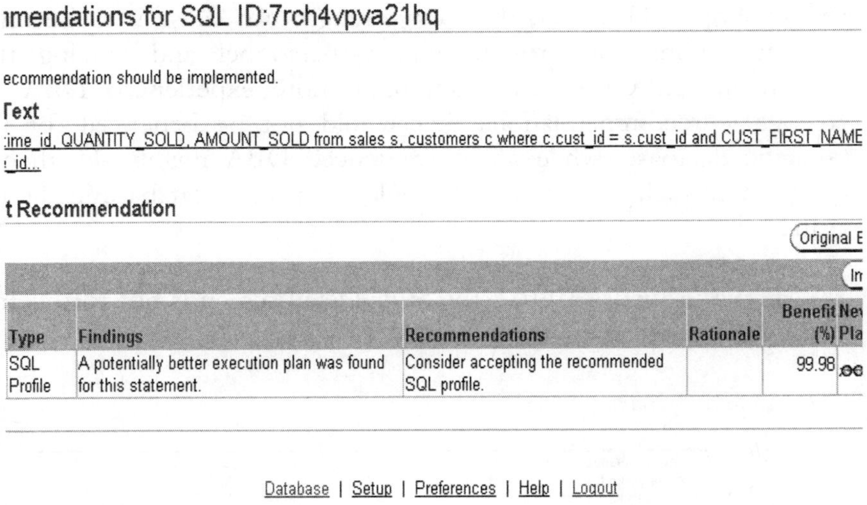

ecommendation should be implemented.

Text

:ime_id, QUANTITY_SOLD, AMOUNT_SOLD from sales s, customers c where c.cust_id = s.cust_id and CUST_FIRST_NAME
:_id...

t Recommendation

Original E

In

Type	Findings	Recommendations	Rationale	Benefit Nev (%) Pla
SQL Profile	A potentially better execution plan was found for this statement.	Consider accepting the recommended SQL profile.		99.98 ,ee

Figure 19.103: *Recommendations Screen*

The OEM allows for multiple statements to be placed together into a single SQL tuning job. Doing so requires the job to usually be run after peak hours.

The closest OEM comes to showing the detail of wait event information is in the Performance section of the interface, as shown in Figure 19.104.

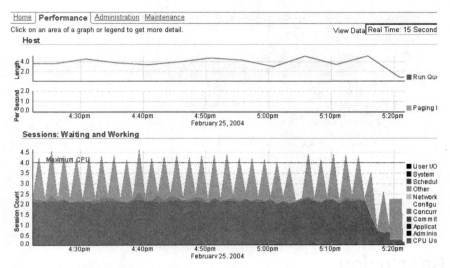

Figure 19.104: *OEM Performance Screen*

This screen only provides the overview of total system waits and requires a time specific drill down to get to more detailed data.

One nice feature of the OEM interface is before and after looks at problem statement explain plans based on the implementation of tuning suggestions. A New Explain Plan is show in Figure 19.105.

Any experienced DBA will likely explain that sometimes explain plans and cost figures do not actually represent the best performing SQL statements in the real work. For example, the explain plan in Figure 19.105, based on taking Oracle advice, shifts from a hash join, to a nest loop, which may or may not provide better performance. The reality is that OEM does not always make the best recommendations about improving SQL performance. This is why the skilled DBA will always be in high demand.

New Explain Plan

Expand All | Collapse All

Operation	Line ID	Order	Rows	KB	Cost	Time (seconds)	CPU Cost	IO Cost	Object
▼ SELECT STATEMENT	0	6	2	0.064	5	1	44468	5	
▼ NESTED LOOPS	1	5	2	0.064	5	1	44468	5	
▼ TABLE ACCESS BY GLOBAL INDEX ROWID	2	2	918843	18,843.461	4	1	28955	4	SH.SALES
INDEX FULL SCAN DESCENDING	3	1	1		3	1	21564	3	SH.SALES_TIME_IDX
▼ TABLE ACCESS BY INDEX ROWID	4	4	1	0.012	1	1	15512	1	SH.CUSTOMERS
INDEX UNIQUE SCAN	5	3	1		0	1	8171	0	SH.CUSTOMERS_PK

Figure 19.105: *New Explain Plan Feature of OEM*

Conclusion

Oracle has made a major investment in the development of OEM with the goal of creating a one-stop interface for the myriad of Oracle administration duties. The tuning tools are littered throughout the dozens of complex and confusing screens.

On the other hand, third-party tools such as WISE and DBFlash provide a task-specific tool that provides the experienced DBA with a scalpel for use in surgically finding and correcting poorly performing SQL.

- Intelligent Approach: By utilizing the Oracle wait interface and specific Oracle statistics and tying this information back to their source SQL statements, tools such as DBFlash allow for correction of the specific problems in an Oracle database SQL portfolio, eliminating the tuning of apparently bad SQL which, in fact, is not a problem at all. In contrast, Oracle's SQL Access advisor makes global recommendations only on indexes and materialized views while the SQL Tuning advisor makes specific recommendations; however, these recommendations may be made with limited intelligence. The SQL Access Advisor is a limited tool, and it can only recommend simple solutions such as new indexes and materialized views, ignoring the dozens of other SQL tuning options.

- Less overhead: While AWR, through use of the MMON background process, is more efficient at gathering statistics than the use of the Oracle job interface was for STATSPACK, it still has more performance impact than some third-party tools.

- Less expensive: Oracle ASH is a component of Oracle Enterprise Manager Diagnostic Pack and the Oracle Tuning Pack. These are extra cost features, and they must be licensed separately. The costs of these tuning packs can be prohibitively expensive for some shops.

- Tightly Focused: The OEM screens are not focused on performance management, but rather the entire database, or databases being monitored and their overall status. The OEM user can presented with a bewildering array of options.

- Fast problem identification: In comparison to OEM, problem SQL can be quickly found by tools like WISE and DBFlash within a few mouse clicks. The OEM interface and SQL Analyzer the DBA may face an ordeal of scheduled analysis and correction jobs. The OEM interface practices an extreme amount of hand holding, while reassuring to the inexperienced DBA, which can be annoying to the more experienced DBA. The DBFlash interface assumes an experienced DBA is at the helm.

- Fast tuning Solutions: Savvy DBAs know that long-term workload tests do not help tune most SQL. Oracle claims that many Oracle SQL statements will change execution plans as the workload changes. While this is true for a small number of shops, the vast majority of Oracle shops will find that there is one, and only one, optimal execution plan for any SQL statement.

This chapter has focused on the Oracle10g Enterprise Manager tuning components and on how OEM displays AWR and ASH data in a visual form.

While the OEM performance screens are built-in to the OEM console, many Oracle professionals are not aware that using these screens may require additional Oracle licenses. Third-party tools that bypass the AWR and ASH views can sometimes provide a more cost-effective solution.

Finally, it is noteworthy that many senior DBA's eschew GUI tools and use customized scripts to expose Oracle performance issues.

The next chapter will explore techniques for tuning Oracle Cluster Systems and investigate Real Application Clusters (RAC) and tuning for Oracle10g grid systems.

Oracle RAC and Grid Tuning

I know Grid, RAC, Streams and three other Oracle words.

Introduction to Tuning with RAC

The use of Oracle Real Application Clusters (RAC) is a complex and robust Oracle solution that provides infinite scalability and instant failover. Originally, this approach was named Oracle Parallel Server (OPS).

Oracle RAC is the flagship Oracle product, designed to provide high availability and scalability for large, mission-critical applications. Oracle RAC technology is the foundation of Oracle Grid computing. Grid computing contributes the "g" in Oracle 10g. When combined with the Transparent Application Failover (TAF) option, Oracle RAC can reconnect failed connections to a failover node without the client even being aware of a server failure.

Highly available and scalable server- based computer systems and applications are an essential part of today's internet-based business environment. This availability and scalability are achieved by clustering technology and fault tolerant systems that allow seamless addition of computing resources to Oracle. This chapter will provide a closer look at high performance computing trends for Oracle RAC database systems.

Oracle RAC and Oracle10g Grid are unique and complex technologies and have very different tuning procedures. This chapter will cover the following RAC tuning topics:

- RAC and Grid in a nutshell

- Inside Oracle 10g Grid computing

- Configuring RAC and Grid for top performance

- RAC node load balancing for optimal performance

- RAC parallelism for high performance

- Monitoring RAC performance

A quick look into the Oracle10g RAC and Grid architecture is presented in the next section.

Oracle RAC in a Nutshell

In a nutshell, Oracle RAC is a complex database architecture where multiple RAM memory regions and processes and Oracle instances share a common set of database files. Figure 20.1 is an illustration of the complex RAC structure in Oracle.

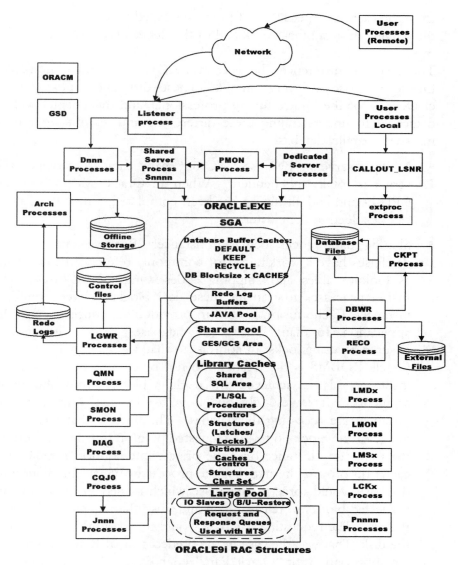

Figure 20.1: *The complex Oracle RAC architecture*

Because there are many Oracle instances sharing the same data files, a large component of Oracle RAC is managing concurrency between the database instances. These concurrencies are called nodes in RAC terminology. In order for the multiple Oracle instances to share data from the caches, a special set of processes called cache fusion" manage the pinging of data blocks back and forth between the instances.

The essential differences between a RAC cluster and a non-RAC Oracle database are very simple. These differences pose unique challenges for the Oracle tuning professional, and this chapter will be dedicated to understanding these differences and learning to tune a massively parallel database:

- Multiple servers: Because RAC has many database servers, each server is totally independent. When an Oracle system becomes CPU-bound and all tuning has been completed, a new RAC node can be added to the cluster.

- Sharing data blocks between instances: Because many Oracle databases have a working set of commonly referenced rows, such as lookup tables and shipping codes, Oracle RAC uses cache fusion processes to transfer these data blocks between multiple instances. Cache fusion is used to provide read consistency to the application. In many non-Oracle databases, read consistency is ensured by using locks. In contrast to that, the main mantra of the Oracle RDBMS is that readers do not block writers. On a single instance, this is achieved by reading blocks from the undo segments. It is less obvious how to do that when multiple instances are accessing the database. The process that creates the image of the block up to the requested point in time and ships it to the requesting instance over the private interconnect is called the cache fusion. An alternative is the process by which the requesting database would force the database which owned the locks on the requested blocks to release them and flush the requested blocks to the disk. The requesting database would then read the blocks from the disk. That was the case in the predecessor of RAC, called OPS (an abbreviation for "Oracle Parallel Server").

- Dynamic resource allocation: This ability to have many instances allows the RAC DBA to add additional servers, with a new instance on each server, whenever Oracle requires more processing power. Oracle10g Grid technology is all about the intelligent allocation of RAC server resources via the Oracle10g Enterprise Manager Grid control screens.

These differences appear simple on the surface, but there are some extremely complex techniques that are used to ensure the top performance of a RAC or Grid database.

It is critical to understand that Oracle RAC is not for every Oracle database, and it is almost always used in super large, mission-critical systems and web database that must support thousands of transactions per second. Oracle RAC is primarily used in these types of shops:

- Low tolerance for downtime: By having many servers, a failure on one node will not cause an outage because Oracle Transparent Application Failover (TAF) will resume all transactions on surviving nodes. This continuous availability feature is used by shops where downtime cost is greater than $100k per minute, and shops with more tolerance for downtime may use other Oracle failover technologies such as Oracle Streams and Oracle Dataguard.

- High scalability: For smaller databases, scale up scalability is best using a large monolithic server with 32 or 64 processors and hundreds of gigabytes of RAM. However, super large Oracle shops need more horsepower, and RAC provides them with the ability to scale out, adding additional servers to RAC cluster whenever they need more hardware resources.

For many systems, Oracle RAC and Grid allows the DBA true transparent scalability. In order to increase the number of servers in OPS, data and application changes were required and the scaling was far from transparent.

The following advantages come with Oracle10g RAC and Grid:

- No physical data partitioning is required

- Vendor applications (SAP, Peoplesoft) will scale without modification.

This automatic, transparent scaling is due almost entirely to the cache fusion layer and the unique parallel architecture of RAC and Grid.

Table 20.1 summarizes the main features of the single instance stand alone database and the multi-instance RAC database.

SINGLE INSTANCE DATABASE	MULTI-INSTANCE RAC DATABASE
Only one instance to access and process database requests	Multiple instances accessing same database
One set of datafiles, redo files, undo and control files etc.	One set of datafiles and control files, but separate redo log files and undo for each instance
Locking and Concurrency Maintenance is confined to one instance	Locking and Concurrency Maintenance is extended to multiple instances
Dedicated Storage Structures for the instance	Multiple instances access the same shared storage structures
Weak on High Availability and Scalability	Provides High Availability and Scalability Solution

Table 20.1: *Stand-alone versus Multi-Instance RAC Database*

By providing the multiple instances such as a host and its associated resources to access the same database, a RAC System creates multiple database computing centers and improves scalability, but it is done at the cost of additional complexity.

Oracle Scalability and Grid Technology

Most savvy Oracle shops practice the scale up approach first, and then scale out after they reach the maximum capacity of their single server. Due to the advances in server technology, the concept of using a large server has become very popular. The following sections outline an approach used by many forward-thinking Oracle shops.

First Scale Up with SMP Servers

This scale up yields the following benefits:

- On demand resource allocation by sharing CPU and RAM between many resources.

- Less maintenance and human resources required to manage fewer servers.

- Optimal utilization of RAM and CPU resources.

- High availability through fault tolerant components.

Next Scale Out with Multiple SMP Servers

This subsequent scale out will yield the following additional benefits:

- High availability through clustering servers with RAC.

- Optimal utilization of servers.

- Quicker implementation and easier maintenance with fewer servers.

The scale out approach using RAC and Grid are designed for super large Oracle databases that support many thousands of concurrent users. Unless a system has a need to support more than 10,000 transactions per second, it is likely that the scale up approach will be more than adequate.

Amazon is an excellent example of a scale out Oracle shop. Amazon announced plans to move their 14 trillion byte Oracle database to Oracle RAC on Linux. Amazon uses load-balanced Linux Web servers to horizontally scale its Web presence.

Large-scale RAC database use large servers, each with 32 or 64 processors and over a hundred gigabytes of RAM. As the capacities of the large servers are exceeded, a new server is genned into the RAC cluster. Figure 20.2 is an illustration of large scale RAC databases with these large servers.

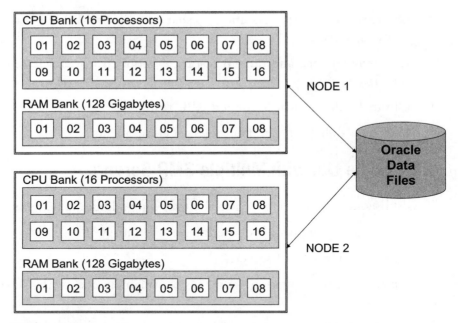

Figure 20.2: *Large scale RAC databases with super large servers*

Large RAC is different!

Large RAC clusters use large SMP servers and do not have the need for dynamic Grid facilities that are used in smaller clustered system with server blades.

The next section will introduce how RAC is used within Oracle10g Grid for high performance database computing.

Oracle10g Grid in a Nutshell

At a high level, Oracle Grid computing is the on-demand sharing of computing resources within a tightly coupled network. For those old enough to remember data processing in the 1980s, the IBM mainframes were a primitive example of Grid computing. These mainframes had several CPUs, each independent, and the MVS/ESA operating system allocated work to the processors based on least recently used algorithms and customized task dispatching priorities. Of course, RAM and disk resources were available to all programs executing on the huge server.

However, Grid computing is fundamentally different from mainframes. In the 21st century, Grid computing performs a virtualization of distributed computing resources and allows for the automated allocation of resources as system demand changes. Each server is independent, yet ready to participate in a variety of processing requests from many types of applications.

Unlike large RAC deployments, Oracle Grid systems often employ small server blades, which are tiny servers with two to four processors and four to eight gigabytes of RAM as illustrated in Figure 20.3.

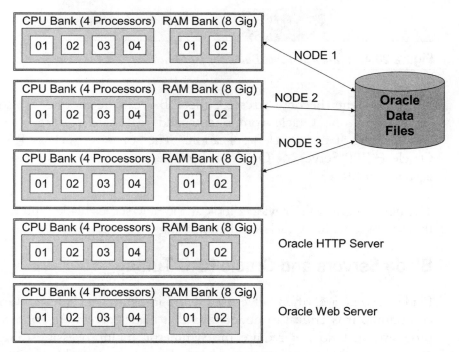

Figure 20.3: *Small scale Grid databases with server blades*

Oracle10g Grid computing also employs special software infrastructure using Oracle Streams to monitor resource usage and allocate requests to the most appropriate resource. This enables a distributed enterprise to function as if it were a single supercomputer as shown in Figure 20.4.

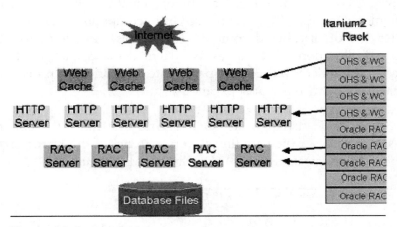

Figure 20.4: *Hardware Load Balancing for Oracle Application Server*

As components become stressed, the DBA can de-allocate a blade server from one Oracle components and reallocate that server to another part of the Oracle application. The software, such as RAC, Oracle HTTP Server, or Oracle web cache, must be pre-installed on each server blade.

The next section will provide a look at the new server blades and how they are used within Oracle Grid computing.

Blade Servers and Oracle RAC Tuning

Blade servers are often advertised hand-in-hand with Oracle Grid computing. It is critical to understand that blade servers are good for programs that do not require the symmetric multiprocessing (SMP) capabilities of large mid-range servers. For example, a blade server would not be appropriate for a RAC node that performs parallel query operations. That is because blade servers are normally small, one to four CPU servers, and Oracle parallel query works best when there are 32 or 64 CPUs for fast full-table scans on very large tables.

On the other hand, blade servers and RAC may be appropriate for small scale OLTP applications because the nature of individual queries does not require multiple CPU resources.

Blade Servers and Oracle App Servers

Blade servers are also an option for Oracle Application Server 10g web cache servers or Oracle HTTP servers, because a new server can easily be added into the Oracle Application Server 10g server farm. In Oracle Application Server 10g, a rack of blade servers can be used and Oracle Web Server and Oracle HTTP server (OHS) software can be pre-installed. At runtime, the Oracle Application Server 10g administrator can add these server blades to their Oracle Application Server 10g farm, using each blade as either a Web cache server or an HTTP server, depending upon the stress on the system.

At this point, it should be very clear that there are a myriad of options for Oracle configurations. Given the complexity of cluster and Grid management, the best migration path may be to first scale up onto a large 64-bit server and add resources to the SMP on the server. Then, for additional high availability and increased flexibility, the scale out option can be explored.

Oracle RAC and Grid are complex technologies for complex applications. Even standard performance monitoring is challenging because multiple servers and instances must be monitored within the common database.

Now that the concepts of RAC and Grid have been presented, the following section will present information on Oracle cache fusion and how it manages inter-instance data block transfer.

The Revolution of Cache Fusion

Until later versions of Oracle8i, an Oracle Parallel Server (OPS) database had to use a laborious process of copying blocks into and out of memory and to and from disks in order to share information in a single block between the multiple instances.

This complex and slow disk-to-disk OPS data sharing mechanism resulted in serious performance issues if the database did not practice some kind of application partitioning, data partitioning and localized use.

Oracle 9i Real Application Clusters (RAC) relieved the limitations of the OPS disk-based block transfer method, but there are still performance issues related to the cache fusion layer.

Cache fusion has several important jobs. The foremost job is being able to maintain cache coherency and read consistency between database instances.

This cache coherency is maintained through the Global Services Directory and the various Global Enqueue processes. These processes monitor each data cache and transfer data block, RAM to RAM across the high-speed cluster interconnect. The architecture of Cache Fusion is illustrated in Figure 20.5.

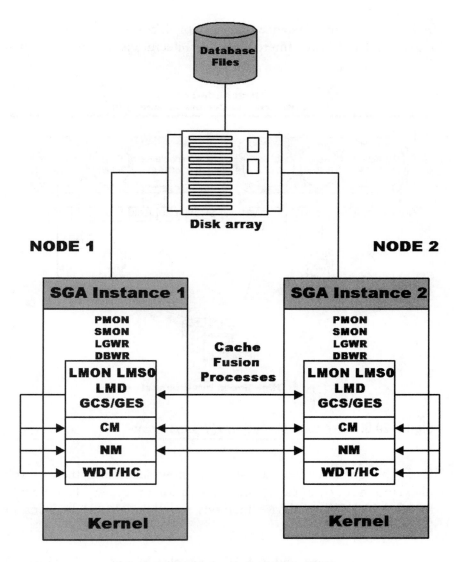

Cache Fusion Architecture

Figure 20.5: *The cache fusion background processes*

The cluster interconnect is the heart of cache fusion. Oracle has global directory services to manage data blocks inside the multiple instances and the use of intra-instance transportable locks to speed up data block transfers. The Cluster Interconnect architecture is illustrated in Figure 20.6.

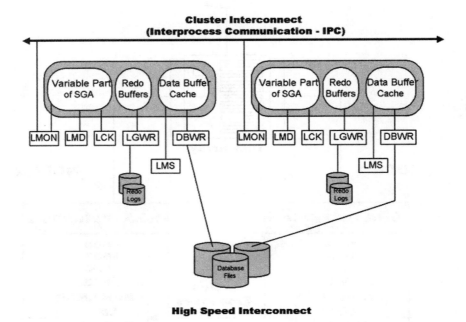

Figure 20.6: *The Cluster Interconnect IPC architecture*

Even though data block transfers are now super fast, there is still a high amount of overhead in the cache fusion processes. It is the job of the Oracle DBA to devise methods to minimize this inter-instance block transfer.

The disk subsystems within RAC must also be managed. Most RAC databases use Storage Area Networks (SAN) and use tools like the IBM FastT storage manager for the RAC nodes as shown in Figure 20.7:

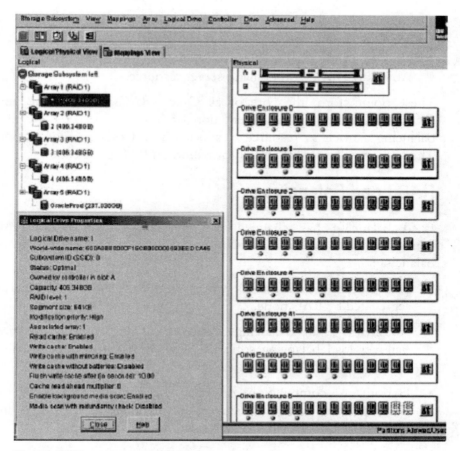

Figure 20.7: *The FastT Storage Manager*

Now that the basics of Oracle cache fusion have been presented, the following sections include information on how to tune Oracle RAC by load balancing traffic between the nodes.

Overview of RAC and Grid Tuning

There are only a few differences between an ordinary Oracle database and a Grid/RAC database. RAC and Grid yield some of the following superb abilities:

- Ability to load balance the transaction load between instances

---

- Ability to adjust inter-instance cache communication

- Ability to leverage parallel nodes

- Ability to provide on-demand server resources

These points form the core of all Oracle RAC tuning. The next section will start with a presentation of information on RAC load balancing as well as resource re-allocation and cache fusion tuning. The section will wrap up with information on RAC parallel tuning

RAC Load Balancing

Load balancing has changed radically between OPS and RAC databases, but there are still two accepted approaches to RAC load balancing:

- Data Localization: Business processes and the associated data are segregated by RAC node.

- Automatic Load Balancing: Using the Transparent Application Failover load balancing software, new connections are routed to the least loaded RAC node.

- Hybrid: A combination of data localization and automatic techniques are used, dedicating a set of nodes to the processing area, and load-balancing connections within that group.

In OPS days, the expensive disk-to-disk data transfers meant that the DBA would carefully partition the application such that different types of applications would connect to different nodes. For example, in a database with order entry, inventory maintenance and customer management functions, clients from each of these areas would be directed to a separate node. The data localization load balancing method is illustrated in Figure 20.8.

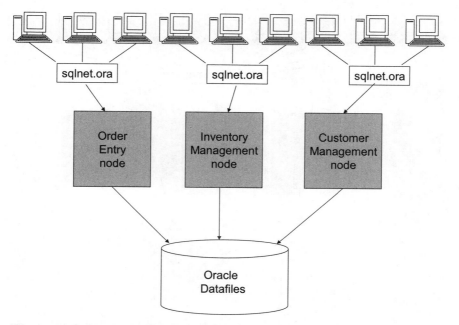

Figure 20.8: *The data localization load balancing method*

This application-level partitioning ensured that all related data blocks were cached on the appropriate instance, and that the expensive disk-to-disk pinging of shared blocks between instances was minimized.

With the introduction of Oracle9i RAC and TAF, another load balancing scheme called automatic load balancing became available. With this scheme, a centralized Oracle RAC listener with a virtual IP address can be created, and the RAC listener will automatically direct transactions to the least loaded Oracle instance. This scheme is illustrated in Figure 20.9.

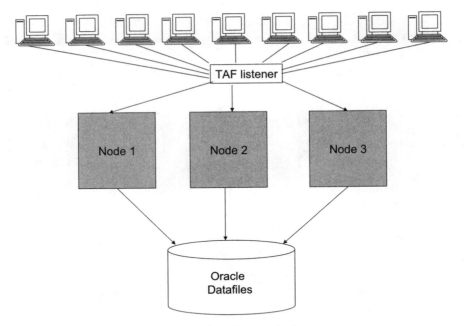

Figure 20.9: *The automatic load balancing method*

The automatic load balancing approach has several advantages for scalability and resources consumption because the Oracle RAC software manages instance load. On the other hand, databases with a large shared working set of frequently referenced data will find high data block transfers within the cache fusion processes. Oracle Grid databases almost exclusively use the automatic load balancing techniques.

There is a third approach that uses a hybrid of the automatic and localization approaches. This load balancing approach is used by large RAC shops where they want to load balance between a group of related nodes, thereby getting the automatic load balancing as well as the reduced cache fusion stress resulting from data localization. This hybrid scheme is illustrated in Figure 20.10.

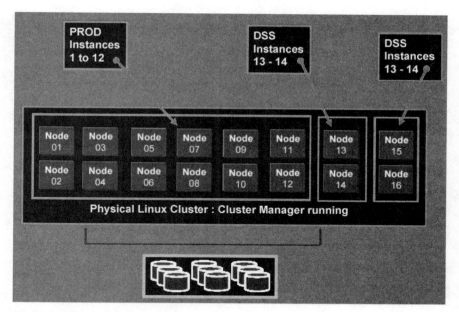

Figure 20.10: *The hybrid load-balancing approach*

The DBA's choice of load balancing techniques depends on their database application. If the application does not share many common data blocks, automatic load balancing is the best choice. However, if the application has transactions that all share the same table rows, the client-based load balancing might be the better choice.

Managing Inter-instance Data Block Transfers

The same data block may reside inside many SGA regions, so it is easy to run queries against the v$bh views on each node to find the data blocks that have been pinged via cache fusion.

The size of this working set of frequently referenced data blocks is important, and minimizing the amount of inter-instance block transfers can greatly improve RAC performance, especially if the working set is frequently updated.

The following script can be run on each instance to identify the data blocks that currently reside within each SGA. This is from Mike Ault's book, *Oracle 10g Grid & Real Application Clusters - Oracle10g Grid Computing with RAC*. Oracle RAC scripts are also available from www.oracle-script.com.

```
break on report

compute sum of distinct_blocks on report

compute sum of blocks on report
set lines 132 pages 57
@title132 'Block Usage Inside SGA Block Buffers'

spool rep_out\&db\block_usage
SELECT a.INST_ID,
decode(b.tablespace_name,null,'UNUSED',b.tablespace_name) ts_name,
       a.file# file_number,
       COUNT(a.block#) Blocks,
       COUNT (DISTINCT a.file# || a.block#) Distinct_blocks
   FROM GV$BH a, dba_data_files b
   WHERE a.file#=b.file_id(+)
   GROUP BY a.INST_ID,
a.file#,decode(b.tablespace_name,null,'UNUSED',b.tablespace_name)
   order by a.inst_id
/
spool off
ttitle off
```

Some inter-instance pinging is unavoidable due to the shared nature of almost all Oracle applications. However, there are many tricks that can be used by the Oracle DBA to minimize the work of the cache fusion layer. The following list shares some of these tricks:

- Block spreading: Small lookup tables can be spread across many data blocks to reduce the likelihood that another instance will need them.

- Blocksize adjustment: Many RAC databases that share large amounts of data blocks will perform better with a 2k blocksize because less data will be transferred between nodes.

- Read only tablespaces: The intelligent use of read only tablespaces allows the DBA to minimize inter-instance communication, because Oracle does not have to maintain read consistency mechanisms.

The following sections provide a more in-depth look at each of these methods.

Block Spreading

Oracle RAC databases that have small, frequently referenced lookup tables can spread the rows across more data blocks. This can be illustrated with a simple example. Suppose that there is a State code lookup table with entries for all 50 states. Even on a 2k blocksize, all 50 rows fit into a single data block.

As competing instances access the lookup table, the same data block must be transferred between all of the nodes, and this can cause a huge overhead for the cache fusion background processes and slow down the entire database.

The solution is to adjust the *pctfree* threshold for the lookup table so that only a single row resides on each data block. Now, instead of consuming one data block, the lookup table resides on 50 separate blocks, and inter-instance communication is greatly minimized. This solution is illustrated in Figure 20.11.

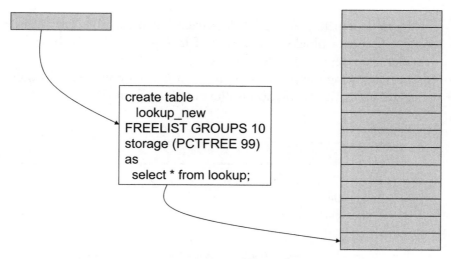

Figure 20.11: *The block spreading approach to relieve RAC contention*

Of course, space is being wasted on each data block, but spreading out the table blocks makes a huge difference in overall performance. The *freelist groups* parameter allows multiple segment header blocks. Multiple *freelist groups* speed up *insert* operations because each node can acquire a separate header block, each with its own *freelist.*

The *freelist groups* object parameter should be set to the number of Oracle RAC nodes that update any table and index simultaneously. For partitioned objects and cases of segment header contention, *freelist groups* may be set for non-RAC systems. This will relieve the database from *buffer busy waits* caused by segment header contention.

Blocksize Adjustment

As a general rule, the RAC DBA should define all inter-instance shared blocks such that only the minimum amount of space is transferred across the cache fusion layer.

For example, if a shared shipping table with 80-byte rows will be frequently referenced by all nodes, a transaction will only want a single row in the table.

If the table is placed in a 32k blocksize, the entire table might fit onto only a few data blocks. However, if it is placed in a 2k blocksize, a smaller number of adjacent rows are transferred by cache fusion, thereby reducing the probability that another node will have to wait for the data block. This solution is illustrated in Figure 20.11.

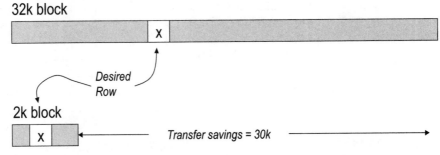

Figure 20.12: *Blocksize adjustment to reduce cache fusion contention*

Oracle RAC supports multiple blocksizes, and the savvy Oracle DBA will adjust the data buffers according to the demands of their application.

Read only Tablespaces

The Oracle RAC DBA can also minimize the cache fusion overhead by using Oracle read only tablespaces. If Oracle is aware that a data block is read only, a great amount of overhead is saved because Oracles does not have to monitor for competing DML and read consistency.

In larger RAC databases, the DBA may take the trouble to locate and segregate those blocks that are always read only. This can be achieved with partitioned tables with only the most current partition being updatable.

Parallel Processing and RAC Performance

Parallel execution involves dividing a task into several smaller tasks and working on each of those smaller tasks in parallel. Oracle Parallel Query (OPQ), where multiple CPUs on a single instance can speed up large-table full-table scans, is already a familiar concept; however, RAC opens up a new area of inter-instance parallelism.

There are two ways to speed up tasks:

- Increasing the number of CPUs and use Oracle Parallel Query (OPQ), parallel DML, etc.

- Manually break down a complex task into multiple sub tasks and assign each component to multiple processors to execute them concurrently.

In the first scenario of OPQ, a single user task, such as a SQL query, can be parallelized to achieve higher speed and throughput by using multiple processors. Generally, Oracle's Intra-query parallel execution improves performance for:

- Queries with large object full-scans

- Creation of large indexes

- Bulk *insert*s, *update*s, and *delete*s

- Data Aggregations such as computing sums and averages

- DBA maintenance such as table and index reorganizations

Parallel processing involves the use of multiple processors to reduce the time needed to complete a given task. Instead of one processor executing an entire task, several processors work on separate tasks that are subordinate to the main task.

There are two types of parallelism that database users can utilize. They are: inter-query parallelism and intra-query parallelism. The differences between these two types of parallelism are outlined below:

- Inter-Query Parallelism: This can be done when individual transactions are independent and no transaction requires the output of other transactions to complete. Many CPUs can be kept busy by assigning each task or each query to a separate CPU. This is accomplished automatically by the server when the application submits the tasks and waits for each subsection to report back its results.

- Intra-Query Parallelism: - To speed up execution of a large, complex query, it must first be decomposed into smaller problems. These smaller problems must be executed concurrently, in parallel, by assigning each subproblem concurrently to its CPUs. This intra-query parallelism is implemented with the Oracle parallel features such as Oracle parallel query.

Inter-query parallelism is an application design issue and is rare in Oracle RAC and Grid databases because most problems cannot be serialized into independent subproblems.

Conclusion

This chapter focused on detailed information on the Oracle RAC and Grid architectures and showing ways to improve the performance of these massively parallel database systems.

The information showed that Oracle Grid provides infinite scalability via on-demand generation of new servers into the RAC cluster, but limitations from the cache fusion layer were examined as were the requirement to transfer data blocks between instances. The main points of this chapter include:

- RAC is not for every system: Most small shops do not need RAC for scalability; although, they may use RAC for continuous availability. RAC for scalability is only for large Oracle systems with more demands than can be met by a single server.

- Oracle Grid uses smaller servers: Unlike traditional RAC implementations with large servers, Oracle Grid computing uses small server blades.

- Cache fusion is the key: The Oracle RAC tuning expert is always concerned with minimizing the work of the cache fusion processes. The most common techniques involve block spreading, application partitioning, using small blocksizes and read only tablespaces.

- Load balancing is important: The choice of data localization or automatic load balancing is an important RAC design consideration.

This completes the information on Oracle RAC and Grid tuning. What follows is a summation of the Automated Work Repository as it was presented in this book.

Book Conclusion

As noted at the outset of this text, Oracle database tuning is an extremely complex subject. The purpose of this book was to provide an outline of the foundations of Oracle proactive tuning so that you will understand how to detect and correct sub-optimal components at the hardware level, Oracle instance, object and SQL levels.

The main thrust of our book has been on the proactive tuning approach and leveraging upon the historical performance data within the Oracle 10g Automatic Workload Repository to detect and repair repeating patterns of database stress. The Oracle 10g historical performance metrics form the foundation for a true predictive model where we can analyze historical stress on all Oracle components, especially the SGA regions (shared pool, data buffer caches), disk access and network utilization.

By applying the proactive techniques described in this book and executing the pre-written scripts in the code depot you should be able to understand the unique characteristics of your database and refine the signatures for all of your important metrics. This knowledge of the shifting bottlenecks within your database will allow you to locate and address the root cause of even the most difficult performance issue. Most important of all, this text lays the foundation for holistic performance tuning whereby you can identify repeating changes in resources and schedule corrective actions before they impact the overall response time.

Remember, those who do not remember the past are condemned to repeat it! Any book is this scope will have opportunities for improvement and we welcome your feedback. All errata and enhancements and published on the Rampant TechPress book detail page for this book, and we continuously strive to address new tuning techniques and methods. If you have errata, comments or suggestion, please send an e-mail to info@rampant.cc.

Index

X

About Don Burleson

Don Burleson is one of the world's top Oracle Database experts with more than 20 years of full-time DBA experience. He specializes in creating database architectures for very large online databases and he has worked with some of the world's most powerful and complex systems.

A former Adjunct Professor, Don Burleson has written 32 books, published more than 100 articles in National Magazines, and serves as Editor-in-Chief of Oracle Internals and Senior Consulting Editor for DBAZine and Series Editor for Rampant TechPress. Don is a popular lecturer and teacher and is a frequent speaker at OracleWorld and other international database conferences.

As a leading corporate database consultant, Don has worked with numerous Fortune 500 corporations creating robust database architectures for mission-critical systems. Don is also a noted expert on eCommerce systems, and has been instrumental in the development of numerous Web-based systems that support thousands of concurrent users.

In addition to his services as a consultant, Don also is active in charitable programs to aid visually impaired individuals. Don pioneered a technique for delivering tiny pigmy horses as guide animals for the blind and manages a non-profit corporation called the Guide Horse Foundation dedicated to providing Guide horses to blind people free-of-charge. The Web Site for The Guide Horse Foundation is www.guidehorse.org.

About Alexey B. Danchenkov

Alexey B. Danchenkov holds a Master's Degree in Computer Science from St. Petersburg State University of Aerospace Instrumentation. He started work as an Oracle Database Administrator at Leaves, Inc. He also worked for several years as a Principal Oracle DBA at a large telecommunications company, where he managed very large databases and billing systems. Alexey is the creator of the Workload Interface Statistics Engine (WISE), a popular Oracle tuning tool.

Alexey lives in St. Petersburg, Russia where he enjoys sailing in the Baltic Sea with his wife Julia, and his two sons Michael and Daniel.

About Mike Reed

When he first started drawing, Mike Reed drew just to amuse himself. It wasn't long, though, before he knew he wanted to be an artist. Today he does illustrations for children's books, magazines, catalogs, and ads.

He also teaches illustration at the College of Visual Art in St. Paul, Minnesota. Mike Reed says, "Making pictures is like acting — you can paint yourself into the action." He often paints on the computer, but he also draws in pen and ink and paints in acrylics. He feels that learning to draw well is the key to being a successful artist.

Mike is regarded as one of the nation's premier illustrators and is the creator of the popular "Flame Warriors" illustrations at www.flamewarriors.com, a website devoted to Internet insults. "To enter his Flame Warriors site is sort of like entering a hellish Sesame Street populated by Oscar the Grouch and 83 of his relatives." – Los Angeles Times.
(http://redwing.hutman.net/%7Emreed/warriorshtm/lat.htm)

Mike Reed has always enjoyed reading. As a young child, he liked the Dr. Seuss books. Later, he started reading biographies and war stories. One reason why he feels lucky to be an illustrator is because he can listen to books on tape while he works. Mike is available to provide custom illustrations for all manner of publications at reasonable prices. Mike can be reached at www.mikereedillustration.com.